Business Ethics

Business Ethics

Concepts and Cases

FIFTH EDITION

Manuel G. Velasquez
Santa Clara University

Prentice Hall

Pearson Education International

Editor-in-Chief: Charlyce Jones Owen
Acquisitions Editor: Ross Miller
Assistant Editor: Katie Janssen
Production Editor: Joseph Scordato
Prepress and Manufacturing Buyer: Sherry Lewis
Copy Editor: Write With, Inc.
Cover Design: Bruce Kenselaar

This book was set in 10.5/12.5 Times Roman by D. M. Cradle Associates, and was printed and bound by Courier Companies, Inc.
The cover was printed by Phoenix Color Corp.

Printed in the United States of America
10 9 8 7 6 5 4 3 2

ISBN 0-13-122726-2

Prentice-Hall International (UK) Limited
Prentice-Hall of Australia Pty. Limited
Prentice-Hall Canada Inc.
Prentice-Hall Hispanoamericana
Prentice-Hall of India Private Limited
Prentice-Hall of Japan, Inc.
Pearson Education Asia Pte. Ltd.
Editora Prentice-Hall do Brasil, Ltda.
Prentice-Hall International, Upper Saddle River, New Jersey

Dedicated
to the memory
of Jerry Kenkel:
Husband, Father, Friend, Lawyer

Contents

Preface

Business Ethics: Concepts and Cases remains a popular and widely-used text. Nevertheless, a revision seemed useful, especially in light of several significant developments in business, particularly in those focused on information technologies. In spite of the demise of many so-called "dot-com" businesses, the World Wide Web has now become a completely familiar and pervasive medium. The rapid evolution of the Web has made a number of ethical issues salient, including issues related to privacy, the ownership of information and, more generally, intellectual property issues. Discussion of these and other issues related to new technologies have been incorporated into this edition. Although this new edition updates the contents of its predecessor, it retains both the basic organization and the conceptual framework of previous versions. For the teacher who would like to know what precise substantive changes have been made to the text, I have appended a paragraph detailing these changes at the end of this preface.

The primary aims of the text remain the same as in earlier editions. They are: (1) to introduce the reader to the ethical concepts that are relevant to resolving moral issues in business; (2) to impart the reasoning and analytical skills needed to apply ethical concepts to business decisions; (3) to identify the moral issues involved in the management of specific problem areas in business; (4) to provide an understanding of the social technological, and natural environments within which moral issues in business arise; and (5) to supply case studies of actual moral dilemmas faced by businesses.

Although the author of a text on business ethics need not apologize for writing on this subject, he or she does owe readers at least some indication of the normative assumptions that underlie what has been written. In the hopes of partially discharging this debt and in order to outline the structure of this book, I will describe its major parts and some key underlying assumptions.

The text is organized into four parts each containing two chapters. Part One provides an introduction to basic ethical theory. A fundamental perspective developed here is the view that ethical behavior is the best long-term business strategy for a company. By this I do not mean that ethical behavior is never costly. Nor do I mean that ethical behavior is always rewarded or that unethical behavior is always punished. It is obvious, in fact, that unethical behavior sometimes pays off, and that ethical behavior can impose serious losses on a company. When I argue that ethical behavior is the best long-range business strategy, I mean merely that over the long run, and for the most part, ethical behavior can give a company significant competitive advantages over companies that are not ethical. I present this idea and argue for it in Chapter 1, where I also indicate how we come to accept ethical standards and how such standards can be incorporated into our moral reasoning processes. Chapter 2 critically discusses four kinds of moral principles: utilitarian principles, principles based on moral rights, principles of justice, and the principles of an ethic of care. These four kinds of moral principles, it is argued, provide a framework for resolving most of the kinds of ethical dilemmas and issues that arise in business. In addition, Chapter 2 discusses virtue theory as an alternative to a principles-based approach.

Having defined the nature and significance of ethical standards and having identified four basic criteria for resolving moral issues in business, I then bring the resulting theory to bear on specific moral issues. Thus, Part Two examines the ethics of markets and price; Part Three discusses environmental and consumer issues; and Part Four looks at employee issues. I assume in each part that in order to apply a moral theory to the real world we must have some information (and theory) about what that world is really like. Consequently, each chapter in these last three parts devotes several pages to laying out the empirical information that the decision-maker must have if he or she is to apply morality to reality. The chapter on market ethics, for example, provides a neoclassical analysis of market structure; the chapter on discrimination presents several statistical and institutional indicators of discrimination; the chapter on the individual in the organization relies on two models of organizational structure.

Each chapter of the text contains two kinds of materials. The main body of the chapter sets out the conceptual materials needed to understand some particular moral issue. This is followed by discussion cases that describe real business situations in which these moral issues are raised. I have provided these discussion cases on the pedagogical assumption that a person's ability to reason about moral matters will improve if the person attempts to think through some concrete moral problems and allows himself or herself to be challenged by others who resolve the issue on the basis of different moral standards. These kinds of challenges, when they arise in dialogue and discussion with others, force us to confront the adequacy of our moral norms and motivate us to search for more adequate principles when our own are shown to be inadequate. Some of the rationale for these pedagogical assumptions is discussed in chapter 1 in the section on moral development and moral reasoning. I hope that I have provided sufficient materials to allow the reader to develop, in discussion and dialogue with others, a set of ethical norms that they can accept as adequate.

Like every other textbook author, I owe a very large debt of gratitude to the numerous colleagues and friends around the world from whom I have shamelessly borrowed ideas and materials. They all, I hope, have been duly recognized in the notes. I owe a special debt to my colleagues in the Management Department where I now teach, especially to Dennis Moberg. My original discipline (and my doctoral training) are in the field of philosophy, but a few years ago I accepted an endowed chair in the Management Department of Santa Clara University. Working closely with the business school faculty there has not only given me a deeper understanding of the special needs that business school instructors have for pedagogical materials in business ethics, it has also deepened my awareness of the significant links between business ethics and business strategy. This deepened awareness permeates this edition.

Although large and small revisions have been made in virtually all the chapters of this edition, the following changes from the previous edition should be noted by previous users of this text. Almost all of the chapters contain new end-of-chapter cases that replace some of the cases in the previous edition. The new cases include: "Napster's Revolution," "Publius," "Accolade versus Sega," "Playing Monopoly: Microsoft," "Genetic Engineering at Monsanto/Pharmacia," and "AIDS and Needles." In addition, the case "Philip Morris' Troubles" has been considerably updated. Those instructors who have used previous editions and who would like to continue using cases from previous editions will be able to find cases through the *Business Ethics: Concepts and Cases* Companion Website (www.prenhall.com/velazquez). Every chapter now also has, at the end of the main text, a section on "Web Resources." While some of these Web materials were available in the endnotes of the previous edition, it seemed best now to place them in a separate section. Chapter 1 includes a few but very brief paragraphs on the ontological nature of corporate organizations based on the work of John Searle and a new section on "Technology and Business Ethics." Chapter 2 includes a new illustrative discussion of Microsoft and human rights in China. Chapters 3 includes new discussions of the views of Locke and Marx on property, and of the theory of property implicit in Smith and in other utilitarian philosophers, as well as a new section on "Property Systems and New Technologies." The examples and tables of Chapter 4 have been updated. Section 5.1 of Chapter 5, on the environment, has been updated, slightly reorganized, and incorporates new data and developments about a number of issues such as acid rain and global warming. Chapter 6 includes several new illustrations and a new section entitled "Consumer Privacy" which discusses new invasive technologies and which uses a theory of privacy that the previous edition had elaborated in chapter 8. In Chapter 7 the section entitled "Discrimination: It's Extent" has been updated to include recent statistics and studies on discrimination. In chapter 8 the section on employee theft has been retitled "Employee Theft and Computers" to make its contents clearer.

Acknowledgments

I would like to acknowledge my gratitude for permission to reprint the following material: Except on pages 266–268 is from Lester R. Brown et al., *State of the World, 2000* (New York: W.W. Norton & Company, 2000). Reprinted by permission of Worldwatch Institute. Copyright © 2000 by Worldwatch Institute. All Rights Reserved. www.worldwatch.com

In addition, I would like to thank those who reviewed the manuscript for this Fifth Edition: Richard J. McGowan of Butler University, Indiana, and Paul L. Schumann of Minnesota State University, Mankato, Minnesota.

Manuel G. Velasquez
Aptos, California

PART ONE

Basic Principles

Business ethics is applied ethics. It is the application of our understanding of what is good and right to that assortment of institutions, technologies, transactions, activities, and pursuits that we call *business*. A discussion of business ethics must begin by providing a framework of basic principles for understanding what is meant by the terms *good* and *right*; only then can one proceed to profitably discuss the implications these have for our business world. These first two chapters provide such a framework. Chapter 1 describes what business ethics is in general and explains the general orientation of the book. Chapter 2 describes several specific approaches to business ethics, which together furnish a basis for analyzing ethical issues in business.

1

Ethics and Business

Introduction

There's no better way to begin an investigation into the relationship between ethics and business than by looking at how real companies have actually tried to incorporate ethics into business. Consider then how one company, Merck and Company, dealt with the issue of "river blindness."

River blindness is an agonizing disease that afflicts some 18 million impoverished people living in remote villages along the banks of rivers in tropical regions of Africa and Latin America. The disease is caused by a tiny parasitic worm that is passed from person to person by the bite of the black fly, which breeds in river waters. The tiny worms burrow under a person's skin, where they grow as long as 2 feet curled up inside ugly round nodules half an inch to an inch in diameter. Inside the nodules, the worms reproduce by releasing millions of microscopic offspring called *microfilaria* that wriggle their way throughout the body moving beneath the skin, discoloring it as they migrate, and causing lesions and such intense itching that victims sometimes commit suicide. Eventually, the microfilaria invade the eyes and blind the victim.

Spraying pesticides to eradicate the black fly faltered when it developed an immunity to the pesticides. Moreover, the only drugs available to treat the parasite in humans have been so expensive, have such severe side effects, and require such lengthy hospital stays that the treatments are impractical for the destitute victims who live in isolated villages. In many countries, people have fled the areas along the rivers, abandoning large tracts of rich fertile land. Many of them, however, eventually return because distant lands prove difficult to farm. Most villagers along the rivers come to accept the nodules, the torturous itching, and eventual blindness as an inescapable part of life.

In 1979, Dr. William Campbell, a research scientist working for Merck and Company, an American drug company, discovered evidence that one of the company's best-selling animal drugs, Ivermectin, might kill the parasite that causes river blindness. Closer analysis indicated that Ivermectin might provide a low-cost, safe, and simple cure for river blindness. Therefore, Campbell and his research team petitioned Merck's chairman, Dr. P. Roy Vagelos, to allow them to develop a human version of the drug, which up to then was only used on animals.

Merck managers quickly realized that if the company succeeded in developing a human version of the drug, the victims of the disease were too poor to afford it. The medical research and large-scale clinical testing required to develop a version of the drug for humans could cost over $100 million. It was unlikely the company could recover these costs or that a viable market could develop in the poverty-stricken regions where the disease was rampant. Moreover, even if the drug were affordable, it would be virtually impossible to distribute it because victims lived in remote areas and had no access to doctors, hospitals, clinics, or commercial drug outlets. Some managers also pointed out that if the drug had adverse side effects when administered to humans, ensuing bad publicity might taint the drug and adversely affect sales of the animal version of the drug, which were about $300 million a year.[1] The risk of harmful side effects was heightened by the possibility that incorrect use of the drug in underdeveloped nations could increase the potential for harm and bad publicity. Finally, if a cheap version of the drug were made available, it might be smuggled to black markets and sold for use on animals, thereby undermining the company's lucrative sales of Ivermectin to veterinarians.

Merck managers were undecided what to do. Although the company had worldwide sales of $2 billion a year, its net income as a percent of sales was in decline due to the rapidly rising costs of developing new drugs, the increasingly restrictive and costly regulations being imposed by government agencies, a lull in basic scientific breakthroughs, and a decline in the productivity of company research programs. Congress was getting ready to pass the Drug Regulation Act, which would intensify competition in the drug industry by allowing competitors to more quickly copy and market drugs originally developed by other companies.[2] As a result of increasing public concerns over rising health costs, government programs such as Medicare and Medicaid had recently put caps on reimbursements for drugs and required cheaper generic drugs in place of the branded name drugs that were Merck's major source of income. In the face of these worsening conditions in the drug industry, Merck managers were reluctant to undertake expensive projects that showed little economic promise, such as the suggested development of a drug for river blindness. Yet without the drug, millions would be condemned to lives of intense suffering and partial or total blindness.

After many earnest discussions among Vagelos and his management team, they came to the conclusion that the potential human benefits of a drug for river blindness were too significant to ignore. Many of the managers felt, in fact, that because of these human benefits the company was morally obligated to proceed despite the costs and the slim chance of economic reward. In late 1980, Vagelos and his fellow managers approved a budget that provided the sizable funding needed to develop a human version of Ivermectin.

After 7 years of expensive research and numerous clinical trials, Merck succeeded in developing a human version of Ivermectin: A single pill of the new drug taken once a year would eradicate from the human body all traces of the parasite that caused river blindness and prevent new infections. Unfortunately, exactly as the company had earlier suspected, no one stepped forward to buy the miraculous new pill. Merck officials pleaded with the World Health Organization (WHO), the U.S. government, and the governments of nations afflicted with the disease, asking that someone—anyone—come forward to buy the drug to protect the 85 million people who were at risk for the disease. None responded to the company's pleas. Merck decided, therefore, that it would give the drug away for free to potential victims.[3] However, this plan proved difficult to implement because, as the company had earlier feared, there were no established distribution channels to get the drug to the people who desperately needed it. Working with the WHO, therefore, the company financed an international committee to provide the infrastructure to distribute the drug safely to people in the Third World and to ensure it would not be diverted into the black market to be sold for use on animals. By 1996, the committee, working with government and private voluntary organizations, had provided the drug to millions of people, effectively transforming their lives and relieving the intense sufferings and potential blindness of the disease.

When asked why the company had invested so much money and effort into researching, developing, manufacturing, and distributing a drug that made no money, Dr. Roy Vagelos replied that, once the company suspected that one of its animal drugs might cure a severe human disease that was ravaging people, the only ethical choice was to develop it. Moreover, people in the Third World "will remember" that Merck helped them, he commented, and would respond favorably to the company in the future.[4] Over the years, the company had learned that such actions have strategically important long-term advantages. "When I first went to Japan 15 years ago, I was told by Japanese business people that it was Merck that brought streptomycin to Japan after World War II to eliminate tuberculosis which was eating up their society. We did that. We didn't make any money. But it's no accident that Merck is the largest American pharmaceutical company in Japan today."[5]

Having looked at how Merck and Company dealt with its discovery of a cure for river blindness, let us now reflect on the relationship between ethics and business. Pundits sometimes quip that *business ethics* is a contradiction in terms because there is an inherent conflict between ethics and the self-interested pursuit of profit. When ethics conflicts with profits, they imply, businesses always choose profits over ethics. Yet the case of Merck and Company suggests a somewhat different perspective—a perspective that many companies are increasingly taking. The management of this company spent tens of millions of dollars developing a product that they knew had little chance of ever being profitable because they felt they had an ethical obligation to make its potential benefits available to people. In this case, at least, a large and very successful business chose ethics over profits. Moreover, the comments of Vagelos at the end of the case suggest that, in the long run, there may be no inherent conflict between ethical behavior and the pursuit of profit. On the contrary, the comments of Vagelos suggest that ethical behavior creates the kind of goodwill and reputation that expand opportunities for profit.

Not all companies, of course, operate like Merck. Many—perhaps even most—companies will not invest in a research and development (R&D) project that they have good reason to suspect will prove unprofitable. A glance at the headlines of newspapers, in fact, will reveal many cases of companies that choose profits over ethics and enough cases of companies that have profited through unethical behavior. Although companies often engage in unethical behavior, however, habitually unethical behavior is not necessarily a good long-term business strategy for a company. For example, ask yourself whether, as a customer, you are more likely to buy from a business that you know is honest and trustworthy or one that has earned a reputation for being dishonest and crooked? Ask yourself whether, as an employee, you are more likely to loyally serve a company whose actions toward you are fair and respectful or one that habitually treats you and other workers unjustly and disrespectfully? Clearly, when companies are competing against each other for customers and for the best workers, the company with a reputation for ethical behavior has an advantage over one with a reputation for being unethical.

This book takes the view that ethical behavior is the best long-term business strategy for a company—a view that has become increasingly accepted during the last few years.[6] This does not mean that occasions never arise when doing what is ethical will prove costly to a company. Such occasions are common in the life of a company, and we see many examples in this book. Nor does it mean that ethical behavior is always rewarded or that unethical behavior is always punished. On the contrary, unethical behavior sometimes pays off, and the good guy sometimes loses. To say that ethical behavior is the best long-range business strategy means merely that, over the long run and for the most part, ethical behavior can give a company significant competitive advantages over companies that are not ethical. The example of Merck and Company suggests this view, and a bit of reflection over how we, as consumers and employees, respond to companies that behave unethically supports it. Later we see what more can be said for or against the view that ethical behavior is the best long-term business strategy for a company.

The more basic problem is, of course, that the ethical course of action is not always clear to a company's managers. In the Merck case, some company managers, including Dr. Roy Vagelos, the company's CEO, felt it was clear that the company had an ethical obligation to proceed with the development of the drug. Yet the issue was perhaps not as clear as it claimed. Don't the managers of a company have a duty toward investors and shareholders to invest their funds in a profitable manner? Indeed, if a company spent all of its funds on charitable projects that lost money, wouldn't it soon be out of business? Then wouldn't its shareholders be justified in claiming that the company's managers had spent their money unethically? Is it so clear, then, that Merck had an ethical obligation to invest in an unprofitable drug? Can any good reasons be given for the claim that Merck had an obligation to develop the drug? Can any good reasons be given for the claim that Merck had no such obligation? Which view is supported by the strongest reasons?

Although ethics may be the best policy, the ethical course of action is not always clear. The purpose of this book is to help the reader deal with this lack of clarity. Although many ethical issues remain difficult and obscure even after a great deal of study, nevertheless gaining a better understanding of ethics will help the manager deal with ethical uncertainties in a more adequate and informed manner.

This text aims to clarify the ethical issues that managers of modern business organizations must face. This does not mean that it is designed to give moral advice to people in business nor that it is aimed at persuading people to act in certain moral ways. The main purpose of the text is to provide a deeper knowledge of the nature of ethical principles and concepts and an understanding of how these apply to the ethical problems encountered in business. This type of knowledge and understanding should help managers more clearly see their way through the ethical uncertainties that confront them in their business lives—uncertainties such as those faced by the managers of Merck.

The first two chapters introduce the reader to methods of moral reasoning and fundamental moral principles that can be used to analyze moral issues in business. The following chapters apply these principles and methods to the kinds of moral dilemmas that confront people in business. We begin in this chapter by discussing four preliminary topics: (a) the nature of business ethics, (b) moral reasoning, (c) the legitimacy of business ethics, and (d) moral responsibility. Once these notions have been clarified, we devote the next chapter to a discussion of some basic theories of ethics and how they relate to business.

1.1 The Nature of Business Ethics

In a now-classic study of the ethics of business managers, Raymond Baumhart asked more than 100 businesspeople, "What does *ethical* mean to you?" Typical of their replies were the following:[7]

> Before coming to the interview, to make sure that I knew what we would talk about, I looked up *ethics* in my dictionary. I read it and can't understand it. I don't know what the concept means. . . .
>
> *Ethical* is what my feelings tell me is right. But this is not a fixed standard, and that makes problems.
>
> *Ethical* means accepted standards in terms of your personal and social welfare; what you believe is right. But what confuses me . . . is the possibility that I have been misguided, or that somebody else has been poorly educated. Maybe each of us thinks he knows what is ethical, but we differ. How can you tell who is right then?

Of the businesspeople Baumhart interviewed, 50 percent defined *ethical* as "what my feelings tell me is right," 25 percent defined it in religious terms as what is "in accord with my religious beliefs," and 18 percent defined it as what "conforms to the golden rule."[8] Yet feelings are a notoriously inadequate basis on which to make decisions of any sort, and religious authority and the golden rule have been rather devastatingly criticized as inadequate foundations for judging the ethics of business companies.[9] What then do *ethics* and *ethical* mean?

According to the dictionary, the term *ethics* has a variety of different meanings. One of the meanings given to it is: "the principles of conduct governing an individual or a group."[10] We sometimes use the term *personal ethics*, for example, when referring to the rules by which an individual lives his or her personal life. We use the term *accounting ethics* when referring to the code that guides the professional conduct of accountants.

A second—and more important—meaning of *ethics* according to the dictionary is this: Ethics is "the study of morality." Ethicists use the term *ethics* to refer primarily to the study of morality, just as chemists use the term *chemistry* to refer to a study of the properties of chemical substances. Although ethics deals with morality, it is not quite the same as morality. Ethics is a kind of investigation—and includes both the activity of investigating as well as the results of that investigation—whereas morality is the subject matter that ethics investigates.

Morality

So what, then, is morality? We can define *morality* as the standards that an individual or a group has about what is right and wrong, or good and evil. To clarify what this means, let us consider a concrete case.

Several years ago, B. F. Goodrich, a manufacturer of vehicle parts, won a military contract to design, test, and manufacture aircraft brakes for the A7D, a new airplane the Air Force was designing. To conserve weight, Goodrich guaranteed that its compact brake would weigh no more than 106 pounds, contain no more than four small braking disks or "rotors," and stop the aircraft within a certain distance. The contract was potentially quite lucrative for the company and so managers were anxious to deliver a brake that "qualified" by successfully passing tests showing it could stop the aircraft as required. Kermit Vandivier, a Goodrich employee, was given the job of working with Goodrich engineers to write up the report of the tests run on the brake, which the government was unlikely to question and even less likely to repeat. Unfortunately, Vandivier later wrote, when the small brake was tested, the brake linings on the rotors repeatedly "disintegrated" because "there simply was not enough surface area on the disks to stop the aircraft without generating the excessive heat that caused the linings to fail."[11] His superiors, however, told him that, "Regardless of what the brake does on tests, we're going to qualify it."[12] After several tests were run, Vandivier was told to write up a report stating that the brake had passed the tests. Vandivier explained to his superior that, "the only way such a report could be written was to falsify test data," to which his superior replied that "he was well aware of what was required, but that he had been ordered to get a report written regardless of how or what had to be done."[13] Therefore, Vandivier had to decide whether he would participate in writing up the false report. He later stated:

> My job paid well, it was pleasant and challenging, and the future looked reasonably bright. My wife and I had bought a home. . . . If I refused to take part in the A7D fraud, I would have to either resign or be fired. The report would be written by someone anyway, but I would have the satisfaction of knowing I had had no part in the matter. But bills aren't paid with personal satisfaction, nor house payments with ethical principles. I made my decision. The next morning I telephoned [my superior and told him I was ready to begin the qualification report.[14]

As he worked on the report, Vandivier said, he talked with the senior executive assigned to the project and asked him "if his conscience would hurt him if such a thing caused the death of a pilot, and this is when he replied that I was worrying about too many things that did not concern me and advised me to 'do what you're told.' "[15]

In this B. F. Goodrich case, Vandivier's beliefs that it is right to tell the truth and wrong to endanger the lives of others, and his beliefs that integrity is good and dishonesty is bad, are examples of moral standards that he held. Moral standards include the norms we have about the kinds of actions we believe are morally right and wrong as well as the values we place on the kinds of objects we believe are morally good and morally bad. Moral norms can usually be expressed as general rules or statements, such as "Always tell the truth," "It is wrong to kill innocent people," or "Actions are right to the extent that they produce happiness." Moral values can usually be expressed as statements describing objects or features of objects that have worth, such as "Honesty is good" and "Injustice is bad."

Where do these standards come from? Typically a person's moral standards are first absorbed as a child from family, friends, and various societal influences such as church, school, television, magazines, music, and associations. Later, as the person grows up, experience, learning, and intellectual development may lead the maturing person to revise these standards. Some are discarded, and new ones may be adopted to replace them. Hopefully, through this maturing process, the person will develop standards that are more intellectually adequate and so more suited for dealing with the moral dilemmas of adult life. As Vandivier's own statements make clear, however, we do not always live up to the moral standards we hold; that is, we do not always do what we believe is morally right nor do we always pursue what we believe is morally good.

Moral standards can be contrasted with standards we hold about things that are not moral. Examples of nonmoral standards include the standards of etiquette by which we judge manners as good or bad, the standards we call *the law* by which we judge legal right and wrong, the standards of language by which we judge what is grammatically right and wrong, the standards of aesthetics by which we judge good and bad art, and the athletic standards by which we judge how well a game of football or basketball is being played. In fact, whenever we make judgments about the right or wrong way to do things, or judgments about what things are good or bad, our judgments are based on standards of some kind. In Vandivier's case, we can surmise that he probably believed that reports should be written with good grammar, that getting fired from a well-paid, pleasant, and challenging job took precedence over a truthful report, and that it is right to follow the law. The norms of good grammar, the value of a well-paid, pleasant, and challenging job, and the laws of government are also standards, but these standards are not moral standards. As the case of Vandivier also demonstrates, we sometimes choose nonmoral standards over our moral standards.

What are the characteristics that distinguish moral standards from standards that are not moral? This is not an easy question to answer. However, ethicists have suggested five characteristics that help pin down the nature of moral standards. First, moral standards deal with matters that we think can seriously injure or seriously benefit human beings.[16] For example, most people in American society hold moral standards against theft, rape, enslavement, murder, child abuse, assault, slander, fraud, lawbreaking, and so on. All of these plainly deal with matters that people feel are quite serious forms of injury. In the Vandivier case, it was clear that lying in the government report and endangering the lives of pilots were both felt to be serious harms and so both were moral matters, whereas adhering to grammatical standards was not.

Second, moral standards are not established or changed by the decisions of particular authoritative bodies. Laws and legal standards are established by the authority of a legislature or the decisions of voters. Moral standards, however, are not established by authority nor does their validity rest on voting procedures. Instead, the validity of moral standards rests on the adequacy of the reasons that are taken to support and justify them; so long as these reasons are adequate, the standards remain valid.

Third, and perhaps most striking, we feel that moral standards should be preferred to other values including (especially?) self-interest.[17] That is, if a person has a moral obligation to do something, then he or she is supposed to do it even if this conflicts with other nonmoral values or self-interest. In the Vandivier case, for example, we feel that Vandivier should have chosen the moral values of honesty and respect for life over the nonmoral value of keeping his well-paid, pleasant, and challenging job. This does not mean, of course, that it is always wrong to act on self-interest; it only means that it is wrong to choose self-interest over morality.

Fourth, and generally, moral standards are based on impartial considerations.[18] The fact that you will benefit from a lie and that I will be harmed is irrelevant to whether lying is morally wrong. Recent philosophers have expressed this point by saying that moral standards are based on "the moral point of view"—that is, a point of view that does not evaluate standards according to whether they advance the interests of a particular individual or group, but one that goes beyond personal interests to a "universal" standpoint in which everyone's interests are impartially counted as equal.[19] Other philosophers have made the same point by saying that moral standards are based on the kinds of impartial reasons that an "ideal observer" or an "impartial spectator" would accept, or that in deciding moral matters "each counts for one and none for more than one."[20] As we see in the next chapter, however, although impartiality is a characteristic of moral standards, it must be balanced with certain kinds of partiality, in particular, with the partiality that arises from legitimate caring and preference for those individuals with whom we have a special relationship such as family members and friends. Although morality says that we should be impartial in those contexts where justice is called for, such as assigning salaries in a public company, it also identifies certain contexts, such as taking care of family members, where preferential caring for individuals may be morally legitimate and perhaps even morally required.

Last, moral standards are associated with special emotions and a special vocabulary.[21] For example, if I act contrary to a moral standard, I will normally feel guilty, ashamed, or remorseful; I will characterize my behavior as "immoral" or "wrong" and I will feel bad about myself and experience a loss of self-esteem. A careful reading of Vandivier's statements, for example, suggests that he later felt shame and remorse about what he did (as a matter of fact, Vandivier later testified before Congress in an attempt to make things right). However, if we see others acting contrary to a moral standard we accept, we normally feel indignation, resentment, or even disgust toward those persons; we say that they are not "living up" to their "moral obligations" or their "moral responsibilities" and we esteem them less. This is perhaps the reader's own response to reading the Vandivier case.

Moral standards, then, are standards that deal with matters that we think are of serious consequence, are based on good reasons and not on authority, override self-interest, are based on impartial considerations, and whose transgression is associated with feelings of guilt and shame and with a special moral vocabulary. We absorb these standards as children from a variety of influences and revise them as we mature.

Ethics

What, then, is ethics? Ethics is the discipline that examines one's moral standards or the moral standards of a society. It asks how these standards apply to our lives and whether these standards are reasonable or unreasonable—that is, whether they are supported by good reasons or poor ones. Therefore, a person starts to do ethics when he or she takes the moral standards absorbed from family, church, and friends and asks: What do these standards imply for the situations in which I find myself? Do these standards really make sense? What are the reasons for or against these standards? Why should I continue to believe in them? What can be said in their favor and what can be said against them? Are they really reasonable for me to hold? Are their implications in this or that particular situation reasonable?

Take Vandivier and the B. F. Goodrich case as an example. Vandivier had apparently been raised to accept the moral standard that one has an obligation to tell the truth, and so he felt that in his particular situation it would be wrong to write a false report on the brake. But we might ask whether writing what he felt was a false report was really wrong in his particular circumstances. Vandivier had several important financial obligations both toward himself and other people. He states, for example, that he had just married and bought a house, so he had mortgage payments to make each month and had to provide support for his family. If he did not write the report as he was ordered to do, then he would be fired and not be able to live up to these obligations. Don't these moral obligations toward himself and his family outweigh his obligation not to write a false report? What is the basis of his obligation to tell the truth, and why is the obligation to tell the truth greater or lesser than a person's obligations toward himself and his family? Consider next Vandivier's obligations toward his employer, B. F. Goodrich. Doesn't an employee have a moral obligation to obey his employer? Does the obligation to obey one's employer outweigh the obligation not to write a false report? What is the source of both of these obligations and what makes one greater or lesser than another? Consider, also, that the company and all its managers insisted that the best course of action was to write the report qualifying the brake. If something went wrong with the brake or the contract, the company, B. F. Goodrich, would be held accountable, not Vandivier, who was a lower level employee. Because the company, not Vandivier, would be held accountable, did the company have the moral right to make the final decision about the report, instead of Vandivier, who was a lower level employee? Does the moral right to make a decision belong to the party that will be held accountable for the decision? What is the basis of such a right, and why should we accept it? Consider, finally, that Vandivier states that, in the end, his personal refusal to participate in writing the report would have given him some "satisfaction," but would have made no difference to what happened because someone else would have been hired to write the report. Because the consequences would be the same whether he agreed or refused, did he really have a moral obligation to refuse? Does one have a moral obligation to do something that will make no difference?

Notice the sort of questions that Vandivier's case leads us to ask. They are questions about whether it is reasonable to apply various moral standards to his situation, whether it is reasonable to say that one moral standard is more or less important than another, and what reasons we might have to hold these standards. When a person asks these kinds of questions about his or her moral standards or about the moral standards of his or her society, the person has started to do ethics. Ethics is the study of moral standards—the process of examining the moral standards of a person or society to determine whether these standards are reasonable or unreasonable in order to apply them to concrete situations and issues. The ultimate aim of ethics is to develop a body of moral standards that we feel are reasonable to hold—standards that we have thought about carefully and have decided are justified standards for us to accept and apply to the choices that fill our lives.

Ethics is not the only way to study morality. The social sciences—such as anthropology, sociology, and psychology—also study morality, but do so in a way that is quite different from the approach to morality that is characteristic of ethics. Although ethics is a *normative* study of ethics, the social sciences engage in a *descriptive* study of ethics. A normative study is an investigation that attempts to reach normative conclusions—that is, conclusions about what things are good or bad or about what actions are right or wrong. In short, a normative study aims to discover what should be. As we have seen, ethics is the study of moral standards whose explicit purpose is to determine as far as possible which standards are correct or supported by the best reasons, and so it attempts to reach conclusions about moral right and wrong and moral good and evil.

A descriptive study is one that does not try to reach any conclusions about what things are truly good or bad or right or wrong. Instead, a descriptive study attempts to describe or explain the world without reaching any conclusions about whether the world is as it should be. Anthropologists and sociologists, for example, may study the moral standards that a particular village or culture holds. In doing so, they attempt to develop accurate descriptions of the moral standards of that culture and perhaps even to formulate an explanatory theory about their structure. As anthropologists or sociologists, however, it is not their aim to determine whether these moral standards are correct or incorrect.

Ethics, in contrast, is a study of moral standards whose explicit purpose is to determine as far as possible whether a given moral standard (or moral judgment based on that standard) is more or less correct. Whereas the sociologist asks, "Do Americans believe that bribery is wrong?" the ethician asks, "Is bribery wrong?" The ethician then is concerned with developing reasonable normative claims and theories, whereas an anthropological or sociological study of morality aims at providing descriptive characterizations of people's beliefs.

Business Ethics

This characterization of ethics has been intended to convey an idea of what ethics is. Our concern here, however, is not with ethics in general, but with a particular field of ethics: *business* ethics. Business ethics is a specialized study of moral right and wrong. It concentrates on moral standards as they apply to business policies, institutions, and behavior. A brief description of the nature of business institutions should clarify this.

A society consists of people who have common ends and whose activities are organized by a system of institutions designed to achieve these ends. That men, women, and children have common ends is obvious. There is the common end of establishing, nurturing, and protecting family life; producing and distributing the materials on which human life depends; restraining and regularizing the use of force; organizing the means for making collective decisions; and creating and preserving cultural values such as art, knowledge, technology, and religion. The members of a society achieve these ends by establishing the relatively fixed patterns of activity that we call *institutions*: familial, economic, legal, political, and educational.

The most influential institutions within contemporary societies may be their economic institutions. These are designed to achieve two ends: (a) production of the goods and services the members of society want and need, and (b) distribution of these goods and services to the various members of society. Thus, economic institutions determine who will carry out the work of production, how that work will be organized, what resources that work will consume, and how its products and benefits will be distributed among society's members.

Business enterprises are the primary economic institutions through which people in modern societies carry on the tasks of producing and distributing goods and services. They provide the fundamental structures within which the members of society combine their scarce resources—land, labor, capital, and technology—into usable goods, and they provide the channels through which these goods are distributed in the form of consumer products, employee salaries, investors' return, and government taxes. Mining, manufacturing, retailing, banking, marketing, transporting, insuring, constructing, and advertising are all different facets of the productive and distributive processes of our modern business institutions.

The most significant kinds of modern business enterprises are corporations: organizations that the law endows with special legal rights and powers. Today large corporate organizations dominate our economies. At the beginning of the 21st century, General Motors, the world's largest automobile company, had revenues of $189 billion and employed more than 388,000 workers; Wal Mart, the world's largest retailer, had sales of $165 billion and 1,140,000 employees; General Electric, the world's largest maker of electrical equipment, had sales of $111 billion and 340,000 employees; and IBM, the world's largest computer company, had revenues of $87.5 billion and 307,000 employees.[22] Of the world's 190 nations, only a handful (e.g., Canada, France, Germany, Italy, Japan, United States, Russia, United Kingdom) had government budgets larger than any one of these companys' sales revenues, and most of the world's nations had fewer workers engaged in their entire auto, retailing, electrical, or computer industries than did these gigantic companies. About half of America's combined industrial profits and earnings are in the hands of about 100 such large corporations, each of which has assets worth over $1 billion. The 195,000 smaller firms, each with assets of less than $10 million, control only about 10 percent of the nation's assets and profits. As reported in *Fortune* magazine's annual summary, the 500 largest American corporations at the turn of this century had combined sales of $6.3 trillion (more than the gross domestic product of Japan and Germany combined), total profits of $410 billion (47 percent of the U.S. total), and a combined labor force of 22 million employees (more than 10 percent of the U.S. workforce).

These 500 corporations account for about 65 percent of all industrial sales, 80 percent of all industrial profits, 80 percent of all industrial assets, and about 75 percent of all industrial employees. Yet they comprise only about 0.2 percent of the total number of industrial firms operating in the United States.

The business corporation in its present form is a relatively new kind of institution (as institutions go). Although it developed from the 16th-century "joint stock company," most of its current characteristics were acquired during the 19th century. Modern corporations are organizations that the law treats as immortal fictitious "persons" who have the right to sue and be sued, own and sell property, and enter into contracts, all in their own name. As an organization, the modern corporation consists of (a) stockholders who contribute capital and who own the corporation but whose liability for the acts of the corporation is limited to the money they contributed, (b) directors and officers who administer the corporation's assets and who run the corporation through various levels of "middle managers," and (c) employees who provide labor and who do the basic work related directly to the production of goods and services. To cope with their complex coordination and control problems, the officers and managers of large corporations adopt formal bureaucratic systems of rules that link together the activities of the individual members of the organization so as to achieve certain outcomes or objectives. So long as the individual follows these rules, the outcome can be achieved even if the individual does not know what it is and does not care about it.

Business ethics is a study of moral standards and how these apply to the systems and organizations through which modern societies produce and distribute goods and services, and to the people who work within these organizations. Business ethics, in other words, is a form of applied ethics. It includes not only the analysis of moral norms and moral values, but also attempts to apply the conclusions of this analysis to that assortment of institutions, technologies, transactions, activities, and pursuits that we call *business*.

As this description of business ethics suggests, the issues that business ethics covers encompass a wide variety of topics. To introduce some order into this variety, it helps if we distinguish three different kinds of issues that business ethics investigates: systemic, corporate, and individual. Systemic issues in business ethics are ethical questions raised about the economic, political, legal, and other social systems within which businesses operate. These include questions about the morality of capitalism or of the laws, regulations, industrial structures, and social practices within which American businesses operate. One example would be questions about the morality of the government contracting system through which B. F. Goodrich was allowed to test the adequacy of its own brake design for the A7D. Another example would be questions about the morality of the international economic system with which Merck was forced to deal.

Corporate issues in business ethics are ethical questions raised about a particular company. These include questions about the morality of the activities, policies, practices, or organizational structure of an individual company taken as a whole. One set of examples of this kind of issue would be questions about the morality of B. F. Goodrich's corporate culture or questions about the company's corporate decision to "qualify" the A7D brake. Another set would be questions about the morality of Merck's corporate decision to invest so many millions of dollars on a project that the company knew would probably not generate any profits.

Finally, individual issues in business ethics are ethical questions raised about a particular individual or particular individuals within a company. These include questions about the morality of the decisions, actions, or character of an individual. An example would be the question of whether Vandivier's decision to participate in writing a report on the A7D brake, which he believed to be false, was morally justified. A second example would be the question of whether it was moral for Merck's chairman, Dr. P. Roy Vagelos, to allow his researchers to develop a drug that would probably not generate any profits.

It is helpful when analyzing the ethical issues raised by a particular decision or case to sort out the issues in terms of whether they are systemic, corporate, or individual issues. Often the world presents us with decisions that involve a large number of extremely complicated interrelated kinds of issues that can cause confusion unless the different kinds of issues are first carefully sorted out and distinguished from each other.

Do Moral Standards Apply to Corporations or Only to Individuals?

Corporate organizations pose major problems for anyone who tries to apply moral standards to business activities. Can we say that the acts of these organizations are moral or immoral in the same sense that the actions of human individuals are? Can we say that these organizations are morally responsible for their acts in the same sense that human individuals are? Or must we say that it makes no sense to apply moral terms to organizations as a whole but only to the individuals who make up the organization? In a recent case, the Justice Department charged E. F. Hutton Corporation with operating an elaborate fraud in which employees wrote overdrafts on bank accounts that allowed E. F. Hutton to derive interest earnings that rightly belonged to the banks. Critics afterward claimed that the Justice Department should have charged the individual managers of E. F. Hutton, not the corporation, because "Corporations don't commit crimes, people do."[23] Can moral notions like *responsibility, wrongdoing,* and *obligation* be applied to groups such as corporations, or are individual people the only real moral agents?

Two views have emerged in response to this problem.[24] At one extreme is the view of those who argue that, because the rules that tie organizations together allow us to say that corporations act as individuals and have "intended objectives" for what they do, we can also say that they are "morally responsible" for their actions and that their actions are "moral" or "immoral" in exactly the same sense that a human being's are. The major problem with this view is that organizations do not seem to "act" or "intend" in the same sense that individual humans do, and organizations differ from human beings in morally important ways: Organizations feel neither pain nor pleasure and they cannot act except through human beings. At the other extreme is the view of philosophers who hold that it makes no sense to hold business organizations "morally responsible" or to say that they have "moral" duties. These philosophers argue that business organizations are the same as machines whose members must blindly and undeviatingly conform to formal rules that have nothing to do with morality. Consequently, it makes no more sense to hold organizations "morally responsible" for failing to follow moral standards than it makes to criticize a machine for failing to act morally. The major problem with this second view is that, unlike machines, at least some of the members of organizations usually know what they are doing and are free to choose whether to follow the organization's rules or even to change these rules. When an organization's members collectively, but freely and knowingly, pursue immoral objectives, it ordinarily makes perfectly good sense to say that the actions they perform for the organization are "immoral" and that the organization is "morally responsible" for this immoral action.

Which of these two extreme views is correct? Perhaps neither. The underlying difficulty with which both views are trying to struggle is this: Although we say that corporate organizations "exist" and "act" like individuals, they obviously are not human individuals. Yet our moral categories are designed to deal primarily with individual humans who feel, reason, and deliberate, and who act on the basis of their own feelings, reasonings, and deliberations. Therefore, how can we apply these moral categories to corporate organizations and their "acts"? We can see our way through these difficulties only if we first see that corporate organizations and their acts depend on human individuals: Organizations are composed of related human individuals that we conventionally agree to treat as a single unit, and they "act" only when we conventionally agree to treat the actions of these individuals as the actions of that unit. We can express this precisely in two somewhat technical claims that build on the work of philosopher John Searle:[25]

I. *A corporate organization "exists" only if (1) there exist certain human individuals who are in certain circumstances and relationships, and (2) our linguistic and* *social conventions lay down that when those kinds of individuals exist in those kinds of circumstances and relationships, they shall count as a corporate organization.*

II. *A corporate organization "acts" only if (1) certain human individuals in the organization performed certain actions in certain circumstances and (2) our linguistic and social conventions lay down that when those kinds of individuals perform those kinds of actions in those kinds of circumstancees, this shall count as an act of their corporate organization.*

Our own social and legal conventions, for example, say that a corporation exists when there exists a properly qualified group of individuals who have agreed among themselves to incorporate and they have performed the necessary legal acts of incorporation. Our social conventions also say that a corporation acts when properly qualified members of the corporation carry out their assigned duties within the scope of their assigned authority.

Because corporate acts originate in the choices and actions of human individuals, it is these individuals who must be seen as the primary bearers of moral duties and moral responsibility: Human individuals are responsible for what the corporation does because corporate actions flow wholly out of their choices and behaviors. If a corporation acts wrongly, it is because of what some individual or individuals in that corporation chose to do; if a corporation acts morally, it is because some individual or individuals in that corporation chose to have the corporation act morally.

Nonetheless, it makes perfectly good sense to say that a corporate organization has moral duties and that it is morally responsible for its acts. However, organizations have moral duties and are morally responsible in a secondary sense: A corporation has a moral duty to do something only if some of its members have a moral duty to make sure it is done, and a corporation is morally responsible for something only if some of its members are morally responsible for what happened (i.e., they acted with knowledge and freedom—topics we discuss later).

The central point that we must constantly keep before our eyes as we apply the standards of ethics to business activities and that we must not let the fiction of "the corporation" obscure is that human individuals underlie the corporate organization. Consequently, these human individuals are the primary carriers of moral duties and moral responsibilities. This is not to say, of course, that the human beings who make up a corporation are not influenced by each other and their beliefs about the corporation and its structure. Corporate policies, corporate culture, corporate norms, and corporate design can and do have an enormous influence on the choices, beliefs, and behaviors of corporate employees. However, these corporate artifacts are like the furniture of the social world the corporate employee inhabits. They provide the subject matter of the employee's choices, the obstacles around which the employee might have to maneuver, and the instruments that help the employee act. Yet these corporate artifacts do not make the employee's choices for him or her and so they are not responsible for his or her actions.

The Multinational Corporation and Business Ethics

Most large corporations today are multinationals: firms that maintain manufacturing, marketing, service, or administrative operations in many different host countries. In fact, virtually all of the 500 largest U.S. industrial corporations maintain operations in more than one nation. Because they operate in several different nations, such multinational corporations face a number of ethical issues that deserve special mention.

With a worldwide presence, multinational corporations tend to be very large; draw capital, raw materials, and human labor from wherever in the world they are cheap, skilled, and available; and assemble and market their products in whatever nations offer manufacturing advantages and open markets. General Electric, for example, which is headquartered in Schenectady, New York, has operations in more than 100 countries around the world and derives almost half of its revenues from outside the United States. It has metallurgy plants in Prague; software operations in India; product design offices in Budapest, Tokyo, and Paris; and manufacturing operations in Mexico. Non-Americans make up a large part of GE's employee base, and an equivalent proportion of its top management team is from outside the United States. Designers engineer the company's products all over the world, much of the work being done over the Internet in different countries; raw materials for its products came from all over the world. Components for its products are manufactured all over the world, assembled in different countries, and marketed in countless countries outside the United States.

The fact that multinationals operate in more than one country produces ethical dilemmas for their managers that managers of firms limited to a single country do not face. First, because the multinational has operations in more than one country, it has the ability to shift its operations out of any country that becomes inhospitable and relocate in another country that offers it cheaper labor, less stringent laws, or more favorable treatment. This ability to shift its operations sometimes enables the multinational to escape the social controls that a single nation might attempt to impose on the multinational and can allow the multinational to play one country against another. Environmental laws, for example, which can ensure that domestic companies operate in the responsible manner that a country deems right for its people, may not be effective constraints on a multinational that can simply move or threaten to move to a country without such laws. Again, union rules that can ensure fair treatment of workers or decent wages may be ineffective against a multinational that can go or threaten to go anywhere in the world to look for cheap labor. Thus, the managers of multinationals are sometimes confronted with the dilemma of choosing between the economic needs and interests of their business, on the one hand, and the local needs and interests of their host country, on the other hand.

Governments, however, are not completely powerless, and many have developed highly effective means of controlling the multinationals they allow within their borders. For example, once a multinational invests in a foreign country and starts a profitable operation, it becomes a hostage of the local government because that government can threaten to confiscate all or part of the multinational's local investment and profits. If its investment is large or if it depends heavily on the foreign profits, the multinational will find it difficult to disagree with any demands of the local government, including ethically questionable demands, such as a Muslim government's demand that companies in effect discriminate against local Jewish minorities. This situation creates additional moral dilemmas for multinational managers: that of either refusing to do what they believe is wrong and risking their business investment or saving their business by going along with what they believe is an unethical practice. Moreover, the objectives of the governments of different countries can result in conflicting demands on the multinational. A multinational may have invested heavily in South Africa during the last century, while apartheid was still practiced, and then found itself pressured by the U.S. government to eliminate all discriminatory practices in its South African subsidiaries and simultaneously commanded by the South African government to maintain discriminatory practices in its South African operations. Mexico can require a General Motors subsidiary located within its borders to export more and import less, while the governments of Brazil, Korea, Europe, and elsewhere are also telling their General Motors subsidiaries to export more and import less.

Another set of dilemmas is created by the following: Because the multinational operates plants in several countries, it can sometimes transfer raw materials, goods, and capital among its plants in different countries at terms that enable it to escape taxes and fiscal obligations that companies limited to a single nation must bear. Suppose, for example, that a multinational manufactures goods in plants in Nation *H*, where taxes on profits are high, by using raw materials from one of its mines in Nation *L*, where taxes are low. Suppose it ships the manufactured goods to its stores in a third country, *S*, where taxes are low and the goods are ultimately marketed. Clearly, the multinational will want to maximize its profits at its mine and store in the low-tax Countries *L* and *S* and minimize its profits at its plant in high-tax Country *H*. To accomplish this, it will have its mine in Country *L* sell raw materials to its plant in Country *H* at high, inflated prices; this increases profits at its mine in low-tax Country *L* while reducing profits at its plant in high-tax Country *H*. Then it will have its plant in Country *H* sell its finished goods to its store in Country *S* at low, deflated prices. This further reduces its profits in high-tax Country *H* while increasing its profits in low-tax

Country *S*. Because the multinational is thus able to set the prices for the materials it transfers and exchanges among its network of plants and operations, it can, in effect, transfer income, expenses, and profits to whatever country it chooses, always seeking the most favorable tax treatment it can. Thus, the managers of a multinational often are faced with the choice of whether they will escape from carrying the share of the tax burden that a local regime believes is morally just. Local governments, of course, will try to control such practices by imposing regulations on the multinational's pricing policies, but such regulations are difficult to frame and even more difficult to enforce.

Yet another group of dilemmas is faced by multinationals: Because they operate in several countries, they often have the opportunity to transfer a new technology or set of products from a more developed country into nations that are less developed. The multinational wants to carry out the transfer, of course, because it perceives an opportunity for profit, and the host country wants and allows the transfer because it perceives these technologies and products as keys to its own development. However, the transfer of new technologies and products into a developing country can create risks when the country is not ready to assimilate them. A chemical company, for example, may import a new toxic pesticide into a developing agrarian nation whose farm workers are neither knowledgeable about nor able to protect themselves against the injuries it will inflict on their health when they apply the foreign-made pesticide by hand to their plants. Yet if the chemical company refuses to supply the pesticide, the local government may object that it is withholding a technology that it judges to be critically needed by its farmers. The advertising campaigns of a food company can motivate consumers in Third World nations to spend their meager food budgets on "foods" such as carbonated soft drinks, sweets, or cigarettes, which provide few or no nutritional benefits and may impose some long-range health costs. Yet, again, the local government may object if the food company holds back some foods that it makes available to consumers of other advanced nations. Thus, the managers of multinationals are often faced with the dilemma of choosing between the benefits that both the company and its host country can derive from a product or technology transfer and the risks and hazards that such transfers can produce.

Finally, because the multinational operates in different nations and because countries have different national standards, it is often faced with the quandary of deciding which of these different norms and standards it should implement in its many operations. For example, when a nation headquartered in a highly developed country such as the United States operates in a less developed nation such as Trinidad, should it pay workers U.S. wages or the lower wages prevalent among Trinidad businesses? Should it use U.S. workplace safety standards for its workers or the lower standards prevalent among Trinidad businesses? If it uses U.S. wages and U.S. safety standards, the result may be that it unfairly draws the best workers away from local Trinidad businesses that cannot afford to do the same. If it uses the wages and safety standards prevalent in Trinidad, it may in effect be exploiting workers.

Thus, because they operate in many different countries, multinationals are faced with a number of unique ethical dilemmas. Their presence in different countries may allow them to escape the taxes and other legal and social constraints through which local governments seek to control their activities. Because they operate in countries at different levels of development and with different standards and norms, they must determine which risks and standards are ethically appropriate for a given country. Because their foreign operations become hostage to the governments of their host countries, they must choose whether to go along with the many conflicting and sometimes morally questionable demands of these governments or risk losing some or all of their foreign investment.

Do the Same Moral Standards Apply to Multinationals Everywhere?

Ethical relativism is the theory that, because different societies have different ethical beliefs, there is no rational way of determining whether an action is morally right or wrong other than by asking whether the people of this or that society believe it is morally right or wrong. To put it another way: Ethical relativism is the view that there are no ethical standards that are absolutely true and that apply or should be applied to the companies and people of all societies. Instead, relativism holds that something is right for the people or companies in one particular society if it accords with their moral standards and wrong for them if it violates their moral standards. The people of certain Arab societies, for example, hold that business bribery is morally acceptable, although Americans believe it is immoral. The ethical relativist will conclude that, although it is wrong for an American company to bribe in America, it is not wrong for Arabs or their companies to bribe in their own society. The company or businessperson who operates in several different countries, then, and who encounters societies with many different moral standards are advised by the theory of ethical relativism in this way: In one's moral reasoning, one should always follow the moral standards prevalent in whatever society one finds oneself. After all, because moral standards differ and since there are no other criteria of right and wrong, the best one can do is follow the old adage, "When in Rome, do as the Romans do." However, is this view—ethical relativism—a reasonable view to hold?

Clearly, there are numerous practices that are judged immoral by some societies that other societies have deemed morally acceptable, including polygamy, abortion, infanticide, slavery, homosexuality, racial and sexual discrimination, genocide, patricide, and the torture of animals. Yet critics of ethical relativism have pointed out that it does not follow that there are no moral standards that are binding on people everywhere.[26] Critics of ethical relativism have argued, in fact, that there are certain moral standards that the members of any society must accept if that society is to survive and if its members are to interact with each other effectively. Thus, all societies have norms against injuring or killing other members of the society, norms about using language truthfully when communicating with members of one's society, and norms against taking the personal goods of other members of one's society.

In addition, many apparent moral differences among societies turn out on closer examination to mask deeper underlying similarities. For example, anthropologists tell us that in some Alaskan Inuit societies it was morally acceptable for families to abandon their aged to die outdoors during times of hardship, whereas other societies felt they had a moral obligation to protect and nurture their aged at all times. Yet on closer examination, it can turn out that underlying the different practices of both kinds of societies is a belief in the same ethical standard: the moral duty of ensuring the long-term survival of the community. In their harsh environment, Inuit people may have had no way of ensuring their community's survival when food supplies ran short other than by abandoning their aged. Other communities ensured their long-term survival by protecting the elders who carried within them the knowledge and experience they needed.

Moreover, other critics of the theory of ethical relativism point out that, because different people have different moral beliefs about some issue, it does not follow logically that there is no objective truth about that issue nor that all beliefs about that issue are equally acceptable. When two people or two groups have different beliefs, philosophers are fond of pointing out, at least one of them is wrong. For example, Philosopher James Rachels put the matter quite succinctly.

> The fact that different societies have different moral codes proves nothing. There is also disagreement from society to society about scientific matters: in some cultures it is believed that the earth is flat, and that disease is caused by evil spirits. We do not on that account conclude that there is no truth in geography or in medicine. Instead, we conclude that in some cultures people are better informed than in others. Similarly, disagreement in ethics might signal nothing more than that some people are less enlightened than others. At the very least, the fact of disagreement does not, by itself, entail that truth does not exist. Why should we assume that, if ethical truth exists, everyone must know it?[27]

Perhaps the most telling criticisms against ethical relativism are those that point to the incoherent consequences of the theory. If ethical relativism were true, then it would make little sense to criticize the practices of other societies so long as they conformed to their own standards. For example, we could not say that the slavery of our pre-Civil War Southern societies was wrong, that the discrimination practiced in the societies of the American South before the 1950s was unjust, or that the Germans' treatment of Jews in the Nazi society of the 1930s was immoral. Moreover, if ethical relativism were correct, it would also make no sense—in fact it would be morally wrong—to criticize any of the moral standards or practices accepted by our own society. If our society accepts that a certain practice—such as torturing animals—is morally right, then as members of this society, we too must accept that practice as morally right, and it is immoral for us to tell others in our society to go against this belief because right and wrong for us must be determined by the standards of our society. Thus, the theory of ethical relativism implies that whatever the majority in our society believes about morality is automatically correct.

Thus, the fundamental problem with ethical relativism is that it holds that the moral standards of a society are the only criteria by which actions in that society can be judged. The theory gives the moral standards of each society a privileged place that is above all criticism by members of that society or by anyone else: They cannot be mistaken. Clearly, this implication of ethical relativism indicates that the theory is mistaken. We recognize that the moral standards of our own society as well as those of other societies can be mistaken. This recognition that our own moral standards as well as those of other societies might be wrong implies that the moral standards a society happens to accept cannot be the only criteria of right and wrong.

The ethical relativist correctly reminds us that different societies have different moral beliefs, and we should not simply dismiss the moral beliefs of other cultures when they do not match our own. However, the ethical relativist is wrong to conclude that all moral beliefs are equally acceptable and that the only criteria of right and wrong are the moral standards prevalent in a given society.

Technology and Business Ethics

Technology consists of all those methods, processes, and tools that humans invent to manipulate their environment. To an extent never before realized in history, contemporary business is being continuously and radically transformed by the rapid evolution of new technologies that raise new ethical issues for business.

This is not the first time that new technologies have had a revolutionary impact on business and society. Several thousand years ago, during what is sometimes called the *Agricultural Revolution,* humans developed the farming technologies that enabled them to stop relying on foraging and on the luck of the hunt and to develop, instead, reasonably constant supplies of food. The invention of irrigation, the harnessing of water and wind power, and the development of levers, wedges, hoists, and gears during this period eventually allowed humans to accumulate more goods than they could consume, and out of this surplus grew trade, commerce, and the first businesses.

In the 18th century, the technology of the Industrial Revolution again transformed Western society and business, primarily through the introduction of electromechanical machines powered by fossil fuels such as the steam engine, automobile, railroad, and cotton gin. Prior to the Industrial Revolution, most businesses were small organizations that operated in local markets and that were managed by owners who oversaw relatively few workers who assembled goods by hand. The Industrial Revolution brought with it new forms of machine production that enabled businesses to make massive quantities of goods to ship and sell in national markets. These changes in turn required large organizations to manage the enormous armies of people that had to be mobilized to process the output of these machines on long assembly lines in huge factories. The result was the large corporation that came to dominate our economies and that brought with it a host of ethical issues for business, including the possibilities of exploiting the workers who labored at the new machines, manipulating the new financial markets that financed these large enterprises, and producing massive damage to the environment.

New technologies developed in the closing decades of the 20th century are again transforming society and business and creating the potential for new ethical problems. Foremost among these developments are the revolutions in biotechnology and in what is sometimes called *information technology*, including not only the development of extremely powerful and compact computers, but also the development of the Internet, wireless communications, digitalization, and numerous other technologies that have enabled us to capture, manipulate, and move information in new and creative ways. These new technologies have spurred a number of changes, such as increasingly rapid globalization and the decreasing importance of distance; the rise of new ways to communicate and transfer any kind of media—movies, newspapers, music, books, mail—instantaneously from one place to another; the acceleration of change as product life cycles get shorter and revolutionary new products are invented and marketed ever more quickly; and the ability to create new life forms whose benefits and risks are unpredictable. To cope with these rapid changes, business organizations have had to become smaller, flatter, and more nimble—they have had to deal with a host of intriguing new ethical issues.

Almost all ethical issues raised by new technologies are related in one way or another to questions of risk: Are the risks of a new technology predictable? How large are the risks and are they reversible? Are the benefits worth the potential risks, and who should decide? Do those persons on whom the risks will fall know about the risk and have they consented to bear these risks? Will they be justly compensated for their losses? Are the risks fairly distributed among the various parts of society including poor and rich, young and old, future generations and present ones?

Many of the ethical issues new technologies have created—especially information technologies like the computer—are related to privacy. Computers enable us to collect detailed information on individuals on a scale that was never possible before (by tracking users on the Internet, gathering information on customers at cash registers, collecting information on credit card purchases, retrieving information from applications for licenses, bank accounts, credit cards, e-mail, monitoring employees working at computers, etc.), they have the power to quickly link this information to other databases (containing financial information, purchase histories, addresses, phone numbers, driving record, arrest records, credit history, medical and academic records, memberships), and they can quickly sift, sort, or retrieve any part of this information for anyone who has access to the computer. Because these technologies enable others to gather such detailed and potentially injurious information about ourselves, many people have argued that they violate our right to privacy: the right to prohibit others from knowing things about us that are private.

Information technologies have also raised difficult ethical issues about the nature of the right to property when the property in question is information (such as computer software, computer code, or any other kind of data—text, numbers, pictures, sounds—that have been encoded into a computer file) or computer services (access to a computer or a computer system). Computerized information (such as a software program or digitized picture) can be copied perfectly countless times without in any way changing the original. What kind of property rights does one have when one owns one of these copies? What kind of property rights does the original creator of the information have and how does it differ from the property rights of someone who buys a copy? Is it wrong for me to make a copy without the permission of the original creator when doing so in no way changes the original? What, if any, harms will society or individuals suffer if people are allowed to copy any kind of computerized information at will? Will people stop creating information? For example, will they stop writing software and stop producing music? What kind of property rights does one have over computer systems? Is it wrong to use my company's computer system for personal business, such as to send personal e-mail or to log onto websites that have nothing to do with my work? Is it wrong for me to electronically break into another organization's computer system if I do not change anything on the system but merely "look around"?

Finally, biotechnology has created yet another host of troubling ethical issues. *Genetic engineering* refers to a large variety of new techniques that let us change the genes in the cells of humans, animals, and plants. Genes, which are composed of deoxyribonucleic acid (DNA), contain the blueprints that determine what characteristics an organism will have. Through recombinant DNA technology, for example, the genes from one species are removed and inserted into the genes of another species to create a new kind of organism with the combined characteristics of both species. Businesses have used genetic engineering to create and market new varieties of vegetables, grains, sheep, cows, rabbits, bacteria, viruses, and numerous other organisms. Bacteria have been engineered to consume oil spills and detoxify waste, wheat has been engineered to be resistant to disease, grass has been engineered to be immune to herbicides, and a French laboratory is said to have inserted the fluorescent genes from a jellyfish into a rabbit embryo that was born glowing in the dark just like the jellyfish. Is this kind of technology ethical? Is it wrong for a business to change and manipulate nature in this way? When a company creates a new organism through genetic engineering, should it be able to patent the new organism so that it in effect *owns* this *new* form of life? Often the consequences of releasing genetically modified organisms into the world cannot be predicted. Engineered animals may drive out natural species, and engineered plants may poison wild organisms. The pollen of a species of corn that had been engineered to kill certain pests, for example, was later found to also be killing off certain butterflies. Is it ethical for businesses to market and distribute such unpredictable engineered organisms throughout the world?

1.2 Moral Development and Moral Reasoning

We have said that ethics is the study of morality and that a person begins to do ethics when he or she turns to look at the moral standards that have been absorbed from family, church, friends, and society, and begins asking whether these standards are reasonable or unreasonable and what these standards imply for situations and issues. In this section, we examine more closely this process of examining one's moral standards and of applying them to concrete situations and issues. We begin by describing how a person's ability to use and critically evaluate his or her moral standards develops in the course of a person's life, and then we describe the reasoning processes through which these moral standards are employed and evaluated.

Moral Development

We sometimes assume that a person's values are formed during childhood and do not change after that. In fact, a great deal of psychological research, as well as one's own personal experience, demonstrates that as people mature, they change their values in very deep and profound ways. Just as people's physical, emotional, and cognitive abilities develop as they age, so also their ability to deal with moral issues develops as they move through their lives. In fact, just as there are identifiable stages of growth in physical development, so the ability to make reasoned moral judgments also develops in identifiable stages. As children we are simply told what is right and what is wrong, and we obey so as to avoid punishment: The child's adherence to moral standards is essentially based on a self-absorbed avoidance of pain. As we mature into adolescence, these conventional moral standards are gradually internalized. Adherence to moral standards is now based on living up to the expectations of family, friends, and surrounding society. We do what is right because it is what our groups expect of us. It is only as rational and experienced adults that we acquire the capacity to critically reflect on the conventional moral standards bequeathed to us by our families, peers, culture, or religion. We then begin to rationally evaluate these moral standards and their consequences, and to revise them where they are inadequate, inconsistent, or unreasonable. We begin, in short, to do ethics, and our morality now increasingly consists of moral standards that are more impartial and that take into account more of the interests of others, or that more adequately balance taking care of others with taking care of ourselves.

There is a good deal of psychological research that shows that people's moral views develop more or less in this manner. The psychologist Lawrence Kohlberg, for example, who pioneered research in this field, concluded on the basis of over 20 years of research that there is a sequence of six identifiable stages in the development of a person's ability to deal with moral issues.[28] Kohlberg grouped these stages of moral development into three levels, each containing two stages, the second of which is the more advanced and organized form of the general perspective of each level. The sequence of the six stages can be summarized as follows.

Level One: Preconventional Stages[29]

At these first two stages, the child is able to respond to rules and social expectations and can apply the labels *good, bad, right,* and *wrong*. These rules, however, are seen as something externally imposed on the self. Right and wrong are interpreted in terms of the pleasant or painful consequences of actions or in terms of the physical power of those who set the rules. If one were to ask a 5-year-old, for example, whether stealing is wrong, she or he will say it is; if one then asks the child why it is wrong, the answer will be something like, "Because Mommy will punish me if I steal." The child can see situations only from his or her own point of view; because the child does not yet have the ability to identify with others to any great extent, the primary motivation is self-centered.

Stage One: Punishment and Obedience Orientation At this stage, the physical consequences of an act wholly determine the goodness or badness of that act. The child's reasons for doing the right thing are to avoid punishment or defer to the superior physical power of authorities. There is little awareness that others have needs and desires similar to one's own.

Stage Two: Instrument and Relativity Orientation At this stage, right actions become those that can serve as instruments for satisfying the child's own needs or the needs of those for whom the child cares. The child is now aware that others have needs and desires similar to his or her own and begins to defer to them to get them to do what he or she wants.

Level Two: Conventional Stages

Maintaining the expectations of one's own family, peer group, or nation is now seen as valuable in its own right, regardless of the consequences. The person at this level of development does not merely conform to expectations but exhibits loyalty to the group and its norms. If one were to ask an adolescent at this level about why something is wrong or why it is right, for example, the adolescent would probably answer in terms of "what my friends think," "what my family has taught me," "what we Americans hold," or even "what our laws say." The adolescent at this stage is now able to see situations from the point of view of others, but the only perspectives the adolescent can take up are the familiar viewpoints of the people who belong to the adolescent's own social groups, such family, peers, organizations, nation, and social class, and she assumes that everyone is like them. The person is motivated to conform to the group's norms and subordinates the needs of the individual to those of the group.

Stage Three: Interpersonal Concordance Orientation Good behavior at this early conventional stage is living to the expectations of those for whom one feels loyalty, affection, and trust, such as family and friends. Right action is conformity to what is generally expected in one's role as a good son, daughter, brother, friend, and so on. Doing what is right is motivated by the need to be seen as a good performer in one's own eyes and in the eyes of others.

Stage Four: Law and Order Orientation Right and wrong at this more mature conventional stage now come to be determined by loyalty to one's own larger nation or surrounding society. Laws are to be upheld except where they conflict with other fixed social duties. The person is now able to see other people as parts of a larger social system that defines individual roles and obligations, and he or she can separate the norms generated by this system from his or her interpersonal relationships and motives.

Level Three: Postconventional, Autonomous, or Principled Stages

At these stages, the person no longer simply accepts the values and norms of the groups to which he or she belongs. Instead the person now tries to see situations from a point of view that impartially takes everyone's interests into account. The person questions the laws and values that society has adopted and redefines them in terms of self-chosen moral principles that can be justified in rational terms. If an adult at this stage is asked why something is wrong, the person will respond in terms of what has been decided through processes that are "fair to everyone" or in terms of "justice," "human rights," or "society's overall welfare." The proper laws and values are those that conform to principles to which any reasonable person would be motivated to commit him or herself.

Stage Five: Social Contract Orientation At this first postconventional stage, the person becomes aware that people hold a variety of conflicting personal views and opinions and emphasizes fair ways of reaching consensus by agreement, contract, and due process. The person believes that all values and norms are relative and that, apart from this democratic consensus, all should be tolerated.

Stage Six: Universal Ethical Principles Orientation At this final stage, right action comes to be defined in terms of moral principles chosen because of their logical comprehensiveness, universality, and consistency. These ethical principles are not concrete like the ten commandments, but abstract general principles dealing with justice, society's welfare, the equality of human rights, respect for the dignity of individual human beings, and the idea that persons are ends in themselves and must be treated as such. The person's reasons for doing what is right are based on a commitment to these moral principles, and the person sees them as the criteria for evaluating all other moral rules and arrangements including democratic consensus.

Kohlberg's theory is useful because it helps us understand how our moral capacities develop and reveals how we can become increasingly sophisticated and critical in our use and understanding of the moral standards we hold. Research by Kohlberg and others has shown that, although people generally progress through the stages in the same sequence, not everyone progresses through all the stages. Kohlberg found that many people remain stuck at one of the early stages throughout their lives. For those who remain at the preconventional level, right and wrong always continues to be defined in the egocentric terms of avoiding punishment and doing what powerful authority figures say. For those who reach the conventional level but never get any further, right and wrong continues to be defined in terms of the conventional norms of their social groups or the laws of their nation or society. However, for those who reach the postconventional level and take a reflective and critical look at the moral standards they have been raised to hold, moral right and wrong is defined in terms of moral principles they have chosen for themselves as more reasonable and adequate.

It is important to notice that Kohlberg implies that the moral reasoning of people at the later stages of moral development are better than the reasoning of those at earlier stages. First, people at the later stages have the ability to see things from a wider and fuller perspective than those at earlier stages. The person at the preconventional level can see situations only from one's own egocentric point of view; the person at the conventional level can see situations only from the familiar viewpoints of people in the person's own social groups; and the person at the postconventional point of view has the ability to look at situations from a perspective that tries to take into account everyone affected by the decision. Second, people at the later stages have better ways of justifying their decisions to others than those at earlier stages. The person at the preconventional level can justify decisions only in terms of how one's own interests will be affected, and therefore justifications are ultimately only persuasive to oneself. The person at the conventional level can justify decisions in terms of the norms of the groups to which one belongs, and therefore justifications are ultimately persuasive only to members of one's groups. Finally, the person at the postconventional level can justify what one does on the basis of moral principles that are impartial and reasonable, and that therefore can appeal to any reasonable person.

Kohlberg's theory, however, has been subjected to a number of criticisms.[30] First, Kohlberg has been criticized for claiming that the higher stages are morally preferable to the lower stages. This criticism is surely right. Although the higher Kohlberg levels incorporate broader perspectives and widely acceptable justifications, it does not follow that these perspectives are morally better than the lower ones. To establish that the higher stages are morally better will require more argument than Kohlberg provides. In later chapters, we see what kind of reasons can be given for the view that the perspectives and justifications of the moral principles characteristic of the later Kohlberg stages are morally preferable to those of the earlier stages.

A second significant criticism of Kohlberg is one that arises from the work of Carol Gilligan, a psychologist. She suggests that, although Kohlberg's theory correctly identifies the stages through which men pass as they develop, it fails to adequately trace out the pattern of development of women.[31] Because most of Kohlberg's subjects were male, Gilligan has argued, his theory failed to take into account the patterns of moral thinking of women.

There are, Gilligan claimed, two different ways to approach moral issues. First, there is a "male" approach that Kohlberg's theory emphasizes. According to Gilligan, males tend to deal with moral issues in terms of impersonal, impartial, and abstract moral rules—exactly the kind of approach that is exemplified by the principles of justice and rights that Kohlberg says are characteristic of postconventional thinking. However, Gilligan claimed, there is a second, "female" approach to moral issues that Kohlberg does not recognize. Females, Gilligan claimed, tend to see themselves as part of a "web" of relationships with family and friends; when females encounter moral issues, they are concerned with sustaining these relationships, avoiding hurt to others in these relationships, and caring for their well-being. For women, morality is primarily a matter of "caring" and "being responsible" for others with whom one is involved in personal relationships, and not a matter of adhering to impartial and impersonal rules. In addition to defining this new "female" approach to morality, Gilligan claimed that women who take this approach to morality follow somewhat different stages as they mature and develop their moral views. Moral development for women is marked by progress toward more adequate ways of caring and being responsible for oneself and others. In her theory, the earliest or preconventional level of moral development for women is one marked by caring only for oneself. Women move to a second or conventional level when they internalize conventional norms about caring for others and in doing so come to neglect themselves. As women move to the postconventional or most mature level, however, they become critical of the conventional norms they had earlier accepted, and they come to achieve a balance between caring for others and caring for oneself.

Is Gilligan right? Although additional research has shown that male and female moral development do not differ in the ways that Gilligan originally suggested, that same research has confirmed the claim that Gilligan has identified an approach or perspective toward moral issues that is different from the approach that Kohlberg emphasizes.[32] Moral issues can be dealt with from a perspective of impersonal impartiality or from a perspective of caring for persons and relationships, and these two perspectives are distinct. However, women as well as men sometimes approach moral issues from the perspective of impartial and impersonal moral rules, and men as well as women sometimes approach moral issues from the perspective of care and responsibility in relationships.[33] Although research on the *care perspective* that Gilligan described is still in its infancy, it is clearly an important moral perspective that both men and women should take into account. We look more carefully at this new and exciting perspective in the next chapter and assess its relevance to business.

For our purposes, however, what is important to note at this point is that both Kohlberg and Gilligan agreed that there are stages of growth in our moral development. Both also agreed that moral development moves from a preconventional stage focused on the self, through a conventional stage in which we uncritically accept the conventional moral standards of the groups to which we belong, and on to a mature stage in which we learn to critically and reflectively examine the adequacy of the conventional moral standards we earlier accepted and to fashion more adequate standards of our own, both standards of caring for particular persons, as well as standards of impartiality toward all persons.

We said earlier that one begins to do ethics when one begins to critically examine the moral standards one has accepted from family, friends, and society, and asks whether these standards are reasonable or unreasonable. In terms of the stages of moral development that Kohlberg and Gilligan proposed, ethics begins when one moves from a simple acceptance of the conventional moral standards that one has absorbed from society and tries to critically and reflectively develop more mature standards that are based on more adequate reasons and that are capable of dealing with a wider range of moral issues in a more adequate manner. The study of ethics is the process of developing one's ability to deal with moral issues—a process that should enable the individual to acquire the more reflective understanding of "right" and "wrong" that characterizes the later postconventional stages of moral development. Therefore, one of the central aims of the study of ethics is the stimulation of this moral development.

This is an important point—one that should not be lost on the reader. The text and cases that follow are designed to be read and discussed with others—students, teachers, friends—to stimulate in ourselves the kind of moral development that we have been discussing. Intense interaction and discussion of moral issues with others develops our ability to move beyond a simple acceptance of the moral standards we may have uncritically absorbed from family, peers, organization, nation, or culture. By discussing, analyzing, and criticizing the moral judgments we and others make, we come to acquire the habits of thinking that are needed to develop and determine for ourselves a set of moral principles to which we can reasonably assent.

The moral principles that are produced by the kind of analysis and reflection that are characteristic of the latter stages of moral development in both Kohlberg and Gilligan, then, are "better" but not because they come at a later stage. One set of moral principles is "better" than another only when it has been carefully examined and found to be supported by better and stronger reasons—a process that is enhanced through discussion and challenge with others. The moral principles that appear in the later stages of moral development, then, are better because and to the extent that they are the product of the kind of reasoned examination and reasoned discussion with others that tends to emerge as people improve their reasoning skills, grow in their understanding and knowledge of human life, and interact with others to develop a firmer and more mature moral perspective.

Moral Reasoning

We have used the term *moral reasoning* repeatedly. What does the term mean? Moral reasoning refers to the reasoning process by which human behaviors, institutions, or policies are judged to be in accordance with or in violation of moral standards. Moral reasoning always involves two essential components: (a) an understanding of what reasonable moral standards require, prohibit, value, or condemn; and (b) evidence or information that shows that a particular person, policy, institution, or behavior has the kinds of features that these moral standards require, prohibit, value, or condemn. Here is an illustration of moral reasoning whose author is offering us his reasons for claiming that American social institutions are unjust.

> The nonwhite . . . live in American society, fight for American society in disproportionate numbers, and contribute cheap labor to American society, thereby enabling others to live disproportionately well. But the nonwhite . . . do not share in the benefits of the American society in which they live and for which they fight and to which they contribute. Forty-one percent of Negroes fall below the poverty line as compared with 12 percent of whites. Infant mortality is three times as high

> among nonwhite babies as among white. Whereas, Negroes make up 11 percent of the nation's work force, they have but 6 percent of the nation's technical and professional jobs, 3 percent of the managerial jobs, and 6 percent of jobs in skilled trades. Discrimination which prevents people from getting out of their society what they contribute is unjust.[34]

In this example, the author has in mind a moral standard that he sets out at the end of the paragraph: "Discrimination which prevents people from getting out of their society what they contribute is unjust." The rest of the paragraph is devoted to citing evidence showing that American society exhibits the kind of discrimination proscribed by this moral principle. The author's moral judgment that American society is unjust, then, is based on a chain of reasoning that appeals to a moral standard and to evidence that American society has the features condemned by this standard. Schematically, then, moral or ethical reasoning usually has the kind of structure indicated in Fig. 1.1.[35]

In many cases, one or more of the three components involved in a person's moral reasoning are not expressed. More often than not, in fact, people will fail to make explicit the moral standards on which their moral judgments are based. For example, a person might say, "American society is unjust because it allows 41 percent of Negroes to fall below the poverty line as compared with 12 percent of whites." Here the unspoken moral standard on which the judgment "American society is unjust" is based on something such as "A society is unjust if it does not treat minorities equal to the majority." The disproportionate number of Blacks that fall below the poverty line is being cited as evidence that minorities in America are not treated equally to the White majority. The main reason that moral standards are often not made explicit is that they are generally presumed to be obvious. People put more of their efforts into producing evidence that a given policy, institution, or action conforms to, or violates, their unexpressed standards than they put into identifying or explaining the moral standards on which their judgments rely. Failure to make one's moral standards explicit leaves one vulnerable to all the problems created by basing critical decisions on unexamined

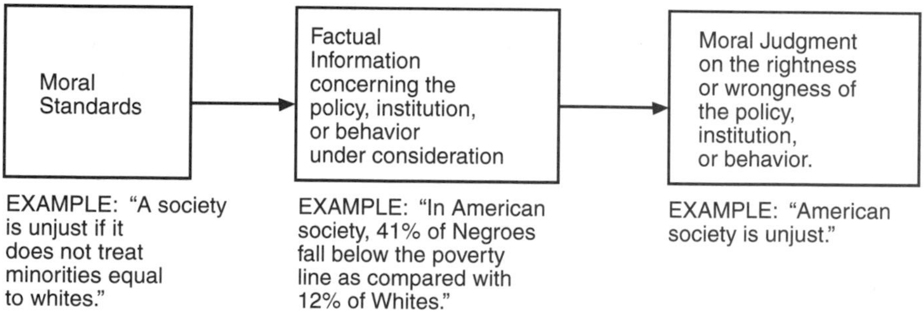

Figure 1.1

assumptions: The assumptions may be inconsistent, they may have no rational basis, and they may lead the decision maker into unwittingly making decisions with undesirable consequences. We saw at the end of the last section two arguments that tried to show that managers should not be ethical but both of which were based on assumed moral standards that were unacceptable once they were made explicit.

To uncover the implicit moral standards on which a person's moral judgments are founded, one has to retrace the person's moral reasoning back to its bases. This involves asking (a) What factual information does the person accept as evidence for this moral judgment? (b) What moral standards are needed to relate this factual information (logically) to the moral judgment?[36] For example, suppose I judge that capital punishment is morally wrong. Further, suppose I base my judgment on the factual evidence that capital punishment occasionally results in the death of innocent people. Then, in order to relate this factual information to my judgment, I must accept this general moral principle: Whatever occasionally results in the death of innocent people is morally wrong. This general moral principle is needed if there is to be a (logical) connection between the factual information ("capital punishment occasionally results in the death of innocent people") and the moral judgment that is based on this fact ("capital punishment is morally wrong"). Without the moral principle, the factual information would have no logical relation to the judgment and would therefore be irrelevant.

The moral standards on which adults base their moral judgments are usually much more complex than this simple example suggests. Developed moral standards (as we see) incorporate qualifications, exceptions, and restrictions that limit their scope. Also they may be combined in various ways with other important standards. However, the general method of uncovering unexpressed moral standards remains roughly the same whatever their complexity. One asks: What general standards relate a person's factual evidence to his or her moral judgments?

Hopefully this account of ethical reasoning has not suggested that it is always easy to separate factual information from moral standards in a piece of moral reasoning; nothing could be farther from the truth. In practice, the two are sometimes intertwined in ways that are difficult to disentangle. There are several theoretical difficulties in trying to draw a precise line separating the two.[37] Although the difference between the two is usually clear enough for practical purposes, the reader should be aware that sometimes they cannot be clearly distinguished.

Analyzing Moral Reasoning

There are various criteria that ethicians use to evaluate the adequacy of moral reasoning. First and primarily, moral reasoning must be logical. The analysis of moral reasoning requires that the logic of the arguments used to establish a moral judgment be rigorously examined, all the unspoken moral and factual assumptions be made explicit, and both assumptions and premises be displayed and subjected to criticism.

Second, the factual evidence cited in support of a person's judgment must be *accurate*, *relevant*, and *complete*.[38] For example, the illustration of moral reasoning quoted cites several statistics ("Whereas Negroes make up 11 percent of the nation's work force, they have but 6 percent of the nation's technical and professional jobs, 3 percent of . . . ") and relationships ("The nonwhite contribute cheap labor which enables others to live disproportionately well") that apparently exist in America. If the moral reasoning is to be adequate, these statistics and relationships must be *accurate*: They must rest on reliable statistical methods and well-supported scientific theory. In addition, evidence must be *relevant*: It must show that the behavior, policy, or institution being judged has precisely those characteristics that are proscribed by the moral standards involved. For instance, the statistics and relationships in the illustration of moral reasoning given must show that some people are "prevented from getting out of [American] society what they contribute," the precise characteristic that is condemned by the moral standard cited in the illustration. Evidence must be *complete*: It must take into account all relevant information and must not selectively advert only to the evidence that tends to support a single point of view.

Third, the moral standards involved in a person's moral reasonings must be *consistent*. They must be consistent with each other and with the other standards and beliefs the person holds. Inconsistency between a person's moral standards can be uncovered and corrected by examining situations in which these moral standards require incompatible things. Suppose that I believe that (1) it is wrong to disobey an employer whom one has contractually agreed to obey, and I also believe that (2) it is wrong to help someone who is endangering innocent people's lives. Then suppose that one day my employer insists that I work on a project that might result in the deaths of several innocent people. The situation now reveals an inconsistency between these two moral standards: I can either obey my employer and avoid disloyalty, or I can disobey him and avoid helping endanger people's lives, but I cannot do both.

When inconsistencies between one's moral standards are uncovered in this way, one (or both) of the standards must be modified. In this example, I might decide that orders of employers have to be obeyed *except* when they threaten human life. Notice that, to determine what kinds of modifications are called for, one has to examine the *reasons* one has for accepting the inconsistent standards and weigh these reasons to see what is more important and worth retaining and what is less important and subject to modification. In this example, for instance, I may have decided that the reason that employee loyalty is important is that it safeguards property, but the reason that the refusal to endanger people is important is that it safeguards human life. Human life, I then decide, is more important than property. This sort of criticism and adjustment of one's moral standards is an important part of the process through which moral development takes place.

There is another kind of consistency that is perhaps even more important in ethical reasoning. Consistency also refers to the requirement that one must be willing to accept the consequences of applying one's moral standards consistently to all persons in similar circumstances.[39] This consistency requirement can be phrased as follows:

> *If I judge that a certain person is morally justified (or unjustified) in doing A in circumstances C, then I must accept that it is morally justified (or unjustified) for any other person*
>
> ***(a)*** *to perform any act relevantly similar to A*
>
> ***(b)*** *in any circumstances relevantly similar to C.*

That is, I must apply the same moral standards to one situation that I applied to another one that was relevantly similar. (Two situations are "relevantly similar" when all those factors that have a bearing on the judgment that an action is right or wrong in one situation are also present in the other situation.) For example, suppose that I judge that it is morally permissible for me to fix prices because I want the high profits. If I am to be consistent, I must hold that it is morally permissible for my *suppliers* to fix prices when they want high profits. If I am not willing to consistently accept the consequences of applying to other similar persons the standard that price fixing is morally justified for those who want high prices, I cannot rationally hold that the standard is true in my own case.

The consistency requirement is the basis of an important method of showing that a given moral standard must be modified or rejected: the use of counterexamples or hypotheticals. If a moral standard is inadequate or unacceptable, we can often show it is inadequate by showing that its implications in a certain hypothetical example are unacceptable. For instance, suppose someone should advance the claim that we should always do only what will benefit ourselves—that is, that we should act only egoistically. We might want to attack this view by proposing the hypothetical example of an individual who is made happy only when he or she does what will benefit *others* and *not* him or herself. According to the egoistic standard, this individual should to do only what will make him or her unhappy! This, we might want to hold, is clearly unacceptable. The egoist, of course, may want to modify his or her view (by saying, "What I *really* meant by 'benefit ourselves' was . . . "), but that is another story. The point is that hypothetical counterexamples can be used effectively to show that a moral standard must be rejected or at least modified.

1.3 Arguments for and Against Business Ethics

We have described business ethics as the process of rationally evaluating our moral standards and applying them to business situations. However, many people have raised objections to the very idea of applying moral standards to business activities. In this section, we address some of these objections and also look at what can be said in favor of bringing ethics into business.

Three Objections to Bringing Ethics into Business

Occasionally people object to the view that ethical standards should be applied to the behavior of people in business organizations. Persons involved in business, they claim, should single mindedly pursue the financial interests of their firm and not sidetrack their energies or their firm's resources into "doing good works." Three different kinds of arguments are advanced in support of this view.

First, some have argued that in perfectly competitive free markets, the pursuit of profit will by itself ensure that the members of society are served in the most socially beneficial ways.[40] To be profitable, each firm has to produce only what the members of society want and has to do this by the most efficient means available. The members of society will benefit most, then, if managers do not impose their own values on a business, but instead devote themselves to the single-minded pursuit of profit, and thereby devote themselves to producing efficiently what the members of society value.

Arguments of this sort conceal a number of assumptions that require a much lengthier discussion than we can provide at this stage. Because we examine many of these claims in greater detail in the chapters that follow, here we only note some of the more questionable assumptions on which the argument rests.[41] First, most industrial markets are not "perfectly competitive" as the argument assumes, and to the extent that firms do not have to compete they can maximize profits despite inefficient production. Second, the argument assumes that any steps taken to increase profits will necessarily be socially beneficial, when in fact several ways of increasing profits actually injure society: allowing harmful pollution to go uncontrolled, deceptive advertising, concealing product hazards, fraud, bribery, tax evasion, price fixing, and so on. Third, the argument assumes that, by producing whatever the buying public wants (or values), firms are producing what all the members of society want, when in fact the wants of large segments of society (the poor and disadvantaged) are not necessarily met because they cannot participate fully in the marketplace. Fourth, the argument is essentially making a normative judgment ("managers should devote themselves to the single-minded pursuit of profits") on the basis of some assumed but unproved moral standards ("people should do whatever will benefit those who participate in markets"). Thus, although the argument tries to show that ethics does not matter, it can do this only by assuming an unproved moral standard that at least appears mistaken.

A second kind of argument sometimes advanced to show that business managers should single mindedly pursue the interests of their firms and should ignore ethical considerations is embodied in what Alex C. Michales called the "loyal agent's argument."[42] The argument can be paraphrased as follows:

> *As a loyal agent of his or her employer, the manager has a duty to serve his or her employer as the employer would want to be served (if the employer had the agent's expertise).*
>
> *An employer would want to be served in whatever ways will advance his or her self-interests.*
>
> *Therefore, as a loyal agent of his or her employer, the manager has a duty to serve his or her employer in whatever ways will advance the employer's self-interests.*

The argument can be, and often has been, used to justify a manager's unethical or illegal conduct. For example, the officer of a corporation may plead that, although he engaged in certain illegal or unethical conduct (e.g., price fixing), he should be excused because he did it not for himself, but to protect the best interests of his company, its shareholders, or its workers. The loyal agent's argument underlies this kind of excuse. More generally, if we replace *employer* with *government* and *manager* with *officer*, we get the kind of argument that Nazi officers used after World War II to defend their involvement in Hitler's morally corrupt government.

The loyal agent's argument relies on several questionable assumptions. First, the argument tries to show, again, that ethics does not matter by assuming an unproved moral standard ("the manager *should* serve his or her employer in whatever way the employer wants to be served"). But there is no reason to assume that this moral standard is acceptable as it stands, and some reason to think that it would be acceptable only if it were suitably qualified (e.g., "the manager should serve his or her employer in whatever *moral* way the employer wants to be served"). Second, the loyal agent's argument assumes that there are no limits to the manager's duties to serve the employer, when in fact such limits are an express part of the legal and social institutions from which these duties arise. An agent's duties are defined by what is called *the law of agency,* (i.e., the law that specifies the duties of persons [agents] who agree to act on behalf of another party and who are authorized by the agreement so to act). Lawyers, managers, engineers, stockbrokers, and so on all act as agents for their employers in this sense. By freely entering an agreement to act as someone's agent, then, a person accepts a legal (and moral) duty to serve the client loyally, obediently, and in a confidential manner as specified in the law of agency.[43] Yet the law of agency states that, "in determining whether or not the orders of the [client] to the agent are reasonable . . . business or professional ethics are to be considered," and "in no event would it be implied that an agent has a duty to perform acts which are illegal or unethical."[44] The manager's duties to serve his employer, then, are limited by the constraints of morality, because it is with this understanding that his duties as a loyal agent are defined. Third, the loyal agent's argument assumes that if a manager agrees to serve a firm, then this agreement automatically justifies whatever the manager does on behalf of the firm. However, this assumption is false: Agreements to serve other people do not automatically justify doing wrong on their behalf. For example, it is clearly wrong for me to kill an innocent person to advance my own interests. Suppose that one day I enter an agreement to serve your interests and that later it turns out that your interests require that I kill an innocent person for you. Does the agreement now justify my killing the innocent person? Obviously it does not because agreements do not change the moral character of wrongful acts. If it is morally wrong, then, for a manager to do something out of self-interest, it is also morally wrong for him to do it in the interests of his company even though he has agreed to serve the company. The assumptions of the loyal agent's argument, then, are mistaken.

A third kind of objection is sometimes made against bringing ethics into business. This is the objection that to be ethical it is enough for business people merely to obey the law: Business ethics is essentially obeying the law. For example, when an accountant was asked to prepare a business ethics report for the board of directors of 7-Eleven Stores, his report excluded allegations that a store manager was trying to bribe New York tax officials. When asked why the alleged bribery attempt was excluded from the report, he replied that he did not feel the incident was unethical because it was not illegal, implying that *unethical* and *illegal* are the same.[45]

It is wrong, however, to see law and ethics as identical. It is true that some laws require behavior that is the same as the behavior required by our moral standards. Examples of these are laws that prohibit murder, rape, theft, fraud, and so on. In such cases, law and morality coincide, and the obligation to obey such laws is the same as the obligation to be moral.

However, law and morality do not always coincide. Some laws have nothing to do with morality because they do not involve serious matters. These include parking laws, dress codes, and other laws covering similar matters. Other laws may even violate our moral standards so that they are actually contrary to morality. Our own pre-Civil War slavery laws, for example, required us to treat slaves like property, and the laws of Nazi Germany required antisemitic behavior. The laws of Saudi Arabia today require that businesses discriminate against women and Jews in ways that most people would say are clearly immoral. Thus, it is clear that ethics is not simply following the law.

This does not mean, of course, that ethics has nothing to do with following the law.[46] Our moral standards are sometimes incorporated into the law when enough of us feel that a moral standard should be enforced by the pressures of a legal system. In contrast, laws are sometimes criticized and eliminated when it becomes clear that they blatantly violate our moral standards. Our moral standards against bribery in business, for example, were incorporated into the Foreign Corrupt Practices Act, and only a few decades ago it became clear that laws permitting job discrimination—like earlier laws permitting slavery—were blatantly unjust and had to be eliminated. Morality, therefore, has shaped and influenced many of the laws we have.

Moreover, most ethicists agree that all citizens have a moral obligation to obey the law so long as the law does not require clearly unjust behavior. This means that, in most cases, it is immoral to break the law. Tragically, the obligation to obey the law can create terrible conflicts when the law requires something that the businessperson believes is immoral. In such cases, a person will be faced with a conflict between the obligation to obey the law and the obligation to obey his or her conscience.

The Case for Ethics in Business

We have looked at several arguments attempting to establish that ethics should not be brought into business and we found them all wanting. Is there anything to be said for the opposite claim—that ethics should be brought into business? One way to argue that ethics should be brought into business is simply by pointing out that, because ethics should govern all voluntary human activities and because business is a voluntary human activity, ethics should also govern business. In short, there is nothing about business that would prevent us from applying the same standards of ethics to business activities that should be applied to all voluntary human activities.

Another argument for the view that ethics should be part of business points out that business activities, like any other human activities, cannot exist unless the people involved in the business and its surrounding community adhere to some minimal standards of ethics. Business is a cooperative activity whose very existence requires ethical behavior. First, any individual business will collapse if all of its managers, employees, and customers come to think that it is morally permissible to steal from, lie to, or break their agreements with the company. Because no business can exist entirely without ethics, the pursuit of business requires at least a minimal adherence to ethics on the part of those involved in business. Second, all businesses require a stable society in which to carry on their business dealings. Yet the stability of any society requires that its members adhere to some minimal standards of ethics. In a society without ethics, as the philosopher Hobbes once wrote, distrust and unrestrained self-interest would create "a war of every man against every man," and in such a situation life would become "nasty, brutish, and short." The impossibility of conducting business in such a society—one in which lying, theft, cheating, distrust, and unrestrained self-interested conflict became the norm—is shown by the way in which business activities break down in societies torn by strife, conflict, distrust, and civil war. Because businesses cannot survive without ethics, then, it is in the best interests of business to promote ethical behavior both among its own members as well as within its larger society.[47]

Another persuasive way to argue that ethics should be brought into business is by showing that ethical considerations are consistent with business pursuits, in particular with the pursuit of profit. That ethics is consistent with the pursuit of profit can be shown by simply finding examples of companies where a history of good ethics has existed side by side with a history of profitable operations. As we saw, Merck is renowned for its long-standing ethical culture and yet it is one of the most spectacularly profitable companies of all time. Other companies that have combined a good history of profit with exemplary ethical climates include: Xerox, Home Depot, Odwalla, Hewlett-Packard, Silicon Graphics, Levi Strauss, Polaroid, Patagonia, Johnson & Johnson, and Starbucks Coffee.[48]

Yet pointing to individual companies in which the pursuit of ethics has existed side by side with the pursuit of profit does not fully demonstrate that ethics is consistent with the pursuit of profits. Many chance factors affect profitability (overcapacity in a particular industry, recessions, weather patterns, interest rates, changing consumer tastes, etc.). Consequently, these companies may be nothing more than the few companies in which ethics by chance happened to coincide with profits for a period of time. Is there any evidence that ethics in business is systematically correlated with profitability? Are ethical companies more profitable than other companies?

There are many difficulties involved in trying to study whether ethical companies are more profitable than unethical ones. There are many different ways of defining *ethical*, many different ways of measuring profit, many different ways of deciding whose actions count as the actions of the company, many different factors that can affect a company's profits, and many different dimensions along which companies can be compared. Despite these difficulties, several studies have examined whether profitability is correlated with ethical behavior. The results have been mixed. Although several studies have found a positive relationship between socially responsible behavior and profitability,[49] some have found no such relationship.[50] No studies, however, have found a negative correlation, which would have indicated that ethics is a drag on profits. Other studies have looked at how socially responsible firms perform on the stock market and have concluded that ethical companies provide higher returns than other companies.[51] Together, all these studies suggest that, by and large, ethics does not detract from profit and seems to contribute to profits.

Are there any other reasons to think that ethics should be brought into business? Consider an argument based on the prisoner's dilemma.[52] A prisoner's dilemma is a situation in which two parties are each faced with a choice between two options: Either cooperate with the other party or do not cooperate.[53] If both parties cooperate, they will both gain some benefit. If both choose not to cooperate, neither gets the benefit. If one cooperates while the other chooses not to cooperate, the one who cooperates suffers a loss while the one who chooses not to cooperate gains a benefit.[54] The story that gives the prisoner's dilemma its name is a good illustration of this kind of dilemma. Two men who are arrested for robbing a store secretly agree that neither will confess that they committed the crime. The police commissioner separates the two men and tells each *prisoner* the same thing. If neither admits that the two of them robbed the store, they will both be kept in jail for a year. If both prisoners confess to robbing the store, each will get 2 years in jail. If one of them keeps quiet while the other confesses, the one who keeps quiet will get 3 years in jail while the one who confesses will go free. The options are summed up in Fig. 1.2.

From the joint standpoint of the parties involved, the best outcome in a prisoner's dilemma is for both parties to cooperate in their agreement. Mutual cooperation will leave them each better off (only 1 year in jail) than if both do not cooperate (2 years in jail). However, if the parties to a single prisoner's dilemma are rational and self-interested, they will inevitably choose not to cooperate. A rational self-interested party will reason like this: "The other party has only two choices: to cooperate or not cooperate. Suppose he chooses to cooperate.

	Prisoner B cooperates with prisoner A	Prisoner B does not cooperate with prisoner A
Prisoner A cooperates with prisoner B	A gets 1 year B gets 1 year	A gets 3 years B goes free
Prisoner A does not cooperate with prisoner B	A goes free B gets 3 years	A gets 2 years B gets 2 years

Figure 1.2

Then I will be better off if I do not cooperate. Suppose he chooses not to cooperate. Then again it is clearly better for me not to cooperate. So in either case, it is better for me not to cooperate than to cooperate." Because both parties will reason this way, both parties will end up not cooperating (and both will go to jail for 2 years). In short, when people must choose between cooperating or not cooperating in rules or agreements, and when each has more to gain by not cooperating, then rational self-interest suggests that people should not cooperate in keeping the rules or agreements.

If the reader takes a moment to think about it, it becomes clear that we encounter prisoner's dilemmas in every part of our lives. In fact, wherever there are agreements or mutual expectations, competitions or games, rules or norms, there are prisoner's dilemmas. Our lives are filled with situations in which we can cooperate with others by sticking to an agreement or a rule, or we can choose not to cooperate and instead try to take advantage of the other party by breaking the agreement or rule by which the other party continues to abide. In such cases, rational self-interest seems to tell us that we can gain an advantage by not cooperating and that, consequently, noncooperation is better than cooperation.

Much of ethics, of course, consists of rules that each of us can choose to follow or not to follow and so ethics, too, creates a prisoners' dilemma. If everyone cooperates in following the rules of ethics—do not steal, do not lie, do not injure, keep your promises, do not cheat—we will each be better off. Because a person can often gain an advantage over others by breaking the rules of ethics (e.g., by stealing or cheating), it seems that it is more rational to not cooperate in the rules of ethics than to cooperate. The prisoner's dilemma, then, seems to show that the rational self-interested person should be unethical in business when there is something to be gained through unethical behavior.

However, this conclusion is based on a false assumption. We have assumed so far that prisoner's dilemma situations are isolated interactions between people who never interact again. In real life, individuals have to deal with each other repeatedly or have ongoing relationships with each other. When individuals have to deal with each other in repeated prisoner's dilemma situations, and one individual takes advantage of the other in one interaction, the victim can retaliate by doing the same in the next interaction.[55] This threat of future retaliation makes it more rational for the parties in a series of repeated exchanges to cooperate than to try to take advantage of each other. Through cooperation, the parties will gain the advantages conferred by mutually beneficial activities, whereas noncooperation will lead to a deteriorating series of costly clashes. The most important lesson of the prisoner's dilemma, then, is that when people deal with each other repeatedly, so that each can later retaliate against or reward the other party, cooperation is more advantageous than continuously trying to take advantage of the other party.

The prisoner's dilemma analysis of ethics has significant implications for ethics in business. Business interactions with employees, customers, suppliers, and creditors are repetitive and ongoing. If a business tries to take advantage of employees, customers, suppliers, or creditors through unethical behavior today, then the latter will likely find a way to retaliate against the business when they meet again tomorrow. The retaliation may take a simple form, such as refusing to buy from, refusing to work for, or refusing to do business with the unethical party. Or retaliation may be more complex, such as sabotage, getting others to boycott the unethical party, or getting even by inflicting other kinds of costs on the business. A business can sometimes, even often, get away with unethical behavior. In the long run, however, if interactions are repeated and retaliation is a real threat, unethical behavior tends to impose costs on the business, whereas ethical behavior can set the stage for mutually advantageous interactions with cooperative parties.

The prisoner's dilemma argument, then, implies that, over the long run and for the most part, it is better to be ethical in business than to be unethical. Although being unethical toward another party in business may sometimes pay off, over the long run unethical behavior in business tends to be a losing proposition because it undermines the long-term cooperative relationships with customers, employees, and community members on which business success ultimately depends.

We should note that the prisoner's dilemma argument is sometimes criticized because it assumes that people are isolated individuals motivated only by self-interest.[56] This criticism is correct, but it misses the point of the prisoner's dilemma argument. The prisoner's dilemma argument tries to show that *even if people were individualistically motivated only by self-interest*, they would still have a good reason to be ethical in business. In reality, of course, most people seem to be social and so are also motivated by a concern for the welfare of others. To the extent that people are motivated by a concern for others, they will probably behave ethically. However, it is not clear how far concern for others extends nor is it clear that everyone is motivated by a concern for the welfare of others. What the prisoner's dilemma argument shows is that even those who have no concern for the welfare of others—even self-interested individualists—still have a good reason to bring ethics into their business dealings.

Finally, we should note that there is also a good deal of evidence that most people so value ethical behavior that they will punish those whom they perceive to be behaving unethically and reward those who are perceived to be ethical.[57] In particular, a large body of research in social psychology has concluded that people in all kinds of social situations react to perceived injustices with distress and will attempt to eliminate their distress by restoring justice, whereas they will be attracted to just organizations and will reward the just organization with loyalty and commitment. Customers will turn against a company if they perceive a gross injustice in the way it conducts its business and will lower their willingness to buy its products.[58] Employees who feel their company's decision-making processes are unjust will exhibit higher absenteeism, higher turnover, lower productivity, and demand higher wages.[59] In contrast, when employees feel that an organization's decision-making processes are just, they exhibit lower levels of turnover and absenteeism, show higher levels of trust and commitment to the organization and its management, and demand lower wages.[60] When employees believe an organization is just, they are more willing to follow the organization's managers, do what managers say, and see managers' leadership as legitimate.[61] In short, ethics is a key component of effective management.

There are, then, a number of strong arguments supporting the view that ethics should be brought into business. Taken together, the arguments—some philosophical and some more empirical—suggest that businesses are short-sighted when they fail to take the ethical aspects of their activities into consideration.

1.4 Moral Responsibility and Blame

Up to now, our discussion has focused on judgments of right and wrong and of good and evil. Moral reasoning, however, is sometimes directed at a related but different kind of judgment: determining whether a person is *morally responsible*, or culpable, for having done something wrong or for having wrongfully injured someone.[62] A judgment about a person's moral responsibility for a wrongful injury is a judgment about the extent to which the person deserves blame or punishment, or should pay restitution for the injury. For example, if an employer deliberately injures the health of her employees, we would judge the employer morally responsible for those injuries. We are then saying the employer is to blame for those injuries and perhaps deserves punishment and should compensate the victims.

It is important not to confuse this meaning of *moral responsibility* with a second meaning that the words sometimes have. The term *moral responsibility* is sometimes used as an equivalent to *moral duty* or *moral obligation.* For example, if we say that "Vandiver had a moral responsibility not to lie," we use the term *moral responsibility* to mean *moral obligation.* This is not the kind of moral responsibility that we are presently discussing. The term *moral responsibility* sometimes is also used to express that a person is to blame for an action. For example, if we say that "Vandiver was morally responsible for the deaths of five pilots who crashed when trying to land the A7D airplane," we use the term *morally responsible* to mean "to blame." It is this second meaning of *morally responsible* that we discuss here.

People are not always morally responsible for their wrongful or injurious acts. A person, for example, may inflict an injury on an innocent human being, but do so without knowing what he or she was doing (perhaps the person did it by accident). We would not hold the person morally responsible for that injury: What the person did was wrong, but the person is *excused* by virtue of his or her ignorance. When is a person morally responsible—or to blame—for having done something?

A person is morally responsible only for those acts and their forseen injurious effects (a) which the person knowingly and freely performed or brought about and which it was morally wrong for the person to perform or bring about, or (b) which the person knowingly and freely failed to perform or prevent and which it was morally wrong for the person to fail to perform or prevent. For example, Stefan Golab, a 59-year-old Polish immigrant who spoke little English, died from cyanide poisoning after working for 2 months over open vats of fuming cyanide for Film Recovery Systems, a company that recovered silver from old film. In a landmark case, Steven O'Neil, president of the company, together with Charles Kirschbaum, the plant supervisor, and Daniel Rodriguez, the plant foreman, were judged responsible by a court for Golab's death on charges of murder.[63] The judgment was based on testimony that the managers maintained the hazardous working conditions knowing the life-threatening dangers of breathing the cyanide fumes, that they failed to warn or protect workers like Golab who could not read English, and that they had skull-and-crossbones warning symbols scraped off cyanide drums. Thus, they were held responsible for knowingly and freely maintaining the dangerous workplace and for defacing the pictorial warnings, both of which were wrongful actions. They were also held responsible for Golab's death because it was held that they "knew there was a strong probability of bodily harm" resulting from their actions.

One can also be held morally responsible for failing to act or failing to prevent an injury if one's omission is free and knowledgeable and if one could and should have acted, or could and should have prevented the injury. Several manufacturers of asbestos, for example, were recently judged responsible for the lung diseases suffered by some of their workers.[64] The judgment was based in part on the finding that the manufacturers had a special duty (a duty they were assigned by their position) to warn their workers of the known dangers of working with asbestos, but that they knowingly failed to perform this duty, and the lung diseases were a foreseen injury that they could have prevented had they acted as they had a duty to act.

There is wide agreement that two conditions completely eliminate a person's moral responsibility for causing a wrongful injury: (1) ignorance and (2) inability.[65] These are called *excusing* conditions because they fully excuse a person from being held responsible for something. If a person was ignorant of, or unable to avoid, what he or she did, then that person did not act knowingly and freely and cannot be blamed for what he or she did. Asbestos manufacturers, for example, have claimed that they did not know that conditions in their plants would cause lung cancer in their workers. If this is true, then it would be wrong to blame them for the diseases that resulted. Other asbestos manufacturers have said that they tried to prevent these diseases by trying to get their workers to wear protective masks and clothing, but they were unable to enforce these protective measures because the workers refused to adhere to them. If these manufacturers truly tried everything they could to prevent these diseases, but they were unable to do so because of circumstances they could not control, then again they are not morally responsible for these injurious effects.

It is important to understand exactly when ignorance and inability remove a person's responsibility. Ignorance and inability do not always excuse a person. One exception is when a person deliberately keeps himself ignorant of a certain matter to escape responsibility. For example, if an asbestos manufacturer told the company's doctors *not* to tell him the results of the medical examinations they carried out on his workers so that he would not be legally liable for leaving conditions in his factory unchanged, he would still be morally responsible for any injuries if the tests turned out positive. A second exception is when a person negligently fails to take adequate steps to become informed about a matter that is of known importance. A manager in an asbestos company, for example, who has reason to suspect that asbestos may be dangerous, but who fails to inform himself on the matter out of laziness, cannot later plead ignorance as an excuse.

A person may be ignorant of either the relevant facts or the relevant moral standards. For example, I may be sure that bribery is wrong (a moral standard) but may not have realized that in tipping a customs official I was actually bribing him into canceling certain import fees (a fact). In contrast, I may be genuinely ignorant that bribing government officials is wrong (a moral standard), although I know that in tipping the customs official I am bribing him into reducing the fees I owe (a fact).

Ignorance of *fact* generally eliminates moral responsibility completely for the simple reason that a person cannot be obligated to do something over which he or she has no control: Moral obligation requires freedom.[66] Because people cannot control matters of which they are ignorant, they cannot have any moral obligations with respect to such matters, and their moral responsibility for such matters is consequently nonexistent. Negligently or deliberately created ignorance is an exception to this principle because such ignorance can be controlled. Insofar as we can control the extent of our ignorance, we become morally responsible for it and, therefore, also for its injurious consequences. Ignorance of the relevant *moral standards* generally also removes responsibility because a person is not responsible for failing to meet obligations of whose existence he or she is genuinely ignorant. However, to the extent that our ignorance of moral standards is the result of freely choosing not to ascertain what these standards are, we are responsible for our ignorance and for its wrongful or injurious consequences.

Inability can be the result of either internal or external circumstances that render a person unable to do something or unable to keep from doing something. A person may lack sufficient power, skill, opportunity, or resources to act; a person may be physically constrained or prevented from acting; or a person's mind may be psychologically impaired in a way that prevents him or her from controlling his or her actions. A manager working under extremely stressful circumstances, for example, may be so tense that one day he is overcome by rage at a subordinate and genuinely is unable to control his actions toward that subordinate. An engineer who is part of a larger operating committee may be unable to prevent the other committee members from making a decision that the engineer feels will wrongfully injure other parties. An assembly-line worker with an undiagnosed malady may suffer muscle spasms that cause the assembly line to malfunction in a way that inflicts physical injuries on other workers. In all of these cases, the person is not morally responsible for the wrong or the injury as a result of the person's inability to control events.

Inability eliminates responsibility because, again, a person cannot have any moral obligation to do (or forbear from doing) something over which the person has no control. Insofar as circumstances render a person unable to control his or her actions or to prevent a certain injury, it is wrong to blame the person.

In addition to the two *excusing* conditions (ignorance and inability) that completely remove a person's moral responsibility for a wrong, there are also several mitigating factors that can lessen a person's moral responsibility depending on the severity of the wrong. Mitigating factors include (a) circumstances that leave a person *uncertain* but not altogether unsure about what he or she is doing (these affect the person's knowledge); (b) circumstances that make it *difficult* but not impossible for the person to avoid doing it (these affect the person's freedom); and (c) circumstances that minimize but not completely remove a person's *involvement* in an act (these affect the degree to which the person actually caused or helped to cause the wrongful injury). These can lessen a person's responsibility for wrongdoing depending on a fourth factor: the seriousness of the wrong. To clarify these, we can discuss each of them in turn.

First, circumstances can produce *uncertainty* about a variety of matters. A person may be fairly convinced that doing something is wrong, yet may still be doubtful about some important *facts*, or may have doubts about the *moral standards* involved or doubts about how *seriously wrong* the action is. For example, an office worker who is asked to carry proprietary information to a competitor might feel fairly sure that doing so is wrong yet may also have some genuine uncertainty about how serious the matter is. Such uncertainties can lessen a person's moral responsibility for a wrongful act.

Second, a person may find it *difficult* to avoid a certain course of action because he or she is subjected to threats or duress of some sort or because avoiding that course of action will impose heavy costs on the person. Middle managers, for example, are sometimes intensely pressured or threatened by their superiors to reach unrealistic production targets or to keep certain health information secret from workers or the public, although it is clearly unethical to do so.[67] If the pressures on managers are great enough, then their responsibility is correspondingly diminished. Although they are to blame for the wrong, their blame is mitigated (those who knowingly and freely impose pressures on subordinates that can be expected to issue in wrongful acts are also responsible for those wrongful acts).

Third, a person's responsibility can also be mitigated by circumstances that diminish the person's *active involvement* in the act that caused or brought about an injury. An engineer may contribute to an unsafe product, for example, by knowingly drawing up the unsafe design and thus being actively involved in causing the future injuries. In contrast, the engineer may be aware of the unsafe features in somebody else's design, but passively stand by without doing anything about it because "that's not my job." In such a case, the engineer is not actively involved in causing any future injuries. In general, the less one's actual actions contribute to the outcome of an act, the less one is morally responsible for that outcome (depending, however, on the seriousness of the act). However, if a person has a special (an officially assigned) duty to report or try to prevent certain wrongdoings, then that person is morally responsible for acts he or she refrains from reporting or trying to prevent even if the person is not otherwise involved in the act. An accountant, for example, who was hired to report any fraudulent activity observed cannot plead diminished responsibility for a fraud the accountant knowingly failed to report by pleading that she did not actively carry out the fraudulent act. In such cases where a person has a special (specifically assigned) duty to prevent an injury, freely and knowingly *failing* to prevent it is wrong. One is responsible for it (along with the other guilty party or parties) if one should and could have prevented it but did not.

Fourth, the extent to which these three mitigating circumstances can diminish a person's responsibility for a wrongful injury depends on the seriousness of the wrong. For example, if doing something is very seriously wrong, then even heavy pressures and minimal involvement may not substantially reduce a person's responsibility for the act. If my employer, for example, threatens to fire me unless I sell a used product that I know will kill someone, it would be wrong for me to obey him even though loss of a job will impose some heavy costs on me. However, if only a relatively minor matter is involved, then the threat of a job loss might substantially mitigate my responsibility. In determining one's moral responsibility for a wrongful act, therefore, one must judge one's uncertainties, the pressures to which one is subjected, and the extent of one's involvement and then weigh these against the seriousness of the wrong. Obviously such judgments are often extremely difficult and tragically painful to make.

It may be helpful to summarize here the essential points of this somewhat lengthy and complicated discussion of an individual's moral responsibility for a wrong or an injury. First, an individual is morally responsible for those wrongful acts he performed (or wrongly omitted) and for those injurious effects he brought about (or wrongly failed to prevent) when this was done knowingly and freely. Second, moral responsibility is completely eliminated (excused) by ignorance and inability. Third, moral responsibility for a wrong or an injury is mitigated by (a) uncertainty, (b) difficulty, and (c) minimal involvement (although failure to act does not mitigate if one has a specific duty to prevent the wrong), but the extent to which these lessen one's responsibility depends on (d) the seriousness of the wrong or the injury: The greater the seriousness, the less the first three factors mitigate.

Before leaving this topic, we should note that critics have contested whether all of the mitigating factors really affect a person's responsibility. Some have claimed that evil may never be done no matter what personal pressures are exerted on a person.[68] Other critics have claimed that I am as responsible when I refrain from stopping a wrong as I am when I perform the wrong myself because passively *allowing* something to happen is morally no different from actively *causing* it to happen.[69] If these critics are correct, then mere passive involvement in something does not mitigate moral responsibility. Although neither of these criticisms seems to be correct, the reader should make up his or her own mind on the matter. Discussing all the issues the criticisms raise would take us too far afield.

Corporate Responsibility

Within the modern corporation, responsibility for a corporate act is often distributed among a number of cooperating parties. Corporate acts normally are brought about by several actions or omissions of many different people all cooperating together so that their linked actions and omissions jointly produce the corporate act. For example, one team of managers designs a car, another team tests it, and a third team builds it; one person orders, advises, or encourages something and others act on these orders, advice, or encouragement; one group knowingly defrauds buyers and another group knowingly but silently enjoys the resulting profits; one person contributes the means and another person accomplishes the act; one group does the wrong and another group conceals it. The variations on cooperation are endless.

Who is morally responsible for such jointly produced acts? The traditional view is that those who knowingly and freely did what was necessary to produce the corporate act are each morally responsible.[70] On this view, situations in which a person needs the actions of others to bring about a wrongful corporate act are no different in principle from situations in which a person needs certain external circumstances to commit a wrong. For example, if I want to shoot an innocent person, I must rely on my gun going off (an external circumstance). If I want to defraud the stockholders of a corporation, I must rely on others to do their part in the fraud. In both cases, I can bring about the wrongful injury only by relying on something or someone other than myself. In both cases, if I am knowingly and freely trying to bring about the fraud, then I am equally morally responsible for the wrongful injury. Bringing about a wrongful act with the help of others, then, does not differ in a morally significant way from deliberately bringing about a wrongful act with the help of inanimate instruments: The person is fully responsible for the wrong or the injury even if this responsibility is shared with others. If, for example, as a member of the board of directors of a corporation, with full knowledge and complete freedom, I act on insider information to vote for some stock options that will benefit me but unfairly injure the other stockholders, then I am morally responsible for the wrongful corporate act of the board even if I share this responsibility with other members of the board. By my vote, I was trying to bring about the illegal corporate act and I did so knowingly and freely.

Critics of this traditional view of the individual's responsibility for corporate acts have claimed that when an organized group such as a corporation acts together, their corporate act may be described as the act of the group and, consequently, the corporate group and not the individuals who make up the group must be held responsible for the act.[71] For example, we normally credit the manufacture of a defective car to the corporation that made it and not to the individual engineers involved in its manufacture. The law typically attributes the acts of a corporation's managers to the corporation (so long as the managers act within their authority) and not to the managers as individuals. Traditionalists, however, can reply that, although we sometimes attribute acts to corporate groups, this linguistic and legal fact does not change the moral reality behind all such corporate acts: Individuals had to carry out the particular actions that brought about the corporate act. Because individuals are morally responsible for the known and intended consequences of their free actions, any individual who knowingly and freely joins his actions together with those of others, intending thereby to bring about a certain corporate act, will be morally responsible for that act.[72]

More often than not, however, employees of large corporations cannot be said to have "knowingly and freely joined their actions together" to bring about a corporate act or to pursue a corporate objective. Employees of large-scale organizations follow bureaucratic rules that link their activities together to achieve corporate outcomes of which the employee may not even be aware. The engineers in one department may build a component with certain weaknesses, for example, not knowing that another department plans to use that component in a product that these weaknesses will render dangerous. Employees may feel pressured to conform to company rules with whose corporate outcomes they may not agree, but which they feel they are not in a position to change. A worker on an assembly line, for example, may feel there is no choice but to stay at the job even though knowing that the cars he or she built with the help of others are dangerous. Obviously, then, a person working within the bureaucratic structure of a large organization is not necessarily morally responsible for every corporate act he or she helps to bring about. If I am working as a secretary, clerk, or janitor in a corporation, or if I become a stockholder in a corporation, then my actions may help the officers of the corporation commit a fraud. If I know nothing about the fraud or if I am in no way able to prevent it (e.g., by reporting it), then I am not morally responsible for the fraud. Here, as elsewhere, the excusing factors of ignorance and inability, which are endemic to large-scale bureaucratic corporate organizations, will completely eliminate a person's moral responsibility.

Moreover, depending on the seriousness of the act, the mitigating factors of uncertainty, difficulty, and minimal involvement can also diminish a person's moral responsibility for a corporate act. Sometimes employees in a corporation go along with a wrongful corporate act although they know (to some extent) that it is wrong and they have the ability (to some extent) to withdraw their cooperation: They unwillingly go along because of pressures placed on them. Traditional moralists have argued that a person's responsibility for unwillingly cooperating with others in a wrongful act should be determined by weighing the various factors that *mitigate* individual responsibility. That is, one must weigh the seriousness of the wrongful act against the uncertainty, difficulty, and degree of involvement that were present (but again, those who have a moral duty to prevent a wrong cannot plead that their omission constitutes "minimal involvement"). The more seriously wrong a corporate act is, the less my responsibility is mitigated by uncertainty, pressures, and minimal involvement.

Subordinates' Responsibility

In a corporation, employees often act on the basis of their superiors orders. Corporations usually have a hierarchical structure of authority in which orders and directives pass from those higher in the structure to a variety of agents at lower levels. A vice president tells several middle managers that they must reach certain production goals and the middle managers try to attain them. A plant manager tells the foremen to close down a certain line and the foremen do it. An engineer tells a clerk to write up a certain report and the clerk does it. Who is morally responsible when a superior orders a subordinate to carry out an act that both of them know is wrong?

People sometimes suggest that when a subordinate acts on the orders of a legitimate superior, the subordinate is absolved of all responsibility for that act: Only the superior is morally responsible for the wrongful act even though the subordinate was the agent who carried it out. Several years ago, for example, the managers of a national semiconductor plant allegedly ordered their employees to write a government report that falsely stated that certain computer components sold to the government had been tested for defects.[73] Some employees objected, but when the managers allegedly insisted, the employees complied with their orders. When the falsified reports were discovered, the managers argued that only the corporation as a whole should be held responsible for the falsified reports. No individual employee should be held morally responsible, they argued, because each employee was simply an agent who was following orders.

It is clearly mistaken, however, to think that an employee who freely and knowingly does something wrong is absolved of all responsibility when he or she is "following orders." Moral responsibility requires merely that one act freely and knowingly, and it is irrelevant that one's wrongful act is that of freely and knowingly choosing to follow an order. For example, if I am ordered by my superior to murder a competitor and I do so, I can hardly later claim that I am totally innocent because I was merely "following orders." The fact that my superior ordered me to perform what I knew was an immoral act in no way alters the fact that in performing that act I knew what I was doing and I freely chose to do it anyway and so I am morally responsible for it. As we noted when discussing the "loyal agent's argument," there are limits to an employee's obligation to obey his or her superior: An employee has no obligation to obey an order to do what is immoral. Of course, a superior can put significant economic pressures on an employee and such pressures can mitigate the employee's responsibility but they do not totally eliminate it.

Thus, when a superior orders an employee to carry out an act that both of them know is wrong, the employee is morally responsible for that act if he or she carries it out. Is the superior also morally responsible? Obviously, the superior is also morally responsible because in ordering the employee, the superior is knowingly and freely bringing about the wrongful act through the instrumentality of the employee. The fact that a superior uses a human being to bring about the wrongful act does not change the fact that the superior brought it about.

Questions for Review and Discussion

1. Define the following concepts: ethics, business ethics, preconventional morality, conventional morality, autonomous morality, moral reasoning, consistency requirement, ethical relativism, moral responsibility.

2. "Ethics has no place in business." Discuss this statement.
3. In your judgment, did the managers of Merck have a moral obligation to spend the money needed to develop the drug for river blindness? Can you state the general moral standard or standards on which you base your judgment? Are you willing to apply the "consistency requirement" to your moral standard or standards?
4. "Kohlberg's views on moral development show that the more morally mature a person becomes, the more likely it is that the person will obey the moral norms of his or her society." Discuss this statement.

Web Resources

Readers who would like to research the general topic of business ethics on the Internet might want to begin by accessing the following websites:

The website of Santa Clara University's Markkula Center for Applied Ethics (http://www.scu.edu/SCU/Centers/Ethics) has outstanding articles and other content plus hundreds of annotated links to other web resources on ethics; Depaul University's Ethics Institute provides links to several ethics resources on the Internet plus its own collection of materials (http://condor.depaul.edu/ethics); the Essential Organization provides links to numerous organizations and data resources, both radical and conservative, that deal with corporate social responsibility (http://essential.org); Wall Street Research Net has links and data on publicly traded companies and the economy (http://www.wsrn.com); the Stern School of Business at New York University provides searchable access to all SEC company filings (http://edgar.stern.nyu.edu/edgar.html); Resources for Activists has info on companies (http://violet.berkeley.edu/~orouke/LINKS.htm), as does Corporate Watch (http://www.corpwatch.org), World Watch (http://www.worldwatch.org), and Ethical Business (http://www.arq.co.uk/ethicalbusiness).

Notes

1. *Wall Street Journal*, "Merck to Donate Drug for River Blindness," October 22, 1987, p. 42.
2. Standard & Poor's Corporation, *Standard & Poor's Industry Surveys*, vol. 1, April 1979, pp. H13–H16.
3. *Wall Street Journal*, "Merck to Donate Drug for River Blindness," October 22, 1987, p. 42.
4. David Bollier, "Merck & Company" (The Business Enterprise Trust: Stanford, CA, 1991), p. 5.
5. Bollier, *ibid.*, p. 16.
6. Thomas J. Peters and Robert H. Waterman, Jr., for example, made this point in their popular book, *In Search of Excellence* (New York: Harper and Row, 1982).

7. Raymond Baumhart, *An Honest Profit: What Businessmen Say About Ethics in Business* (New York: Holt, Rinehart and Winston, 1968), pp. 11–12; for a later update of the Baumhart study, see Steven N. Brenner and Earl A. Molander, "Is the Ethics of Business Changing?" *Harvard Business Review*, 55, no. 1 (January/February 1977): 57–71.

8. *Ibid.*, p. 13.

9. See, for example, James Rachels' criticisms of religious authority and feeling as the basis of ethical reasoning in *The Elements of Moral Philosophy* (New York: McGraw-Hill, Inc., 1986), pp. 25–38 and 39–52; Craig C. Lundberg criticizes the golden rule in "The Golden Rule and Business Management: Quo Vadis?" *Journal of Economics and Business* 20 (January 1968): 36–40.

10. "Ethic," *Webster's Third New International Dictionary*, Unabridged (Springfield, MA: Merriam-Webster Inc., 1986), p. 780. Similar definitions can be found in any recent dictionary.

11. Kermit Vandivier, "Why Should My Conscience Bother Me?" in *In the Name of Profit* (Garden City, NY: Doubleday & Co., Inc., 1972), p. 8.

12. U.S. Congress, *Air Force A-7D Brake Problem: Hearing before the Subcommittee on Economy in Government of the Joint Economic Committee, 91st Congress, 1st session*, 13 August 1969, p. 2.

13. *Ibid.*, p. 5.

14. Vandivier, "Why Should My Conscience Bother Me?" p. 4.

15. U.S. Congress, *Air Force A-7D Brake Problem*, pp. 5 and 6.

16. H. L. A. Hart, *The Concept of Law* (London: Oxford University Press, 1961), pp. 84–85. See also Charles Fried, *An Anatomy of Values* (Cambridge: Harvard University Press, 1970), pp. 91–142.

17. The point is made in Michael Scriven, *Primary Philosophy* (New York: McGraw-Hill Book Company, 1966), pp. 232–33.

18. See, for example, Rachels, *Elements of Moral Philosophy*, pp. 9–10.

19. Baier, *Moral Point of View* (New York: Random House, 1965), p. 107.

20. The point is made in Peter Singer, *Practical Ethics*, 2nd ed. (New York: Cambridge University Press, 1993), pp. 10–11.

21. Richard B. Brandt, *A Theory of the Good and the Right* (New York: Oxford University Press, 1979), pp. 166–69.

22. See www.hoovers.com for these and more recent figures.

23. "Corporate Criminals or Criminal Corporations?" *Wall Street Journal*, 19 June 1985; "Who Pays for Executive Sins?" *New York Times*, 4 March 1984.

24. For the first view, see Peter A. French, *Collective and Corporate Responsibility* (New York: Columbia University Press, 1984); Kenneth E. Goodpaster and John B. Matthews, Jr., "Can a Corporation Have a Conscience?" *Harvard Business Review*, 60 (1982): 132–41; Thomas Donaldson, "Moral Agency and Corporations," *Philosophy in Context*, 10 (1980): 51–70; David T. Ozar, "The Moral Responsibility of Corporations," in *Ethical Issues in Business*, Thomas Donaldson and Patricia Werhane, eds. (Englewood Cliffs, NJ: Prentice-Hall, 1979), pp. 294–300. For the second, see John Ladd, "Morality and the Ideal of Rationality in Formal Organizations," *The Monist*, 54, no. 4 (1970): 488–516, and "Corporate Mythology and Individual Responsibility," *The International Journal of Applied Philosophy*, 2, no. 1 (Spring 1984): 1–21; Patricia H. Werhane, "Formal

Organizations, Economic Freedom and Moral Agency," *Journal of Value Inquiry*, 14 (1980): 43–50. The author's own views are more fully developed in Manuel Velasquez, "Why Corporations Are Not Morally Responsible for Anything They Do," *Business & Professional Ethics Journal*, 2, no. 3 (Spring 1983): 1–18; also similar to the author's views are those in Michael Keeley, "Organizations as Non-Persons," *Journal of Value Inquiry*, 15 (1981): 149–55.

25. John R. Searle, *The Construction of Social Reality* (New York: Oxford Press, 1995). Searle convincingly argues that the development of human social institutions depends on three "primitive" elements: collective intentionality (the ability humans have to act and think in cooperation with others), the assignment of function (the ability humans have to give objects functions that are not instrinsic properties of the object), and constitutive rules (social conventions of the form "X counts as Y in circumstances C," which do not merely regulate antecedently existing activities, but constitute that activity, such as playing chess, which is an activity created by following the rules of chess). When combined, these three elements make possible a "status function," which is a function that cannot be performed in virtue of physical or natural properties, but instead requires the collective acceptance or recognition of the status. In Claims I and II, I am implicitly appealing to Searle's theory and am claiming that the concept of a corporate organization and a corporate act are status functions that rely on the collective acceptance of a system of constitutive rules that assign certain functions to individuals in certain circumstances and in certain relations.

26. The arguments for and against ethical relativism are surveyed in Manuel Velasquez, "Ethical Relativism and the International Business Manager," *Studies in Economic Ethics and Philosophy* (Berlin: Springer-Verlag, 1997).

27. James Rachels, "Can Ethics Provide Answers," *The Hastings Center Report*, vol. 10, no. 3 (June 1980): pp. 33–39; a more recent presentation of this argument can be found in James Rachels, *The Elements of Moral Philosophy* (New York: Random House, 1986).

28. See Donald R. C. Reed, *Following Kohlberg: Liberalism and the Practice of Democratic Community* (Notre Dame, Indiana: University of Notre Dame Press, 1997), which provides a useful summary and critical analysis of Kohlberg's theory, how that theory developed over the years, and the kinds of criticisms to which it has been subjected.

29. This summary is based on Lawrence Kohlberg, "Moral Stages and Moralization: The Cognitive-Developmental Approach," in Thomas Lickona, ed., *Moral Development and Behavior: Theory, Research, and Social Issues* (New York: Holt, Rinehart and Winston, 1976), pp. 31–53; other papers collected in Lickona's book survey the literature both in support of and critical of Kohlberg. For a more recent overview of the research and literature on Kohlberg and his relevance to teaching, see Edward J. Conry and Donald R. Nelson, "Business Law and Moral Growth," *American Business Law Journal*, vol. 27, no. 1 (Spring 1989): pp. 1–39. Kohlberg's work was built on the theories of Piaget; see Jean Piaget, *The Moral Judgment of the Child*, Marjorie Grabain, trans. (New York: The Free Press, 1965).

30. See Reed, *ibid.*, for a comprehensive overview of the criticisms that have been lodged against Kohlberg's theory and research.

31. See Carol Gilligan, *In a Different Voice: Psychological Theory and Women's Development* (Cambridge, MA: Harvard University Press, 1982).

32. For reviews of the literature surrounding Kohlberg and the Gilligan critique, see Norman Sprinthall and Richard Sprinthall, *Educational Psychology*, 4th ed. (New York: Random House, 1987), pp. 157–77; and Nancy Eisenberg, Richard Fabes, and Cindy Shea, "Gender Differences in Empathy and Prosocial Moral Reasoning: Empirical Investigations," in Mary M. Brabeck, *Who Cares? Theory, Research, and Educational Implications of the Ethic of Care* (New York: Praeger, 1989).

33. Among the studies that have failed to find significant gender differences in moral reasoning are Robbin Derry, "Moral Reasoning in Work Related Conflicts," in *Research in Corporate Social Performance and Policy*, William Frederick, ed., vol. 9 (Greenwich, CT: JAI, 1987): pp. 25–49; Freedman, Robinson, and Freedman, "Sex Differences in Moral Judgment? A Test of Gilligan's Theory," *Psychology of Women Quarterly*, vol. 37 (1987); for some recent studies that explore the two different perspectives, see Eva Feder Kittay and Diana T. Meyers, eds., *Women and Moral Theory* (Totowa, NJ: Rowman and Littlefield, 1987). An attempt to work out an ethic of care is Nell Noddings, *Caring: A Feminine Approach to Ethics and Moral Education* (Berkeley, CA: University of California Press, 1984).

34. Edward J. Stevens, *Making Moral Decisions* (New York: Paulist Press, 1969), pp. 123–25.

35. For a fuller discussion of this approach, see Stephen Toulmin, Richard Rieke, and Allan Janik, *An Introduction to Reasoning* (New York: Macmillan Inc., 1979), pp. 309–37.

36. See Richard M. Hare, *Freedom and Reason* (New York: Oxford University Press, 1965), pp. 30–50, 86–111.

37. The difficulties are discussed in John R. Searle, *Speech Acts* (New York: Cambridge University Press, 1969), pp. 182–88.

38. An excellent and compact account of these features may be found in Lawrence Habermehl "The Susceptibility of Moral Claims to Reasoned Assessment," in *Morality in the Modern World*, Lawrence Habermehl, ed. (Belmont, CA: Dickenson Publishing Co., Inc., 1976), pp. 18–32.

39. See Marcus G. Singer, *Generalization in Ethics* (New York: Alfred A. Knopf, Inc., 1961), p. 5; Hare, *Freedom and Reason*, p. 15.

40. See, for example, the long discussion of these issues in LaRue Tone Hosmer, *The Ethics of Management*, 2nd ed. (Homewood, IL: Richard D. Irwin, Inc., 1991), pp. 34–55.

41. For these and other criticisms, see Alan H. Goldman, "Business Ethics: Profits, Utilities, and Moral Rights," *Philosophy and Public Affairs*, 9, no. 3 (Spring 1980): 260–86.

42. Alex C. Michales, *A Pragmatic Approach to Business Ethics* (Thousand Oaks, CA: Sage Publications, 1995), pp. 44–53. See also Milton Friedman, "The Social Responsibility of Business Is to Increase Its Profits," *New York Times Magazine*, 13 (September 1970).

43. See Phillip I. Blumberg, "Corporate Responsibility and the Employee's Duty of Loyalty and Obedience: A Preliminary Inquiry," in *The Corporate Dilemma: Traditional Values Versus Contemporary Problems*, Dow Votaw and S. Prakash Sethi, eds. (Englewood Cliffs, NJ: Prentice Hall, 1973), pp. 82–113.

44. Quoted in *Ibid.*, p. 86.

45. "The Complex Case of the *U.S. vs. Southland*," *Business Week*, 21 November 1983.

46. See John Finnis, *Natural Law and Natural Rights* (Oxford: Clarendon Press, 1980), pp. 295–350; John Rawls, *A Theory of Justice* (Cambridge, MA: Harvard University Press, 1971), pp. 108–14; Alan Donagan, *The Theory of Morality* (Chicago: University of Chicago Press, 1977), pp. 108–11.

47. For a similar version of this argument, see Alex C. Michalos, *A Pragmatic Approach to Business Ethics*, pp. 54–57.

48. These are some of the more well-known companies cited over several years in the Business Ethics Awards list. See *Business Ethics*, November/December 1995, pp. 30–31.

49. Jean B. McGuire, Alison Sundgren, and Thomas Schneewels, "Corporate Social Responsibility and Firm Financial Performance," *Academy of Management Journal*, December 1988, p. 869.

50. For a review of these studies and a new study that found no correlation one way or another, see Kenneth E. Alpperle, Archie B. Carroll, and John D. Hatfield, "An Empirical Examination of the Relationship Between Corporate Social Responsibility and Profitability," *Academy of Management Journal*, June 1985, pp. 460–61.

51. "Responsible Investing in a Changing World," *Business Ethics*, November/December, 1995, p. 48.

52. See Manuel Velasquez,"Why Ethics Matters: A Defense of Ethics in Business Organizations," *Business Ethics Quarterly*, vol. 6, no. 2 (April 1996): pp. 201–22.

53. Anatol Rapaport and A. Chammah, *Prisoner's Dilemma* (Ann Arbor: University of Michigan Press, 1965).

54. For a nontechnical and fascinating overview of the history and significance of prisoner's dilemma research, see William Poundstone, *Prisoner's Dilemma* (New York: Anchor Books Doubleday, 1992).

55. Through mutual retaliation, the parties can enforce cooperation, and a stable pattern of mutual cooperation can emerge. This phenomenon has been extensively studied in contemporary game theory. Robert Axelrod, in particular, has shown that in a series of repeated prisoner's dilemma encounters, the best strategy—called TIT FOR TAT—is for a party to cooperate, but to retaliate with noncooperation each time the other party fails to cooperate. See Robert Axelrod, *The Evolution of Cooperation* (New York: Basic Books, Inc., 1984).

56. See, for example, Daniel R. Gilbert, Jr., "The Prisoner's Dilemma and the Prisoners of the Prisoner's Dilemma," *Business Ethics Quarterly*, vol. 6, no. 2 (April 1996), 165–78.

57. This research is summarized and reviewed in Velasquez, *ibid.*

58. J. Brockner, T. Tyler, and R. Schneider, "The higher they are, the harder they fall: The effect of prior commitment and procedural injustice on subsequent commitment to social institutions," paper presented at the annual academy of management meeting, Miami Beach, FL (1991, August).

59. In addition to Velasquez, *ibid.*, which reviews the literature and research in this area, consult Blair H. Sheppard, Roy J. Lewicki, and John W. Minton, *Organizational Justice* (New York: Lexington Books, 1992), pp. 101–103; on the higher wages workers demand to work for a firm they see as socially responsible in comparison to one they see as socially irresponsible, see R. H. Frank, "Can Socially Responsible Firms Survive in a Competitive Environment?" in D. M. Messick and

A. E. Tenbrunsel, eds., *Research on Negotiations in Organizations* (Greenwich, CT: JAI Press, 1997).

60. R. Folger and M. A. Konovsky, "Effects of procedural and distributive justice on reactions to pay raise decisions," *Academy of Management Journal*, 32 (1989): 115–30; S. Alexander and M. Ruderman, "The Role of Procedural and Distributive Justice in Organizational Behavior," *Social Justice Research*, vol. 1 (1987): pp. 177–98; see also Tyler, T. R., "Justice and Leadership Endorsement," in R. R. Lau and D. O. Sears, eds., *Political Cognition* (Hillsdale, NJ: Erlbaum, 1986), pp. 257–78.

61. T. R. Tyler and E. A. Lind, "A relational model of authority in groups," in M. Zanna, ed., *Advances in Experimental Social Psychology*, vol. 25 (New York: Academic Press, 1992); J. Greenberg, "Cultivating an Image of Justice: Looking Fair on the Job," *Academy of Management Executive*, vol. 2 (1988), pp. 155–58; Organ, D. W., *Organizational Citizenship Behavior: The Good Soldier Syndrome* (Lexington, MA: Lexington Books, 1988).

62. A person can also be morally responsible for good acts. But because we are concerned with determining when a person is excused from doing wrong, we discuss moral responsibility only as it relates to wrongdoing and to being excused therefrom.

63. "Job Safety Becomes a Murder Issue," *Business Week*, 6 August 1984; "3 Executives Convicted of Murder for Unsafe Workplace Conditions," *New York Times*, 15 June 1985; "Working Them to Death," *Time*, 15 July 1985; "Murder Case a Corporate Landmark," part I, *Los Angeles Times*, 15 September 1985; "Trial Makes History," part II, *Los Angeles Times*, 16 September 1985. Their conviction was later overturned.

64. Jim Jubak, "They Are the First," *Environmental Action* (February 1983); Jeff Coplon, "Left in the Dust," *Voice*, 1 March 1983; George Miller, "The Asbestos Cover-Up," *Congressional Record*, 17 May 1979.

65. This agreement goes back to Aristotle, *Nicomachean Ethics*, Martin Ostwald, trans. (New York: The Bobbs-Merrill Company, 1962), bk. III, ch. 1. Recent discussions of moral responsibility have questioned this agreement, but this recent discussion raises issues that are too complex to examine here. Readers interested in the issue may want to consult the essays collected in John Martin Fischer and Mark Ravizza, eds., *Perspectives on Moral Responsibility* (Ithaca, NY: Cornell University Press, 1993), especially the editors' "Introduction" and their essay, "Responsibility for Consequences."

66. See the discussion of this in Hare, *Freedom and Reason*, pp. 50–60.

67. "Overdriven Execs: Some Middle Managers Cut Corners to Achieve High Corporate Goals," *Wall Street Journal*, 8 November 1979.

68. Alan Donagan, *The Theory of Morality* (Chicago: University of Chicago Press, 1977), pp. 154–57, 206–207.

69. Singer, *Practical Ethics*, p. 152.

70. See W. L. LaCroix, *Principles for Ethics in Business* (Washington, DC: University Press of America, 1976), pp. 106–7; Thomas M. Garrett, *Business Ethics*, 2nd ed. (Englewood Cliffs, NJ: Prentice Hall, 1986), pp. 12–13; Henry J. Wirtenberger, S. J., *Morality and Business* (Chicago: Loyola University Press, 1962), pp. 109–14; Herbert Jone, *Moral Theology*, Urban Adelman, trans. (Westminster, MD: The Newman Press, 1961), p. 236.

71. Peter A. French, "Corporate Moral Agency," in Tom L. Beauchamp and Norman E. Bowie, eds. *Ethical Theory and Business* (Englewood Cliffs, NJ: Prentice Hall, 1979), pp. 175–86; see also Christopher D. Stone, *Where the Law Ends* (New York: Harper & Row, Publishers, Inc., 1975), pp. 58–69, for the legal basis of this view.

72. See Manuel Velasquez, "Why Corporations Are Not Morally Responsible for Anything They Do," *Business & Professional Ethics Journal*, 2, no. 3 (Spring 1983): pp. 1–18; see also the two commentaries on this article appearing in the same journal by Kenneth E. Goodpaster, *ibid.*, 2, no. 4, pp. 100–103; and Thomas A. Klein, *ibid.*, 3, no. 2, pp. 70–71.

73. David Sylvester, "National Semi May Lose Defense Jobs," *San Jose Mercury News*, 31 May 1984.

Cases for Discussion

Napster's Revolution[1]

Eighteen-year-old Shawn "Napster" Fanning, then a freshman at Northeastern University, dropped out of school and founded Napster Inc. (website was at www.napster.com) in San Mateo, California in May 1999. Two months earlier, working in his college dorm room, he had developed both a website that let users locate other users who were willing to share whatever music files they had in MP3 format on the hard drives of their computers and a software program (called "Napster") that let users copy these music files from each other over the Internet. When an early free version of the program he posted on Download.com received more than 300,000 hits and was named "Download of the Week," he decided to devote himself full time to developing his program and website. The final version of his program was officially released in August 1999, and in May 2000, with more than 10 million people—most of them students on college campuses where Napster was especially popular—signed up at its website, Shawn's company received $15 million of start-up funds from venture capital firms in California's "Silicon Valley."

Fanning grew up in Brockton, Massauchettes, the son of a nurse's aid and the stepson of a truck driver, in a family of four half-brothers and half-sisters. He got the nickname "Napster" during a basketball game when a player commented on his closely cropped sweaty head of hair. Fanning had taught himself programming and had held several summer programming jobs.

The company Shawn helped establish gave the Napster program away for free and charged users nothing to use its website to post the URL addresses where personal copies of music could be downloaded. Nevertheless, a month later, Shawn found himself embroiled in a legal and ethical controversy when two record labels, two musicians (Metallica and Dr. Dre), and two industry trade groups of music companies (the National Music Publishers Association and the Recording Industry Association of America) filed suits against his young company claiming that Napster's software was enabling others to make and distribute copies of copyrighted music that the musicians and companies owned.

On June 12, the two industry trade groups filed preliminary injunctions against the company demanding that it remove all the songs owned by their member companies from Napster's song directories. According to the two groups, a survey of 2555 college students showed a correlation between Napster use and decreased CD purchases. College students were outraged, especially fans of Metallica and Dr. Dre. Supporters of Napster argued that Napster allowed people to hear music that they then went out and purchased, so Napster actually helped the music companies. Music sales had increased by over $500 million a year since Napster had started to operate, but the music companies claimed that this was a result of a booming economy. Supporters of Napster also argued that individuals had a moral and legal right to lend other individuals a copy of the music on the CDs that they had purchased. After all, they argued, the law explicitly stated that an individual could make a copy of copyrighted music he or she had purchased to hear the music on another player. Moreover, according to Fanning, Napster was not doing anything illegal, and the company was not responsible if other people used its software and website to copy music in violation of copyright law anymore than a car company was responsible when its autos were used by thieves to rob banks. Much of the music that was downloaded using Napster, they claimed, was in the public domain (i.e., not legally owned by anyone) and was being legally copied. The music companies countered that an individual had no right to give multiple copies of their music to others even if the individual had paid for the original CD. If everyone was allowed to copy music without paying for it, they charged, eventually the music companies would stop producing music and musicians would stop creating it. Other musicians claimed, however, that Napster and the Web gave them a way to put their music before millions of potential fans without having to beg the music companies to sponser them.

In March 2000, the band Metallica hired consultant PDNet to electronically "evesdrop" on users who assumed they were anonymously accessing Napster's website. The following week the band's lawyers handed Napster a list with the names of 300,000 people that Metallica claimed had violated its copyrights using Napster's service and that Metallica now wanted removed from Napster's services. Fanning complied with the demand of Metallica, whose drummer, Lars Ulrich, was one of his musical heros. "If they want to steal our music," said Ulrich, "why don't they just go down to Tower Records and grab them off the shelves?" Many young people protested that the bands should not be alienating their own fans in this way. One fan posted a note on an MP3 chat room: "Give me a break! I have been dropping 16 bucks an album for Metallica's music since I was a teenager. They made a fortune off us and now they accuse us of stealing from them. What nerve!" Howard King, a Los Angeles lawyer for Metallica and Dr. Dre, stated that "I don't know Shawn Fanning but he seems to be a pretty good kid who came up with a sensational program. But this sensational program has allowed people to take music without paying. . . . Shawn probably had no idea of the legal ramifications of what he created. I'm sure the thought never crossed his mind."

In August 2000, a federal judge in San Francisco, Marilyn Patel, responded to the suit against Napster. Judge Patel called Shawn's company a "monster" and charged that the only purpose of Napster was to copy pirated music without paying for it. The judge ordered Napster to remove all URLs from its website that referenced material that was copyrighted.

Judge Patel's ruling would have shut down the company's website immediately. But a few days later, an appeals court reversed Judge Patel and allowed the company to continue operating. The reprieve was only temporary. On Monday Febrary 12, 2001, the Ninth Circuit Court of Appeals in San Francisco affirmed Judge Patel's ruling. The company attempted to circumvent the ruling by negotiating agreements with the music companies that would pay them certain annual fees in return for withdrawing the suit.

Napster was not the only software that allowed individuals to swap files from one personal computer to another over the Internet. The software program named "Gnutella" let individuals swap any kind of files—music, text, or visuals—over the Internet, but Gnutella did not operate a centralized index like the website that Napster had established. Observers predicted that if Napster was put out of business, numerous underground websites would be created providing the kind of listing service that the company had earlier provided on its website. Already a website named zeropaid.com provided free copies of Gnutella and many other Napster clones that users could download and use to share digital music files with each other. Unlike Napster, these software products did not require a central website to connect users to each other, making it impossible for music companies to find and target a single entity whom they could sue. Many observers predicted that Napster was only the beginning of an upheaval that would revolutionize the music industry, forcing music companies to lower their prices, make their music easily available on the Internet, and completely change their business models.

Questions

1. What are the legal issues involved in this case, and what are the moral issues? How are the two different kinds of issues different from each other, and how are they related to each other? Identify and distinguish the "systemic, corporate, and individual issues" involved in this case.

2. In your judgment, was it morally wrong for Shawn Fanning to develop and release his technology to the world given its possible consequences? Was it morally wrong for an individual to use Napster's website and software to copy for free the copyrighted music on another person's hard drive? If you believe it was wrong, then explain exactly why it was wrong. If you believe it was not morally wrong, then how would you defend your views against the claim that such copying is stealing? Assume that it was not illegal for an individual to copy music using Napster. Would there be anything immoral with doing so? Explain.
3. Assume that it is morally wrong for a person to use Napster's website and software to make a copy of copyrighted music. Who, then, would be morally responsible for this person's wrongdoing? Would only the person himself be morally responsible? Was Napster, the company, morally responsible? Was Shawn Fanning morally responsible? Was any employee of Napster, the company, morally responsible? Was the operator of the server or that portion of the Internet that the person used morally responsible? What if the person did not know that the music was copyrighted or did not think that it was illegal to copy copyrighted music?
4. Do the music companies share any of the moral responsibility for what has happened? How do you think technology like Napster is likely to change the music industry? In your judgment, are these changes ethically good or ethically bad?

Notes

1. This Napster case is entirely drawn from the following sources: Stephen Pizzo, "The Napster That Ate Hollywood," *Metro Santa Cruz*, July 12–19, 2000, pp. 5–9; Lynda Gorov, "You Say You Want a Revolution?" *San Jose Mercury News*, Sunday July 2, 2000, pp. 1F-2F; Brad Stone, "The Day the Music (Almost) Died," *Newsweek* (August 7, 2000), pp. 60–62.

H. B. Fuller and the Street Children of Central America

The article was one of many published on street children in Latin American cities during the early 1990s. The issue on which it focused was one that children's advocates had brought to the attention of H. B. Fuller Company repeatedly over many years. The article read:

> On a sidewalk in San Pedro Sula, Honduras . . . a lanky, dark-haired boy [is] sitting with arms curled around his folded legs, staring at the passing traffic. The boy, a nineteen-year-old named Marvin, has been sniffing glue for ten years. Once the leader of a gang of street kids, he now has slurred speech and vacant eyes. A year ago, Marvin began to lose feeling in his legs. Now he can no longer walk. He slides on his butt, spiderlike, through gutters, across streets, and along the sidewalks. Still loyal to their chief, the younger kids in his gang bring Marvin food,

carry him to a news stand to spend the night, and make sure he has enough glue to stay high. . . . Doctors offer no hope that Marvin will ever walk again. Toluene, the solvent in the glue he sniffs, is a neurotoxin known to cause irreparable nerve damage. . . . In Honduras, the drug of choice for children is H. B. Fuller's Resistol, a common shoe-glue made with toluene. Toluene creates the high the children come to crave. . . . Sniffing the glue is so common . . . that the common name for street kids is Resistoleros.[1]

Marvin was not the only casualty of the toluene-based glue. Toluene, a sweet-smelling chemical used as a solvent for the ingredients in adhesives, destroys the thin layers of fat that surround nerves, causing them to die. Occasional inhalation will produce nosebleeds and rashes while habitual use produces numerous disorders including: severe neurological dysfunction, brain atrophy, loss of liver and kidney functions, loss of sight and hearing, leukemia, and muscle atrophy. Prolonged use can result in eventual death. For over a decade, thousands of homeless children throughout Latin America, but most visibly in Guatemala and Honduras, had become addicted to inhaling the glue. Many of them were thought to have died while many more were now severely disabled by blindness, diminished brain functioning, and crippling muscle atrophy.

H. B. Fuller had total revenues of $1.243 billion in 1995, up from $1.097 billion in 1994. Profits had totaled $392 million in 1995 and $354 million in 1994. Founded in 1887, the company was now a global manufacturer of adhesives, sealants, and other specialty chemicals, and had operations in over 40 countries in North America, Europe, Asia, and Latin America. Although 15 percent of its sales revenues came from its Latin American operations, those operations accounted for 27 percent of its profits, indicative of the fact that its Latin American operations were much more lucrative than its operations elsewhere around the world. According to the company, it has profits of about $450,000 a year from glue sales in Central America.[2]

The company's adhesive products are made and distributed in Central America by H. B. Fuller S.A., a subsidiary of Kativo Chemical Industries, which is a wholly owned subsidiary of H. B. Fuller Company of St. Paul, Minnesota. "Resistol" is a brand name that H. B. Fuller puts on over a dozen of the adhesives it manufactures in Latin America including its toluene-based glues. These toluene-based adhesives have qualities that water-based adhesives cannot duplicate: They set very rapidly, they adhere strongly, and they are resistant to water. The glues are widely used throughout Latin America by shoe manufacturers, leather workers, carpenters, furniture makers, and small shoe repair shops.[3]

Both Honduras and Guatemala, two countries where Fuller markets its glue products and the two countries where Resistol abuse is most pronounced, are mired in poverty. In 1993, Honduras had a per capita gross domestic product (GDP) of only $1950 and unemployment of approximately 20 percent. Guatemala was doing slightly better with a per capita GDP of $3000 and an unemployment rate of about 15 percent. More than a third of the population of each country is below poverty. For several years, both countries have had large deficit budgets, forcing them to take on an ever larger debt burden and to sharply curtail all social services. Migration from the countryside into the major cities had exacerbated urban crowding and created large impoverished populations in every large city. In these impoverished, insecure, and stressful conditions, family life often became unstable: Husbands abandoned their wives, and both abandoned the children they were too poor or too sickly to care for. The countless children that roamed city streets begging for handouts, for the most part, had been abandoned by their families, although a good number were runaways from what they felt was an intolerable home life.

For years, H. B. Fuller had been pressured by child advocate groups in Central America and the United States that were concerned about the rising use of the company's glues by homeless children in Latin America. A number of child advocates and social workers argued that Fuller should follow the lead of Testors—a company that makes and markets glues in the United States. Criticized in the late 1960s for marketing glues that American teenagers had started sniffing, the company ran a number of tests and decided that a safe way keep kids from sniffing its glues was by adding minute amounts of mustard-seed oil (allyl isothiocyanate), a common food additive. Inhaling glue containing the mustard-seed additive produced tearing and gagging that discouraged inhalation. Testors reported that the use of mustard-seed oil had virtually eliminated abuse of its glues and that it had never had reports of any kind of injury deriving from the addition of the oil from users nor from employees in its plants.[4]

In response to the urging of Honduran social workers, the legislature of Honduras in March 1989 passed Decree 36–89, which banned importing or manufacturing solvent-based adhesives that did not contain mustard-seed oil. However, the general manager and other executives from the local H. B. Fuller subsidiary lobbied the government to have the law revoked. "Possibly," observers noted, "because it might reduce the glue's effectiveness, possibly because the smell would be irritating to legitimate users."[5] Company officials in Fuller's Honduras subsidiary argued that they had data showing that mustard-seed oil had a short shelf life and that studies on rats in the United States had shown that the substance was potentially carcinogenic. They urged that, instead of requiring additives, the government should attempt to control distribution of the glue by prohibiting its sale to children and should educate street kids on the dangers of inhaling it. In November 1989, a Honduran government commission recommended that the new law be scrapped and that the government should concentrate on controlling distribution of the glue and providing education on the dangers of inhaling glue. Two years later, a journalist investigating the incident reported, however, that "there is no official study" showing a decline in the effectiveness of mustard-seed oil in adhesives as they sat on store shelves and that, far from being carcinogenic, "the Food and Drug Administration lists the additive on its 'Generally Regarded as Safe' list" and it is consumed daily in products such as horseradish and pickles.[6]

Honduran law already prohibited sale of toluene-based products to children, although the law was rarely enforced. To reduce the availability of the glue to children, the company now discontinued selling the glue in small jars. Fuller also began paying for the support of several social workers to work with street children. The company began providing information to distributors warning of the dangers of Resistol addiction.

Children's advocates, however, who had worked with street children for several years did not feel the programs were working. The terrible economic conditions afflicting the country that led parents to abandon their children also made life on the streets a painful, unceasing nightmare for a child from which the only available escape was the cheap intoxication offered by inhaling glue. Casa Alianza, the Latin American wing of Covenant House, an international Catholic charity based in New York, would later release a report on Central American street children stating that, "Living on the edge of survival they are often swept in an undertow of beatings, illegal detention, torture, sexual abuse, rape, and murder."[7] The report detailed numerous cases of children detained and beaten by police for sniffing glue. In one case, the mutilated bodies of four street boys were found in 1990, their eyes were burned out, ears and tongues severed, some had had boiling liquid poured over their bodies, and all were shot in the head, some with bullets that were later traced to a government-issued gun. In such conditions, the lure of the hallucinogenic glue was irresistible. Said one social worker about an abandoned child who habitually sniffed glue, "When he inhales Resistol, he hallucinates about his mother caressing him."[8]

Although criticisms of the company continued, the company argued that the problem did not lie with its glue, but with the "social conditions" that led children to misuse it, particularly the terrible economic conditions afflicting the countries. The company insisted that it was not responsible for the way its glues were being misused and that if it were to remove Resistol from the market, the street children would merely begin to use one of the toluene-based products of the other companies selling glues in the region. The company insisted, in fact, that by continuing to sell its glue in Central America, it was helping to improve the economic conditions that were at the root of the problem. Commenting on its reasons for staying, a company spokesperson stated that, "We believe those little [shoe] businesses need to survive. They provide employment, help relieve the issue of poverty, and we're willing to do whatever we can."[9]

On July 16, 1992, however, the company's board of directors met and voted unanimously to "stop selling . . . Resistol adhesives" in Central America.

According to the company's 1992 annual report: "Faced with the realization that a suitable replacement product would not be available in the near future and that the illegitimate distribution was continuing, the Board of Directors decided that our Central American operations should stop selling those solvent-based Resistol adhesives that were commonly being abused by children."[10]

The company sent press releases announcing its decision to newspapers around the country, and the board's decision was widely publicized and highly praised. However, in September 1993, the company revealed that, although it had stopped selling its glue to retailers, it had continued to sell the glue to industrial customers who were willing to buy it in large tubs and barrels.[11]

The new controls restricting distribution of the product into retail markets, however, did not take it off the streets. Large quantities of the glue still continued to flow into the hands of street children, presumably from the supplies of Fuller's industrial customers.[12]

In 1994, the company decided to change the chemical formula of its glue to make it less attractive to children. The toluene in the glue was replaced with the chemical cyclohexane, which smells less sweet and is less volatile than toluene, although like toluene it too produces an intoxicating high and has similar toxic effects on the body. However, because it does not evaporate as quickly as toluene, it takes much longer for cyclohexane to produce similar concentrations of fumes. The company also announced that it would increase the price of its glue by 30 percent to price it further out of the reach of children. Both of these moves, the company said, would discourage use of its glues among street children. However, Dr. Tim Rohrig, a toxicologist, said that he doubted the formula change had led children to stop sniffing Resistol: "I doubt the kids are that sophisticated that they can differentiate by odor. If it can get them high, then they will use it. . . . They may have to take more sniffs with cyclohexane than they would with toluene but they still can get the desired intoxication."

In 1995, the company issued a statement claiming that, in reality, it "neither manufactured nor sold Resistol." Instead, the company asserted, it was a subsidiary of a subsidiary of the company in Central America that had actually made and sold Resistol, and claims that the company was responsible for the deaths of children "are nothing more than an attempt to hold Fuller liable for acts and omissions of its second-tier Guatemalan subsidiary."[13]

QUESTIONS

1. In your judgment, is H. B. Fuller morally responsible for the addiction of street children to its Resistol products? Do you agree or disagree with the statement that the social conditions in Honduras and Guatemala are ultimately responsible for misuse of H. B. Fuller's products and that neither the product nor the company is to blame?

Do you agree or disagree that a parent company is not responsible for the activities of its subsidiaries? Explain your answers fully.

2. In your judgment, did H. B. Fuller conduct itself in a morally appropriate manner? Explain your answer. Suppose that H. B. Fuller was not a multinational company, but was a domestic company operating only in the United States, and that the events outlined in the case had all occurred in the United States on the streets of an American city. How would this change your moral evaluation of H. B. Fuller's conduct? Explain.

3. What, if anything, should the company have done that it did not do?

Notes

1. Ed. Griffin-Nolan, "Dealing Glue to Third World Children," *The Progressive*, December 1991, p. 26.

2. Diana B. Henriques, "Black Mark for a 'Good Citizen'," *New York Times*, 26 November 1995, section 3, p. 1.

3. Norman Bowie and Stefanie Ann Lenway, "H. B. Fuller in Honduras: Street Children and Substance Abuse," in Thomas Donaldson and Al Gini, eds., *Case Studies in Business Ethics*, 3rd ed. (Englewood Cliffs, NJ: Prentice Hall, 1993), p. 287.

4. Griffin-Nolan, "Dealing Glue," p. 26.

5. Henriques, "Black Mark for a 'Good Citizen'."

6. Griffin-Nolan, "Dealing Glue," p. 27.

7. Paul McEnroe, "Glue Abuse in Latin America Haunts Fuller Co.," *Star Tribune*, 21 April 1996.

8. Griffin-Nolan, "Dealing Glue," p. 28.

9. McEnroe, "Glue Abuse."

10. H. B. Fuller, *Annual Report*, 1992.

11. Diana B. Henriques, "Black Mark for a 'Good Citizen'," *New York Times*, 26 November 1995, section 3, p. 1.

12. McEnroe, "Glue Abuse."

13. McEnroe, "Glue Abuse."

2

Ethical Principles in Business

Introduction

It was the middle of the last century, 1948, when the Whites-only National Party won control of the South African government and passed the first Apartheid legislation. Apartheid laws established the supremacy of Whites, who comprised 20 percent of the population, over Blacks, who made up the other 80 percent. The Apartheid system legalized racial discrimination in all aspects of life. Apartheid deprived the entire Black population of all political and civil rights: They could not vote, could not hold significant political office, could not unionize nor bargain collectively, had no right to freedom of assembly, nor right to habeas corpus. Blacks had to live in racially segregated areas, they received grossly discriminatory wages, they could not intermarry with Whites, could not oversee Whites, had to attend separate and inferior schools, used separate bathrooms, used separate entrances, ate in separate dining rooms, and were prohibited from socializing with Whites. Over the years, as Blacks repeatedly demonstrated against the increasingly brutal regime, the White South African government responded with widespread killings, arrests, and repression. The White government killed hundreds of young Black activists and jailed thousands of others. Nelson Mandela, the charismatic and brave son of a Black tribal chief, was among those imprisoned. Opposition Black political parties were outlawed and their leaders imprisoned. The policies of the cruel Apartheid government remained in place until the early 1990s.

During the 1980s, at the very height of the Apartheid regime, Caltex, an American oil company, operated several oil refineries in South Africa. Jointly owned by Texaco and Standard Oil, Caltex had repeatedly expanded its refinery operations in South Africa. Each expansion gave the South African government greater access to the petroleum it desperately needed. The South African economy relied on oil for 25 percent of its energy needs, and South African law required refineries to set aside some of their oil for the government. In addition, stiff corporate taxes ensured that a high percentage of Caltex annual revenues went to the government.

Many stockholders of Texaco and Standard Oil bitterly opposed allowing Caltex to continue its refinery operations in South Africa. In 1983, 1984, and 1985, they introduced shareholder resolutions requiring Caltex to either break off relations with the South African government or leave South Africa altogether.[1] A leader of the dissident stockholders had earlier stated why Caltex and other American companies should leave South Africa:

> Nonwhites in South Africa are rightless persons in the land of their birth . . . [The black South African] has no rights in "white areas." He cannot vote, cannot own land, and may not have his family with him unless he has government permission. . . . The two major political parties have been banned and hundreds of persons detained for political offenses . . . strikes by Africans are illegal and meaningful collective bargaining is outlawed. . . . By investing in South Africa, American companies inevitably strengthen the status quo of white supremacy. . . . The leasing of a computer, the establishment of a new plant, the selling of supplies to the military all have political overtones. . . . And among the country's white community, the overriding goal of politics is maintenance of white control. In the words of Prime Minister John Vorster . . . "We are building a nation for whites only."[2]

The management of Caltex, however, did not feel that it should stop selling petroleum products to the South African government nor that it should leave South Africa. The company acknowledged that its operations provided a strategic resource for the racist South African government. Nevertheless, the company claimed that its operations ultimately helped Black South Africans, particularly the company's own Black workers toward whom the company had special responsibilities. In an early statement opposing one of the many resolutions that stockholders would repeatedly put forward over the years, Caltex managers made their position clear:

> Texaco believes that continuation of Caltex's operations in South Africa is in the best interests of Caltex's employees of all races in South Africa. . . . In management's opinion, if Caltex were to withdraw from South Africa in an attempt to achieve political changes in that country, as the proposal directs, . . . such withdrawal would endanger prospects for the future of all Caltex employees in South

> Africa regardless of race. We are convinced that the resulting dislocation and hardship would fall most heavily on the nonwhite communities. In this regard, and contrary to the implications of the stockholders' statement, Caltex employment policies include equal pay for equal work and the same level of benefit plans for all employees as well as a continuing and successful program to advance employees to positions of responsibility on the basis of ability, not race.[3]

Caltex managers argued that foreign corporations in South Africa had helped Black incomes rise by more than 150 percent during the 1970s. Moreover, they claimed, American corporations, with their own internal policies of "equal pay for equal work," had helped narrow the gap between Black and White incomes by a significant amount.

Among those who vigorously supported the resolutions asking American companies to leave South Africa was Desmond Tutu, an outspoken Anglican bishop who won the Nobel Peace Prize in 1984. Described as a modest, cheerful man of faith, with a great passion for justice, Tutu advocated nonviolent opposition to Apartheid and led many peaceful protests, marches, and boycotts against the racist regime. Although in constant danger for his life, Tutu courageously called on the world's nations to exert economic pressure on South Africa's White government by threatening to leave and not return until Apartheid was ended. To say that American companies should stay in South Africa because they paid higher wages and provided other economic benefits, Tutu said, was to "attempt to polish my chains and make them more comfortable. I want to cut my chains and cast them away."

The debate over whether Caltex should continue to operate in South Africa was a moral debate. The debate was not about what the law of South Africa required: The requirements of the law were quite clear. Instead, the debate centered on whether these laws were morally appropriate and whether companies should operate in a nation whose government supported such laws. The arguments on both sides of these issues appealed to moral considerations. They appealed, in fact, to four basic kinds of moral standards: utilitarianism, rights, justice, and caring. At several points, moreover, the debate referred to the moral character of people involved in the issue.

Those who argued that Caltex should leave South Africa, for example, argued that Caltex was actively supporting policies that were unjust because they laid burdens on Blacks that Whites did not have to bear. They also argued that these policies violated Black people's civil and political rights. These arguments were appeals to two distinct kinds of moral principles. Judgments about *justice* are based on moral principles that identify fair ways of distributing benefits and burdens among the members of a society. Judgments about violations of people's *rights* are based on moral principles that indicate the areas in which people's rights to freedom and well-being must be respected.

The arguments of Caltex managers also appealed to moral considerations. Caltex managers argued that if the company stayed in South Africa, the welfare of Blacks and Whites would improve, but if the company left Blacks would suffer greatly. Such arguments were an implicit appeal to what is called a *utilitarian* standard of morality; a moral principle, that is, that claims that something is right to the extent that it diminishes social costs and increases social benefits. Caltex managers also argued that they took special care of their Black workers, and that the company's special responsibility for the well-being of its workers implied that they should not abandon them. Such considerations are closely linked to what is called an *ethic of care*: an ethic that emphasizes caring for the concrete well-being of those near to us.

Finally, embedded in the debate were numerous references to the moral character of various persons and groups. Archbishop Tutu, for example, was characterized as courageous, nonviolent, cheerful, and possessing a passion for justice. The Apartheid government was said to be cruel and brutal. Nelson Mandela was characterized as thoughtful, brave, and charismatic. These kinds of evaluations of the moral character of persons or groups are based on what is called an *ethic of virtue*.

These various kinds of approaches to moral evaluation constitute some of the most important types of ethical standards studied by moral philosophers. As the discussion of business in South Africa demonstrates, these approaches are the common and natural ways by which we discuss and debate the morality of what we are doing. Each approach to moral evaluation employs distinct moral concepts, and each emphasizes aspects of moral behavior that are neglected or at least not emphasized by the others. The purpose of this chapter is to explain each of these approaches to moral judgments. We describe each approach, explain the kinds of concepts and information that each employs, identify their strengths and weaknesses, and explain how these approaches can be used to clarify the moral issues that confront people in business.

2.1 Utilitarianism: Weighing Social Costs and Benefits

We begin by looking at that approach to moral decision making that the Caltex managers took when they claimed that they should remain in South Africa because that course of action would have the most beneficial consequences. This approach is sometimes referred to as a *consequentialist* approach and sometimes as a *utilitarian* approach. To see more clearly what the approach involves, let us look at a situation where this approach was a basic consideration in a business decision that had a dramatic impact on the lives of many people.

In the early 1960s, Ford's position in the automobile market was being heavily eroded by competition from foreign automakers, particularly from

Japanese companies making compact, fuel-efficient cars. Lee Iaccoca, president of Ford at that time, was desperately trying to regain Ford's share of the automobile market. His strategy centered on quickly designing, manufacturing, and marketing a new car to be called the "Pinto."[4] The Pinto was to be a low-cost subcompact that would weigh less than 2000 pounds, cost less than $2000, and be brought to market in 2 years instead of the normal 4. Because the Pinto was a rush project, styling considerations dictated engineering design to a greater degree than usual. In particular, the Pinto's styling required that the gas tank be placed behind the rear axle, where it was more vulnerable to being punctured in case of a rear-end collision. When an early model of the Pinto was crash-tested, it was found that, when struck from the rear at 20 miles per hour or more, the gas tank would sometimes rupture and gas would spray out and into the passenger compartment. In a real accident, stray sparks might explosively ignite the spraying gasoline and possibly burn any trapped occupants.

Ford managers decided, nonetheless, to go ahead with production of the Pinto for several reasons. First, the design met all the applicable legal and government standards then in effect. At the time, government regulations required that a gas tank only remain intact in a rear-end collision of less than 20 miles per hour. Second, Ford managers felt that the car was comparable in safety to several other cars then being produced by other auto companies. Third, according to an internal cost–benefit study that Ford carried out, the costs of modifying the Pinto would not be balanced by the benefits. The study showed that modifying the gas tank of the 12.5 million autos that would eventually be built would cost about $11 a unit for $137 million:

Costs:

$11 × 12.5 million autos = $137 million

However, statistical data showed that the modification would prevent the loss of about 180 burn deaths, 180 serious burn injuries, and 2100 burned vehicles. At the time, the government officially valued a human life at $200,000, insurance companies valued a serious burn injury at $67,000, and the average residual value on subcompacts was $700. So in monetary terms, the modification would have the benefit of preventing losses with a total value of only $49.15 million:

Benefits:

(180 deaths × $200,000) + (180 injuries × $67,000) + (2100 vehicles × $700)
= $49.15 million

Thus, a modification that would ultimately cost customers \$137 million (because the costs of the modification would be added to the price of the car) would result in the prevention of customer losses valued at only \$49.15 million. It was not right, the study argued, to spend \$137 million of society's money to provide a benefit society valued at only \$49.15 million.

Ford subsequently went ahead with production of the unmodified Pinto. It is estimated that in the decade that followed at least 60 persons died in fiery accidents involving Pintos and that at least twice that many suffered severe burns over large areas of their bodies, many requiring years of painful skin grafts. Ford eventually phased out the Pinto model.

The kind of analysis that Ford managers used in their cost–benefit study is a version of what has been traditionally called *utilitarianism. Utilitarianism* is a general term for any view that holds that actions and policies should be evaluated on the basis of the benefits and costs they will impose on society. In any situation, the "right" action or policy is the one that will produce the greatest net benefits or the lowest net costs (when all alternatives have only net costs).

The Ford managers reduced costs and benefits primarily to economic costs and benefits (such as medical costs, loss of income, and damage to buildings) and these were measured in monetary terms. But the benefits of an action may include any desirable goods (pleasures, health, lives, satisfactions, knowledge, happiness) produced by the action, and costs may include any of its undesirable evils (pain, which the Ford study did take into account, sickness, death, dissatisfaction, ignorance, unhappiness). The inclusive term used to refer to the net benefits of any sort produced by an action is *utility*. Hence, the name *utilitarianism* is used for any theory that advocates selection of that action or policy that maximizes benefits (or minimizes costs).

Many business analysts hold that the best way to evaluate the ethical propriety of a business decision—or any other decision—is by relying on utilitarian cost–benefit analysis.[5] The socially responsible course for a business to take is the one that will produce the greatest net benefits for society or impose the lowest net costs. Several government agencies, many legal theorists, numerous moralists, and a variety of business analysts advocate utilitarianism.[6] We begin our discussion of ethical principles by examining this popular approach.

Traditional Utilitarianism

Jeremy Bentham (1748–1832) is generally considered the founder of traditional utilitarianism.[7] Bentham sought an objective basis for making value judgments that would provide a common and publicly acceptable norm for determining social policy and social legislation. The most promising way to reach such an objective ground of agreement, he believed, is by looking at the various policies a legislature could enact and comparing the beneficial and harmful consequences of each. The right course of action from an ethical point of view would be to choose the policy that would produce the greatest amount of utility. Summarized, the utilitarian principle holds that

> *An action is right from an ethical point of view if and only if the sum total of utilities produced by that act is greater than the sum total of utilities produced by any other act the agent could have performed in its place.*

The utilitarian principle assumes that we can somehow measure and add the quantities of benefits produced by an action and subtract from them the measured quantities of harm the action will have, and thereby determine which action produces the greatest total benefits or the lowest total costs. That is, the principle assumes that all the benefits and costs of an action can be measured on a common numerical scale and then added or subtracted from each other.[8] The satisfactions that an improved work environment imparts to workers, for example, might be equivalent to 500 positive units of utility, whereas the resulting bills that arrive the next month might be equivalent to 700 negative units of utility. Therefore, the total combined utility of this act (improving the work environment) would be 200 units of *negative* utility.

When the utilitarian principle says that the right action for a particular occasion is the one that produces more utility than any other possible action, it does not mean that the right action is the one that produces the most utility for the person performing the action. Rather, an action is right if it produces the most utility for *all* persons affected by the action (including the person performing the action).[9] Nor does the utilitarian principle say that an action is right so long as its benefits outweigh its costs. Rather, utilitarianism holds that, in the final analysis, only one action is right: that one action whose net benefits are greatest by comparison to the net benefits of all other possible alternatives. A third misunderstanding is to think that the utilitarian principle requires us to consider only the direct and immediate consequences of our actions. Instead, both the immediate and all foreseeable future costs and benefits that each alternative will provide for each individual must be taken into account as well as any significant indirect effects.

Consequently, to ascertain what I should do on a particular occasion, I must do three things. First, I must determine what alternative actions or policies are available to me on that occasion. The Ford managers, for example, were implicitly considering two alternatives: to redesign the Pinto by putting a rubber bladder around the gas tank or leave it as originally designed. Second, for each alternative action, I must estimate the direct and indirect benefits and costs that the action would produce for each and every person affected by the action in the foreseeable future. Ford's calculations of the costs and benefits that all affected parties would have to bear if the Pinto design were changed, and those that all parties would have to bear if it were not changed, are examples of such estimates. Third, the alternative that produces the greatest sum total of utility must be chosen as the ethically appropriate course of action. The Ford managers, for example, decided that the course of action that would impose the lowest costs and the greatest benefits would be to leave the Pinto design unchanged.

Utilitarianism is in many respects an attractive theory. For one thing, it matches fairly nicely the views that we tend to advocate when discussing the choice of government policies and public goods. Most people agree, for example, that when the government is trying to determine on which public projects it should spend tax monies, the proper course of action would be for it to adopt those projects that objective studies show will provide the greatest benefits for the members of society at the least cost. Of course, this is just another way of saying that the proper government policies are those that would have the greatest measurable utility for people—or, in the words of a famous slogan, those that will produce "the greatest good for the greatest number."

Utilitarianism also seems to fit in rather neatly with the intuitive criteria that people employ when discussing moral conduct.[10] For example, when people explain why they have a moral obligation to perform some action, they often proceed by pointing to the benefits or harms the action will impose on human beings. Moreover, morality requires that one impartially take everyone's interest equally into account. Utilitarianism meets this requirement insofar as it takes into account the effects actions have on everyone and insofar as it requires one to impartially choose the action with the greatest net utility regardless of who gets the benefits.

Utilitarianism also has the advantage of being able to explain why we hold that certain types of activities are generally morally wrong (lying, adultery, killing) while others are generally morally right (telling the truth, fidelity, keeping one's promises). The utilitarian can say that lying is generally wrong because of the costly effects lying has on our human welfare. When people lie to each other, they are less apt to trust each other and cooperate with each other. The less trust and cooperation, the more our welfare declines. Telling the truth is generally right because it strengthens cooperation and trust, and thereby improves everyone's well-being. In general, then, it is a good rule of thumb to tell the truth and to refrain from lying. Traditional utilitarians would deny, however, that any kinds of actions are always right or always wrong. They would deny, for example, that dishonesty or theft is necessarily always wrong. If in a certain situation more good consequences would flow from being dishonest than from any other act a person could perform in that situation, then, according to traditional utilitarian theory, dishonesty would be morally right in that particular situation.

Utilitarian views have also been highly influential in economics.[11] A long line of economists, beginning in the 19th century, argued that economic behavior could be explained by assuming that human beings always attempt to maximize their utility and that the utilities of commodities can be measured by the prices people are willing to pay for them. With these and a few other simplifying assumptions (such as the use of indifference curves), economists were able to derive the familiar supply and demand curves of sellers and buyers in markets and explain why prices in a perfectly competitive market gravitate toward an equilibrium. More important, economists were also able to demonstrate that a system of perfectly competitive markets would lead to a use of resources and price variations that would enable consumers to maximize their utility (defined in terms of Pareto optimality) through their purchases.[12] On utilitarian grounds, therefore, these economists concluded that such a system of markets is better than any other alternative.

Utilitarianism is also the basis of the techniques of economic cost–benefit analysis.[13] This type of analysis is used to determine the desirability of investing in a project (such as a dam, factory, or public park) by figuring whether its present and future economic benefits outweigh its present and future economic costs. To calculate these costs and benefits, discounted monetary prices are estimated for all the effects the project will have on the present and future environment and on present and future populations. Carrying out these sorts of calculations is not always an easy matter, but various methods have been devised for determining the monetary prices of even such intangible benefits as the beauty of a forest (e.g., we might ask how much people pay to see the beauty of a similar privately owned park). If the monetary benefits of a certain public project exceed the monetary costs and if the excess is greater than the excess produced by any other feasible project, then the project should be undertaken. In this form of utilitarianism, the concept of utility is restricted to monetarily measurable economic costs and benefits.

Finally, we can note that utilitarianism fits nicely with a value that many people prize: efficiency. Efficiency can mean different things to different people, but for many it means operating in such a way that one produces the most one can with the resources at hand. That is, an efficient operation is one that produces a desired output with the lowest resource input. Such efficiency is precisely what utilitarianism advocates because it holds that one should always adopt the course of action that will produce the greatest benefits at the lowest cost. If we read "desired output" in the place of "benefits" and "resource input" in place of "cost," utilitarianism implies that the right course of action is always the most efficient one.

Problems of Measurement

One major set of problems with utilitarianism is centered on the difficulties encountered when trying to measure utility.[14] One problem is this: How can the utilities different actions have for different people be measured and compared as utilitarianism requires? Suppose you and I would both enjoy getting a certain job: How can we figure out whether the utility you would get out of having the job is more or less than the utility I would get out of having it? Each of us may be sure that he or she would benefit most from the job, but because we cannot get into each other's skin, this judgment has no objective basis. Comparative measures of the values things have for different people cannot be made, the critics argue, thus there is no way of knowing whether utility would be maximized by giving me the job or giving you the job. If we cannot know which actions will produce the greatest amounts of utility, then we cannot apply the utilitarian principle.

A second problem is that some benefits and costs seem intractable to measurement. How, for example, can one measure the value of health or life?[15] Suppose that installing an expensive exhaust system in a workshop will eliminate a large portion of certain carcinogenic particles that workers might otherwise inhale. Suppose that as a result some of the workers probably will live 5 years longer. How is one to calculate the value of those years of added life, and how is this value to be quantitatively balanced against the costs of installing the exhaust system? The Ford managers, when considering the deaths that the Pinto design would cause, decided that a human life was worth $200,000 (in 1970 dollars). But doesn't the price they assigned to a life seem arbitrary and doesn't the attempt to price life seem morally inappropriate?

A third problem is that, because many of the benefits and costs of an action cannot be reliably predicted, they also cannot be adequately measured.[16] The beneficial or costly consequences of basic scientific knowledge, for example, are notoriously difficult to predict. Yet suppose that one has to decide how much to invest in a research program that will probably uncover some highly theoretical, but not immediately usable, information about the universe. How is the future value of that information to be measured, and how can it be weighed against either the present costs of funding the research or the more certain benefits that would result from putting the funds to an alternative use, such as adding a new wing to the local hospital or building housing for the poor?

Yet a fourth problem is that it is unclear exactly what is to count as a benefit and what is to count as a cost.[17] This lack of clarity is especially problematic with respect to social issues that are given significantly different evaluations by different cultural groups. Suppose a bank must decide, for example, whether to extend a loan to the manager of a local pornographic theater or to the manager of a bar that caters to homosexuals. One group of people may see the increased enjoyment of pornography connoisseurs or the increased enjoyment of homosexuals as benefits accruing to society. Another group, however, may see these as harmful and hence as costs.

Finally, the utilitarian assumption that all goods are measurable implies that all goods can be traded for equivalents of each other: For a given quantity of any specific good, there is some quantity of each other good that is equal in value to it. For example, if you are willing to trade the enjoyment of eating two slices of pizza for the enjoyment of a half hour of listening to your favorite CD recording and vice versa, then these two quantifities of goods are equal in value to you. Utilitarianism must assume that all goods are tradable for some quantity of each other good because it holds that there is some scale on which all goods can be measured, and so by using this scale we can discover what quantity of any good is equivalent to a given quantity of any other good. However, critics have argued that there are some noneconomic goods—such as life, freedom, equality, health, beauty—whose value is such that no quantity of any economic good is equal in value to the value of the noneconomic good.[18] No amount of money—or pizzas or CDs—can be equal in value to life, freedom, equality, health, or beauty.

The critics of utilitarianism contend that these measurement problems undercut whatever claims utilitarian theory makes to providing an objective basis for determining normative issues. These problems have become especially obvious in debates over the feasibility of corporate social audits.[19] Although business firms have been increasingly pressured to produce an "audit" or report measuring the social costs and benefits resulting from their business activities, their efforts have been stymied by their inability to place quantitative measures on their various programs and by differences of opinion over what should be counted as a benefit.[20] The only way of resolving these problems is by arbitrarily accepting the valuations of one social group or another. But this in effect bases utilitarian cost–benefit analysis on the subjective biases and tastes of that group.

Utilitarian Replies to Measurement Objections

The defender of utilitarianism has an array of replies ready to counter the measurement objections enumerated.

First, the utilitarian may argue that, although utilitarianism ideally requires accurate quantifiable measurements of all costs and benefits, this requirement can be relaxed when such measurements are impossible.[21] Utilitarianism merely insists that the consequences of any projected act be expressly stated with as much clarity and accuracy as is humanly possible, and that all relevant information concerning these consequences be presented in a form that will allow them to be systematically compared and impartially weighed against each other. Expressing this information in quantitative terms facilitates such comparisons and weighings. However, where quantitative data are unavailable, one may legitimately rely on shared and common-sense judgments of the comparative values things have for most people. For example, we know that, by and large, cancer is a greater injury than a cold no matter who has the cancer and who has the cold. Similarly, a steak has a greater value as food than a peanut no matter whose hunger is involved.

The utilitarian can also point to several common-sense criteria that can be used to determine the relative values that should be given to various categories of goods. One criterion, for example, depends on the distinction between *intrinsic* and *instrumental* goods.[22] Instrumental goods are things that are considered valuable only because they lead to other good things. A painful visit to the dentist, for example, is only an instrumental good (unless I happen to be a masochist): It is desired only as a means to health. Intrinsic goods, however, are things that are desirable independent of any other benefits they may produce. Thus, health is an intrinsic good: It is desired for its own sake. (Many things, of course, have both intrinsic and instrumental value. I may use a skateboard, for example, not only because skateboarding is a means to health and rapid transportation, but also because I enjoy skateboarding for itself.) Now it is clear that intrinsic goods take priority over instrumental goods. Under most circumstances, for example, money, which is an instrumental good, must not take priority over life and health, which have intrinsic values.

A second common-sense criterion that can be used to weigh goods turns on the distinction between needs and wants.[23] To say that someone needs something is to say that without it he or she will be harmed in some way. People's "basic" needs consist of their needs for things without which they will suffer some fundamental harm such as injury, illness, or death. Among a person's basic needs are the food, clothing, and housing required to stay alive; the medical care and hygienic environment required to remain healthy; and the security and safety required to remain free from injury. However, to say that a person wants something is to say that the person desires it: The person believes it will advance his or her interests in some way. A need, of course, may also be a want: If I know I need something, then I may also want it. Many wants, however, are not needs but simply desires for things without which the individual would not suffer any fundamental harm. I may want something simply because I enjoy it, even though it is a luxury I could as well do without. Desires of this sort that are not also needs are called mere wants. In general, satisfying a person's basic needs is more valuable than satisfying his or her mere wants. If people do not get something for which they have a basic need, they may be injured in a way that makes it impossible for them to enjoy the satisfaction of any number of mere wants. Because the satisfaction of a person's basic needs makes possible not only the intrinsic values of life and health but also the enjoyment of most other intrinsic values, satisfaction of the basic needs has a value that is greater than that of satisfying mere wants.

However, these common-sense methods of weighing goods are only intended to aid us in situations where quantitative methods fail. In actual fact, the consequences of many decisions are relatively amenable to quantification, the convinced utilitarian will claim. This constitutes the utilitarian's second major reply to the measurement objections as previously outlined.

The most flexible method of providing a common quantitative measure for the benefits and costs associated with a decision, the utilitarian may hold, is in terms of their monetary equivalents.[24] Basically, this implies that the value a thing has for a person can be measured by the price the person is willing to pay for it. If a person will pay twice as much for one thing as for another, then that thing has exactly twice the value of the other for that person. To determine the average values items have for a group of people, then, one need merely look at the average prices given to those items when everyone is allowed to bid for them on open markets. In short, market prices can serve to provide a common quantitative measure of the various benefits and costs associated with a decision. In general, to determine the value of a thing, one need merely ask what it sells for on an open market. If the item does not sell on an open market, then one can ask what is the selling price for similar items.

The use of monetary values also has the advantage of allowing one to take into account the effects of the passage of time and the impact of uncertainty. If the known monetary costs or benefits lie in the future, then their present values can be determined by discounting them at the appropriate rate of interest. If the monetary costs or benefits are only probable and not certain, then their expected values can be computed by multiplying the monetary costs or benefits by the appropriate probability factor.

A standard objection against using monetary values to measure all costs and benefits is that some goods, in particular health and life, cannot be priced. The utilitarian may argue, however, that not only is it possible to put a price on health and life, but that we do so almost daily. Anytime people place a limit on the amount of money they are willing to pay to reduce the risk that some object poses to their lives, they have set an implicit price on their own lives. For example, suppose that people are willing to pay $5 for a piece of safety equipment that will reduce the probability of their being killed in an auto accident from .00005 to .00004, but they are unwilling to pay any more than that. Then, in effect, they have implicitly decided that .00001 of a life is worth $5—or, in other words, that a life is worth $500,000. Such pricing is inevitable and necessary, the utilitarian may hold, so long as we live in an environment in which risks to health and life can be lowered only by giving up (trading off) other things that we may want and on which we set a clear price.

Finally, the utilitarian may say, where market prices are incapable of providing quantitative data for comparing the costs and benefits of various decisions, other sorts of quantitative measures are available.[25] Should people disagree, for example, as they often do, over the harmful or beneficial aspects of various sexual activities, then sociological surveys or political votes can be used to measure the intensity and extensiveness of people's attitudes. Economic experts can also provide informed judgments of the relative quantitative values of various costs and benefits. Thus, the utilitarian will grant that the problems of measurement encountered by utilitarianism are real enough. They are at least partially soluble by the various methods enumerated. There are, however, other criticisms of utilitarianism.

Problems with Rights and Justice

The major difficulty with utilitarianism, according to some critics, is that it is unable to deal with two kinds of moral issues: those relating to rights and those relating to justice.[26] That is, the utilitarian principle implies that certain actions are morally right when in fact they are unjust or violate people's rights. Some examples may serve to indicate the sort of difficult counterexamples critics pose for utilitarianism.

First, suppose that your uncle has an incurable and painful disease, so that he is quite unhappy but does not choose to die. Although he is hospitalized and will die within a year, he continues to run his chemical plant. Because of his own misery, he deliberately makes life miserable for his workers and has insisted on not installing safety devices in his chemical plant, although he knows that as a result one worker will certainly lose his life over the next year. You, his only living relative, know that on your uncle's death you will inherit his business and will not only be wealthy and immensely happy, but also intend to prevent any future loss of life by installing the needed safety devices. You are cold-blooded and correctly judge that you could secretly murder your uncle without being caught and without your happiness being in any way affected by it afterward. If it is possible for you to murder your uncle without in any way diminishing anyone else's happiness, then according to utilitarianism you have a moral obligation to do so. By murdering your uncle, you are trading his life for the life of the worker, and you are gaining your happiness while doing away with his unhappiness and pain: The gain is obviously on the side of utility. However, the critics of utilitarianism claim, it seems quite clear that the murder of your uncle would be a gross violation of his right to life. Utilitarianism has led us to approve an act of murder that is an obvious violation of an individual's most important right.

Second, utilitarianism can also go wrong, according to the critics, when it is applied to situations that involve social justice. For example, suppose that subsistence wages force a small group of migrant workers to continue doing the most undesirable agricultural jobs in an economy but produce immense amounts of satisfaction for the vast majority of society's members, because they enjoy cheap vegetables and savings that allow them to indulge other wants. Suppose also that the amounts of satisfaction thereby produced, when balanced against the unhappiness and pain imposed on the small group of farm workers, results in a greater net utility than would exist if everyone had to share the burdens of farm work. Then, according to the utilitarian criterion, it would be morally right to continue this system of subsistence wages for farm workers. However, to the critics of utilitarianism, a social system that imposes such unequal sharing of burdens is clearly immoral and offends against justice. The great benefits the system may have for the majority does not justify the extreme burdens that it imposes on a small group. The shortcoming this counterexample reveals is that utilitarianism allows benefits and burdens to be distributed among the members of society in any way whatsoever, so long as the total amount of benefits is maximized. In fact, some ways of distributing benefits and burdens (like the extremely unequal distributions involved in the counterexample) are unjust regardless of how great the store of benefits such distributions produce. Utilitarianism looks only at how much utility is produced in a society and fails to take into account how that utility is distributed among the members of society.

To see more clearly how utilitarianism ignores considerations of justice and rights, consider how Ford's managers dealt with the Pinto's design. Had they decided to change the Pinto's design and add $11 to the cost of each Pinto, they would, in effect, have forced all the buyers of the Pinto to share in paying the $137 million that the design change would cost. Each buyer would pay an equal share of the total costs necessitated by this aspect of the Pinto design. However, by not changing the Pinto's design, the Ford managers were in effect forcing the 180 people who would die to absorb all the costs of this aspect of the Pinto design. So we should ask: Is it more just to have 180 buyers bear all the costs of the Pinto design by themselves, or is it more just to distribute the costs equally among all buyers? Which is the fairest way of distributing these costs?

Consider, next, that when Ford's managers decided to make no change to the Pinto's design, they were not only making the Pinto cheaper, they were also building a car with a certain amount of risk (to life): Those who drove the Pinto would be driving a car that posed a slightly greater risk to life than they might have reasonably assumed it posed. It is possible that drivers of the Pinto would have gladly accepted this slightly added risk to life in exchange for the lower price of the car. But they had no choice in the matter, because they did not know the car carried this added risk. So we should ask: Do people have the right to know what they are buying when they choose to purchase a product? Do people have a right to choose whether to have greater risk added to their lives? Did the makers of the Pinto violate this basic right of customers to freely choose for themselves whether to accept a riskier car in return for a lower price?

Thus, the Pinto case makes clear that utilitarianism seems to ignore certain important aspects of ethics. Considerations of justice (which look at how benefits and burdens are distributed among people) and rights (which look at individual entitlements to freedom of choice and well-being) seem to be ignored by an analysis that looks only at the costs and benefits of decisions.

Utilitarian Replies to Objections on Rights and Justice

To deal with the sorts of counterexamples that critics of traditional utilitarianism have offered, utilitarians have proposed an important and influential alternative version of utilitarianism called *rule-utilitarianism.*[27] The basic strategy of the rule-utilitarian is to limit utilitarian analysis to the evaluations of moral rules. According to the rule-utilitarian, when trying to determine whether a particular action is ethical, one is never supposed to ask whether that particular action will produce the greatest amount of utility. Instead, one is supposed to ask whether the action is required by the correct moral rules that everyone should follow. If the action is required by such rules, then one should carry out the action. But what are the "correct" moral rules? It is only this second question, according to the rule-utilitarian, that is supposed to be answered by reference to maximizing utility. The correct moral rules are those that would produce the greatest amount of utility if everyone were to follow them. An example may make this clear.

Suppose I am trying to decide whether it is ethical for me to fix prices with a competitor. Then, according to the rule-utilitarian, I should not ask whether this particular instance of price-fixing will produce more utility than anything else I can do. Instead, I should first ask myself: What are the correct moral rules with respect to price-fixing? Perhaps I might conclude, after some thought, that the following list of rules includes all the candidates:

1. Managers are never to meet with competitors for the purpose of fixing prices.
2. Managers may always meet with competitors for the purpose of fixing prices.
3. Managers may meet with competitors for the purpose of fixing prices when they are losing money.

Which of these three is the correct moral rule? According to the rule-utilitarian, the correct moral rule is the one that would produce the greatest amount of utility for everyone affected. Let us suppose that after analyzing the economic effects of price-fixing, I conclude that within our economic and social circumstances people would benefit much more if everyone followed Rule 1 than if everyone followed Rule 2 or 3. If this is so, then Rule 1 is the correct moral rule concerning price-fixing. Now that I know what the correct moral rule on price-fixing is, I can go on to ask a second question: Should I engage in this particular act of fixing prices? To answer this second question, I only have to ask: What is required by the correct moral rules? As we have already noted, the correct rule is to never fix prices. Consequently, even if on this particular occasion, fixing prices actually would produce more utility than not doing so, I am, nonetheless, ethically obligated to refrain from fixing prices because this is required by the rules from which everyone in my society would most benefit.

The theory of the rule-utilitarian, then, has two parts, which we can summarize in the following two principles:

I. *An action is right from an ethical point of view if and only if the action would be required by those moral rules that are correct.*

II. *A moral rule is correct if and only if the sum total of utilities produced if everyone were to follow that rule is greater than the sum total utilities produced if everyone were to follow some alternative rule.*

Thus, according to the rule-utilitarian, the fact that a certain action would maximize utility on one particular occasion does not show that it is right from an ethical point of view.

For the rule-utilitarian, the flaw in the counterexamples that the critics of traditional utilitarianism offer is that in each case the utilitarian criterion is applied to particular actions and not to rules. Instead, the rule-utilitarian would urge that we must use the utilitarian criterion to find out what the correct moral rule is for each counterexample and then evaluate the particular actions involved in the counterexample only in terms of this rule. Doing this allows utilitarianism to escape the counterexamples undamaged.

The counterexample involving the rich uncle and the murderous heir, for example, is a situation that deals with killing a sick person. In such situations, the rule-utilitarian might argue, it is clear that a moral rule that forbids killing without the due process of law will, in the long run, have greater utility for society than other kinds of rules. Therefore, such a rule is the correct one to apply to the case. It would be wrong for the heir to kill his uncle because doing so would violate a correct moral rule, and the fact that murder would on this particular occasion maximize utility is irrelevant.

The case dealing with subsistence wages, the rule-utilitarian would argue, should be treated similarly. It is clear that a rule that forbade unnecessary subsistence wages in societies would in the long run result in more utility than a rule that allowed them. Such a rule would be the correct rule to invoke when asking whether practicing *wage slavery* is morally permissible, and the practice would then be rejected as ethically wrong even if it would maximize utility on a particular occasion.

The ploy of the rule-utilitarian, however, has not satisfied the critics of utilitarianism, who have pointed out an important difficulty in the rule-utilitarian position: According to its critics, rule-utilitarianism is traditional utilitarianism in disguise.[28] These critics argue that rules that allow (beneficial) exceptions will produce more utility than rules that do not allow any exceptions. However, once a rule allows these exceptions, the critics claim, it will allow the same injustices and violations of rights that traditional utilitarianism allows. Some examples may help us see more clearly what these critics mean. The critics claim that if a rule allows people to make an exception whenever an exception will maximize utility, then it will produce more utility than it would if it allowed no exceptions. For example, more utility would be produced by a rule that says, "People are not to be killed without due process *except when doing so will produce more utility than not doing so*," than would be produced by a rule that simply says, "People are not to be killed without due process." The first rule will *always* maximize utility, whereas the second rule will maximize utility only *most of the time* (because the second rule rigidly requires due process even when it would be more beneficial to dispense with due process). Because the rule-utilitarian holds that the correct moral rule is the one that produces more utility, he must hold that the correct moral rule is the one that allows exceptions when exceptions will maximize utility. Once the exception clause is made part of the rule, the critics point out, then applying the rule to an action will have exactly the same consequences as applying the traditional utilitarian criterion directly to the action because the utilitarian criterion is now part of the rule. In the case of the sick uncle and murderous heir, for example, the rule that "People are not to be killed without due process *except when doing so will produce more utility than not doing so*" will now allow the heir to murder his uncle exactly as traditional utilitarianism did before. Similarly, more utility would be produced by a rule that says, "Subsistence wages are prohibited *except in those situations where they will maximize utility*," than would be produced by a rule that simply says, "Subsistence wages are prohibited." Therefore, the rule that allows exceptions will be the "correct" one. But this "correct" rule will now allow the society we described earlier to institute wage slavery exactly as traditional utilitarianism did. Rule-utilitarianism, then, is a disguised form of traditional utilitarianism, and the counterexamples that set difficulties for one seem to set similar difficulties for the other.

Many rule-utilitarians do not admit that rules produce more utility when they allow exceptions. Because human nature is weak and self-interested, they claim, humans would take advantage of any allowable exceptions, and this would leave everyone worse off. Other utilitarians refuse to admit that the counterexamples of the critics are correct. They claim that if killing a person without due process really would produce more utility than all other feasible alternatives, then all other alternatives must have greater evils attached to them. If this is so, then killing the person without due process really would be morally right. Similarly, if in certain circumstances subsistence wages really are the least (socially) injurious means to employ in getting a job done, then in those circumstances subsistence wages are morally right exactly as utilitarianism implies.

There are two main limits to utilitarian methods of moral reasoning, therefore, although the precise extent of these limits is controversial. First, utilitarian methods are difficult to use when dealing with values that are difficult and perhaps impossible to measure quantitatively. Second, utilitarianism by itself seems to deal inadequately with situations that involve rights and justice, although some have tried to remedy this deficiency by restricting utilitarianism to the evaluation of rules. To clarify our ideas on these issues, the next two sections examine methods of moral reasoning that explicitly deal with the two moral issues on which utilitarianism seems to fall short: rights and justice.

2.2 Rights and Duties

In April 2000, executives of Microsoft, the world's largest software company, were confronted with a group of stockholders who were concerned with the company's operations in China and who wanted Microsoft's stockholders to require Microsoft to respect certain human rights. In 1999, the U.S. State Department had reported that the Chinese "government's human rights record deteriorated sharply" in 1998 and that "the government continues to restrict tightly worker rights and forced labor remains a problem."[29] Earlier, in 1994, China's Ministry of Labor had issued a set of "Regulations on the Labor Management of Foreign-Funded Enterprises" covering some employee rights. These regulations recognized the right of workers to bargain collectively, but only through China's one government-sanctioned labor union. More problematic was the fact that China's economy still made massive use of prison or forced labor. China's prisons contained large numbers of political dissidents and persons with "suspicious" class backgrounds. These prisoners were forced to engage in unpaid, exhausting, and dangerous labor—often being detained to work beyond their sentences—to "reform" or "reeducate" them. In addition, regular workers were sometimes paid such low wages (an average of 30 cents an hour in manufacturing) that they could not meet their basic needs. Poor health and safety standards were so widespread that China had one of the highest rates of industrial accidents in the world, and overseers were sometimes abusive to workers. Microsoft operated a Research and Development center in Beijing, where it employed nearly 100 researchers, and a customer support center in Shanghai—its largest in Asia—where it planned to double its workforce from 300 to 600. Microsoft also planned to establish a joint venture with Beijing Centergate Technologies, a Chinese company, to develop Chinese language software.

A group of Microsoft stockholders who collectively owned more than 70,000 shares proposed at the company's annual shareholder meeting that shareholders vote in favor of having Microsoft adopt the "U.S. Business Principles for

Human Rights of Workers in China," a statement supported by several organizations and businesses including Levi Strauss, Mattel, and Reebok. If more than half of the company's shareholders voted for it, the statement would commit the company to the following human rights principles:[30]

1. No goods or products produced within our company-owned facilities or those of our suppliers shall be manufactured by bonded labor, forced labor within prison camps, or as part of reform-through-labor or reeducation-through-labor programs.
2. Our facilities and suppliers shall adhere to wages that meet workers' basic needs, and to fair and decent working hours.
3. Our facilities and suppliers shall prohibit the use of corporal punishment, as well as any physical, sexual, or verbal abuse or harassment of workers.
4. Our facilities and suppliers shall use production methods that do not negatively affect the occupational safety and health of workers.
5. Our facilities and suppliers shall not call on the police or military to enter their premises to prevent workers from exercising their rights.
6. We shall undertake to promote the following freedoms among our employees and the employees of our suppliers: freedom of association and assembly, including the rights to form unions and to bargain collectively freedom of expression, and freedom from arbitrary arrest or detention. . . .

These principles, their proponents claimed, were based on basic human rights, including the right to not be enslaved, the right to have one's basic human needs met, the right to decent and safe working conditions, the right to unionize, the right to freedom of association, the right to freedom of expression, and the right to freedom from arbitrary arrest or detention.

Microsoft's managers, however, did not want to endorse these principles on the grounds that it already had a code of ethics that ensured "compliance with the laws of the countries in which the Company operates" and that promoted a "healthy environment" and "prohibited harassment." In addition, Microsoft claimed, the principles were "vague and over broad." Microsoft managers urged stockholders to vote against the principles. Other companies argued that U.S. businesses in China should not promote human rights, anyway, because doing so would make them abandon a position of political neutrality, which, they claimed, was essential to doing business in China. Companies also argued that it was wrong of them to "impose" American ideas about human rights on foreign countries and claimed, like Microsoft, that they should merely comply with the laws of the countries in which they operated. The issue of human rights in China and questions about how U.S. businesses would deal with human rights violations promised to become more important in future years since the U.S. Congress voted in 2000 to establish permanent "normal trading relations" with China. Already several companies had established strong operations in China, including Motorola, IBM, Kodak, Boeing,

McDonald's, Coca-Cola, Procter & Gamble, General Motors, Chevron, Texaco, Occidental Petroleum, and Amoco. Investors, employees, and customers were all raising questions to these companies about how they were handling human rights issues in their China operations.

The concept of a *right* obviously appears in many of the moral arguments and moral claims invoked in business discussions. Employees, for example, argue that they have a "right to equal pay for equal work"; managers assert that unions violate their "right to manage"; investors complain that taxation violates their "property rights"; and consumers claim that they have a "right to know." Moreover, public documents often employ the notion of a right. The American Constitution enshrines a long Bill of Rights, defined largely in terms of the duties the federal government has to not interfere in certain areas of its citizens' lives. The Declaration of Independence was based on the idea that "all men . . . are endowed by their Creator with certain unalienable rights . . . among these are life, liberty, and the pursuit of happiness." In 1948, the United Nations adopted a "Universal Declaration of Human Rights," which claimed that "all human beings" are entitled, among other things, to:

> the right to own property alone as well as in association with others . . .
>
> the right to work, to free choice of employment, to just and favorable conditions of work, and to protection against unemployment . . .
>
> the right to just and favorable remuneration ensuring for [the worker] and his family an existence worthy of human dignity . . .
>
> the right to form and to join trade unions . . .
>
> the right to rest and leisure, including reasonable limitation of working hours and periodic holidays with pay . . .

The concept of a right and the correlative notion of duty, then, lie at the heart of much of our moral discourse. This section is intended to provide an understanding of these concepts and of some of the major kinds of ethical principles and methods of analysis that underlie their use.

The Concept of a Right

In general, a right is an individual's entitlement to something.[31] A person has a right when that person is entitled to act in a certain way or is entitled to have others act in a certain way toward him or her. The entitlement may derive from a legal system that permits or empowers the person to act in a specified way or that requires others to act in certain ways toward that person; the entitlement is then called a *legal right*. The American Constitution, for example, guarantees all citizens the right to freedom of speech, and commercial statutes specify that each party to a valid contract has a right to whatever performance the contract requires from the other person. Legal rights are limited, of course, to the particular jurisdiction within which the legal system is in force.

Entitlements can also derive from a system of moral standards independently of any particular legal system. The right to work, for example, is not guaranteed by the American Constitution, but many argue that this is a right that all human beings possess. Such rights, which are called *moral rights* or *human rights*, are based on moral norms and principles that specify that all human beings are permitted or empowered to do something or are entitled to have something done for them. Moral rights, unlike legal rights, are usually thought of as being universal insofar as they are rights that all human beings of every nationality possess to an equal extent simply by virtue of being human beings. Unlike legal rights, moral rights are not limited to a particular jurisdiction. If humans have a moral right not to be tortured, for example, then this is a right that human beings of every nationality have regardless of the legal system under which they live.

Rights are powerful devices whose main purpose is to enable the individual to choose freely whether to pursue certain interests or activities and to protect those choices. In our ordinary discourse, we use the term *right* to cover a variety of situations in which individuals are enabled to make such choices in very different ways. First, we sometimes use the term *right* to indicate the mere absence of prohibitions against pursuing some interest or activity. For example, I have a right to do whatever the law or morality does not positively forbid me to do. In this weak sense of a right, the enabling and protective aspects are minimal. Second, we sometimes use the term *right* to indicate that a person is authorized or empowered to do something either to secure the interests of others or to secure one's interests. An army or police officer, for example, acquires legal rights of command over subordinates that enable the officer to pursue the security of others, whereas a property owner acquires legal property rights that enable doing as one wishes with the property. Third, the term *right* is sometimes used to indicate the existence of prohibitions or requirements on others that enable the individual to pursue certain interests or activities. For example, the American Constitution is said to give citizens the right to free speech because it contains a prohibition against government limits on speech, and federal law is said to give citizens the right to an education because it contains a requirement that each state must provide free public education for all its citizens.[32]

The most important moral rights—and those that will concern us in this chapter—are rights that impose prohibitions or requirements on others and that thereby enable individuals to choose freely whether to pursue certain interests or activities. These moral rights (we mean these kinds of rights when we use the term *moral rights*) identify those activities or interests that the individual is empowered to pursue, or must be left free to pursue, or must be helped to pursue, as he or she chooses; and they protect the individual's pursuit of those interests and activities within the boundaries specified by the rights. These kinds of moral rights have three important features that define these enabling and protective functions.

First, moral rights are tightly correlated with duties.[33] This is because one person's moral right generally can be defined—at least partially—in terms of the moral duties other people have toward that person. To have a moral right necessarily implies that others have certain duties toward the bearer of that right. My moral right to worship as I choose, for example, can be defined in terms of the moral duties other people have to not interfere in my chosen form of worship. The moral right to a suitable standard of living can be defined in terms of the duty that governments (or some other agents of society) have to ensure a suitable standard of living for their citizens. Duties, then, are generally the other side of moral rights: If I have a moral right to do something, then other people have a moral duty not to interfere with me when I do it; if I have a moral right to have someone do something for me, then that other person (or group of persons) has a moral duty to do it for me. Thus, moral rights impose correlative duties on others—either duties of noninterference or duties of positive performance.

In some cases, the correlative duties imposed by a right may fall not on any specific individual, but on all the members of a group. For example, if a person has the "right to work" (a right mentioned in the United Nations' Universal Declaration of Human Rights), this does not necessarily mean that any specific employer has a duty to provide that person with a job. Rather, it means that all the members of society, through their public agencies, have the duty of ensuring that jobs are available to workers.

Second, moral rights provide individuals with autonomy and equality in the free pursuit of their interests.[34] That is, a right identifies activities or interests that people must be left free to pursue or not pursue as they choose (or must be helped to pursue as they freely choose) and whose pursuit must not be subordinated to the interests of others except for special and exceptionally weighty reasons. If I have a right to worship as I choose, for example, then this implies that I am free to worship if and as I personally choose, and that I am not dependent on anyone's permission to worship. It also implies that I cannot generally be forced to stop worshipping on the grounds that society will gain more benefits if I am kept from worshipping: The gains of others do not generally justify interference with a person's pursuit of an interest or an activity when that pursuit is protected by a moral right. To acknowledge a person's moral right, then, is to acknowledge that there is an area in which the person is not subject to my wishes and in which the person's interests are not subordinate to mine. There is an area, in short, within which we stand as autonomous equals.

Third, moral rights provide a basis for justifying one's actions and for invoking the protection or aid of others.[35] If I have a moral right to do something, then I have a moral justification for doing it. Moreover, if I have a right to do something, then others have no justification for interfering with me. On the contrary, others are justified in restraining any persons who try to prevent me from exercising my right or others may have a duty to aid me in exercising my right. When a stronger person helps a weaker one defend his or her rights, for example, we generally acknowledge that the act of the stronger person was justified.

Because moral rights have these three features, they provide bases for making moral judgments that differ substantially from utilitarian standards. First, moral rights express the requirements of morality from the point of view of the *individual*, whereas utilitarianism expresses the requirements of morality from the point of view of *society as a whole*. Moral standards concerned with rights indicate what is due to the individual from others, promote the individual's welfare, and protect the individual's choices against encroachment by society. Utilitarian standards promote society's aggregate utility, and they are indifferent to the individual's welfare except insofar as it affects this social aggregate. Second, rights limit the validity of appeals to social benefits and to numbers. That is, if a person has a right to do something, then it is wrong for anyone to interfere, although a large number of people might gain much more utility from such interference. If I have a right to life, for example, then it is morally wrong for someone to kill me even if many others would gain much more from my death than I will ever gain from living. If the members of a minority group have a right to free speech, then the majority must leave the minority free to speak even if the majority is much more numerous and intensely opposed to what the minority will say.

Although rights generally override utilitarian standards, they are not immune from all utilitarian considerations: If the utilitarian benefits or losses imposed on society become great enough, they might be sufficient to breach the protective walls the right sets up around a person's freedom to pursue his or her interests. In times of war or major public emergencies, for example, it is generally acknowledged that civil rights may legitimately be restricted for the sake of "the public welfare." The property rights of factory owners may be restricted to prevent pollution that is imposing major damages on the health of others. The more important the interest protected by a right, the larger the utilitarian tradeoffs must be: Rights erect higher walls around more important interests, and so the level of social benefits or costs needed to breach the walls must be greater.

Negative and Positive Rights

A large group of rights called *negative rights* is distinguished by the fact that its members can be defined wholly in terms of the duties others have to not interfere in certain activities of the person who holds a given right.[36] For example, if I have a right to privacy, this means that every other person, including my employer, has the duty not to intervene in my private affairs. If I have a right to use, sell, or destroy my personal business assets, this means that every other person has the duty not to prevent me from using, selling, or destroying my business property as I choose.

In contrast, *positive rights* do more than impose negative duties. They also imply that some other agents (it is not always clear who) have the positive duty of providing the holder of the right with whatever he or she needs to freely pursue his or her interests.[37] For example, if I have a right to an adequate standard of living, this does not mean merely that others must not interfere: It also means that if I am unable to provide myself with an adequate income, then I must be provided with such an income (perhaps by the government). Similarly, the right to work, the right to an education, the right to adequate health care, and the right to social security are all rights that go beyond noninterference to also impose a positive duty of providing people with something when they are unable to provide it for themselves.

Positive rights were not emphasized until the 20th century. Negative rights were often employed in the 17th and 18th centuries by writers of manifestos (such as the Declaration of Independence and the Bill of Rights), who were anxious to protect individuals against the encroachments of monarchical governments. Positive rights became important in the 20th century when society increasingly took it on itself to provide its members with the necessities of life that they were unable to provide for themselves. The United Nations declaration, for example, is influenced by this trend when it provides for the rights "to food, clothing, housing, and medical care." The change in the meaning of the phrase "the right to life" is another indication of the rising importance of positive rights. Whereas the 18th century interpreted the "right to life" as the negative right to not be killed (this is the meaning the phrase has in the Declaration of Independence), the 20th century has reinterpreted the phrase to refer to the positive right to be provided with the minimum necessities of life.

Much of the debate over moral rights has concentrated on whether negative or positive rights should be given priority. So-called "conservative" writers, for example, have claimed that government efforts should be limited to enforcing negative rights and not expended on providing positive rights.[38] This is the crux of the debate over whether government efforts should be restricted to protecting property and securing law and order (i.e., protecting people's negative rights) or whether government should also provide the needy with jobs, job training, housing, medical care, and other welfare benefits (i.e., provide for people's positive rights). So-called "liberal" authors, in contrast, hold that positive rights have as strong a claim to being honored as negative rights and that, consequently, government has a duty to provide for both.[39]

Contractual Rights and Duties

Contractual rights and duties (sometimes called *special rights and duties* or *special obligations*) are the limited rights and correlative duties that arise when one person enters an agreement with another person.[40] For example, if I contract to do something for you, then you are entitled to my performance: You acquire a contractual *right* to whatever I promised, and I have a contractual *duty* to perform as I promised.

Contractual rights and duties are distinguished, first, by the fact that they attach to *specific* individuals and the correlative duties are imposed only on other *specific* individuals. If I agree to do something for you, everyone else does not thereby acquire new rights over me, nor do I acquire any new duties toward them. Second, contractual rights arise out of a specific transaction between particular individuals. Unless I actually make a promise or enter some other similar arrangement with you, you do not acquire any contractual rights over me.

Third, contractual rights and duties depend on a publicly accepted system of rules that define the transactions that give rise to those rights and duties.[41] Contracts, for example, create special rights and duties between people only if these people recognize and accept a system of conventions that specifies that, by doing certain things (such as signing a paper), a person undertakes an obligation to do what he or she agrees to do. When a person goes through the appropriate actions, other people know that person is putting him or herself under an obligation because the publicly recognized system of rules specifies that such actions count as a contractual agreement. Because the publicly recognized system obligates or requires the person to do what he or she says, or suffer the appropriate penalties, everyone understands that the person can be relied on to keep the contract and that others can act in accordance with this understanding.

Without the institution of contract and the rights and duties it can create, modern business societies could not operate. Virtually every business transaction at some point requires one of the parties to rely on the word of the other party to the effect that the other party will pay later, will deliver certain services later, or will transfer goods of a certain quality and quantity. Without the social institution of contract, individuals in such situations would be unwilling to rely on the word of the other party, and the transactions would never take place. The institution of contracts provides a way of ensuring that individuals keep their word, and this in turn makes it possible for business society to operate. Employers, for example, acquire contractual rights to the services of their employees in virtue of the work contract that employees enter, and sellers acquire contractual rights to the future cash that credit buyers agree to give them.

Contractual rights and duties also provide a basis for the special duties or obligations that people acquire when they accept a position or role within a legitimate social institution or an organization. For example, married parents have a special duty to care for the upbringing of their children, doctors have a special duty to care for the health of their patients, and managers have a special duty to care for the organization they administer. In each of these cases, there is a publicly accepted institution (such as a familial, medical, or corporate institution) that defines a certain position or role (such as parent, doctor, or manager) on which the welfare of certain vulnerable persons (such as the parents' children, the doctor's patients, the manager's corporate constituencies) depends. Society attaches to these institutional roles special duties of caring for these vulnerable dependents and protecting them from injury—duties that the person who enters the role knows he or she is expected to fulfill. When a person freely enters the role knowing what duties society attaches to the acceptance of the role, that person in effect enters an agreement to fulfill those duties. The existence of a system of contractual obligations ensures that individuals fulfill these agreements by laying on them the public obligations that all agreements carry. As a result, these familial, medical, and corporate institutions can continue to exist, and their vulnerable members are protected against harm. We should recall here that a person's institutional duties are not unlimited. In the first chapter, we noted that, as a "loyal agent," the manager's duties to care for the corporation are limited by the ethical principles that govern any person. Similarly, a doctor cannot murder other people to obtain vital organs for the patients whom he or she has a duty to care.

What kind of ethical rules govern contracts? The system of rules that underlies contractual rights and duties has been traditionally interpreted as including several moral constraints:[42]

1. Both of the parties to a contract must have full knowledge of the nature of the agreement they are entering.
2. Neither party to a contract must intentionally misrepresent the facts of the contractual situation to the other party.
3. Neither party to the contract must be forced to enter the contract under duress or coercion.
4. The contract must not bind the parties to an immoral act.

Contracts that violate one or more of these four conditions have traditionally been considered void.[43] The basis of these sorts of conditions is discussed next.

A Basis for Moral Rights: Kant

How do we know that people have rights? This question can be answered in a fairly straightforward way when it is asked about legal rights: A person has certain legal rights because the person lives within a legal system that guarantees those rights. However, what is the basis of moral rights?

Utilitarians have suggested that utilitarian principles can provide a satisfactory basis for moral rights: People have moral rights because the possession of moral rights maximizes utility. It is doubtful, however, that utilitarianism can serve as an adequate basis for moral rights. To say that someone has a moral right to do something is to say that he or she is entitled to do it regardless of the utilitarian benefits it provides for others. Utilitarianism cannot easily support such a nonutilitarian concept.

A more satisfactory foundation for moral rights is provided by the ethical theory developed by Immanuel Kant (1724–1804).[44] Kant in fact attempts to show that there are certain moral rights and duties that all human beings possess regardless of any utilitarian benefits that the exercise of those rights and duties may provide for others.

Kant's theory is based on a moral principle that he calls the *categorical imperative* and that requires that everyone should be treated as a free person equal to everyone else. That is, everyone has a moral right to such treatment, and everyone has the correlative duty to treat others in this way. Kant provides at least two ways of formulating this basic moral principle; each formulation serves as an explanation of the meaning of this basic moral right and correlative duty.

The First Formulation of Kant's Categorical Imperative

Kant's first formulation of the categorical imperative is as follows: "I ought never to act except in such a way that I can also will that my maxim should become a universal law."[45] A *maxim* for Kant is the reason a person in a certain situation has for doing what he or she plans to do. A maxim would "become a universal law" if every person in a similar situation chose to do the same thing for the same reason. Kant's first version of the categorical imperative, then, comes down to the following principle:

> *An action is morally right for a person in a certain situation if, and only if, the person's reason for carrying out the action is a reason that he or she would be willing to have every person act on, in any similar situation.*

An example may help to clarify the meaning of Kant's principle. Suppose that I am trying to decide whether to fire an employee because I do not like the employee's race. According to Kant's principle, I must ask myself whether I would be willing to have an employer fire any employee whenever the employer does not like the race of his or her employee. In particular, I must ask myself whether I would be willing to be fired myself should my employer not like my race. If I am not willing to have everyone act in this way, even toward me, then it is morally wrong for me to act in this way toward others. A person's reasons for acting, then, must be "reversible": One must be willing to have all others use those reasons even against oneself. There is an obvious similarity, then, between the categorical imperative and the so-called *golden rule*: "Do unto others as you would have them do unto you."

Kant points out that sometimes it is not even possible to *conceive* of having everyone act on a certain reason, much less be *willing* to have everyone act on that reason.[46] For example, suppose that I am considering breaking a contract because it has committed me to do something I do not want to do. Then I must ask whether I would be willing to have everyone break any contract that one did not want to keep. But it is impossible to even conceive of everyone making and then breaking contracts in this way because if everyone knew that any contract could be broken, then people would cease making contracts altogether (what possible purpose would they serve?) and contracts would no longer exist. Consequently, because it is impossible to conceive of everyone making and breaking contracts in this way, it is also impossible for me to be willing to have everyone act like this (how can I want something I cannot even conceive?). It would be wrong, therefore, for me to break a contract simply because I do not want to keep it. A person's reasons for acting, then, must also be universalizable: It must be possible, at least in principle, for everyone to act on those reasons.

The first formulation of the categorical imperative, then, incorporates two criteria for determining moral right and wrong—universalizability and reversibility:

UNIVERSALIZABILITY: The person's reasons for acting must be reasons that everyone could act on at least in principle.

REVERSIBILITY: The person's reasons for acting must be reasons that he or she would be willing to have all others use, even as a basis of how they treat him or her.

This formulation of Kant's categorical imperative is attractive for a number of reasons, not the least of which is that it seems to capture some fundamental aspects of our moral views. Frequently, for example, we say to a person who has done something wrong or who is about to do something wrong: How would you like it if he did that to you? or How would you like it if you were in her place? thereby invoking something like reversibility. Or we may ask, What if everybody did that? and thereby invoke universalizability.

Unlike the principle of utilitarianism, Kant's categorical imperative focuses on a person's interior motivations and not on the consequences of one's external actions. Moral right and wrong, according to Kantian theory, are distinguished not by what a person accomplishes, but by the reasons the person has for what he tries to do. Kant argues that, to the extent that a person performs an action merely because it will advance the person's own future interests or merely because the person finds the action pleasurable, the action "has no moral worth." A person's action has "moral worth" only to the degree that it is *also* motivated by a sense of "duty," that is, a belief that it is the right way for all people to behave. Therefore, Kant claims, to be motivated by a sense of "duty" is to be motivated by reasons that I wish everyone would act on. Consequently, my action has "moral worth" (i.e., it is morally right) only to the extent that it is motivated by reasons that I would be willing to have every person act on. Hence, the categorical imperative.

The Second Formulation of Kant's Categorical Imperative

The second formulation Kant gives of the categorical imperative is this: "Act in such a way that you always treat humanity, whether in your own person or in the person of any other, never simply as a means, but always at the same time as an end."[47] Or never treat people only as means, but always also as ends.

What Kant means by "treating humanity as an end" is that everyone should treat each human being as a being whose existence as a free rational person should be promoted. For Kant, this means two things: (a) respect each person's freedom by treating people only as they have freely consented to be treated beforehand, and (b) develop each person's capacity to freely choose for him or herself the aims he or she will pursue.[48] However, to treat a person only as a means is to use the person only as an instrument for advancing one's own interests and involves neither respect for nor development of the person's capacity to choose freely. Kant's second version of the categorical imperative can be expressed in the following principle:

> *An action is morally right for a person if, and only if, in performing the action, the person does not use others merely as a means for advancing his or her own interests, but also both respects and develops their capacity to choose freely for themselves.*

This version of the categorical imperative implies that human beings have an equal dignity that sets them apart from things such as tools or machines and that is incompatible with their being manipulated, deceived, or otherwise unwillingly exploited to satisfy the self-interests of another. The principle in effect says that people should not be treated as objects incapable of free choice. By this principle, an employee may legitimately be asked to perform the unpleasant (or even dangerous) tasks involved in a job if the employee freely consented to take the job knowing that it would involve these tasks. But it would be wrong to subject an employee to health risks without the employee's knowledge. In general, deception, force, and coercion fail to respect people's freedom to choose and are therefore immoral (unless, perhaps, a person first freely consented to have force used against him or herself).

Kant argues that making fraudulent contracts by deceiving others is wrong and that deliberately refraining from giving others help when they need it is also wrong. By deceiving a person into making a contract that that person would not otherwise freely choose to make, I fail to respect that person's freedom to choose and merely use the person to advance my own interests. By failing to lend needed and easily extended help to another person, I limit what that person is free to choose to do.

The second formulation of the categorical imperative, according to Kant, is really equivalent to the first.[49] The first version says that what is morally right for me must be morally right for others: Everyone is of equal value. If this is so, then no person's freedom should be subordinated to that of others so that the person is used merely to advance the interests of others. Because I am of value, I cannot sacrifice myself to mere self-interest. This, of course, is what the second version of the categorical imperative requires. Both formulations come down to the same thing: People are to treat each other as free and equal in the pursuit of their interests.

Kantian Rights

A large number of authors have held that the categorical imperative (in one or the other of its formulations) explains why people have moral rights.[50] As we have seen, moral rights identify interests that individuals must be left free to pursue as they autonomously choose (or which we must help them pursue as they choose) and whose free pursuit must not be subordinated to our own interests. That is precisely what both formulations of Kant's categorical imperative require in holding that people must be respected as free and equal in the pursuit of their interests. In short, moral rights identify the specific major areas in which persons must deal with each other as free equals, and Kant's categorical imperative implies that persons should deal with each other in precisely this way. The categorical imperative, however, cannot by itself tell us what particular moral rights human beings have. To know what particular rights human beings have, one first must know what interests humans have and whether there are good reasons for giving the free pursuit of one interest, rather than another, the protected status of a right (clearly, not all interests can be turned into rights, because interests can conflict with each other). For example, to establish that humans have a right to free speech, one has to show that freedom to say what one chooses is critically important to human beings and that it is more important than the free pursuit of other conflicting interests that humans may have (such as an interest in repressing ideas that we find distasteful, offensive, or disturbing). Insofar as free speech is critically important, humans must leave each other equally free to speak as they choose: Everyone has a moral right to freedom of speech. However, insofar as free speech conflicts with another human interest that can be shown to be of equal or greater importance (such as our interest in not being libeled or defamed), the right to freedom of speech must be limited.

Although later chapters present various arguments in support of several particular rights, it might be helpful here to give a rough sketch of how some rights have been plausibly defended on the basis of Kant's two formulations of the categorical imperative. First, human beings have a clear interest in being helped by being provided with the work, food, clothing, housing, and medical care they need to live on when they cannot provide these for themselves. Suppose we agree that we would not be willing to have everyone (especially ourselves) deprived of such help when it is needed, and that such help is necessary if a person's capacity to choose freely is to develop and even survive.[51] If so, then no individual should to be deprived of such help. That is, human beings have *positive* rights to the work, food, clothing, housing, and medical care they need to live on when they cannot provide these for themselves and when these are available.

Second, human beings also have a clear interest in being free from injury or fraud and in being free to think, associate, speak, and live privately as they choose. Suppose we agree that we would be willing to have everyone be free of the interference of others in these areas, and that interference in these areas fails to respect a person's freedom to choose for him or herself.[52] If so, then everyone should be free of the interference of others in these areas. That is, human beings have these negative rights: the right to freedom from injury or fraud, the right to freedom of thought, freedom of association and freedom of speech, and the right to privacy.

Third, as we have seen, human beings have a clear interest in preserving the institution of contracts. Suppose we agree that we would end up dropping the institution of contracts (which we are unwilling to do) if everyone stopped honoring their contracts or if everyone had to honor even contracts that were made under duress or without full information. Suppose we agree that we show respect for people's freedom by honoring the contracts they freely make with us and by leaving them free and fully informed about any contracts they make with us.[53] If so, then everyone should honor his or her contracts and everyone should be fully informed and free when making contracts. That is, human beings have a contractual right to what they have been promised in contracts, and everyone also has a right to be left free and fully informed when contracts are made.

Each of the rights just described has been sketched in barest outline, and each one requires a great deal more in the way of qualifications, adjustments with other (conflicting) interests, and full supporting arguments. Crude as it is, however, the list provides some idea of how Kant's categorical imperative might be used in establishing positive, negative, and contractual rights.

Problems with Kant

Despite the attractiveness of Kant's theory, critics have argued that, like utilitarianism, it has its limitations and inadequacies. A first problem that critics have traditionally pointed out is that Kant's theory is not precise enough to always be useful. One difficulty lies in trying to determine whether one would (as the first formulation requires) "be willing to have everyone follow" a certain policy. Although the general thrust of this requirement is usually clear, it sometimes leads to problems. For example, suppose I am a murderer: Would I then be willing to have everyone follow the policy that all murderers should be punished? In a sense I would be willing to because I would want to be protected from other murderers, but in another sense I would not be willing because I do not want to be punished myself. Which sense is correct?[54] It is also sometimes difficult to determine whether (as the second formulation states) one person is using another "merely as a means." Suppose, for example, that Ms. Jones, an employer, only pays minimum wages to her employees and refuses to install the safety equipment they want, yet she says she is "respecting their capacity to freely choose for themselves" because she is willing to let them work elsewhere if they choose. Is she then treating them merely as means or also as ends? Critics complain that they cannot answer such questions because Kant's theory is too vague.[55] There are cases, then, where the requirements of Kant's theory are unclear.

Second, some critics claim that, although we might be able to agree on the kinds of interests that have the status of moral rights, there is substantial disagreement concerning what the limits of each of these rights are and concerning how each of these rights should be balanced against other conflicting rights.[56] Kant's theory does not help us resolve these disagreements. For example, we all agree that everyone should have a right to associate with whomever one wants, as well as a right not to be injured by others. However, how should these rights be balanced against each other when a certain association of people begins to injure others? For example, suppose the loud music of a group of trombone players disturbs others, or suppose a corporation (which is an association of people) pollutes the air and water on which the health of others depends. Kant's categorical imperative does not tell us how the conflicting rights of these persons should be adjusted to each other: Which right should be limited in favor of the other?

A defender of Kant, however, can counter this second criticism by holding that Kant's categorical imperative is not intended to tell us how conflicting rights should be limited and adjusted to each other. To decide whether one right should be curtailed in favor of a second right, one has to examine the relative importance of the interests that each right protects. What arguments can be given to show, for example, that a corporation's interest in financial gains is more or less important than the health of its neighbors? The answer to this question determines whether a corporation's right to use its property for financial gains should be limited in favor of its neighbors' right not to have their health injured. All that Kant's categorical imperative is meant to tell us is that everyone must have equal moral rights and everyone must show as much respect for the protected interests of others as he or she wants others to show for his or her own. It does not tell us what interests people have nor what their relative importance is.

A third group of criticisms that have been made of Kant's theory is that there are counterexamples that show the theory sometimes goes wrong. Most counterexamples to Kant's theory focus on the criteria of universalizability and reversibility.[57] Suppose that an employer can get away with discriminating against Blacks by paying them lower wages than Whites for the same work. Suppose also that he is so fanatical in his dislike of Blacks that he is willing to accept the proposition that if his own skin were Black employers should also discriminate against him. Then, according to Kant's theory, the employer would be acting morally. According to the critics, this is wrong because discrimination is obviously immoral.

Defenders of a Kantian approach to ethics, of course, would reply that it is the critics, not Kant, who are mistaken. If the employer genuinely and conscientiously would be willing to universalize the principles on which he or she is acting, then the action is in fact morally right for him or her.[58] For us, who would be unwilling to universalize the same principle, the action would be immoral. We may also find that it would be morally right for us to impose sanctions on the employer to make him or her stop discriminating. Insofar as the employer is trying to remain true to one's own universal principles, he or she is acting conscientiously and, therefore, in a moral manner.

The Libertarian Objection: Nozick

Some important views on rights that are different from the ones we sketched have been proposed recently by several *libertarian philosophers.* Libertarian philosophers go beyond the general presumption that freedom from human constraint is usually good; they claim that such freedom is necessarily good and that all constraints imposed by others are necessarily evil except when needed to prevent the imposition of greater human constraints. The American philosopher Robert Nozick, for example, claims that the only basic right that every individual possesses is the negative right to be free from the coercion of other human beings.[59] This negative right to freedom from coercion, according to Nozick, must be recognized if individuals are to be treated as distinct persons with separate lives, each of whom has an equal moral weight that may not be sacrificed for the sake of others. The only circumstances under which coercion may be exerted on a person is when it is necessary to keep him or her from coercing others.

According to Nozick, prohibiting people from coercing others constitutes a legitimate moral constraint that rests on "the underlying Kantian principle that individuals are ends and not merely means; they may not be sacrificed or used for achieving of other ends without their consent."[60] Thus, Nozick seems to hold that Kant's theory supports his own views on freedom.

Nozick goes on to argue that the negative right to freedom from the coercion of others implies that people must be left free to do what they want with their own labor and with whatever products they manufacture by their labor.[61] This in turn implies that people must be left free to acquire property, to use it in whatever way they wish, and to exchange it with others in free markets (so long as the situation of others is not thereby harmed or "worsened"). Thus, the libertarian view that coercive restrictions on freedom are immoral (except when needed to restrain coercion) is also supposed to justify the free use of property, freedom of contract, the institution of free markets in which individuals can exchange goods as they choose without government restrictions, and the elimination of taxes for social welfare programs. However, there is no basis for any positive rights nor for the social programs they might require.

Nozick and other libertarians, however, pass too quickly over the fact that the freedom of one person necessarily imposes constraints on other persons. Such constraints are inevitable because when one person is granted freedom, other persons must be constrained from interfering with that person. If I am to be free to do what I want with my property, for example, other people must be constrained from trespassing on it and taking it from me. Even the "free market system" that Nozick advocates depends on an underlying system of coercion: I can sell something only if I first own it, and ownership depends essentially on an enforced (coercive) system of property laws. Consequently, because granting a freedom to one person necessarily imposes constraints on others, it follows that if constraints require justification, freedom will also always require justification.

The same point can be made in a different way. Because there are many different kinds of freedoms, the freedom one group of agents is given to pursue some of its interests will usually restrict the freedom other agents have to pursue other conflicting interests. For example, the freedom of corporations to use their property to pollute the environment as they want can restrict the freedom of individuals to breathe clean air whenever they want. The freedom of employees to unionize as they want can conflict with the freedom of employers to hire whatever nonunion workers they want. Consequently, allowing one kind of freedom to one group entails restricting some other kind of freedom for some other group: A decision in favor of the freedom to pursue one interest implies a decision against the freedom to pursue another kind of interest. This means that we cannot argue in favor of a certain kind of freedom by simply claiming that constraints are always evil and must always be replaced by freedom. Instead, an argument for a specific freedom must show that the interests that can be satisfied by that kind of freedom are somehow better or more worth satisfying than the interests that other opposing kinds of freedoms could satisfy. Neither Nozick nor other libertarians supply such arguments.

Moreover, it is not obvious that Kantian principles can support libertarian views the same as those of Nozick. Kant holds, as we saw, that the dignity of each person should be respected and that each person's capacity to choose freely should be developed. Because we have these duties to each other, government coercion is legitimate whenever it is needed to ensure that the dignity of citizens is being respected or when it is needed to secure the full development of people's capacity to choose. This, as Kant argues, means that government may legitimately place limits on the use of property and on the making of contracts and impose market restrictions and compulsory taxes when these are needed to care for the welfare or development of persons "who are not able to support themselves."[62] We have no reason to think that only negative rights exist. People can also have positive rights, and Kant's theory supports these as much as it supports negative rights.

2.3 Justice and Fairness

Several years ago, a Senate subcommittee heard the testimony of several workers who had contracted "brown lung" disease by breathing cotton dust while working cotton mills in the south.[63] Brown lung is a chronic disabling respiratory disease with symptoms similar to asthma and emphysema and is a cause of premature death. The disabled workers were seeking a federal law that would facilitate the process of getting disability compensation from the cotton mills, similar to federal laws covering "black lung" disease contracted in coal mines.

Senator Strom Thurmond:

A number of people have talked to me about this and they feel that if the federal government enters the field of black lung, it should enter the field of brown lung; and if those who have suffered from black lung are to receive federal consideration, then it seems fair that those who have suffered from brown lung receive federal consideration. . . . If our [state's cotton mill] workers have been injured and have not been properly compensated, then steps should be taken to see that is done. We want to see them treated fairly and squarely and properly, and so we look forward to . . . the testimony here today.

Mrs. Beatrice Norton:

I started in the mill when I was fourteen years old and I had to get out in 1968. . . . I worked in the dust year after year, just like my mother. I got sicker and sicker . . . I suddenly had no job, no money, and I was sick, too sick to ever work in my life again. . . . State legislators have proven in two successive sessions that they are not going to do anything to help the brown lung victims, so now we come to you in Washington and ask for help. We've waited a long time, and many of us have died waiting. I don't want to die of injustice.

Mrs. Vinnie Ellison:

My husband worked for twenty-one years [in the mill] in Spartanburg, and he worked in the dustiest parts of the mill, the opening room, the cardroom, and cleaning the air-conditioning ducts. . . . In the early sixties he started having trouble keeping up his job because of his breathing. His bossman told him that he had been a good worker, but wasn't worth a damn anymore, and fired him. . . . He had no pension and nothing to live on and we had to go on welfare to live. . . . My husband worked long and hard and lost his health and many years of pay because of the dust. It isn't fair that [the mill] threw him away like so much human garbage after he couldn't keep up his job because he was sick from the dust. We are not asking for handouts; we want what is owed to my husband for twenty-five years of hard work.

Disputes among individuals in business are often interlaced with references to *justice* or *fairness.* This is the case, for example, when one person accuses another of unjustly discriminating against him or her, showing unjust favoritism toward someone else, or not taking up a *fair* share of the burdens involved in some cooperative venture. Resolving disputes like these requires that we compare and weigh the conflicting claims of each of the parties and strike a balance between them. Justice and fairness are essentially comparative. They are concerned with the comparative treatment given to the members of a group when benefits and burdens are distributed, when rules and laws are administered, when members of a group cooperate or compete with each other, and when people are punished for the wrongs they have done or compensated for the wrongs they have suffered. Although the terms *justice* and *fairness* are used almost interchangeably, we tend to reserve the word *justice* for matters that are especially serious, although some authors have held that the concept of fairness is more fundamental.[64]

Standards of justice are generally taken to be more important than utilitarian considerations.[65] If a society is unjust to some of its members, then we normally condemn that society, even if the injustices secure more utilitarian benefits for everyone. If we think that slavery is unjust, for example, then we condemn a society that uses slavery even if slavery makes that society more productive. Greater benefits for some cannot justify injustices for others. Nonetheless, we also seem to hold that if the social gains are sufficiently large, a certain level of injustice may legitimately be tolerated.[66] In countries with extreme deprivation and poverty, for example, we seem to hold that some degree of equality may be traded off for major economic gains that leave everyone better off.

Standards of justice do not generally override the moral rights of individuals. Part of the reason for this is that, to some extent, justice is based on individual moral rights. The moral right to be treated as a free and equal person, for example, is part of what lies behind the idea that benefits and burdens should be distributed equally.[67] More important, however, is the fact that, as we saw, a moral right identifies interests people have, the free pursuit of which may not be subordinated to the interests of others except where there are special and exceptionally weighty reasons. This means that, for the most part, the moral rights of some individuals cannot be sacrificed merely in order to secure a somewhat better distribution of benefits for others. However, correcting extreme injustices may justify restricting some individuals' rights. Property rights, for example, might be legitimately redistributed for the sake of justice. We discuss trade-offs of this sort more fully after we have a better idea of what *justice* means.

Issues involving questions of justice and fairness are usually divided into three categories. *Distributive justice*, the first and basic category, is concerned with the fair distribution of society's benefits and burdens. In the brown lung hearings, for example, Senator Thurmond pointed out that if federal law helped workers afflicted by black lung, then it was only "fair" that it also help workers afflicted by brown lung. *Retributive justice*, the second category, refers to the just imposition of punishments and penalties on those who do wrong: A just penalty is one that in some sense is deserved by the person who does wrong. Retributive justice would be at issue, for example, if we were to ask whether it would be fair to penalize cotton mills for causing brown lung disease among their workers. *Compensatory justice*, the third category, concerns the just way of compensating people for what they lost when they were wronged by others: A just compensation is one that in some sense is proportional to the loss suffered by the person being compensated (such as loss of livelihood). During the brown lung hearings, for example, both Mrs. Norton and Mrs. Ellison claimed that, in justice, they were owed compensation from the cotton mills because of injuries inflicted by the mills.

This section examines each of these three kinds of justice separately. The section begins with a discussion of a basic principle of distributive justice (equals should be treated as equals) and then examines several views on the criteria relevant to determining whether two persons are equal. The section then turns to a brief discussion of retributive justice and ends with a discussion of compensatory justice.

Distributive Justice

Questions of distributive justice arise when different people put forth conflicting claims on society's benefits and burdens and all the claims cannot be satisfied.[68] The central cases are those where there is a scarcity of benefits—such as jobs, food, housing, medical care, income, and wealth—as compared with the numbers and desires of the people who want these goods. The other side of the coin is that there may be too many burdens—unpleasant work, drudgery, substandard housing, health injuries of various sorts—and not enough people willing to shoulder them. If there were enough goods to satisfy everyone's desires and enough people willing to share society's burdens, then conflicts between people would not arise and distributive justice would not be needed.

When people's desires and aversions exceed the adequacy of their resources, they are forced to develop principles for allocating scarce benefits and undesirable burdens in ways that are just and that resolve the conflicts in a fair way. The development of such principles is the concern of distributive justice.

The fundamental principle of distributive justice is that equals should be treated equally and unequals treated unequally.[69] More precisely, the fundamental principle of distributive justice may be expressed as follows:

> *Individuals who are similar in all respects relevant to the kind of treatment in question should be given similar benefits and burdens, even if they are dissimilar in other irrelevant respects; and individuals who are dissimilar in a relevant respect ought to be treated dissimilarly, in proportion to their dissimilarity.*

For example, if Susan and Bill are both doing the same work for me and there are no relevant differences between them or the work they are doing, then in justice I should pay them equal wages. However, if Susan is working twice as long as Bill and if length of working time is the relevant basis for determining wages on the sort of work they are doing, then, to be just, I should pay Susan twice as much as Bill. To return to our earlier example, if the federal government rightly helps workers who have suffered from black lung and there are no relevant differences between such workers and workers who have suffered from brown lung, then, as Senator Thurmond said, it is "fair that those who have suffered from brown lung [also] receive federal consideration."

This fundamental principle of distributive justice, however, is purely formal.[70] It is based on the purely logical idea that we must be consistent in the way we treat similar situations. The principle does not specify the "relevant respects" that may legitimately provide the basis for similarity or dissimilarity of treatment. For example, is race relevant when determining who should get what jobs? Most of us would say no, but then what characteristics are relevant when determining what benefits and burdens people should receive? We turn now to examine different views on the kinds of characteristics that may be relevant when determining who should get what. Each of these views provides a material principle of justice (i.e., a principle that gives specific content to the fundamental principle of distributive justice). For example, one simple principle that people often use to decide who should receive a limited or scarce good is the "first come, first served" principle that operates when waiting in line to receive something as well as in the seniority systems that businesses use. The "first come, first served" principle assumes that being first is a relevant characteristic for determining who should be the first party served when not all can be served at once. The reader can undoubtedly think of many other such simple principles that we use. However, here we will concentrate on several principles that are often thought to be more fundamental than principles such as "first come, first served."

Justice as Equality: Egalitarianism

Egalitarians hold that there are no relevant differences among people that can justify unequal treatment.[71] According to the egalitarian, all benefits and burdens should be distributed according to the following formula:

> *Every person should be given exactly equal shares of a society's or a group's benefits and burdens.*

Egalitarians base their view on the proposition that all human beings are equal in some fundamental respect and that, in virtue of this equality, each person has an equal claim to society's goods.[72] According to the egalitarian, this implies that goods should be allocated to people in equal portions.

Equality has been proposed as a principle of justice not only for entire societies, but also within smaller groups or organizations. Within a family, for example, it is often assumed that children should, over the course of their lives, receive equal shares of the goods parents make available to them. In some companies and in some workgroups, particularly when the group has strong feelings of solidarity and is working at tasks that require cooperation, workers feel that all should receive equal compensation for the work they are doing. Interestingly, when workers in a group receive equal compensation, they tend to become more cooperative with each other and to feel greater solidarity with each other.[73] Also interestingly, workers in countries such as Japan, which is characterized as having a more collectivist culture, prefer the principle of equality more than workers in countries such as the United States, which is characterized as having a more individualistic culture.[74]

Equality has, of course, appeared to many as an attractive social ideal and inequality, as a defect. "All men are created equal," says our Declaration of Independence, and the ideal of equality has been the driving force behind the emancipation of slaves; the prohibition of indentured servitude; the elimination of racial, sexual, and property requirements on voting and holding public office; and the institution of free public education. Americans have long prided themselves on the lack of overt status consciousness in their social relations.

Despite their popularity, however, egalitarian views have been subjected to heavy criticisms. One line of attack has focused on the egalitarian claim that all human beings are equal in some fundamental respect.[75] Critics claim that there is no quality that all human beings possess in precisely the same degree: Human beings differ in their abilities, intelligence, virtues, needs, desires, and all other physical and mental characteristics. If this is so, then human beings are unequal in all respects.

A second set of criticisms argues that the egalitarian ignores some characteristics that should be taken into account in distributing goods both in society and in smaller groups: need, ability, and effort.[76] If everyone is given exactly the same things, critics point out, then the lazy person will get as much as the industrious one, although the lazy one does not deserve as much. If everyone is given exactly the same, then the sick person will get only as much as healthy ones, although the sick person needs more. If everyone is given exactly the same, the handicapped person will have to do as much as more able persons, although the handicapped person has less ability. If everyone is given exactly the same, then individuals will have no incentives to exert greater efforts in their work. As a result, society's productivity and efficiency will decline.[77] Because the egalitarian formula ignores all these facts, and because it is clear that they should be taken into account, critics allege, egalitarianism must be mistaken.

Some egalitarians have tried to strengthen their position by distinguishing two different kinds of equality: political equality and economic equality.[78] *Political equality* refers to an equal participation in, and treatment by, the means of controlling and directing the political system. This includes equal rights to participate in the legislative process, equal civil liberties, and equal rights to due process. *Economic equality* refers to equality of income and wealth and equality of opportunity. The criticisms leveled against equality, according to some egalitarians, only apply to economic equality and not to political equality. Although everyone will concede that differences of need, ability, and effort may justify some inequalities in the distribution of income and wealth, everyone will also agree that political rights and liberties should not be unequally distributed. Thus, the egalitarian position may be correct with respect to political equality even if it is mistaken with respect to economic equality.

Other egalitarians have claimed that even economic equality is defensible if it is suitably limited. Thus, they have argued that every person has a right to a minimum standard of living and that income and wealth should be distributed equally until this standard is achieved for everyone.[79] The economic surplus that remains after everyone has achieved the minimum standard of living can then be distributed unequally according to need, effort, and so on. A major difficulty that this limited type of economic egalitarianism must face, however, is specifying what it means by *minimum standard of living.* Different societies and cultures have different views as to what constitutes the necessary minimum to live on. A relatively primitive economy will place the minimum at a lower point than a relatively affluent one. Nonetheless, most people would agree that justice requires that affluent societies satisfy at least the basic needs of their members and not let them die of starvation, exposure, or disease.

Justice Based on Contribution: Capitalist Justice

Some writers have argued that a society's benefits should be distributed in proportion to what each individual contributes to a society and/or to a group. The more a person contributes to a society's pool of economic goods, for example, the more that person is entitled to take from that pool; the less an individual contributes, the less that individual should get. The more a worker contributes to a project, the more he or she should be paid. According to this capitalist view of justice, when people engage in economic exchanges with each other, what a person gets out of the exchange should be at least equal in value to what he or she contributed. Justice requires, then, that the benefits a person receives should be proportional to the value of his or her contribution. Quite simply:

> *Benefits should be distributed according to the value of the contribution the individual makes to a society, a task, a group, or an exchange.*

The principle of contribution is perhaps the most widely used principle of fairness used to establish salaries and wages in American companies. In workgroups, particularly when relationships among the members of the group are impersonal and the product of each worker is independent of the efforts of the others, workers tend to feel that they should be paid in proportion to the work they have contributed.[80] Sales people out on the road, for example, or workers at individual sewing machines sewing individual garments or doing other piecework tend to feel that they should be paid in proportion to the quantity of goods they have individually sold or made. Interestingly, when workers are paid in accordance with the principle of contribution, this tends to promote among them an uncooperative and even competitive atmosphere in which resources and information are less willingly shared and in which status differences emerge.[81] Workers in countries that are characterized as having a more individualistic culture, such as the United States, prefer the principle of contribution more than workers in countries that are characterized as having a more collectivist culture, such as Japan.[82]

The main question raised by the contributive principle of distributive justice is how the "value of the contribution" of each individual is to be measured. One long-lived tradition has held that contributions should be measured in terms of *work effort*. The more effort people put forth in their work, the greater the share of benefits to which they are entitled. The harder one works, the more one deserves. This is the assumption behind the *Puritan ethic*, which held that every individual had a religious obligation to work hard at his *calling* (the career to which God summons each individual) and that God justly rewards hard work with wealth and success, while He justly punishes laziness with poverty and failure.[83] In the United States, this Puritan ethic has evolved into a secularized *work ethic*, which places a high value on individual effort and which assumes that, whereas hard work does and should lead to success, loafing is and should be punished.[84]

However, there are many problems with using effort as the basis of distribution.[85] First, to reward a person's efforts without any reference to whether the person produces anything worthwhile through these efforts is to reward incompetence and inefficiency. Second, if we reward people solely for their efforts and ignore their abilities and relative productivity, then talented and highly productive people will be given little incentive to invest their talent and productivity in producing goods for society. As a result, society's welfare will decline.

A second important tradition has held that contributions should be measured in terms of *productivity*: The better the quality of a person's contributed product, the more he or she should receive. (*Product* here should be interpreted broadly to include services rendered, capital invested, commodities manufactured, and any type of literary, scientific, or aesthetic works produced.)[86] A major problem with this second proposal is that it ignores people's needs. Handicapped, ill, untrained, and immature persons may be unable to produce anything worthwhile; if people are rewarded on the basis of their productivity, the needs of these disadvantaged groups will not be met. The main problem with this second proposal is that it is difficult to place any objective measure on the value of a person's product, especially in fields such as the sciences, the arts, entertainment, athletics, education, theology, and health care. Who would want to have their products priced on the basis of someone else's subjective estimates?

To deal with the last difficulty mentioned, some authors have suggested a third and highly influential version of the principle of contribution: They have argued that the value of a person's product should be determined by the market forces of supply and demand.[87] The value of a product would then depend not on its intrinsic value, but on the extent to which it is both relatively scarce and is viewed by buyers as desirable. In other words, the value of a person's contribution is equal to whatever that contribution would sell for in a competitive market. People then deserve to receive in exchange with others whatever the market value of their product is worth. Unfortunately, this method of measuring the value of a person's product still ignores people's needs. Moreover, to many people, market prices are an unjust method of evaluating the value of a person's product precisely because markets ignore the intrinsic values of things. Markets, for example, reward entertainers more than doctors. Also markets often reward a person who, through pure chance, has ended with something (e.g., an inheritance) that is scarce and that people happen to want. This, to many, seems the height of injustice.

Justice Based on Needs and Abilities: Socialism

Because there are probably as many kinds of socialism as there are socialists, it is somewhat inaccurate to speak of "the" socialist position on distributive justice. Nonetheless, the dictum proposed first by Louis Blanc (1811–1882) and then by Karl Marx (1818–1883) and Nikolai Lenin (1870–1924) is traditionally taken to represent the socialist view on distribution: "From each according to his ability, to each according to his needs."[88] The socialist principle, then, can be paraphrased as follows:

> *Work burdens should be distributed according to people's abilities, and benefits should be distributed according to people's needs.*

This socialist principle is based first on the idea that people realize their human potential by exercising their abilities in productive work.[89] Because the realization of one's full potentiality is a value, work should be distributed in such a way that a person can be as productive as possible, and this implies distributing work according to ability. Second, the benefits produced through work should be used to promote human happiness and well-being. This means distributing them so that people's basic biological and health needs are met, and then using what is left over to meet people's other nonbasic needs. Perhaps most fundamental to the socialist view is the notion that societies should be communities in which benefits and burdens are distributed on the model of a family. Just as able family members willingly support the family, and just as needy family members are willingly supported by the family, so also the able members of a society should contribute their abilities to society by taking up its burdens while the needy should be allowed to share in its benefits.

As the example of the family suggests, the principle of distribution according to need and ability is used within small groups as well as within larger society. In athletics, for example, the members of a team will distribute burdens according to each athlete's ability and will tend to stand together and help each other according to each one's need. The principle of need and ability, however, is the principle that tends to be least acknowledged in business. Managers sometimes invoke the principle when they pass out the more difficult jobs among the members of a workgroup to those who are stronger and more able, but they often retreat when these workers complain that they are being given larger burdens without higher compensation. Managers also sometimes invoke the principle when they make special allowances for workers who seem to have special needs. (This was, in fact, a key consideration when Congress passed the Americans with Disabilities Act.) However, they rarely do so and are often criticized for showing favoritism when they do this.

Nevertheless, there is something to be said for the socialist principle: Needs and abilities certainly should be taken into account when determining how benefits and burdens should be distributed among the members of a group or society. Most people would agree, for example, that we should make a greater contribution to the lives of cotton mill workers with brown lung disease who have greater needs than to the lives of healthy persons who have all they need. Most people would also agree that individuals should be employed in occupations for which they are fitted, and that this means matching each person's abilities to his or her job as far as possible. Vocational tests in high school and college, for example, are supposed to help students find careers that match their abilities.

However, the socialist principle has also had its critics. First, opponents have pointed out that, under the socialist principle, there would be no relation between the amount of effort a worker puts forth and the amount of remuneration one receives (because remuneration would depend on need, not on effort). Consequently, opponents conclude, workers would have no incentive to put forth any work efforts at all knowing that they will receive the same regardless of whether they work hard. The result, it is claimed, will be a stagnating economy with a declining productivity (a claim, however, that does not seem to be borne out by the facts).[90] Underlying this criticism is a deeper objection—namely, that it is unrealistic to think that entire societies could be modeled on familial relationships. Human nature is essentially self-interested and competitive, the critics of socialism hold, and so outside the family people cannot be motivated by the fraternal willingness to share and help that is characteristic of families. Socialists have usually replied to this charge by arguing that human beings are trained to acquire the vices of selfishness and competitiveness by modern social and economic institutions that inculcate and encourage competitive and self-interested behavior, but that people do not have these vices by nature. By nature, humans are born into families where they instinctively value helping each other. If these instinctive and "natural" attitudes continued to be nurtured, instead of being eradicated, humans would continue to value helping others even outside the family and would acquire the virtues of being cooperative, helpful, and selfless. The debate on what kinds of motivations human nature is subject to is still largely unsettled.

A second objection that opponents of the socialist principle have urged is that, if the socialist principle were enforced, it would obliterate individual freedom.[91] Under the socialist principle, the occupation each person entered would be determined by the person's abilities and not by his or her free choice. If a person has the ability to be a university teacher but wants to be a ditch-digger, the person will have to become a teacher. Similarly, under the socialist principle, the goods a person gets will be determined by the person's needs and not by his or her free choice. If a person needs a loaf of bread but wants a bottle of beer, he or she will have to take the loaf of bread. The sacrifice of freedom is even greater, the critics claim, when one considers that in a socialist society some central government agency has to decide what tasks should be matched to each person's abilities and what goods should be allotted to each person's needs. The decisions of this central agency will then have to be imposed on other persons at the expense of their freedom to choose for themselves. The socialist principle substitutes paternalism for freedom.

Justice as Freedom: Libertarianism

The last section discussed libertarian views on moral rights; libertarians also have some clear and related views on the nature of justice. The libertarian holds that no particular way of distributing goods can be said to be just or unjust apart from the free choices individuals make. Any distribution of benefits and burdens is just if it is the result of individuals freely choosing to exchange with each other the goods each person already owns. Robert Nozick, a leading libertarian, suggests this principle as the basic principle of distributive justice:

> *From each according to what he chooses to do, to each according to what he makes for himself (perhaps with the contracted aid of others) and what others choose to do for him and choose to give him of what they've been given previously (under this maxim) and haven't yet expended or transferred.*[92]

Quite simply, "From each as they choose, to each as they are chosen." For example, if I choose to write a novel or carve a statue out of a piece of driftwood, then I should be allowed to keep the novel or statue if I choose to keep it. If I choose, I should be allowed to give them away to someone else or exchange them for other objects with whomever I choose. In general, people should be allowed to keep everything they make and everything they are freely given. Obviously, this means it would be wrong to tax one person (i.e., take the person's money) to provide welfare benefits for someone else's needs.

Nozick's principle is based on the claim (which we have already discussed) that every person has a right to freedom from coercion that takes priority over all other rights and values. The only distribution that is just, according to Nozick, is one that results from free individual choices. Any distribution that results from an attempt to impose a certain pattern on society (e.g., imposing equality on everyone or taking from the have's and giving to the have nots) will therefore be unjust.

We have already noted some of the problems associated with the libertarian position. The major difficulty is that the libertarian enshrines a certain value—freedom from the coercion of others—and sacrifices all other rights and values to it without giving any persuasive reasons why this should be done. Opponents of the libertarian view argue that other forms of freedom must also be secured, such as freedom from ignorance and freedom from hunger. In many cases, these other forms of freedom override freedom from coercion. If a man is starving, for example, his right to be free from the constraints imposed by hunger is more important than the right of a satisfied man to be free of the constraint of being forced to share his surplus food. To secure these more important rights, society may impose a certain pattern of distribution even if this means that, in some cases, some people will have to be coerced into conforming to the distribution. Those with surplus money, for example, may have to be taxed to provide for those who are starving.

A second related criticism of libertarianism claims that the libertarian principle of distributive justice will generate unjust treatment of the disadvantaged.[93] Under the libertarian principle, a person's share of goods will depend wholly on what the person can produce through his or her own efforts or what others choose to give the person out of charity (or some other motive). Both of these sources may be unavailable to a person through no fault of the person. A person may be ill, handicapped, unable to obtain the tools or land needed to produce goods, too old or too young to work, or otherwise incapable of producing anything through his or her own efforts. Other people (perhaps out of greed) may refuse to provide that person with what he or she needs. According to the libertarian principle, such a person should get nothing. But this, say the critics of libertarianism, is surely mistaken. If people through no fault of their own happen to be unable to care for themselves, their survival should not depend on the outside chance that others will provide them with what they need. Each person's life is of value, and consequently each person should be cared for, even if this means coercing others into distributing some of their surplus to the person.

Justice as Fairness: Rawls

These discussions have suggested several different considerations that should be taken into account in the distribution of society's benefits and burdens: political and economic equality, a minimum standard of living, needs, ability, effort, and freedom. What is needed, however, is a comprehensive theory capable of drawing these considerations together and fitting them together into a logical whole. John Rawls provides one approach to distributive justice that at least approximates this ideal of a comprehensive theory.[94]

John Rawls' theory is based on the assumption that conflicts involving justice should be settled by first devising a fair method for choosing the principles by which the conflicts are resolved. Once a fair method of choosing principles is devised, the principles we choose by using that method should serve us as our own principles of distributive justice.

Rawls proposes two basic principles that, he argues, we would select if we were to use a fair method of choosing principles to resolve our social conflicts.[95] The principles of distributive justice that Rawls proposes can be paraphrased by saying that the distribution of benefits and burdens in a society is just if and only if:

1. *each person has an equal right to the most extensive basic liberties compatible with similar liberties for all, and*
2. *social and economic inequalities are arranged so that they are both*
   a. *to the greatest benefit of the least advantaged persons, and*
   b. *attached to offices and positions open to all under conditions of fair equality of opportunity.*

Rawls tells us that Principle 1 is supposed to take priority over Principle 2 should the two of them ever come into conflict, and within Principle 2, Part *b* is supposed to take priority over Part *a*.

Principle 1 is called the *principle of equal liberty*. Essentially it says that each citizen's liberties must be protected from invasion by others and must be equal to those of others. These basic liberties include the right to vote, freedom of speech and conscience and the other civil liberties, freedom to hold personal property, and freedom from arbitrary arrest.[96] If the principle of equal liberty is correct, then it implies that it is unjust for business institutions to invade the privacy of employees, pressure managers to vote in certain ways, exert undue influence on political processes by the use of bribes, or otherwise violate the equal political liberties of society's members. According to Rawls, moreover, because our freedom to make contracts would diminish if we were afraid of being defrauded or were afraid that contracts would not be honored, the principle of equal liberty also prohibits the use of force, fraud, or deception in contractual transactions and requires that just contracts should be honored.[97] If this is true, then contractual transactions with customers (including advertising) should morally be free of fraud, and employees have a moral obligation to render the services they have justly contracted to their employer.

Part *a* of Principle 2 is called the *difference principle*. It assumes that a productive society will incorporate inequalities, but it then asserts that steps must be taken to improve the position of the most needy members of society, such as the sick and the disabled, unless such improvements would so burden society that they make everyone, including the needy, worse off than before.[98] Rawls claims that the more productive a society is, the more benefits it will be able to provide for its least advantaged members. Because the difference principle obliges us to maximize benefits for the least advantaged, this means that business institutions should be as efficient in their use of resources as possible. If we assume that a market system such as ours is most efficient when it is most competitive, then the difference principle will in effect imply that markets should be competitive and that anticompetitive practices such as price-fixing and monopolies are unjust. In addition, because pollution and other environmentally damaging external effects consume resources inefficiently, the difference principle also implies that it is wrong for firms to pollute.

Part *b* of Principle 2 is called the *principle of fair equality of opportunity.* It says that everyone should be given an equal opportunity to qualify for the more privileged positions in society's institutions.[99] This means not only that job qualifications should be related to the requirements of the job (thereby prohibiting racial and sexual discrimination), but that each person must have access to the training and education needed to qualify for the desirable jobs. A person's efforts, abilities, and contribution would then determine his or her remuneration.

The principles that Rawls proposes are quite comprehensive and bring together the main considerations stressed by the other approaches to justice that we have examined. However, Rawls not only provides us with a set of principles of justice, he also proposes a general method for evaluating in a fair way the adequacy of any moral principles. The method he proposes consists of determining what principles a group of rational self-interested persons would choose to live by if they knew they would live in a society governed by those principles but they did not yet know what each of them would turn out to be like in that society.[100] We might ask, for example, whether such a group of rational self-interested persons would choose to live in a society governed by a principle that discriminates against Blacks when none of them knows whether he or she will turn out to be a Black person in that society. The answer, clearly, is that such a racist principle would be rejected and consequently, according to Rawls, the racist principle would be unjust. Thus, Rawls claims that a principle is a morally justified principle of justice if, and only if, the principle would be acceptable to a group of rational self-interested persons who know they will live in a society governed by the principles they accept but who do not know what sex, race, abilities, religion, interests, social position, income, or other particular characteristics each of them will possess in that future society.

Rawls refers to the situation of such an imaginary group of rational persons as the *original position*, and he refers to their ignorance of any particulars about themselves as the *veil of ignorance*.[101] The purpose and effect of decreeing that the parties to the original position do not know what particular characteristics each of them will possess is to ensure that none of them can protect his or her own special interests. Because they are ignorant of their particular qualities, the parties to the original position are forced to be fair and impartial and to show no favoritism toward any special group: They must look after the good of all.

According to Rawls, the principles that the imaginary parties to the original position accept will *ipso facto* turn out to be morally justified.[102] They will be morally justified because the original position incorporates the Kantian moral ideas of reversibility (the parties choose principles that will apply to themselves), universalizability (the principles must apply equally to everyone), and treating people as ends (each party has an equal say in the choice of principles). The principles are further justified, according to Rawls, because they are consistent with our deepest considered intuitions about justice. The principles chosen by the parties to the original position match most of the moral convictions we already have; where they do not, according to Rawls, we would be willing to change them to fit Rawls' principles once we reflect on his arguments.

Rawls goes on to claim that the parties to the original position would in fact choose his (Rawls') principles of justice—that is, the principle of equal liberty, the difference principle, and the principle of fair equality of opportunity.[103] The principle of equal liberty would be chosen because the parties will want to be free to pursue their major special interests whatever these might be. In the original position, each person is ignorant of what special interests he or she will have, thus everyone will want to secure a maximum amount of freedom so that he or she can pursue whatever interests he or she has on entering society. The difference principle will be chosen because all parties will want to protect themselves against the possibility of ending in the worst position in society. By adopting the difference principle, the parties will ensure that even the position of the most needy is cared for. The principle of fair equality of opportunity will be chosen, according to Rawls, because all parties to the original position will want to protect their interests should they turn out to be among the talented. The principle of fair equality of opportunity ensures that everyone has an equal opportunity to advance through the use of his or her own abilities, efforts, and contributions.

If Rawls is correct in claiming that the principles chosen by the parties to the original position are morally justified, and if he is correct in arguing that his own principles would be chosen by the parties to the original position, then it follows that his principles are in fact morally justified to serve as our own principles of justice. These principles would then constitute the proper principles of distributive justice.

Critics, however, have objected to various parts of Rawls' theory.[104] Some have argued that the original position is not an adequate method for choosing moral principles. According to these critics, the mere fact that a set of principles is chosen by the hypothetical parties to the original position tells us nothing about whether the principles are morally justified. Other critics have argued that the parties to the original position would not choose Rawls' principles at all. Utilitarians, for example, have argued that the hypothetical parties to the original position would choose utilitarianism and not Rawls' principles. Still other critics have claimed that Rawls' principles are mistaken. According to these critics, Rawls' principles are opposed to our basic convictions concerning what justice is.

Despite the many objections that have been raised against Rawls' theory, his defenders still claim that the advantages of the theory outweigh its defects. For one thing, they claim, the theory preserves the basic values that have become embedded in our moral beliefs: freedom, equality of opportunity, and concern for the disadvantaged. Second, the theory fits easily into the basic economic institutions of Western societies: It does not reject the market system, work incentives, nor the inequalities consequent on a division of labor. Instead, by requiring that inequalities work for the benefit of the least advantaged and by requiring equality of opportunity, the theory shows how the inequalities that attend the division of labor and free markets can be compensated for and thereby made just. Third, the theory incorporates both the communitarian and individualistic strains that are intertwined in Western culture. The difference principle encourages the more talented to use their skills in ways that will rebound to the benefit of fellow citizens who are less well off, thereby encouraging a type of communitarian or fraternal concern.[105] The principle of equal liberty leaves the individual free to pursue whatever special interests the individual may have. Fourth, Rawls' theory takes into account the criteria of need, ability, effort, and contribution. The difference principle distributes benefits in accordance with need, whereas the principle of fair equality of opportunity in effect distributes benefits and burdens according to ability and contribution.[106] Fifth, the defenders of Rawls argue that there is the moral justification that the original position provides. The original position is defined so that its parties choose impartial principles that take into account the equal interests of everyone, and this, they claim, is the essence of morality.

Retributive Justice

Retributive justice concerns the justice of blaming or punishing persons for doing wrong. Philosophers have long debated the justification of blame and punishment, but we need not enter these debates here. More relevant to our purposes is the question of the conditions under which it is just to punish a person for doing wrong.

The first chapter discussed some major conditions under which a person could not be held morally responsible for what he or she did: ignorance and inability. These conditions are also relevant to determining the justice of punishing or blaming someone for doing wrong: If people do not know or freely choose what they are doing, they cannot justly be punished or blamed for it. For example, if the cotton mill owners mentioned at the beginning of this section did not know that the conditions in their mills would cause brown lung disease, then it would be unjust to punish them when it turns out that their mills caused this disease.

A second kind of condition of just punishments is certitude that the person being punished actually did wrong. For example, many firms use more or less complex systems of due process that are intended to ascertain whether the conduct of employees was really such as to merit dismissal or some other penalty.[107] Penalizing an employee on the basis of flimsy or incomplete evidence is rightly considered an injustice.

A third kind of condition of just punishments is that they must be consistent and proportioned to the wrong. Punishment is consistent only when everyone is given the same penalty for the same infraction; punishment is proportioned to the wrong when the penalty is no greater in magnitude than the harm that the wrongdoer inflicted.[108] It is unjust, for example, for a manager to impose harsh penalties for minor infractions of rules or to be lenient toward favorites but harsh toward all others. If the purpose of a punishment is to deter others from committing the same wrong or to prevent the wrongdoer from repeating the wrong, then punishment should not be greater than what is consistently necessary to achieve these aims.

Compensatory Justice

Compensatory justice concerns the justice of restoring to a person what the person lost when he or she was wronged by someone else. We generally hold that when one person wrongfully harms the interests of another person, the wrongdoer has a moral duty to provide some form of restitution to the person he or she wronged. For example, if I destroy someone's property or injure him bodily, I will be held morally responsible for paying him damages.

There are no hard and fast rules for determining how much compensation a wrongdoer owes the victim. Justice seems to require that the wrongdoer as far as possible should restore whatever he or she took, and this would usually mean that the amount of restitution should be equal to the loss the wrongdoer knowingly inflicted on the victim. However, some losses are impossible to measure. If I maliciously injure someone's reputation, for example, how much restitution should I make? Some losses, moreover, cannot be restored at all: How can the loss of life or the loss of sight be compensated? In cases such as the Ford Pinto case, where the injury is such that full restoration of the loss is not possible, we seem to hold that the wrongdoer should at least pay for the material damages the loss inflicts on the injured person and his or her immediate family.

Traditional moralists have argued that a person has a moral obligation to compensate an injured party only if three conditions are present:[109]

1. *The action that inflicted the injury was wrong or negligent. For example, if by efficiently managing my firm I undersell my competitor and run her out of business, I am not morally bound to compensate her since such competition is neither wrongful nor negligent; but if I steal from my employer, then I owe him compensation, or if I fail to exercise due care in my driving, then I owe compensation to those whom I injure.*
2. *The person's action was the real cause of the injury. For example, if a banker loans a person money and the borrower then uses it to cheat others, the banker is not morally obligated to compensate the victims; but if the banker defrauds a customer, the customer must be compensated.*
3. *The person inflicted the injury voluntarily. For example, if I injure someone's property accidentally and without negligence, I am not morally obligated to compensate the person. (I may, however, be legally bound to do so depending on how the law chooses to distribute the social costs of injury.)*

The most controversial forms of compensation undoubtedly are the preferential treatment programs that attempt to remedy past injustices against groups. For example, if a racial group has been unjustly discriminated against for an extended period of time in the past and its members consequently now hold the lowest economic and social positions in society, does justice require that members of that group be compensated by being given special preference in hiring, training, and promotion procedures? Would such special treatment be a violation of justice by violating the principle of equal treatment? Does justice legitimize quotas even if this requires turning down more highly qualified nonminorities? These are complex and involved questions that we are not able to answer at this point. We return to them in a later chapter.

2.4 The Ethics of Care

At 8 p.m. on the night of December 11, 1995, an explosion near a boiler room rocked the Malden Mills factory in Lawrence, Massachusetts.[110] Fires broke out in the century-old brick textile factory. Fanned by winds, the fires quickly gutted three factory buildings, injuring 25 workers, destroying nearly all of the plant, and putting nearly 1400 people out of work 2 weeks before Christmas.

Founded in 1906, Malden Mills, a family-owned company, was one of the few makers of textiles still operating in New England. Most other textile manufacturers had relocated to the south and then to Asia in their search for cheap nonunion labor. President and major owner of the company, Aaron Feuerstein, however, had refused to abandon the community and its workers who he said were "the most valuable asset that Malden Mills has, . . . not an expense that can be cut." Emerging from a brush with bankruptcy in 1982, Feuerstein had refocused the company on the pricier end of the textile market, where state-of-the-art technology and high-quality goods are more important than low costs. Shunning low-margin commodity fabrics such as plain polyester sheets, the company focused on a new synthetic material labeled *Polartec* that company workers had discovered how to make through trial and error during the early 1980s. The new material was a fleecy, lightweight, warm material that could wick away perspiration and that required precise combinations of artificial yarns, raising and shaving the pile, and weaving at specially invented (and patented) machines operated at exactly the right temperature, humidity, and speed. Workers had to develop special skills to achieve the correct weave and quality. Soon recognizing Polartec as the highest quality and most technically advanced fabric available for performance outdoor clothing, Patagonia, L.L Bean, Eddie Bauer, Lands' End, North Face, Ralph Lauren, and other upscale outfitters adopted the high-priced material. Polartec sales climbed from $5 million in 1982 to over $200 million by 1995. With additional revenues from high-quality upholstery fabrics, Malden Mills' revenues in 1995 had totaled $403 million, and its employees, who now numbered nearly 3200, were the highest paid in the country. Feuerstein, who frequently provided special help to workers with special needs, kept an open-door policy with workers.

The morning after the December fire, however, with the factory in smouldering ruins, newspapers predicted that owner Aaron Feuerstein would do the smart thing and collect over $100 million that insurers would owe him, sell off the remaining assets, and either shut down the company or rebuild in a Third World country where labor was cheaper. Instead, Feuerstein announced that the company would rebuild in Lawrence. In a move that confounded the industry, he promised that every employee forced out of work by the fire would continue to be paid full wages, would receive full medical benefits, and would be guaranteed a job when operations restarted in a few months. Rebuilding in Lawrence would cost over $300 million while keeping 1400 laid-off workers on full salaries for a period of up to 3 months would cost an additional $20 million. "I have a responsibility to the worker, both blue-collar and white-collar," Feuerstein later said. "I have an equal responsibility to the community. It would have been unconscionable to put 3000 people on the streets and deliver a death blow to the cities of Lawrence and Methuen. Maybe on paper our company is [now] worth less to Wall Street, but I can tell you it's [really] worth more."

The Malden Mills incident suggests a perspective on ethics that is not adequately captured by the moral views we have so far examined. Consider that from a utilitarian perspective Feuerstein had no obligation to rebuild the factory in Lawrence nor to continue to pay his workers while they were not working. Moreover, relocating the operations of Malden Mills to a Third World country where labor is cheaper would not only have benefited the company, it would also have provided jobs for Third World workers who are more desperately needy than American workers. From an impartial utilitarian perspective, then, more utility would have been produced by bringing jobs to Third World workers than by spending the money to preserve the jobs of current Malden Mills employees in Lawrence, Massachusetts. It is true that the Malden Mills workers were close to Feuerstein and that over the years they had remained loyal to him and had built a close relationship with him. However, from an impartial standpoint, the utilitarian would say such personal relationships are irrelevant and should be set aside in favor of whatever maximizes utility.

A rights perspective would also not provide any support for the decision to remain in Lawrence nor to continue to pay workers full wages while the company rebuilt. Workers certainly could not claim to have a moral right to be paid while they were not working. Nor could workers claim to have a moral right to have a factory rebuilt for them. The impartial perspective of a rights theory, then, does not suggest that Feuerstein had any special obligations to his employees after the fire.

Nor, finally, could one argue that justice demanded that Feuerstein rebuild the factory and continue to pay workers while they were not working. Although workers were pivotal to the success of the company, the company had rewarded them by paying them very generous salaries over many years. Impartial justice does not seem to require that the company support people while they are not working nor does it seem to require that the company build a factory for them. In fact, if one is impartial, then it seems more just to move the factory to a Third World country where people are more needy than to keep the jobs in the United States where people are relatively well off.

Partiality and Care

The approaches to ethics that we have seen, then, all assume that ethics should be impartial and that, consequently, any special relationships that one may have with particular individuals, such as relatives, friends, or one's employees, should be set aside when determining what one should do.[111] Some utilitarians have claimed, in fact, that if a stranger and your parent were both drowning and you could save only one of them, and if saving the stranger would produce more utility than saving your parent (perhaps the stranger is a brilliant surgeon who would save many lives), then you would have a moral obligation to save the stranger and let your parent drown.[112] Such a conclusion, many people have argued, is perverse and mistaken.[113] In such a situation, the special relationship of love and caring that you have with your parents gives you a special obligation to care for them in a way that overrides obligations you may have toward strangers. Similarly, in the Malden Mills incident, Feuerstein had a special obligation to take care of his workers precisely because they were his workers and had built concrete relationships with him, helping him build his business and create the revolutionary new fabrics that gave Malden Mills its amazing competitive advantage in the textile industry. This obligation toward his own particular workers, who were to a large extent dependent on his company, it could be argued, overrode any obligations he may have had toward strangers in the Third World.

This view—that we have an obligation to exercise special care toward those particular persons with whom we have valuable close relationships, particularly relations of dependency—is a key concept in an "ethic of care," an approach to ethics that many feminist ethicists have recently advanced. We briefly discussed this approach to ethics in the first chapter when we noted the new approach to moral development worked out by psychologist Carol Gilligan. A morality of care "rests on an understanding of relationships as response to another in their terms."[114] According to this "care" view of ethics, the moral task is not to follow universal and impartial moral principles, but instead to attend and respond to the good of particular concrete persons with whom we are in a valuable and close relationship.[115] Compassion, concern, love, friendship, and kindness are all sentiments or virtues that normally manifest this dimension of morality. Thus, an ethic of care emphasizes two moral demands:

1. *We each exist in a web of relationships and should preserve and nurture those concrete and valuable relationships we have with specific persons.*
2. *We each should exercise special care for those with whom we are concretely related by attending to their particular needs, values, desires, and concrete well-being as seen from their own personal perspective, and by responding positively to these needs, values, desires, and concrete well being, particularly of those who are vulnerable and dependent on our care.*

For example, Feuerstein's decision to remain in the community of Lawrence and care for his workers by continuing to pay them after the fire was a response to the imperative of preserving the concrete relationships he had formed with his employees, and of exercising special care for the specific needs of these particular individuals who were economically dependent on him. This requirement to take care of this specific group of individuals is more significant than any moral requirement to care for strangers in Third World countries.

It is important not to restrict the notion of a concrete relationship to relationships between two individuals or to relationships between an individual and a specific group. The examples of relationships that we have given so far have been of this kind. Many advocates of an ethic of care have noted that an ethic of care should also encompass the larger systems of relationships that make up concrete communities. An ethic of care, therefore, can be seen as encompassing the kinds of obligations that a so-called *communitarian ethic* advocates. A communitarian ethic is an ethic that sees concrete communities and communal relationships as having a fundamental value that should be preserved and maintained.[116] What is important in a communitarian ethic is not the isolated individual, but the community within which individuals discover who they are by seeing themselves as integral parts of a larger community with its traditions, culture, practices, and history.[117] The concrete relationships that make up a particular community, then, should be preserved and nurtured just as much as the more interpersonal relationships that spring up between people.

What kind of argument can be given in support of an ethic of care? An ethic of care can be based on the claim that the identity of the self—who I am—is based on the relationships the self has with other selves: The individual cannot exist, cannot even be who he or she is, in isolation from caring relationships with others.[118] I need others to feed and care for me when I am born; I need others to educate me and care for me as I grow; I need others as friends and lovers to care for me when I mature; and always I must live in a community on whose language, traditions, culture, and other benefits I depend and that come to define me. It is in these concrete relationships with others that I form my understanding of who and what I am. Therefore, to whatever extent the self has value, to that same extent the relationships that are necessary for the self to exist and be what it is must also have value and so should be maintained and nurtured. The value of the self, then, is ultimately derivative from the value of the community.

It is also important in this context to distinguish three different forms of caring: caring about something, caring after someone, and caring for someone.[119] The kind of caring demanded by an ethic of care is the kind expressed by the phrase "caring for someone." Ethicists have suggested that the paradigm example of caring for someone is the kind of caring that a mother extends toward her child.[120] Such caring is focused on persons and their well-being, not on things; it does not seek to foster dependence, but nurtures the development of the person so that one becomes capable of making one's own choices and living one's own life. It is not detached, but is "engrossed" in the person and attempts to see the world through the eyes and values of the person. In contrast, caring about something is the kind of concern and interest that one can have for things or ideas where there is no second person in whose subjective reality one becomes engrossed. Such caring for objects is not the kind of caring demanded by an ethics of care. One can also become busy taking care of people in a manner that looks after their needs but remains objective and distant from them as, for example, often happens in bureaucratic service institutions such as the post office or a social welfare office. Caring after people in this way, although often necessary, is not the kind of caring demanded by an ethic of care.

Two additional issues are important to note. First, not all relationships have value, and so not all would generate the duties of care. Relationships in which one person attempts to dominate, oppress, or harm another, relationships that are characterized by hatred, violence, disrespect, and viciousness, and relationships that are characterized by injustice, exploitation, and harm to others lack the value that an ethic of care requires. An ethic of care does not obligate us to maintain and nurture such relationships. However, relationships that exhibit the virtues of compassion, concern, love, friendship, and loyalty do have the kind of value that an ethic of care requires, and an ethic of care implies that such relationships should be maintained and nurtured.

Second, it is important to recognize that the demands of caring are sometimes in conflict with the demands of justice. Consider two examples. First, suppose that one of the employees whom a female manager supervises is a friend of hers. Suppose that one day she catches her friend stealing from the company. Should she turn in her friend as company policy requires or should she say nothing to protect her friend? Second, suppose that a female manager is supervising several people, one of whom is a close friend of hers. Suppose that she must recommend one of these subordinates for promotion to a particularly desirable position. Should she recommend her friend simply because she is her friend, or should she be impartial and follow company policy by recommending the subordinate who is most qualified even if this means passing over her friend? Clearly, in each of these cases, justice would require that the manager not favor her friend. The demands of an ethic of care would seem to require that the manager favor her friend for the sake of their friendship. How should conflicts of this sort be resolved?

First, notice that there is no fixed rule that can resolve all such conflicts. One can imagine situations in which the manager's obligations of justice toward her company would clearly override the obligations she has toward her friend. (Imagine that her friend stole several million dollars and was prepared to steal several million more.) One can imagine situations in which the manager's obligations toward her friend override her obligations toward the company. (Imagine, for example, that what her friend stole was insignificant, that her friend desperately needed what she stole, and that the company would react by imposing an excessively harsh punishment on the friend.)

Although no fixed rule can resolve all conflicts between the demands of caring and the requirements of justice, nevertheless, some guidelines can be helpful in resolving such conflicts. Consider that when the manager was hired, she voluntarily agreed to accept the position of manager along with the duties and privileges that would define her role as a manager. Among the duties she promised to carry out is the duty to protect the resources of the company and abide by company policy. Therefore, the manager betrays her relationships with the people to whom she made these promises if she now shows favoritism toward her friend in violation of the company policies she voluntarily agreed to uphold. The institutional obligations we voluntary accept and to which we voluntarily commit ourselves, then, can require that we be impartial toward our friends and that we pay more attention to the demands of impartial justice than to the demands of an ethic of care. What about situations in which there is a conflict between our institutional obligations and the demands of a relationship, and the relationship is so important to us that we feel we must favor the relationship over our institutional obligations? Then morality would seem to require that we relinquish the institutional role that we have voluntarily accepted. Thus, the manager who feels that she must favor her friend and that she cannot be impartial as she voluntarily agreed to be when she accepted her job must resign her job. Otherwise the manager is in effect living a lie: By keeping her job while favoring her friend, she would imply that she was living up to her voluntary agreement of impartiality when in fact she was being partial toward her friend.

It was noted that the care approach to ethics has been developed primarily by feminist ethicists. The care approach, in fact, originated in the claim of psychologist Carol Gilligan that women and men approach moral issues from two different perspectives: Men approach moral issues from an individualistic focus on rights and justice, whereas women approach moral issues from a nonindividualistic focus on relationships and caring. Empirical research, however, has shown that this claim is, for the most part, mistaken, although there are some differences evident in the way that men and women respond to moral dilemmas.[121] Most ethicists have abandoned the view that an ethic of care is for women only, and have argued, instead, that just as women must recognize the demands of justice and impartiality, so men must recognize the demands of caring and partiality.[122] Caring is not the task of women, but a moral imperative for both men and women.

Objections to Care

The care approach to ethics has been criticized on several grounds. First, it has been claimed that an ethic of care can degenerate into unjust favoritism.[123] Being partial, for example, to members of one's own ethnic group, to a sexist *old boy* network, to members of one's own race, or to members of one's own nation can all be unjust forms of partiality. Proponents of an ethic of care, however, can respond that, although the demands of partiality can conflict with other demands of morality, this is true of all approaches to ethics. Morality consists of a wide spectrum of moral considerations that can conflict with each other: Utilitarian considerations can conflict with considerations of justice, and these can conflict with moral rights. In the same way, the demands of partiality and caring can also conflict with the demands of utility, justice, and rights. What morality requires is not that we get rid of all moral conflicts, but that we learn to weigh moral considerations and balance their different demands in specific situations. The fact that caring can sometimes conflict with justice, then, does not make an ethic of caring less adequate than any other approach to ethics, but simply points out the need to weigh and balance the relative importance of caring versus justice in specific situations.

A second important criticism of an ethic of care is that its demands can lead to "burnout." In demanding that people exercise caring for children, parents, siblings, spouses, lovers, friends, and other members of the community, an ethic of care seems to demand that people sacrifice their own needs and desires to care for the well-being of others. However, proponents of caring can respond that an adequate view of caring will balance caring for the caregiver with caring for others.[124]

The advantage of an ethic of care is that it forces us to focus on the moral value of being partial toward those concrete persons with whom we have special and valuable relationships, and the moral importance of responding to such persons as particular individuals with characteristics that demand a response to them that we do not extend to others. In these respects, an ethic of care provides an important corrective to the other approaches to ethics that we have examined, which all emphasize impartiality and universality. An ethic of care, with its focus on partiality and particularity, is an important reminder of an aspect of morality that cannot be ignored.

2.5 Integrating Utility, Rights, Justice, and Caring

The last three sections have described the four main kinds of moral standards that today lie at the basis of most of our moral judgments and that force us to bring distinctive kinds of considerations into our moral reasonings. Utilitarian standards must be used when we do not have the resources to attain everyone's objectives, so we are forced to consider the net social benefits and social costs consequent on the actions (or policies or institutions) by which we can attain these objectives. When these utilitarian considerations are employed, the person must bring into his or her moral reasoning measurements, estimates, and comparisons of the relevant benefits and costs. Such measurements, estimates, and comparisons constitute the information on which the utilitarian moral judgment is based.

Our moral judgments are also partially based on standards that specify how individuals must be treated or respected. These sorts of standards must be employed when our actions and policies will substantially affect the welfare and freedom of specifiable individuals. Moral reasoning of this type forces consideration of whether the behavior respects the basic rights of the individuals involved and whether the behavior is consistent with one's agreements and special duties. These sorts of considerations require information concerning how the behavior affects the basic needs of the humans involved, the freedom they have to choose, the information available to them, the extent to which force, coercion, manipulation, or deception are used on them, and the tacit and explicit understandings with which they entered various roles and agreements.

Third, our moral judgments are also in part based on standards of justice that indicate how benefits and burdens should be distributed among the members of a group. These sorts of standards must be employed when evaluating actions whose distributive effects differ in important ways. The moral reasoning on which such judgments are based will incorporate considerations concerning whether the behavior distributes benefits and burdens equally or in accordance with the needs, abilities, contributions, and free choices of people as well as the extent of their wrongdoing. These sorts of considerations in turn rely on comparisons of the benefits and burdens going to different groups (or individuals) and comparisons of their relative needs, efforts, and so forth.

Fourth, our moral judgments are also based on standards of caring that indicate the kind of care that is owed to those with whom we have special concrete relationships. Standards of caring are essential when moral questions arise that involve persons embedded in a web of relationships, particularly persons with whom one has close relationships, particularly relationships of dependency. Moral reasoning that invokes standards of caring will incorporate considerations concerning the particular characteristics and needs of those persons with whom one has a concrete relationship, the nature of one's relationships with those persons, and the forms of caring and partiality that are called for by those relationships and that are needed to sustain those relationships.

Our morality, therefore, contains four main kinds of basic moral considerations, each of which emphasizes certain morally important aspects of our behavior, but no one of which captures all the factors that must be taken into account in making moral judgments. Utilitarian standards consider only the aggregate social welfare, but ignore the individual and how that welfare is distributed. Moral rights consider the individual but discount both aggregate well-being and distributive considerations. Standards of justice consider distributive issues, but they ignore aggregate social welfare and the individual as such. Although standards of caring consider the partiality that must be shown to those close to us, they ignore the demands of impartiality. These four kinds of moral considerations do not seem to be reducible to each other yet all seem to be necessary parts of our morality. That is, there are some moral problems for which utilitarian considerations are decisive, whereas for other problems the decisive considerations are the rights of individuals or the justice of the distributions involved, and for others the most significant issue is how those close to us should be cared for. This suggests that moral reasoning should incorporate all four kinds of moral considerations, although only one or the other may turn out to be relevant or decisive in a particular situation. One simple strategy for ensuring that all four kinds of considerations are incorporated into one's moral reasoning is to inquire systematically into the utility, rights, justice, and caring involved in a given moral judgment, as in Fig. 2.1. One might, for example, ask a series of questions about an action that one is considering: (a) Does the action, as far as possible, maximize social benefits and minimize social injuries? (b) Is the action consistent with the moral rights of those whom it will affect? (c) Will the action lead to a just distribution of benefits and burdens? (d) Does the action exhibit appropriate care for the well-being of those who are closely related to or dependent on oneself?

Bringing together different moral standards in this way, however, requires that one keep in mind how they relate to each other. As we have seen, moral rights identify areas in which other people generally may not interfere even if they can show that they would derive greater benefits from such interference. Generally speaking, therefore, standards concerned with moral rights have greater weight than either utilitarian standards or standards of justice. Similarly, standards of justice are generally accorded greater weight than utilitarian considerations. Standards of caring seem to be given greater weight than principles of impartiality in situations that involve close relationships (such as family and friends) and privately owned resources.

But these relationships hold only in general. If a certain action (or policy or institution) promises to generate sufficiently large social benefits or prevent sufficiently large social harm, the enormity of these utilitarian consequences may justify limited infringements of the rights of some individuals. Sufficiently large social costs and benefits may also be significant enough to justify some departures from standards of justice. The correction of large and widespread injustices may be important enough to justify limited infringements on some individual rights. When a large injustice or large violation of rights, or even large social costs, are at stake, the demands of caring may have to give way to the demands of impartiality.

At this time, we have no comprehensive moral theory capable of determining precisely when utilitarian considerations become sufficiently large to outweigh narrow infringements on a conflicting right, a standard of justice, or the demands of caring. Nor can we provide a universal rule that will tell us when considerations of justice become important enough to outweigh infringements

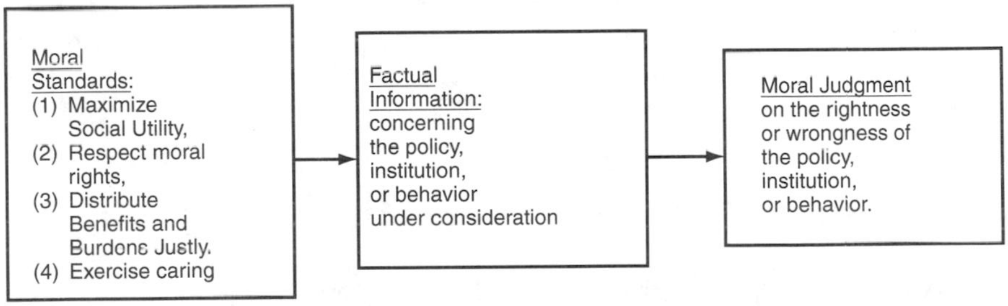

Figure 2.1

on conflicting rights or on the demands of caring. Moral philosophers have been unable to agree on any absolute rules for making such judgments. However, there are a number of rough criteria that can guide us in these matters. Suppose, for example, that only by invading my employees' right to privacy (with hidden cameras and legal on-the-job phone taps) will I be able to stop the continuing theft of several life-saving drugs that some of them are clearly stealing. How can I determine whether the utilitarian benefits here are sufficiently large to justify infringing on their right? First, I might ask whether the kinds of utilitarian values involved are clearly more important than the kinds of values protected by the right (or distributed by the standard of justice). The utilitarian benefits in the present example include the saving of human life, whereas the right to privacy protects (let us suppose) the values of freedom from shame and blackmail and of freedom to live one's life as one chooses. Considering this, I might decide that human life is clearly the more important kind of value because without life freedom has little value. Second, I might then ask whether the more important kind of value also involves substantially more people. For example, because the recovered drugs will (we assume) save several hundred lives, whereas the invasion of privacy will affect only a dozen people, the utilitarian values do involve substantially more people. Third, I can ask whether the actual injuries sustained by the persons whose rights are violated (or to whom an injustice is done) will be minor. For example, suppose that I can ensure that my employees suffer no shame, blackmail, or restriction on their freedom as a result of my uncovering information about their private lives (I intend to destroy all such information). Fourth, I can ask whether the potential breakdown in trusting relationships that surveillance risks is more or less important than the theft of life-saving resources. Let us suppose, for example, that the potential harm that surveillance will inflict on employee relationships of trust is not large. Then it would appear that my invasion of the privacy of employees is justified.

Hence, there are rough criteria that can guide our thinking when it appears that, in a certain situation utilitarian, considerations might be sufficiently important to override conflicting rights, standards of justice, or the demands of caring. Similar criteria can be used to determine whether, in a certain situation, considerations of justice should override an individual's rights, or when the demands of caring are more or less significant than the requirements of justice. But these criteria remain rough and intuitive. They lie at the edges of the light that ethics can shed on moral reasoning.

2.6 An Alternative to Moral Principles: Virtue Ethics

Ivan F. Boesky, born into a family of modest means, moved to New York City when, as a young lawyer, he was turned down for jobs by Detroit's top law firms. By the mid-1980s, the hard-working Boesky had accumulated a personal fortune estimated at over $400 million and was CEO of a large financial services company. He was famous in financial circles for his extraordinary skills in arbitrage, the art of spotting differences in the prices at which financial securities are selling on different world markets, and profiting by buying the securities where they are priced low and selling them where they are priced high. As a prominent member of New York society, Boesky enjoyed a reputation as an honest citizen and a generous philanthropist. He once wrote, "My life has been profoundly influenced by my father's spirit and commitment to the well-being of humanity, and by his emphasis on learning as the most important means to justice, mercy and righteousness."[125]

However, on December 18, 1987, Boesky was sentenced to 3 years in prison and paid a penalty of $100 million for illegally profiting from *insider information.* According to court records, Boesky paid David Levine, a friend who worked inside a firm that arranged mergers and acquisitions, to provide him with information about companies that were about to be purchased by another party (usually a corporation) for much more than the current price of their stock on the stock market. Relying on this insider's information and before it became public, Boesky would buy up the stock of the companies on the stock market—in effect buying the stock from stockholders who did not realize that their companies were about to be purchased for much more than the current stock market price. When the purchase of the company was announced, the stock price rose and Boesky would sell his stock at a handsome profit. Although buying and selling stock on the basis of insider information is legal in many countries (e.g., Italy, Switzerland, Hong Kong) and many economists argue that the economic benefits of the practice (it tends to make the price of a company's stock reflect the true value of the company) outweigh its harms (it tends to discourage noninsiders from participating in the stock market), nevertheless, the practice is illegal in the United States.

What drove a man who already had hundreds of millions of dollars, and everything else most people could ever want or need, to become so obsessed with making money that he deliberately broke the law? Much of the answer, it has been claimed, lay in his character. A former friend is quoted as saying, "Maybe he's greedy beyond the wildest imaginings of mere mortals like you and me."[126] Boesky once described his obsession to accumulate ever more money as "a sickness I have in the face of which I am helpless."[127] Others said of him that:

> He was driven by work, overzealous, and subject to severe mood swings. Intimates of Mr. Boesky say he vacillated between "being loud, and harsh and aggressive, to mellifluously soft-spoken, charming and courtly." He was also fiendish about his pursuit of information. "When somebody got an edge on something, he would go bananas." When it came to money and business dealings, he was quite ruthless and pursued his goal with a single-minded purpose. . . . Although his first love was money, he hankered for the genteel respectability and status that are generally denied the nouveau riche.[128]

The story of the fall of Ivan Boesky is the story of a man brought down by greed. What stands out in this story are the descriptions of his moral character—the character of a man driven by an obsessive "love" of money. Boesky is described as being "greedy," "sick," "aggressive," "fiendish," and "ruthless." Because what he said of himself did not match his secret dealings, some said he "lacked integrity" and others that he was "hypocritical" and "dishonest." All of these descriptions are judgments about the moral character of the man, not judgments about the morality of his actions. In fact, although it is clear that trading on insider information is illegal, the fact that the practice is legal in many countries and that many economists support it suggest that the practice is not inherently immoral.

As the Boesky case makes clear, we evaluate the morality of people's character as well as their actions. The approaches to ethics that we have examined so far all focus on action as the key subject matter of ethics and ignore the character of the agent who carries out the action. Utilitarianism, for example, tells us that "*actions* are right in proportion as they tend to promote happiness," while Kantian ethics tells us that "I ought never to *act* except in such a way that I can also will that my maxim should become a universal law." However, the central issue that emerges in the case of Boesky, and in many similar stories of men and women in business, is not the wrongness of their actions, but the flawed nature of their character.

Many ethicists have criticized the assumption that actions are the fundamental subject matter of ethics. Ethics, they have argued, should look not only at the kinds of actions an agent ought to perform, but should pay attention to the kind of person an agent ought to be. An "agent-based" focus on what one ought to be, in contrast to an "action-based" focus on how one ought to act, would look carefully at a person's moral character, including, in particular, whether a person's moral character exhibits virtue or vice. A more adequate approach to ethics, according to these ethicists, would take the virtues (such as honesty, courage, temperance, integrity, compassion, self-control) and the vices (such as dishonesty, ruthlessness, greed, lack of integrity, cowardliness) as the basic starting point for ethical reasoning.

Although virtue ethics looks at moral issues from a very different perspective than action-based ethics, it does not follow that the conclusions of virtue ethics will differ radically from the conclusions of an action-based ethic. As we see, there are virtues that are correlated with utilitarianism (e.g., the virtue of benevolence), virtues that are correlated with rights (e.g., the virtue of respect), and virtues that are correlated with justice and caring. The virtues, then, should not be seen as providing a fifth alternative to utility, rights, justice, and caring. Instead, the virtues can be seen as providing a perspective that surveys the same ground as the four approaches, but from an entirely different perspective. What the principles of utility, rights, justice, and caring do from the perspective of action evaluations, an ethic of care does from the perspective of character evaluations.

The Nature of Virtue

What exactly is a moral virtue? A *moral virtue* is an acquired disposition that is valued as part of the character of a morally good human being and that is exhibited in the person's habitual behavior. A person has a moral virtue when the person is disposed to behave habitually in the way and with the reasons, feelings, and desires that are characteristic of a morally good person. Honesty, for example, is valued as a character trait of morally good people. A person possesses the virtue of honesty when the person is disposed to habitually tell the truth and does so because he believes telling the truth is right, feels good when he tells the truth and uncomfortable when he lies, and always wants to tell the truth out of respect for the truth and its importance in human communication. If a person told the truth on occasion, or did so for the wrong reasons or with the wrong desires, we would not say that the person is honest. We would not say a person is honest, for example, if the person frequently lies, if the person tells the truth only because he or she thought it was the way to get people to like him or her, or if the person told the truth out of fear and reluctantly. Moreover, a moral virtue must be acquired, and not merely a natural characteristic such as intelligence, or beauty, or natural strength. A moral virtue is praiseworthy in part because it is an achievement: Its development requires effort.

The Moral Virtues

The most basic issue, from the perspective of virtue ethics, is the question: What are the traits of character that make a person a morally good human being? Which traits of character are moral virtues? On this issue, there have been numerous views. The most significant and influential theory of virtue was that proposed by the Greek philosopher Aristotle who argued that a moral virtue is a habit that enables a human being to act in accordance with the specific purpose of human beings. What distinguishes humans from all other creatures, Aristotle held, is the ability to reason, and so the distinguishing purpose of human beings is to exercise reason in all their activities. Moral virtues, then, are habits that enable a person to live according to reason. A person lives according to reason, Aristotle argued, when the person knows and chooses the reasonable middle ground between going too far and not going far enough in his actions, emotions, and desires: "Moral virtue is . . . a mean between two vices, one of excess and the other of deficiency, and . . . it aims at hitting the mean in feelings, [desires,] and actions." With respect to the emotion of fear, for example, courage is the virtue of responding to fear with the reasonable amount of daring, whereas cowardliness is the vice of not being daring enough in response to fear, and recklessness is the vice of being too daring in response to fear. With respect to the desire for food, temperance is the virtue of being reasonable by indulging the desire neither too much nor too little, whereas gluttony is the vice of indulging to unreasonable excess, and austerity is the vice of unreasonably indulging too little. With respect to the action of giving people the external goods they deserve, justice is the virtue of giving people exactly what they deserve, whereas injustice is the vice of either giving them more or less than they deserve. Virtues, then, are habits of dealing with one's emotions, desires, and actions in a manner that seeks the reasonable midle ground and avoids unreasonable extremes, whereas vices are habits of going to the extreme of either excess or deficiency. How does one determine what is reasonable? Prudence, Aristotle held, is the virtue that enables one to know what is reasonable in a given situation.

St. Thomas Aquinas, a Christian philosopher of the middle ages, followed Aristotle in holding that the moral virtues enable people to follow reason in dealing with their desires, emotions, and actions and in accepting that the four pivitol or cardinal moral virtues are courage, temperance, justice, and prudence. But as a Christian, and so unlike Aristotle, Aquinas held that the purpose of a person is not merely the exercise of reason in this world, but union with God in the next. Therefore, to Aristotle's list of the moral virtues, Aquinas added the "theological" or Christian virtues of faith, hope, and charity—the virtues that enable a person to achieve union with God. Moreover, Aquinas expanded Aristotle's list of the moral virtues to include others that make sense within the life of a Christian but would have been foreign to the life of the Greek aristocratic citizen on whom Aristotle had focused. For example, Aquinas held that humility is a Christian virtue and that pride is a vice for the Christian, whereas Aristotle had argued that for the Greek aristocrat pride is a virtue and humility is a vice.

More recently, the American philosopher Alasdair MacIntyre has claimed that a virtue is any human disposition that is praised because it enables a person to achieve the good at which human "practices" aim:

> The virtues . . . are to be understood as those dispositions which will not only sustain practices and enable us to achieve the goods internal to practices, but which will also sustain us in the relevant kind of quest for the good, by enabling us to overcome the harms, dangers, temptations and situations which we encounter, and which will furnish us with increasing self-knowledge and increasing knowledge of the good.[129]

Critics have argued, however, that MacIntyre's approach does not seem to get things quite right. When Ivan Boesky, for example, was criticized as "greedy," "dishonest," "ruthless," and so on, people were not faulting him for failing to have the virtues proper to the practices within which he was pursuing his vision of the good. The moral defects for which Boesky was criticized were his alleged failings as a human being, regardless of how well or poorly he did in the various human practices in which he was engaged. The moral virtues seem to be those dispositions that enable one to live a morally good human life in general and not merely those that enable one to engage successfully in some set of human practices.

Edmund L. Pincoffs, in particular, criticizes MacIntyre for claiming that virtues include only those traits required by some set of social practices. Instead, Pincoffs suggests that virtues include all those dispositions to act, feel, and think in certain ways that we use as the basis for choosing between persons or between potential future selves.[130] When deciding, for example, whom to choose as a friend, spouse, employee, or manager, we look to people's dispositions: Are they honest or dishonest, sincere or insincere, greedy or selfish, reliable or unreliable, trustworthy or untrustworthy, dependable or undependable? Similarly, when thinking about a moral decision, we often think not so much of what we are obligated to do, but instead of the kind of person we would be by doing it: In carrying out the action, would I be honest or dishonest, sincere or insincere, selfish or unselfish?

However, what makes one disposition a moral virtue and another a moral vice? There is no simple answer to this question, Pincoffs claims. Some dispositions, he points out, provide specific grounds for preferring a person because they make a person good or bad at specific tasks such as painting houses. Such specific dispositions are not virtues. But other dispositions are generally desirable because they make a person good at dealing with the kinds of situations that frequently and typically arise in human life. The virtues consist of such "generally desirable dispositions" that it is desirable for people to have in view of the "human situation, of conditions, that is, under which human beings must (given the nature of the physical world and of human nature and human association) live." Because the human situation often requires concerted effort, for example, it is desirable that we have persistence and courage. Because tempers often flare, we need tolerance and tact. Because goods must often be distributed by consistent criteria, we need fairness and nondiscrimination. However, selfishness, deceptiveness, cruelty, and unfairness are vices: They are generally undesirable because they are destructive to human relationships. The moral virtues, then, are those dispositions that it is generally desirable for people to have in the kinds of situations they typically encounter in living together. They are desirable because they are useful either "for everyone in general or for the possessor of the quality."

Pincoff's theory of virtue seems more adequate than a theory, like MacIntyre's, which confines virtue to traits connected with practices. For the virtues seem to be dispositions that enable us to deal well with all of the exigencies of human life and not merely the exigencies of practices. Both Aristotle and Aquinas, for example, felt that, in articulating the moral virtues, they were articulating those habits that enable a person to live a human life well and not merely to do well in social practices.

As we have seen, however, Aristotle and Aquinas had different views on exactly what human life required. This suggests that to some extent what counts as a moral virtue will depend on one's beliefs about the kinds of situations that humans will face. Nevertheless, as Pincoff suggests, "we share a good deal of well-grounded agreement on the question of who is the right sort of person in general," because people in all societies have to face similar problems in living together. Catholics, for example, can recognize when a Buddhist is not just a good Buddhist, but also a person of good moral character: "Courage is not more a Catholic than it is a Buddhist virtue; honesty commends itself to Presbyterian and Coptic Christian alike." The moral virtues, then, include that wide variety of dispositions that people in all societies recognize as desirable because they "serve as reasons for preference in the ordinary and not-so-ordinary exigencies of life." The four classical virtues on which Aristotle and Aquinas both agreed—courage, temperance, justice, and prudence—fall in this class. However, the three theological virtues—faith, hope, and charity—that Aquinas added because of their special importance for a Christian life would not count as moral virtues because they are desirable only within a special kind of life devoted to the pursuit of special religious objectives. Similarly, pride, which was a quality admired in Greek society, would not count as a moral virtue because it too is desirable only within a specific kind of society.

Virtues, Actions, and Institutions

So far we have ignored a key aspect of virtue theory: How does it help us decide what we are to do? Can an ethic of virtue do more than tell us the kind of people we should be? Is an ethic of virtue able to provide us with little guidance about how we should live our lives, how we should behave? One of the major criticisms made against virtue theory, in fact, is that it fails to provide us with guidance on how we are to act. When a woman is trying to decide whether to have an abortion, for example, she may ask a friend, "What should I do?" In such situations, it does not help to be told what kind of character one should have. In such situations, one needs advice about what kinds of actions are appropriate in one's situation, and virtue theory seems incapable of providing such advice. This criticism—that virtue theory provides no guidance for action—is natural because virtue theory deliberately turns away from action and focuses on moral character as the fundamental moral category. Nevertheless, although virtue is the foundation of virtue theory, this does not mean that virtue theory can provide no guidance for action.

Virtue theory argues that the aim of the moral life is to develop those general dispositions we call the *moral virtues*, and to exercise and exhibit them in the many situations that human life sets before us. Insofar as we exercise the virtues in our actions, insofar as our actions exhibit the virtues, or insofar as our actions make us virtuous, those actions are morally right actions. Yet insofar as our actions are the exercise of vice or insofar as our actions develop a vicious character, to that extent the actions are morally wrong. The key action-guiding implication of virtue theory, then, can be summed up in the claim that:

> *An action is morally right if in carrying out the action the agent exercises, exhibits, or develops a morally virtuous character, and it is morally wrong to the extent that by carrying out the action the agent exercises, exhibits, or develops a morally vicious character.*

From this perspective, then, the wrongfulness of an action can be determined by examining the kind of character the action tends to produce or the kind of character that tends to produce the action. In either case, the ethics of the action depends on its relationship to the character of the agent. For example, it has been argued that the morality of abortion, adultery, or any other action should be evaluated by attending to the kind of character evidenced by people who engage in such actions. If the decision to engage in such actions tends to develop a person's character by making them more responsible, caring, principled, honest, open, and self-sacrificing, then such actions are morally right. However, if the decision to engage in such actions tends to make people more self-centered, irresponsible, dishonest, careless, and selfish, then such actions are morally wrong. Actions are not only evaluated by the kind of character they develop; we also condemn certain actions precisely because they are the outcome of a morally vicious character. For example, we condemn cruel actions because they exhibit a vicious character, and we condemn lies because they are products of a dishonest character.

Virtue theory not only provides a criterion for evaluating actions, it also provides a useful criterion for evaluating our social institutions and practices. For example, it has been argued that some economic institutions make people greedy, large bureaucratic organizations make people less responsible, and the practice of providing government "handouts" to people makes them lazy and dependent. All such arguments, at bottom, evaluate institutions and practices on the basis of a theory of virtue. Although such arguments may be false, they all appeal to the idea that institutions are morally defective when they tend to form morally defective characters.

Perhaps there is no simple way to classify all the virtues. We have suggested that moral virtues are dispositions that are generally desirable because they are required by the human situation with which all people everywhere must cope. Some dispositions are moral virtues, for example, because people everywhere are tempted by their emotions and desires to not do what they know they should do. Courage, temperance, and, in general, the virtues of self-control are of this sort. Some virtues are dispositions to willingly engage in specific kinds of moral action that are valued in all societies, such as honesty. Pincoffs suggests that some dispositions can be classified as "instrumental virtues" because they enable people everywhere to pursue their goals effectively as individuals (persistence, carefulness, determination) or as part of a group (cooperativeness), whereas some are "noninstrumental virtues" because they are desirable everywhere for their own sake (serenity, nobility, wittiness, gracefulness, tolerance, reasonableness, gentleness, warmth, modesty, civility). Some virtues are cognitive and consist of understanding the requirements of morality toward ourselves and others, such as wisdom and prudence. Other virtues are dispositions that incline one to act according to general moral principles. The virtue of benevolence, for example, inclines one to maximize people's happiness, the virtue of respect for others inclines one to exercise consideration for the rights of individuals, the virtue of fairness inclines one to behave according to the principles of justice, and the virtue of caring inclines one to live up to the tenets of care.

Virtues and Principles

What is the relationship between a theory of virtue and the theories of ethics that we have considered (utilitarian theories, rights theories, justice theories, and care theories)? As a glance at the many kinds of dispositions that count as virtues suggests, there is no single simple relationship between the virtues and a morality based on principles. Some virtues enable people to do what moral principles require. Courage, for example, enables us to stick to our moral principles even when fear of the consequences tempts us to do otherwise. Some virtues consist of a readiness to act on moral principles. Justice, for example, is the virtue of being disposed to follow principles of justice. Some virtues are dispositions that our moral principles require us to develop. Utilitarianism, for example, requires us to develop dispositions such as kindness and generosity that will lead us to enhance the happiness of people.

Hence, there is no conflict between theories of ethics that are based on principles and theories of ethics based on virtues. That is, an ethic of virtue does not advocate actions that differ from those advocated by an ethic of principles (e.g., utilitarian principles may require actions that differ from those required by principles of justice). Nor does an ethic of principles advocate different moral dispositions than does an ethic of virtue. Instead, a theory of virtue differs from an ethic of principles in the perspective from which it approaches moral evaluations. A theory of virtue judges actions, for example, in terms of the dispositions that are associated with those actions, whereas an ethic of principles judges dispositions in terms of the actions associated with those dispositions. For an ethic of principles actions are primary, whereas for an ethic of virtue dispositions are primary. We may say, then, that both an ethic of principles and an ethic of virtue identify what the moral life is about. However, principles look at the moral life in terms of the actions that morality obligates us to perform, whereas the virtues look at the moral life in terms of the kind of person morality obligates us to be. An ethic of virtue, then, covers much of the same ground as an ethic of principles, but from a very different standpoint.

An ethic of virtue, then, is not a fifth kind of moral principle that should take its place alongside the principles of utilitarianism, rights, justice, and caring. Instead, an ethics of virtue fills out and adds to utilitarianism, rights, justice, and caring by looking not at the actions people are required to perform, but at the character they are required to have. An adequate ethics of virtue, then, will look at the virtues that are associated with utilitarianism, the virtues associated with rights, those associated with justice, and those associated with caring. In addition, it will (and in this respect an ethic of virtue goes beyond an ethic of principles) look at the virtues people need to stick to their moral principles when their feelings, desires, and passions tempt them to do otherwise. It will look at the many other virtues that the principles of utilitarianism, rights, justice, and caring require a person to cultivate. An ethic of virtue, then, addresses the same landscape of issues that an ethic of principles does, but in addition it also addresses issues related to motivation and feeling that are largely ignored by an ethic of principles.

2.7 Morality in International Contexts

We noted in Chapter 1 that multinational corporations operate in foreign host countries whose laws or government decrees, common practices, levels of development, and cultural understandings are sometimes much different from those of their home country. These differences, we argued, do not provide adequate justification for the theory of ethical relativism. How should the moral principles of utilitarianism, rights, justice, and caring be applied in foreign countries that differ in so many ways from our own?[131]

For example, the laws and decrees of government that the managers of Dow Chemical Company find prevalent in the company's home country, the United States, are very different from those they confront in Mexico and other host countries. Legal safety standards regulating worker exposure to workplace toxins and other hazards are quite explicit and stringent in the United States, whereas they are vague, lax, or altogether lacking in Mexico. Consumer product safety and labeling laws, which require careful quality controls, rigorous product tests, and warnings of risk for end users in the United States, are very different in Mexico, which allows lower levels of quality control, much less testing of products, and fewer warnings directed at end users. The environmental pollution laws of the U.S. government are strict and set at very high levels, whereas those of Mexico are virtually nonexistent. Moreover, the very legitimacy of government decrees differs from country to country because governments differ in the extent to which they are truly representative of the needs and aspirations of their people. Although the U.S. government is deficient in many respects, it is to a relatively high degree responsive to the needs of American citizens. This is not so of the governments of other nations, such as the former government of Haiti, which was notoriously corrupt and consistently promoted the interests and wealth of a small group of government elites at the expense of the general population's needs.

Common practices can also differ markedly among nations. Whereas all forms of bribery of government personnel are considered wrong in the United States, many forms of petty bribery of lower level government personnel are not only openly engaged in in Mexico but are universally accepted there as standard practices even if officially frowned on. Nepotism and sexism, although condemned in public companies in the United States, are accepted as a matter of course in some Arab public business environments. Manufacturing wages of $2 an hour without benefits are accepted as common practice in Jamaica, whereas manufacturing wages in the United States average close to $12 an hour plus benefits.

Multinationals also often operate in countries at very different levels of development.[132] Some countries have very high levels of technological, social, and economic resources available, whereas the resources of other countries in these and other areas are quite undeveloped. Technological sophistication, unions, financial markets, unemployment insurance, social security, and public education are widespread in more developed nations but are virtually unknown in Third World countries. Dow Chemical, for example, has been accused periodically of introducing pesticides whose safe use requires a literate worker with access to technologically sophisticated protective gear into developing nations whose uneducated laborers are ill prepared to handle such pesticides safely. Again, the Swiss company Nestle Corporation has been accused of marketing powdered infant formula whose safe use requires a literate consumer who has a clean supply of water available in less developed nations where illiterate mothers have used unsanitary water to mix and dilute the formula, which they have fed to their babies, many of whom have subsequently died.

Most strikingly, the cultural practices of nations may differ so radically that the same action may mean something very different in two different cultures. In the United States, for example, it would be considered a lie for a company to provide the government with income statements that would understate the company's actual earnings for tax purposes. In some periods of Italy's history, however, it was accepted as a matter of course that all businesses would understate their annual earnings by one third when they reported their tax liability to the government at the end of the year. Knowing this, the government would automatically inflate each company's income statements by one third and levy taxes on this more accurate estimate, which companies willingly paid. Thus, because of a cultural practice that was known to both the business community and the government, Italian companies did not actually lie to their government when they understated their income: What looked like a lie to an outsider was, in the cultural context, a clearly understood signal of a company's true income.

When confronted with a foreign context, in which laws and government decrees, prevailing practices, levels of development, and cultural understandings are very different from those of the manager's home country, what should the manager of a multinational do? For example, when operating in a foreign country, should the manager of the multinational adopt the practices of its home country or those prevalent in the host country?

Some have claimed that, when operating in less developed countries, multinationals from more developed home countries should always follow those practices prevalent in the more developed country, which set higher or more stringent standards.[133] But this claim ignores that introducing practices that have evolved in a highly developed country into one that is less developed may produce more harm than good—a violation of utilitarian standards of ethics. For example, if an American company operating in Mexico pays local workers U.S. wages, it may draw all the skilled workers away from local Mexican companies that cannot afford to pay the same high salaries. As a consequence, Mexico's efforts to develop local companies may be crippled while havoc is wreaked in local labor markets. Again, if American companies operating in Mexico are required to operate in Mexico according to the more costly wage, consumer, environmental, and safety standards prevalent in the United States, they will have no reason to invest in Mexico, and Mexico's development will be retarded. Precisely because they need and want foreign investment and technology, the governments of many less developed nations, genuinely interested in advancing the interests of their people, have insisted on less costly standards that can attract foreign companies. Thus, it is clear that local conditions, particularly developmental conditions, must at least be considered when determining whether to import practices from a developing country into a less developed one, and that it is a mistake to accept the blanket claim that one must always adopt the "higher" practices of the more developed home country.

Some have gone to the opposite extreme and argued that multinationals should always follow local practices, whatever they might be, or that they should do whatever the local government wants, because it is the representative of the people. But it is often as unethical to go along with local practices or government requirements as it sometimes is to oppose them. The lower environmental standards of Mexico, for example, may be so low that they permit pollution levels that cripple the health of or even kill those living near chemical plants, producing flagrant violations of these people's basic human rights. The Apartheid policies of the South African government may require levels of discrimination against South African Blacks that are deep violations of justice. Again, the self-interest of government elites in Haiti may lead them to support policies that enrich them while harming the citizens they are supposed to represent. Therefore, the blanket claim that local practices should always be adopted is also mistaken.

It is clear, then, that while local laws or government decrees, common practices, levels of development, and cultural understandings all must be taken into account when evaluating the ethics of business policies and actions in a foreign country, the local status quo cannot simply be adopted without question by the multinational manager, but must still be subjected to ethical analysis. What factors should be considered when evaluating the ethics of an action or policy in a foreign context? The foregoing discussion suggests that the following questions should be asked about any corporate action or policy under consideration by a company operating in a foreign country:

1. *What does the corporate policy or action really mean in the context of the local culture? When viewed in terms of its local cultural meaning, is the policy or action ethically acceptable, or does it violate the ethical standards of utilitarianism, rights, justice, and caring to such an extent that it should not be undertaken? From the perspective of virtue, does the action or policy encourage the exercise or the development of morally good character?*
2. *Taking into account the nation's level of technological, social, and economic development and what its government is doing to promote this development, does the corporate policy or action produce consequences that are ethically acceptable from the point of view of utilitarianism, rights, justice, and caring, or from the point of view of moral character? Can the more stringent legal requirements or practices common in more developed nations be implemented without damage to the host country and its development, and in context would such implementation be more consistent with the ethical standards of utilitarianism, rights, justice, and caring? Would such implementation encourage the exercise or the development of morally good character?*
3. *If the corporate action or policy is allowed or required by the laws or the decrees of the local government, does this government truly represent the will of all its people? Does the corporate action or policy nevertheless violate the principles of utilitarianism, rights, justice, or caring, or is it condemnable from the perspective of moral character? If so, and if the action or policy is legally required to do business in the host country, then is the ethical violation significant enough to require withdrawal from that country?*
4. *If the corporate action or policy involves a local common practice that is morally questionable by home country standards (such as sexual discrimination or bribery of government personnel), is it possible to conduct business in the host country without engaging in the practice?*[134] *If not, then does the practice violate the principles of utilitarianism, rights, justice, and caring to a degree significant enough to require withdrawal from that country? Is the practice so pernicious from the perspective of moral character as to require withdrawal from the country?*

Answering these questions, of course, will not automatically solve all the ethical dilemmas encountered in international contexts. However, the questions indicate the kinds of issues that must be considered when applying ethical principles in international contexts.

Questions for Review and Discussion

1. Define the following concepts: utilitarianism, utility, intrinsic good, instrumental good, basic need, mere wants, rule-utilitarianism, rights, legal rights, moral rights, negative rights, positive rights, contractual rights, categorical imperative (both versions), the libertarian view on rights, distributive justice, the fundamental (or formal) principle of distributive justice, material principle of justice, egalitarian justice, capitalist justice, socialist justice, libertarian justice, justice as fairness, principle of equal liberty, difference principle, principle of fair equality of opportunity, the "original position," retributive justice, compensatory justice, caring, ethic of caring, concrete relationship, virtue, ethics of virtue.
2. A student incorrectly defined *utilitarianism* this way: "Utilitarianism is the view that so long as an action provides me with more measurable economic benefits than costs, the action is morally right." Identify all of the mistakes contained in this definition of utilitarianism.
3. In your view, does utilitarianism provide a more objective standard for determining right and wrong than moral rights do? Explain your answer fully. Does utilitarianism provide a more objective standard than principles of justice? Explain.
4. "Every principle of distributive justice, whether that of the egalitarian, or the capitalist, or the socialist, or the libertarian, or of Rawls, in the end is illegitimately advocating some type of equality." Do you agree or disagree? Explain.
5. "An ethic of caring conflicts with morality because morality requires impartiality." Discuss this criticism of an ethic of caring.
6. "An ethic of virtue implies that moral relativism is correct, while an action-centered ethic does not." Do you agree or disagree? Explain.

Web Resources

Readers who would like to conduct research on ethics through the Internet may want to begin with the website of the Markkula Center for Applied Ethics at Santa Clara University (http://scuish.scu.edu/Ethics), which, in addition to its own resources, also provides annotated links to all the other major ethics sites on the Internet; the DePaul University Ethics Institute provides links to ethics resources (http://condor.depaul.edu/ethics); other ethics resources are the Communication Department at California State University at Fullerton (http://www5.fullerton.edu/les/ethics_list.html); the Students for Responsible Business (http://www.srbnet.org); the Business Ethics Organization (http://www.businessethics.org); the Business Social Responsibility Organization (http://www.bsr.org); the University of San Diego (http://ethics.acusd.edu/index.html); Indiana University (http://www.indiana.edu/~asanl/web-phil.html); Antioch (http://college.antioch.edu/~smauldin); and the World Guide (http://www.theworld.com/HUMANITI/PHILOSOP/SUBJECT.HTM).

Notes

1. Investor Responsibility Research Center, Inc., *U.S. Corporate Activity in South Africa, 1986*, Analysis B, 28 January 1986.
2. Timothy Smith, "South Africa: The Churches vs. the Corporations," *Business and Society Review*, 1971, pp. 54, 55, 56.
3. *Texaco Proxy Statement*, 1977, item 3.
4. The details of this well-known case are derived from the findings of fact stated by the court in *Grimshaw v. Ford Motor Co*., App., 174 Cal. Rptr. 348. Grimshaw was a young teenager when he was traumatically seared over much of his body and face in a Pinto fire that resulted from a rear-end collision in San Bernardino, California. Details of the cost–benefit study are based on Ralph Drayton, "One Manufacturer's Approach to Automobile Safety Standards," *CTLA News*, VIII, no. 2 (February 1968): 11; and Mark Dowie, "Pinto Madness," *Mother Jones* (September/October 1977), p. 28. A book-length treatment of the case is Lee P. Strobel, *Reckless Homicide? Ford's Pinto Trial* (South Bend, IN: And Books, 1980).
5. Thomas A. Klein, *Social Costs and Benefits of Business* (Englewood Cliffs, NJ: Prentice-Hall, 1977).
6. Among the more well-known utilitarian moralists are Peter Singer, *Practical Ethics*, 2nd ed. (London: Cambridge University Press, 1993); and Richard B. Brandt, *A Theory of the Good and the Right* (New York: Oxford University Press, 1979).
7. Jeremy Bentham, *The Principles of Morals and Legislation* (Oxford, 1789); Henry Sidgwick, *Outlines of the History of Ethics*, 5th ed. (London, 1902), traces the history of utilitarian thought to Bentham's predecessors. Some modern expositions of utilitarian thought may be found in Michael D. Bayles, ed., *Contemporary Utilitarianism* (Garden City, NY: Doubleday & Co., Inc., 1968); J. J. C. Smart and Bernard Williams, *Utilitarianism: For and Against* (London: Cambridge University Press, 1973); Amartya Sen and Bernard Williams, eds., *Utilitarianism and Beyond* (New York: Cambridge University Press, 1982); and Harlan B. Miller and William H. Williams, eds., *The Limits of Utilitarianism* (Minneapolis: University of Minnesota Press, 1982).
8. Henry Sidgwick, *Methods of Ethics*, 7th ed. (Chicago: University of Chicago Press, 1962), p. 413.
9. John Stuart Mill, *Utilitarianism* (Indianapolis: The Bobbs-Merrill Co., Inc., 1957), p. 22.
10. Richard Brandt, *Ethical Theory* (Englewood Cliffs, NJ: Prentice-Hall, 1959), p. 386; see also Dan W. Brock, "Utilitarianism," in Tom Regan and Donald Van DeVeer, eds., *And Justice for All* (Totowa, NJ: Rowman and Littlefield, 1982), pp. 217–40.
11. For example, William Stanley Javons, *Theory of Political Economy* (1871); Alfred Marshall, *Principles of Economics* (1890); Cecil Arthur Pigou, *Wealth and*

Welfare (1912); for a contemporary defense of utilitarianism in economics, see J. A. Mirrlees, "The Economic Uses of Utilitarianism," in Sen and Williams, eds., *Utilitarianism and Beyond*, pp. 63–84.

12. See Paul Samuelson, *Foundations of Economic Analysis* (Cambridge: Harvard University Press, 1947). A system is "Pareto optimal" if no one in the system can be made better off without making some other person worse off; an "indifference curve" indicates the quantities of one good a person would willingly trade for greater or lesser quantities of another good.

13. E. J. Mishan, *Economics for Social Decisions: Elements of Cost-Benefit Analysis* (New York: Praeger Publishers, Inc., 1973), pp. 14–17. See also E. J. Mishan, ed., *Cost-Benefit Analysis*, 3rd. ed. (London: Cambridge University Press, 1982).

14. For example, Wesley C. Mitchell, "Bentham's Felicific Calculus," in *The Backward Art of Spending Money and Other Essays* (New York: Augustus M. Kelley, Inc., 1950), pp. 177–202; but see the replies to these measurement objections in Paul Weirch, "Interpersonal Utility in Principles of Social Choice," *Erkenntnis*, 21 (November 1984): 295–318.

15. For a discussion of this problem, see Michael D. Bayles, "The Price of Life," *Ethics*, 89, no. 1 (October 1978): 20–34; Jonathan Glover, *Causing Death and Saving Lives* (New York: Penguin Books, 1977); Peter S. Albin, "Economic Values and the Value of Human Life," in Sidney Hook, ed., *Human Values and Economic Policy* (New York: New York University Press, 1967).

16. G. E. Moore, *Principia Ethica*, 5th ed. (Cambridge: Cambridge University Press, 1956), p. 149.

17. Alastair MacIntyre, "Utilitarianism and Cost-Benefit Analysis: An Essay on the Relevance of Moral Philosophy to Bureaucratic Theory," in Kenneth Syre, ed., *Values in the Electric Power Industry* (Notre Dame, IN: University of Notre Dame Press, 1977).

18. For example, Mark Sagoff, "Some Problems with Environmental Ethics," and Steven Kelman, "Cost-Benefit Analysis: An Ethical Critique," both in Christine Pierce and Donald VanDeVeer, eds., *People, Penguins, and Plastic Trees*, 2nd ed. (Belmont, CA: Wadsworth, 1995).

19. David H. Blake, William C. Frederick, and Mildred S. Myers, "Measurement Problems in the Social Audit," in Tom L. Beauchamp and Norman E. Bowie, eds., *Ethical Theory and Business* (Englewood Cliffs, NJ: Prentice-Hall, 1979), pp. 246–52; an excellent review of the literature is contained in Task Force on Corporate Social Performance, *Corporate Social Reporting in the United States and Western Europe* (Washington, DC: U.S. Government Printing Office, 1979), pp. 2–36; see also the more accessible Harold L. John, *Disclosure of Corporate Social Performance: Survey, Evaluation and Prospects* (New York: Praeger Publishers, Inc., 1979).

20. Raymond A. Bauer and Dan H. Fenn, Jr., *The Corporate Social Audit* (New York: Sage Publications, Inc., 1972), pp. 3–14; John J. Corson and George A. Steiner, *Measuring Business's Social Performance: The Corporate Social Audit* (New York: Committee for Economic Development, 1974), p. 41; Thomas C. Taylor, "The Illusions of Social Accounting," *CPA Journal*, 46 (January 1976), 24–28; Manuel A. Tipgos, "A Case Against the Social Audit," *Management Accounting* (August 1976), pp. 23–26.

21. Tom L. Beauchamp, "Utilitarianism and Cost-Benefit Analysis: A Reply to MacIntyre," in Beauchamp and Bowie, eds., *Ethical Theory*, pp. 276–82; and

Herman B. Leonard and Richard J. Zeckhauser, "Cost-Benefit Analysis Defended," *QQ-Report from the Center for Philosophy and Public Policy*, 3, no. 3 (Summer 1983): 6–9.

22. See Amitai Etzioni and Edward W. Lehman, "Dangers in 'Valid' Social Measurements," *Annals of the American Academy of Political and Social Sciences*, 373 (September 1967): 6; also William K. Frankena, *Ethics*, 2nd ed. (Englewood Cliffs, NJ: Prentice-Hall, 1973), pp. 80–83.

23. See Kenneth Arrow, *Social Choice and Individual Values*, 2nd ed. (New York: John Wiley & Sons, Inc., 1951), p. 87; and Norman E. Bowie, *Towards a New Theory of Distributive Justice* (Amherst: The University of Massachusetts Press, 1971), pp. 86–87.

24. Steven Edwards, "In Defense of Environmental Economics," and William Baster, "People or Penguins," both in Christine Pierce and Donald VanDeVeer, eds., *People, Penguins, and Plastic Trees*, 2nd ed. (Belmont, CA: Wadsworth, 1995). See also the techniques enumerated in Mishan, *Economics for Social Decisions*.

25. E. Bruce Frederickson, "Noneconomic Criteria and the Decision Process," *Decision Sciences*, 2, no. 1 (January 1971): 25–52.

26. Bowie, *Towards a New Theory of Distributive Justice*, pp. 20–24.

27. See J. O. Ormson, "The Interpretation of the Philosophy of J. S. Mill," *Philosophical Quarterly*, 3 (1953): 33–40; D. W. Haslett, *Equal Consideration: A Theory of Moral Justification* (Newark, DL: University of Delaware Press, 1987).

28. David Lyons, *Forms and Limits of Utilitarianism* (Oxford: Oxford University Press, 1965). Some ethicians hold, however, that act utilitarianism and rule utilitarianism are not really equivalent; see Thomas M. Lennon, "Rules and Relevance: The Act Utilitarianism-Rule Utilitarianism Equivalence Issue," *Idealistic Studies: An International Philosophical Journal*, 14, (May 1984): 148–58.

29. U.S. State Department, *Country Reports on Human Rights Practices for 1998* (February 1999).

30. See Meg Voorhes, "2000 Company Report-B1, Microsoft U.S. Business Operations in China," October 20, 2000, © 2000 by the Investor Responsibility Research Center (at www.irrc.org).

31. H. J. McCloskey, "Rights," *The Philosophical Quarterly*, 15 (1965): 115–27; several book-length discussions of rights are available including Alan R. White, *Rights* (Oxford: Clarendon Press, 1984); Samuel Stoljar, *An Analysis of Rights* (New York: St. Martin's Press, 1984); and Henry Shue, *Basic Rights* (Princeton: Princeton University Press, 1981); for a review of the literature on rights, see Jeremy Waldron, "Rights," in Robert E. Goodin and Philip Pettit, eds., *A Companion to Contemporary Political Philosophy* (Oxford: Blackwell, 1995); an outstanding historical account of the evolution of the concept of a right is Richard Tuck, *Natural Rights Theories, Their Origin and Development* (New York: Cambridge University Press, 1979).

32. For a more technical but now widely accepted classification of legal rights, see Wesley Hohfeld, *Fundamental Legal Conceptions* (New Haven: Yale University Press, 1919, rpt. 1964), pp. 457–84.

33. There are different ways of characterizing the relation between rights and duties, not all of them equally sound. For example, some authors claim that a person is granted rights only if the person accepts certain duties toward the community that grants those rights. Other authors claim that all my rights can be defined wholly in terms of the duties of others. Both of these claims are probably mistaken, but neither claim is being advanced in this paragraph. The view of this paragraph is that moral rights of the kind identified in the previous paragraph always can be defined at least in part in terms of duties others have toward the bearer of the right. To have a moral right of this kind always implies that others have certain moral duties toward me; but it does not follow that if others have those duties, then I have the corresponding right. Thus, the claim is that the imposition of certain correlative moral duties on others is a necessary but not sufficient condition for one's possession of a moral right.

34. See Richard Wasserstrom, "Rights, Human Rights, and Racial Discrimination," *The Journal of Philosophy*, 61 (29 October 1964): 628–41.

35. *Ibid.*, p. 62.

36. Feinberg, *Social Philosophy*, pp. 59–61.

37. *Ibid.*

38. See, for example, Milton Friedman, *Capitalism and Freedom* (Chicago: The University of Chicago Press, 1962), pp. 22–36; Friedrich Hayek, *The Road to Serfdom* (Chicago: The University of Chicago Press, 1944), pp. 25–26.

39. Peter Singer, "Rights and the Market," in John Arthur and William Shaw, eds., *Justice and Economic Distribution* (Englewood Cliffs, NJ: Prentice-Hall, 1978), pp. 207–21.

40. H. L. A. Hart, "Are There Any Natural Rights," *Philosophical Review*, 64 (April 1955): 185.

41. J. R. Searle, *Speech Acts* (Cambridge: The University Press, 1969), pp. 57–62.

42. Thomas M. Garrett, *Business Ethics*, 2nd ed. (Englewood Cliffs, NJ: Prentice-Hall, 1986), pp. 88–91.

43. *Ibid.*, p. 75. See also John Rawls, *A Theory of Justice* (Cambridge: Harvard University Press, The Belknap Press, 1971), pp. 342–50.

44. An excellent explanation of Kant's moral theory is Roger J. Sullivan, *Immanuel Kant's Moral Theory* (New York: Cambridge University Press, 1989). Onora O'Neill has recently articulated a refreshingly clear interpretation of Kant in a series of essays collected in Onora Oneill, *Constructions of Reason: Explorations of Kant's Practical Philosophy* (Cambridge: Cambridge University Press, 1989); for an accessible overview of Kant's philosophy, see Paul Guyer, ed., *The Cambridge Companion to Kant* (New York: Cambridge University Press, 1992).

45. Immanuel Kant, *Groundwork of the Metaphysics of Morals*, H. J. Paton, trans. (New York: Harper & Row, Publishers, Inc., 1964), p. 70.

46. *Ibid.*, p. 91.

47. *Ibid.*, p. 96.

48. See Feldman, *Introductory Ethics* (Englewood Cliffs, NJ: Prentice-Hall, 1978), pp. 119–28; and Rawls, *A Theory of Justice*, pp. 179–80.

49. Kant, *Groundwork*, p. 105. On the equivalence of the two versions of the categorical imperative, see Sullivan, *ibid.*, pp. 193–194.

50. p. 93 in Gregory Vlastos, "Justice and Equality," p. 48 in Richard Brandt, ed., *Social Justice* (Englewood Cliffs, NJ: Prentice Hall, 1964), pp. 31–72. See, for example, A. K. Bierman, *Life and Morals: An Introduction to Ethics* (New York: Harcourt Brace Jovanovich, Inc., 1980), pp. 300–301; Charles Fried, *Right and*

Wrong (Cambridge: Harvard University Press, 1978), p. 129; Dworkin, *Taking Rights Seriously*, p. 198; Thomas E. Hill, Jr., "Servility and Self-Respect," *The Monist*, 57, no. 1 (January 1973): 87–104; Feinberg, *Social Philosophy.*

51. For a similar argument based on Kant's first formulation of the categorical imperative, see Marcus Singer, *Generalization in Ethics* (New York: Alfred A. Knopf, Inc., 1961), pp. 267–74; for one based on Kant's second formulation, see Alan Donagan, *The Theory of Morality* (Chicago: The University of Chicago Press, 1977), p. 85; also see I. Kant, *Metaphysical Elements of Justice* (New York: Bobbs-Merrill Co., Inc., 1965), pp. 91–99.

52. See Alan Gewirth, *Reason and Morality* (Chicago: The University of Chicago Press, 1978), who argues for these rights (p. 256) on the basis of a principle that, although different from Kant's first formulation in some important respects, is nonetheless very much like it: "Every agent must claim that he has rights to freedom and well-being for the reason that he is a prospective purposive agent . . . it follows, by the principle of universalizability, that all prospective purposive agents have rights to freedom and well-being" (p. 133); Donagan, *The Theory of Morality*, pp. 81–90, argues for these on the basis of Kant's second formulation.

53. See Singer, *Generalization in Ethics*, pp. 255–57, for a discussion of how Kant's first formulation provides a basis for the obligation to keep one's promises and for truthfulness in the making of promises; see Donagan, *Theory of Morality* pp. 90–94, for a discussion of the same subject in terms of the second formulation.

54. See Jonathan Harrison, "Kant's Examples of the First Formulation of the Categorical Imperative," in Robert Paul Wolff, ed., *Kant, A Collection of Critical Essays* (Garden City, NY: Doubleday & Co., Inc., 1967), pp. 228–45; see also in the same work the reply by J. Kemp and the counterreply by J. Harrison, both of which focus on the meaning of "is willing."

55. Fred Feldman, *Introductory Ethics*, pp. 123–28; Robert Paul Wolff, *The Autonomy of Reason* (New York: Harper Torch Books, 1973), p. 175.

56. For example, J. B. Mabbott, *The State and the Citizen* (London: Arrow, 1958), pp. 57–58.

57. Feldman, *Introductory Ethics*, pp. 116–17.

58. For example, Richard M. Hare, *Freedom and Reason* (New York: Oxford University Press, 1965), who uses Kant's first formulation (p. 34), defends himself against the example of the "fanatic" in this way.

59. Robert Nozick, *Anarchy, State, and Utopia* (New York: Basic Books, Inc., Publishers, 1974), p. ix.

60. *Ibid.*, pp. 30–31.

61. *Ibid.*, p. 160; see also pp. 160–62.

62. Kant, *The Metaphysical Elements of Justice*, p. 93.

63. U.S. Congress, Senate, *Brown Lung: Hearing Before a Subcommittee of the Committee on Appropriations, 95th Congress, 1st Session*. 9 December 1977, pp. 3, 52, 53, 54, 59, and 60.

64. John Rawls, "Justice as Fairness," *The Philosophical Review*, 67 (1958): 164–94; R. M. Hare, "Justice and Equality," in Arthur and Shaw, eds., *Justice and Economic Distribution*, p. 119. An excellent collection of readings on the nature of justice and fairness is Robert C. Solomon and Mark C. Murphy, *What Is*

Justice? Classic and Contemporary Readings (New York: Oxford University Press, 1990).

65. Rawls, *A Theory of Justice*, pp. 3–4.

66. See, for example, Rawls, *A Theory of Justice*, p. 542; and Joel Feinberg, "Rawls and Intuitionism," pp. 114–16 in Norman Daniels, ed. *Reading Rawls* (New York: Basic Books, Inc., Publishers, n.d.), pp. 108–24; and T. M. Scanlon, "Rawls' Theory of Justice," pp. 185–91 in *ibid.*, pp. 160–205.

67. See, for example, Vlastos, "Justice and Equality."

68. Rawls, *A Theory of Justice*, pp. 126–30.

69. William K. Frankena, "The Concept of Social Justice," in Brandt, ed., *Social Justice*, pp. 1–29; C. Perelman, *The Idea of Justice and the Problem of Argument* (New York: Humanities Press, Inc., 1963), p. 16.

70. Feinberg, *Social Philosophy*, pp. 100–102; Perelman, *Idea of Justice*, p. 16.

71. Christopher Ake, "Justice as Equality," *Philosophy and Public Affairs*, 5, no. 1 (Fall 1975): 69–89.

72. Kai Nielsen, "Class and Justice," in Arthur and Shaw, eds., *Justice and Economic Distribution*, pp. 225–45; see also Gregory Vlastos, *Justice and Equality*. Vlastos interprets "equality" in a much different sense than I do here.

73. Morton Deutsch, "Egalitarianism in the Laboratory and at Work," in Melvin J. Lerner and Riel Vermunt, eds., *Social Justice In Human Relations*, vol. 1 (New York: Plenum Publishing Corporation, 1991); Morton Deutsch, "Equity, Equality, and Need: What Determines Which Value Will Be Used as the Basis of Distributive Justice?" *Journal of Social Issues*, vol. 31 (1975): 221–79.

74. Leung, K., and Bond, M. H., "How Chinese and Americans Reward Task-Related Contributions: A Preliminary Study," *Psychologia*, vol. 25 (1982): 32–39; Leung, K., and Bond, M. H., "The Impact of Cultural Collectism on Reward Allocation," *Journal of Personality and Social Psychology*, vol. 47 (1984): 793–804; Kwok Leung and Iwawaki Saburo, "Cultural Collectivism and Distributive Behavior," *Journal of Cross-Cultural Psychology*, vol. 19, no. 1 (March 1988). 35–49.

75. Bernard Williams, "The Idea of Equality," in Laslett and Runciman, eds., *Philosophy and Society*, 2nd series (London: Blackwell, 1962), pp. 110–31.

76. Feinberg, *Social Philosophy*, pp. 109–11.

77. The evidence does not seem, however, to support this view. See Lane Kenworthy, *In Search of National Economic Success* (Thousand Oaks, CA: Sage Publications, 1995), who shows that societies with greater degrees of equality seem to be more productive than others; see Morton Deutsch, "Egalitarianism in the Laboratory and at Work," *ibid.*, for evidence that even in small work groups equality does not seem to result in lowered productivity.

78. See Bowie, *A New Theory of Distributive Justice*, pp. 60–64.

79. See D. D. Raphael, "Equality and Equity," *Philosophy*, 21 (1946): 118–32. See also, Bowie, *A New Theory of Distributive Justice*, pp. 64–65.

80. See Manuel Velasquez, "Why Ethics Matters," *Business Ethics Quarterly*, vol. 6, no. 2, (April 1996): 211.

81. *Ibid.*

82. See K. Leung, and M. H. Bond, *ibid.*, and K. Leung, and S. Iwawaki, *ibid.*

83. See Francis X. Sutton, Seymour E. Harris, Carl Kaysen, and James Tobin, *The American Business Creed* (Cambridge: Harvard University Press, 1956), pp. 276–78; the classic source is Max Weber, *The Protestant Ethic and the Spirit of Capitalism*, Talcott Parsons, trans. (London: 1930); see also, Perry Miller, *The New England Mind: From Colony to Province* (Cambridge: Harvard University Press, 1953), pp. 40–52.

84. See A. Whitner Griswold, "Three Puritans on Prosperity," *The New England Quarterly*, 7 (September 1934): 475–88; see also Daniel T. Rodgers, *The Work Ethic in Industrial America* (Chicago: The University of Chicago Press, 1978).

85. John A. Ryan, *Distributive Justice*, 3rd ed. (New York: The Macmillan Co., 1941), pp. 182–83; Nicholas Rescher, *Distributive Justice* (New York: The Bobbs-Merrill Co., Inc., 1966), pp. 77–78.

86. Rescher, *Distributive Justice*, pp. 78–79; Ryan, *Distributive Justice*, pp. 183–85.

87. Rescher, *Distributive Justice*, pp. 80–81; Ryan, *Distributive Justice*, pp. 186–87.

88. Karl Marx, *Critique of the Gotha Program* (London: Lawrence and Wishart, Ltd., 1938), pp. 14 and 107; Louis Blanc, *L'Organization du Travail* (Paris, 1850), cited in D. O. Wagner, *Social Reformers* (New York: The Macmillan Co., 1946), p. 218; Nikolai Lenin, "Marxism on the State," pp. 76–77; on the question of whether Marx had a theory of distributive justice, see Ziyad I. Husami, "Marx on Distributive Justice," in Marshall Cohen, Thomas Nagel, and Thomas Scanlon, eds., *Marx, Justice, and History* (Princeton: Princeton University Press, 1980), pp. 42–79.

89. Marx, *Critique of the Gotha Program*; see also John McMurtry, *The Structure of Marx's World View* (Princeton: Princeton University Press, 1978), ch. I.

90. Bowie, *A New Theory of Distributive Justice*, pp. 92–93. See also Norman Daniels, "Meritocracy," in Arthur and Shaw, eds., *Justice and Economic Distribution*, pp. 167–78. For an interesting examination of international data that suggest that equality does not undermine work incentive, see Kenworthy, *In Search of National Economic Success*, pp. 48–49.

91. Bowie, *ibid.*, pp. 96–98.

92. Robert Nozick, *Anarchy, State, and Utopia*, p. 160.

93. Rawls, *A Theory of Justice*, pp. 65–75.

94. *Ibid.*, pp. 577–87.

95. *Ibid.*, pp. 298–303.

96. *Ibid.*, p. 61.

97. *Ibid.*, pp. 108–14 and 342–50.

98. *Ibid.*, pp. 75–83 and 274–84.

99. *Ibid.*, pp. 83–90.

100. *Ibid.*, pp. 17–22.

101. *Ibid.*, pp. 136–42.

102. *Ibid.*, pp. 46–53.

103. The core of the argument is at *ibid.*, pp. 175–83, but parts may also be found at pp. 205–209, 325–32, 333–50, 541–48.

104. See the articles collected in *Reading Rawls*, Daniels, ed.; see also Brian Barry, *The Libal Theory of Justice* (Oxford: Clarendon Press, 1973); Robert Paul Wolff, *Understanding Rawls* (Princeton: Princeton University Press, 1977).

105. Rawls, *A Theory of Justice*, pp. 105–108.

106. *Ibid.*, p. 276.

107. On the relation between justice and due process, see David Resnick, "Due Process and Procedural Justice," in J. Roland Pennock and John W. Chapman, eds., *Due Process* (New York: New York University Press, 1977), pp. 302–10; employee due process procedures are discussed in Maurice S. Trotta and Harry R. Gudenberg, "Resolving Personnel Problems in Non-union Plants," in Alan F. Westin and Stephen Salisbury, eds., *Individual Rights in the Corporation* (New York: Pantheon Books, Inc., 1980), pp. 302–310.

108. On the relation between justice and consistency in the application of rules, see Perelman, *The Idea of Justice*, pp. 36–45; proportionality in punishment is discussed in John Kleinig, *Punishment and Desert* (The Hague: Martinus Nijoff, 1973), pp. 110–33; and C. W. K. Mundle, "Punishment and Desert," *Philosophical Quarterly*, IV (1954): 216–28.

109. Henry J. Wirtenberger, *Morality and Business* (Chicago: Loyola University Press, 1962), pp. 109–19; see also Herbert Jone, *Moral Theology*, Urban Adelman, trans. (Westminster, MD: The Newman Press, 1961), pp. 225–47.

110. This account of the Malden Mills incident is based on stories in: *Parade Magazine*, September 8, 1996; *Boston Globe*, December 5, 1995, December 13, 1995, January 12, 1996, and January 16, 1996; *Sun* (Lowell, MA), December 17, 1995 and November 5, 1995; *The New York Times*, July 24, 1994, December 16, 1995, July 14, 1996, and Penelope Washbourn, " 'When All Is Moral Chaos, This Is the Time for You to Be a Mensche': Reflections on Malden Mills for the Teaching of Business Ethics," unpublished paper presented at The Society for Business Ethics Annual Meeting, August 10, 1996, Quebec City, Quebec.

111. See, for example, Cottingham, "Ethics and Impartiality," *Philosophical Studies*, 43 (1983): 90–91.

112. See William Godwin, in K. Codell Carter, ed., *Enquiry Concerning Political Justice* (Oxford: Clarendon House, 1971), p. 71; and Peter Singer, *Practical Ethics*, 2nd ed. (Cambridge U. Press, 1993), pp. 10–12, 21.

113. See Lawrence Blum, *Moral Perception and Particularity* (Cambridge: Cambridge University Press, 1994); Lawrence Blum, *Friendship, Altruism, and Morality* (London: Routledge & Kegan Paul, 1980); John Kekes, "Morality and Impartiality," *American Philosophical Quarterly*, 18 (October 1981).

114. N. Lyons, "Two Perspectives: On Self, Relationships and Morality," *Harvard Educational Review*, 53(2) (1983): 136.

115. Lawrence A. Blum, *Moral Perception and Particularity* (Cambridge University Press, 1994), p. 12; Robin S. Dillon, "Care and Respect," in Eve Browning Cole and Susan Coultrap-McQuin, eds., *Explorations in Feminist Ethics: Theory and Practice* (Bloomington and Indianapolis, Indiana University Press, 1992), pp. 69–81; see also Mary C. Raugust, "Feminist Ethics and Workplace Values" in Eve Browning Cole and Susan Coultrap-McQuin, ed., *Explorations in Feminist Ethics: Theory and Practice* (Bloomington and Indianapolis, Indiana University Press, 1992), p. 127.

116. See the essays collected in Shlomo Avineri and Avner de-Shalit, eds., *Individualism and Communitarianism* (Oxford: Oxford University Press, 1992).

117. Michael Sandel, *Liberalism and the Limits of Justice* (Cambridge: Cambridge University Press, 1982) p. 150.

118. See Sandel, *Liberalism*, p. 179; MacIntyre, *After Virtue* (Notre Dame, IN: University of Notre Dame Press), pp. 204–205.

119. Nell Noddings, *Caring* (Berkeley: University of California Press, 1984), distinguishes between caring for and caring about on pp. 21–2; she refers to what I have called "caring after" as "institutional" caring on pp. 25–26.

120. See Sara Ruddick, *Maternal Thinking* (New York: Ballantine Books, 1989).

121. Lawrence Walker, "Sex Differences in the Development of Moral Reasoning: A Critical Review," and Catherine G. Greeno and Eleanor E. Maccoby, "How Different is the 'Different Voice'?" both in Mary Jeanne Larrabee, ed., *An Ethic of Care: Feminist and Interdisciplinary Perspectives* (New York: Routledge, 1993); for some evidence of some differences between men and women in how they deal with moral dilemmas, see T. White, "Business Ethics and Carol Gilligan's 'Two Voices'," *Business Ethics Quarterly*, vol. 2, no. 1, pp. 51–59. White provides some highly provocative suggestions about the implications of an ethic of care to business ethics.

122. See Joan C. Tronto, "Beyond Gender Difference to a Theory of Care," in *Ibid.*; and Debra Shogan, *Care and Moral Motivation* (Toronto: The Ontario Institute for Studies in Education Press, 1988).

123. See Alan Gewirth, "Ethical Universalism and Particularism," *Journal of Philosophy*, 85 (June 1988); John Cottingham, "Partiality, Favoritism, and Morality," *Philosophical Quarterly*, 36, no. 144 (1986).

124. This balancing of caring for self versus caring for others is a central theme in Carol Gilligan, *In a Different Voice: Psychological Theory and Women's Development* (Cambridge: Harvard University Press, 1982).

125. Ivan F. Boesky (Jeffrey Madrick, ed.), *Merger Mania* (New York: Holt, Rinehart and Winston, 1985), p. v.

126. Tim Metz and Michael W. Miller, "Boesky's Rise and Fall Illustrate a Compulsion to Profit by Getting Inside Track on Market," *The Wall Street Journal*, 17 November, 1986, p. 28.

127. *Ibid.*

128. S. Prakash Sethi and Paul Steidlmeier, *Up Against the Corporate Wall: Cases in Business and Society* (Upper Saddle River, NJ: Prentice-Hall, 1997), p. 47.

129. Alasdair MacIntyre, *After Virtue* (Notre Dame, IN: University of Notre Dame Press, 1981), p. 204.

130. See Edmund L. Pincoffs, *Quandaries and Virtues* (Lawrence, KS: University Press of Kansas, 1986). All quotes in the following paragraphs are from this work.

131. Business ethics in the international arena is a topic that is not well developed in the literature on business ethics, and a great deal of work remains to be done in these areas. See my discussion of the problems with current approaches in Manuel Velasquez, "International Business Ethics," *Business Ethics Quarterly*, vol. 5, no. 4 (October 1995): 865–82; and "International Business, Morality, and the Common Good," *Business Ethics Quarterly*, vol. 2., no. 1 (January 1992): 27–40. Among the better books on this topic, and from which I draw, are: Thomas Donaldson, *The Ethics of International Business* (New York: Oxford University Press, 1989); R. T. DeGeorge, *Competing with Integrity in International Business* (New York: Oxford University Press, 1993); G. Elfstrom, *Moral Issues and Multinational Corporations* (New York: St. Martin's Press, 1991). An older but still useful compendium of the ethical issues multinationals face is Thomas N.

Gladwin and Ingo Walter, *Multinationals Under Fire: Lessons in the Management of Conflict* (New York: John Wiley & Sons, 1980). Two pessimistic evaluations of multinational activities are David C. Korten, *When Corporations Rule the World* (San Francisco: Berrett-Koehler Publishers, 1995), and Richard J. Barnet and John Cavanagh, *Global Dreams* (New York: Simon & Schuster, 1994).

132. The importance of singling out issues of development is a point made by Thomas Donaldson in *op. cit.*, pp. 102–103.

133. Arnold Berleant, "Multinationals and the Problem of Ethical Consistency," *Journal of Business Ethics*, vol. 3 (August 1982): 185–95.

134. This is a suggestion of Thomas Donaldson in *op. cit.*, pp. 104–105.

CASES FOR DISCUSSION

Publius[1]

Although many people believe that the World Wide Web is anonymous and secure from censorship, the reality is very different. Governments, law courts, and other officials who want to censor, examine, or trace a file of materials on the Web need merely go to the server (the online computer) where they think the file is stored. Using their subpoena power, they can comb through the server's drives to find the files they are looking for and the identity of the person who created the files.

On Friday June 30, 2000, however, researchers at AT&T Labs announced the creation of Publius, a software program that enables Web users to encrypt (translate into a secret code) their files—text, pictures, or music—break them up like the pieces of a jigsaw puzzle, and store the encrypted pieces on many different servers scattered all over the globe on the World Wide Web. As a result, anyone wanting to examine or censor the files or wanting to trace the original transaction that produced the file would find it impossible to succeed because they would have to examine the contents of dozens of different servers all over the world, and the files in the servers would be encrypted and fragmented in a way that would make the pieces impossible to identify without the help of the person who created the file. A person authorized to retrieve the file, however, would look through a directory of his files posted on a Publius-affiliated website, and the Publius network would reassemble the file for him at his request. Researchers published a description of Publius at www.cs.nyu.edu/waldman/publius.

Although many people welcomed the way that the new software would enhance freedom of speech on the Web, many others were dismayed. Bruce Taylor, an antipornography activist for the National Law Center for Children and Families, stated: "Its nice to be anonymous, but who wants to be more anonymous than criminals, terrorists, child molesters, child pornographers, hackers, and e-mail virus punks." Aviel Rubin and Lorrie Cranor, the creators of Publius, however, hoped that their program would help people in countries where freedom of speech was repressed and individuals were punished for speaking out. The ideal user of Publius, they stated, was "a person in China observing abuses of human rights on a day-to-day basis."

Questions

1. Analyze the ethics of marketing Publius using utilitarianism, rights, justice, and caring. In your judgment, is it ethical to market Publius? Explain.
2. Are the creators of Publius in any way morally responsible for any criminal acts that criminals are able to carry out and keep secret by relying on Publius? Is AT&T in any way morally responsible for these? Explain your answers.
3. In your judgment, should governments allow the implementation of Publius? Why or why not?

Notes

1. This case is based on John Schwartz, "Publius Aims to Bring Net Freedom," *San Jose Mercury News*, July 1, 2000, pp. 1C, 13C.

Philip Morris' Troubles

Each day cigarettes cause or contribute to the deaths of about 1000 Americans. An average of five and a half minutes of life are lost for each cigarette smoked. Although smoking among adult men has been declining, smoking among adult women and children has been on the rise; today lung cancer kills more women than breast cancer. Smoking illnesses now account for 11percent of the aggregate costs of all illness in the United States; 25 percent of disability days for men between ages 45 and 64 are associated with cigarette smoking. Indirect economic losses from reduced productivity and lost earnings are estimated at $37 billion per year, and total economic losses are estimated conservatively at $65 billion a year.

Nevertheless, the tobacco industry has continued to increase its revenues by 2 percent to 3 percent a year, and profits have generally continued to rise. Although the total number of cigarettes sold in the United States peaked in 1981, the industry continued to increase its profits by cutting costs, raising prices, and expanding into foreign markets. Philip Morris, the world's largest manufacturer of cigarettes, reported profits of $5.4 billion in 1998 on revenues to $74.4 billion.[1] As the company looked ahead, its managers realized that it would have to deal with a number of ethical issues.

Philip Morris, with a labor force of over 144,000 employees, is the nation's largest cigarette manufacturer, its largest food company, and its second largest beer company. Before the 1970s, virtually all of Philip Morris' revenues were derived from tobacco sales. Then accelerating a long-term strategy of diversifying away from the U.S. tobacco industry (a strategy that would become common in the tobacco industry), Philip Morris acquired Miller Brewing company in 1970. In 1985, it bought General Foods for $5.7 billion; in 1988, it paid $13 billion for Kraft, then the largest U.S. food company; in 1990, it acquired Suchard, a Swiss coffee and confectionery company, for $3.8 billion; in 1993, it acquired the ready-to-eat cereal businesses of RJR Nabisco for $448 million; and in 1994, it acquired Cirkel AB, a Swedish coffee and spices company. Activists accused the company of laundering the "dirty money" it had made in the cigarette business by using it to buy up clean food businesses—in effect protecting these funds from any potential liability that might strike its tobacco business.

Tobacco products, however, continued to be the company's largest business. Among the company's well-known cigarette brands were: Alpine, Benson & Hedges, Cambridge, Marlboro, Merit, Parliament, Players, PM, and Virginia Slims. Its beer brands included Genuine Draft, High Life, Leinenkugel, Lowenbrau, Lite, Meister Brau, Miller, and Milwaukee's Best. The company's food brands included Post cereals, Entenmann and Freihofer's bakery products, Jell-O desserts, Birds Eye frozen foods, Maxwell House coffee, Velveeta, Cracker Barrel and Churny cheeses, Oscar Mayer meat products, and Claussen pickles. In 1998, the company's tobacco operations accounted for 57 percent of its profits; food products accounted for 37 percent, and beer for 4 percent. The company's food and beer businesses were a net drag on the large profits its cigarette operations threw off.

Philip Morris' food companies, while not losing money, were also not substantially increasing their market share. Maxwell House, their basic coffee brand, had earlier lost market share to Procter & Gamble's Folgers, and Post Cereals had lost market share to cereals made by Kellogg's and General Mills. Part of the company's difficulties in the food industry could be traced to the fact that their food division was not a single business, but a complex bundle of different companies each with its own distinct set of agricultural suppliers, government regulations, manufacturing processes, distribution channels, and special set of competitors. Used to the simpler and more traditional dynamics of the cigarette industry, Philip Morris' managers found the food business difficult at best. In addition, the food industry was buffeted by a number of social concerns. As the population aged and became more health-conscious, consumers became more concerned about the high-fat and high-cholesterol content of the packaged foods that were the core of its food business and that created health risks for some consumers. Phillip Morris' food companies also were trying to convince consumers that they should not be concerned about new technologies the company was using—such as irradiation, which was used to preserve foods, and genetic engineering, which was the basis of some of the new crops that its food companies used as ingredients. Although some food companies informed consumers about which products were made of genetically modified organisms or about which products had been irradiated, Philip Morris did not.

Philip Morris owned and operated eight beer breweries in the United States. The beer industry was highly competitive. Since 1991, volume growth had averaged less than 1 percent annually, and brewers had tried to gain market share through lower prices and innovative promotions. The three top brewers, who controlled 79 percent of the beer industry in 1998, included: Anheuser-Busch with 46.6 percent of the market, Miller Brewing with 21 percent, and Adolph Coors with 11 percent. Total volume sales of beer had decreased from 202.1 million barrels in 1997 to 200.3 million barrels in 1998. Miller Brewing Company sold only 42.7 million barrels in 1998, down 2.3 percent from 1997, and its market share had declined from 21.8 percent in 1997 to 21.2 percent in 1998. The number of consumers reaching legal drinking age in the United States had increased in 1998 and 1999, but many brewers were turning to China, Eastern Europe, and Latin America to increase their sales. By 1999, China was already the world's second-largest beer market and had overtaken the U.S. market in 2000; Eastern Europe was an established beer stronghold, and favorable demographics combined with rising economies made Latin America an attractive option for Philip Morris.

Philip Morris' most successful business, however, was still its cigarette business. In 1998, tobacco was a $53 billion industry in the United States, and cigarettes accounted for 94 percent of this total. About one in four Americans smokes, with the average smoker spending over $260 a year on tobacco. In 1998, the nation smoked 470 billion cigarettes. Philip Morris' "Marlboro" brand, the world's best-selling cigarette, held 34 percent of the U.S. market—8.1 billion packs—down from 35 percent in 1997. Together with its other brands, Philip Morris held 49.4 percent of the U.S. cigarette market. Since 1981, when the nation smoked 640 billion cigarettes, however, U.S. consumption had fallen about 2 percent a year. Four companies controlled approximately 98 percent of the domestic market in 1998: Philip Morris (49.5 percent), R. J. Reynolds Tobacco Company (24 percent), Brown & Williamson (15.3 percent), and Lorillard (9 percent). Competition among the four companies was intense.

But competition was not the main factor threatening Philip Morris' tobacco business. Since the 1950s, the tobacco industry had been buffeted repeatedly by studies linking heavy smoking with high rates of lung cancer and other chronic lung diseases, heart disease, and birth defects. In 1966, 1969, and 1985, Congress passed laws requiring health warnings on cigarette packages.

A new concern had surfaced in 1986 when the U.S. Surgeon General and the National Academy of Sciences reported that nonsmokers were at increased risk of lung cancer when exposed the second-hand smoke produced by smokers. In 1991, the U.S. Environmental Protection Agency issued a report on the risks of second-hand smoke. Reacting to the new findings, several local governments enacted legislation restricting or banning cigarette smoking in public places and workplaces, and the airlines had banned smoking on all commercial flights within the United States.

In 1994, the government turned its attention to the addictive nature of cigarettes. The U.S. Surgeon General had already issued a report in 1988 summarizing research that nicotine was addictive. In 1994, Congress held hearings on the question of whether the nicotine in cigarettes is an addictive drug and whether the cigarette industry was manipulating the nicotine levels of cigarettes. The executives of all the tobacco companies were called to testify. At the hearings, William Campbell, head of Philip Morris' tobacco unit, denied under oath that nicotine was addictive and said that the company "does not manipulate nor independently control the level of nicotine in our cigarettes."[2] On April 1, 1994, Congressman Henry A. Waxman announced that a committee he headed had found evidence that Philip Morris had suppressed a 1983 study by Dr. Victor DeNoble that had produced definitive evidence of the addictive qualities of tobacco in rats, and that Philip Morris had, therefore, known since that time that tobacco was addictive. Waxman stated that the discovery "goes to the basic question that was raised in our hearing: 'Have the American people been manipulated into thinking that smoking is a matter of choice, or in fact is it a choice denied them because of the possible intentional manipulation of nicotine levels to keep them addicted?' "[3] Waxman's findings were corroborated when, on March 19, 1996, the FDA released sworn statements from two Philip Morris research scientists and a Philip Morris plant manager contradicting Campbell's testimony.[4] Jerome Rivers, the plant manager, outlined a sophisticated manufacturing process in which the levels of nicotine in tobacco were carefully monitored and during which tobacco, whose nicotine levels were "out of spec," was pulled out and reprocessed. Ian Uydess, one of the research scientists, testified that, "Nicotine levels were routinely targeted and adjusted by Philip Morris in its various products at least in part" and that "Dr. DeNoble's research on nicotine analogues" was known in the company where "there was a growing concern among Philip Morris management" about the use of the term *addictive* and where "internal reports were increasingly scrutinized by Philip Morris management." Dr. W. Farone, former director of the company's applied research, also testified to the company's "sequestering of much good science."

Litigation had also become a significant issue for Philip Morris. At the end of 1998, approximately 510 cases were pending against Philip Morris (up from 375 cases in 1997 and 185 in 1996) seeking compensatory and, in some cases, punitive damages for cancer and other health effects claimed to have resulted from cigarette smoking or exposure to cigarette smoke. Although sick customers had sued the company hundreds of times, it had never lost a major case before 1998, although it had often only won on appeal. Among the defenses used in litigation by Philip Morris was the argument that complying with the 1965 Federal Cigarette Labeling and Advertising Act, particularly as amended in 1969 and 1985, protected the company from claims that it failed to warn smokers that cigarettes were dangerous—a defense that five federal courts of appeal had upheld.[5]

In February 1999, however, a San Francisco jury awarded a woman with inoperable lung cancer $51.5 million in a lawsuit she had brought against Philip Morris. The judge cut the award to $26.5 million. In March 1999, a jury in Portland, Oregon, awarded $80.3 million to the family of a man who had died of lung cancer in 1997 after a lifetime smoking Marlboros. This award was reduced to $32.8 million by the judge. In July 1999, in the first phase of a three-phase class-action lawsuit in Florida filed on behalf of 500,000 sick Florida smokers, a six-person jury concluded that cigarette companies had produced a "defective product" that caused emphysema, lung cancer, heart disease, and other sicknesses. The plaintiffs sought at least $200 billion in damages, but any award would have to wait until the second and third phases of the trial were concluded, during which Philip Morris and other tobacco companies would argue that smokers voluntarily and knowingly assume the risks of smoking and so were personally responsible for their health problems.

Philip Morris first responded to the rising tide of health concerns by arguing through advertisements that the studies linking smoking to lung cancer were not conclusive. In particular, the company claimed that, because not all smokers got lung cancer, there was no demonstrable cause–effect relationship between smoking and lung cancer. The company also argued that smoking was not addictive and, consequently, smokers were free to quit smoking any time they wanted. Smoking, the company argued, was a matter of personal choice, and all individuals should be left free to exercise their personal right to smoke when, where, and as much as they choose. Moreover, even if cigarette smoking were dangerous, the company claimed, the warnings on cigarettes required by the federal government gave smokers a knowledge of the risks associated with smoking and so it could not be argued that they did not willingly assume those risks. These views were advanced in the pages of a free quarterly magazine that the company had been mailing to smokers since the late 1980s. In 1999, however, for the first time the company acknowledged the link between smoking and cancer. The company continued to insist, however, that smoking was not addictive, but was a matter of free choice and personal responsibility.

In November 1998, Philip Morris and the other leading tobacco companies reached a settlement with 46 states whose governments had threatened to sue the companies for recovery of smoking-related health care costs. The companies agreed to pay $206 billion over 25 years to the states, to not engage in any advertising targeted at young people, to not use cartoon characters in advertisements, to not engage in outdoor advertising, and to provide other smoking cessation programs. In a separate agreement with four states that had not participated in the November 1998 settlement, the companies agreed to provide an additional $40 billion in payments, for a total of almost $250 billion. Each cigarette company was liable for a percentage of these annual payments equal to its market share in a given year—an arrangement that placed the heaviest burden on Philip Morris. Although the settlements banned all future lawsuits by state governments, it did not provide any protection from any lawsuits brought against cigarette companies by any other parties. Anticipating the settlement, cigarette companies had raised the wholesale price of cigarettes by 50 percent since January 1998. On November 23, the day the settlement was reached, two companies raised their wholesale prices by 45 cents a pack—the greatest cigarette price increase in history.

In his state of the union address in January 1999, President Clinton announced that he would instruct the Department of Justice to prepare a lawsuit against the tobacco companies to recover health care-related costs carried by Medicare, using the 1962 Medical Care Recovery Act, which granted the government the right to recover taxpayer money spent on illnesses caused by a negligent party. Although the tobacco companies vowed to fight the lawsuit, observers argued that the industry would probably enter a settlement in the range of $150 billion to $200 billion in return for protection from any future federal litigation.

Although health concerns had affected sales in the United States, governments of other countries, especially those in the Third World, did not spend much money on antismoking campaigns, and many were reluctant to give up the tax revenues associated with cigarettes. Consequently, tobacco companies, particularly Philip Morris, had begun to push vigorously into foreign markets, especially into Third World and, more recently, East European markets. Although U.S. consumption of cigarettes declined, U.S. tobacco exports rose. In 1998, Philip Morris shipped 717 billion cigarettes outside of the United States, compared with total U.S. shipments of 228 billion. Philip Morris had modernized and expanded its factories in Germany, the Netherlands, Switzerland, Poland, Romania, Russia, Lithuania, the Ukraine, Turkey, Malaysia, and Brazil. The company held over 15 percent of the market in 25 countries, including France, Germany, Italy, and Mexico, and had been one of the first American companies to market its cigarettes in Japan, Taiwan, and China. Turkey was the fourth biggest importer of cigarettes (after Japan, Belgium-Luxembourg, and Hong Kong). Turkey was, in fact, considered a key location because it borders the former Soviet Union and is a stepping stone to Asia. Moreover, Turks are heavy smokers, and Turkish cigarette consumption was expected to grow substantially. In a joint venture with Sabanci Holdings (the second largest industrial conglomerate in Turkey),

Philip Morris had built a $400 million cigarette factory in Turkey that went into production in 1993. This was the largest plant Philip Morris had built recently outside the United States.

Philip Morris' beer business was also under pressure. A number of interest groups had formed around the issue of drunk driving, including SADD (Students Against Driving Drunk) and MADD (Mothers Against Drunk Driving), the latter of which was a particularly effective lobby for raising the drinking age, increasing penalties on drunk driving, and limiting the availability of alcohol to minors. Another group, SMART (Stop Marketing Alcohol on Radio and Television), was lobbying hard for legislation to restrict advertising of beer both on the grounds that alcohol was associated with health problems and that television and radio advertising appealed to minors. Congress was now considering restricting the advertising of alcoholic beverages.

The beer industry was also being buffeted by rising health and dietary concerns. Growing awareness of the long-term effects of alcohol on internal organs, especially the liver and heart, were becoming significant concerns. The Alcoholic Beverage Labeling Act of 1988 already required all alcoholic beverages to carry warnings associating the consumption of alcohol with health problems, the risk of birth defects, and a lowered ability to drive a car or operate machinery. In addition, the high-calorie content of alcoholic beverages had spurred a growing health trend toward nonalcoholic or low-alcohol beverages, which contained fewer calories. Light beers now account for about a third of the total beer market. Sharp's, a nonalcoholic beer from Miller, was the leader among nonalcoholic beers, followed by Anheuser Busch and O'Doul's.

The fifth largest selling beer, Miller's Magnum, had bucked these health trends, but had run into other social problems. Miller's Magnum was a malt liquor—a type of beer that typically contains up to 50 percent more alcohol than other beer. Malt liquors were under fire from community organizations who argued that these beers, with their high alcoholic content, were targeted at Blacks and Hispanics and encouraged inner-city violence. Malt liquors like Magnum were top sellers among ghetto youth. Promotions for malt liquors often used rap music, and their advertisements used pictures suggestive of inner-city gang culture that subtly associated the beer with feelings of being powerful and masterful. The U.S. Surgeon General had charged that, in targeting young Black males, makers of malt liquors had singled out "a group with a level of cirrhosis of the liver more prevalent than others." The *New York Times* editorialized that beer companies should "stop targeting a population already devastated by alcohol and drug problems." Black ministers assailed the malt beers from their church pulpits.

Looking over the issues facing the company's various businesses, Philip Morris managment realized that developing a strategy for the future would require a very delicate hand. The company would have to come up with corporate and business level strategies for the new century that would enable it to deal with the many threats it faced around the globe. What should the company do?

Questions

1. Identify all the moral issues that are raised by Philip Morris' activities in the tobacco, beer, and food industries. Discuss these issues in terms of utilitarianism, rights, justice, and care.
2. Both the tobacco and beer industries have been characterized as "sin industries." Comment on the extent to which virtue theory sheds light on the company's activities in these industries.
3. What, in your judgment, would be a morally appropriate course of action for the government agencies involved in the case?

Notes

1. Philip Morris, *Annual Report*, 1999
2. Alix M. Freedman, "Philip Morris Memo Likens Nicotine to Such Drugs as Cocaine, Morphine," *Wall Street Journal*, 8 December 1995.
3. Philip J. Hilts, "Philip Morris Blocked '83 Paper Showing Tobacco Is Addictive, Panel Finds," *New York Times*, 1 April 1994, p. A21.
4. Tim Friend, "New Heat on Tobacco Firm," *USA Today*, 19 March 1996, p. A1; "Tobacco Industry Under Fire," *USA Today*, 19 March 1996, p. B2; Dough Henry, "Whistleblowers Wreak Havoc," *USA Today*, 19 March 1996, p. B2.
5. Philip Morris Companies, Inc., Securities and Exchange Commission Form10-K, 1991, p. 4.

Pepsi's Burma Connection

On April 23, 1996, PepsiCo announced that it had decided to sell its 40 percent stake in a bottling plant in Burma in part because of criticisms that by remaining in Burma the company was helping to support the repressive military regime that now ruled the country. [1] In a letter to a shareholder who had been one of many pressuring the company to get out of Burma, the company's corporate secretary wrote:

> When we first spoke about Burma I promised to stay in touch with you on the subject. In that spirit, I wanted to let you now about a change in our business there. We've decided to sell PepsiCo's minority stake in

our franchise bottler and we expect to finalize the divestiture soon. As a result we will have no employees and no assets in the country.

We're taking this action for a number of reasons, including the sentiment expressed by you and others about investing in Burma at this time. Having said that, let me reiterate our belief that free trade leads to free societies.[2]

The letter, however, made no mention of the fact that PepsiCo would continue to sell its syrup concentrate to the bottler in Burma and would continue to allow the bottler to sell Pepsi in Burma.

Burma is an Asian country with a population of 42 million and an area about the size of Texas; it is bounded by India, China, Thailand, and the ocean. The country is poor, with a per capita gross domestic product of only $408, a high infant mortality rate (95 deaths for every 1000 live births), a low life expectancy (53 years for males and 56 for females), and inflation above 20 percent.

Burma gained its independence from British rule in 1948. In July 1988, as economic conditions declined, large-scale and bloody rioting broke out in the cities of Burma. In September 1988, the army under General U. Saw Maung assumed control and brutally repressed dissent, killing, it is believed, thousands of students and civilians. General Maung replaced the government with the State Law and Order Restoration Council (SLORC), a group of military officers. In 1990, the SLORC, believing it had the support of the people, called for a new government and allowed free elections, confident it would win. However, the overwhelming majority of seats in the proposed new government (80 percent) was won by the civilian opposition party led by Suu Kyi. Refusing to turn over power to a civilian government, the SLORC annulled the election, outlawed the opposition party, and arrested its leaders, including Suu Kyi. The SLORC invited foreign private investors and companies to invest in Burma with the hopes of improving the economy.

PepsiCo was one of many American companies that responded favorably to the invitations of the SLORC. Others included apparel manufacturers such as Eddie Bauer, Liz Claiborne, Spiegel's, and Levi Strauss; shoe manufacturers such as Reebok; and oil companies such as Amoco, Unocal, and Texaco. The United States was the fifth largest foreign investor in Burma.

The country was attractive for several reasons. Not only was labor extremely cheap, but because the culture placed a high value on education, worker literacy rates were very high. The country's oil resources were an irresistible lure to the oil companies, and its many other untapped resources presented major opportunities. Burma not only offered a potentially large market, it also occupied a strategic location that could serve as a link to markets in China, India, and other countries in Southeast Asia. Also, with the military dictatorship to maintain law and order, the political environment was extremely stable.

The military, however, presented a problem. Many groups, including the U.S. Department of State, accused the SLORC of numerous human rights abuses. The U.S. Department of State reported:

> The Government's unacceptable record on human rights changed little in 1994. Burmese citizens continued to live subject at any time and without appeal to the arbitrary and sometimes brutal dictates of the military. The use of porters by the army—with all the attendant maltreatment, illness, and even death for those compelled to serve—remained a standard practice. . . . The Burmese military forced hundreds of thousands, if not millions, of ordinary Burmese (including women and children) to "contribute" their labor, often under harsh working conditions, to construction projects throughout the country. The forced resettlement of civilians also continued. Four hundred or more political prisoners remained in detention, including approximately 40 parliamentarians elected in 1990. . . . The SLORC continued to restrict severely basic rights to free speech, association and assembly. In July and August the authorities arrested five persons for trying to smuggle out information on conditions in Burma to the outside world. . . . Throughout 1994, the Government continued to rule by decree and was not bound by any constitutional provisions guaranteeing fair public trials or any other rights. . . . The security services continued to clamp down on those who expressed opposition political views. . . . Workers were not free to form [trade unions] and leaders of unofficial labor associations remained subject to arrest. Surplus labor conditions and lack of protection by government authorities continue to dictate substandard conditions for workers.[3]

Nevertheless, the management of PepsiCo was intrigued by the government's invitation to invest in Burma. In 1991, PepsiCo decided to enter a joint venture with Myanmar Golden Star Co., a Burmese company owned by a Burmese businessman named Thein Tun. Myanmar Golden Star would own 60 percent of the venture while PepsiCo would own 40 percent. The venture would set up a bottling plant with a 10-year license to bottle and distribute PepsiCo-owned products in Burma, including Pepsi Cola, 7 Up, and Miranda soft drinks.

The bottling venture did well. In 1995, PepsiCo reported that the revenues made by the Burma bottler totaled $20 million, of which PepsiCo's share was $8 million. The company announced that in 1996 revenues in Burma increased by 25 percent. Pepsi products had become the main source of income for Thein Tun, who was a very close friend of the generals who made up the SLORC. Tun's close ties with the military junta was one of the factors that had led PepsiCo to choose him as a partner.

Back in the United States, however, critics were questioning the ethics of doing business in Burma. On numerous campuses, students were pressing universities to purge their portfolios of any companies doing business in Burma. Several cities had passed bans on city purchases of any goods or services from companies doing business in Burma. A network of students on about 100 campuses had launched a boycott of Pepsi products. Harvard students had pressured that university to refuse to give PepsiCo a contract (valued at $1 million) to sell Pepsi on campus. Company shareholders had submitted resolutions urging PepsiCo to leave Burma. The company had received hundreds of letters demanding that the company leave Burma.

Critics claimed that, by doing business in Burma, American companies were helping prop up the repressive military government of that county through taxes and other means. If foreign companies were to abandon Burma, the military would fail in its attempts to create a vibrant market economy. Declining economic conditions would pressure the military into instituting democratic reforms to attract foreign investment back into the country.

Moreover, many of the American companies in Burma engaged in a practice called *countertrade*, which according to critics was associated with the forced labor now rampant in rural areas. Burmese money was worthless outside of the country, making it virtually impossible for an American company to transfer its profits out of Burma and into the United States. To get around this problem, many companies traded their Burmese profits for Burmese agricultural commodities. They would then export the agricultural commodities to countries outside of Burma, sell them there, and transfer those monies to the United States. PepsiCo had admitted to engaging in countertrade, as had many other companies. The problem with countertrade, critics claimed, was that forced labor was widely used throughout the agricultural sector, particularly on the many farms now controlled by the military. The military had confiscated much of the best farmland in Burma, evicted the farmers, and then forced them to return to provide slave labor to grow the crops that the military then harvested and sold, keeping the proceeds. A good portion of the agricultural commodities that American companies purchased and sold abroad were thus likely to have been produced by forced labor.

PepsiCo and other companies, however, argued for a policy they called *constructive engagement*. The best way to get the military to institute reforms, they argued, was by staying in Burma and pressuring the military to change its ways. Improving economic conditions would develop a flourishing middle class that would bring about democracy. "Free trade leads to free societies" was a favorite slogan of PepsiCo and others.

In 1992, however, Levi Strauss withdrew from Burma, saying, "it is not possible to do business in [Burma] without directly supporting the military government and its pervasive violations of human rights." In 1994, Reebok and Liz

Claiborne withdrew, saying they could not do business in Burma until "significant improvements in human rights conditions" were enacted. In 1995, Eddie Bauer and Amoco pulled out, citing growing opposition at home to company involvement in Burma.

The growing pressures being put on PepsiCo to leave Burma finally convinced the company in 1996 that it should divest itself of its holdings in the Burmese bottling plant. In 1997, the company sold its holdings in the plant to its partner, Thein Tun. But PepsiCo had decided to continue to honor its 10-year license allowing the bottler to sell Pepsi in Burma and continue to provide the bottler with the necessary syrup used to mix Pepsi soft drinks. Critics objected that the half-way move meant that PepsiCo was still doing business in Burma and vowed to keep up the pressure on the company.

Questions

1. In your judgment, did PepsiCo have a moral obligation to divest itself of all its Burmese assets? Explain your answer. Which approach to ethics—utilitarianism, rights, justice, caring, or virtue—is most appropriate for analyzing the events in this case?
2. In your judgment, does PepsiCo have a moral obligation to now pull its products and brand name out of Burma? Explain your answer.

Notes

1. "PepsiCo to Exit From Burma Bottling Joint-Venture," *Bloomberg Business News*, 23 April, 1996.
2. Letter dated April 22, 1996, sent to Father Joseph La Mar of the Maryknoll Order, one of several shareholders petitioning Pepsico to leave Burma.
3. Department of State, *Country Reports on Human Rights Practices for 1994* (Washington, DC: U.S. Government Printing Office, 1995), pp. 539–48.

PART TWO

The Market and Business

American business transactions are for the most part carried out within market structures. Businesses acquire supplies, raw materials, and machinery in industrial markets; they go to labor markets to find workers; they transfer their finished products to retailers in wholesale markets; and the final transfer to consumers is made in retail markets. The next two chapters examine the ethical aspects of these market activities. Chapter 3 discusses the morality of the market system as a whole: How is it justified and what are its strengths and weaknesses from an ethical point of view? Chapter 4 discusses the ethics of various market practices. There the emphasis is no longer on the ethics of the market system considered as a whole, but on the ethics of particular practices within the market system: price-fixing, manipulation of supply, price discrimination, bribery, and market concentration.

3

The Business System

Introduction

The American economy during the closing decades of the 20th century suffered severely turbulent shocks, partly as a result of the United States' declining ability to compete with other nations in certain key markets. The economy suffered from declining productivity (e.g., in the textile, automobile, and steel industries), high unemployment, increasing international competition (especially from the Japanese), record-setting trade deficits, repeated economic recessions (in the early 1980s and again in the early 1990s), and stubbornly high poverty rates. As the century drew to a close, foreign nations had become dominant in several segments of the high-technology and information industries that the United States had pioneered. These challenges to America's international economic leadership sparked a national debate on the need for a "new industrial policy" that would strengthen domestic industries so that they can compete more vigorously abroad.[1]

Proponents of industrial policy have repeatedly urged the government to adopt coherent economic measures to help declining industries and their workers adjust to new economic conditions, and to nurture and protect newly emerging technological industries until they are strong enough to compete abroad. Proposals have included the passage of laws to restrict foreign imports; development of planning agencies in which business, government, and labor representatives can negotiate coherent industrial plans; and creation of public financial institutions to oversee direct loans to selected industries. Only these kinds of coordinating mechanisms, it has been argued, can deal with the economic problems posed by rising competition from other countries, declining industries, and unemployment. Economist Ray Marshall, testifying during one of several congressional hearings held on these issues, said:

> The solutions to economic problems should be built on a sensible division of labor between government, the market, and mechanisms that promote cooperative problem solving. And I would give heavy weight to the latter, because I think it's one of the main disadvantages the United States faces relative to other countries. While the market can be a marvel of promoting short-run efficiency, it cannot solve larger problems. It cannot prevent recession, inflation, or create open and fair trade and competition. Markets by themselves cannot protect the environment, promote equal opportunities and adequate income for our people, foster our long-run basic research and innovation, and insure the national security. Indeed, without government intervention to preserve competitive conditions, markets would be less effective than they are. While we must rely primarily on market forces, there can be little doubt about the need for positive government partnership with the private sector in addressing important national problems. There is an important range of problems, particularly in fighting inflation and in strengthening the international competitiveness of American industry, that will not yield to the uncoordinated actions of either the public or private sector alone. Public and private partnership must be forged, establishing a new institution of governance.[2]

Opponents of these "industrial policy" proposals, however, have held that government should not intervene in the economy in this manner because such intervention is not a proper function of government. Many business people are especially antagonistic to the proposals, holding that in the long run free market competition would create stronger industries while government intervention would inevitably fail. Robert Anderson, chairman of Rockwell International Corporation, for example, testified at another congressional hearing:

> The full revitalization of the American economy . . . will occur only if those improvements contribute to increasing America's ability to compete in the new world we are in. . . . Given the emergence of a global marketplace, a turn inward [through protectionist limits on foreign imports] would be self-defeating in the long run. Our mandate must not be to punish or retard the competitive gains made by other nations, but to do a better job of competing ourselves. . . . Just as we must avoid the pitfall of protectionism, so we must avoid the peril of increased Government intervention into the activities of the private sector. If industrial policy simply means centralized Government planning, count us out. Such a course would be inconsistent with our historic free market traditions and counterproductive in this new era.[3]

The controversy over "industrial policy" is but a single episode in a great and centuries-long debate over the American business system: Should government regulate and coordinate the activities of business firms, or should business firms be left free to pursue their own interests within unregulated markets? Should the business system be a "planned" economy, or should it be a "free market" economy? The arguments that Marshall and Anderson advanced are clear examples of the two opposing viewpoints on this critical issue. One side argues that unregulated market systems are defective because they cannot deal with the problems of recession, inflation, ensuring open and fair trade and competition, the environment, equal opportunities, poverty, the need to foster long-run basic research and innovation, and ensuring national security. The other side argues that regulation is defective because it violates the right to freedom and leads to an inefficient allocation of resources. This chapter examines these arguments for and against free markets and government regulation.

Ideologies

In analyzing these arguments on free markets and government, we in effect analyze what sociologists refer to as *ideologies*. An ideology is a system of normative beliefs shared by members of some social group. The ideology expresses the group's answers to questions about human nature (e.g., are human beings only motivated by economic incentives?), the basic purpose of our social institutions (e.g., what is the purpose of government? of business? of the market?), how societies actually function (e.g., are markets free? does big business control government?), and the values society should try to protect (e.g., freedom? productivity? equality?). A business ideology, then, is a normative system of beliefs on these matters, but specifically one that is held by business groups such as managers.

The importance of analyzing business ideologies is obvious: A business person's ideology often determines the business decisions he or she makes; through these decisions, the ideology influences the person's behavior. The businessperson's ideology, for example, will color the person's perceptions of the groups with whom he or she has to deal (employees, government officials, the poor, competitors, consumers); it will encourage the person to give in to certain pressures from these groups (perhaps even to support them) and oppose others; it will make him or her look on some actions as justified and legitimate and other actions (both those of the person and those of other groups) as unjustified and illegitimate. If a person's ideology is never examined, it will nonetheless have a deep and pervasive influence on the person's decision making—an influence that may go largely unnoticed and that may derive from what is actually a false and ethically objectionable ideology.

In a widely read analysis of the business ideologies that tend to dominate in American society, and of the need to make these ideologies more appropriate for the highly competitive environment in which U.S. businesses now operate,

George Lodge, of the Harvard Business School, identified two important ideologies—"individualistic" and "communitarian"—that are characteristic of different societies:

> In an individualistic society, the role of government is limited. Its fundamental purposes are to protect property, enforce contracts, and keep the marketplace open so that competition among firms may be as vigorous and as free as possible. Government is essentially separate from business. It intervenes in the affairs of business only when the national health and safety are involved. Intervention thus hinges on crisis—epidemics, pollution, economic disaster, war—and is temporary, an exception to the normal state of individual and business autonomy. . . . An individualistic society is inherently suspicious of government, anxious about centralized power, and reluctant to allow government to plan, especially over the long term.
>
> The role of government in a communitarian society is quite different. Here, government is prestigious and authoritative, sometimes authoritarian. Its function is to define the needs of the community over the long as well as the short term, and to see that those needs are met (although not necessarily through its offices). It sets a vision for the community; it defines and ensures the rights and duties of community membership, and it plays a central role in creating—sometimes imposing—consensus to support the direction in which it decides the community should move. Consensus-making often requires coercion of one sort or another, which may occur in either a centralized or decentralized fashion, flowing down from an elite or up from the grass roots. Communitarian societies may be hierarchical or egalitarian. . . .
>
> To oversimplify, among the so-called capitalist countries, the United States has tended traditionally to be the most individualistic, Japan the most communitarian. Other nations can be placed somewhere along the continuum between these two extremes. Germany is more communitarian than the United Kingdom, but still less so than Japan. France is a complex mix. . . .
>
> Traditional Western economics is rooted in individualism, holding that free trade among independent firms unconstrained by the hand of government results in the best outcome for all concerned. Firms benefit from their country's natural endowments or its comparative advantage.
>
> The dramatic success of Japan and other Asian countries in the past twenty years, however, has called this ideology into question. These nations and their companies have benefited greatly by acting contrary to the tenets of individualism. Their governments and companies practice neither free trade nor free enterprise, as traditionally conceived, and they are quite prepared to restrict the freedom of the market when it serves their purposes.[4]

Lodge, like many others, is suggesting that businesspeople in the United States must change the individualistic ideology they espouse because this ideology obstructs their ability to accept the many changes they must make if U.S. businesses are to regain their competitive edge in the world economy. The individualistic ideology that Lodge identifies incorporates various ideas drawn from the thinking of Adam Smith, John Locke, and other influential thinkers whose normative views we examine and evaluate in this chapter.[5] We discuss these ideas not only because of the significant influence they have on businesspeople's ideologies, but also because of the rising insistence with which many Americans are urging that these ideologies be adapted to the contemporary needs of business. It would be a valuable exercise for the reader to identify the ideology he or she holds and to examine and criticize its elements as he or she reads this chapter.

Market Systems versus Command Systems

Markets are meant to solve a fundamental economic problem that all societies face: coordinating the economic activities of society's many members.[6] Who will produce what goods for what people? Modern societies solve this problem in two main ways: by a command system or by a market system.[7]

In a command system, a single authority (a person or committee) makes the decisions about what is to be produced, who will produce it, and who will get it. The authority then communicates these decisions to the members of the system in the form of enforcible commands or directives, and transfers among the members then take place in accordance with the commands. This is the way in which the internal economic activities of vertically integrated business corporations are coordinated. In the integrated corporation, a management group decides what the various divisions will produce and what products each division will supply to the other divisions. These decisions are then communicated to the organization, perhaps in the form of a "budget." Command systems can also be extended to an entire economy. For 5 years during World War II, the United States and Great Britain both employed command systems to coordinate production among war-related industries.[8] From 1928 to 1953, the Soviet Union imposed a series of plans on its entire economy that told each firm exactly what labor and material resources it was to acquire, what goods it was to produce from these, and how it was to allocate its finished products among other firms and consumers.[9] The purpose of the USSR's "central planning system" was to industrialize the economy as rapidly as possible: In 1928, the Soviet Union was the fifth largest producer of industrial goods, whereas by the 1960s, it ranked second after the United States.

The modern alternative to command is the "free market."[10] Within a free market system, individual firms—each privately owned and each desirous of making a profit—make their own decisions about what they will produce and how they will produce it. Each firm then exchanges its goods with other firms and with consumers at the most advantageous prices it can get. Price levels serve to coordinate production by encouraging investment in highly profitable industries and discouraging it in unprofitable ones.

Free market systems, in theory, are based on two main components: a private property system and a voluntary exchange system.[11] If a society is to employ a market system, it must maintain a system of property laws (including contract law) that will assign to private individuals the right to make decisions about the goods they own, and that reassigns these rights when individuals exchange their goods with each other. Of course, a free market system cannot exist unless individuals are legally free to come together in "markets" to voluntarily exchange their goods with each other.

In a pure free market system, there would be no constraints whatsoever on the property one could own and what one could do with the property one owns, nor on the voluntary exchanges one could make. Slavery would be entirely legal, as would prostitution and all drugs including hard drugs. There are, however, no pure market systems. In all economies, there are some things that may not be owned (such as slaves), some things that may not be done with one's own property (such as pollution), some exchanges that are illegal (children's labor), and some exchanges that are imposed (through taxation). Such limitations on free markets are, of course, intrusions of a command system: Government concern for the public welfare leads it to issue directives concerning which goods may or may not be produced or exchanged. The result is government regulation in one form or another.

Since the 18th century, debates have raged over whether government should intervene in the market or whether market systems should remain free of all government intervention.[12] Should economies be partially or wholly coordinated by a government-authored command system? Or should private property rights and free exchanges be allowed to operate with few or no restrictions? The debate over industrial policy was essentially a debate over these issues.

Two main arguments are usually advanced in favor of the free market system. The first argument, which originated with John Locke, is based on a theory of moral rights that employs many of the concepts examined in the second section of Chapter 2. The second, which was first clearly proposed by Adam Smith, is based on the utilitarian benefits that free markets provide to society—an argument that rests on the utilitarian principles discussed in the first section of Chapter 2. A third important but opposing argument is that of Karl Marx, who held that capitalist systems promote injustice. All of these arguments are examined in what follows. As we see, entwined in all of these arguments are claims about the kind of moral character that free market systems encourage.

3.1 Free Markets and Rights: John Locke

One of the strongest cases for an unregulated market derives from the idea that human beings have certain "natural rights" that only a free market system can preserve. The two natural rights that free markets are supposed to protect are the right to freedom and the right to private property. Free markets are supposed to preserve the right to freedom insofar as they enable each individual to voluntarily exchange goods with others free from the coercive power of government. They are supposed to preserve the right to private property insofar as each individual is free to decide what will be done with what he or she owns without interference from government.

John Locke (1632–1704), an English political philosopher, is generally credited with developing the idea that human beings have a "natural right" to liberty and a "natural right" to private property.[13] Locke argued that if there were no governments, human beings would find themselves in a *state of nature*. In this state of nature, each man would be the political equal of all others and would be perfectly free of any constraints other than the *law of nature*—that is, the moral principles that God gave to humanity and that each man can discover by the use of his own God-given reason. As he puts it, in a state of nature, all men would be in:

> A *state of perfect freedom* to order their actions and dispose of their possessions and persons as they think fit, within the bounds of the law of nature, without asking leave, or depending upon the will of any other man. A state also of equality, wherein all the power and jurisdiction is reciprocal, no one having more than another . . . without subordination or subjection [to another]. . . . But . . . the state of nature has a law of nature to govern it, which obliges everyone: and reason, which is that law, teaches all mankind, who will but consult it, that being all equal and independent, no one ought to harm another in his life, health, liberty, or possessions.[14]

According to Locke, the law of nature "teaches" each man that he has a right to liberty and that, consequently, "no one can be put out of this [natural] estate and subjected to the political power of another without his own consent."[15] The law of nature also informs us that each man has rights of ownership over his own body, his own labor, and the products of his labor, and that these ownership rights are "natural"—that is, they are not invented or created by government nor are they the result of a government grant:

> Every man has a property in his own person: This nobody has a right to but himself. The labor of his body, and the work of his hands, we may say, are properly his. Whatsoever then he removes out of the state that nature has provided and left it in, he has mixed his labor with, and joined to it something that is his own, and thereby makes it his property. . . . [For] this labor being the unquestionable property of the laborer, no man but he can have a right to what that [labor] is once joined to, at least where there is enough, and as good, left in common for others.[16]

The state of nature, however, is a perilous state in which individuals are in constant danger of being harmed by others, "for all being kings as much as he, every man his equal, and the greater part no strict observers of equity and justice, the enjoyment of the property he has in this state is very unsafe, very insecure."[17] Consequently, individuals inevitably organize themselves into a political body and create a government whose primary purpose is to provide the protection of their natural rights that is lacking in the state of nature. Because the citizen consents to government "only with an intention . . . to preserve himself, his liberty and property . . . the power of the society or legislature constituted by them can never be supposed to extend farther" than what is needed to preserve these rights.[18] Government cannot interfere with any citizen's natural right to liberty and natural right to property except insofar as such interference is needed to protect one person's liberty or property from being invaded by others.

Although Locke never explicitly used his theory of natural rights to argue for free markets, several 20th-century authors have employed his theory for this purpose.[19] Friedrich A. Hayek, Murray Rothbard, Gottfried Dietze, Eric Mack, and many others have claimed that each person has the right to liberty and property that Locke credited to every human being and that, consequently, government must leave individuals free to exchange their labor and their property as they voluntarily choose.[20] Only a free private enterprise exchange economy, in which government stays out of the market and in which government protects the property rights of private individuals, allows for such voluntary exchanges. The existence of the Lockean rights to liberty and property, then, implies that societies should incorporate private property institutions and free markets.

It is also important to note that Locke's views on the right to private property have had a significant influence on American institutions of property even in today's computer society. First, and most important, throughout most of its early history, American law has held to the theory that individuals have an almost absolute right to do whatever they want with their property and that government has no right to interfere with or confiscate an individual's private property even for the good of society. The Fifth Amendment to the U.S. Constitution states that, "No person shall be . . . deprived of life, liberty, or property without due process of law; nor shall private property be taken for public use, without just compensation." This view (which quotes Locke's phrase, "life, liberty, and property") ultimately derives from Locke's view that private property rights are established "by nature" (when an individual "mixes" his labor into a thing) and so are prior to government. Government does not grant or create private property rights. Instead, it must respect and protect the property rights that are naturally generated through labor and trade. It is only relatively recently, in the late 19th and 20th centuries, that this Lockean view began to give way in the United States to the more "socialist" view that government may limit an individual's private property rights for the good of society. Even today in the United States there is a strong presumption that government does not create property rights, but must respect and enforce the property rights that individuals create through their own efforts. It is important to see that this American and Lockean view of property is not universal. In some countries, such as Japan, resources are not seen as things over which individuals have an absolute private property right. Instead, in Japan, as in other Asian societies, resources are seen as functioning primarily to serve the needs of society as a whole, and so the property rights of individuals should give way to the needs of society when there is a conflict between the two.

Second, underlying many American laws regarding property and ownership is Locke's view that, when a person expends his or her labor and effort to create or improve a thing, he or she acquires property rights over that thing. If a person writes a book or software program, for example, then that book or software program is the property of the person who "mixed" his or her labor into it. A person may, of course, agree to "sell" his labor to an employer, and thereby agree that he will give his employer ownership of whatever he creates. However, even such employee agreements assume that the employee has the right to "sell" his labor, and this means that the employee must have been the original owner of the labor used to create the object. Software developers, for example, are the rightful owners of the software programs they develop not only because they have invested a great deal of time and energy into developing these programs, but also because they have paid the software engineers who "sold" them their labor to produce these programs. We should notice that these views on property, of course, all assume that a private property right is really a bundle of rights. To say that X is my private property is to say that I have a right to use it, consume it, sell it, give it away, loan it, rent it, keep anything of value it produces, change it, destroy it, and, most important, exclude others from doing any of these things without my consent.

Criticisms of Lockean Rights

Criticisms of the Lockean defense of free markets have focused on four of its major weaknesses: (a) the assumption that individuals have the "natural rights" Locke claimed they have, (b) the conflict between these negative rights and positive rights, (c) the conflict between these Lockean rights and the principles of justice, and (d) the individualistic assumptions Locke makes and their conflict with the demands of caring.

First, the Lockean defense of free markets rests on the unproven assumption that people have rights to liberty and property that take precedence over all other rights. If humans do not have the overriding rights to liberty and property, then the fact that free markets would preserve the rights does not mean a great deal. Neither Locke nor his 20th-century followers, however, have provided the arguments needed to establish that human beings have such "natural" rights. Locke merely asserted that, "reason . . . teaches all mankind, who will but consult it" that these rights exist.[21] Instead of arguing for these rights, therefore,

Locke had to fall back on the bare assertion that the existence of these rights is "self-evident": All rational human beings are supposed to be able to intuit that the alleged rights to liberty and to property exist. Unfortunately, many rational human beings have tried and failed to have this intuition.[22]

The problem emerges most clearly if we look more closely at Locke's views on the natural right to property. Locke claims that when a person "mixes" his labor into some object that is unclaimed, the object becomes that person's property. For example, if I find a piece of driftwood on a seashore and whittle it into a pretty statue, the statue becomes my property because I have taken something of mine—my labor—and "mixed" it into the wood so as to make it more valuable. Investing effort and work into making something more valuable makes that thing mine. But why should this be? As the philosopher Robert Nozick has asked, if I "mix" my labor into something that is not yet mine, then why isn't this just a way of losing my labor?[23] Suppose that I own a cup of water and I throw my cup of water into the ocean so that I mix my water with the *unowned* water of the ocean. Does the ocean become "mine"? Clearly, in this case at least, mixing something of mine into something that is not mine is merely a way of losing what was mine, not a way of acquiring something that was not mine. Why is it that when I invest my work at improving or changing some object so as to make it more valuable, that object becomes my "property"? Locke provides no answer to this question, apparently thinking that it is "self-evident."

Second, even if human beings have a natural right to liberty and property, it does not follow that this right must override all other rights. The right to liberty and property is a "negative" right in the sense defined in Chapter 2. As we saw there, negative rights can conflict with people's positive rights. For example, the negative right to liberty may conflict with someone else's positive right to food, medical care, housing, or clean air. Why must we believe that in such cases the negative right has greater priority than the positive right? Critics argue, in fact, that we have no reason to believe that the rights to liberty and property are overriding. Consequently, we also have no reason to be persuaded by the argument that free markets must be preserved because they protect this alleged right.[24]

The third major criticism of the Lockean defense of free markets is based on the idea that free markets create unjust inequalities.[25] In a free market economy, a person's productive power is proportioned to the amount of labor or property he or she already possesses. Those individuals who have accumulated a great deal of wealth and who have access to education and training will be able to accumulate even more wealth by purchasing more productive assets. Individuals who own no property, who are unable to work, or who are unskilled (such as the handicapped, infirm, poor, aged) will be unable to buy any goods at all without help from the government. As a result, without government intervention, the gap between the richest and poorest will widen until large disparities of wealth emerge. Unless government intervenes to adjust the distribution of property that results from free markets, large groups of citizens will remain at a subsistence level while others grow ever wealthier.

To prove their point, critics cite the high poverty levels and large inequalities of "capitalist" nations such as the United States. In 1995, for example, during a period of relative economic prosperity when the wealth of the richest Americans increased, 36.4 million Americans or about 13.8 percent of the population continued living in poverty (as defined by the Council of Economic Advisors).[26] About 40.6 million people lacked health insurance coverage (15.4 percent of the population). Between 300,000 and 3 million were estimated to be homeless and living on the streets.[27] One out of every five American children under the age of 18 lived in poverty. In contrast, the top 1 percent of the population held one fourth of all U.S. personal wealth, controlled more than half of all of America's stocks, and owned 60 percent of its wealth in bonds.[28] Critics point to the highly unequal distribution of income and wealth among each fifth of the population that has emerged during the last two decades, as Table 3.1 summarizes. By standard measures of inequality, such as the so-called "Gini Index," American inequality has been rising steeply in the United States, as Fig. 3.1 shows.[29] Figure 3.2 shows the steadily growing gap between the *haves* and the *have nots,* and Fig. 3.3 shows how the richest 20 percent of U.S. households have come close to having as much income as all the rest combined.

Finally, critics have argued, Locke's argument assumes human beings are atomistic individuals with personal rights to liberty and property that

TABLE 3.1 DISTRIBUTION OF INCOME AND WEALTH AMONG AMERICAN FAMILIES

	Percent of Total U.S. Income	Percent of Total U.S. Wealth	Percent of Total U.S. Net Worth	Median Family Net Worth
Group	(1996)	(1983)	(1993)	(1993)
Poorest Fifth	3.7%	–0.2%	7.20%	$4249
Second Fifth	9.0%	1.8%	12.20%	$20,230
Third Fifth	15.1%	5.9%	15.90%	$30,788
Fourth Fifth	23.3%	13.6%	20.60%	$50,000
Richest Fifth	49.0%	78.8%	44.10%	$118,996

Sources: U.S. income figures from Bureau of the Census, *Current Population Reports,* P60–189. U.S. wealth from Levy, *The Economic Future of American Families,* 1991. Net worth and median net worth from Bureau of the Census, *Current Population Reports,* P70–47.

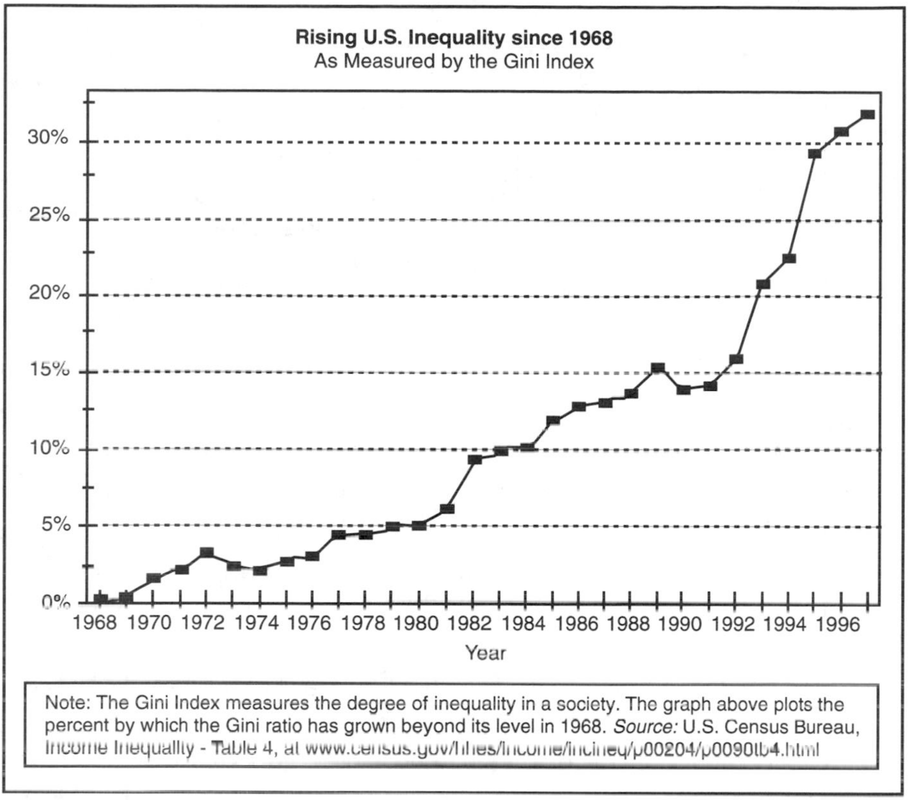

Figure 3.1

flow from their personal nature independently of their relations to the larger community. Because these rights are assumed to be prior to and independent of the community, the community can make no claims on the property or freedom of the individual. However, critics claim that these individualistic assumptions are completely false: They ignore the key role of caring relationships in human societies and the demands of caring that arise from these relationships. Critics of Locke point out that humans are born dependent on the care of others; as they grow, they remain dependent on the care of others to acquire what they need to become able adults. Even when they become adults, they depend on the caring cooperation of others in their communities for virtually everything they do or produce. The degree of liberty a person has depends on what the person can do: The less a person can do, the less he is free to do. But a person's abilities depend on what he learns from those who care for him as well as on what others care to help him to do or allow him to do.

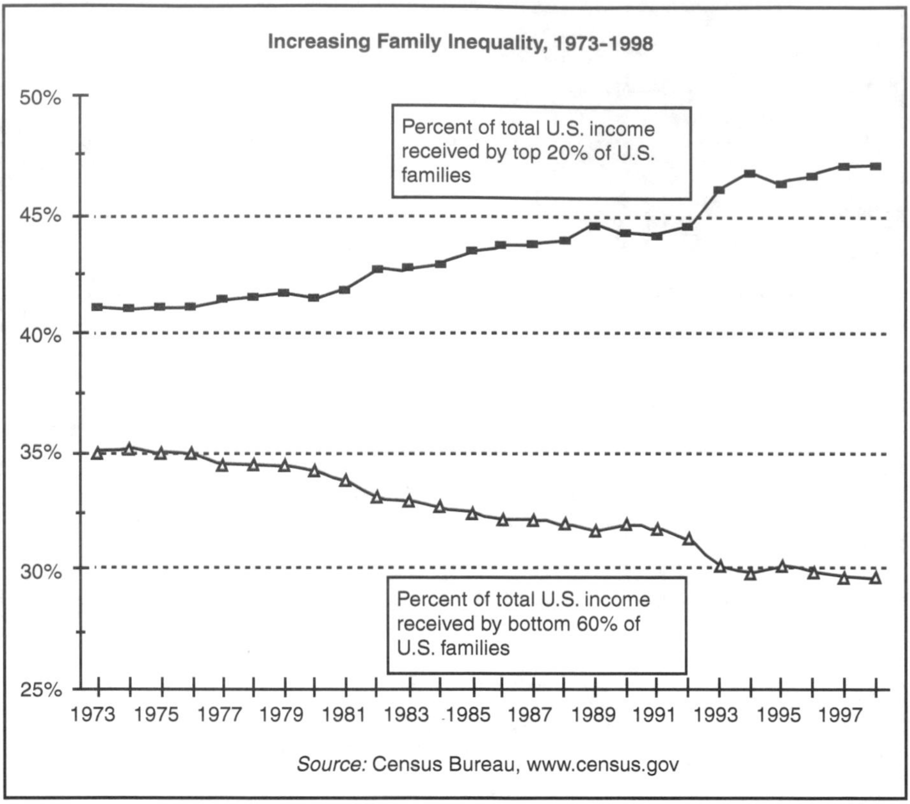

Figure 3.2

Similarly, the "property" that a person produces through his labor depends ultimately on the skills he acquired from those who cared for him, and on the cooperative work of others in the community such as employees. Even one's identity—one's sense of who one is as a member of the various communities and groups to which one belongs—depends on the one's relationships with others in the community. In short, the invidualistic assumptions built into Locke's view of human beings ignores the concrete caring relationships from which a person's identity and the possibility of individual rights arise. Humans are not atomistic individuals with rights that are independent of others: Instead, they are persons embedded in caring relationships that make those rights possible and that make the person who and what he or she is. Moreover, critics continue, persons are morally required to sustain these relationships and to care for others as others have cared for them. The community can legitimately make claims on the property of individuals and can restrict the freedom of individuals precisely because

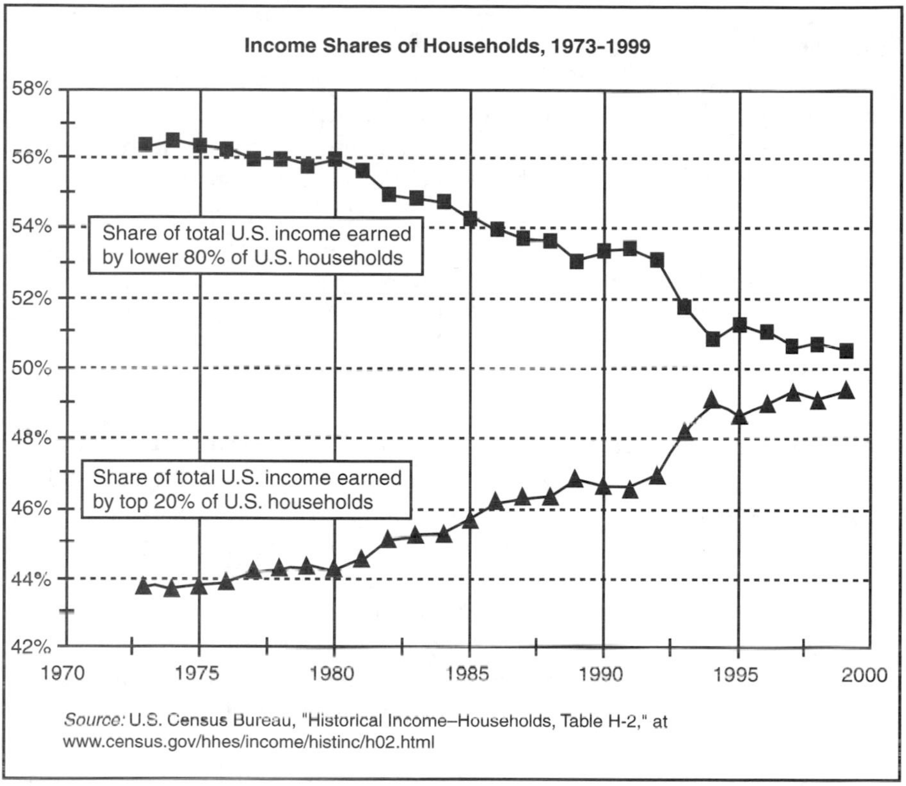

Figure 3.3

the community and the caring it has provided are the ultimate source of that property and freedom.

3.2 The Utility of Free Markets: Adam Smith

The second major defense of unregulated markets rests on the utilitarian argument that unregulated markets and private property will produce greater benefits than any amount of regulation could. In a system with free markets and private property, buyers will seek to purchase what they want for themselves at the lowest prices they can find. Therefore, it will pay private businesses to produce and sell what consumers want and it will do this at the lowest possible prices. To keep their prices down, private businesses will try to cut back on the costly resources they consume. Thus, the free market, coupled with private property, ensures that the economy is producing what consumers want, that prices are at the lowest levels possible, and that resources are efficiently used. The economic utility of society's members is thereby maximized.

Adam Smith (1723–1790), the "father of modern economics," is the originator of this utilitarian argument for the free market.[30] According to Smith, when private individuals are left free to seek their own interests in free markets, they will inevitably be led to further the public welfare by an "invisible hand":

> By directing [his] industry in such a manner as its produce may be of the greatest value, [the individual] intends only his own gain, and he is in this, as in many other cases, led by an invisible hand to promote an end that was no part of his intention. . . . By pursuing his own interest he frequently promotes that of society more effectively than when he really intends to promote it.[31]

The "invisible hand," of course, is market competition. Every producer seeks to make a living by using his or her private resources to produce and sell those goods that he or she perceives people want to buy. In a competitive market, a multiplicity of such private businesses must all compete with each other for the same buyers. To attract customers, therefore, each seller is forced not only to supply what consumers want, but to drop the price of goods as close as possible to "what it really costs the person who brings it to market."[32] To increase one's profits, each producer must pare his or her costs, thereby reducing the resources he or she consumes. The competition produced by a multiplicity of self-interested private sellers serves to lower prices, conserve resources, and make producers respond to consumer desires. Motivated only by self-interest, private businesses are led to serve society. As Smith put the matter in a famous passage:

> It is not from the benevolence of the butcher, the baker, and the brewer that we expect our dinner, but from their regard for their own self-interest. We address ourselves not to their humanity, but to their self-love, and never talk to them of our own necessities, but of their advantages.[33]

Smith also argued that a system of competitive markets allocates resources efficiently among the various industries of a society.[34] When the supply of a certain commodity is not enough to meet the demand, buyers bid the price of the commodity upward until it rises above what Smith called the *natural price* (i.e., the price that just covers the costs of producing the commodity, including the going rate of profit obtainable in other markets). Producers of that commodity then reap profits higher than those available to producers of other commodities. The higher profits induce producers of those other products to switch their resources into the production of the more profitable commodity. As a result, the shortage of that commodity disappears and its price sinks back to its natural level. Conversely, when the supply of a commodity is greater than the quantity demanded, its price falls, inducing its producers to switch their resources into the production of other, more profitable commodities. The fluctuating prices of commodities in a system of competitive markets then forces producers to allocate their resources to those industries where they are most in demand and to withdraw resources from industries where there is a relative oversupply of commodities. The market, in short, allocates resources so as to most efficiently meet consumer demand, thereby promoting social utility.

The best policy of a government that hopes to advance the public welfare, therefore, is to do nothing: to let each individual pursue his or her self-interest in "natural liberty."[35] Any interventions into the market by government can only serve to interrupt the self-regulating effect of competition and reduce its many beneficial consequences.

In the early 20th century, economists Ludwig von Mises and Friedrich A. Hayek supplemented Smith's market theories by an ingenious argument.[36] They argued that not only does a system of free markets and private ownership serve to allocate resources efficiently, but it is in principle impossible for the government or any human being to allocate resources with the same efficiency. Human beings cannot allocate resources efficiently because they can never have enough information nor calculate fast enough to coordinate in an efficient way the hundreds of thousands of daily exchanges required by a complex industrial economy. In a free market, high prices indicate that additional resources are needed to meet consumer demand, and they motivate producers to allocate their resources to those consumers. The market thereby allocates resources efficiently from day to day through the pricing mechanism. If a human agency were to try to do the same thing, von Mises and Hayek argued, the agency would have to know from day to day what things each consumer desired, what materials each producer would need to produce the countless things consumers desired, and would then have to calculate how best to allocate resources among interrelated producers so as to enable them to meet consumer desires. The infinite quantity of detailed bits of information and the astronomical number of calculations that such an agency would need, von Mises and Hayek claimed, were beyond the capacity of any human beings. Thus, not only do free markets allocate goods efficiently, but it is quite impossible for government planners to duplicate their performance.

Finally, it is important to note that, although Adam Smith did not discuss the notion of private property at great length, it is a key assumption of his views. Before individuals can come together in markets to sell things to each other, they must have some agreement about what each individual "owns" and what each individual has the right to "sell" to others. Unless a society has a system of private property that allocates its resources to individuals, that society cannot have a free market system. For this reason, Adam Smith assumed that a society with free markets would have a private property system, although he gave no explicit utilitarian arguments showing that a system of private property was better than, say, a system where all productive resources were "owned" in common by everyone. Earlier philosophers, however, had provided utilitarian arguments in support of a private property system. In the 13th century, for example, philosopher Thomas Aquinas argued that society should not use a system in which all things were owned by everyone "in common." Instead, society would prosper only if its resources were owned by individuals who would then take an interest in improving and caring for those resources. A private property system, he argued,

> . . . is necessary to human life for three reasons. First because every man is more careful to procure what is for himself alone than that which is common to many or to all: since each one would shirk the labor and leave to another that which concerns the community. . . . Secondly, because human affairs are conducted in more orderly fashion if each man is charged with tâking care of some particular thing himself, whereas there would be confusion if everyone had to look after any one thing indeterminately. Thirdly, because a more peaceful state is ensured to man if each one is contented with his own. Hence it is to be observed that quarrels arise more frequently where there is no division of the things possessed.[37]

In the view Aquinas proposed, private property is not something that is "naturally" produced when labor is "mixed" into things. Instead, private property is a social construct, an artificial, but useful social arrangement, that can be shaped in numerous ways. These utilitarian arguments in favor of a private property system over a system of common ownership have often been repeated. In particular, many philosophers have repeated the argument that, without a private property system in which the individual gets the benefits that come from caring for the resouces she owns, individuals would stop working because they would have no incentive to work.[38] A private property system is best because it provides incentives for individuals to invest their time, work, and effort in improving and exploiting the resources they own and whose benefits they know they will personally receive.

Criticisms of Adam Smith

Critics of Smith's classic utilitarian argument in defense of free markets and private property have attacked it on a variety of fronts. The most common criticism is that the argument rests on unrealistic assumptions.[39] Smith's arguments assume, first, that the impersonal forces of supply and demand will force prices down to their lowest levels because the sellers of products are so numerous and each enterprise is so small that no one seller can control the price of a product. This assumption was perhaps true enough in Smith's day, when the largest firms employed only a few dozen men and a multitude of small shops and petty merchants competed for the consumer's attention. However, today many industries and markets are completely or partially monopolized, and the small firm is no longer the rule. In these monopolized industries, where one or a few large enterprises are able to set their own prices, it is no longer true that prices necessarily move to their lowest levels. The monopoly power of the industrial giants enables them prices at artificially high levels and production at artificially low levels.

Second, critics claim, Smith's arguments assume that all the resources used to produce a product will be paid for by the manufacturer and that the manufacturer will try to reduce these costs to maximize his profits. As a result, there is a tendency toward a more efficient utilization of society's resources. This assumption is also proved false when the manufacturer of a product consumes resources for which he or she does not have to pay and on which he or she, therefore, does not try to economize. For example, when manufacturers use up clean air by polluting it, or when they impose health costs by dumping harmful chemicals into rivers, lakes, and seas, they are using resources of society for which they do not pay. Consequently, there is no reason for them to attempt to minimize these costs, and social waste is the result. Such waste is a particular instance of a more general problem that Smith's analysis ignored. Smith failed to take into account the external effects that business activities often have on their surrounding environment. Pollution is one example of such effects, but there are others, such as the effects on society of introducing advanced technology, the psychological effects increased mechanization has had on laborers, the harmful effects that handling dangerous products has on the health of workers, and the economic shocks that result when natural resources are depleted for short-term gains. Smith ignored these external effects of the firm and assumed that the firm is a self-contained agent whose activities affect only itself and its buyers.

Third, critics claim, Smith's analysis wrongly assumes that every human being is motivated only by a "natural" and self-interested desire for profit. Smith, at least in The Wealth of Nations, assumes that in all his dealings a person "intends only his own gain."[40] Human nature follows the rule of "economic rationality": Give away as little as you can in return for as much as you can get. Because a human being "intends only his own gain" anyway, the best economic arrangement is one that recognizes this "natural" motivation and allows it free play in competitive markets that force self-interest to serve the public interest. However, this theory of human nature, critics have claimed, is clearly false. First, human beings regularly show a concern for the good of others and constrain their self-interest for the sake of the rights of others. Even when buying and selling in markets, the constraints of honesty and fairness affect our conduct. Second, the critics claim, it is not necessarily "rational" to follow the rule "give away as little as you can for as much as you can get." In numerous situations, everyone is better off when everyone shows concern for others, and it is then rational to show such concern. Third, critics have argued, if human beings often behave like "rational economic men," this is not because such behavior is natural, but because the widespread adoption of competitive market relations forces humans to relate to each other as "rational economic men." The market system of a society makes humans selfish, and this widespread selfishness then makes us think the profit motive is "natural."[41] It is the institutions of capitalism that engender selfishness, materialism, and competitiveness. In actual fact, human beings are born with a natural tendency to show concern for other members of their species (e.g., in their families). A major moral defect of a society built around competitive markets, in fact, is that within such societies this natural benevolent tendency toward virtue is gradually replaced by self-interested tendencies toward vice. In short, such societies are morally defective because they encourage morally bad character.

As for the argument of von Mises and Hayek—that human planners cannot allocate resources efficiently—the examples of French, Dutch, and Swedish planning have demonstrated that planning within some sectors of the economy is not quite as impossible as von Mises and Hayek imagined.[42] Moreover, the argument of von Mises and Hayek was answered on theoretical grounds by the socialist economist Oskar Lange, who demonstrated that a "central planning board" could efficiently allocate goods in an economy without having to know everything about consumers and producers and without engaging in impossibly elaborate calculations.[43] All that is necessary is for the central planners to receive reports on the sizes of the inventories of producers and price their commodities accordingly. Surplus inventories would indicate that lowering of prices was necessary, whereas inventory shortages would indicate that prices should be raised. By setting the prices of all commodities in this way, the central planning board could create an efficient flow of resources throughout the economy. It must be acknowledged, however, that the kind of large-scale planning that has been attempted in some communist nations—particularly the former Soviet Union—has resulted in large-scale failure. Planning is possible so long as it remains but one component within an economy in which exchanges are for the most part based on market forces.

The Keynesian Criticism

The most influential criticism of Adam Smith's classical assumptions came from John Maynard Keynes (1883–1946), an English economist.[44] Smith assumed that without any help from the government, the automatic play of market forces would ensure full employment of all economic resources including labor. If some resources are not being used, then their costs drop and entrepreneurs are induced to expand their output by using these cheapened resources. The purchase of these resources in turn creates the incomes that enable people to buy the products made from them. Thus, all available resources are used and demand always expands to absorb the supply of commodities made from them (a relationship that is now called *Say's Law*). Since Keynes, however, economists have argued that, without government intervention, the demand for goods may not be high enough to absorb the supply. The result is unemployment and a slide into economic depression.

Keynes argued that the total demand for goods and services is the sum of the demand of three sectors of the economy: households, businesses, and government.[45] The aggregate demand of these three sectors may be less than the aggregate amounts of goods and services supplied by the economy at the full employment level. This mismatch between aggregate demand and aggregate supply will occur when households prefer to save some of their income in liquid securities instead of spending it on goods and services. When, as a consequence, aggregate demand is less than aggregate supply, the result is a contraction of supply. Businesses realize they are not selling all their goods, so they cut back on production and thereby cut back on employment. As production falls, the incomes of households also fall, but the amounts households are willing to save fall even faster. Eventually, the economy reaches a stable point of equilibrium at which demand once again equals supply, but at which there is widespread unemployment of labor and other resources.

Government, according to Keynes, can influence the propensity to save, which lowers aggregate demand and creates unemployment. Government can prevent excess savings through its influence on interest rates, and it can influence interest rates by regulating the money supply: The higher the supply of money, the lower the rates at which it is lent. Second, government can directly affect the amount of money households have available to them by raising or lowering taxes. Third, government spending can close any gap between aggregate demand and aggregate supply by taking up the slack in demand from households and businesses (and, incidentally, creating inflation).

Thus, contrary to Smith's claims, government intervention in the economy is a necessary instrument for maximizing society's utility. Free markets alone are not necessarily the most efficient means for coordinating the use of society's resources. Government spending and fiscal policies can serve to create the demand needed to stave off unemployment. These views were the kernels of Keynesian economics.

Keynes' views, however, have fallen on hard times. During the 1970s, the United States (and other Western economies) were confronted with the simultaneous occurrence of inflation and unemployment, termed *stagflation*. The standard Keynesian analysis would have led us to believe that these two should not have occurred together: Increased government spending, although inflationary, should have enlarged demand and thereby alleviated unemployment. However, during the 1970s, the standard Keynesian remedy for unemployment (increased government spending) had the expected effect of creating increasing inflation but did not cure unemployment.

Various diagnoses have been offered for the apparent failure of Keynesian economics to deal with the twin problems of inflation and stubborn unemployment particularly during the 1970s.[46] Notable among these are the new Keynesian approaches being pioneered by the so-called *post-Keynesian school*.[47] John Hicks, a long-time Keynesian enthusiast and a "post-Keynesian," for example, has suggested that in many industries today prices and wages are no longer determined by competitive market forces as Keynes assumed. Instead, they are set by conventional agreements among producers and unions.[48] The ultimate effect of these price-setting conventions is continuing inflation in the face of continued unemployment. Regardless of whether Hicks' analysis is correct, a flourishing post-Keynesian school has lately been developing new approaches to Keynes that can more adequately account for the problems of stagflation. Post-Keynesian theories, like those of Hicks, retain the key claim of Keynes that unemployment can be cured by increasing aggregate demand (the "principle of effective demand") through government expenditures. Unlike Keynes, however, Hicks and other post-Keynesians take more seriously the oligopolistic nature of most modern industries and unionized labor markets, as well as the role that social conventions and agreements play in these oligopolistic markets as large unions and large companies struggle over income shares. The role for government, then, is even larger than that envisioned by Keynes. Not only must government boost aggregate demand through increased spending, it must also curb the power of large oligopolistic groups.

The Utility of Survival of the Fittest: Social Darwinism

Nineteenth-century social Darwinists added a new twist to utilitarian justifications of free markets by arguing that free markets have beneficial consequences over and above those that Adam Smith identified. They argued that economic competition produces human progress. The doctrines of social Darwinism were named after Charles Darwin (1809–1882), who argued that the various species of living things were evolving as the result of the action of an environment that favored the survival of some things while destroying others: "This preservation of favorable individual differences and variations, and the destruction of those which are injurious, I have called natural selection or the survival of the fittest."[49] The environmental factors that resulted in the *survival of the fittest* were the competitive pressures of the animal world. As a result of this competitive "struggle for existence," Darwin held, species gradually change because only the "fittest" survive to pass their favorable characteristics on to their progeny.

Even before Darwin published his theories, philosopher Herbert Spencer (1820–1903) and other thinkers had already begun to suggest that the evolutionary processes that Darwin described were also operative in human societies. Spencer claimed that just as competition in the animal world ensures that only the fittest survive, so free competition in the economic world ensures that only the most capable individuals survive and rise to the top. The implication is that:

> Inconvenience, suffering, and death are the penalties attached by Nature to ignorance as well as to incompetence and are also the means of remedying these. Partly by weeding out those of lowest development, and partly by subjecting those who remain to the never-ceasing discipline of experience, Nature secures the growth of a race who shall both understand the conditions of existence, and be able to act up to them.[50]

Those individuals whose aggressive business dealings enable them to succeed in the competitive world of business are the "fittest" and therefore the best. Just as survival of the fittest ensures the continuing progress and improvement of an animal species, so the free competition that enriches some individuals and reduces others to poverty result in the gradual improvement of the human race. Government must not be allowed to interfere with this stern competition because this would only impede progress. In particular, government must not lend economic aid to those who fall behind in the competition for survival. If these economic misfits survive, they will pass on their inferior qualities and the human race will decline.

It was easy enough for later thinkers to revise Spencer's views so as to rid them of their apparent callousness. Modern versions of Spencerism hold that competition is good not because it destroys the weak individual, but because it weeds out the weak firm. Economic competition ensures that the "best" business firms survive and, as a result, the economic system gradually improves. The lesson of modern social Darwinism is the same: Government must stay out of the market because competition is beneficial.

The shortcomings of Spencer's views were obvious even to his contemporaries.[51] Critics were quick to point out that the skills and traits that help individuals and firms advance and "survive" in the business world are not necessarily those that help humanity survive on the planet. Advancement in the business world might be achieved through a ruthless disregard for other human beings. The survival of humanity, however, may well depend on the development of cooperative attitudes and the mutual willingness of people to help each other.

The basic problem underlying the views of the social Darwinist, however, is the fundamental normative assumption that *survival of the fittest* means *survival of the best.* That is, whatever results from the workings of nature is necessarily good. The fallacy, which modern authors call the *naturalistic fallacy,* implies, of course, that whatever happens naturally is always for the best. It is a basic failure of logic, however, to infer that what is should be or that what nature creates is necessarily for the best.

3.3 Marxist Criticisms

Karl Marx (1818–1883) is undoubtedly the harshest and most influential critic of the inequalities that private property institutions and free markets are accused of creating.[52] Writing at the height of the Industrial Revolution, Marx was an eyewitness of the wrenching and exploitative effects that industrialization had on the laboring peasant classes of England and Europe. In his writings, he detailed the suffering and misery that capitalism was imposing on its workers: exploitative working hours, pulmonary diseases and premature deaths caused by unsanitary factory conditions, seven-year-olds working 12 to 15 hours a day; 30 seamstresses working 30 hours without a break in a room made for 10 people.[53]

Marx claimed, however, that these instances of worker exploitation were merely symptoms of the underlying extremes of inequality that capitalism necessarily produces. According to Marx, capitalist systems offer only two sources of income: sale of one's own labor and ownership of the means of production (buildings, machinery, land, raw materials). Because workers cannot produce anything without access to the means of production, they are forced to sell their labor to the owner in return for a wage. The owner, however, does not pay workers the full value of their labor, only what they need to subsist. The difference ("surplus") between the value of their labor and the subsistence wages they receive is retained by the owner and is the source of the owner's profits. Thus, the owner is able to exploit workers by appropriating from them the surplus they produce, using as leverage his ownership of the means of production. As a result, those who own the means of production gradually become wealthier, and workers become relatively poorer. Capitalism promotes injustice and undermines communal relationships.

Alienation

The living conditions that capitalism imposed on the lower working classes contrasted sharply with Marx's view of how human beings should live. Marx held that human beings should be enabled to realize their human nature by freely developing their potential for self-expression and satisfying their real human needs.[54] To develop their capacity for expressing themselves in what they make and in what they do, people should be able to engage in activities that develop their productive potential and should have control over what they produce. To satisfy their needs, they must know what their real human needs are and be able to form satisfying social relationships. In Marx's view, capitalism "alienated" the lower working classes by neither allowing them to develop their productive potential nor satisfying their real human needs.

According to Marx, capitalist economies produce four forms of alienation in workers—that is, four forms of "separation" from what is essentially theirs.[55] First, capitalist societies give control of the worker's products to others. The objects that the worker produces by his or her labor are taken away by the capitalist employer and used for purposes that are antagonistic to the worker's own interests. As Marx wrote:

> The life that he has given to the object sets itself against him as an alien and hostile force. . . . Labor certainly produces marvels for the rich, but it produces privation for the worker. It produces palaces, but hovels for the worker. It produces beauty, but deformity for the worker. It replaces human labor with machines, but it casts some of the workers back into a barbarous kind of work and turns others into machines. It produces intelligence, but also stupidity and cretinism for the workers.[56]

Second, capitalism alienates the worker from one's own activity. Labor markets force people into earning their living by accepting work that they find dissatisfying, unfulfilling, and that is controlled by someone else's choices. Marx asks:

> What constitutes the alienation of laboring? That working is external to the worker, that it is not part of his nature and that, consequently, he does not fulfill himself in his work, but denies himself, has a feeling of misery rather than well-being, does not develop freely his mental and physical energies but is physically exhausted and mentally debased . . . its alien character is clearly shown by the fact that as soon as there is no physical or other compulsion it is avoided like a plague . . . it is not his own work but work for someone else.[57]

Third, capitalism alienates people from themselves by instilling in them false views of what their real human needs and desires are. Marx describes this alienation from one's own true self in a graphic portrait of the character traits of the capitalist economist:

> [His] principal thesis is the renunciation of life and of human needs. The less you eat, drink, buy books, go to the theater or to balls, or to the public house, and the less you think, love, theorize, sing, paint, play, etc., the more you will be able to save and the greater will become your treasure which neither moth nor dust will

> corrupt—your capital. The less you are, the less you express your life, the more you have, the greater is your alienated life, and the greater is the saving of your alienated being.[58]

Fourth, capitalist societies alienate human beings from each other by separating them into antagonistic and unequal social classes that break down community and caring relationships.[59] According to Marx, capitalism divides humanity into a "proletariat" laboring class and a "bourgeois" class of owners and employers: "Society as a whole is more and more splitting up into two great hostile camps, into two great classes directly facing each other: bourgeoisie and proletariat."[60]

Capitalist ownership and unregulated markets, then, necessarily produce inequalities of wealth and power: a "bourgeois" class of owners who own the means of production and accumulate ever greater amounts of capital, and a "proletariat" class of workers who must sell their labor to subsist and are alienated from what they produce, from their own work, from their own human needs, and from the fellow human beings with whom they should constitute a caring community. Although private property and free markets may secure the "freedom" of the wealthy owner class, they do so by creating an alienated laboring class in which caring relationships break down. Such alienation is unjust and in conflict with the demands of caring.

Marx did not hesitate to make clear that his views implied that private property systems were wrong. Private property systems, he held, were the basis of the great inequalities that characterized capitalist societies:

> You are horrified at our intending to do away with private property. But in your exisiting society private property is already done away with for nine-tenths of the population; its existence for the few is solely due to its non-existence in the hands of those nine-tenths. You reproach us, therefore, with intending to do away with a form of property, the necessary condition for whose existence is the non-existence of any property for the immense majority of society.[61]

To the utilitarian argument that without private property there would be no incentive for individuals to work, Marx replied:

> It has been objected that upon the abolution of private property all work will cease and universal laziness will overtake us. According to this, bourgeois society ought long ago to have gone to the dogs through sheer ideleness; for those of its members who work, acquire nothing, and those who acquire anything, do not work.[62]

Marx's argument here is that the working class, who performs all of the work in a capitalist society, does not own any property, whereas the capitalists who do not work are the ones who own all of society's productive property. Consequently, the claim that private property provides an incentive to work cannot be correct.

The Real Purpose of Government

The actual function that governments have historically served, according to Marx, is that of protecting the interests of the ruling economic class. It may be a popular belief that government exists to protect freedom and equality and that it rules by consent (as Locke suggested), but in fact such beliefs are ideological myths that hide the reality of the control the wealthiest class exercises over the political process. To back up his claim, Marx offered a breathtakingly comprehensive analysis of society, which we can only sketch here.

According to Marx, every society can be analyzed in terms of its two main components: its economic substructure and its social superstructure.[63] The economic substructure of a society consists of the materials and social controls that society uses to produce its economic goods. Marx refers to the materials (land, labor, natural resources, machinery, energy, technology) used in production as the *forces of production.* Societies during the Middle Ages, for example, were based on agricultural economies in which the forces of production were primitive farming methods, manual labor, and hand tools. Modern societies are based on an industrial economy that uses assembly-line manufacturing techniques, electricity, and factory machinery.

Marx called the social controls used in producing goods (i.e., the social controls by which society organizes and controls its workers) the *relations of production.* There are, Marx suggests, two main types of relations of production: (a) control based on ownership of the materials used to produce goods, and (b) control based on authority to command. In medieval society, for example, the feudal lords controlled their serfs through the (a) ownership the lords exercised over the manor farms on which the serfs worked, and (b) legal authority the lords exercised over their serfs who were legally bound to live on the manor lands and to obey the lord of the manor. In modern industrial society, capitalist owners control their factory laborers because (a) the capitalists own the machinery on which laborers must work if they are to survive, and (b) the laborer must enter a wage contract by which he or she gives the owner (or his or her manager) the legal authority to command. According to Marx, a society's relations of production define the main classes that exist in that society. In medieval society, for example, the relations of production created the ruling class of lords and the exploited serf class, whereas in industrial society, the relations of production created the capitalist class of owners (whom Marx called the *bourgeoisie*) and the exploited working class of wage earners (whom Marx called the *proletariat*).

Marx also claims that the kinds of production relations a society adopts depends on the kinds of forces of production that society has. That is, the methods a society uses to produce goods determine the way that society organizes and controls its workers. For example, the fact that medieval society had to depend on manual farming methods to survive forced it to adopt a social system in which a small class of lords organized and directed the large class of serfs who provided the manual labor society needed on its farms. Similarly, the fact that modern society depends on mass production methods has forced us to adopt a social system in which a small class of owners accumulates the capital needed to build large factories, and in which a large class of workers provides the labor these mechanized factory assembly lines require. In short, a society's production forces determine its relations of production, and these relations of production then determine its social classes.

So much for the economic substructure: What is the "social superstructure" of a society and how is it determined? A society's superstructure consists of its government and its popular ideologies. Marx claims that the ruling class created by the economic substructure inevitably controls this superstructure. That is, the members of the ruling class will control the government and ensure that it uses its force to protect their privileged position. At the same time, they will popularize those ideologies that justify their position of privilege. Medieval kings, for example, were selected from the class of lords and they enforced feudal law, even while the lords helped spread the ideology that their noble status was justified because of the aristocratic blood that ran in their veins. Similarly, in modern societies, Marx suggests, the class of owners is instrumental in the selection of government officials and the government then enforces the property system on which the wealth of this class depends. Moreover, the ownership class, through its economists and its popularizing writers, inculcates the ideologies of free enterprise and of respect for private property, both of which support their privileged positions. Modern government, then, is not created by consent, as Locke had claimed, but by a kind of economic determination.

According to Marx, a society's government and its ideologies are designed to protect the interests of its ruling economic classes. These classes, in turn, are created by the society's underlying relations of production, and these relations of production in their turn are determined by the underlying forces of production. In fact, Marx claimed, all major historical changes are ultimately produced by changes in society's forces of production: Economic or "material" forces determine the course of history because they determine the functions of government. As new material forces of production are found or invented (such as the steam engine or assembly line), the old forces are pushed out of the way (such as water power and hand crafts), and society reorganizes itself around the newly fashioned economic methods of production. New legal structures and social classes are created (such as the corporation and the managerial class), and the old legal structures and social classes are demolished (such as the manor and the aristocracy). Great ideological battles took place for men's minds during these periods of transformation, but the new ideas always triumph: History always follows the lead of the newest forces of production. This Marxist view of history as determined by changes in the economic methods by which humanity produces the materials on which it must live is now generally referred to as *historical materialism.*

Immiseration of Workers

Marx also claims that so long as production in modern economies is not planned but is left to depend on private ownership and unrestrained free markets, the result could only be a series of related disasters that would all tend to harm the working class. This claim rested on his analysis of two basic features of modern capitalism.[64]

First, in modern capitalist systems, productive assets (factories, land, technology, etc.) are privately controlled by self-interested owners who seek to increase their assets by competing in free markets against other self-interested owners. Second, in modern capitalist systems, commodities are mass produced in factories by a highly organized group of laborers who, if they are to live, must work on the modern factory assembly lines controlled by the self-seeking owners. Such economic systems, in which self-interested owners compete in free markets while their organized workers combine to produce massive amounts of goods, Marx argues, is a "contradiction" that will inevitably generate three tendencies that collectively leave the worker in a *miserable* state. First, such societies will exhibit an increasing concentration of industrial power in a relatively few hands.[65] As self-interested private owners struggle to increase the assets they control, little businesses will gradually be taken over by larger firms that will keep expanding in size. As time passes, Marx predicted, the small businessperson will become less important and the owners of a few large firms will come to control the bulk of society's markets and assets. The rich, that is, will get richer.

Second, capitalist societies will experience repeated cycles of economic downturns or crises.[66] Because the production of workers is highly organized, the firm of each owner can produce large amounts of surplus. Because owners are self-interested and competitive, they each will try to produce as much as they can in their firms without coordinating their production with that of other owners. As a result, firms will periodically produce an oversupply of goods. These will flood the market, and a depression or recession will result as the economy slows down to absorb the surplus.

Third, Marx argues, the position of the worker in capitalist societies will gradually worsen.[67] This gradual decline will result from the self-interested desire of capitalist owners to increase their assets at the expense of their workers. This self-interest will lead owners to replace workers with machines, thereby creating a rising level of unemployment, which society will be unable to curb. Self-interest will also keep owners from increasing their workers' wages in proportion to the increase in productivity that mechanization makes possible. The combined effects of increased concentration, cyclic crises, rising unemployment, and declining relative compensation are what Marx refers to as the *immiseration* of the worker. The solution to all these problems, according to Marx, is collective ownership of society's productive assets and the use of central planning to replace unregulated markets.[68]

Marx's theory has, of course, been subjected to intense and detailed criticism. The most telling criticism is that the immiseration of workers that he predicted did not in fact occur. Workers in capitalist countries are much better off now than their fathers were a century ago. Nonetheless, contemporary Marxist writers point out that many of Marx's predictions have turned out correct. Factory workers today continue to find their work alienating insofar as it is dehumanizing, meaningless, and lacking in personal satisfaction.[69] Unemployment, inflation, recessions, and other "crises" continue to plague our economy.[70] Advertisements incessantly attempt to instill in us desires for things that we do not really need.[71] Inequality and discrimination persist.[72] Our societies continue to be characterized by the breakdown of community.[73]

The Replies

Proponents of the free market have traditionally answered the criticisms that free markets generate injustices by arguing that the criticisms wrongly assume that justice means either equality or distribution according to need. This assumption is unprovable, they claim.[74] There are too many difficulties in the way of establishing acceptable principles of justice. Should distributive justice be determined in terms of effort, ability, need? These questions cannot be answered in any objective way, they claim, so any attempt to replace free markets with some distributive principle will, in the final analysis, be an imposition of someone's subjective preferences on the other members of society. This, of course, will violate the (negative) right every individual has to be free of the coercion of others.

Other defenders of free markets argue that justice can be given a clear meaning but one that supports free markets. Justice really means distribution according to contribution.[75] When markets are free and functioning competitively, some have argued, they will pay each worker the value of his or her contribution because each person's wage will be determined by what the person adds to the output of the economy. Consequently, they argue, justice requires free markets.

A third kind of reply that free market proponents have made to the criticism that markets generate unjust inequalities is that, although inequalities may be endemic to private ownership and free markets, the benefits that private ownership and free markets make possible are more important.[76] The free market enables resources to be allocated efficiently without coercion, and this is a greater benefit than equality.

Free market proponents also have replied to the criticism that free market structures break down communities. Free markets, they have argued, are based on the idea that the preferences of those in government should not determine the relationships of citizens. Government may not, for example, favor one kind of religious community or church relationships, over another, nor may it favor one community's values or forms of relationships over those of others. In societies characterized by such freedom, people are able to join together in associations in which they can pursue whatever values—religious or nonreligious—they choose.[77] In such free associations—supported by the right to freedom of association—true community and communal relationships can flourish. The freedom that underlies free markets, in short, provides the opportunity to freely form plural communities. Such communities are not possible in societies, such as the former Soviet Union, in which those in government decide which associations are allowed and which are prohibited.

Thus, the persuasiveness of the argument that unregulated markets should be supported because they are efficient and protect the right to liberty and property depends, in the end, on the importance attributed to several ethical factors. How important are the rights to liberty and to property as compared with a just distribution of income and wealth? How important are the negative rights of liberty and property as compared with the positive rights of needy workers and of those who own no property? How important is efficiency as compared with the claims of justice? How important are the goods of community and of caring as compared with the rights of individuals?

3.4 Conclusion: The Mixed Economy

The debate for and against free markets, government intervention, and private property still rages on. In fact, the debate has been spurred on by recent world events, particularly the collapse of several communist regines such as the former Soviet Union and the emergence of strong competitors in several Asian nations such as Japan. Some people have claimed that the collapse of communist regimes around the world has shown that capitalism, with its emphasis on free markets, is the clear winner.[78] Other observers, however, have held that the emergence of strong economies in nations that emphasize government intervention and collectivist property rights, such as Japan, shows that free markets alone are not the key to prosperity.[79] It is inevitable, perhaps, that the controversy has led many economists to advocate retention of market systems and private ownership but modification of their workings through government regulation so as to rid them of their most obvious defects. The resulting amalgam of government regulation, partially free markets, and limited property rights is appropriately referred to as the *mixed economy.*[80]

Basically, a mixed economy retains a market and private property system but relies heavily on government policies to remedy their deficiencies. Government transfers (of private income) are used to get rid of the worst aspects of inequality by drawing money from the wealthy in the form of income taxes and distributing it to the disadvantaged in the form of welfare. Minimum wage laws, safety laws, union laws, and other forms of labor legislation are used to protect workers from exploitation. Monopolies are regulated, nationalized, or outlawed. Government monetary and fiscal policies attempt to ensure full employment. Government regulatory agencies police firms to ensure they do not engage in socially harmful behavior.

How effective are these sorts of policies? A comparison of the American economy with other economies that have gone much farther down the road toward implementing the policies of a "mixed economy" may be helpful. Sweden, Germany, Denmark, Japan, the Netherlands, Belgium, Norway, Finland, and Switzerland are all mixed economies with high levels of government intervention. Several studies have compared the performance of the economies of these countries to that of the United States and other countries that have lower levels of government intervention.[81] The conclusions are interesting. To begin with, the United States has much greater inequality than any of these countries: The top 10 percent of all U.S. households, for example, receive 15 times as much income as the bottom 10 percent, whereas in Sweden the ratio is 7 times, in Germany it is 7 times, and in Japan it is 10 times. Although inequality in the United States is comparatively high, productivity had, until recently, been on a comparative decline, and since the 1970s productivity has been significantly lower in the United States than in many of these countries. During the 1970s, for example, Sweden's productivity growth rate was 11 percent more than ours, and Japan's was 25 percent more than ours. In terms of per capita GNP, the United States has been surpassed periodically by Japan, Sweden, Switzerland, Denmark, Norway, and Germany. Although unemployment often has been higher in the United States than in these countries, average inflation also has been higher. At the present time, of course, the performance of the United States is superior to that of most other nations.

Although these brief comparisons do not tell the whole story, they indicate at least that a mixed economy may have some advantages. Moreover, if we compare the performance of the U.S. economy at different periods in its history, the same conclusion is indicated. Prior to the intrusion of government regulation and social welfare programs, the highest per capita growth rate in GNP that the

United States experienced during a single decade was the 22 percent rate of growth that occurred between 1900 and 1910. During the 1940s, when the U.S. economy was run as a command wartime economy, the growth rate in per capita GNP climbed to 36 percent (the highest ever); during the 1960s, when the United States introduced its major social welfare programs, the per capita GNP growth rate was at a 30 percent level. Again, these comparisons do not tell the whole story, but they strongly suggest that the mixed economy is not altogether a bad thing.

The desirability of the policies of the mixed economy also continues to be subject to the same debates that swirl around the concepts of free markets, private property, and government intervention. Since the 1980s, these debates have tended to focus on the "productivity crisis" that the United States is still undergoing as it competes with other nations in global markets.[82] Between 1948 and 1968, worker output per hour increased at a rate of 3.2 percent each year; then between 1968 and 1973, the annual rate of increase slipped to 1.9 percent; and from 1970 to the early 1990s, it averaged about 0.5 percent.[83] Thus, U.S. productivity growth continued to lag until the mid-1990s, when it improved considerably. Some have blamed the productivity crisis on excessive government intervention in the marketplace. According to these critics, environmental legislation and worker health laws forced companies to invest heavily in nonproductive pollution-control equipment and in worker safety and have thereby drained off capital that should have been used to upgrade or replace inefficient plants and machines. Others have argued that much of the problem can be traced to the short-term strategies of business managers who were reluctant to invest in risky research and development and in retooling programs that might hurt their short-run profit picture, and who have been more interested in expanding their companies through mergers and acquisitions that create no new value.[84]

Property Systems and New Technologies

Debates have also swirled around the proper balance between property systems that emphasize Lockean notions of private individual ownership and socialist notions that emphasize collective ownership of resources. Nowhere has this debate been more acute than in regard to the new forms of intellectual property that modern technology—such as the computer and genetic engineering—have created. Intellectual property is property that consists of an abstract and nonphysical object, such as a software program, a song, an idea, an invention, a recipe, a digital image or sound, a genetic code, or any form of information. Unlike physical objects, intellectual property is nonexclusive. That is, unlike physical objects, one person's use of intellectual property does not exclude other people's simultaneous use of that property. A physical object such as a house, a pizza, a car, or a square yard of land can be used only by one or a few parties at any single time, and what one party uses or consumes of the object cannot be used or consumed by another person. In contrast, intellectual property such as a song, an idea, or a piece of information can be copied, used, or consumed by countless individuals at the same time. If you create a digital program or image and store it on your computer, others can come along and make millions of exact copies of that program or image that work and look exactly like your original. Those millions of exact copies can be used and enjoyed by millions of people without limiting your own ability to use or enjoy your original copy.

What sort of property systems should societies adopt to determine ownership rights for intellectual property? On one side are those who take the Lockean or the utilitarian view that intellectual property should be treated like private property. Those who take a Lockean view argue that if I create a software program or an image then it should be treated as my private property simply because it is a product of my own mental labor. So if anyone tries to use or copy my program or image without my permission, they should be seen as violating my property rights. Utilitarians may also argue for private ownership of intellectual property, but for different reasons. Utilitarians argue that private ownership of intellectual property provides a neccessary incentive for people to work hard at generating new intellectual creations. It takes a lot of hard work for a company like Microsoft to create a word processing program or for a musician to create an original piece of music. Companies and individuals would not put forth these efforts nor make these investments if they could not profit from their creations by being given rights of ownership that allow them the exclusive right to copy their creations and that prevent others from making copies without their permission. Without such private property rights, intellectual creation would dry up.

On the other side of this debate are those who take a Marxist or socialist position that supports the collective or common ownership of intellectual property. Like Marx, many modern critics of private ownership of intellectual property claim that intellectual creativity does not require the financial incentives of a private property system. Before the modern period of history, the stories, poems, songs, and information that people created were all considered to become common property that anyone had a right to use or copy. Despite the lack of any financial returns, these artists, writers, and thinkers continued to produce their works. Even today many people write software or music and make it freely available to others—perhaps on the Internet under the slogan "Information Wants To Be Free!"—despite receiving no financial incentives for their creativity. There is, in fact, a large group of computer software writers who promote "open source software," like the Linux Operating System, which is software that anyone can freely copy, use, or change. Others argue that the common good of society will be better served if intellectual property is treated as public or communal property that is freely available for others to use to develop new intellectual products or otherwise produce benefits for society. New scientific discoveries or new engineering developments should not be hoarded and hidden under the guise of *private property*, but should be freely available to benefit society. This is the position of many developing countries, where intellectual property is conceived as the common property of everyone in society. Ethicist Paul Steidlmeir, for example, writes that "developing countries argue that individual claims on intellectual property are subordinated to more fundamental claims of social well-being . . . [and] that while people may have a right to the fruit of their labor, they have a duty to reward society which made the very fruitfulness of labor possible."[85] Not surprisingly, software "piracy" is rampant in many developing countries where copies of software that is priced at three, four, and five hundred dollars in the United States is available from street vendors for five or ten dollars.

The property system for intellectual property in the United States is still evolving, although in many respects it tends more toward a Lockean/utilitarian system than a Marxist/socialist one. In the United States, an important distinction is made between an *idea* and the *expression* of the idea. Ideas cannot be owned nor become private property, but remain the common property of everyone. However, a particular *expression* of an idea, such as the text or words used to express the idea, can be granted a *copyright*, and that particular expression of the idea then becomes the private property of an individual or a company. Any tangible writing (writing that can be physically seen) can be copyrighted, including books, magazines, newspapers, speeches, music, plays, movies, radio and television shows, maps, paintings, drawings, photos, greeting cards, sound recordings on tapes or compact disks, software programs, and the masks used to imprint computer circuits. In a Lockean fashion, the law says that registering a copyright with the government does not create the copyright, but that mere authorship of a work creates a copyright (i.e., ownership) in the work. Nevertheless, copyrights expire after 95 years and then, like ideas, become common or public property.[86] A second way of creating property rights in intellectual property is through a *patent*. New inventions of machines, drugs, chemicals or other "compositions of matter," processes, software programs, nonsexually reproduced plants, living material invented by a person, and product designs can also become private property by being granted a "patent." Patents, however, expire after 14 or 20 years and then also become the common property of everyone.[87] Many people criticize this system, arguing that patents and copyrights prevent others from developing improved versions of protected software or from taking advantage of key new drug discoveries—a criticism that appeals to a Marxist view that property should serve the good of the community. Yet others counter that patents expire too quickly and that new inventions should remain the private property of the inventor for much longer—a view with Lockean connotation. The debate between Locke and Marx thus continues to simmer.

The End of Marxism?

Defenders of free markets have been greatly encouraged by what some have called the complete abandonment of communism in several formerly communist nations, particularly the U.S.S.R. On September 24, 1990, the Soviet legislature voted to switch to a free market economy and to scrap 70 years of communist economics that had led to inefficiencies and consumer shortages. Then during the summer of 1991, the communist party was outlawed after party leaders botched an attempt to take over the Soviet government. The Soviet Union fragmented and its reorganized states discarded their radical Marxist–Leninist ideologies in favor of worldviews that incorporated both socialist and capitalist elements. The new nations embarked on experimental attempts to integrate private property and free markets into their still heavily socialist economies. These developments were hailed by some observers, such as Francis Fukuyama, as indicating "The End of History."[88] What Fukuyama and others were suggesting is that, with the end of communism, there will be no more "progress" toward a better or more perfect economic system: The whole world now agrees that the best system is capitalism.

These historic communist reforms, however, have not signaled the "complete abandonment" of Marx or socialism. Without exception, all of these reforms have been aimed at moving communist systems toward economies that are based on the best features of both socialist and free market ideologies. They have, in short, been aimed at moving the communist countries toward the same ideology of the mixed economy that dominates Western nations. The debate today in the formerly communist world as in the United States is over the best mix of government regulation, private property rights, and free markets.

Followers of Smith and Locke continue to insist that the level of government intervention tolerated by the mixed economy does more harm than good. Their opponents continue to counter that, in our mixed economy, government favors business interests and that allowing businesses to set their own policies exacerbates our economic problems. On balance, however, it may be that the mixed economy comes closest to combining the utilitarian benefits of free markets with the respect for human rights, justice, and caring that are the characteristic strengths of planned economies.

Questions for Review and Discussion

1. Define the following: ideology, individualistic ideology, communitarian ideology, command economy, free market system, private property system, state of nature, natural rights, Locke's natural right to property, surplus value, alienation, bourgeois, proletariat, economic substructure, social superstructure, forces of production, relations of production, historical materialism, immiseration of workers, invisible hand,

natural price, natural liberty, aggregate demand, aggregate supply, Keynesian economics, survival of the fittest, social Darwinism, naturalistic fallacy, mixed economy, productivity crisis, intellectual property.

2. Contrast the views of Locke, Marx, Smith, Keynes, and Spencer on the nature and proper functions of government and on its relationship to business. Which views seem to you to provide the most adequate analysis of contemporary relations between business and government? Explain your answer fully.
3. "Locke's views on property, Smith's views on free markets, and Marx's views on capitalism obviously do not hold true when applied to the organizational structure and the operations of modern corporations." Comment on this statement. What reforms, if any, would Locke, Smith, and Marx advocate with respect to current corporate organization and performance?
4. "Equality, justice, and a respect for rights are characteristics of the American economic system." Would you agree or disagree with this statement? Why?
5. "Free markets allocate economic goods in the most socially beneficial way and ensure progress." To what extent is this statement true? To what extent do you think it is false?

Web Resources

Readers interested in researching the general topic of market ideologies on the Internet might want to begin by accessing the web page of the Essential Organization, which lists a number of organizations, both radical and not so radical, that take opposing views on capitalism and corporate organizations, such as the Multinational Monitor (http://www.essential.org); the Environmental fund provides opposing views (http://www.efund.com/investors_action.html); the web has stuff on Locke, Marx, and Smith (http://www.knuten.liu.se/~bjoch509/philosophers), on general philosophical resources (http://www.univie.ac.at/philosophie/phr/philrcs.htm), guides to philosophy on the Internet (http://www.carlham.edu/~peters/philinks.htm), and guides to political philosophy (http://a2z.lycos.com/Government/Politics/Political_Philosophy/index-random.html, and http://www.library.ubc.ca/poli/theory.html).

Notes

1. Among the many books written on the subject are Gar Alperovitz and Jeff Faux, *Rebuilding America* (New York: Pantheon Books, 1984); George C. Lodge, *Perestroika for America: Restructuring Business-Government Relations for World Competitiveness* (Boston, MA: Harvard Business School Press, 1990); Stephen S. Cohen and John Zysman, *Manufacturing Matters: The Myth of the Post Industrial Economy* (New York: Basic Books, 1987); Robert B. Reich, *The Next American Frontier* (New York: Times Books, 1983); Robert Reich, *The Work of Nations* (New York: Alfred A. Knopf, Inc., 1991).
2. Joint Economic Committee, *The Unemployment Crisis and Policies for Economic Recovery, Hearings Before the Joint Economic Committee of the Congress of the*

United States, 97th Congress, 2nd session, October 15, 20, and November 24, 1982 (Washington, DC: U.S. Government Printing Office, 1983), p. 34.

3. House Committee on Banking, Finance, and Urban Affairs, *Industrial Policy, Hearings Before the Subcommittee on Economic Stabilization of the Committee on Banking, Finance and Urban Affairs of the House of Representatives*, 98th Congress, 1st session, part I, June 9, 14, 21, 22, 28, and 30, 1983 (Washington, DC: U.S. Government Printing Office, 1983), p. 12.
4. George C. Lodge, *Perestroika for America: Restructuring Business-Government Relations for World Competitiveness* (Boston, MA: Harvard Business School Press, 1990), pp. 15, 16, 17.
5. For interesting research on individualistic societies and collectivist societies, see Geertz Hofstede, *Culture's Consequences: International Differences in Work-related Values* (Beverly Hills, CA: Sage, 1980); Geertz Hofstede, *Cultures and Organizations: Software of the Mind* (London: McGraw Hill, 1991). For recent research on individualism versus collectivism, see U. Kim, H. Triandis, C. Kagitcibasi, S. Choi, G. Yoon, eds., *Individualism and Collectivism* (Thousand Oaks, CA: Sage, 1994).
6. Robert L. Heilbroner, *The Economic Problem*, 3rd ed. (Englewood Cliffs, NJ: Prentice-Hall, 1972), pp. 14–28; see also Paul A. Samuelson, *Economics*, 9th ed. (New York: McGraw-Hill Book Company, 1973), pp. 17–18.
7. See Charles E. Lindblom, *Politics and Markets* (New York: Basic Books Inc., Publishers, 1977), chapters 2, 3, 5, and 6 for a discussion contrasting these two abstractions and for a subtle criticism of their adequacy.
8. George Dalton, *Economic Systems and Society: Capitalism, Communism, and the Third World* (New York: Penguin Books, 1974), pp. 122–24; Otis L. Graham, Jr., *Toward a Planned Society: From Roosevelt to Nixon* (New York: Oxford University Press, 1976), pp. 69–86.
9. *Ibid.,* pp. 121–31.
10. Lindblom, *Politics and Markets*, p. 33.
11. Milton Friedman, *Capitalism and Freedom* (Chicago: The University of Chicago Press, 1962), p. 14; see also John Chamberlain, *The Roots of Capitalism* (New York: D. Van Nostrand Company, 1959), pp. 7–42.
12. Joseph Schumpeter, *A History of Economic Analysis* (New York: Oxford University Press, 1954), pp. 370–72 and 397–99. For a treatment of 20th-century controversies, see Graham, *Toward a Planned Society.*
13. The literature on Locke is extensive; see Richard I. Aaron, *John Locke*, 3rd ed. (London: Oxford University Press, 1971), pp. 352–76 for bibliographic materials.
14. John Locke, *Two Treatises of Government*, rev. ed., Peter Laslett, ed. (New York: Cambridge University Press, 1963), pp. 309, 311.
15. *Ibid.*, p. 374.
16. Ibid., pp. 328–29.
17. *Ibid.*, p. 395.
18. *Ibid* ., p. 398.
19. C. B. Macpherson, however, argues that Locke was attempting to establish the morality and rationality of a capitalist system; see his *The Political Theory of Possessive Individualism: Hobbes to Locke* (Oxford: The Clarendon Press, 1962).
20. Friedrich A. Hayek, *The Road to Serfdom* (Chicago: University of Chicago Press, 1944); Murray N. Rothbard, *For a New Liberty* (New York: Collier Books, 1978);

Gottfried Dietz, *In Defense of Property* (Baltimore: The Johns Hopkins Press, 1971); Eric Mack, "Liberty and Justice," in John Arthur and William Shaw, eds., *Justice and Economic Distribution* (Englewood Cliffs, NJ: Prentice-Hall, 1978), pp. 183–93; John Hospers, *Libertarianism* (Los Angeles: Nash, 1971); T. R. Machan, *Human Rights and Human Liberties* (Chicago: Nelson-Hall, 1975).

21. Locke, *Two Treatises*, p. 311; for a fuller treatment of Locke's views on the law of nature, see John Locke, W. von Leyden, ed., *Essays on the Law of Nature* (Oxford: The Clarendon Press, 1954).

22. William K. Frankena, *Ethics*, 2nd ed. (Englewood Cliffs, NJ: Prentice-Hall, 1973), pp. 102–5.

23. Robert Nozick, *Anarchy, State, and Utopia* (New York: Basic Books, Inc., 1974).

24. For versions of this argument, see Lindblom, *Politics and Markets*, pp. 45–51.

25. Arthur M. Okun, *Equality and Efficiency* (Washington, DC: The Brookings Institution, 1975), pp. 1–4; see also Paul Baron and Paul Sweezy, *Monopoly Capitalism* (New York: Monthly Review, 1966), ch. 10; Frank Ackerman and Andrew Zimbalist, "Capitalism and Inequality in the United States," in Richard C. Edwards, Michael Reich, Thomas E. Weisskopf, eds., *The Capitalist System*, 2nd ed. (Englewood Cliffs, NJ: Prentice-Hall, 1978), pp. 297–307; Jonathan H. Turner and Charles E. Starnes, *Inequality: Privilege & Poverty in America* (Pacific Palisades, CA: Goodyear Publishing Company, Inc., 1976), pp. 44–45, 134–38.

26. See U.S. Census Bureau, "Press Briefing on 1995 Income, Poverty, and Health Insurance Estimates," by Daniel H. Weinberg, September 26, 1996. Accessible at http://www.census.gov/Press-Release/speech.html.

27. Nancy Gibbs, "The Homeless: Answers at Last," *Time*, 17 December 1990, p. 44.

28. Lars Osberg, *Economic Inequality in the United States* (New York: M. E. Sharpe, Inc., 1984), p. 41.

29. See Daniel H. Weinberg, "Income Inequality, A Brief Look at Postwar U.S. Income Inequality," Census Bureau, P60, No. 191 (1996). Accessible on the Internet at http://www.census.gov.

30. See Patricia Werhane, *Adam Smith and His Legacy for Modern Capitalism* (New York: Oxford University Press, 1991); S. Hollander, The Economics of Adam Smith (Toronto: University of Toronto Press, 1973).

31. Adam Smith, *An Inquiry into the Nature and Causes of the Wealth of Nations* [1776]. (New York: The Modern Library, n.d.), p. 423.

32. *Ibid.*, p. 55.

33. *Ibid.*, p. 14.

34. *Ibid.*, pp. 55–58.

35. *Ibid.*, p. 651.

36. Friedrich A. Hayek, "The Price System as a Mechanism for Using Knowledge," and Ludwig von Mises, "Economic Calculation in Socialism," both in Morris Bornstein, ed., *Comparative Economic Systems: Models and Cases* (Homewood, IL: Richard D. Irwin, Inc., 1965), pp. 39–50 and 79–85.

37. Thomas Aquinas, *Summa Theologica*, II–II, q. 66, a. 2.

38. For example, David Hume, Essay XLI, *An Inquiry Concerning the Principles of Morals*, part II, pp. 423–429, in *Essays, Literary, Moral, and Political*, by David Hume, Esq. (New York: Ward, Lock, & Co., Warwick House, no date).

39. These criticisms can be found in any standard economic textbook, but see especially Frank J. B. Stilwell, *Normative Economics* (Elmsford, NY: Pergamon Press, 1975).

40. But see Werhane, *op. cit.*, who argues that Smith did not hold that individuals are motivated only by self-interest. Instead, she argues, Smith's views in *The Wealth of Nations* must be supplemented with his views on "sympathy," "approbation," "propriety," "virtue," and "sentiment," which are spelled out in his earlier treatise, *Theory of the Moral Sentiments*.

41. See, for example, J. Philip Wogaman, *The Great Economic Debate: An Ethical Analysis* (Philadelphia: The Westminster Press, 1977), pp. 61 and 85.

42. See Vaclav Holesovsky, *Economic Systems, Analysis, and Comparison* (New York: McGraw-Hill Book Company, 1977), chs. 9 and 10.

43. Oskar Lange, "On the Economic Theory of Socialism," in Bornstein, ed., *Comparative Economic Systems*, pp. 86–94.

44. The standard work on Keynes is Alvin H. Hansen, *A Guide to Keynes* (New York: McGraw-Hill Book Company, 1953).

45. John Maynard Keynes, *The General Theory of Employment, Interest, and Money* (London: Macmillan & Co., Ltd., 1936). For an accessible summary of Keynes' views, see his article, "The General Theory of Employment," *Quarterly Journal of Economics*, 51 (September 1937): 209–23.

46. For an overview of the so-called "Post Keynesian School," see the collection of papers in J. Pheby, ed., *New Directions in Post Keynesian Economics* (Aldershot: Edward Elgar, 1989), and M. C. Sawyer, *Post Keynesian Economics, Schools of Thought in Economics Series 2*, (Aldershot: Edward Elgar, 1988).

47. See Sheila C. Dow, "The Post-Keynesian School," in Douglas Mair and Anne G. Miller, eds., *A Modern Guide to Economic Thought* (Aldershot: Edward Elgar, 1991).

48. John Hicks, *The Crisis in Keynesian Economics* (Oxford: Basil Blackwell, 1974), p. 25.

49. Charles Darwin, *The Origin of Species by Means of Natural Selection* (New York: D. Appleton and Company, 1883), p. 63.

50. Herbert Spencer, *Social Statics, Abridged and Revised* (New York: D. Appleton and Company, 1893), pp. 204–5; for an account of Spencerism in America, see Richard Hofstadter, *Social Darwinism in American Thought* (Boston: Beacon Press, 1955).

51. See the essays collected in R. J. Wilson, *Darwinism and the American Intellectual* (Homewood, IL: The Dorsey Press, 1967); see also Donald Fleming, "Social Darwinism," in Arthur Schlesinger, Jr. and Morton White, eds., *Paths of American Thoughts* (Boston: Houghton Mifflin Company, 1970), pp. 123–46.

52. The current interest in Marx has resulted in a number of excellent studies: David McLellan, *Karl Marx: His Life and Thought* (New York: Harper and Row Publishers, Inc., 1973); John McMurtry, *The Structure of Marx's World-View* (Princeton: Princeton University Press, 1978); Anthony Cutler, Barry Hindess, Paul Hirst, and Arthur Hussain, *Marx's Capital and Capitalism Today* (London: Routledge and Kegan Paul, 1977); Ernest Mandel, *An Introduction to Marxist Economic Theory* (New York: Pathfinder Press, 1970); Shlomo Avineri, *The Social and Political Thought of Karl Marx* (New York: Cambridge University Press, 1968); Robert Heilbroner, *Marxism: For and Against* (New York: W. W. Norton & Co., Inc., 1980).

53. For these and other illustrations cited by Marx, see his *Capital*, vol. I, Samuel Moore and Edward Aveling, trans. (Chicago: Charles H. Kerr & Company, 1906), pp. 268–82.

54. McMurtry, *Structure of Marx's World-View*, pp. 19–37.

55. Karl Marx, "Estranged Labor," in Dirk Struik, ed., *The Economic and Philosophic Manuscripts of 1844*, Martin Milligan, trans. (New York: International Publishers, 1964), pp. 106–19.

56. *Ibid.*, pp. 108–9.

57. *Ibid.*, pp. 110–11.

58. *Ibid.*, p. 150.

59. *Ibid.*, p. 116.

60. Karl Marx and Friedrich Engels, *Manifesto of the Communist Party* (New York: International Publishers, 1948), p. 9.

61. Karl Marx and Frederich Engels, *Manifesto of the Communist Party* [1848] (Moscow: Progress Publishers, 1971), p. 48.

62. Marx and Engels, *Ibid.*

63. The classic expression of this distinction is Karl Marx, *A Contribution to the Critique of Political Economy*, N. I. Stone, ed. (New York: The International Library Publishing Co., 1904), pp. 11–13.

64. See McMurtry, *Structure of Marx's World-View*, pp. 72–89.

65. Marx, *Capital*, vol. I, pp. 681–89.

66. Marx, *Capital*, vol. II, pp. 86–87.

67. Marx, *Capital,* vol. I, pp. 689 ff.

68. Marx and Engels, *Manifesto*, p. 30.

69. See *Work in America: Report of the Special Task Force to the Secretary of Health, Education and Welfare* (Cambridge, MA: MIT Press, 1973).

70. See Thomas E. Weisskopf, "Sources of Cyclical Downturns and Inflation" and Arthur MacEwan, "World Capitalism and the Crisis of the 1970s," in Richard C. Edwards, Michael Reich, and Thomas E. Weisskopf, eds., *The Capitalist System*, 2nd ed. (Englewood Cliffs, NJ: Prentice-Hall, 1978), pp. 441–61.

71. Herbert Marcuse, *One Dimensional Man* (Boston: Beacon Press, 1964), pp. 225–46.

72. Frank Ackerman and Andrew Zimbalist, "Capitalism and Inequality in the United States," in Edwards, Reich, Weisskopf, eds., *The Capitalist System*, pp. 297–307; and Michael Reich, "The Economics of Racism," in *ibid.*, pp. 381–88.

73. See D. Miller, "In What Sense Must Socialism Be Communitarian?" *Social Philosophy and Policy*, 6 (1989): pp. 51–73.

74. Irving Kristol, "A Capitalist Conception of Justice," in Richard T. DeGeorge and Joseph A. Pickler, eds., *Ethics, Free Enterprise and Public Policy* (New York: Oxford University Press, 1978), p. 65; see also H. B. Acton, *The Morals of Markets* (London: Longman Group Limited, 1971), pp. 68–72.

75. John Bates Clark, *The Distribution of Wealth* (New York: The Macmillan Co., 1899), pp. 7–9, 106–7; for a critique of this argument, see Okun, *Equality and Efficiency*, pp. 40–47.

76. Milton Friedman, *Capitalism and Freedom*, pp. 168–72.

77. See, for example, the arguments in John Rawls, *Political Liberalism* (New York: Columbia University Press, 1993), pp. 37–43; and *A Theory of Justice* (Boston: Harvard University Press, 1971).

78. See, for example, Richard Rorty, "For a More Banal Politics," *Harper's*, vol. 284 (May 1992): 16–21.

79. See Lodge, *ibid.*

80. See, for example, Paul Samuelson, *Economics*, 9th ed. (New York: McGraw-Hill Book Company, 1973), p. 845.

81. See, for example, Lane Kenworthy, *In Search of National Economic Success: Balancing Competition and Cooperation* (Thousand Oaks, CA: Sage Publications, 1995); Lester C. Thurow, *The Zero-Sum Society* (New York: Basic Books, Inc., 1980).

82. See "The Productivity Crisis," *Newsweek* (8 September 1980): 50–69, especially the debate between Friedman and Samuelson capsulized on pp. 68–69.

83. For the earlier data, see "The Reindustrialization of America," *Business Week* (30 June 1980): 65; for later data to 1990, see Lane Kenworthy, *In Search of National Economic Success* (Thousand Oaks, CA: Sage, 1995), p. 50.

84. For analyses of these viewpoints, see James Fallows, "American Industry, What Ails It, How to Save It," *The Atlantic*, September 1980, pp. 35–50.

85. Paul Steidlmeier, "The Moral Legitimacy of Intellectual Property Claims: American Business and Developing Country Perspectives," *The Journal of Business Ethics*, December 1993, pp. 161–62.

86. More exactly, the U.S. *Copyright Term Extension Act* (CTEA) of 1998 says that a copyright held by the individual author lasts for the life of the author plus 70 years, whereas if a business owns a copyright it lasts for 95 years from the year of first publication or 120 years from the year of its creation, whichever is shorter.

87. More exactly, patents on manufactured articles and processes expire after 20 years, whereas design patents expire after 14 years. Patents are granted only when the invention is novel, useful, and nonobvious.

88. See Francis Fukuyama, *The End of History and The Last Man* (New York: The Free Press, 1992).

Cases for Discussion

The Health Business[1]

In August 1992, Christy deMeurers, a 32-year-old Los Angeles school teacher and the happily married mother of two small children, discovered a lump in her breast. It was cancer. Two months earlier, she had signed up to become a member of Health Net, a health maintenance organization (HMO) that provides medical care for its members and that was one of the medical insurance plans offered by the school where she taught. Health Net paid for a radical mastectomy as well as radiation therapy and chemotherapy treatments. In May 1993, however, a bone scan revealed that her cancer had recurred and spread into her bone marrow. Her doctor, Dr. Gupta, now suggested she consider a bone-marrow transplant and arranged for her to see Dr. McMillan, a specialist who would evaluate whether she was a suitable candidate for a transplant—a treatment that probably would cost at least $100,000. When Christy and her family visited Dr. McMillan, however, he declined even to describe what was involved in a bone-marrow transplant, saying she would first have to undergo preliminary drug treatments to determine whether her tumor would respond to the drugs used in a bone-marrow transplant.

Suspicious that Health Net, which paid both Dr. Gupta and Dr. McMillan, might be unduly influencing their decisions to avoid paying for the transplant, Christy and her family flew to Denver the next day to consult Dr. Roy B. Jones, a leading bone-marrow transplant specialist. On June 8, 1993, Dr. Jones recommended a transplant, indicating that the research showed that "its efficacy in breast cancer is at least equivalent to many other procedures that we do every day." That same day, however, back in Los Angeles, Health Net determined it would not pay for a transplant for Christy because it had decided to classify such transplants as *investigational* or *experimental*, and Health Net was not contractually required to pay for investigational procedures. When the deMeurers returned to Los Angeles, they found Dr. Gupta now unwilling to recommend a transplant.

Health Net was founded as an independent company in 1979 by Blue Cross of Southern California. The new company made $17,000 its first year and $17 million the second year. Health Net operated as an independent company until 1994, when it was sold to another HMO named QualMed. As an HMO, Health Net collects monthly premiums from employers in return for providing their employees with medical care. In 1995, Health Net collected $2 billion from employers. The HMO enters contracts with doctors and hospitals whom it pays to provide the actual care. Each patient is assigned to a hospital as well as to a primary care doctor whom the patient regularly visits and who must approve any medical services the patient receives. Any specialists seen by the patient must be approved by the primary care doctor and must have a contract with the HMO. To keep costs low, the HMOs use a system called *capitation*.

In a capitation system, an HMO pays doctors, specialists, groups of doctors, and hospitals a fixed monthly fee for each patient assigned to them. If the doctor, specialist, doctors' group, or hospital spends less than the capitation fee for medical services for the patient, they can keep the difference; if they spend more than the capitation fee, they must cover the loss themselves. The capitation system thus provides an economic incentive to provide reduced levels of medical care. As one former Health Net doctor commented: "Understand, every time a patient comes into the doctor's office, it's a liability, not an asset—because he's on a fixed income."

The capitation system is, in fact, partly responsible for putting a brake on medical costs that had skyrocketed during the 1980s and that had in turn made medical insurance premiums rise astronomically. Rising medical costs had precipitated a crisis as companies increasingly found they could no longer afford insurance for their employees and as growing numbers of people found they could no longer afford medical care for serious illnesses. HMOs and the capitation system brought the crisis under control. For example, a survey of HMOs found that HMO premiums had actually declined between 1994 and 1995, and that the number of days HMO patients spent in the hospital declined from 315 per 1000 patients to 275.

By using the capitation system and by introducing other kinds of cost controls from the world of business into the world of medicine, HMOs had been turned into very profitable businesses. Consider Dr. Malik M. Hasan, for example, the founder of QualMed, a for-profit company that owns several HMOs and that acquired Health Net in 1994. When he founded QualMed, he found that, by imposing tight cost controls and corporate management systems designed to force doctors and hospitals to become economically efficient, he could take over failing HMOs and turn them into lucrative profit centers. When QualMed went public, for example, his stock in the company was suddenly worth $150 million. He commented, "We all got very rich."

In December 1995, Health Net was accredited by the National Committee for Quality Assurance (NCQA), an industry group that provides accreditation to HMOs that meet certain standards. The NCQA also publishes comparative surveys of HMOs. According to a survey report issued by NCQA, Health Net spent less than the others on medical care and more than the others on marketing, salaries, and other administrative expenses.

When Dr. Gupta refused to recommend a transplant for her, Christy petitioned to see another cancer specialist, Dr. Schinke, who was also a Health Net doctor. Dr. Schinke examined Christy and agreed that a transplant should be considered; he recommended she be evaluated for a transplant at the UCLA Medical Center. Dr. Schinke, however, later received a telephone call from a Health Net administrator and, he later said, "I didn't understand an administrator calling up and in an abrupt tone saying, 'Why in the world, what was your thinking, why are you recommending this patient consider such an option?' " Nevertheless, Dr. Schinke did not withdraw his recommendation. The UCLA Medical Center to which Dr. Schinke sent Christy was one of the hospitals with which Health Net had a contract.

Extremely distrustful now, Christy did not reveal that she was a Health Net patient when she visited Dr. John Glaspy, a cancer specialist at UCLA Medical Center on June 25, 1993. Unaware that Christy was a Health Net member, Dr. Glaspy agreed that a transplant was "on the rational list" of options for her. However, he, too, said that she would have to undergo an initial drug treatment to test the responsiveness of her cancer to the drugs. Two months later, when tests showed that she was responding favorably to the drugs, Christy and her family signed an agreement promising to pay the hospital $92,000 from their own pockets for the full costs of the transplant.

Christy and her family appealed to Health Net to reconsider its policy of classifying transplants as investigatory and so refusing to pay for them. In

1990, in fact, Health Net's chief medical officer had commissioned a study to evaluate the status of transplants, and the study had concluded that three out of four insurers paid for such transplants, and that by 1991 such transplants would become "prevailing practice among practitioners, providers, and payers." However, Dr. Ossorio, a Health Net administrator, again refused to allow payment for the transplant. Then, according to the findings of an arbitration panel that eventually reviewed the case, Dr. Ossorio called the head of the UCLA Medical Clinic's cancer unit and, in a statement made to "influence or intimidate" the hospital, demanded why UCLA was allowing a transplant to deMeurers in violation of Health Net guidelines. Shaken, the head of the cancer unit said he was unfamiliar with the case, but would look into it. Under the terms of its contract, Health Net could terminate its contract with the hospital with 90 days warning—a move that could create a substantial financial crisis for UCLA because a large fraction of its money comes from Health Net. A week later, UCLA Medical Center notified Health Net that it would swallow the costs of the expensive treatment because it had already been approved.

On September 23, 1993, Christy finally began her treatment in the UCLA hospital. By now she hardly had enough strength to walk from one room to another. A few weeks after her release from the hospital, she felt healthy enough to mow the lawn. She remained cancer-free for 4 more months, then discovered in spring 1994 that the cancer had recurred. That summer she and her family went on a camping trip across the United States. Her family has fond memories of that period and the subsequent Christmas. On Friday, March 10, 1995, she died.

Questions

1. Should medical care be subjected to the competitive forces of the free market? Explain how Locke, Smith, and Marx might answer this question. Should the provision of medical care be turned into a business? Explain your answer by reference to the views of Locke, Smith, or Marx.
2. In your judgment, is it morally appropriate for an HMO to use a capitation system that provides economic incentives to increase efficiency in the delivery of medical care? Explain your answer.
3. Evaluate the ethics of the activities of the various individuals involved in this case.

Note

1. The information for this case is drawn from Erik Larson, "The Soul of an HMO," *Time*, vol. 147, no. 4 (22 January, 1996): 44–52.

Accolade versus Sega[1]

Accolade, Inc. is a small software company located in San Jose, California, that had prospered by making and marketing games that could be played on Sega game consoles. Its most popular game was a game cartridge called "Ishido: The Way of Stones," which could be inserted into a Sega console and played. Sega had not granted Accolade a license to do this, and Sega derived no income from sales of Accolade's games.

In the early 1990s, Sega marketed a new game console called "Genesis," and Accolade engineers discovered that their games would no longer work on the new console because Sega had inserted new secret codes and security devices into its Genesis consoles that prevented any other cartridges from working on the console except those made by Sega.

To get around this problem, Accolade engineers set to work reverse engineering Sega's new console and several of its game cartridges. Reverse engineering is the process of analyzing a product to discover how it was made and how it works. First Accolade took several Genesis consoles apart to learn how its security mechanisms worked. Then Accolade decompiled several of Sega's game cartridges.

To understand what this involved, it is necessary to understand that the software that makes up a game is produced in a two-step process. First, engineers write the program for the game using a software language that is easily understood by an engineer who knows the language and that consists of a series of comprehensible instructions such as "GOTO line 5." This version of the program is called the *source code*. Second, once they have finished writing the source code, the engineers enter the source code into a computer that compiles the code, essentially translating it into a machine language consisting of zeros and ones (such as "00011011001111001010"). Although the new compiled code is virtually impossible for a human to understand, the series of zeros and ones that make up a compiled code can be read by the game console computer and provide the basic instructions that make the game operate.

Game cartridges (and, in fact, all software programs) that are sold in retail stores consist of such compiled code. Decompiling is an attempt to reverse the two-step process through which the program was originally produced. Basically, the compiled or "machine" code that makes up the software program is fed into a computer that attempts to translate the machine language (i.e., the series of zeros and ones) back into the original source code language (i.e., instructions such as "GOTO line 5") that can be understood by the engineer. The engineer can then examine the new source code and discover exactly how the program works and how it was put together. The process of decompiling is not always completely accurate, and sometimes engineers have to work hard to figure out exactly what the original source code was. Many engineers believe that reverse engineering, particularly decompiling, is inherently unethical.

Nevertheless, Accolade engineers succeeded in getting the information they wanted, and with this knowledge they were soon able to write games that would work on Sega's new Genesis consoles. Sega, however, immediately sued Accolade, claiming that Accolade had infringed on its copyright. Initially the U.S. District Court in San Francisco agreed with Sega and issued an injunction forcing Accolade to withdraw its Sega-compatible games from the market.

Sega lawyers argued that when Accolade reversed engineered its software programs, Accolade had illegally made copies of Sega's source code. Because this source code was owned by Sega, Accolade had no right to copy it nor did it have a right to reverse engineer it, and Accolade in effect had stolen Sega's property by doing so. In addition, the new games that Accolade wrote had to include secret codes that were required to allow the software to work on the Genesis console. These secret codes, Sega claimed, were also owned and copyrighted by Sega and so could not be copied by Accolade and inserted into its game programs.

Accolade, however, appealed the decision of the U.S. District Court to a higher court, the Ninth Circuit Court of Appeals. Accolade claimed that the secret codes and security devices that Sega had used and that had to be known to allow games to play on the Genesis console, were in effect a public interface standard. An *interface standard* is a standardized mechanism that one kind of product must use if it is to be able to work on another product. (The standard prongs that an electric cord must have if it is to fit into a standard outlet are an example of a simple interface standard.) Such interface standards cannot be privately owned by anyone, but are public property that can be used and duplicated by everyone. It was permissible, Accolade lawyers argued, to duplicate the source code because this was merely a way of getting access to the interface standard on the Genesis consoles. It was permissible for Accolade to include copies of these secret codes in its games because these were public property. Accolade's arguments eventually won out when it appealed the decision of the U.S. District Court in the Ninth Circuit Court of Appeals. The Ninth Circuit Court of Appeals overturned the earlier decision and essentially agreed with Accolade.

However, many legal experts disagreed with the Ninth Circuit Court of Appeals. They felt that Accolade's arguments were wrong and that Accolade had really stolen Sega's property. The security devices and secret codes that Sega had developed were not like the interface standards that different companies must agree on when working on products that must be compatible with each other. It is true that when companies are working on products that must be compatible with each other—like tires that must fit on cars, electric plugs that must fit into electric sockets, or tape cassettes that must fit on tape players—they need to agree on a public standard interface that no one will own but that everyone will be able to freely use. But Sega's Genesis console was a product that belonged to Sega alone and for which Sega wanted to be the sole provider of games. Thus, this was not a case of different companies having to reach an agreement over a public standard: It was a case of a single company making use of its own private technology to make its own games. Thus, there was no public interface standard involved.

QUESTIONS

1. Analyze this case from the perspective of each of the theories of private property described in this chapter (i.e., from the perspective of Locke's theory of private theory, the utilitarian theory of private property, and the Marxist theory of private property). Which of these views do you most agree with and which do you think is most appropriate for this case?
2. Do you agree that Accolade had "really stolen" Sega's property? Explain why or why not.
3. In your judgment, did Accolade go too far in trying to discover the underlying source code of Sega's programs? Does a company have a right to reverse engineer any product it wants?

NOTES

1. This case is based on Richard A. Spinello, "Software Compatibility and Reverse Engineering," in Richard A. Spinello, *Case Studies in Information and Computer Ethics* (Upper Saddle River, NJ: Prentice Hall, 1997), pp. 142–145.

Brian's Franchise

Brian, a well-off American in his twenties, is now living in Amsterdam. Until a few years ago, he was the owner of a large franchise chain of small indoor farms specializing in growing marijuana. Having become expert in breeding and raising marijuana indoors while in college, he dropped out of school in 1989 and set up a chain of small indoor marijuana gardens that he tended in rented houses in and around Washington, DC. His personally bred variety of marijuana—"Potomac Indica"—soon became well known, and he hit on the idea of selling his expertise and his plants to others. He found several local partners in towns along the East Coast whom he provided with the necessary equipment and plants, instructions on how to cultivate marijuana indoors, and regular onsite consultations. In return, partners gave him a percentage of the profits from each crop. In effect, Brian had set up a franchise chain modeled on other decentralized organizations such as McDonald's.[1]

Marijuana is the nation's largest cash crop. Estimated at $32 billion a year in 1995, it dwarfs other U.S. crops such as corn ($14 billion) or soybeans ($11 billion). Unlike other agricultural industries, however, a large portion—perhaps the majority—of marijuana produced in America is now grown indoors and is not sold through traditional agricultural distribution channels.

Marijuana production in the United States originated in the early 1970s when hippies left cities such as San Francisco and Berkeley and migrated to rural communities in northern California.[2] Until the mid-1970s, most marijuana smoked in the United States was imported from Mexico. In 1975, however, the federal government cracked down on the smuggling of marijuana across the Mexican border. The hippie communities in rural northern California responded by starting to cultivate their own marijuana, first in small amounts for their personal use and then increasingly in larger amounts to sell to others. The fledgling new domestic industry created by government restrictions of foreign supplies eventually spread into several northern California counties, including Mendocino, Humboldt, and Siskiyou Counties, an area now known as the "Emerald Triangle"—an analogy with Southeast Asia's Golden Triangle, where much of the world's opium is grown.[3]

The climate in rural, forested northern California was particularly favorable for growing cannabis indica, a frost-tolerant species of marijuana. As the marijuana business grew from a few small plots in 1975 to become a $300 million industry in Humboldt County alone by 1979 (hay, the second largest crop, was valued at $7 million, and only the timber industry was estimated to be larger), the jobless rate in the county fell from a high of 22 percent in 1975 to 9 percent in 1979.

California's clandestine marijuana industry created a considerable political stir. Because of its economic importance, local governments tended to discourage police efforts to restrict marijuana growers by vetoing funding for such efforts. As one county supervisor said in 1979: "Some responsible businessmen think it [the marijuana industry] is very important to the economy. You know: people who sell cars, hardware, fencing and garden tools."[4]

Government efforts to eradicate the industry, however, stepped up considerably during the Reagan era, when the federal government launched the "Campaign Against Marijuana Planting" (CAMP). With annual CAMP outlays of up to $2 million in California, the federal government also used helicopters to hunt down the farmers as well as roadblocks to sever their distribution systems. In addition, "asset forfeiture" laws were passed that allowed authorities to confiscate and keep any property related to the production, sale, or possession of marijuana, regardless of whether the actual owner of the property was found guilty of a crime. The confiscating agency was allowed to keep the proceeds from the sale of the confiscated property and spend the money on whatever it wanted.

Pressured by CAMP efforts to eradicate American marijuana farms, intensive research by marijuana farmers led to even smaller, more potent varieties of the plant that could be grown indoors and that could be harvested quickly, as well as the development of technologically advanced methods of manipulating the indoor environment to maximize production in minimal spaces, and new cloning methods that removed the unpredictability of growing from seed. By 1989, the new indoor strains of marijuana contained an average of 10 percent THC compared with the 0.5 percent that was common during the 1970s. Within the space of a phone booth, using carefully controlled amounts of light, water, air circulation, carbon dioxide, and nutrients, 100 of the new dwarf plants could be grown and forced to produce the same yields as had earlier been produced on half an acre.

It was at this point that Brian left college and set up his franchise operation, having played a role in the research that led to the development of the new breeds and the new indoor farming technology. On October 26, 1989, however, the government launched a new offensive named *Green Merchant*, which was aimed at eradicating the new indoor marijuana gardens. New federal laws were passed imposing heavier sentences on growers (5 years for having 100 plants, 10 years for 1000). The government was now spending as much as $1.7 billion on antimarijuana programs. As government antimarijuana efforts intensified during the early 1990s, Brian sold off his business and moved to Amsterdam, where police do not enforce marijuana laws.

In Amsterdam, Brain turned to developing self-contained indoor garden units that were operated completely by a computer and that could be monitored from a distance through the Internet. In this way, a marijuana farmer could set up garden units in isolated areas, visiting them only to plant and harvest the crop. The computer in the unit would send a message through the Internet if anyone broke in and would then automatically destroy the garden and all computer data. The farmer would then know that the garden should be abandoned and never revisited. Brian felt that computerization would revolutionize the still growing industry.

QUESTIONS

1. How would Marx analyze the events recounted in the case? How would Smith analyze these events? How would Locke analyze these events? To what extent, if at all, are these analyses correct?
2. "When government interferes with free market activities it distorts the market, forces consumer prices to rise, and rarely achieves its objectives." Comment on this statement in light of the history of the marijuana industry in the United States.
3. In your view, should government prohibit consumer actitivies like using marijuana products they freely choose to use, or economic activities like growing and selling

marijuana? Why or why not? What sorts of business activities should government prohibit? What sort should it not prohibit? Justify your position fully. Identify the ideology implied by your position.

4. From an ethical point of view, what recommendations would you make to Brian? Explain your recommendations in terms of the moral principles that you feel are involved.

NOTES

1. Michael Pollan, "America's No. 1 Cash Crop," *New York Times Magazine* (February 19, 1995).
2. Ed Pope, "Grower Brings New Life to Land," *San Jose Mercury* (21 October 1979): 3A.
3. Bill Weinberg, "Into the Emerald Triangle," *High Times,* vol. 248 (April 1996).
4. Ed Pope, "Marijuana Is Cash Crop for North Coast Farmers," *San Jose Mercury News* (21 October 197): 3A.

4

Ethics in the Marketplace

INTRODUCTION

Consider the following recent news stories:

> Antitrust lawsuits filed by 28 states against 18 major record companies Tuesday charge that fixed prices have robbed consumers of an estimated $480 million, according to Federal Trade Commission tallies. . . . Five major music companies—Capitol Records, Sony Music, BMG Music, Universal Music and Warner Music—adopted price-fixing to counter price-cutting efforts from discount chains. Minimum advertised prices were established in all music retail outlets, costing consumers an estimated $2 to $5 per CD.[1]
>
> Since 1985, state attorneys general have filed or investigated at least 70 antitrust cases in the healthcare industry, according to the preliminary results of a recent study. . . . Of those cases, 34 involved allegations of illegal group boycotts or concerted efforts by competitors against a third party. Seventeen cases involved allegations of price fixing; eleven cases involved allegations of anticompetitive mergers; and eight cases involved various other suspected antitrust violations.[2]
>
> ADM's unofficial motto—the competitors are our friends and the customers are our enemies—laid the cultural groundwork for price-fixing crimes that cost consumers worldwide more than $1 billion. Relying heavily on [an informant's] work for the FBI—his video and audio tapings of hundreds of hours of meetings between executives from ADM and its competitors in which they fixed prices and volume—the Justice department forced ADM to plead guilty to price-fixing crimes. The company was fined $100 million.[3]

> Six foreign vitamin companies agreed to pay $335 million to settle a lawsuit accusing them of conspiring to fix prices. The lawsuit alleged that the companies, which produce vitamin pills and supplements for fortified foods and agricultural feed, secretly met to fix prices from 1989 to 1998. F. Hoffmann-La Roche of Switzerland, BASF of Germany, Aventis of France, and Japanese companies Takeda Chemical Industries Ltd., Eisai Co. And Daiichi Pharmaceutical Co. took part in the settlement. Last year Hoffman-La Roche and BASF were ordered to pay $725 million in criminal fines for colluding to divide up markets and set wholesale prices. Four former executives of BASF and Hoffman-La Roche agreed this year to plead guilty, pay fines, and serve time in U.S. prisons for sheming to fix vitamin prices.[4]

In view of the key role of competition in the American economy, both factually and from a normative point of view, it is surprising that anticompetitive practices are so common. A report on New York Stock Exchange companies showed that 10 percent of the companies had been involved in antitrust suits during the previous 5 years.[5] A survey of major corporate executives indicated that 60 percent of those sampled believed that many businesses engage in price fixing.[6] One study found that in a period of 2 years alone over 60 major firms were prosecuted by federal agencies for anticompetitive practices.

If free markets are justified, it is because they allocate resources and distribute commodities in ways that are just, that maximize the economic utility of society's members, and that respect the freedom of choice of both buyers and sellers. These moral aspects of a market system depend crucially on the competitive nature of the system. If firms join together and use their combined power to fix prices, drive out competitors with unfair practices, or earn monopolistic profits at the expense of consumers, the market ceases to be competitive and the results are injustice, a decline in social utility, and a restriction of people's freedom of choice. This chapter examines the ethics of anticompetitive practices, the underlying rationales for prohibiting them, and the moral values that market competition is meant to achieve.

Before studying the ethics of anticompetitive practices, it is essential that we have before us a clear understanding of the meaning of *market competition*. Of course, we all have an intuitive understanding of competition: It is a rivalry between two or more parties trying to obtain something that only one of them can possess. Competition exists in political elections, in football games, on the battlefield, and in courses in which grades are distributed on the curve. Market competition, however, involves more than mere rivalry between two or more firms. To get a clearer idea of the nature of market competition, we examine three abstract models describing three degrees of competition in a market: perfect competition, pure monopoly, and oligopoly. We also examine the ethical issues raised by each type of competition.

4.1 Perfect Competition

A market is any forum in which people come together for the purpose of exchanging ownership of goods or money. Markets can be small and very temporary (two friends trading clothes can constitute a tiny transient market) or quite large and relatively permanent (the oil market spans several continents and has been operating for decades).

A perfectly competitive free market is one in which no buyer or seller has the power to significantly affect the prices at which goods are being exchanged.[7] Perfectly competitive free markets are characterized by the following seven features:

1. There are numerous buyers and sellers, none of whom has a substantial share of the market.
2. All buyers and sellers can freely and immediately enter or leave the market.
3. Every buyer and seller has full and perfect knowledge of what every other buyer and seller is doing, including knowledge of the prices, quantities, and quality of all goods being bought and sold.
4. The goods being sold in the market are so similar to each other that no one cares from whom each buys or sells.
5. The costs and benefits of producing or using the goods being exchanged are borne entirely by those buying or selling the goods and not by any other external parties.
6. All buyers and sellers are utility maximizers: Each tries to get as much as possible for as little as possible.
7. No external parties (such as the government) regulate the price, quantity, or quality of any of the goods being bought and sold in the market.

The first two features are the basic characteristics of a "competitive" market because they ensure that buyers and sellers are roughly equal in power and none can force the others to accept its terms. The seventh feature is what makes a market qualify as a "free" market: It is one that is free of any externally imposed regulations on price, quantity, or quality. (So-called *free* markets, however, are not necessarily free of all constraints, as we see later.)

In addition to these seven characteristics, free competitive markets also need an enforceable private property system (otherwise buyers and sellers would not have any ownership rights to exchange), an underlying system of contracts (which allows buyers and sellers to forge agreements that transfer ownership), and an underlying system of production (that generates goods or services whose ownership can be exchanged).

In a perfectly competitive free market, the price buyers are willing to pay for goods rises when fewer goods are available, and these rising prices induce sellers to provide greater quantities of goods. Thus, as more goods are made available, prices tend to fall, and these falling prices lead sellers to decrease the quantities of goods they provide. These fluctuations produce a striking outcome: In a perfectly competitive market, prices and quantities always move toward what is called the *equilibrium point.* The equilibrium point is the point at which the amount of goods buyers want to buy exactly equals the amount of goods sellers want to sell, and at which the highest price buyers are willing to pay exactly equals the lowest price sellers are willing to take. At the equilibrium point, every seller finds a willing buyer and every buyer finds a willing seller. Moreover, this surprising result of perfectly competitive free markets has an even more astonishing outcome: It satisfies three of the moral criteria: justice, utility, and rights. That is, perfectly competitive free markets achieve a certain kind of justice, they satisfy a certain version of utilitarianism, and they respect certain kinds of moral rights.

Why do perfectly competitive markets achieve these three surprising moral outcomes? The well-known supply and demand curves can be used to explain the phenomenon. Our explanation proceeds in two stages. First, we see why perfectly competitive free markets always move toward the equilibrium point. Then we see why markets that move toward equilibrium in this way achieve these three moral outcomes.

Equilibrium in Perfectly Competitive Markets

A demand curve is a line on a graph indicating the most that consumers (or buyers) would be willing to pay for a unit of some product when they buy different quantities of those products. As we mentioned, the fewer the units of a certain product consumers buy, the more they are willing to pay for those units, so the demand curve slopes down to the right. In the imaginary curve in Fig. 4.1, for example, buyers are willing to pay $1 per basket of potatoes if they buy 600 million tons of potatoes, but they are willing to pay as much as $5 per basket if they buy only 100 million tons of potatoes.

Notice that the demand curve slopes downward to the right, indicating that consumers are willing to pay less for each unit of a good as they buy more of those units: The value of a potato falls for consumers as they buy up more potatoes. Why is this? This phenomenon is explained by a principle we assume human nature always follows—the so-called *principle of diminishing marginal utility.* This principle states that each additional item a person consumes is less satisfying than each of the earlier items the person consumed: The more we consume, the less utility or satisfaction we get from consuming more. The second pizza a person eats at lunch, for example, is much less satisfying than the first one; the third will be substantially less tasty than the second; while the fourth may be positively disgusting. Because of the principle of diminishing marginal utility, the more goods consumers purchase in a market, the less satisfying additional

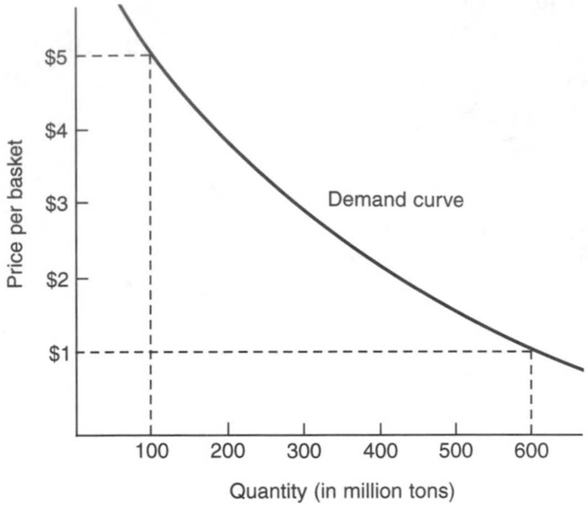

Figure 4.1 Demand curve for potatoes.

goods are to them and the less value they place on each additional good. Thus, the buyer's demand curve slopes downward to the right because the principle of diminishing marginal utility ensures that the price consumers are willing to pay for goods diminishes as the quantity they buy increases.

The demand curve thus indicates the value consumers place on each unit of a product as they purchase more units. Consequently, if the price of a product were to rise above their demand curve, average buyers would see themselves as losers—that is, as paying out more for the product than what it is worth to them. At any point below the demand curve, they would see themselves as winners—that is, as paying out less for a product than what it is worth to them. Therefore, if prices should rise above the demand curve, buyers would have little motive to buy, and they would tend to leave the market to spend their money in other markets. However, if prices were to fall below the demand curve, new buyers would tend to flock into the market because they would perceive a chance to buy the product for less than what it is worth to them.

Now let us look at the other side of the market: the supply side. A supply curve is a line on a graph indicating the prices producers must charge to cover the average costs of supplying a given amount of a commodity. Beyond a certain point (which we explain shortly), the more units producers make, the higher the average costs of making each unit, so the curve slopes upward to the right. In the sample curve traced in Fig. 4.2, for example, it costs farmers on average $1 a basket to grow 100 million tons of potatoes, but it costs them $4 per basket to grow 500 million tons.

At first sight, it may seem odd that producers or sellers must charge higher prices when they are producing large volumes than when producing smaller

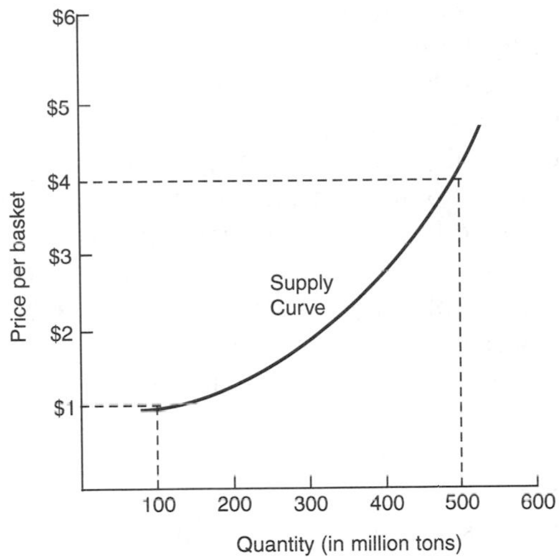

Figure 4.2 Supply curve for potatoes.

quantities. We are accustomed to thinking that it costs less to produce goods in large quantities than in small quantities. However, the increasing costs of production are explained by a principle that we call the *principle of increasing marginal costs*. This principle states that, after a certain point, each additional item the seller produces costs him more to produce than earlier items. Why? Because of an unfortunate feature of our physical world: Its productive resources are limited. A producer will use the best and most productive resources to make his first few goods and at this point his costs will indeed decline as he expands his production. A potato grower farming in a valley, for example, will begin by planting the level fertile acres in the floor of the valley where the more acreage he plants the more his costs per unit decline. But as the farmer continues to expand his farm, he eventually runs out of these highly productive resources and must turn to using less productive land. As the potato farmer uses up the acreage on the floor of the valley, he is forced to start planting the sloping and less fertile land at the edges of the valley, which may be rocky and may require more expensive irrigation. If he continues increasing his production, he will eventually have to start planting the land on the mountainsides and his costs will rise even higher. Eventually, the farmer reaches a situation where the more he produces the more it costs him to produce each unit because he is forced to use increasingly unproductive materials. The predicament of the potato farmer illustrates the principle of increasing marginal costs: After a certain point, added production always entails increasing costs per unit. That is the situation illustrated by the supply curve. The supply curve rises upward to the right because it pictures the point at which sellers must begin to charge more per unit to cover the costs of supplying additional goods.

The supply curve, then, indicates how much producers must charge per unit to cover the costs of producing given amounts of a good. To avoid misunderstandings, it is extremely important to note that the "costs" of producing a good include more than the "ordinary" costs of labor, materials, distribution, and so on. The "costs" of producing a commodity also include the "normal" profits sellers must make to motivate them to invest their resources in producing the commodity and to forgo the opportunity of making profits by investing in other markets. The "costs" of producing a commodity, then, include the ordinary costs of production, plus a normal profit. What is a "normal" profit? For our purposes, we can say that a "normal" profit is the average profit producers could make in other markets that carry similar risks. The prices on the supply curve, then, are sufficient to cover the ordinary costs of production plus a normal profit. Profits are counted as part of the necessary "costs" of bringing a product to the market.

The prices on the supply curve, then, represent the minimum producers must receive to cover their ordinary costs and make a normal profit. When prices fall below the supply curve, producers see themselves as losers: They are receiving less than what it costs them to produce the product (keep in mind that "costs" include ordinary costs plus a normal profit). Consequently, if prices fall below the supply curve, producers will tend to leave the market and invest their resources in other, more profitable markets. However, if prices rise above the supply curve, then new producers will come crowding into the market, attracted by the opportunity to invest their resources in a market where they can derive higher profits than in other markets.

Sellers and buyers, of course, trade in the same markets, so their respective supply and demand curves can be superimposed on the same graph. Typically when this is done, the supply and demand curves will meet and cross at some point. The point at which they meet is the point at which the price buyers are willing to pay for a certain amount of goods exactly matching the price sellers must take to cover the costs of producing that same amount (i.e., the "equilibrium price"). This point of intersection, as indicated in Fig. 4.3, where the point, "E," at which the supply and demand curves meet, is the so-called *point of equilibrium* or *equilibrium price*. It is at $2 on the graph.

We mentioned that in a perfectly competitive free market, prices, the amounts supplied, and the amounts demanded all tend to move toward the point of equilibrium. Why does this happen? Notice in Fig. 4.3 that if the prices of potatoes rise above the point of equilibrium, say to $4 per basket, producers will supply more goods (500 million tons) than at the equilibrium price level (300 million tons). But at that high price, consumers will purchase fewer goods (only 100 million tons) than at the equilibrium price. The result will be a surplus of unsold goods (500 – 100 = 400 million tons of unsold potatoes). To get rid of their unsold surplus, sellers will be forced to lower their prices and

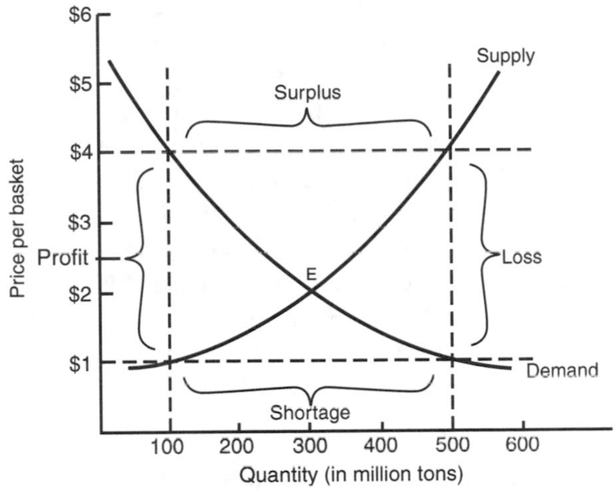

Figure 4.3 Supply and demand curves for potatoes.

decrease production. Eventually, equilibrium prices and amounts will be reached.

In contrast, if the price drops below the point of equilibrium in Fig. 4.3, say to $1 per basket, then producers will start losing money and so will supply less than consumers want at that price. The result will be an excessive demand and shortages will appear. The shortages will lead buyers to bid up the price. Subsequently, prices will rise and the rising prices will attract more producers into the market, thereby raising supplies. Eventually, again, equilibrium will reassert itself.

Notice also what happens in Fig. 4.3 if the amount being supplied, say 100 million tons, for some reason is less than the equilibrium amount. The cost of supplying such an amount ($1 per basket) is below what consumers are willing to pay ($4 per basket) for that same amount. Producers will be able to raise their prices up to the level the consumer is willing to pay ($4) and pocket the difference ($3) as abnormally high profits (i.e., profits far above the normal profit as defined). The abnormally high profits, however, will attract outside producers into the market, thereby increasing the quantities supplied and bringing about a corresponding decrease in the price consumers are willing to pay for the larger quantities. Gradually, the amounts supplied will increase to the equilibrium point, and prices will drop to equilibrium prices.

The opposite happens if the amount being supplied, say 500 million tons, is for some reason more than the equilibrium amount. Under these circumstances, sellers will have to lower their prices to the very low levels that consumers are willing to pay for such large amounts. At such low price levels, producers will leave the market to invest their resources in other, more profitable markets, thereby lowering the supply, raising the price, and once again reestablishing equilibrium levels.

At this point, the reader may be trying to think of an industry that fits the description of perfect competition we have just given. The reader will have some difficulty finding one. Only a few agricultural markets such as grain and potato markets come close to embodying the six features that characterize a perfectly competitive market.[8] The fact is that the model of perfect competition is a theoretical construct of the economist that does not exist. Although the model does not describe many real markets, it does provide us with a clear understanding of the advantages of competition and an understanding of why it is desirable to keep markets as competitive as possible.

Ethics and Perfectly Competitive Markets

As we have seen, perfectly competitive free markets incorporate forces that inevitably drive buyers and sellers toward the so-called *point of equilibrium*. In doing so, they achieve three major moral values: (a) they lead buyers and sellers to exchange their goods in a way that is just (in a certain sense of *just*); (b) they maximize the utility of buyers and sellers by leading them to allocate, use, and distribute their goods with perfect efficiency; and (c) they bring about these achievements in a way that respects buyers' and sellers' right of free consent. As we examine each of these moral achievements, it is important to keep in mind that they are characteristics only of the perfectly competitive free market—that is, of markets that have the seven features we listed. Markets that fail to have one or the other of these features do not necessarily achieve these three moral values.

To understand why perfectly competitive free markets lead buyers and sellers to make exchanges that are just, we begin by recalling the capitalist meaning of *justice* described in Chapter 2. According to the capitalist criterion of justice, benefits and burdens are distributed justly when a person receives in return at least the value of the contribution he or she made to an enterprise: Fairness is getting paid fully in return for what one contributes. It is this form of justice (and only this form) that is achieved in perfectly competitive free markets.

Perfectly competitive free markets embody capitalist justice because such markets necessarily converge on the equilibrium point, and the equilibrium point is the one (and only) point at which buyers and sellers on average receive the value of what they contribute. Why is this true? Consider the matter, first, from the seller's point of view. The supply curve indicates the price producers must receive to cover what it costs them to produce given quantities of a good. Consequently, if prices (and quantities) fall below the seller's supply curve, consumers are unfairly shortchanging the seller because they are paying him less than he contributed to produce those goods in those quantities. If prices rise above the seller's supply curve, the average seller is unfairly overcharging consumers because he is charging them more than what he knows those goods are worth in terms of what it costs to produce them. Thus, from the standpoint of the seller's contribution, the price is fair (i.e., the price equals the costs of his contribution) only if it falls somewhere on the seller's supply curve.

Next consider the matter from the standpoint of the average buyer. The demand curve indicates the highest price consumers are willing to pay for given quantities of goods. So if the prices (and quantities) of goods were to rise above the consumer's demand curve, the average consumer would be contributing more for those goods than what the goods (in those quantities) are worth to him. If prices (and quantities) fall below the consumer's demand curve, the average consumer unfairly contributes less to sellers than the value (to him) of the goods he is receiving. Thus, from the standpoint of the value the average consumer places on different quantities of goods, the contribution is fair (i.e., the price is equal to what the goods are worth to the consumer) only if it falls somewhere on the consumer's demand curve.

Obviously, there is only a single point at which the price and quantity of a commodity lies both on the buyer's demand curve (and is thus fair from the standpoint of the value the average buyer places on the goods) and on the seller's supply curve (and is thus fair from the standpoint of what it costs the average seller to bring those goods to market): the equilibrium point. Thus, the equilibrium point is the one and only point at which prices on average are just both from the buyer's and seller's points of view. When prices or quantities deviate from the equilibrium point, either the average buyer or the average seller is unjustly being shortchanged: One or the other has to contribute more than what he or she is receiving.

The perfectly competitive market thus continually—almost magically—reestablishes capitalist justice for its participants by continually leading them to buy and sell goods at the one quantity and the one price at which each receives the value of what he contributes, whether this value is calculated from the average buyer's or the average seller's point of view.[9]

In addition to establishing a form of justice, competitive markets also maximize the utility of buyers and sellers by leading them to allocate, use, and distribute their goods with perfect efficiency. To understand this aspect of perfectly competitive markets, we must consider what happens not in a single isolated market, but in an economy that consists of a system of many markets. A market system is perfectly efficient when all the goods in all the markets are allocated, used, and distributed in a way that produces the highest level of satisfaction possible from these goods. A system of perfectly competitive markets achieves such efficiency in three main ways.[10]

First, a perfectly competitive market system motivates firms to invest resources in those industries where consumer demand is high and to move resources away from industries where consumer demand is low. Resources will be attracted into markets where high consumer demand creates shortages that raise prices above equilibrium, and they will flee markets where low consumer demand leads to surpluses that lower prices below equilibrium. The perfectly competitive market system allocates resources efficiently in accordance with consumer demands and needs: The consumer is "sovereign" over the market.

Second, perfectly competitive markets encourage firms to minimize the amount of resources consumed in producing a commodity and use the most efficient technology available. Firms are motivated to use resources sparingly because they want to lower their costs and thereby increase their profit margin. Moreover, to not lose buyers to other firms, each firm will reduce its profits to the lowest levels consistent with the survival of the firm. The perfectly competitive market encourages an efficient use of the seller's resources as well.

Third, perfectly competitive markets distribute commodities among buyers in such a way that all buyers receive the most satisfying bundle of commodities they can purchase, given the commodities available to them and the money they can spend on these commodities. When faced by a system of perfectly competitive markets, each buyer will buy up those proportions of each commodity that correspond with the buyer's desire for the commodity when weighed against the buyer's desires for other commodities. When buyers have completed their buying, they will know that they cannot improve on their purchases by trading their goods with other consumers because all consumers can buy the same goods at the same prices. Thus, perfectly competitive markets enable consumers to attain a level of satisfaction on which they cannot improve given the constraints of their budgets and the range of available goods. An efficient distribution of commodities is thereby achieved.

Finally, perfectly competitive markets establish capitalist justice and maximize utility in a way that respects buyers' and sellers' negative rights.

First, in a perfectly competitive market, buyers and sellers are free (by definition) to enter or leave the market as they choose. That is, individuals are neither forced into nor prevented from engaging in a certain business, provided they have the expertise and the financial resources required.[11] Perfectly competitive markets thus embody the negative right of freedom of opportunity.

Second, in the perfectly competitive free market, all exchanges are fully voluntary. That is, participants are not forced to buy or sell anything other than what they freely and knowingly consent to buy or sell. In a competitive free market, all participants have full and complete knowledge of what they are buying or selling, and no external agency (such as the government) forces them to buy or sell goods they do not want at prices they do not choose in quantities they do not desire.[12] Moreover, buyers and sellers in a perfectly competitive free market are not forced to pay for goods that others enjoy. In a perfectly competitive free market, by definition, the costs and benefits of producing or using goods are borne entirely by those buying or selling the goods and not by any other external parties. Free competitive markets thus embody the negative right of freedom of consent.

Third, no single seller or buyer will so dominate the perfectly competitive free market that he is able to force the others to accept his terms or go without.[13] In a perfectly competitive market, industrial power is decentralized among numerous firms so that prices and quantities are not dependent on the whim of one or a few businesses. In short, perfectly competitive free markets embody the negative right of freedom from coercion.

Thus, perfectly competitive free markets are perfectly moral in three important respects: (a) Each continuously establishes a capitalist form of justice; (b) together they maximize utility in the form of market efficiency; and (c) each respects certain important negative rights of buyers and sellers.

Several cautions are in order, however, when interpreting these moral features of perfectly competitive free markets. First, perfectly competitive free markets do not establish other forms of justice. Because they do not respond to the needs of those outside the market or those who have little to exchange, for example, they cannot establish a justice based on needs. Moreover, perfectly competitive free markets impose no restrictions on how much wealth each participant accumulates relative to the others, so they ignore egalitarian justice and may incorporate large inequalities.

Second, competitive markets maximize the utility of those who can participate in the market given the constraints of each participant's budget. However, this does not mean that society's total utility is necessarily maximized. The bundle of goods distributed to each individual by a competitive market system depends ultimately on that individual's ability to participate in the market and on how much that individual has to spend in the market. But this way of distributing goods may not produce the most satisfaction for everyone in society. Society's welfare might be increased, for example, by giving more goods to those who cannot participate in the market because they have nothing to exchange (perhaps they are too poor, too old, too sick, too disabled, or too young to have anything to trade in markets); or the overall welfare might be increased by distributing more goods to those who have only a little to spend or by limiting the consumption of those who can spend a lot.

Third, although free competitive markets establish certain negative rights for those within the market, they may actually diminish the positive rights of those outside (those, e.g., who cannot compete) or of those whose participation is minimal. People who have the money to participate in markets may consume goods (such as food or educational resources) that people outside the market, or those with very little money, need to develop and exercise their own freedom and rationality. Thus, although perfectly competitive free markets secure capitalist justice, although they maximize economic utility, and respect certain negative rights, they largely do this only for those who have the means (the money or the goods) to participate fully in those markets, and they necessarily ignore the needs, utility, and rights of those who are left out of the marketplace.

Fourth, free competitive markets ignore and even conflict with the demands of caring. As we have seen, an ethic of care implies that people exist in a web of interdependent relationships and should care for those who are closely related to them. A free market system, however, operates as if individuals are completely independent of each other and takes no account of the human relationships that may exist among them. Moreover, as we mentioned, a free market pressures individuals to spend their resources (time, labor, money) efficiently: A system of competitive markets pressures individuals to invest, use, and distribute goods in ways that will produce the maximum economic returns. If individuals do not invest, use, and distribute their resources efficiently, they will lose out in the competition that free markets create. This means that if individuals divert their resources to spend them on caring for those with whom they have close relationships, instead of investing, using, and distributing them efficiently, they will lose out. For example, when an employer who likes and cares for his or her workers gives them higher wages than other employers are paying, his or her costs will rise. Then he or she must either charge more for goods than other employers, which will drive customers away, or accept lower profits than other employers, which will allow other employers to make more money that they can then invest in improvements and may eventually enable them to drive him or her out of business. In short, the pressures toward economic efficiency that a system of perfectly competitive free markets creates not only ignore but can regularly conflict with the demands of caring.[14]

Fifth, free competitive markets may have a pernicious effect on people's moral character. The competitive pressures that are present in perfectly competitive markets can lead people to attend constantly to economic efficiency. Producers are constantly pressured to reduce their costs and increase their profit margins. Consumers are constantly pressured to patronize sellers that provide the highest value at the lowest cost. Employees are constantly pressured to seek out employers that pay higher wages and to abandon those with lower wages. Such pressures, it has been argued, lead people to develop character traits associated with maximizing individual economic well-being and neglect character traits associated with building close relationships to others. The virtues of loyalty, kindness, and caring all diminish, whereas the vices of being greedy, self-seeking, avaricious, and calculating are encouraged.

Finally, and most important, we should note that the three values of capitalist justice, utility, and negative rights are produced by free markets only if they embody the seven conditions that define perfect competition. If one or more of these conditions are not present in a given real market, then the claim can no longer be made that these three values are present. As we see in the remainder of this chapter—and, in fact, throughout the rest of this book—this is the most crucial limitation of free market morality because real markets are not perfectly competitive, and consequently they do not achieve the three moral values that characterize perfect competition. Despite this critical limitation, however, the perfectly competitive free market provides us with a clear idea of how economic exchanges in a market economy should be structured if relationships among buyers and sellers are to secure the three moral achievements we indicated. We turn next to see what happens when some of the defining characteristics of perfect competition are absent.

4.2 Monopoly Competition

What happens when a free market (i.e., one without government intervention) ceases to be perfectly competitive? We begin to answer this question in this section by examining the opposite extreme of a perfectly competitive market: the free (unregulated) monopoly market. We then examine some less extreme varieties of noncompetition.

We noted earlier that a perfectly competitive market is characterized by seven conditions. In a monopoly, two of these conditions are not present.[15] First, instead of "numerous sellers, none of whom has a substantial share of the market," the monopoly market has only one seller, and that single seller has a substantial (100 percent) share of the market. Second, instead of being a market that other sellers "can freely and immediately enter or leave," the monopoly market is one that other sellers cannot enter. Instead, there are barriers to entry such as patent laws, which give only one seller the right to produce a commodity, or high capitalization costs, which make it too expensive for a new seller to start a business in that industry.

The classic and standard example of a monopoly is the market in aluminum that developed during the first few decades of this century.[16] Alcoa (the Aluminum Company of America) held the patents for the production of virgin aluminum in the United States until 1909, by which time it was firmly entrenched as the sole domestic producer of aluminum. Moreover, although its patents ran out in 1909, other manufacturers were never able to enter successfully into the production of aluminum because their start-up costs would have been too high and they lacked Alcoa's experience, trade connections, and trained personnel. Alcoa remained the sole domestic producer of virgin aluminum until the 1940s, when it was successfully prosecuted under the Sherman Antitrust Act. For similar reasons, Western Electric emerged during the 1960s as the sole monopoly producer of certain telephone products.

Monopolies can also be created through mergers. At the turn of the century, for example, the leading oil refineries merged into a "holding company" (then called "Standard Oil," now named "Exxon"), which acquired monopoly control over oil refining. The monopoly was broken into 34 separate companies when the Supreme Court charged the company with monopolization in 1911. A policy of forced mergers during the closing decades of the 19th century enabled the American Tobacco Company to absorb all the major cigarette manufacturing companies in the United States so that by the turn of the century the combine controlled the American cigarette market. In 1911, the company was ordered broken up into several smaller firms.

Monopoly markets, then, are those in which a single firm is the only seller in the market and which new sellers are barred from entering. A seller in a monopoly market, therefore, can control the prices of the available goods. Figure 4.4 illustrates the situation in a monopoly market: The monopoly firm is able to fix its output at a quantity that is less than equilibrium and at which demand is so high that it allows the firm to reap an excess monopoly profit by charging prices that are far above the supply curve and above the equilibrium price. A monopoly seller, for example, can set prices above their equilibrium level—at, say, $3. By limiting supply to only those amounts buyers will purchase at the monopolist's high prices (300 units), the monopoly firm can ensure that it sells all its products and reaps substantial profits from its business. The monopoly firm will, of course, calculate the price-amount ratios that will secure the highest total profits (i.e., the profit-per-unit multiplied by the number of units) and will then fix its prices and production at those levels. At the turn of the century, for example, the American Tobacco Company, which earlier had managed to

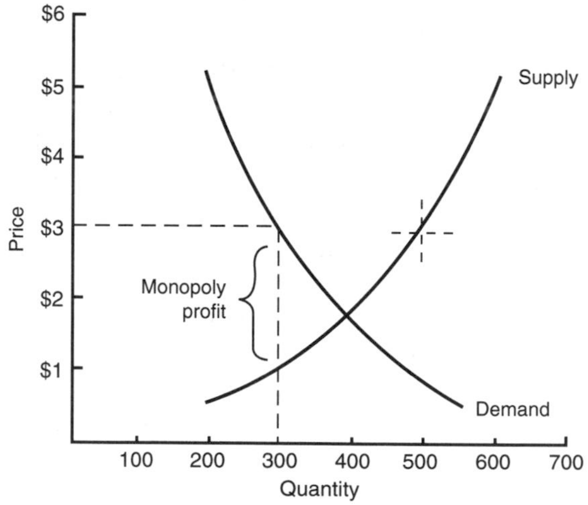

Figure 4.4

acquire a monopoly in the sale of cigarettes, was making profits equal to about 56 percent of its sales.

If entry into the market were open, of course, these excess profits would draw other producers into the market, resulting in an increased supply of goods and a drop in prices until equilibrium was attained. In a monopoly market, where entry is closed or prohibitive, this does not happen, and prices remain high.

Monopoly Competition: Justice, Utility, and Rights

How well does a free monopoly market succeed in achieving the moral values that characterize perfectly competitive free markets? Not well. Unregulated monopoly markets can fall short of the three values of capitalist justice, economic efficiency, and respect for negative rights that perfect competition achieves.

The most obvious failure of monopoly markets lies in the high prices they enable the monopolist to charge and the high profits they enable him to reap—a failure that violates capitalist justice.[17] Why do the high prices and profits of the monopolist violate capitalist justice? Capitalist justice says that what each person receives should equal the value of the contribution he or she makes. As we saw, the equilibrium point is the one (and only) point at which buyers and sellers each receive in return the exact value of what each contributes to the other, whether this value is determined from the average buyer's or the average seller's point of view. In a monopoly market, however, prices for goods are set above the equilibrium level, and quantities are set at less than the equilibrium amount. As a result, the seller charges the buyer far more than the goods are worth (from the average seller's point of view) because he charges far more than it costs him to make those goods. Thus, the high prices the seller forces the buyer to pay are unjust, and these unjustly high prices are the source of the seller's excess profits.

A monopoly market also results in a decline in the efficiency with which it allocates and distributes goods. First, the monopoly market allows resources to be used in ways that will produce shortages of those things buyers want and cause them to be sold at higher prices than necessary. The high profits in a monopoly market indicate a shortage of goods. However, because other firms are blocked from entering the market, their resources cannot be used to make up the shortages indicated by the high profits. This means that the resources of these other firms are deflected into other nonmonopoly markets that already have an adequate supply of goods. Shortages, therefore, continue to exist. Moreover, the monopoly market allows the monopoly firm to set its prices well above costs instead of forcing the firm to lower its prices to cost levels. The result is an inflated price for the consumer—a price that the consumer is forced to accept because the absence of other sellers has limited his or her choices. These excess profits absorbed by the monopolist are resources that are not needed to supply the amounts of goods the consumer is getting.

Second, monopoly markets do not encourage suppliers to use resources in ways that will minimize the resources consumed to produce a certain amount of a commodity. A monopoly firm is not encouraged to reduce its costs and is therefore not motivated to find less costly methods of production. Because profits are high anyway, there is little incentive for it to develop new technology that might reduce costs or that might give it a competitive edge over other firms for there are no other competing firms.

Third, a monopoly market allows the seller to introduce price differentials that block consumers from putting together the most satisfying bundle of commodities they can purchase given the commodities available and the money they can spend. Because everyone must buy from the monopoly firm, the firm can set its prices so that some buyers are forced to pay a higher price for the same goods than others. For example, the monopoly firm can adjust its prices so that those consumers who have a greater desire for its goods must pay a higher price for the same goods than those consumers who have a lesser desire for them. As a consequence, those who have the greater desire now buy less, and those who have the lesser desire now buy more, than either would buy at an equal price. The result is that some consumers are no longer able to purchase the most satisfying bundle of goods they could buy.

Monopoly markets also embody restrictions on the negative rights that perfectly free markets respect. First, monopoly markets by definition are markets that other sellers are not free to enter. Second, monopoly markets enable the monopoly firm to force on its buyers goods that they may not want in quantities they may not desire. The monopoly firm, for example, can force consumers to purchase Commodity X only if they also purchase Commodity Y from the firm. Third, monopoly markets are dominated by a single seller whose decisions determine the prices and quantities of a commodity offered for sale. The monopoly firm's power over the market is absolute.

A monopoly market, then, is one that deviates from the ideals of capitalist justice, economic utility, and negative rights. Instead of continually establishing a just equilibrium, the monopoly market imposes unjustly high prices on the buyer and generates unjustly high profits for the seller. Instead of maximizing efficiency, monopoly markets provide incentives for waste, misallocation of resources, and profit gouging. Instead of respecting negative rights of freedom, monopoly markets create an inequality of power that allows the monopoly firm to dictate terms to the consumer. The producer then replaces the consumer as "sovereign" of the market.

4.3 Oligopolistic Competition

Few industries are monopolies. Most major industrial markets are not dominated by a single firm, but more usually by as many as four firms or more. Such markets lie somewhere on the spectrum between the two extremes of the perfectly competitive market with innumerable sellers and the pure monopoly market with only one seller. Market structures of this "impure" type are referred to collectively as *imperfectly competitive markets*, of which the most important kind is the "oligopoly."[18]

In an oligopoly, two of the seven conditions that characterize the purely competitive market are once again not present. First, instead of many sellers, there are only a few significant sellers. That is, most of the market is shared by a relatively small number of large firms that together can exercise some influence on prices. The share each firm holds may be somewhere between 25 percent and 90 percent of the market, and the firms controlling this share may range from 2 to 50 depending on the industry. Second, other sellers are not able to freely enter the market. Although more than one seller is present in an oligopoly market, new sellers find it difficult to break into the industry. This may be because of the prohibitively high costs of starting a business in that industry, it may be as a result of long-term contracts that have tied all the buyers to the firms already in the industry, or it may be because of enduring loyalties created by brand-name advertising.

Oligopoly markets, which are dominated by a few (e.g., four to eight) large firms, are said to be *highly concentrated*. Examples of such oligopoly markets are not hard to find because they include many of the largest manufacturing industries. Table 4.1 lists several highly concentrated U.S. industries, as indicated by the large share of the market that the biggest firms control.

The firms that dominate the highly concentrated American industries tend, by and large, to be among the largest corporations in the United States. Table 4.2 lists several major corporations dominant in various oligopoly industries, together with the approximate percentage of the markets controlled by these firms. As you can see, these include many of the most well-known and largest American firms operating in several of the most basic American industries.

Although oligopolies can form in a variety of ways, the most common causes of an oligopolistic market structure are horizontal mergers.[19] A horizontal merger is simply the unification of two or more companies that were formerly competing in the same line of business. If enough companies in a competitive industry merge, the industry can become an oligopoly composed of a few very large firms. During the 1950s, for example, the 108 competing banks in Philadelphia began to merge until, by 1963, the number of bank firms had been reduced to 42.[20] The Philadelphia National Bank emerged as the second largest bank (as a result of nine mergers), and the Girard Bank emerged as the third largest (as a result of six mergers). In the early 1960s, the Philadelphia National Bank and the Girard Bank proposed to merge into a single firm. If the merger had been approved (it was stopped through legal action), the two banks together would have controlled well over one third of the banking activities of metropolitan Philadelphia.

TABLE 4.1 MARKET SHARES OF LARGEST FIRMS BY PRODUCT, 1989

	Percent of Market Controlled by Largest Firms		
Product	4 Largest	8 Largest	Herfindahl–Hirschman Index
Cereal breakfast foods	87	99	2207
Cane sugar refining	87	99	2310
Vegetable oil	74	92	1736
Malt beverages	87	98	(NA)
Cigarettes	92	99	(NA)
Tire cord	91	99	(NA)
Greetings cards	85	89	2830
House slippers	77	88	2208
Glass containers	78	89	2126
Primary aluminum	74	95	1934
Small gun ammunition	88	96	(NA)
Turbines	80	95	2162
Refrigerators and freezers	85	98	2256
Washers and driers	93	(NA)	2855
Electric bulbs	91	94	(NA)
Batteries	88	94	(NA)
Automobiles	90	95	(NA)
Photographic equipment	77	84	2241
Hard floor coverings	82	99	2550

Source: U.S. Bureau of the Census, Census of Manufacturing, *Concentration Ratios in Manufacturing*, February 1992, Table 4. The Herfindahl–Hirschman index is a measure of market concentration calculated by squaring the individual market share (in percent) of the firms in the market and adding the squares together. An industry with a 4-firm combined share above 80% or a Herfindahl–Hirschman number above 1800 is considered to be highly concentrated.

How do oligopoly industries affect the market? Because a highly concentrated oligopoly has a relatively small number of firms, it is relatively easy for the managers of these firms to join forces and act as a unit. By explicitly or tacitly agreeing to set their prices at the same levels and to restrict their output accordingly, the oligopolists can function much like a single giant firm. This uniting of forces, together with the barriers to entry that are characteristic of oligopoly industries, can result in the same high prices and low supply levels characteristic of monopoly markets. As a consequence, oligopoly markets, like monopolies, can fail to exhibit just profit levels, can generate a decline in social utility, and can fail to respect basic economic freedoms. It has been shown, for example, that generally the more highly concentrated an oligopoly industry is, the higher the profits it is able to extract.[21] Studies also have estimated that the

TABLE 4.2 DOMINANT BRANDS AND COMPANIES IN OLIGOPOLY MARKETS, 2000

Brand/Company	Market	Market Share (%)
Gerber	Baby Food	73%
Campbell's	Canned Soup	70%
Kelloggs	Toaster Pastry	72%
A-1	Marinades	79%
Gatorade	Sports Drinks	82%
Levi's	Jeans	52%
Procter & Gamble	Laundry Soap	57%
Clorox	Chlorine Bleach	59%
Kiwi	Shoe Polish	76%
General Electric	Light Bulbs	79%
Tyco	Plastic Pipe	60%
Reynolds	Aluminum Foil	64%
3 Com	Personal Digital Assistants	85%
Iomega	Zip Drives	75%
Hewlett Packard	Desktop Laser Printers	61%
KitchenAid	Stand-alone Mixers	83%
In-Sink-Erator	Garbage Disposal	77%
Sony	Digital Camcorders	68%
Kodak	Single-use Cameras	61%
Sony	Video Game Consoles	66%
Sony	Video Game	64%
H&B	Wooden Bats	65%

Source: Robert S. Lazich, *Market Share Reporter* 2001 (Detroit, MI: Gale Research, 2001).

overall decline in utility as a result of inefficient allocation of resources by highly concentrated oligopoly industries ranges between 0.5 percent and 4.0 percent of the nation's gross national product or between $10 billion and $80 billion per year.[22]

Explicit Agreements

Prices in an oligopoly can be set at profitable levels through explicit agreements that restrain competition. The managers of the few firms operating in an oligopoly can meet and jointly agree to fix prices at a level much higher than what each would be forced to take in a perfectly competitive market. The greater the degree of market concentration present in an industry, the fewer the managers that have to be brought into such a price-fixing agreement, and the easier it is for them to come to an agreement, as the data in Table 4.3 suggests. Such

TABLE 4.3 SELECTED PRICE-FIXING CONSPIRACIES IN U.S. INDUSTRIES, 1961–1970

Market	Geographical Scope	Percent of Market Controlled by Four Largest Firms	Number of Conspirators	Their Share of Sales	Number of Firms in Market
Wrought steel wheels	National	85%	7	100%	5
Bed springs	National	61	10		20
Metal library shelving	National	60	7	78	9
Self-locking nuts	National	97	4	97	6
Refuse collection	Local		86		102
Steel products	Regional	66	5	72	
Gasoline	Regional	49	12		
Milk	Local	90	11	80	13
Concrete pipe	Regional	100	4	100	4
Drill jig bushings	National	56	9	82	13
Linen supplies	Local	49	31	90	
Plumbing fixtures	National	76	7	98	15
Class rings	Regional	100	3	90	5
Tickets	Regional	78	9	91	10
Athletic equipment	Local	90	6	100	6
Dairy products	Regional	95	3	95	13
Vending machines	Local	93	6	100	6
Ready-mix concrete	Local	86	9	100	9
Carbon steel sheets	National	59	10		
Liquid asphalt	Regional	56	20	95	

Source: William G. Shepherd, *The Economics of Industrial Organization* (Englewood Cliffs, NJ: Prentice-Hall, Inc., 1979), p. 306.

agreements, of course, reproduce the effects of a monopoly and consequently curtail market justice, market efficiency, and market rights as defined in the first section of this chapter.

If the justice, freedom, and social utility that competitive markets achieve are important values for society, then it is crucial that the managers of oligopoly firms refrain from engaging in practices that restrict competition. Only if markets function competitively will they exhibit the justice, freedom, and utility that justify their existence. These beneficial aspects of a free market are reaped by society only as long as monopoly firms refrain from engaging in collusive arrangements that do away with competition and reproduce the effects of monopoly markets. In particular, the following sorts of market practices have been identified as unethical.

Price Fixing When firms are operating in an oligopoly market, it is easy enough for their managers to meet secretly and agree to set their prices at artificially high levels. This is straightforward price fixing. In 1978, for example, several managers of firms manufacturing paper bags used for packaging foods, coffee, and other goods were fined for getting together and conspiring to fix the prices of those paper bags.[23] The managers worked for Continental Group, Inc., Chase Bag Co., American Bag and Paper Corp., and Harley Corp., four of the dominant firms in paper bag markets.

Manipulation of Supply Firms in an oligopoly industry might agree to limit their production so that prices rise to levels higher than those that would result from free competition. When hardwood manufacturers met periodically in trade associations early in this century, they would often agree on output policies that would secure high profits.[24] The American Column and Lumber Company was eventually prosecuted under the Sherman Antitrust law to force it to desist from this practice. Such a "manipulation of supply" would also result in market shortages.

Exclusive Dealing Arrangements A firm institutes an exclusive dealing arrangement when it sells to a retailer on condition that the retailer will not purchase any products from other companies and/or will not sell outside of a certain geographical area. During the 1940s, for instance, American Can Company would lease its can-closing machines (at very low prices) only to those customers who agreed not to purchase any cans from Continental Can Company, its major competitor.[25] Exclusive dealing arrangements tend to remove competition between retailers who are all selling the same company's products and to this extent they conflict with the values of free competition. However, an exclusive dealing arrangement can also motivate those retailers who are selling the products of a single company to become more aggressive in selling the products of that company. In this way, an exclusive dealing arrangement can actually increase competition between retailers selling the products of different companies. For this reason, exclusive dealing arrangements must be examined carefully to determine whether their overall effect is to dampen or promote competition.[26]

Tying Arrangements A firm enters into a tying arrangement when it sells a buyer a certain good only on condition that the buyer agrees to purchase certain other goods from the firm. Chicken Delight, for example, franchises home delivery and pick-up food stores whose major product is chicken cooked in a special mix. In 1970, Chicken Delight would sell a franchise license to a person only if the person also agreed to purchase a certain number of cookers, fryers, and other supplies.[27] The firm was subsequently forced to stop the practice through legal action.

Retail Price Maintenance Agreements If a manufacturer sells to retailers only on condition that they agree to charge the same set retail prices for its goods, it is engaging in "retail price maintenance." Eastman Kodak Company, for example, until stopped by the Federal Trade Commission, used to establish the prices at which retailers had to sell its "Kodachrome" and

"Magazine Cine-Kodak Film" and would not sell to retailers unless they agreed to abide by these prices.[28] A manufacturer may publish suggested retail prices and may even refuse to sell to retailers who regularly sell their goods at lower prices. It is illegal, however, for retailers to enter an agreement to abide by the manufacturer's prices and illegal for manufacturers to force retailers to enter such an agreement. Retail price maintenance dampens competition between retailers and removes from the manufacturer the competitive pressure to lower prices and cut costs.

Price Discrimination To charge different prices to different buyers for identical goods or services is to engage in price discrimination. Price discrimination was used by Continental Pie Company during the 1960s in an attempt to undersell Utah Pie Company, which had managed to take away much of the Salt Lake City business of Continental Baking Company. For several years, Continental sold its pies to Salt Lake City customers at prices substantially lower than those it charged for the same goods sold to customers in other areas. The Supreme Court found such pricing practices "predatory." Price differences are legitimate only when based on volume differences or other differences related to the true costs of manufacturing, packaging, marketing, transporting, or servicing goods.

Why do businesspeople engage in such anticompetitive practices? In a detailed study of several companies whose employees had been implicated in price-fixing arrangements, researchers Sonnenfeld and Lawrence found that several industry and organizational factors tended to lead to price fixing, including the following:[29]

A Crowded and Mature Market When large numbers of new entrants or declining demand create overcapacity in a market, the resulting decline in revenues and profits creates pressures on middle-level managers. They may respond by allowing, encouraging, and even ordering their sales teams to engage in price fixing.

Job-Order Nature of Business If orders are priced individually so that pricing decisions are made frequently and at low levels of the organization, collusion among low-level salespeople is more likely.

Undifferentiated Products When the product offered by each company in an industry is so similar to those of other companies that they must compete on price alone by continually reducing prices, salespeople come to feel that the only way to keep prices from collapsing is by getting together and fixing prices.

Culture of the Business When an organization's salespeople feel that price fixing is a common practice and is desired, condoned, accepted, rationalized, and even encouraged by the organization, price fixing is more likely. Top managers should counter this through personal example, consistent communication of a commitment to ethical practices, and development of a code of ethics that explicitly addresses price fixing in clear detail, is backed by sanctions, and is checked through regular corporate audits.

Personnel Practices When managers are evaluated and rewarded solely or primarily on the basis of profits and volume, so that bonuses, commissions, advancement, and other rewards are dependent on these objectives, they will come to believe that the company wants them to achieve these objectives regardless of the means. Compensation should be based on other factors, and the organization should strive to instill in employees a professional pride in the company's adherence to ethics.

Pricing Decisions When organizations are decentralized so that pricing decisions are pushed down into the hands of a lower part of the organization, price fixing is more likely to happen. Price decisions should be made at higher organizational levels.

Trade Associations Allowing salespeople to meet with competitors in trade association meetings will encourage them to talk about pricing and to begin to engage in price-setting arrangements with their counterparts in competing firms. Salespeople should be prohibited from meeting with competitors.

Corporate Legal Staff When legal departments fail to provide guidance to sales staff until after a problem has occurred, price-fixing problems are more likely. The legal staff should regularly provide one-on-one training in the legal aspects of price fixing for those who make pricing and sales decisions.

The failure of top managers to deal with these industry and organizational factors can put significant pressures on individuals who are otherwise striving to do what is best for a company. One chief executive officer describes the pressures that an irresponsible management can place on young new salespeople:

> I think we are particularly vulnerable where we have a salesman with two kids, plenty of financial demands, and a concern over the security of his job. There is a certain amount of looseness to a new set of rules. He may accept questionable practices feeling that he may just not know the system. There are no specific procedures for him to follow other than what other salesmen tell him. At the same time, he is in an industry where the acceptance for his product and the level of profitability are clearly dropping. Finally, we add to his pressures by letting him know who will take his job from him if he doesn't get good price and volume levels. I guess this will bring a lot of soul-searching out of an individual.[30]

Tacit Agreements

Although most of the forms of explicit market agreements enumerated are illegal, the more common types of price setting in oligopolies are accomplished through some unspoken form of cooperation against which it is difficult to legislate. How does this take place? The managers of the major firms in an oligopoly can learn by hard experience that competition is not in their personal financial interests. Price-cutting competition, they find, will only lead to minimal profits. The firms in an oligopoly, therefore, may each come to the conclusion that cooperation is in the best interests of all. Each firm may then reach the independent conclusion that they will all benefit if, when one major firm raises its prices, all other firms set their prices at the same high levels. Through this process of "price setting," all the major firms will retain their share of the market and they will all gain by the higher price. Since the 1930s, for example, the major tobacco companies have charged identical list prices for cigarettes. When one company decides it has a reason to raise or lower its cigarette prices, the other companies will always follow suit within a short period of time. The officials of these companies, however, have made no explicit agreement to act in concert; without ever having talked the matter over among themselves, each realizes that all will benefit so long as they continue to act in a unified fashion. In 1945, incidentally, the U.S. Supreme Court found the dominant cigarette companies guilty of tacit collusion, but the companies reverted to identical pricing after the case was settled.

To coordinate their prices, some oligopoly industries will recognize one firm as the industry's "price leader."[31] Each firm will tacitly agree to set its prices at the levels announced by the price leader, knowing that all other firms will also follow its price leadership. Because each oligopolist knows it will not have to compete with another firm's lower prices, it is not forced to reduce its margin of profit to the levels to which open competition would reduce them. There need be no overt collusion involved in this form of price setting, only an unspoken understanding that all firms will follow the price leadership of the dominant firm and will not engage in the price-lowering tactics of competition.

Whether prices in an oligopoly market are set by explicit agreements or implicit understandings, it is clear that social utility declines to the extent that prices are artificially raised above the levels that would be set by a perfectly competitive market. Consumers must pay the unjust prices of the oligopolists, resources are no longer efficiently allocated and used, and the freedom of both consumers and potential competitors diminishes.

Bribery

When used to secure the sale of a product, political bribery can also introduce diseconomies into the operations of markets. This is a form of market defect that received a great deal of public attention during the late 1970s, when it was discovered that a sizable group of companies had attempted to land contracts with overseas governments by paying bribes to various government officials. Lockheed Aircraft Corporation, for example, paid several million dollars to government officials in Saudi Arabia, Japan, Italy, and Holland to influence aircraft sales in those countries.[32]

When bribes are used to secure the purchase of a commodity, the net effect is a decline in market competition.[33] The product of the briber no longer competes equally with the product of other sellers on the basis of its price or merits. Instead, the bribe serves as a barrier to prevent other sellers from entering the briber's government market. Because of the bribe, the government involved buys only from the firm who supplies the bribe and the briber becomes in effect a monopoly seller.

If a briber succeeds in preventing other sellers from receiving equal entry into a government market, it becomes possible for the briber to engage in the inefficiencies characteristic of monopolies. The bribing firm can impose higher prices, engage in waste, and neglect quality and cost controls because the monopoly secured by the bribe will secure a sizable profit without need of making the price or quality of its products competitive with those of other sellers.

Bribes used to secure the sale of products by shutting out other sellers differ, of course, from bribes used for other purposes. An official may insist on being paid to perform his or her legal duties on behalf of a petitioner as when, for example, a customs officer asks for a "tip" to expedite the processing of an import permit. A government official may offer to lower a costly tariff in return for an under-the-table payment. The previous analysis would not apply to bribes of this sort, which are being used for a purpose other than to erect market barriers.

In determining the ethical nature of payments used for purposes other than to shut out other competitors from a market, the following considerations are relevant:

1. Is the offer of a payment initiated by the payer (the one who pays the money), or does the payee (the one who receives the money) demand the payment by threatening injury to the payer's interests? In the latter case, the payment is not a bribe but a form of extortion. If the threatened injury is large enough, the payer may not be morally responsible for his or her act, or the moral responsibility may at least be diminished.
2. Is the payment made to induce the payee to act in a manner that violates his or her official sworn duty to act in the best interests of the public? Or is the payment made to induce the payee to perform what is already his or her official duty? If the payee is being induced to violate his or her official duty, then the payer is cooperating in an immoral act because the payee has entered an agreement to fulfill these duties.
3. Are the nature and purpose of the payment considered ethically unobjectionable in the local culture? If a form of payment is a locally accepted public custom and there is a proportionately serious reason for making the payment (it is not intended to erect a market barrier nor to induce an official to violate his or her public duties), then it would appear to be ethically permissible on utilitarian grounds. (It might, however, constitute a legal violation of the Foreign Corrupt Practices Act of 1977.)

4.4 Oligopolies and Public Policy

It is the high degree of market concentration in oligopoly industries that places a great deal of economic power in the hands of a small number of firms and that enables them to collude, overtly or tacitly. It is not clear, however, how great this economic power is or how much it is used. Some authors have argued that the economic power held by oligopoly corporations is actually quite small and insufficient to affect society, whereas others have claimed that several social factors inhibit the use of this power. One's opinion of what, if anything, should be done about the high degree of market concentration in oligopoly industries depends largely on one's views concerning the extent and the use of oligopoly power.

The Do-Nothing View

Some economists hold that nothing should be done about the economic power held by oligopoly corporations. Some have claimed that the power of large oligopoly corporations is actually not as large as it may first appear. Several arguments have been given to support this claim. First, it is argued that, although competition within industries has declined, it has been replaced by competition between industries with substitutable products.[34] The steel industry, for example, is now in competition with the aluminum and cement industries. Consequently, although there may be a high degree of market concentration in a single industry like steel, a high level of competition is still maintained by its relation to other competing industries.

Second, as John Kenneth Galbraith once argued, the economic power of any large corporation may be balanced and restrained by the "countervailing power" of other large corporate groups in society.[35] Government and unions, for example, both restrain the power of big businesses. Although a business corporation may have a large share of an industrial market, it is faced by buyers that are equally large and equally powerful. A large steel company, for example, must sell to equally large automobile companies. This balance of power between large corporate groups, Galbraith claims, effectively reduces the economic power any one corporate giant can exert.

Other economists have very different reasons for urging that we should not worry about the economic power of large oligopoly corporations. The so-called *Chicago School* of antitrust has argued that markets are economically efficient even when there are as few as three significant rivals in a market.[36] Although government should prohibit outright price fixing and mergers that create a single-company monopoly, it should not become involved in trying to break down oligopolies that are providing consumers with products they freely choose to buy and that are, therefore, efficiently using economic resources to improve consumer welfare.[37]

Finally, yet others have argued that big is good particularly in light of the globalization of business that has taken place during recent decades. If American companies are to compete with large foreign companies, they must be able to achieve the same economies of scale that are achievable by large foreign companies. Economies of scale are reductions in the cost of producing goods that result when larger quantities of goods are produced using the same fixed resources, such as the same machines, marketing programs, group of managers, or employees. If a company can make and sell larger quantities of products, it can spread these "fixed costs" over more units, thus reducing the cost of each unit and allowing it to sell its goods at lower prices. Thus, by expanding, companies are able to reduce their prices and thus compete more effectively against similarly large foreign companies. Although research suggests that in most industries expansion beyond a certain point will not lower costs but will instead increase costs, nevertheless many people continue to urge the *big is good* argument.[38]

The Antitrust View

Other observers are less sanguine about the economic power exerted by oligopoly corporations. They argue that prices and profits in concentrated industries are higher than they should be. The solution, they argue, is to reinstate competitive pressures by forcing the large companies to divest themselves of their holdings, thereby breaking them up into smaller firms.

Clearly, the antitrust view is based on a number of assumptions. J. Fred Weston has summarized the basic propositions on which this view is based as follows:

1. If an industry is not atomistic with many small competitors, there is likely to be administrative discretion over prices.
2. Concentration results in recognized interdependence among companies, with no price competition in concentrated industries.
3. Concentration is due mostly to mergers because the most efficient scale of operation is not more than 3 to 5 percent of the industry. A high degree of concentration is unnecessary.
4. There is a positive correlation between concentration and profitability that gives evidence of monopoly power in concentrated industries—the ability to elevate prices and the persistence of high profits. Entry does not take place to eliminate excessive profits.
5. Concentration is aggravated by product differentiation and advertising. Advertising is correlated with higher profits.
6. There is oligopolistic coordination by signaling through press releases or other means.[39]

On the basis of these assumptions, proponents of the antitrust view reach the conclusion that, by breaking up large corporations into smaller units, higher levels of competition will emerge in those industries that are currently highly concentrated. The result is a decrease in explicit and tacit collusion, lower prices for consumers, greater innovation, and the increased development of cost-cutting technologies that will benefit us all.

The Regulation View

A third group of observers holds that oligopoly corporations should not be broken up because their large size has beneficial consequences that would be lost if they were forced to decentralize.[40] In particular, they argue, mass production and mass distribution of goods can be carried out only by using the highly centralized accumulation of assets and personnel that the large corporation makes possible. Moreover, the concentration of assets allows large firms to take advantage of the economies made possible by large-scale production in large plants. These savings are passed onto consumers in the form of cheaper and more plentiful products.

Although firms should not be broken up, it does not follow that they should not be regulated. According to this third view, concentration gives large firms an economic power that allows them to fix prices and engage in other forms of behavior that are not in the public interest. To ensure that consumers are not harmed by large firms, regulatory agencies and legislation should be set up to restrain and control the activities of large corporations.

Some observers, in fact, advocate that where large firms cannot be effectively controlled by the usual forms of regulation, then regulation should take the form of nationalization. That is, the government should take over the operation of firms in those industries[41] where only public ownership can ensure that firms operate in the public interest.

Other advocates of regulation, however, argue that nationalization is not in the public interest. Public ownership of firms, they claim, inevitably leads to the creation of unresponsive and inefficient bureaucracies. Moreover, publicly owned enterprises are not subject to competitive market pressures, and this results in higher prices and higher costs.

Which of these three views is correct: the do-nothing view, the antitrust view, or the regulation view? Readers will have to decide this issue for themselves because at the moment there does not appear to be sufficient evidence to answer this question unequivocably. Whichever of these three views readers may find most persuasive, it is clear that the social benefits generated by free markets cannot be secured unless the managers of firms maintain competitive market relationships among themselves. The ethical rules prohibiting collusion are meant to ensure that markets are structured competitively. These rules may be voluntarily followed or legally enforced. They are justified insofar as society is justified in pursuing the utilitarian benefits, justice, and rights to negative freedom that free competitive markets can secure.

Questions for Review and Discussion

1. Define the following concepts: perfect competition, demand curve, supply curve, equilibrium point, monopoly competition, oligopolistic competition, price fixing, manipulation of supply, tying arrangements, retail price maintenance, price discrimination, price setting, price leadership, extortion, countervailing power, do-nothing view on oligopoly power, antitrust view on oligopoly power, regulation view on oligopoly power.
2. "From an ethical point of view big business is always bad business." Discuss the pros and cons of this statement.
3. What kind of public policy do you think the United States should have with respect to business competition? Develop moral arguments to support your answer (i.e., arguments showing that the kinds of policies you favor will advance the public welfare, or secure certain important rights, or ensure certain forms of justice).
4. In your judgment, should an American company operating in a foreign country in which collusive price fixing is not illegal obey the U.S. laws against collusion? Explain your answer.

Web Resources

Readers who want to conduct research on the market issues in this chapter through the Internet might want to start with the Antitrust Organization, which provides cases, articles, and links on price fixing, mergers, vertical price restraints, and so on (http://www.antitrust.org). The Federal Trade Commission provides access to its antitrust decisions and proceedings (http://www.ftc.gov), and the Justice Department does the same (http://www.usdoj.gov). Additional links and important legal cases relating to all these issues can be found through the excellently organized and copious resources of Hieros Gamos (http://www.hg.org), or through the American Bar Association (http://www.abanet.org). The Federal Legal Research Template provides information on many legal issues including antitrust law (http://www.netrail.net/~sunburst). Yahoo provides numerous useful links about antitrust law (http://www.yahoo.com/Government/Law).

Notes

1. "Record Industry Must Pay for Charging High CD Prices," *University Wire*, Staff Editorial, August 11, 2000.
2. *Modern Healthcare*, 17 December 1990, p. 41.

3. Russell Mokhiber, "Grim Reapers," *The Washington Post*, October 1, 2000, p. 6.
4. "Vitamin Manufacturers Pay Settlement in Price-Fixing Suit," *Minneapolis Star Tribune*, October 11, 2000, p. 3D.
5. Sharen D. Knight, ed., *Concerned Investors Guide*, NYSE Volume 1983 (Arlington, VA: Resource Publishing Group, Inc., 1983), pp. 24–25.
6. Ralph Nader and Mark J. Green, "Crime in the Suites," *New Republic*, 29 April 1972, pp. 17– 21.
7. The elementary account that follows can be found in any standard economics textbook, for instance, Paul A. Samuelson, *Economics*, 11th ed. (New York: McGraw-Hill Book Company, 1980), pp. 52–62.
8. Daniel B. Suits, "Agriculture," in Walter Adams, ed., *The Structure of American Industry*, 5th ed. (New York: Macmillan Inc., 1977), pp. 1–39.
9. The reader may recall that one of the major criticisms leveled at the capitalist conception of justice is that it says people should be paid the exact value of the things they contribute, yet it gives no criterion for determining the "value" of a thing. Because different people place different values on things, this indeterminacy seems to make the capitalist conception of justice hopelessly vague: A price that is "just" in terms of the value one person places on a thing may be "unjust" in terms of the value another person places on that same thing. However, the values given to things by perfectly competitive markets are just from every participant's point of view because at the point of equilibrium all participants (both buyers and sellers) place the same value on commodities and prices converge on this uniquely just value.
10. See Robert Dorfman, *Prices and Markets*, 2nd ed. (Englewood Cliffs, NJ: Prentice-Hall, 1972), pp. 170–226.
11. Russell G. Warren, *Antitrust in Theory and Practice* (Columbus, OH: Grid, Inc., 1975), pp. 58–59.
12. Milton Friedman, *Capitalism and Freedom* (Chicago: The University of Chicago Press, 1962), p. 14.
13. Warren, *Antitrust*, pp. 76–77.
14. It has been argued, however, that a company in which caring flourishes will have a competitive economic advantage over a company in which such caring does not obtain. See Jeanne M. Liedtka, "Feminist Morality and Competitive Reality: A Role for an Ethic of Care?" *Business Ethics Quarterly*, vol. 6, no. 2 (April 1996): 179–200.
15. Again, any standard economics textbook can be consulted for these elementary ideas, for example, H. Robert Heller, *The Economic System* (New York: Macmillan Inc., 1972), p. 109.
16. See Douglas F. Greer, *Industrial Organization and Public Policy* (New York: Macmillan, Inc. 1984), pp. 189–91. Note, however, that some researchers challenge this traditional approach to the Alcoa Case; for example, Dominick T. Armentano, *Antitrust and Monopoly, Anatomy of a Policy Failure* (New York: John Wiley & Sons, Inc. 1982), pp. 100–12.
17. Of course, it is conceivable that the managers of a monopoly firm may be motivated by altruism to forgo potential profits and fix their prices at a low equilibrium level—that is, the level that just covers their costs. But we assume that, in the absence of any external regulatory agencies (such as the government), monopolists are utility

maximizers like everyone else in a market and, therefore, seek to maximize their profits.

18. See Samuelson, *Economics*, pp. 462–63, 481–84.

19. See George J. Stigler, "Monopoly and Oligopoly by Merger," *The American Economic Review* 40 (Proceedings of the American Economic Association, 1950): 23–34.

20. Warren, *Antitrust,* p. 271.

21. The numerous studies confirming this relationship are surveyed in Douglas F. Greer, *Industrial Organization and Public Policy*, 2nd ed. (New York: Macmillan, Inc. 1984), pp. 407–14; Greer also critically evaluates the few studies that seem to show no such relationship.

22. Greer, *Industrial Organization*, pp. 416–17.

23. "Paper Companies Get Heavy Fines for Price-Fixing," *Wall Street Journal*, 21 September 1978, p. 2. For an analysis of price fixing, see Jeffrey Sonnenfeld and Paul R. Lawrence, "Why Do Companies Succumb to Price-Fixing?" *Harvard Business Review*, vol. 56, no. 4 (July–August 1978): 145–57.

24. Almarin Phillips, *Market Structure, Organization, and Performance* (Cambridge: Harvard University Press, 1962), pp. 138–60.

25. Warren, *Antitrust*, pp. 233–35.

26. Newman S. Peery, Jr., *Business, Government, & Society: Managing Competitiveness, Ethics, and Social Issues* (Englewood Cliffs, NJ: Prentice-Hall, 1995), pp. 400–401.

27. *Ibid.*, pp. 218–19.

28. *Ibid.*, pp. 161–62.

29. Jeffrey Sonnenfeld and Paul R. Lawrence, "Why Do Companies Succumb to Price-Fixing?" in Kenneth R. Andrews, ed., *Ethics in Practice* (Boston, MA: Harvard Business School Press, 1989), pp. 71–83.

30. *Ibid.*, p. 75.

31. Jesse W. Markham, "The Nature and Significance of Price Leadership," *The American Economic Review*, vol. 41 (1951): 891–905.

32. Willard F. Mueller, "Conglomerates: A Nonindustry," [pp. 442–81]in Adams, ed., *The Structure of American Industry*, p. 459.

33. Neil H. Jacoby, Peter Nehemkis, and Richard Eells, *Bribery and Extortion in World Business* (New York: Macmillan Inc., 1977), p. 183.

34. See J. M. Clarm, "Toward a Concept of Workable Competition," *American Economic Review*, vol. 30 (1940): 241–56.

35. John Kenneth Galbraith, *American Capitalism: The Concept of Countervailing Power*, rev. ed. (Cambridge, MA: The Riverside Press, 1956), pp. 112–13.

36. Robert H. Bork, *The Antitrust Paradox: A Policy at War with Itself* (New York: Basic Books, 1978), pp. 20–58, 405.

37. Richard Posner, "The Chicago School of Antitrust Analysis," *University of Pennsylvania Law Review*, vol. 925 (1979).

38. See the summary of the research on the claim that size and efficiency are correlated in Douglas F. Greer, *Business, Government, and Society*, 3rd ed. (New York: Macmillan Publishing Company, 1993), pp. 175–78.

39. J. Fred Weston, "Big Corporations: The Arguments For and Against Breaking Them Up," *Business and Its Changing Environment*, proceedings of a conference held by the Graduate School of Management at UCLA, July 24–August 3, 1977, pp. 232–33; see also John M. Blair, *Economic Concentration: Structure, Behavior, and Public Policy* (New York: Harcourt Brace Jovanovich, 1972).
40. J. A. Schumpeter, *Capitalism, Socialism, and Democracy* (New York: Harper, 1943), pp. 79 ff.
41. L. Von Mises, *Planned Chaos* (New York: Foundations for Economic Education, 1947).

CASES FOR DISCUSSION

Playing Monopoly: Microsoft

On November 5, 1999, Bill Gates, then the richest man in the world, learned that a federal judge had just issued "findings of fact" declaring that his company, Microsoft, "enjoys monopoly power," and that it had used its monopoly power to "harm consumers" and crush competitors to maintain its monopoly. On the day the judgment was issued, Microsoft stock began its decline. Five months later, on April 3, 2000, the same judge, Thomas Penfield Jackson, issued a second verdict, concluding on the basis of the findings of fact that Microsoft had violated antitrust law and was subject to the penalties allowed by the law. The price of Microsoft stock plunged, bringing the entire stock market down with it. Two short months later, on June 7, 2000, Judge Jackson ordered that Microsoft should be broken up into two separate companies—one devoted to operating systems and the other to applications such as word processing, spreadsheets, and web browsers. With the price of Microsoft stock now skidding, Gates, who was no longer the richest man in the world, vowed that Microsoft would appeal this verdict and would never be broken apart.[1]

Bill Gates was born in 1955 in Bremerton, Washington. When he was 13 years old, his grammar school acquired a computer terminal, and by the end of the year he had written his first software program (for playing tic-tac-toe). During high school, he held a few entry-level programming jobs, and when he finished high school, he set up his first company, named "Traf-O-Data." Traf-O-Data sold a computer that used the new Intel 8008 microprocessor to count cars being driven past a fixed point. Gates enrolled in Harvard University in 1974, but quickly lost interest in classes and quit to start a software business in Albuquerque, New Mexico, with a friend, Paul Allen, whom he had known since grammar school in Seattle. At the time, the first small but primitive personal computers were being manufactured as kits for hobbyists by small engineering companies. These computers, like the Altair 8080 computer (which used Intel's new 8080 microprocessor, had no keyboard, no screen, and only 256 bytes of memory), had no accompanying software and were extremely difficult to program because they had to use "machine code" (consisting entirely of sequences of zeros and ones) that is virtually incomprehensible to humans. Gates and Allen together revised a program called BASIC (Beginner's All-purpose Symbolic Instruction Code, a program written several years earlier by two engineers who gave it away for free), which allowed users to write their own programs using an understandable set of English instructions, and they adapted it so that it would work on the Altair 8080. They sold the adaptation to the maker of the Altair 8080 for $3000.

In 1977, Apple Computer marketed the first personal computer (PC) aimed at consumers, and by 1978, more than 300 dealers were selling the "Apple II." That year, Gates and Allen began writing software for the Apple II, renamed their company *Microsoft*, and moved it to Seattle, where, with 13 employees, it ended the year with revenues of $1.4 million. In 1979, two hobbyists developed VisiCalc, the first spreadsheet program, for the Apple II, and Microsoft developed "MS Word," a rudimentary word processor for the Apple II. With these new software "applications," sales of the Apple II took off and the personal computer market was born. By 1980, Microsoft's revenues had reached $8 million.

1980 was the year that IBM belatedly decided to enter the rapidly growing market for personal computers. By now many other companies had flocked into the PC market, including Radio Shack, Commodore, COMPAQ, AT&T, Xerox, DEC, Data General, and Wang. By 1984, some 350 companies around the world would be making PCs. Because IBM needed to enter the market quickly, it decided to assemble its computer from components that were already available on the market. A key component that IBM needed for its computer was an operating system. An operating system is the software that allows "application" programs (like a word processor, spread sheet, browser, or game) to run on a particular machine. Every computer must have an operating system or it cannot run any application programs. The operating system coordinates the various components of the computer (keyboard inputs, monitor, printer, ports, etc.) and contains the "applications programming interface" (API), which consists of the codes that applications use to "command" the computer to carry out its functions. Applications programs are written so that they will run on a specific operating system by making use of that operating system's API to make the computer carry out the program's commands, and a program written for one operating system will not work on another operating system. Most of the companies making PCs had developed their own operating systems, although several made use of one called *CP/M*, which was written to work on many different computers. Applications developed to run on CP/M could run on any computer using CP/M. This meant that an application did not have to be rewritten for each different kind of computer, but could be written once for CP/M and would then run on any computer using CP/M.

IBM needed an operating system quickly and approached the maker of CP/M for a license to use CP/M, but was turned down. The somewhat desperate IBM representatives then met with Bill Gates to ask whether Microsoft had one available. Although Microsoft at the time did not own an operating system, Bill Gates told IBM that he could provide one to them. Immediately after the IBM meeting, Bill Gates went to a friend who, he knew, had written an operating system that was a "knock-off of CP/M" and that could work on the computer IBM was planning. Without telling his friend about the meeting with IBM, Gates offered to buy his friend's operating system for $60,000. The friend agreed. After some tweaking, Microsoft licensed the system to IBM as *MS-DOS*, with the proviso that Microsoft could also license MS-DOS to other computer manufacturers. When IBM started mass producing its personal computer in 1981 (IBM's share of the market went from nothing in 1981, to 10 percent in 1983, and 40 percent in 1987) and other computer makers began producing copies of IBM's computer, MS-DOS became the standard operating system for personal computers built according to IBM's standards. Bill Gates' company was on its way to becoming a billion dollar firm.

Because an application program has to be written to work on a specific operating system, and because so many personal computers were now using MS-DOS, software companies were much more willing to produce programs for the large market of MS-DOS users than for the much smaller numbers of people using competing operating systems. Thousands of new software programs were developed for MS-DOS—including Microsoft's own spreadsheet, "Multiplan," and its word processor, "MS Word"—initiating what some have called a *virtuous circle*. In this virtuous circle, the more people that use an operating system, the more that software companies are willing to write programs for that operating system. The more software programs they write for the operating system, the more people want to buy that operating system. Because of this virtuous circle or "network effect," the proportion of computers using MS-DOS gradually increased, and the proportion of computers using other operating systems (such as CP/M, Apple computer's, or Atari's or Commodore's) gradually declined.

However, in 1984, Apple Computer developed an innovative new operating system for its own computers that used intuitive graphics or pictures that let users issue commands to the computer by selecting icons and pull-down menus on the screen using a mouse. The new operating system was tremendously popular, and Apple sales began to climb. In 1987, however, Microsoft began selling *Windows*, a new operating system for IBM-compatible computers that copied Apple's operating system. Unlike MS-DOS, which had used obscure combinations of characters to issue commands to the computer, Windows used graphics that were similar to Apple's, had virtually the same pull-down menus and icons, and the same usage of the same mouse. Apple sued Microsoft on the grounds that, in copying the "look and feel" of their operating system, Microsoft had stolen a key piece of their copyrighted property. Apple lost the suit and, with the loss of its key software advantage, its market share whithered away.

The early versions of Windows still required that MS-DOS be loaded onto the computer, but in 1995 Microsoft issued Widows 95, which was a stand-alone operating system that dispensed with MS-DOS. In 1998, Microsoft issued Windows 98, and in 2000 it issued its Millennium version of Windows. By the end of the century, Microsoft controlled 90 percent of the personal computer operating system market—a virtual monopoly—and Bill Gates was fabulously rich.

In the early 1990s, however, two threats to Microsoft's monopoly had emerged.[2] One was Netscape, an Internet "browser," and the other was Java, a programming language. The Internet is a network through which digital information, pictures, sounds, text, and other digital data can be sent from one computer to another. To make these data usable, a user's computer must be connected to the Internet and must have a software program called a *browser*. The "browser" takes the digital data that come through the Internet and transforms them into an intelligible picture or text that can be displayed on the user's computer screen or into a sound that can be played on the computer's speakers. However, a browser is not only capable of displaying digital data that come over the Internet; it can also execute the instructions of software programs, whether those programs are sent over the Internet or reside in the user's own computer. In this respect, a browser functions much like an operating system. Some people predicted that someday every computer might rely on a browser instead of an operating system to run software programs. Although the browser would still need some rudimentary operating system to run, this operating system did not have to be Windows. Windows could become obsolete. Netscape, a company that began selling a browser named *Navigator* on December 15, 1994, quickly captured 70 percent of the browser market. In May 1995, Bill Gates wrote an internal memo to his executives warning:

> A new competitor "born" on the Internet is Netscape. Their browser is dominant, with a 70% usage share, allowing them to determine which network extensions will catch on. They are pursuing a multi-platform strategy where they move the key API [applications programming interface] into the client to commoditize the underlying operating system.

In addition to the browser threat, Microsoft was also worried about Java, a programming language that Sun Microsystems, a manufacturer of computer hardware and software, had developed in May 1995. Programs that are written in the Java language can operate on any computer equipped with the Java software, regardless of the operating system the computer used. In this respect, Java software also functioned like an operating system and also threatened to make Windows obsolete. In an internal memo, a Microsoft senior executive stated that Java was "our major threat," and in September 1996, Bill Gates wrote an e-mail saying, "This scares the hell out of me," and asked managers to make it a top priority to neutralize Java.

To make matters worse, Java and Netscape joined forces. Netscape agreed to incorporate the Java software into its Navigator browser so that any programs written in Java would work on a computer that was using Netscape. This meant that short programs written in Java could be sent over the Internet and then run on the user's computer through its Netscape browser. This also meant that Java programs did not need Windows, but could run on any computer using any operating system so long as it was also using Netscape's Navigator browser. Because Java was now being distributed together with Netscape, the number of computers equipped with Java rapidly multiplied. A Microsoft executive fearfully wrote in a memo that Netscape's browser had become the "major distribution vehicle" for Java.

According to the "findings of fact" accepted by the judge presiding over the Microsoft antitrust trial, Microsoft quickly embarked on a campaign to undercut the threat that Netscape now posed to its monopoly. First, a team of Microsoft executives met with Netscape's executives in June 1995. Microsoft's people proposed that Microsoft should provide the browser for Windows computers while Netscape should provide browsers for all other computers—essentially the 10 percent of computers that ran on Apple's operating system, on OS/2, or on other relatively minor operating systems. A memo written the next day by a Microsoft executive who was present stated that a goal of the meeting was to "establish Microsoft ownership of the Internet client platform for Win95." Netscape refused to go along with this plan to divide the browser market. Microsoft then refused to share with them the codes for Windows 95 so that Netscape would be unable to develop a browser for Windows 95. Netscape had to wait several months after Windows 95 was released before it finally got hold of its codes and was finally able to develop a new version of Navigator that would take advantage of the Windows 95 applications interface.

Microsoft also developed its own browser by borrowing a browser program it had earlier licensed from Spyglass Inc, naming it *Internet Explorer*, and copying many of Netscape's features onto it. (The chairman of Spyglass later complained that "whenever you license technology to Microsoft, you have to understand it can someday build it itself, drop it into the operating system, and put you out of that business.") Unfortunately, when Microsoft tried to sell its browser in 1995, users felt it was inferior to Netscape and sales lagged.

Microsoft continued working on its browser, and its fourth version, "Internet Explorer 4.0," released in late 1997, finally began to be compared favorably to Netscape's browser. Still, few people were buying Internet Explorer. Microsoft then decided to use its operating system monopoly to undercut Netscape. In February 1997, Christian Wildfeuer, a Microsoft executive, suggested in an internal memo that it would "be very hard to increase browser share on the merits of Internet Explorer 4 alone. It will be more important to leverage our Operating System asset to make people use Internet Explorer instead of Netscape's Navigator." If Internet Explorer was bundled together with Windows, so that when Windows was installed on a computer Internet Explorer was also automatically installed, then users would tend to use Internet Explorer rather than go through the expense and trouble of purchasing and installing Netscape. Accordingly, Microsoft incorporated a copy of Internet Explorer into Windows 95 that automatically installed itself when Windows was installed. Windows 98 went farther by integrating Internet Explorer into the operating system so that it was extremely difficult for a user even to remove Internet Explorer. Moreover, when a user "uninstalled" Internet Explorer, it stayed in the computer and still appeared when Windows 98 was running certain commands. Although this integration made Windows 98 run more slowly and consumed resources on the user's computer, it also made it much more ifficult and risky for users to try to replace Internet Explorer with Netscape Navigator.

Microsoft did more than make users accept Internet Explorer when they purchased Windows. According to the court's "findings of fact," Microsoft required any computer maker that wanted Windows on its computers to agree that it would not remove Windows Explorer and would not promote Netscape's browser. If a computer maker also agreed to not even give its customers a copy of Netscape, Microsoft discounted the price of Windows. Because Microsoft's monopoly meant that computer manufacturers either had to install Windows on their computers or make them virtually useless, manufacturers had no choice but to sign the agreements that shut Netscape out of the market. Although users were still able to buy a copy of Netscape from a retailer, the number of users doing this declined. Not only would purchasing a copy of Netscape require paying extra for software that would do much of what their installed Internet Explorer could already do, but it also required that they perform the tricky task of removing Internet Explorer from their computers and installing Netscape in its place. Not surprisingly, Netscape's share of the market rapidly dropped, and Internet Explorer's rapidly rose—a successful outcome of Wildfeuer's strategy "to leverage our Operating System asset to make people use Internet Explorer instead of Navigator."

Microsoft dealt with its Java threat by asking Sun Microsystems for the right to license and distribute Java with its Windows system. Sun Microsystems gave Microsoft that right, not knowing that Microsoft was planning to change

Java. The version of Java that Microsoft distributed was a version that incorporated several changes that would no longer allow regular Java programs to run on computers using Microsoft's Java. Thus, there were now two versions of Java, and the version that most users were getting installed with their Windows computers was a version that was incompatible with the regular version of Java and that Microsoft now owned. Microsoft had apparently planned this move because an earlier internal Microsoft document stated that it was a "strategic objective" for Microsoft to "kill cross-platform Java" by expanding the "polluted Java market"—a reference to Microsoft's own "polluted" version of Java. Because all Windows-based computers now incorporated a copy of Microsoft's Java, developers began to write programs for Microsoft's Java, not Sun's. Microsoft encouraged these developers by offering them special technical support and other inducements. In effect, Microsoft had turned Java into a part of Windows so that there was now little threat that Windows would be rendered obsolete by Java.

But on May 18, 1998, the U.S. Department of Justice (DOJ) filed an antitrust suit against Microsoft in Judge Jackson's court, claiming that the company had violated the Sherman Antitrust Act by engaging in "a pattern of anticompetitive practices designed to thwart browser competition on the merits, to deprive customers of choice between alternative browsers, and to exclude Microsoft's Internet browser competitors," especially Netscape and Java.[3] The DOJ claimed that Microsoft had violated the antitrust act in four ways: (a) Microsoft had forced computer companies that used its Windows operating system to sign agreements that they would not license, distribute, or promote software products that competed with Microsoft's own software products; (b) Microsoft "tied" its own browser, "Internet Explorer," to its Windows operating system so that customers who purchased Windows also had to get Internet Explorer, although these were separate products and tying the two products together degraded the performance of Windows; (c) Microsoft had attempted to gain a monopoly in the Internet browser market by forcing computer companies that used its Windows operating system to agree to leave Internet Explorer as the default browser and to not preinstall or promote the browser of any other company; and (d) Microsoft had a monopoly in the market for PC operating systems and had used anticompetitive and predatory tactics to maintain its monopoly power.

On June 7, 2000, Judge Jackson found Microsoft guilty of Counts b, c and d, and ordered that the company be broken up into two separate companies—one to develop and market operating systems and the other to develop and market all other Microsoft programs. Although the judge could have simply ordered Microsoft to cease engaging in the illegal practices, he feared that policing such an order would require so much government oversight that it was simply not practical. The judge also ruled that the two new companies would not be allowed to share any technical information with each other that they did not share with all their other customers. Nor could Microsoft punish or threaten any computer manufacturers for distributing or promoting the products or services of its competitors. Finally, Judge Jackson ordered that Microsoft had to let computer manufacturers remove any Microsoft applications from its Windows operating system.[4] The Judge ruled, however, that Microsoft would not have to implement his orders until it had time to appeal his decision.

In a defensive "white paper," Microsoft stated:

> Antitrust policy seeks to promote low prices, high output, and rapid innovaton. On all three measures, the personal computer software industry generally—and Microsoft in particular—is a model of competitiveness. . . . Market share numbers do not reflect the highly dynamic nature of the software industry, where entire business segments can disappear virtually overnight as new technologies are developed.

Microsoft claimed that it was responsible for much of the innovation that characterized the software industry. In addition, it claimed that its actions, including its decision to give Internet Exporer away for free with Windows and its decision to "improve" Java by changing it, were all done to help consumers and give them more value for their money.

QUESTIONS

1. Identify the behaviors that you think are ethically questionable in the history of Microsoft. Evaluate the ethics of these behaviors.
2. What characteristics of the software industry do you think created the monopoly market that Microsoft's operating system enjoyed? Evaluate this market in terms of utilitarianism, rights, and justice (your analysis should make use of the textbook's discussion of the effects of monopoly markets on the utility of participants in the market, on the moral rights of participants in the market, and on the distribution of benefits and burdens among participants in the market), giving explicit examples from the software industry to illustrate your points.
3. In your view, should the government have sued Microsoft for violation of the antitrust laws? In your view, was the final "penalty" of Judge Jackson fair to Microsoft? Explain your answers.
4. Who, if anyone, is harmed by the kind of market that Microsoft's operating system enjoyed? Explain your answer. What kind of public policies, if any, should we have to deal with industries like the operating system industry?

Notes

1. This and the following information is based on Sandy McMurray, "Why Microsoft Lost in Court," *The Toronto Sun*, June 14, 2000, p. 73; Jared Sandberg, "Bill's Many Trials," *Newsweek*, April 17, 2000, p. 48; Eun-Kyung Kim, "Judge Rules Against Microsoft," *Associated Press*, April 3, 2000; David Lawsky, "Judge Finds Microsoft Broke Antitrust Law," *Reuters*, April 3, 2000; James V. Grimaldi, "Judge Says Microsoft Broke Antitrust Law," *Washingon Post*, p. 1. For histories of Microsoft in particular and the software industry in general, see James Wallace and Jim Erickson, *Hard Drive: Bill Gates and the Making of the Microsoft Empire* (New York: Harper Collins, 1992); Michael A. Cusumano and Richard W. Selby, *Microsoft Secrets: How the Worlds' Most Powerful Company Creates Technology, Shapes Markets, and Manages People* (New York: Free Press, 1995); H. W. Brands, *Masters of Enterprise* (New York: The Free Press, 1999).
2. This and the following paragraphs are based on Thomas Penfield Jackson, United States District Court for the District of Columbia, "Findings of Fact," in *United States of America v. Microsoft Corporation*, Civil Action No. 98–1232; posted on November 8, 1999 at http://www.seattletimes.com/microsoft/ruling.html.
3. *United States of America v. Microsoft Corporation*, Civil Action No. 98–1232, Complaint filed in the United States District Court for the District of Columbia, May 18, 1998; posted at http://www.usdoj.gov/atr.
4. "Excerpts From Judge's Order," *Associated Press Online*, June 7, 2000.

A Japanese Bribe

In July 1976, Kukeo Tanaka, former prime minister of Japan, was arrested on charges of taking bribes ($1.8 million) from Lockheed Aircraft Company to secure the purchase of several Lockheed jets. Tanaka's secretary and several other government officials were arrested with him. The Japanese public reacted with angry demands for a complete disclosure of Tanaka's dealings. By the end of the year, they had ousted Tanaka's successor, Takeo Miki, who was widely believed to have been trying to conceal Tanaka's actions.

In Holland that same year, Prince Bernhard, husband of Queen Juliana, resigned from 300 hundred positions he held in government, military, and private organizations. The reason: He was alleged to have accepted $1.1 million in bribes from Lockheed in connection with the sale of 138 F-104 Starfighter jets.

In Italy, Giovani Leone, president in 1970, and Aldo Moro and Mariano Rumor, both prime ministers, were accused of accepting bribes from Lockheed in connection with the purchase of $100 million worth of aircraft in the late 1960s. All were excluded from government.

Scandinavia, South Africa, Turkey, Greece, and Nigeria were also among the 15 countries in which Lockheed admitted to having handed out payments and at least $202 million in *commissions* since 1970.

Lockheed Aircraft's involvement in the Japanese bribes was revealed to have begun in 1958 when Lockheed and Grumman Aircraft (also an American firm) were competing for a Japanese Air Force jet aircraft contract. According to the testimony of Mr. William Findley, a partner in Arthur Young & Co. (auditors for Lockheed), in 1958 Lockheed engaged the services of Yoshio Kodama, an ultra right-wing war criminal and reputed underworld figure with strong political ties to officials in the ruling Liberal Democratic Party. With Kodama's help, Lockheed secured the government contract. Seventeen years later, it was revealed that the CIA had been informed at the time (by an American embassy employee) that Lockheed had made several bribes while negotiating the contract.[1]

In 1972, Lockheed again hired Kodama as a consultant to help secure the sale of its aircraft in Japan. Lockheed was desperate to sell planes to any major Japanese airline because it was scrambling to recover from a series of financial disasters. Cost overruns on a government contract had pushed Lockheed to the brink of bankruptcy in 1970. Only through a controversial emergency government loan guarantee of $250 million in 1971 did the company narrowly avert disaster. Mr. A. Carl Kotchian, president of Lockheed from 1967 to 1975, was especially anxious to make the sales because the company had been unable to get as many contracts in other parts of the world as it had wanted.

> This bleak situation all but dictated a strong push for sales in the biggest untapped market left-Japan. This push, if successful, might well bring in revenues upwards of $400 million. Such a cash inflow would go a long way towards helping to restore Lockheed's fiscal health, and it would, of course, save the jobs of thousands of the firm's employees. [Statement of Carl Kotchian][2]

Kodama eventually succeeded in engineering a contract for Lockheed with All-Nippon Airways, even beating out McDonnell Douglas, which was actively competing with Lockheed for the same sales. To ensure the sale, Kodama asked for and received from Lockheed about $9 million during the period from 1972 to 1975. Much of the money allegedly went to then-prime minister Kukeo Tanaka and other government officials, who were supposed to intercede with All-Nippon Airlines on behalf of Lockheed.

According to Mr. Carl Kotchian, "I knew from the beginning that this money was going to the office of the prime minister."[3] He was, however, persuaded that, by paying the money, he was sure to get the contract from All-Nippon Airways. The negotiations eventually netted over $1.3 billion in contracts for Lockheed.

In addition to Kodama, Lockheed had also been advised by Toshiharu Okubo, an official of the private trading company, Marubeni, which acted as

Lockheed's official representative. Mr. A. Carl Kotchian later defended the payments, which he saw as one of many "Japanese business practices" that he had accepted on the advice of his local consultants. The payments, the company was convinced, were in keeping with local "business practices."[4]

> Further, as I've noted, such disbursements did not violate American laws. I should also like to stress that my decision to make such payments stemmed from my judgment that the (contracts) . . . would provide Lockheed workers with jobs and thus redound to the benefit of their dependents, their communities, and stockholders of the corporation. I should like to emphasize that the payments to the so-called "high Japanese government officials" were all requested by Okubo and were not brought up from my side. When he told me "five hundred million yen is necessary for such sales," from a purely ethical and moral standpoint I would have declined such a request. However, in that case, I would most certainly have sacrificed commercial success. . . . [If] Lockheed had not remained competitive by the rules of the game as then played, we would not have sold [our planes]. . . . I knew that if we wanted our product to have a chance to win on its own merits, we had to follow the functioning system. [Statement of A. Carl Kotchian][5]

In August 1975, investigations by the U.S. government led Lockheed to admit it had made $22 million in secret payoffs.[6] Subsequent Senate investigations in February 1976 made Lockheed's involvement with Japanese government officials public.[7] Japan subsequently canceled their billion dollar contract with Lockheed.

In June 1979, Lockheed pleaded guilty to concealing the Japanese bribes from the government by falsely writing them off as "marketing costs."[8] The Internal Revenue Code states, in part, "No deduction shall be allowed . . . for any payment made, directly or indirectly, to an official or employee of any government . . . if the payment constitutes an illegal bribe or kickback."[9] Lockheed was not charged specifically with bribery because the U.S. law forbidding bribery was not enacted until 1978. Lockheed pleaded guilty to four counts of fraud and four counts of making false statements to the government. Mr. Kotchian was not indicted, but under pressure from the board of directors, he was forced to resign from Lockheed. In Japan, Kodama was arrested along with Tanaka.

QUESTIONS

1. Fully explain the effects that payments like those which Lockheed made to the Japanese have on the structure of a market.

2. In your view, were Lockheed's payments to the various Japanese parties "bribes" or "extortions"? Explain your response fully.
3. In your judgment, did Mr. A. Carl Kotchian act rightly from a moral point of view? (Your answer should take into account the effects of the payments on the welfare of the societies affected, on the rights and duties of the various parties involved, and on the distribution of benefits and burdens among the groups involved.) In your judgment, was Mr. Kotchian morally responsible for his actions? Was he, in the end, treated fairly?
4. In its October 27, 1980, issue, *Business Week* argued that every corporation has a corporate culture—that is, values that set a pattern for its employees' activities, opinions, and actions and that are instilled in succeeding generations of employees (pp. 148–60). Describe, if you can, the corporate culture of Lockheed and relate that culture to Mr. Kotchian's actions. Describe some strategies for changing that culture in ways that might make foreign payments less likely.

Notes

1. James Post, *Corporate Behavior and Social Change* (Reston, VA: Reston Publishing Co., 1978), p. 207.
2. A. Carl Kotchian, "The Payoff: Lockheed's 70–Day Mission to Tokyo," *Saturday Review*, 9 July 1977, p. 8.
3. *Ibid.*
4. "Lockheed Says It Paid $22 Million to Get Contracts," *Wall Street Journal*, 4 August 1975.
5. Kotchian, "The Payoff," p. 12.
6. *Wall Street Journal*, op. cit.
7. "Payoffs: The Growing Scandal," *Newsweek*, 23 February 1976.
8. "Lockheed Pleads Guilty to Making Secret Payoffs," *San Francisco Chronicle*, 2 June 1979.
9. *Internal Revenue Code 1975*, Section 162C.

PART THREE

Business and Its External Exchanges

Ecology and Consumers

The process of producing goods forces businesses to engage in exchanges and interactions with two main external environments: the natural environment and a consumer environment. It is from the natural environment that business ultimately draws the raw materials that it transforms into its finished products. These finished products are then externally promoted and sold to consumers. Thus, the natural environment provides the raw material input of business, whereas the consumer environment absorbs its finished output.

The next two chapters explore the ethical issues raised by these exchanges and interactions. Chapter 5 discusses the two basic problems related to the natural environment: pollution and resource depletion. Chapter 6 discusses several consumer issues, including product quality and advertising.

5

Ethics and the Environment

Introduction

Modern industry has provided us with a material prosperity unequaled in our history. It has also created unparalleled environmental threats to ourselves and to future generations. The very technology that has enabled us to manipulate and control nature has also polluted our environment and rapidly depleted our natural resources. Each year more than 150 million tons of pollutants are pumped into the air we breathe, more than 41 million tons of toxic wastes are produced, and 15 million gallons of pollutants are dumped into the nation's waterways. The total energy consumption of the United States each year is equivalent to about 2,134,960,000 tons of oil.[1] Each U.S. citizen annually accounts for the consumption of more than 1300 pounds of metal and 18,500 pounds of other minerals, and each produces over four pounds of garbage every day of the year.

Although the nation has made significant progress in controlling certain types of pollution and in conserving energy, significant environmental problems still remain, especially at an international level. In its year 2000 report, the Worldwatch Institute, a highly respected research group, concluded:

> As the twenty-first century begins, several well-established environmental trends are shaping the future of civilization. This [includes]: population growth, rising temperature, falling water tables, shrinking cropland per person, collapsing fisheries, shrinking forests, and the loss of plant and animal species.
>
> Between 1950 and 2000, world population increased from 2.5 billion to 6.1 billion, a gain of 3.6 billion. And even though birth rates have fallen in most of the

world, recent projections show that population is projected to grow to 8.9 billion by 2050, a gain of 2.8 billion. . . . [V]irtually all future growth will occur in the developing world, where countries are already overpopulated. . . . Our numbers continue to expand, but Earth's natural systems do not. The amount of fresh water produced by the hydrological cycle is essentially the same today as it was in 1950 and as it is likely to be in 2050. So, too, is the sustainable yield of oceanic fisheries, of forests, and of rangelands. . . .

A second trend that is affecting the entire world is the rise in temperature that results from increasing atmospheric concentrations of carbon dioxide (CO_2). . . . The average global temperature for 1969–71 was 13.99 degrees celsius. By 1996–98, it was 14.43 degrees, a gain of 0.44 celsius (0.8 degrees Fahrenheit). . . . If CO_2 concentrations double pre-industrial levels during this century, as projected, global temperature is likely to rise by at least 1 degree Celsius and perhaps as much as 4 degrees (2–7 degrees Fahrenheit). Meanwhile, sea level is projected ro rise from a minimum of 17 centimeters to as much as 1 meter by 2100. . . . This will alter every ecosystem on Earth. Already, coral reefs are being affected in nearly all the world's oceans. . . . For example, record sea surface temperatures over the last two years may have wiped out 70 percent of the coral in the Indian Ocean.

The modest temperature rise in recent decades is melting ice caps and glaciers. Ice cover is shrinking in the Arctic, the Antarctic, Alaska, Greenland, the Alps, the Andes, and the Quinghai-Tibetan Plateau. A team of U.S. and British scientists reported in mid-1999 that the two ice shelves on either side of the Antarctic peninsula are in full retreat. Over roughly a half-century through 1997, they lost 7,000 square kilometers. But then within a year or so they lost 3,000 square kilometers. The scientists attribute the accelerated ice melting to a regional rise in average temperature of some 2.5 degrees Celsius since 1940.

One of the least visible trends that is shaping our future is falling water tables. . . . According to Sandra Postel of the Global Water Policy Project, overpumping of aquifers in China, India, North Africa, Saudi Arabia, and the United States exceeds 160 billion tons of water per year. Since it takes roughly 1,000 tons of water to produce 1 ton of grain, this is the equivalent of 160 million tons of grain, or half the U.S. grain harvest. In consumption terms, the food supply of 480 million of the world's 6 billion people is being produced with the unsustainable use of water.

Also making it more difficult to feed the projected growth in population adequately over the next few decades is the worldwide shrinkage in cropland per person. Since the mid-twentieth century, grainland area per person has fallen in half, from 0.24 hectares to 0.12 hectares. If the world grain area remains more or less constant over the next half century . . . the area per person will shrink to 0.08 hectares by 2050. . . .

Humanity also depends heavily on the oceans for food. . . . From 1950 until 1997, the oceanic fish catch expanded form 19 million tons to more than 90 million tons. . . . If, as most marine biologists believe, the oceans cannot sustain an annual catch of ore than 95 million tons, the catch per person will decline steadily in the decades ahead as world population continues to grow.

These three parallel trends—falling water tables, shrinking cropland area per person, and the leveling off of the oceanic fish catch—all suggest that it will be far more difficult to keep up with the growth in world demand for food over the next half century. . . .

> Forests, too, are being overwhelmed by human demands. Over the past half-century, the world's forested area has shrunk substantially, with much of the loss occurring in developing countries. And the forested area per person worldwide is projected to shrink from 0.56 hectares today to 0.38 hectares in 2050. . . . In many situations, the rising worldwide demand for forest products—lumber, paper, and fuelwood—is already overwhelming the sustainable yield of forests.
>
> In some ways, the trend that will most affect the human prospect is an irreversible one—the accelerating extinction of plant and animal species. The share of birds, mammals, and fish vulnerable or in immediate danger of extinction is now measured in double digits: 11 percent of the world's 8615 bird species, 25 percent of the world's 4355 mammal species, and an estimated 34 percent of all fish species. The leading cause of species loss is habitat destruction, but habitat alterations from rising temperatures or pollution can also decimate both plant and animal species. . . . As more and more species disappear, local ecosystems begin to collapse; at some point, we will face wholesale ecosystem collapse.[2]

So intractable and difficult are the problems raised by these environmental threats that many observers believe that they cannot be solved. For example, William Pollard, a physicist, despairs of our being able to deal adequately with these problems:

> My own view is that [mankind] will not do so until he has suffered greatly and much that he now relies upon has been destroyed. As the earth in a short few decades becomes twice as crowded with human beings as it is now, and as human societies are confronted with dwindling resources in the midst of mounting accumulations of wastes, and a steadily deteriorating environment, we can only foresee social paroxysms of an intensity greater than any we have so far known. The problems are so varied and so vast and the means for their solutions so far beyond the resources of the scientific and technological know-how on which we have relied that there simply is not time to avoid the impending catastrophe. We stand, therefore, on the threshold of a time of judgment more severe, undoubtedly, than any mankind has ever faced before in history.[3]

Environmental issues, then, raise large and complicated ethical and technological questions for our business society. What is the extent of the environmental damage produced by present and projected industrial technology? How large a threat does this damage pose to our welfare? What values must we give up to halt or slow such damage? Whose rights are violated by pollution and who should be given the responsibility of paying for the costs of polluting the environment? How long will our natural resources last? What obligations do firms have to future generations to preserve the environment and conserve our resources?

This chapter explores these environmental issues. It begins with an overview of various technical aspects of environmental resource use. This is followed by a discussion of the ethical basis of environment protection. The final sections discuss two controversial issues: our obligations to future generations and the prospects for continued economic growth.

5.1 The Dimensions Of Pollution and Resource Depletion

Environmental damage inevitably threatens the welfare of human beings as well as plants and animals. Threats to the environment come from two sources: pollution and resource depletion. *Pollution* refers to the undesirable and unintended contamination of the environment by the manufacture or use of commodities. *Resource depletion* refers to the consumption of finite or scarce resources. In a certain sense, pollution is really a type of resource depletion because contamination of air, water, or land diminishes their beneficial qualities. But for purposes of discussion, we keep the two issues distinct.

Air Pollution

Air pollution is not new—it has been with us since the Industrial Revolution introduced the world to the belching factory smokestack. However, the costs of air pollution increased exponentially as industrialization expanded. Today, air pollutants affect vegetation, decreasing agricultural yields and inflicting losses on the timber industry; they deteriorate exposed construction materials through corrosion, discoloration, and rot; they are hazardous to health and life, raising medical costs and lessening the enjoyment of living; and they threaten catastrophic global damage in the form of global warming and destruction of the stratospheric ozone layer.[4]

Global Warming Greenhouse gases—carbon dioxide, nitrous oxide, methane, and chlorofluorocarbons—are gases that absorb and hold heat from the sun, preventing it from escaping back into space, much like a greenhouse absorbs and holds the sun's heat. Greenhouse gases occur naturally in the atmosphere where they have kept the earth's temperature about 33°C warmer than it would otherwise be, enabling life as we know it to evolve and flourish. However, industrial, agricultural, and other human activities during the last 150 years have released substantially more greenhouse gases into the atmosphere, particularly by the burning of fossil fuels such as oil and coal. Since the beginning of the industrial era, the amount of carbon dioxide in the atmosphere has increased by 25 percent. Measurements at Mauna Loa, Hawaii, indicate that carbon dioxide is currently increasing at the rate of 1.4 percent a year and that this rate accelerates each passing year.[5] Computer models indicate that rising levels of greenhouse gases will trap increasing amounts of heat on earth and so will raise temperatures around the globe. Average global temperatures are now 1°C (1.8°F) higher than in 1900 and are expected to rise by

1.5° to 4.5°C during this century. This rising heat will expand the world's deserts; melt the polar ice caps, causing sea levels to rise; make several species of plants and animals extinct; disrupt farming; and increase the distribution and severity of diseases.[6]

In 1988, the United Nations formed the Intergovernmental Panel on Climate Change (IPCC) to study the issue of global warming. The IPCC issued reports in 1990 and 1992 confirming the forecasts of global warming. In 1997, it began to issue a series of reports assessing the probable regional impacts of climate change.[7] The IPCC predicts large shifts of vegetation into higher latitudes and higher elevations and rapid changes in the mix of species in these areas. Because forest species grow and reproduce much more slowly than the climate will change, entire forests and forest species will likely disappear. Bodies of water such as lakes and oceans will warm, and this will dramatically shift the geographical distribution of fish and other marine species. Currently some 1.3 billion people do not have adequate supplies of drinking water; climate change will increase the frequency and magnitude of droughts, thereby increasing the number of people without water. Currently 800 million people do not have enough food to eat; climate change will decrease agricultural yields in the tropics and subtropics worsening famine in these areas. Currently half of the world's population and many of the world's major cities are located in coastal zones; climate change will melt glaciers causing seas to rise and flood these coastal zones and their population; it is already increasing the frequency and severity of coastal storms and the resulting storm-surges that wreak destruction on these areas. Currently mortality rates in developed and developing countries have been dropping; however, climate change is already bringing about a disturbing and widespread increase in vector-borne and infectious diseases such as dengue, malaria, hantavirus, West Nile virus, and cholera.[8] As termperatures have risen, mosquitoes have invaded previously cool regions, carrying malaria and dengue fever with them. New York City has seen the emergence of West Nile virus, a disease transmitted by mosquitoes; California has seen the outbreak of hantavirus, a lethal infection carried by rodents whose natural predators have been killed by drought.

Global warming is an extremely difficult problem to solve. The IPCC calculates that halting the increase in levels of greenhouse gases would require reducing current emissions of greenhouse gases by 60 to 70 percent—an amount that would seriously damage the economies of both developed and developing nations. This is such a large reduction, in fact, that few governments are likely to attempt it, and many governments, especially China, actually are increasing their carbon dioxide emissions by substantial amounts. In 1992, the United Nations proposed an agreement to stablize "greenhouse gas concentrations in the atmosphere at a level which would prevent dangerous anthropogenic interference with the climate system." More than 160 countries have signed the agreement, and the United States produced its own Climate Change Action Plan in 1993, wherein it pledged to undertake a number of "voluntary" measures to reduce greenhouse gas emissions. These measures will certainly not be sufficient. Some environmentalists have suggested that what is needed is a wholesale change in lifestyles and values.

Ozone Depletion Of equally serious concern is the gradual breakdown of ozone gas in the stratosphere above us caused by the release of chlorofluorocarbons (CFCs) into the air. A layer of ozone in the lower stratosphere screens all life on earth from harmful ultraviolet radiation. This ozone layer, however, is destroyed by CFC gases, which have been used in aerosol cans, refrigerators, air conditioners, industrial solvents, and industrial foam blowers. When released into the air, CFC gases rise; in 7 to 10 years, they reach the stratosphere, where they destroy ozone molecules and remain for 75 to 130 years, continuing all the while to break down additional ozone molecules. Worldwide monitoring data indicate that global average losses of the ozone layer have totaled about 5 percent since the 1960s, with cumulative losses of about 10 percent in the winter and spring and 5 percent in the summer and autumn over Europe, North America, and Australia. Studies predict that the shrinking of the ozone layer and the subsequent increase of ultraviolet rays will cause several hundred thousand new cases of skin cancer and may cause considerable destruction of the 75 percent of the world's major crops that are sensitive to ultraviolet light. Other studies caution that the plankton that float on the surface layers of the earth's oceans and on which the entire food chain of the world's oceans ultimately depends is sensitive to ultraviolet light and may suffer mass destruction. International agreements to which the United States is a party pledged to gradually phase out the use of CFC gases by 2000, and emissions of CFCs have dropped by 87 percent from their peak in 1988.[9] However, scientists warn that even if the use of CFC gases were completely halted, CFC levels in the atmosphere would still continue their dangerous upward climb because those gases already released will continue to rise upward for many years and will persist for perhaps a century.[10] Moreover, not all countries have agreed to cease making and producing CFC gases, and CFC gases are often released when refrigeration or air conditioning systems built many years ago are repaired or disposed of.[11]

Acid Rain Acid rain is a threat to the environment that, like global warming, is closely related to the combustion of fossil fuels (oil, coal, and natural gas), which are heavily used by utilities to produce electricity. Burning fossil fuels, particularly coal containing high levels of sulfur, releases large quantities of sulfur oxides and nitrogen oxides into the atmosphere. Electric utility plants account for 70 percent of annual sulfur oxide emissions and 30 pecent of nitrogen oxides.[12] When these gases are carried into the air, they combine with water vapor in clouds to form nitric acid and sulfuric acid. These acids are then carried down in rain, which often falls hundreds of miles away from the original sources of the oxides. The acidic rainfall—sometimes as acidic as vinegar—is carried into lakes and rivers, where it raises the acidity of the water. It also soaks into soils and falls directly on trees, grasses, and other vegetation. Numerous studies have shown that many fish populations and other aquatic organisms—including algae, zooplankton, and amphibians—are unable to survive in lakes and rivers that have become highly acidic due to acid rain.[13] Other studies have shown that acid rain directly damages or destroys trees, plants, lichens, and mosses, and indirectly destroys the wildlife and species that depend on forests for food and breeding. Acidic rain water can also leach toxic metals—cadmium, nickel, lead, manganese and mercury—from soil and carry these into waterways, where they contaminate drinking water or fish. Finally, acid rain can corrode and damage buildings, statues, and other objects, particularly those made of iron, limestone, and marble. Dozens of people were killed in West Virginia when a steel bridge collapsed as a result of acid rain corrosion, and priceless monuments such as the Acropolis in Athens and the Taj Mahal in India have been corroded by acid rain. Many researchers fear that future emissions will devastate the world's forests, particularly those located near industrial centers.

Acid rain is an international problem. Acid rain that falls on one country often has its origins in sulfur and nigtrogen oxides produced in another country and blown by prevaling rains. Much of Canada and the northeastern part of the United States, for example, are subject to acid rain whose origins lie in industrial areas around the Great Lakes, and the Netherlands have suffered from acid rain that has its origins in Germany.

Airborne Toxics Less catastrophic but highly worrisome air pollution threats are the 2.4 billion pounds of airborne toxic substances released annually into the nation's atmosphere, including phosgene, a nerve gas used in warfare, and methyl isocyanate, which killed more than 2000 Indians in Bhopal. The chemical brew released into the air annually includes 235 million pounds of carcinogens, such as benzene and formaldehyde, and 527 million pounds of such neurotoxins as toluene and trichloroethylene. Although levels of most airborne toxics have been declining gradually across the nation, some states have registered increases in the levels of several carcinogenic toxics in the air.[14] The Environmental Protection Agency (EPA) estimated that 20 of the more than 329 toxics released into the air alone cause more than 2000 cases of cancer each year, and that living near chemical plants raises a person's chances of cancer to more than 1 in 1000. Exceptionally high cancer rates have been found near plants in several states including West Virginia and Louisiana.

Air Quality The most prevalent forms of air pollution, however, are the gases and particulates spewed out by autos and industrial processes, which affect the quality of the air we breathe. The effects of these pollutants were recognized more than two decades ago when a report of the Department of Health, Education and Welfare summarized them as follows:

> At levels frequently found in heavy traffic, carbon monoxide produces headaches, loss of visual acuity, and decreased muscular coordination.
>
> Sulfur oxides, found wherever coal and oil are common fuels, corrode metal and stone and, at concentrations frequently found in our larger cities, reduce visibility, injure vegetation, and contribute to the incidence of respiratory diseases and to premature death.
>
> Besides their contribution to photochemical smog, described below, nitrogen oxides are responsible for the whiskey-brown haze that not only destroys the view in some of our cities, but endangers the takeoff and landing of planes. At concentrations higher than those usually experienced, these oxides can interfere with respiratory function and, it is suspected, contribute to respiratory disease. They are formed in the combustion of all types of fuel.
>
> Hydrocarbons are a very large class of chemicals, some of which, in particle form, have produced cancer in laboratory animals, and others of which, discharged chiefly by the automobile, play a major role in the formation of photochemical smog.
>
> Photochemical smog is a complex mixture of gases and particles manufactured by sunlight out of the raw materials—nitrogen oxides and hydrocarbons—discharged to the atmosphere chiefly by the automobile. Smog, whose effects have been observed in every region of the United States, can severely damage crops and trees, deteriorate rubber and other materials, reduce visibility, cause the eyes to smart and the throat to sting, and, it is thought, reduce resistance to respiratory disease.
>
> Particulate matter not only soils our clothes, shows up on our window sills, and scatters light to blur the image of what we see, it acts as a catalyst in the formation of other pollutants, it contributes to the corrosion of metals, and, in proper particle size, can carry into our lungs irritant gases which might otherwise have been harmlessly dissipated in the upper respiratory tract. Some particulates contain poisons whose effects on humans are gradual, often the result of the accumulation of years.[15]

More recent long-range studies have indicated that the deterioration of lung function in human beings caused by their chronic exposure to air pollutants, whether it be auto smog or industrial smokestack emissions, is long lasting and often irreversible. Some of the 2500 subjects in the studies suffered as much as 75 percent loss of lung capacity during a 10-year period of living in Los Angeles communities—a region with dangerously high levels of air pollution—leaving them vulnerable to respiratory disease, emphysema, and impairment of their stamina. Damage to the still-developing lungs of children was especially problematic.[16]

As Table 5.1 shows, the major sources of the pollution that affects air quality are utilities, industrial smokestacks, and automobiles. In congested urban areas such as Los Angeles, estimates of the proportion of air pollution caused by

TABLE 5.1 EMISSIONS OF POLLUTANTS BY SOURCE, 1998 (IN THOUSANDS OF TONS)

Source	Particulates (10 microns)*	Sulfur Dioxide	Nitrogen Oxide	Volatile Organic Compounds	Carbon Monoxide	Lead
Fuel combustion						
Electric utilities	302	13,217	6103	54	417	68
Industrial	245	2075	2969	161	1114	19
Other fuel combustion	544	609	1117	678	3843	416
Industrial processes						
Chemical manufacturing	65	299	152	396	1,129	175
Metals processing	171	444	88	76	1495	2098
Petroleum industries	32	345	138	496	368	0
Other	339	370	408	450	632	54
Solvent use	6	1	2	5278	2	0
Storage and transport	94	3	7	1324	80	0
Waste disposal and recycling	310	42	97	433	1154	620
Highway vehicles	257	326	7765	5325	50,386	19
Farm & industrial equipment	461	1048	5280	2461	19,914	503
Miscellaneous (fires, farms)	31,916	12	328	786	8920	0
Total	34,741	19,647	24,454	17,917	89,455	3973

Source: U.S. Environmental Protection Agency, National Air Pollutant Emission Trends, 1900–1998 (March 2000), Table 2-1 for all but lead, Table 3–7 for lead.

*Particulate emission figures are for emissions of particulates 10 microns in diameter or smaller.

TABLE 5.2 CHANGES IN AIR POLLUTION EMISSIONS, 1970–1998 (IN THOUSANDS OF TONS)

Year	Particulates	Sulfur Dioxide	Nitrogen Oxides	Volatile Organic Compounds	Carbon Monoxide	Lead
1970	13,042	31,161	20,928	30,982	129,444	220,869
1980	7119	25,905	24,384	26,336	117,434	74,153
1990	29,962	23,660	24,049	20,936	98,523	4975
1996	33,041	19,121	24,676	18,736	95,480	3899
1998	34,741	19,647	24,454	17,917	89,455	3973

Source: U.S. Environmental Protection Agency, National Air Quality and Emissions Trends Report, 1900–1998 (March 2000), Tables 3–2, 3–3, 3–4, 3–5, 3–7.

automobiles rise to as much as 80 percent. Industrial pollution is derived principally from power plants and plants that refine and manufacture basic metals. Electrical power plants that depend on fossil fuels such as oil, coal, or natural gas throw tons of sulfur oxides, nitrogen oxides, and ashes into the air. When taken into the lungs, sulfur oxides form sulfuric acid, which damages the linings of the lungs and causes emphysema and bronchitis. Sulfur oxides have also been found to be a major factor in infant deaths, and particulates have been implicated in deaths from pneumonia and influenza.[17] As mentioned earlier, sulfur oxides and nitrogen oxides also produce acid rain. Copper refineries and smelters produce large quantities of copper oxides and ash while steel, nickel, cement, and chemical plants produce a variety of airborne particulates.

The last decade has seen considerable improvement in the air quality of most regions of the United States, largely as a result of environmental legislation and regulation. Table 5.2 indicates the quantities of various air pollutants emitted from 1970 to 1998. As the table indicates, emissions of four air pollutants have been substantially reduced, particularly of lead (98 percent reduction from 1970 levels) and sulfur dioxide (37 percent reduction), volatile organic compounds (42 percent reduction), and carbon monoxide (31 percent reduction). However, tons of pollution continue to spew into the air we breathe, and in 1995 some 80 million people lived in areas that did not meet national air quality standards. Moreover, emissions of particulates have continued to increase and emissions of nitrogen oxides have also increased above their 1970 levels.

The health costs of low air quality are known to be high. Studies have indicated that when the concentrations of sulfur oxides over our major cities were cut in half from their 1960 levels, this added an average of 1 year to the lives of each of its residents.[18] If air quality in urban areas were similar to the levels of rural regions with clean air, the death rates for asthma, bronchitis, and emphysema would drop by about 50 percent,[19] and deaths from heart disease would drop by about 15 percent.[20] Improvements in air quality since 1970, it is believed, now save about 14,000 lives per year.[21]

Water Pollution

The contamination of water sources is an old problem—one that has been with us since civilization began using water to dispose of its wastes and sewage. Water pollutants today, however, are much more diverse, consisting not only of organic wastes but also dissolved salts, metals, radioactive materials, as well as suspended materials such as bacteria, viruses, and sediments. These can impair or destroy aquatic life, threaten human health, and foul the water. About 40 percent of our surface water today is too polluted to fish or swim in.[22] Water pollutants enter surface water or underground water basins either from a single or point source, such as a pipe or a well carrying sewage or industrial wastes, or they enter from a diffused or nonpoint source covering a large area, such as crop pesticides or animal wastes carried in rainwater or runoff.[23]

Salt brines from mines and oil wells, as well as mixtures of sodium chloride and calcium chloride used to keep winter roads clear of snow, all eventually drain into water sources where they raise the saline content.[24] The high saline levels in ponds, lakes, and rivers kill whatever fish, vegetation, or other organisms inhabit them. Highly salinated water also poses major health hazards when it finds its way into city water supplies and is drunk by persons afflicted with heart disease, hypertension, cirrhosis of the liver, or renal disease.

Water drainage from coal mining operations contains sulfuric acid as well as iron and sulfate particles. Continuous-casting and hot-rolling mills employ acids to scrub metals, and these acids are then rinsed off with water. The acidic water from these sources is sometimes flushed into streams and rivers. The high acid levels produced in waterways by these practices are lethal to most organisms living within the aquatic environment.[25]

Organic wastes in water are comprised in large part of untreated human wastes and sewage, but a substantial amount is also derived from industrial processing of various food products, from the pulp and paper industry, and from animal feedlots.[26] Organic wastes that find their way into water resources are consumed by various types of bacteria, which in the process deplete the water of its oxygen. The oxygen-depleted water then becomes incapable of supporting fish life and other organisms.

Phosphorus compounds also contaminate many of our water sources.[27] Phosphorus compounds are found in cleansing detergents used both domestically and industrially, in fertilizers used for agricultural purposes, and in untreated human and animal sewage. Lakes with high concentrations of phosphorus give rise to explosive expansions of algae populations that choke waterways, drive out other forms of life, deplete the water of its oxygen, and severely restrict water visibility.

Various inorganic pollutants pose serious health hazards when they make their way into water used for drinking and eating purposes. Mercury has been finding its way into fresh water supplies and the oceans, put there by runoff from the combustion of fossil fuels, past pulp mill uses of mercury-based fungicides, and the use of certain pesticides.[28] Mercury is transformed into organic compounds by microorganisms and becomes increasingly concentrated as it moves up the food chain to fish and birds. When consumed by humans, these compounds can cause brain damage, paralysis, and death. Companies have sometimes discharged large quantities of kepone into the nation's rivers.[29] Kepone is a chlorine compound that is toxic to fish life and causes nerve damage, sterility, and possibly cancer in humans. Cadmium from zinc refineries, the agricultural use of certain fertilizers, and disposed electrical batteries also makes its way into water sources, where it becomes concentrated in the tissues of fish and shellfish.[30] Cadmium causes a degenerate bone disease that cripples some victims and kills others; it induces severe cramps, vomiting, and diarrhea, and it produces high blood pressure and heart disease. Mining companies are notorious for depositing asbestos-contaminated wastes into fresh water sources.[31] Asbestos fibers may cause cancer of the gastrointestinal tract.

Heat is also a water pollutant. Water is used as a coolant in various industrial manufacturing processes and by the electrical power industry, a major heat polluter. Transferring heat into water raises the water's thermal energy to levels that decrease its ability to hold the dissolved oxygen that aquatic organisms require. In addition, the alternating rise and fall of temperatures prevents the water from being populated by fish because most water organisms are adapted only to stable water temperatures.

Oil spills are a form of water pollution whose occurrence became more frequent as our dependence on oil increased. Since 1973, the number of oil pollution incidents reported has remained fairly constant, although the volume of oil spilled has been highly variable. Oil spills result from offshore drilling, discharges of sludge from oil tankers, and oil tanker accidents. In 1989, Exxon Corporation ran the supertanker Valdez aground in Alaska's Prince William Sound, spilling 240,000 barrels (a barrel is 42 gallons) of crude oil over 900 square miles within Prince William Sound.[32] Some years earlier, two Standard Oil of California tankers collided in San Francisco Bay, spilling hundreds of thousands of gallons of oil along 50 miles of California coastlines; 8 months later, a Navy tanker spilled 230,000 gallons on the beaches of San Clemente, and the following month a Swedish tanker spilled 15,000 to 30,000 more gallons of oil into San Francisco Bay. The contamination produced by oil spills is directly lethal to sea life, including fish, seals, plants, and aquatic birds; it requires expensive cleanup operations for residents, and it imposes costly losses on nearby tourist and fishing industries. In 1985, about 11,000 oil spills, involving about 24 million gallons of oil, were recorded in and around U.S. waters.[33]

In the past, the oceans have been used as disposal sites for intermediate- and low-level radioactive wastes (which are discussed more fully later). Since the mid-1970s, oceanographers have found in seawater traces of plutonium, cesium, and other radioactive materials that have apparently leaked from the sealed drums in which radioactive wastes are disposed.[34] Coastal estuaries and marine sediments also have been found to contain unusually high concentrations of cadmium, chromium, copper, lead, mercury, and silver. High concentrations of polycyclic aromatic hydrocarbons (PAHs; chemicals given off by the burning of fossil fuels) have also been found in coastal waters such as those around Boston Harbor and Salem Harbor. PAHs cause mutations and cancers in some marine organisms and are acutely toxic to others. Polychlorinated biphenyls (PCBs), which were used as cooling fluids in electrical transformers, as lubricants, and as flame retardants until their production was completely banned in the United States in 1979, have become widespread in the environment and are gradually accumulating in the oceans, especially in coastal areas. Minute amounts of PCBs are deadly to human beings and other life forms, and traces can engender a variety of toxic effects including reproductive failures, birth defects, tumors, liver disorders, skin lesions, and immune suppression. PCBs, which continue to be produced by other countries and still are often improperly disposed of in the United States, are a cause of profound concern because they are persistent and become increasingly concentrated as they move up the food chain.[35] Periodically, parts of New York's Hudson River have been closed to fishing because of PCB contamination.

Underground water supplies are also becoming more polluted. According to a recent government report, "Incidents of ground-water contamination—by organic chemicals, inorganic chemicals, radionuclides [radioactive wastes], or microorganisms—are being reported with increasing frequency and have now occurred . . . in every state in the nation."[36] The sources of contamination have included landfills, waste piles, legal and illegal dumps, and surface reservoirs. More than 50 percent of the U.S. population depends on underground water sources for drinking water. Underground water contaminants have been linked to cancers, liver and kidney diseases, and damage to the central nervous system. Unfortunately, exposure frequently occurs unknowingly over periods of years because contaminated groundwater is usually odorless, colorless, and tasteless.

Today more than 1 billion people lack access to safe water, most of them in poor countries. Although water is essential to human life as well as to industrial growth and development, the world's per capita supplies of water are shrinking and are now 30 percent smaller than 25 years ago.[37] A number of factors have contributed to this decline. Increases in population and economic activity have increased the demands put on our water resources. As urban areas have grown and increased their demands for water, water has been increasingly diverted from agricultural irrigation to provide water for cities.

How much does water pollution cost us, and what benefits might we expect from its removal? One study estimates that the additional annual costs that would have been incurred in the United States in 1985 without water pollution controls ranged from $18 billion to $0.8 billion (in 1990 dollars from about $21.74 billion to $0.96 billion).[38]

Land Pollution

Toxic Substances Hazardous or toxic substances are those that can cause an increase in mortality rates or irreversible or incapacitating illness or those that have other seriously adverse health or environmental effects. Toxic substances released on land include acidic chemicals, inorganic metals (such as mercury or arsenic), flammable solvents, pesticides, herbicides, phenols, explosives, and so on. (Radioactive wastes are also classified as hazardous substances, but these are discussed separately later.) Silvex and 2, 4, 5-T, for example, are two widely used herbicides that contain dioxin—a deadly poison (100 times more deadly than strychnine) and a carcinogen. Until 1979, these herbicides were being sprayed on forests in Oregon, where they are believed to have led to an abnormal number of miscarriages in local women and to have caused a range of reproductive defects in animals. In the late 1970s, toxic chemicals buried by Hooker Chemical Company at sites near Niagara Falls, New York, were found to have leaked from the sites and to have contaminated the surrounding residential areas, including homes, schools, playing fields, and underground water supplies. The chemicals included dioxin, pesticides, carbon tetrachloride, and other carcinogenic or toxic chemicals suspected of having induced spontaneous abortions, nerve damage, and congenital malformations among families living nearby.[39]

The government estimates that over 58,000 different chemical compounds are currently being used in the United States and that their number is growing each year. Ten times more chemicals, many of them toxic, were being used in the mid-1980s than in 1970. Among the most common of the toxic chemicals produced by industry is acrylonitrile, which is used in the manufacture of plastics (used in appliances, luggage, telephones, and numerous common household and industrial products) and whose production is currently rising by 3 percent a year. Acrylonitrile is a suspected carcinogen; it releases the toxic chemical hydrogen cyanide when plastic containing it is burned.[40]

Benzene is a common industrial toxic chemical used in plastics, dyes, nylon, food additives, detergents, drugs, fungicides, and gasoline. Benzene is a cause of anemia, bone marrow damage, and leukemia. Studies have shown that benzene workers are several times more likely than the general population to get leukemia.[41]

Vinyl chloride is another common industrial chemical used in the production of plastics, whose production is rising by 3 percent per year. Vinyl chloride, which is released in small amounts when plastic products deteriorate, causes liver damage; birth anomalies; liver, respiratory, brain, and lymph cancers; and bone damage. Cancer mortality for vinyl chloride workers is 50 percent higher than for the general population, and communities located around plants where it is used also have higher cancer rates than the general population.[42] Phthalates are resins used in industry to produce model cement, paints, and finishes. They damage the central nervous system of humans and are toxic to fish and birdlife.

Although the health effects of some substances are now known, the toxicity of many others is unknown and difficult to determine. Many chemicals cause chronic diseases only after a long period following a person's first exposure to the chemical. For example, most human cancers caused by exposure to toxic chemicals take 15 to 30 years to show up, which makes it difficult to identify the original causes of the disease. Moreover, studies are expensive and take time because rates of illness in large exposed populations must be compared to those of similar but unexposed groups over these long periods of time.

Solid Wastes Americans today produce more residential garbage than do the citizens of any other country in the world. Each year people living in America's cities produce more than 160 million tons of municipal solid waste—enough to fill a 145,000-mile-long convoy of 10-ton garbage trucks, more than half the distance to the moon,[43] or enough to fill the Astrodome in Houston more than twice daily for a year. Each person reading this book produces, on average, almost 4 pounds of garbage a day. Only about 10 percent of residential wastes are recovered through recycling—a disappointingly low proportion that is due to the lack of financial backing for recycling operations, the small size of markets for recycled products, and toxic chemicals present in recyclable garbage.

Although the amount of garbage we produce has been increasing each year, the facilities to handle it have decreased. In 1978, there were about 20,000 municipal garbage dumps in operation; by 1988, there were less than 6,000, and over a third of these were filled by 2000; others have had to be closed for safety reasons. Florida, Massachusetts, New Hampshire, and New Jersey are a few of the states that have closed most of their garbage dumps during the 1990s. Moreover, fewer and fewer dumps are opened. In the early 1970s, 300 to 400 new facilities were opened each year around the country; today that number has dropped to between 50 and 200.

City garbage dumps are significant sources of pollution, containing toxic substances such as cadmium (from rechargeable batteries), mercury, lead (from car batteries and TV picture tubes), vanadium, copper, zinc, and PCBs (from refrigerators, stoves, engines, and appliances built before 1980 and since dumped). Only about one fourth of all city dumps test groundwater for possible contamination, less than 16 percent have insulating liners, only 5 percent collect polluting liquid wastes before they percolate into groundwater, and less than half impose any restrictions on the kinds of liquid wastes that can be poured into them. Not surprisingly, almost one fourth of the sites identified in the Superfund National Priorities List as posing the greatest chemical hazards to public health and the environment are city dumps.[44]

The quantity of residential garbage that Americans produce, however, is dwarfed by the quantities of solid waste produced through industrial, agricultural, and mining processes. Although residential garbage, as mentioned, is estimated at about 160 million tons a year, American industries generate over 7.6 billion tons of solid waste a year while oil and gas producers generate 2 to 3 billion tons and mining operations about 1.4 billion tons.[45] These wastes are dumped into some 220,000 industrial waste heaps, the vast majority of which are unlined surface dumps.

Thousands of abandoned dumps have been discovered containing hazardous wastes, most created by the chemical and petroleum industries.[46] The majority of hazardous waste sites are located in industrial regions. Altogether, about 80 percent of industrial wastes are estimated to have been deposited in ponds, lagoons, and landfills that are not secure.[47] Efforts begun in 1980 to identify all uncontrolled hazardous sites had succeeded by 1986 in identifying over 24,000 uncontrolled hazardous sites. In many places, wastes have been migrating out of the sites and seeping into the ground, where they have contaminated the water supplies of several communities. A sizable number of these required emergency action because they represented immediate threats. The costs of cleaning up these dumps have been estimated at between $28.4 billion and $55 billion.[48]

The net amounts of hazardous wastes currently being produced have been difficult to establish. The EPA has estimated that 10 to 15 percent of the industrial wastes being produced each year were toxic an estimated total of 15 million tons per year. More recently, the agency announced that nearly six times more hazardous waste was being generated each year than it had previously estimated. New studies suggest that in a single year 290 million tons of toxic wastes were produced.[49]

Nuclear Wastes Light-water nuclear reactors contain radioactive materials, including known carcinogens such as strontium 90, cesium 137, barium 140, and iodine 131. Extremely high levels of radiation from these elements can kill a person; lower dosages (especially if radioactive dust particles are inhaled or ingested) can cause thyroid, lung, or bone cancer as well as genetic damage that will be transmitted to future generations. To this date, nuclear plants in this country have operated safely without any catastrophic release of large quantities of radioactive materials. Estimates of the probable risk of such a catastrophic accident are highly controversial, and considerable doubt has been cast on these probability estimates, especially since the accidents at Three Mile Island in the United States and Chernobyl in Russia.[50] Even without catastrophic accidents, however, small amounts of radioactive materials are routinely released into the environment during the normal operations of a nuclear plant and during the mining, processing, and transporting of nuclear fuels. The U.S. government has estimated that, by the year 2000, at least 1000 people will have died of cancer from these routine emissions; other estimates, however, place these figures at substantially higher levels.[51]

Plutonium is produced as a waste by-product in the spent fuel of light-water reactors. A 1000-megawatt reactor, for example, will generate about 265 pounds (120 kilograms) of plutonium wastes each year that must be disposed of. Plutonium is a highly toxic and extremely carcinogenic substance. A particle weighing 10 millionths of a gram, if inhaled, can cause death within a few weeks. Twenty pounds, if properly distributed, could give lung cancer to everyone on earth. Plutonium is also the basic constituent of atomic bombs. Therefore, as nuclear power plants proliferate around the world,the probability has increased that plutonium will fall into the hands of criminal terrorists or other hostile groups, who may use it to construct an atomic weapon or lethally contaminate large populated areas.[52]

Nuclear power plant wastes are of three main types: high-level wastes, transuranic wastes, and low-level wastes. High-level wastes emit gamma rays, which can penetrate all but the thickest shielding. These include cesium 137 and strontium 90, which both become harmless after about 1000 years, and plutonium, which remains hazardous for 250,000 to 1,000,000 years. All of these are highly carcinogenic. Nuclear reactors already produce about 612,000 gallons of liquid and 2300 tons of solid high-level wastes each year. These wastes must be isolated from the environment until they are no longer hazardous. It is unknown at this time whether there is any safe and permanent method for disposing of these wastes.[53]

Transuranic wastes contain smaller quantities of the elements found in high-level wastes. These come from spent fuel processing and various military weapons processes. Until recently, transuranic wastes were buried in shallow trenches. It has been discovered, however, that radioactive materials have been migrating out of these trenches, and they have to be exhumed and redisposed of at a cost of several hundred million dollars.[54]

Low-level wastes consist of the contaminated clothing and used equipment from reactor sites and the tailings from mining and milling uranium. About 16 million cubic feet of these wastes have been produced at reactor sites, and an additional 500 million cubic feet of uranium tailings (about 140 million tons) have accumulated in the open at mine sites. About 10 million additional tons of mill tailings are produced each year. Uranium tailings continue to emit radioactive radon for several hundred thousand years. In addition, all nuclear plants (including equipment, buildings, and land) become low-level nuclear wastes after an operating life of 30 to 35 years. The entire plant must then be decommissioned because it remains radioactive for thousands of years, the dismantled plant and land site must be maintained under constant security for the next several centuries.[55]

More than one author has suggested that the safe disposal of nuclear wastes is soluble only if we assume that none of our descendants will ever accidentally drill into nuclear repositories or enter them during times of war; records of their locations will be preserved for the next several centuries; the wastes will not accidentally flow together and begin reacting; geological events, ice sheets, or other unforeseen earth movements never uncover the wastes; our engineering estimates of the properties of metal, glass, and cement containers are accurate; and our medical predictions concerning safe levels of radiation exposure prove correct.[56] Although no new nuclear power plants have been constructed in the United States for several years, those built decades ago are still producing wastes, and their past wastes have been accumulating. How these are disposed of is uncertain.

Depletion of Species and Habitats

It is well known that human beings have depleted dozens of plant and animal species to the point of extinction. Since 1600 A.D., at least 63 major identifiable species of mammals and 88 major identifiable species of birds are known to have become extinct.[57] Several hundred more species, such as whales and salmon, today find themselves threatened by commercial predators. Forest habitats on which the bulk of species depend are also being decimated by the timber industry. Between the years 1600 and 1900, half of the forested land area in the United States was cleared.[58] Experts estimate that the planet's rain forests are being destroyed at the rate of about 1 percent a year.[59] The loss of forest habitats combined with the effects of pollution is thought to have led to the extinction of a phenomenal number of species. A recent comprehensive study of 18,000 species and subspecies around the world found that 11,046 of them were in danger of disappearing forever.[60] It is estimated that between half a million to two million species—15 to 20 percent of all species on earth—were rendered extinct by 2000.[61]

Depletion of Fossil Fuels

Until the early 1980s, fossil fuels were being depleted at an exponentially rising rate. That is, the rate at which they were being used had doubled with the passage of a regular fixed time period. This type of exponential depletion is illustrated in Fig. 5.1. Several early predictions of resource depletion assumed that fossil fuels would continue to be depleted at these exponentially rising rates. If continued, an exponentially rising rate of depletion would end with the complete and catastrophic depletion of the resource in a relatively short time.[62] Estimated world resources of coal would be depleted in about 100 years, estimated world reserves of oil would be exhausted in about 40 years, and estimated reserves of natural gas would last only about 25 years.[63]

As many researchers argue, however, our consumption of fossil fuels could not continue rising at historical exponential rates.[64] As reserves of any resource shrink, they become increasingly difficult, and therefore more costly, to extract. Consequently, although the rates at which reserves are depleted may rise exponentially for a period, the rising costs of extraction eventually cause the rates to peak and then begin to decline without complete depletion ever being attained. Figure 5.2 illustrates this type of peaked depletion rate, in which consumption of the resource gradually peters out as the resource becomes increasingly difficult to extract, rather than culminating in complete and sudden depletion within a relatively short period of time. Rising energy prices during the 1970s, in fact, led to drastic reductions in worldwide consumption of oil by 1980.[65] This lowered demand, coupled with the breakdown of OPEC, has led to a downward drift in oil prices. During the 1990s, world consumption of oil began increasing again, but many researchers believe that our consumption of fossil fuels will not return to the exponentially rising rates of earlier decades.[66]

Moreover, if we assume that the rate at which we consume our resources is more adequately mirrored by the peaked model than by the exponential model, then fossil fuels will not be depleted within the short time frame predicted by

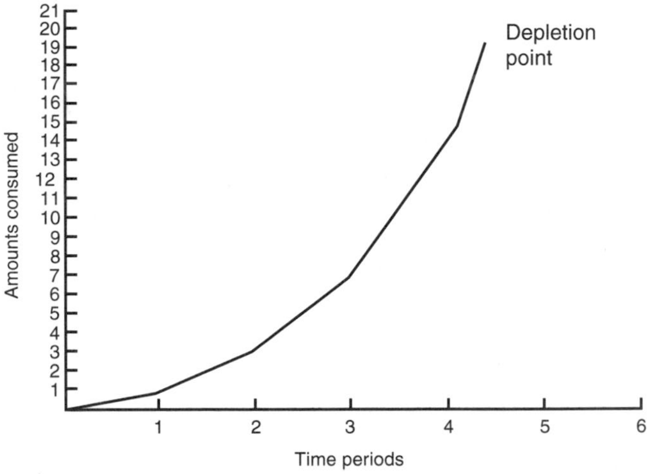

Figure 5.1 Exponential depletion rate.

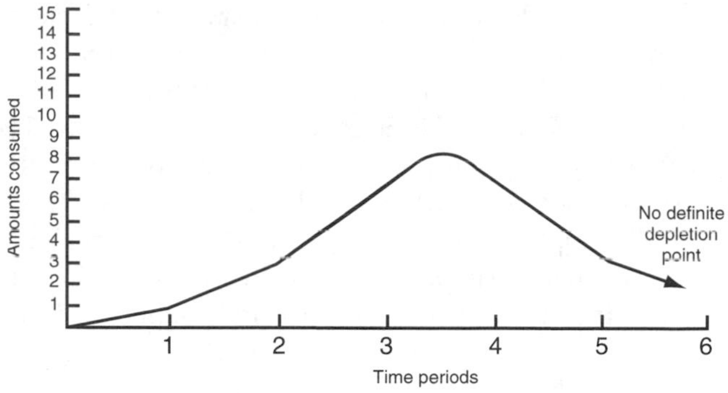

Figure 5.2 Peaked depletion rate.

earlier exponential growth models. The extraction of estimated reserves of coal will probably peak in about 150 years and then continue, but at a declining rate, for another 150 years; the extraction of estimated reserves of oil will probably peak in about 40 years and then gradually decline; the extraction of estimated U.S. reserves of natural gas has already peaked and is expected to decline gradually over the next 30 or 40 years.[67]

Depletion of Minerals

The depletion of mineral reserves, like the depletion of fossil fuels, can also be calculated either on the basis of an exponential growth model or on the basis of a peaked growth model. If earlier exponentially rising rates of depletion continued, then aluminum would be scheduled for exhaustion in the year 2003, iron in 2025, manganese in 2018, molybdenum in 2006, nickel in 2025, tungsten in 2000, zinc in 1990, and copper and lead in 1993.[68] Clearly, if these depletion schedules were correct, the economic consequences would be catastrophic because running out of these essential minerals within these relatively short time frames would lead to a collapse of the numerous industries that rely on them. During the early 1970s, many researchers believed that such an industrial and economic collapse was imminent. However, further research has indicated that such catastrophic depletion schedules were mistaken.

As with fossil fuels, the rate at which minerals are depleted does not continue to grow exponentially, but peaks and then declines as metals become rarer, more difficult, and more expensive to extract. If we use this peaked model analysis and restrict ourselves solely to presently known reserves in the United States, it turns out that, although the extraction rates of some important minerals in the United States have peaked, none has been completely depleted and all continue to be mined. By the turn of the 21st century, the United States had exhausted about

90 percent of its mineable domestic aluminum reserves, 80 percent of its iron, 70 percent of its lead, 90 percent of its manganese, 80 percent of its mercury, 90 percent of its tungsten, and 70 percent of its zinc.[69] Any reserves of these minerals remaining in the United States are difficult to extract, and we have been forced to turn increasingly to recycling, substitutes, and imports from world markets.

World resources, of course, are also limited, and the depletion rates of many of the world's supplies of minerals probably will also peak and then gradually decline as remaining supplies become harder and more expensive to mine.[70] The precise impact the limitations of world supplies will have on us are exceedingly difficult to predict. Mining technologies may continue to develop, which will reduce the difficulty and costs of mineral extraction. This has, in fact, been the case for most minerals up to the present. Increased recycling may reduce the need for intensive mining of remaining mineral reserves. Substitutes may be found for many of the minerals whose supply is limited, and technological development may make many current uses of these minerals obsolete.

Still the most exhaustive and thorough study to date of the world limits of a single mineral—copper—indicates that in the future copper and the other minerals will become increasingly scarce and expensive and that this scarcity will have a noticeable economic impact on our societies.[71] The study, undertaken by Robert B. Gordon and others, indicates that the rate of extraction of the world's copper will rise rapidly over the next 100 years, peak in about 2100, and then slowly decline. Rich copper ores will be exhausted by about 2070. Thereafter, copper must be mined from common rock, an expensive process that will force dramatic exponential rises of copper prices from about $2 per kilogram to $120 per kilogram, even with intense recycling and even assuming other materials can be substituted for all but a handful of the essential uses of copper. According to Gordon and his coauthors: "Similar arguments can be raised for other metals, such as lead, zinc, tin, tungsten, and silver. . . . We have not made a complete analysis for any other scarce metal, but we strongly suspect that if we did a pattern of future use similar to that predicted for copper would emerge."[72]

In a recent study, the U.S. Geological Survey of the U.S. Department of the Interior concluded that world reserves of conventional aluminum resources (bauxite) are sufficient to meet world demand for aluminum "well into the 21st century"[73]; world reserves of manganese total 5 billion tons, which are being mined at the rate of about 7 million tons a year[74]; world reserves of mercury are estimated at nearly 600,000 tons, which are "sufficient for another century or more"[75]; world reserves of copper total 2.3 billion tons which are currently being mined at the rate of 13,000 tons a year[76]; world resources of iron are estimated at more than 250 billion tons which are being mined at a rate of about 1 billion tons a year[77]; and lead world resources total more than 1.5 billion tons, which are being mined at about 3 million tons a year.[78]

There are physical limits, then, to our natural resources: Although many are abundant, they cannot be exploited indefinitely. Eventually they will peter out and the costs of extraction will rise exponentially. More plentiful substitute materials may be found for many of these resources, but it is likely that substitutes cannot be found for all of them. Whatever substitutes are developed will also be limited, so the day of reckoning will only be delayed.

5.2 The Ethics of Pollution Control

For centuries, business institutions were able to ignore their impact on the natural environment, an indulgence created by a number of causes. First, business was able to treat air and water as free goods—that is, as goods that no one owns and that each firm can therefore use without reimbursing anyone for their use. For several years, for example, a DuPont plant in West Virginia had been dumping 10,000 tons of chemical wastes each month into the Gulf of Mexico until it was forced to stop. The waters of the Gulf provided a free dumping site for whose damages DuPont did not have to pay. Because such resources are not privately owned, they lack the protection that a private owner would normally provide, and businesses were able to ignore the damages they inflicted on them. Second, businesses have seen the environment as an unlimited good. That is, the "carrying capacity" of air and water is relatively large, and each firm's contribution of pollution to these resources is relatively small and insignificant.[79] The amount of chemicals DuPont was dumping into the Gulf, for example, might be relatively small compared with the size of the Gulf and the effects viewed as being negligible. When the effects of its activities are seen as so slight, a firm will tend to ignore these effects. However, when every firm reasons in this way, the combined negligible effects of each firm's activities may become enormous and potentially disastrous. The carrying capacity of the air and water is soon exceeded, and these free and unlimited goods rapidly deteriorate.

Of course, pollution problems are not rooted only in business activities. Pollution also results from the use that consumers make of products and human waste products.[80] A primary source of air pollution, for example, is automobile use, and a primary source of water pollution is sewage. We are truly all polluters.[81] Because every human being pollutes, pollution problems have increased as our population has multiplied. The world's population grew from1 billion in 1850 to 2 billion in 1930 to 5.7 billion in 1995; it is projected to grow to between 10 and 12 billion by 2040.[82] This population explosion has put severe strains on the air and water resources into which we dump our share of pollutants. Moreover, these strains have been aggravated by our tendency to concentrate our populations in urban centers. All over the world, urban areas are growing rapidly, and the high-population densities that urbanization has created multiplies the pollution burdens placed on air and water resources.[83]

The problems of pollution, then, have a variety of origins, and their treatment requires a similarly variegated set of solutions. Our focus in what follows, however, concentrates on a single range of problems: the ethical issues raised by pollution from commercial and industrial enterprises.

Ecological Ethics

The problem of pollution (and environmental issues in general) is seen by some researchers as a problem that can best be framed in terms of our duty to recognize and preserve the ecological systems within which we live.[84] An ecological system is an interrelated and interdependent set of organisms and environments, such as a lake—in which the fish depend on small aquatic organisms, which in turn live off decaying plant and fish waste products.[85] Because the various parts of an ecological system are interrelated, the activities of one of its parts will affect all the other parts. Because the various parts are interdependent, the survival of each part depends on the survival of the other parts. Business firms (and all other social institutions) are parts of a larger ecological system, "spaceship earth."[86] Business firms depend on the natural environment for their energy, material resources, and waste disposal, and that environment in turn is affected by the commercial activities of business firms. For example, the activities of 18th-century European manufacturers of beaver hats led to the wholesale destruction of beavers in the United States, which in turn led to the drying up of the innumerable swamp lands that had been created by beaver dams.[87] Unless businesses recognize the interrelationships and interdependencies of the ecological systems within which they operate and unless they ensure that their activities will not seriously injure these systems, we cannot hope to deal with the problem of pollution.

The fact that we are only a part of a larger ecological system has led many writers to insist that we should recognize our moral duty to protect the welfare not only of human beings, but also of other nonhuman parts of this system.[88] This insistence on what is sometimes called *ecological ethics* or *deep ecology* is not based on the idea that the environment should be protected for the sake of human beings. Instead, ecological ethics are based on the idea that nonhuman parts of the environment deserve to be preserved for their own sake, regardless of whether this benefits human beings. Several supporters of this approach have formulated their views in a platform consisting of the following statements:

1. The well-being and flourishing of human and nonhuman life on earth have value in themselves. . . . These values are independent of the usefulness of the nonhuman world for human purposes.

2. Richness and diversity of life forms contribute to the realization of these values and are also values in themselves.
3. Humans have no right to reduce this richness and diversity except to satisfy vital needs.
4. The flourishing of human life and cultures is compatible with a substantial decrease of the human population. The flourishing of nonhuman life requires such a decrease.
5. Present human interference with the nonhuman world is excessive, and the situation is rapidly worsening.
6. Policies must therefore be changed. The changes in policies affect basic economic, technological, and ideological structures. The resulting state of affairs will be deeply different from the present.
7. The ideological change is mainly that of appreciating life quality . . . rather than adhering to an increasingly higher standard of living.
8. Those who subscribe to the foregoing points have an obligation directly or indirectly to participate in the attempt to implement the necessary changes.[89]

An ecological ethic is thus an ethic that claims that the welfare of at least some nonhumans is intrinsically valuable and that, because of this intrinsic value, we humans have a duty to respect and preserve them. These ethical claims have significant implications for those business activities that affect the environment. In June 1990, for example, environmentalists successfully petitioned the U.S. Fish and Wildlife Service to bar the timber industry from logging potentially lucrative old-growth forests of northern California to save the habitat of the spotted owl, an endangered species.[90] The move was estimated to have cost the timber industry millions of dollars, to have lost workers as many as 36,000 lumber jobs, and to have raised the costs of consumer prices for fine wood products such as furniture and musical instruments. Throughout the 1980s, members of the Sea Shepherd Conservation Society sabotaged whale processing plants, sunk several ships, and otherwise imposed costs on the whaling industry.[91] Members of Earth First! have driven nails into randomly selected trees of forest areas scheduled to be logged so that power logging saws are destroyed when they bite into the spiked trees. Supporters of the view that animals have intrinsic value have also imposed substantial costs on cattle ranchers, slaughterhouses, chicken farms, fur companies, and pharmaceutical and cosmetic corporations that use animals to test chemicals.

There are several varieties of ecological ethics, some more radical and far-reaching than others. Perhaps the most popular version claims that, in addition to human beings, other animals have intrinsic value and are deserving of our respect and protection. Some utilitarians have claimed, for example, that pain is an evil whether it is inflicted on humans or on members of other animal species. The pain of an animal must be considered as equal to the comparable pain of a human, and it is a form of *specist* prejudice (akin to racist or sexist bias against members of another race or sex) to think that the duty to avoid inflicting pain on members of other species is not equal to our duty to avoid inflicting comparable pain on members of our own species.[92]

Certain nonutilitarians have reached similar conclusions by a different route. They have claimed that the life of every animal "itself has value" apart from the interests of human beings. Because of the intrinsic value of its life, each animal has certain moral rights, in particular the right to be treated with respect.[93] Humans have a duty to respect this right, although in some cases a human's right might override an animal's right.

Both the utilitarian and the rights arguments in support of human duties toward animals imply that it is wrong to raise animals for food in the crowded and painful circumstances in which agricultural business enterprises currently raise cows, pigs, and chickens. They also imply that it is wrong to use animals in painful test procedures as they are currently used in some businesses (e.g., to test the toxicity of cosmetics).[94]

Broader versions of ecological ethics would extend our duties beyond the animal world to include plants. Thus, some ethicians have claimed that it is arbitrary and hedonistic to confine our duties to creatures that can feel pain. Instead, they urge, we should acknowledge that all living things including plants have "an interest in remaining alive" and that consequently they deserve moral consideration for their own sakes.[95] Other authors have claimed that not only living things but even a natural species—a lake, a wild river, a mountain, and even the entire "biotic community"—has a right to have its "integrity, stability, and beauty" preserved.[96] If correct, these views would have important implications for businesses engaged in strip-mining or logging operations.

Some versions of ecological ethics have turned away from talk of duties and obligations and have instead urged an approach toward nature that is more closely linked to notions of virtue and character. An early version of such an approach was fashioned by Albert Schweitzer, who wrote that when traveling on a river in Africa, "at the very moment when, at sunset, we were making our way through a herd of hippopotamuses, there flashed upon my mind, unforeseen and unsought, the phrase, 'Reverence for Life'."[97] As he later articulated it, to be a person who has reverence for life is to see life itself, in all its forms, as having inherent worth, a worth that inspires an unwillingness to destroy and a desire to preserve:

> The man who has become a thinking being feels a compulsion to give to every will-to-live the same reverence for life that he gives to his own. He experiences that other life in his own. He accepts as being good: to preserve life, to promote life, to raise to its highest value life which is capable of development; and as being evil: to destroy life, to injure life, to repress life which is capable of development. This is the absolute, fundamental principle of the moral.[98]

More recently, the philosopher Paul Taylor has urged a similar approach, writing that "character traits are morally good in virtue of their expressing or embodying a certain ultimate moral attitude, which I call respect for nature."[99] This respect for nature, Taylor argued, is based on the fact that each living thing seeks its own good and so is a "teleological center of a life":

> To say it is a teleological center of a life is to say that its internal functioning as well as its external activities are all goal-oriented, having the constant tendency to maintain the organism's existence through time and to enable it successfully to perform those biological operations whereby it reproduces its kind and continually adapts to changing environmental events and conditions.[100]

The goal-oriented nature of all living things, Taylor argued, implies that all living things have an inherent "good of their own" that should be respected. Such respect is the only attitude consistent with a biocentric outlook that realizes that we ourselves are living members of earth's community of life, that we are part of a system of interdependence with other living things, that living things have their own good, and that we are not inherently superior to other living things within that system.

However, these attempts to extend moral rights to nonhumans or claim that an attitude of respect for all nature is morally demanded are highly controversial, and some authors have labeled them *incredible.*[101] It is difficult, for example, to see why the fact that something is alive implies that it should be alive and that we therefore have a duty to keep it alive or to express respect or even reverence for it. It is also difficult to see why the fact that a river or a mountain exists implies that it should exist and that we have a duty to keep it in existence or revere it. Facts do not imply values in this easy way.[102] It is also controversial whether we can claim that animals have rights or intrinsic value.[103] But we do not have to rely on these unusual views to develop an environmental ethic. For our purposes, we need only examine more traditional approaches to environmental issues.[104] One is based on a theory of human rights, and the other is based on utilitarian considerations.

Environmental Rights and Absolute Bans

In an influential article, William T. Blackstone argued that the possession of a livable environment is not merely a desirable state of affairs, but something to which each human being has a right.[105] That is, a livable environment is not merely something that we would all like to have: It is something that others have a duty to allow us to have. They have this duty, Blackstone argued, because we each have a right to a livable environment, and our right imposes on others the correlative duty of not interfering in our exercise of that right. This is a right, moreover, that should be incorporated into our legal system.

Why do human beings have this right? According to Blackstone, a person has a moral right to a thing when possession of that thing is "essential in permitting him to live a human life" (i.e., in permitting him to fulfill his capacities as a rational and free being).[106] At this time in our history, it has become clear that a livable environment is essential to the fulfillment of our human capacities. Consequently, human beings have a moral right to a decent environment, and it should become a legal right.

Moreover, Blackstone adds, this moral and legal right should override people's legal property rights. Our great and increasing ability to manipulate the environment has revealed that, unless we limit the legal freedom to engage in practices that destroy the environment, we shall lose the very possibility of human life and the possibility of exercising other rights, such as the right to liberty and equality.

Several states have introduced amendments to their constitution that grant to their citizens an environmental right, much like Blackstone advocated. Article One of the Constitution of Pennsylvania, for example, was amended a few years ago to read:

> The people have a right to clean air, pure water, and to the preservation of the natural scenic, historic, and aesthetic values of the environment. Pennsylvania's natural resources . . . are the common property of all the people, including generations yet to come. As trustee of these resources, the commonwealth shall preserve and maintain them for the benefit of all people.

To a large extent, something like Blackstone's concept of *environmental rights* is recognized in federal law. Section 101(b) of the National Environmental Policy Act of 1969, for example, states that one of its purposes is to "assure for all Americans safe, healthful, productive, and aesthetically and culturally pleasing surroundings." Subsequent acts tried to achieve this purpose. The Water Pollution Control Act of 1972 required firms, by 1977, to use the "best practicable technology" to get rid of pollution (i.e., technology used by several of the least polluting plants in an industry); the Clean Water Act of 1977 required that, by 1984, firms must eliminate all toxic and nonconventional wastes with the use of the "best available technology" (i.e., technology used by the one least polluting plant). The Air Quality Act of 1967 and the Clean Air Amendments of 1970 and 1990 established similar limits to air pollution from stationary sources and automobiles, and provided the machinery for enforcing these limits. These federal laws did not rest on a utilitarian cost–benefit analysis. That is, they did not say that firms should reduce pollution so long as the benefits outweigh the costs. Instead they simply imposed absolute bans on pollution regardless of the costs involved. Such absolute restrictions can best be justified by an appeal to people's rights.

Federal statutes in effect impose absolute limits on the property rights of owners of firms, and Blackstone's arguments provide a plausible rationale for limiting property rights in these absolute ways for the sake of a human right to a clean environment. Blackstone's argument obviously rests on a Kantian theory of rights: Because humans have a moral duty to treat each other as ends and not as means, they have a correlative duty to respect and promote the development of another's capacity to freely and rationally choose for him or herself.

The main difficulty with Blackstone's view, however, is that it fails to provide any nuanced guidance on several pressing environmental choices. How much pollution control is really needed? Should we have an absolute ban on pollution? How far should we go in limiting property rights for the sake of the environment? What goods, if any, should we cease manufacturing to halt or slow environmental damage? Who should pay for the costs of preserving the environment? Blackstone's theory gives us no way of handling these questions because it imposes a simple and absolute ban on pollution.

This lack of nuance in the absolute rights approach is especially problematic when the costs of removing certain amounts of pollution are high in comparison to the benefits that will be attained. Consider the situation of a pulp business as reported by its president:

> Surveys conducted along the lower Columbia River since completion of primary treatment facilities at our mills show that water-quality standards are being met and that the river is being used for fishing, swimming, water supply, and recreation. In all respects, therefore, the 1985 goals of the [Federal Water Pollution Control] act are presently being met [in 1975]. But the technical requirements of the act call for installation of secondary treatment facilities at our mills at Camas and Wauna. The cost will be about $20 million and will not result in any measurable improvement of water quality on the river. On the contrary, the total environmental effect will be negative. We calculate that it will take about 57 million kwh of electricity and nearly 8000 tons of chemicals to operate these unnecessary facilities. Total power requirements will involve burning 90,000 bbl/yr of scarce oil, in turn creating 900,000 lb of pollutants at the generating source. . . . Similar trade-offs occur in the field of air-quality control technology. For example, moving from 98 percent to 99.8 percent removal of particulate matter requires four times as much purchased energy as it took to get from zero to 98 percent control.[107]

Also troubling is the possible impact that pollution abatement requirements may have on plant closings and jobs.[108] Some researchers have claimed that pollution control legislation costs as much as 160,000 jobs a year, but such estimates appear both highly inflated and unreliable. The EPA studied the period between 1971 and 1981 and found only 153 plant closings that possibly could be attributed to environmental legislation, and these closings accounted for only 32,611 jobs, for an average of 3,200 jobs lost a year.[109] A Department of Labor study of layoffs during 1987 to 1991 found that of 2546 layoff events only 4 were attributable to environmental and safety regulations.[110] Many, perhaps most, of the workers affected by these closings found other jobs, and many new jobs have been created by companies that design, manufacture, and install pollution control devices. Nevertheless, environmental legislation clearly imposes some minimal level of costs on those workers who are at least temporarily displaced by those layoffs attributable to environmental regulations.

Because of the difficulties raised by absolute bans, the federal government in the early 1980s began to turn to methods of pollution control that tried to balance the costs and benefits of controlling pollution and that did not impose absolute bans. Deadlines for compliance with the standards of the Clean Air Act were extended so that the costs of compliance could be dealt with more adequately. Companies were allowed to increase discharges of pollutants that are costly to control when they agreed to make equivalent reductions of pollutants that are cheaper to control.[111] Executive Order No. 12291, signed into law by President Reagan on February 17, 1981, required all new environmental regulations to be subjected to cost–benefit analysis before they were implemented.[112] These new regulations are not based on the notion that people have absolute environmental rights, but on a utilitarian approach to the environment.

Utilitarianism and Partial Controls

Utilitarianism provides a way to answer the questions that Blackstone's theory of environmental rights leaves unanswered. A fundamentally utilitarian approach to environmental problems is to see them as market defects. If an industry pollutes the environment, the market prices of its commodities will no longer reflect the true cost of producing the commodities; the result is a misallocation of resources, a rise in waste, and an inefficient distribution of commodities. Consequently, society as a whole is harmed as its overall economic welfare declines.[113] Utilitarians, therefore, argue that individuals should avoid pollution because they should avoid harming society's welfare. The following paragraphs explain this utilitarian argument in greater detail, and explain the more nuanced approach to pollution that utilitarian cost–benefit analysis seems to provide.

Private Costs and Social Costs

Economists often distinguish between what it cost a private manufacturer to make a product and what the manufacture of that product cost society as a whole. Suppose, for example, that an electric firm consumes a certain amount of fuel, labor, and equipment to produce one kilowatt of electricity. The cost of these resources is its private cost: The price it must pay out of its own pocket to manufacture one kilowatt of electricity. However, producing the kilowatt of electricity may also involve other external costs for which the firm does not pay.[114] When the firm burns fuel, for example, it may generate smoke and soot that settles on surrounding neighbors, who have to bear the costs of cleaning up the grime and paying for any medical problems the smoke creates. From the viewpoint of society as a whole, then, the costs of producing the kilowatt of electricity include not only the internal costs of fuel, labor, and equipment for which the manufacturer pays, but also the external costs of clean-up and medical care that the neighbors pay. This sum total of costs (the private internal costs plus the neighbors' external costs) are the social costs of producing the kilowatt of electricity: the total price society must pay to manufacture one kilowatt of electricity. Of course, private costs and social costs do not always diverge as in this example: Sometimes the two coincide. If a producer pays for all the costs involved in manufacturing a product, for example, or if manufacturing a product imposes no external costs, then the producer's costs and the total social costs are the same.

Thus, when a firm pollutes its environment in any way, the firm's private costs are always less than the total social costs involved. Whether the pollution is localized and immediate, as in the neighborhood effects described in this example, or whether the pollution is global and long-range, as in the hot-house effects predicted to follow from introducing too much carbon dioxide into the atmosphere, pollution always imposes external costs—that is, costs for which the person who produces the pollution does not have to pay. Pollution is fundamentally a problem of this divergence between private and social costs.

Why should this divergence be a problem? It is a problem because when the private costs of manufacturing a product diverge from the social costs involved in its manufacture, markets no longer price commodities accurately. Consequently, they no longer allocate resources efficiently. As a result, society's welfare declines. To understand why markets become inefficient when private and social costs diverge, let us suppose that the electrical power industry is perfectly competitive (it is not, but let us suppose it is).[115] Suppose, then, that market supply curve, S, in Fig. 5.3 reflects the private costs producers must pay to manufacture each kilowatt of electricity. The market price will then be at the equilibrium point E, where the supply curve based on these private costs crosses the demand curve.

In the hypothetical situation in Fig. 5.3, the curves intersect at the market price of 3.5 cents and at an output of 600 million kilowatt hours. Suppose that, besides the private costs that producers incur in manufacturing electricity, the manufacture of electricity also imposes external costs on their neighbors in the form of environmental pollution. If these external costs were added to the private costs of producers, then a new supply curve, S', would result

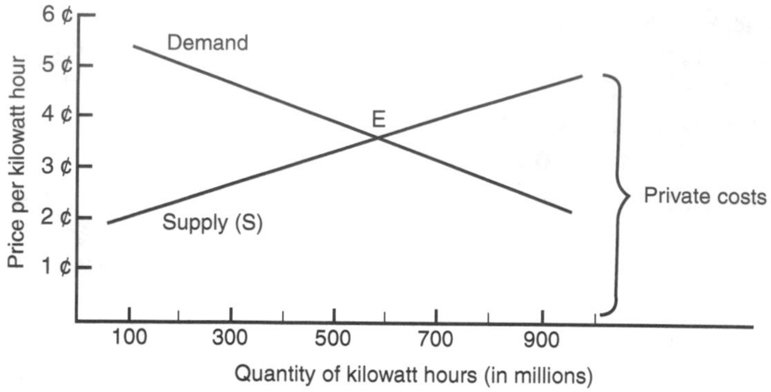

Figure 5.3

that would take into account all the costs of manufacturing each kilowatt hour of electricity, as in Fig. 5.4.

The new supply curve in Fig. 5.4, S', which is above the supply curve, S (which includes only the manufacturer's private costs), shows the quantities of electricity that would be supplied if all the costs of producing the electricity were taken into account and the prices that would have to be charged for each kilowatt hour if all costs were thus taken into account. As the new curve, S', indicates, when all the costs are taken into account, the market price of the commodity, 4.5 cents, will be higher, and the output, 350 million kilowatt hours, will be lower than when only private costs are incorporated. Thus, when only private costs are taken into account, the electricity is underpriced and overproduced. This in turn means that the electricity market is no longer allocating resources and distributing commodities so as to maximize utility. Three deficiencies, in particular, can be noted.

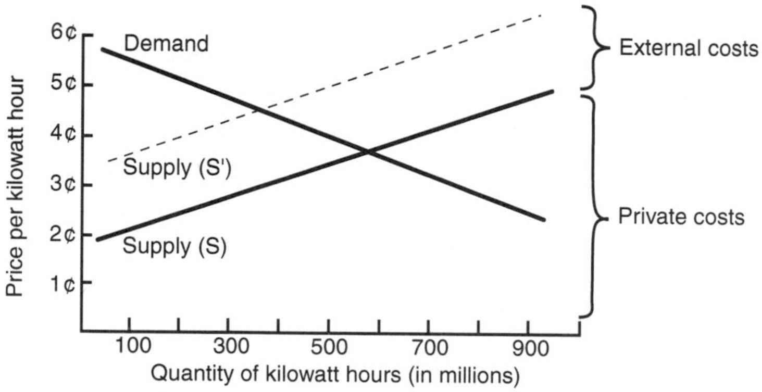

Figure 5.4

First, allocation of resources in markets that do not take all costs into account is not optimal because, from the point of view of society as a whole, more of the commodity is being produced than society would demand if society had available an accurate measure of what it is actually paying to produce the commodity. Because the commodity is being overproduced, more of society's resources are being consumed to produce the commodity than is optimal. The resources being consumed by overproduction of the commodity are resources that could be used to produce other commodities for which there would be greater demand if prices accurately reflected costs. Resources are thereby being misallocated.

Second, when external costs are not taken into account by producers, producers ignore these costs and make no attempt to minimize them. So long as the firm does not have to pay for external costs, it has no incentive to use technology that might decrease or eliminate them. Consequently, the resources being consumed by these external costs (such as clean air) are being unnecessarily wasted. There may be technologically feasible ways of producing the same commodities without imposing as many external costs, but the producer will make no attempt to find them.

Third, when the production of a commodity imposes external costs on third parties, goods are no longer efficiently distributed to consumers. External costs introduce effective price differentials into markets: Everyone does not pay equal prices for the same commodities. The neighbors who live near our imaginary electric plant, for example, pay not only the prices the plant charges everyone else for electricity, but also the costs the smoke from the burning fuel imposes on them in the form of extra cleaning bills, medical bills, painting bills, and so forth. Because they must pay for these extra external costs, of course, they have fewer funds to pay for their share of market commodities. Consequently, their share of goods is not proportioned to their desires and needs as compared with the shares of those who do not have to pay the extra external costs.

Pollution, then, imposes external costs, and this in turn means that the private costs of production are less than the social costs. As a consequence, markets do not impose an optimal discipline on producers, and the result is a drop in social utility. Pollution of the environment, then, is a violation of the utilitarian principles that underlie a market system.

Remedies: The Duties of the Firm

The remedy for external costs, according to the utilitarian argument sketched earlier, is to ensure that the costs of pollution are internalized—that is, that they are absorbed by the producer and taken into account when determining the price of his goods.[116] In this way, goods will be accurately priced, market forces will provide the incentives that will encourage producers to minimize external costs, and some consumers will no longer end up paying more than others for the same commodities.

There are various ways to internalize the external costs of pollution. One way is for the polluting agent to pay to all of those being harmed, voluntarily or by law, an amount equal to the costs the pollution imposes on them. When Union Oil's drilling in the Santa Barbara channel on the California coast led to an oil spill, the total costs that the spill imposed on local residents and state and federal agencies were estimated at about $16,400,000 (including costs of clean-up, containment, administration, damage to tourism and fishing, recreational and property damages, and loss of marine life). Union Oil paid about $10,400,000 of these costs voluntarily by paying for all clean-up and containment of the oil, and it paid about $6,300,000 in damages to the affected parties as the result of litigation.[117] Thus, the costs of the oil spill were internalized, in part through voluntary action and in part through legal action. When the polluting firm pays those on whom its manufacturing processes impose costs, as Union Oil did, it is led to figure these costs into its own subsequent price determinations. Market mechanisms then lead it to come up with ways of cutting down pollution to cut down its costs. Since the Santa Barbara oil spill, for example, Union Oil and other petroleum firms have invested considerable amounts of money in developing methods to minimize pollution damage from oil spills.

A problem with this way of internalizing the costs of pollution, however, is that when several polluters are involved, it is not always clear just who is being damaged by whom. How much of the environmental damage caused by several polluters should be counted as damages to my property and how much should be counted as damages to your property, when the damages are inflicted on things such as air or public bodies of water, and for how much of the damage should each polluter be held responsible? Moreover, the administrative and legal costs of assessing damages for each distinct polluter and granting separate compensations to each distinct claimant can become substantial.

A second remedy is for the polluter to stop pollution at its source by installing pollution-control devices. In this way, the external costs of polluting the environment are translated into the internal costs the firm pays to install pollution controls. Once costs are internalized in this way, market mechanisms again provide cost-cutting incentives and ensure that prices reflect the true costs of producing the commodity. In addition, the installation of pollution-control devices serves to eliminate the long-range and potentially disastrous worldwide effects of pollution.

Justice

This utilitarian way of dealing with pollution (i.e., by internalizing costs) seems to be consistent with the requirements of distributive justice insofar as distributive justice favors equality. Observers have noted that pollution often has the effect of increasing inequality.[118] If a firm pollutes, its stockholders benefit because their firm does not have to absorb the external costs of pollution; this leaves them with greater profits, and those customers who purchase the firm's products also benefit because the firm does not charge them for all the costs involved in making the product. Therefore, the beneficiaries of pollution tend to be those who can afford to buy a firm's stock and its products. However, the external costs of pollution are borne largely by the poor—a phenomenon some have termed *environmental injustice.*[119] Property values in polluted neighborhoods are generally lower, and consequently they are inhabited by the poor and abandoned by the wealthy. Thus, pollution may produce a net flow of benefits away from the poor and toward the well-off, thereby increasing inequality. In addition, several studies have supported claims of environmental racism: claims that pollution levels tend to be correlated with race so that the higher the proportion of racial minorities living in an area, the higher the likelihood that the area is subject to pollution. To the extent that pollution is correlated with income and race, pollution violates distributive justice. Internalizing the costs of pollution, as utilitarianism requires, would rectify matters by removing the burdens of external costs from the backs of minorities and the poor and placing them in the hands of the wealthy: the firm's stockholders and its customers. By and large, therefore, the utilitarian claim that the external costs of pollution should be internalized is consistent with the requirements of distributive justice.

We should note, however, that if a firm makes basic goods (food products, clothing, gasoline, automobiles) for which the poor must allocate a larger proportion of their budgets than the affluent, then internalizing costs may place a heavier burden on the poor than on the affluent because the prices of these basic goods will rise. The poor may also suffer if the costs of pollution control rise so high that unemployment results (although as noted earlier, current studies indicate that the unemployment effects of pollution-control programs are transitory and minimal).[120] There is some rudimentary evidence that tends to show that current pollution-control measures place greater burdens on the poor than on the wealthy.[121] This suggests the need to integrate distributional criteria into our pollution-control programs.

Internalizing external costs also seems to be consistent with the requirements of retributive and compensatory justice.[122] Retributive justice requires that those who are responsible for and benefit from an injury should bear the burdens of rectifying the injury, whereas compensatory justice requires that those who have been injured should be compensated by those who injure them. Taken together, these requirements imply that (a) the costs of pollution control should be borne by those who cause pollution and who have benefited from pollution activities, whereas (b) the benefits of pollution control should flow to those who have had to bear the external costs of pollution. Internalizing external costs seems to meet these two requirements: (a) The costs of pollution control are borne by stockholders and customers, both of whom benefit from the polluting activities of the firm; and (b) the benefits of pollution control flow to those neighbors who once had to put up with the firm's pollution.

Costs and Benefits

The technology for pollution control has developed effective but costly methods for abating pollution. Up to 60 percent of water pollutants can be removed through primary screening and sedimentation processes, up to 90 percent can be removed through more expensive secondary biological and chemical processes, and amounts over 95 percent can be removed through even more expensive tertiary chemical treatment.[123] Air pollution abatement techniques include the use of fuels and combustion procedures that burn more cleanly; mechanical filters that screen or isolate dust particles in the air; scrubbing processes that pass polluted air through liquids that remove pollutants; and, most expensive of all, chemical treatment that transforms gases into more easily removed compounds.

It is possible, however, for a firm to invest too much in pollution control devices. Suppose, for example, that the pollution from a certain firm causes $100 worth of environmental damage, and suppose that the only device that can eliminate this pollution would cost the firm at least $1000. Then obviously the firm should not install the device; if it does so, the economic utility of society will decline: The costs of eliminating the pollution will be greater than the benefits society will reap, thereby resulting in a shrinkage of total utility.

How much should a firm invest in pollution control then? Consider that the costs of controlling pollution and the benefits derived from pollution control are inversely related.[124] As one rises, the other falls. Why is this so? Think for a moment that if a body of water is highly polluted, it will probably be quite easy and consequently quite cheap to filter out a certain limited amount of pollutants. To filter out a few more pollutants, however, will require finer and, therefore, additional and more expensive filters. Costs will keep climbing for each additional level of purity desired, and getting out the last few molecules of impurities would require astronomically expensive additional equipment. However, getting out those last traces of impurities will probably not matter much to people and will therefore be unnecessary. At the other end of the scale, however, getting rid of the first gross amounts of pollutants will be highly beneficial to people: The costs of damages from these pollutants are substantial. Consequently, if we plot as curves on a graph the costs of removing pollution and the benefits of removing pollution (which are equivalent to the external costs removed), the result will be two intersecting curves as illustrated in Fig. 5.5. What is the optimal amount of pollution control? Obviously, the point at which the two lines cross. At this point, the costs of pollution control exactly equal its benefits. If the firm invests additional resources in removing pollution, society's net utility will decline. Beyond this point, the firm should resort to directly or indirectly (i.e., through taxes or other forms of social investment) paying society for the costs of polluting the environment.

To enable the firm to make such cost-benefit analyses, researchers have devised an array of theoretical methods and techniques for calculating the costs and benefits of removing pollution. These make use of estimates of consumer surplus, rents, market prices and *shadow prices*, adjustment for transfers, discounted future values, and recognition of risk factors.[125] Thomas Klein summarized the procedures for cost–benefit analysis as follows:

> **1.** Identify costs and benefits of the proposed program and the person or sectors incurring or receiving them. Trace transfers.
>
> **2.** Evaluate the costs and benefits in terms of their value to beneficiaries and donors. The standard of measure is the value of each marginal unit to demanders and suppliers ideally captured in competitive prices. Useful refinements involve:
>
> **a.** Incorporating time values through the use of a discount rate.
>
> **b.** Recognizing risk by factoring possible outcomes according to probabilities and, where dependent, probability trees.
>
> **3.** Add up costs and benefits to determine the net social benefit of a project or program.[126]

To avoid erratic and costly use of these procedures, Klein recommended that firms introduce a system of social accounting that "routinely measures, records, and reports external effects to management and other parties."[127]

It is at this point, however, that a fundamental difficulty in the utilitarian approach to pollution emerges. The cost–benefit analyses just described assume that the costs and benefits of reducing pollution can be accurately measured.[128]

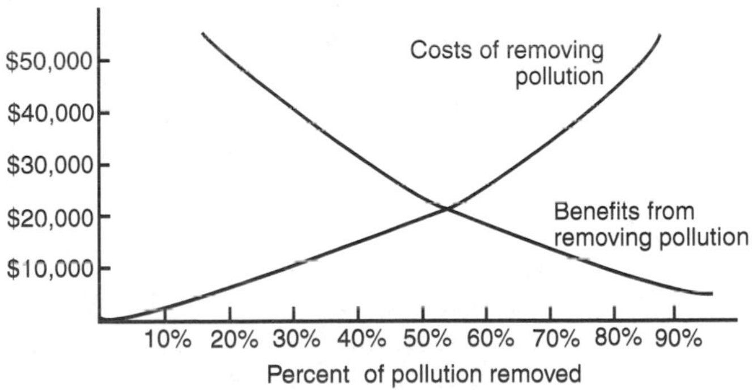

Figure 5.5

In some cases (limited and local in character), cost–benefit measurements are available: The costs and benefits of cleaning up the oil spilled by Union Oil at Santa Barbara several years ago, for example, were more or less measurable. However, the costs and benefits of pollution removal are difficult to measure when they involve damages to human health and loss of life: What is the price of life?[129]

Measurement is also difficult when the effects of pollution are uncertain and, consequently, difficult to predict: What will be the effects of increasing the carbon dioxide content of our atmosphere by burning more coal, as the United States is now starting to do? In fact, perhaps the major problem involved in obtaining the measurements needed to apply cost–benefit analysis to pollution problems is the problem of estimating and evaluating risk (i.e., the probability of future costly consequences).[130] Many new technologies carry with them unknown degrees of risk to present and future generations. The use of nuclear technology, for example, involves some probability of damages to health and loss of life for present and future generations: There are the risks of health damages from mining and the use and disposal of radioactive materials, plus the risks of sabotage and a proliferation of the materials used in atomic weapons. But there are insurmountable obstacles in the way of measuring these risks accurately. For example, we cannot use trial and error (a usual method for learning what the probabilities of an event are) to learn the risk of a nuclear accident because the lesson would obviously be too costly and some of the health effects of radioactivity would not appear until decades after it is too late to correct them. Moreover, the mathematical models that we must rely on to measure risk in the absence of trial and error learning are not useful when all the possible things that can go wrong with a technology are not known. Human error, carelessness, and malice have been involved in most nuclear mishaps. The human factor is notoriously impossible to predict and, therefore, impossible to incorporate into a measurement of the risks associated with using nuclear power. Moreover, even if the numerical risk associated with a new technology were known, it is unclear how much weight it should be given in a social cost–benefit analysis. Imagine, for example, that society currently accepts with some indifference a 0.01 risk of death associated with driving. Does it then follow that society also should be indifferent to accepting a 0.01 risk of death from the introduction of a certain new technology? Obviously not because risk is cumulative: The new technology will *double* society's risk of death to 0.02; while society may be indifferent to carrying a 0.01 risk of death, it may find a 0.02 risk unacceptable. Knowing the risk of a certain costly future event does not, then, necessarily tell us the value that society will place on that risk once it is added to the other risks society already runs. To make matters worse, individuals differ substantially in their aversion to risk: Some individuals like to gamble, whereas others find it extremely distasteful.

The almost insurmountable problems involved in getting accurate pollution measurements are illustrated by the few federal estimates of the benefits produced by pollution control activities. The present financial *costs* of pollution control are fairly easy to obtain by examining reports on expenditures for pollution equipment. However, the *benefits* that these expenditures produce cannot be accurately measured. For example, we know with certainty that total expenditures for pollution control, including government and private expenditures, were $46.7 billion in 1978. Moreover, the federal government estimated that the annual benefits from air pollution control alone were around $21.4 billion in 1978, and earlier studies estimated the annual benefits of water pollution control alone would be $12.3 billion by 1978. Yet these estimates are based on exceedingly unreliable methodologies, and they omit many of the effects of pollution that, today, we are much more aware of, especially long-range global effects such as the effects of carbon dioxide build-up and ozone depletion, as well as the health benefits from the elimination of chemical contamination in drinking water.

The problems involved in getting accurate measurements of the benefits of pollution control are also illustrated by the difficulties businesses have encountered in trying to construct a social audit (a report of the social costs and social benefits of the firm's activities). Those who advocate that a corporation should measure and report the social impacts of its activities have been forced to "recognize that the goal of measuring all impacts of all actions on all conditions and all publics, using standard techniques and units, considerably exceeds current capabilities and that compromises and modifications are inevitable."[131] As a result of this inability to measure benefits, so-called *social audits* are usually nothing more than qualitative descriptions of what a firm is doing. Without definite quantitative measurements of the benefits deriving from its attempts to reduce pollution, a firm has no way of knowing whether its efforts are cost-effective from a social point of view.

These failures of measurement pose significant technical problems for utilitarian approaches to pollution. In addition, the use of utilitarian cost–benefit analysis is sometimes based on assumptions that are inconsistent with people's moral rights. Advocates of utilitarian cost–benefit analysis sometimes assume that if the benefits of a certain technology or manufacturing process clearly outweigh its costs, then it is morally permissible to impose the process on unwilling citizens. For example, a recent government report makes the following recommendations:

> Because nuclear problems are such highly emotional issues and becoming even more so, as evidenced by the states that have indicated an unwillingness to permit nuclear waste disposal within their boundaries, it may be impossible to get the public and political support necessary for a given state to accept nuclear waste.

> Ultimately, if state approval for waste repository sites cannot be obtained within an established time, the federal government might have to mandate selections. While such action would not be easy it may be necessary if the waste problem is to be solved in a reasonable time.[132]

However, recommendations of this type seem to violate the basic moral right that underlies democratic societies: Persons have a moral right to be treated only as they have consented to be treated beforehand (see Chapter 2, second section). If people have not consented to take on the costs of a technology (and indicate this unwillingness, e.g., through local legislation, hearings, or opinion surveys), then their moral right of consent is violated when these costs are imposed on them anyway. Using only cost–benefit analysis to determine whether a new technology or manufacturing process should be used, then, ignores the question of whether the costs involved are voluntarily accepted by those who must bear them or whether they are unilaterally imposed on them by others in violation of their rights.

It should be noted that, although the right of consent seems to imply that decisions concerning pollution control should always be left in the hands of the ordinary citizen, this implication is not necessarily correct. People can give their informed consent to a risky project only if they have an adequate understanding of the project and its attendant risks. However, contemporary technology is often so complex that even experts disagree when estimating and assessing the risks it may involve (e.g., scientists disagree wildly over the safety of using nuclear power). Therefore, it may be impossible for ordinary citizens to understand and assess the risks that a certain polluting technology will impose on them. Consequently, it may be impossible, in principle, for them to give their informed consent to it.

In view of all the problems raised by utilitarian approaches to pollution, it may be that alternative approaches are more adequate. In particular, it may be that the absolute bans on pollution that are still incorporated in many federal laws, and the rights theory on which these absolute bans rest, are, for the present at least, a more adequate approach to pollution issues than utilitarianism. Alternatively, some writers have suggested that when risks cannot be reliably estimated, it is best to choose only those projects that carry no risk of irreversible damages. For example, if there is a probability that the pollution from a certain technology may bring about catastrophic consequences that will continue to plague us forever, then the technology should be rejected in favor of other technologies that will not close off our options in the same permanent way. Others suggest that when risks cannot be assessed, we should, in justice, identify those who are most vulnerable and who would have to bear the heaviest costs if things should go wrong, and then take steps to ensure that they are protected. For example, future generations and children should be protected against our polluting choices. Finally, others suggest that when risks cannot be measured, the only rational procedure is to first assume that the worst will happen and then choose the option that will leave us best off when the worst happens (this is the so-called *maximin rule* of probability theory). It is unclear which, if any, of these alternative approaches should be adopted when utilitarian cost–benefit analysis fails.

Social Ecology, Ecofeminism, and the Demands of Caring

The difficulties inherent in utilitarian and rights-based approaches to the ethical issues raised by environmental degradation have led many to look for alternative approaches. Some have argued, in fact, that utilitarian and rights-based theories embody a kind of calculative and rationalistic way of thinking that is responsible for environmental crises. Utilitarian thinking assumes that nature is to be measured and used efficiently, whereas rights-based theories see humans and other entities in individualistic terms and ignore their relationships with the rest of nature. These ways of thinking, it has been argued, are tightly linked to the kind of society in which we live.

Many thinkers have argued that the environmental crises we face are rooted in the social systems of hierarchy and domination that characterize our society. This view, now referred to as *social ecology*, holds that, until those patterns of hierarchy and domination are changed, we will be unable to deal with environmental crises. In a system of hierarchy, one group holds power over another and members of the superior group are able to dominate those of the inferior group and get them to serve their ends. Examples of such systems of hierarchy include social practices such as racism, sexism, and social classes, as well as social institutions such as property rights, capitalism, bureaucracies, and the mechanisms of government. Such systems of hierarchy and domination go hand in hand with the widespread environmental destruction taking place all around us and with economic ways of managing the environment. Murray Bookchin, the most well-known proponent of this view, wrote:

> We must look into the cultural forms of domination that exist in the family, between generations, sexes, racial and ethnic groups, in all institutions of political, economic, and social management, and very significantly in the way we experience reality as a whole, including nature and nonhuman life forms.[133]

Systems of hierarchy and domination, Bookchin suggested, facilitate the rise of a broad cultural mentality that encourages domination in many forms, including the domination of nature. Success becomes identified with dominance and control: The greater the number of people who work for a person, the greater that person's wealth, power, and status, and the more successful the person is deemed to be. Success also becomes identified with the domination of nature as society comes to identify "progress" with the increasing ability to control and dominate nature and its processes. Science, technology, and agriculture all join hands in this attempt to dominate and control nature. Utilitarian weighing of the costs and benefits of destroying nature are inevitable in this perspective. The widespread destruction of nature that results, then, cannot be halted until our societies become less hierarchical, less dominating, and less oppressive. The ideal society is one that eschews all domination and in which all power is decentralized. Agriculture and technology would be restricted to those that are sustainable and in which humans live in harmony with nature.

Several feminist thinkers have argued that the key form of hierarchy connected to destruction of the environment is the domination of women by men. Ecofeminism has been described as "the position that there are important connections—historical, experiential, symbolic, theoretical—between the domination of women and the domination of nature, an understanding of which is crucial to both feminism and environmental ethics."[134] Ecofeminists have argued that the root of our ecological crisis lies in a pattern of domination of nature that is tightly linked to the social practices and institutions through which women have been subordinated to men. Underlying this subordination of women to men are ways of thinking that justify and perpetuate the subordination. One key pattern of thinking—the "logic of domination"—sets up dualisms (masculine–feminine, reason–emotion, artifact–nature, mind-body, objective–subjective) that are used to characterize men and women. Because of their roles in childbearing, childraising, and human sexuality, women are seen as more emotional, closer to nature and the body, and more subjective and passive, whereas men are masculine, more rational, closer to constructed artifacts and the life of the mind, and more objective and active. The masculine characteristics are then seen as superior to and more valuable than the feminine characteristics (reason, objectivity, and the mind are superior to emotion, subjectivity, and bodily feelings), and this is taken as justifying the subordination of women to men. This subordination of what is feminine in turn is transferred to nature, which is seen as feminine (mother nature) and with which women are felt to be more closely associated. Thus, the domination of nature accompanies the domination of women, and as women are exploited for the interests of men, so too is nature.

If the forms of thinking that accompany hierarchy and domination are responsible for the destruction of the environment, with what should they be replaced? Social ecologists such as Bookchin have argued that humans should see themselves as stewards of nature, not as masters who should dominate nature. Some ecofeminists have argued that women should strive for an androgynous culture, which eradicates traditional gender roles and does away with the distinction between *feminine* and *masculine* that justifies a destructive domination of nature. Many ecofeminists have argued that instead one should try "to remedy ecological and other problems through the creation of an alternative 'women's culture' . . . based on revaluing, celebrating and defending what patriarchy has devalued, including the feminine, nonhuman nature, the body and the emotions."[135] In particular, some have argued, the destructive masculine perspective of domination and hierarchy must be replaced with the feminine perspective of caring.

From the perspective of an ethic of caring, the destruction of nature that has accompanied male hierarchies of domination must be replaced with caring for and nurturing our relationships to nature and living things. Nel Noddings, a feminist proponent of an ethic of care, argued that, "When my caring is directed to living things, I must consider their natures, ways of life, needs, and desires. And, although I can never accomplish it entirely, I try to apprehend the reality of the other."[136] Although Noddings holds that the demands of caring extend only to those parts of nature that are living and with which one is directly related, others have extended the ethic of care to encompass relationships with all of nature. Karen Warren, for example, in discussing the relationship a person can have to a rock or mountain one is climbing, called attention to:

> . . . the difference in attitudes and behaviors toward a rock when one is "making it to the top" and when one thinks of oneself as "friends with" or "caring about" the rock one climbs. These different attitudes and behaviors suggest an ethically germane contrast between two different types of relationship humans or climbers may have toward a rock: an imposed conqueror-type relationship, and an emergent caring-type relationship. . . . Ecofeminism makes a central place for values of care, love, friendship, trust, and appropriate reciprocity—values that presuppose that our relationships to others are central to our understanding of who we are. It thereby gives voice to the sensitivity that in climbing a mountain, one is doing something in relationship with an "other," an "other" whom one can come to care about and treat respectfully.[137]

Ecofeminists like Warren would hold that, although the concepts of utilitarianism, rights, and justice have a limited role to play in environmental ethics, an adequate environmental ethic must also take into account in a central manner the perspectives of an ethic of care. Nature must be seen as an other that can be cared for and with which one has a relationship that must be nurtured and attended to. Nature must not be seen as an object to be dominated, controlled, and manipulated.

Although ecofeminist approaches to the environment are thought provoking, it is unclear what their specific implications may turn out to be. These approaches are too recent to have been fully articulated. The shortcomings of utilitarian and rights-based approaches to the environment, however, may prompt a much fuller development of these approaches in the near future.

5.3 The Ethics of Conserving Depletable Resources

Conservation refers to the saving or rationing of natural resources for later uses. Conservation, therefore, looks primarily to the future: to the need to limit consumption now to have resources available for tomorrow.

In a sense, pollution control is a form of conservation. Pollution "consumes" pure air and water, and pollution control "conserves" them for the future. However, there are basic differences between the problems of pollution and the problems of resource depletion that makes the term *conservation* more applicable to the latter problems than to the former. With some notable exceptions (such as nuclear wastes), most forms of pollution affect present generations, and their control will benefit present generations. The depletion of most scarce resources, however, lies far in the future, and the effects of their depletion will be felt primarily by posterity and not by present generations. Consequently, our concern over the depletion of resources is primarily a concern for future generations and for the benefits that will be available to them. For this reason, conservation is more applicable to the problems of resource depletion than to those of pollution. Moreover (again with notable exceptions), pollution is a problem concerned primarily with "renewable" resources, insofar as air and water can be "renewed" by ceasing to dump pollutants into them and allowing them time to recover. Tomorrow's supply, therefore, will be created anew over and over if we take the proper precautions. Resource depletion, however, is concerned with finite, nonrenewable resources. The only store of a finite, nonrenewable resource that will be around tomorrow is that which is left over from today. Conservation, therefore, is the only way of ensuring a supply for tomorrow's generations.Resource depletion forces two main kinds of questions on us: Why should we conserve resources for future generations? How much should we conserve?

Rights of Future Generations

It might appear that we have an obligation to conserve resources for future generations because they have an equal right to the limited resources of this planet. If future generations have an equal right to the world's resources, then by depleting these resources, we are taking what is actually theirs and violating their equal right to these resources.

A number of writers, however, have claimed that it is a mistake to think that future generations have rights.[138] Consequently, it is a mistake to think that we should refrain from consuming natural resources because we are taking what future generations have a right to. Three main reasons have been advanced to show that future generations cannot have rights.

First, future generations cannot intelligently be said to have rights because they do not now exist and may never exist.[139] I may be able to think about future people, but I cannot hit them, punish them, injure them, or treat them wrongly. Future people exist only in the imagination, and imaginary entities cannot be acted on in any way whatsoever except in imagination. Similarly, we cannot say that future people possess things now when they do not yet exist to possess or have them. Because there is a possibility that future generations may never exist, they cannot "possess" rights.

Second, if future generations did have rights, we might be led to the absurd conclusion that we must sacrifice our entire civilization for their sake.[140] Suppose that each of the infinite number of future generations had an equal right to the world's supply of oil. Then we would have to divide the oil equally among them all, and our share would be a few quarts at the most. We would then be put in the absurd position of having to shut down our entire Western civilization so that each future person might be able to possess a few quarts of oil.

Third, we can say that someone has a certain right only if we know that he or she has a certain interest which that right protects. The purpose of a right, after all, is to protect the interests of the right holder, but we are virtually ignorant of what interests future generations will have. What wants will they have? The men and women of the future may be genetically fabricated to order, with desires, pleasures, and needs vastly different from our own. What kinds of resources will future technology require for supplying their wants? Science might come up with technologies for creating products from raw materials that we have in abundance—minerals in sea water, for example—and might find potentially unlimited energy sources such as nuclear fusion. Moreover, future generations might develop cheap and plentiful substitutes for the scarce resources that we now need. Because we are uncertain about these matters, we must remain ignorant about the interests future generations will want to protect (who could have guessed 80 years ago that uranium rocks would one day be considered a "resource" in which people would have an interest?). Consequently, we are unable to say what rights future people might have.[141]

If these arguments are correct, then to the extent that we are uncertain what future generations will exist or what they will be like, they do not have any rights. It does not follow, however, that we have no obligations to any future generations because our obligations may be based on other grounds.

Justice to Future Generations

John Rawls argued that, although it is unjust to impose disproportionately heavy burdens on present generations for the sake of future generations, it is also unjust for present generations to leave nothing for future generations. To determine a just way of distributing resources between generations, he suggested, the members of each generation should put themselves in the "original position" and, without knowing what generation they belong to, they should:

> ask what is reasonable for members of adjacent generations to expect of one another at each level of (historical) advance. They should try to piece together a just savings schedule by balancing how much at each stage (of history) they would be willing to save for their immediate descendants against what they would feel entitled to claim of their immediate predecessors. Thus, imagining themselves to be parents, say, they are to ascertain how much they would set aside for their children by noting what they would believe themselves entitled to claim of their own parents.[142]

In general, Rawls claims that this method of ascertaining what earlier generations in justice owe to later generations will lead to the conclusion that what justice demands of us is merely that we hand to the next generation a situation no worse than we received from the generation before us:

> Each generation must not only preserve the gains of culture and civilization, and maintain intact those just institutions that have been established, but it must also put aside in each period of time a suitable amount of real capital accumulation. . . . (It should be kept in mind here that capital is not only factories, and machines, and so on, but also the knowledge and culture, as well as the techniques and skills, that make possible just institutions and the fair value of liberty.) This . . . is in return for what is received from previous generations that enables the later ones to enjoy better life in a more just society.[143]

Justice, then, requires that we hand over to our immediate successors a world that is not in worse condition than the one we received from our ancestors.[144]

The demands of caring that arise from an ethic of care would also suggest conservation policies that are similar to those advocated by Rawls' views on justice. Although most people would agree that they have a fairly direct relationship of care and concern with the generation that immediately succeeds their own, such a direct relationship does not exist with more distant and so more abstract generations. The generation that immediately succeeds our own, for example, consists of our own children. The demands of caring, we have seen, imply that one should attempt to see matters from the perspective of those with whom we are thus directly related and that we attempt to care for their specific needs. Such caring would imply that we should at least leave the immediately succeeding generation a world that is not worse than the one we received.

Rawls' conclusion is also supported by some utilitarian reasoning. Robin Attfield, a utilitarian, for example, argued that utilitarianism favors what he called the *Lockean principle* that "each should leave enough and as good for others."[145] Attfield interpreted this principle to mean that each generation must leave for future generations a world whose output capacity is no less than that generation received from previous generations.[146] That is, each generation must leave the world no less productive than it found it. Attfield suggested that leaving the world with the same output capacity does not necessarily mean leaving the world with the same resources. Instead, maintaining the same level of output can be achieved either through conservation, recycling, or technological innovation.

Other utilitarians have reached slightly different but otherwise similar conclusions by relying on other basic utilitarian principles. Utilitarians have argued that each generation has a duty to maximize the future beneficial consequences of its actions and to minimize their future injurious consequences.[147] However, utilitarians have claimed that these future consequences should be "discounted" (given less weight) in proportion to their uncertainty and to their distance in the future.[148] Together these utilitarian principles imply that we at least have an obligation to avoid those practices whose harmful consequences for the generation that immediately follows us are certain to outweigh the beneficial consequences our own generation derives from them. Our responsibility for more distant future generations, however, is diminished especially insofar as we are unable to foresee what effects our present actions will have on them because we do not know what needs or technology they will have.

Unfortunately, we cannot rely on market mechanisms (i.e., price rises) to ensure that scarce resources are conserved for future generations. The market registers only the effective demands of present participants and the actual supplies presently being made available. The needs and demands of future generations, as well as the potential scarcities that lie far in the future, are so heavily "discounted" by markets that they hardly affect prices at all.[149] William Shepherd and Clair Wilcox provided a summary of the reasons that the private choices represented in markets and market prices fail to take into account the future scarcity of resources:

1. *Multiple access* If a resource can be used by several separate extractors, then the shared access will invariably lead the resource to be depleted too fast. . . . As with several people with straws in one milkshake, each owner's private interest is in taking it out as fast as possible. . . .
2. *Time preferences and myopia* Firms often have short time horizons, under the stress of commercial competition. This may underrepresent the legitimate interests of future generations. . . .
3. *Inadequate forecasting* Present users may simply fail to foresee future developments. This may reflect a lack of sufficient research interest and ability to discern future changes. . . .
4. *Special influences* Specific taxes and other incentive devices may encourage overly rapid use of resources. . . .
5. *External effects* There are important externalities in the uses of many resources, so that private users ignore major degrees of pollution and other external costs. . . .

6. *Distribution* Finally, private market decisions are based on the existing pattern of distribution of wealth and income. As resource users vote with their dollars, market demand will more strongly reflect the interests and preferences of the wealthy.[150]

The only means of conserving for the future, then, appear to be voluntary (or politically enforced) policies of conservation.

In practical terms, Rawls' view implies that, although we should not sacrifice the cultural advances we have made, we should adopt voluntary or legal measures to conserve those resources and environmental benefits that we can reasonably assume our immediate posterity will need if they are to live lives with a variety of available choices comparable, at least, to ours. In particular, this would mean that we should preserve wildlife and endangered species; that we should take steps to ensure that the rate of consumption of fossil fuels and minerals does not continue to rise; that we should cut down our consumption and production of those goods that depend on nonrenewable resources; and that we should recycle nonrenewable resources; and that we should search for substitutes for materials that we are too rapidly depleting.

Economic Growth?

However, to many observers, conservation measures fall far short of what is needed. Several writers have argued that if we are to preserve enough scarce resources so that future generations can maintain their quality of life at a satisfactory level, we shall have to change our economies substantially, particularly by scaling down our pursuit of economic growth. E. F. Schumacher, for example, claimed that the industrialized nations will have to convert from growth-oriented capital-intensive technologies to much more labor-intensive technologies in which humans do work machines now do.[151] Others argue that economic systems will have to abandon their goal of steadily increasing production and put in its place the goal of decreasing production until it has been scaled down to "a steady state"—that is, a point at which "the total population and the total stock of physical wealth are maintained constant at some desired levels by a 'minimal' rate of maintenance throughout (that is, by birth and death rates that are equal at the lowest feasible level, and by physical production and consumption rates that are equal at the lowest feasible level)."[152] The conclusion that economic growth must be abandoned if society is to be able to deal with the problems of diminishing resources has been challenged.[153] It is at least arguable that adherence to continual economic growth promises to degrade the quality of life of future generations.[154]

The arguments for this claim are simple, stark, and highly controversial. If the world's economies continue to pursue the goal of economic growth, the demand for depletable resources will continue to rise. Because world resources are finite, at some point supplies will simply run out. At this point, if the world's nations are still based on growth economies, we can expect a collapse of their major economic institutions (i.e., of manufacturing and financial institutions, communication networks, the service industries), which in turn will bring down their political and social institutions (i.e., centralized governments, education and cultural programs, scientific and technological development, health care).[155] Living standards will then decline precipitously in the wake of widespread starvation and political dislocations. Various scenarios for this sequence of events have been constructed, all of them more or less speculative and necessarily based on uncertain assumptions.[156] The most famous and oldest of these are the studies of the Club of Rome, which over two decades ago projected on computers the catastrophic results of continuing the economic growth patterns of the past in the face of declining resources.[157] Later studies came to similar conclusions.[158] Figure. 5.6 reproduces one of the original computer projections of the Club of Rome.

In the computer-based graph of Fig. 5.6, the horizontal axis represents time; as we run from the year A.D. 1900 at the left to the year A.D. 2100 at the

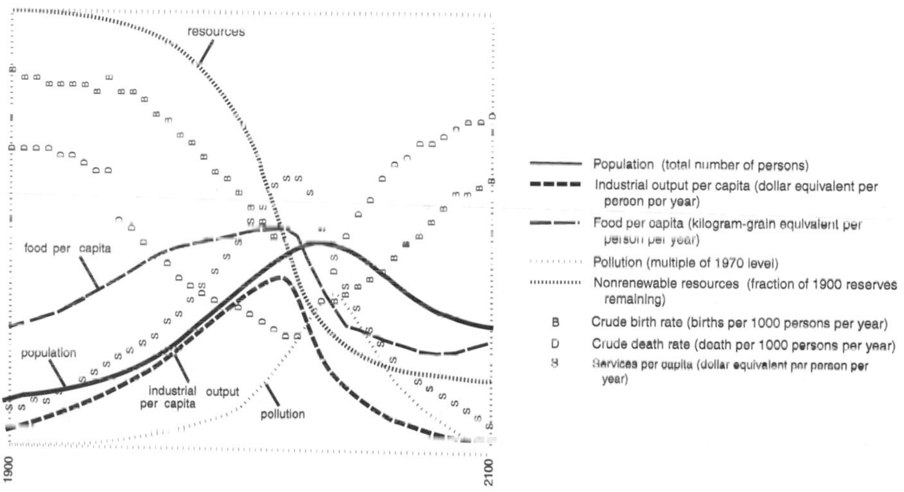

Figure 5.6 The "standard" world model run assumes no major change in the physical, economic, or social relationships that have historically governed the development of the world system. All variables plotted here follow historical values from 1900 to 1970. Food, industrial output, and population grow exponentially until the rapidly diminishing resource base forces a slowdown in industrial growth. Because of natural delays in the system, both population and pollution continue to increase for some time after the peak of industrialization. Population growth is finally halted by a rise in the death rate due to decreased food and medical services. *Source:* From Donella H. Meadows et al., *The Limits to Growth* (New York: Universe Books, 1974), pp. 123–24. Reprinted by permission of Universe Books.

right, we see what will happen to the world's population, industrial output, food, pollution levels, nonrenewable resources, and so on as time passes. During the first half of the 1900s, population, output, food, and services continue to grow while death rates, birth rates, and resources decline. At some point after 2050, however, a catastrophic collapse of output and services occurs as resources run out. Population continues to rise, but a climbing death rate and declining food supply soon brings it down. The decline in industrial output causes a decline in pollution, but food supplies, industrial output, and population by 2100 are below 1900 levels. "We can thus say with some confidence that, under the assumption of no major change in the present system, population and industrial growth will certainly stop within the next century at the latest."[159]

The assumptions on which the doomsday scenarios of the Club of Rome and other groups were based have been repeatedly criticized and "debunked."[160] The computer programs and underlying equations on which the predictions were based made controversial and highly uncertain assumptions about future population growth rates, the absence of future increases in output per unit of input, our inability to find substitutes for depleted resources, and the ineffectiveness of recycling. These assumptions can all be challenged. Although future generations will certainly have fewer of the natural resources on which we depend, we cannot be sure exactly what impact this will have on them. Perhaps the impact will not be as catastrophic nor occur as early as the prognostications of the Club of Rome indicated.[161] We also cannot assume that the impact will be entirely benign, nor that there will be no major environmental disruptions in our lifetimes.[162] Moreover, as the quotation from the year 2000 Report of the Worldwatch Institute with which we opened this chapter suggests, many observers are again coming to the conclusion that the Club of Rome may have been substantially correct even if its timetables and assumptions were to some extent mistaken. The increasing pace of species extinctions, the global rise in temperature attributable to rising levels of greenhouse gases, the continuing decimation of forests, and the still increasing rates of population growth all point to a difficult future for us. Given the extreme uncertainties in our situation, at the very least a commitment to conservation seems to be in order. Whether a wholesale transformation of our economy is also necessary if civilization is to survive is a difficult and disturbing question that we may soon have to face.

Just as troubling are the moral questions raised by the distribution of dwindling energy supplies among the world's peoples. The United States is the world's richest nation and the highest consumer of energy. The 6 percent of the world's population that lives within the United States consumes 35 percent of the world's annual energy supplies, whereas the 50 percent of the world's people who inhabit less developed nations must get along with about 8 percent of its energy supplies. Each person in the United States, in fact, consumes 15 times more energy than a native South American, 24 times more than a native Asian, and 31 times more than a native African.

The high energy consumption rates of Americans are not paralleled by similarly high rates of energy production. In fact, U.S. energy consumption is, subsidized by other countries, in particular by the Caribbean, the Middle East, and Africa. That is, there is a net flow of energy out of these less-consuming populations and into the high-consumption population of the United States. Moreover, Americans use much of the energy supplies available to them for inessentials (unneeded products, unnecessary travel, household comforts, and conveniences), whereas the more frugal nations tend to use their supplies to meet basic needs (food, clothing, housing).

In view of the approaching scarcity of energy resources, these comparisons cannot help but raise the question of whether a high-consumption nation is morally justified in continuing to appropriate for its own use the nonrenewable energy resources of other more frugal nations that are too weak economically to use these resources or too weak militarily to protect them. Any attempt to answer this question obviously requires a detailed inquiry into the nature of the world's social, economic, and political systems—an inquiry that is beyond the scope of this book. The question, however, is one that events may also soon force us to face.[163]

Questions for Review and Discussion

1. Define the following concepts: pollution, toxic substance, nuclear wastes, exponential depletion, peaked depletion, free good, unlimited good, ecological system, ecological ethic, right to a livable environment, absolute ban, private costs, social costs, external costs, to internalize costs, cost–benefit analysis, risk, social audit, right of consent, conservation, rights of future generations, justice toward future generations, multiple access, time preference, doomsday scenario, high-consumption nation.
2. Define the main forms of pollution and resource depletion and identify the major problems associated with each form.
3. Compare and contrast the views of (a) an ecological ethic, (b) Blackstone's ethic of environmental rights, and (c) a utilitarian ethic of pollution control. Which view seems to you to be the more adequate? Explain your answer.
4. Do you agree with the claims that (a) future generations have no rights, and (2) the future generations to which we have obligations actually include only the generation that will immediately succeed us? Explain your answer. If you do not agree with these claims, state your own views and provide arguments to support them.
5. In your judgment, should the major decisions on pollution and resource depletion (especially energy policy) be made by government experts? By scientific experts? By everyone? Provide moral arguments in support of your judgment.
6. "Any pollution law is unjust because it necessarily violates people's right to liberty and right to property." Discuss.
7. In their book *Energy Future*, R. Strobaugh and D. Yergin claimed that, in the debate over nuclear power, "the resolution of differing opinions over how to deal with uncertainty, over how much risk is acceptable, or how safe is safe enough-all require judgments in which values play as large a role as scientific facts" (p. 100). Discuss this claim.

Web Resources

Readers interested in researching environmental issues through the Internet should begin with the Envirolink web page, which has links to numerous Internet resources (http://www.envirolink.com) and to the environmental resources at Indiana University's virtual library (http://www.law.indiana.edu). The EPA also provides numerous links and its own ample database (http://www.epa.gov), as does the Office of Ocean and Coastal Resource Management (http://wave.nos.noaa.gov/ocrm). Several environmental organizations and journals are accessible through the Essential Organization web page (http://essential.org). Other links are provided by the Pacific Net Page (http://www.pacific.net) and the Greenmoney fund (http://www.greenmoney.com/index.htm).

Notes

1. The World Bank, *World Development Indicators, 1999* (Washington, DC: International Bank for Reconstruction and Development, The World Bank, 1999), Table 3.7.
2. Lester R. Brown, "Challenges of the New Century," *State of the World, 2000* (New York: W.W. Norton & Company, 2000) excerpts from pp. 5, 6, 7, 8.
3. William G. Pollard, "The Uniqueness of the Earth," in Ian G. Barbour. ed., *Earth Might Be Fair* (Englewood Cliffs, NJ: Prentice-Hall, 1972), pp. 95–96; see also Robert L. Heilbroner, *An Inquiry into the Human Prospect, Updated for the 1980s* (New York: W. W. Norton & Company, Inc., 1980).
4. The most important study of the health effects of air pollution remains Lester Lave and Eugene Seskind, *Air Pollution and Human Health* (Baltimore: Johns Hopkins University Press, 1977); for a review of the literature, see A. Myrick Freeman, III, *Air and Water Pollution Control* (New York: John Wiley & Sons, Inc., 1982), pp. 36–85.
5. Council on Environmental Quality, *Environmental Trends* (Washington, DC: U.S. Government Printing Office, 1989), pp. 62–63.
6. U.S. Geological Survey, Fact Sheet 002–00, "Sea Level and Climate," January 2000; Tim Beardsley, "Getting Warmer?" *Scientific American* (July 1988): 32; see the EPA website on global warming at http://www.epa.gov/globalwarming/index.html, and access their page on "impacts"; see also the report of the Intergovernmental Panel on Climate Change, *The Regional Impacts of Climate Change—An Assessment of Vulnerability*, edited by R. T. Watson, M. C. Zinyowera, and R. H. Moss (New York: Cambridge University Press, 1997), excerpts of which are also available at www.ipcc.ch/pub/reports.htm and on the EPA website at www.epa.gov/globalwarming/publications/reference/ipcc/index.html. Two other useful websites are www.heatisonline.org and www.med.harvard.edu/chge.
7. *The Regional Impacts of Climate Change*, excerpts are available at http://www.epa.gov/globalwarming/publications/reference/ipcc/index.html.

8. Paul R. Epstein, "Is Global Warming Harmful to Health?" *Scientific American*, vol. 283, no. 2, (August 2000): 50–57.

9. Lester R. Brown, ed., *State of the World, 2000* (New York: W. W. Norton & Company, 2000), p. 200; see, more generally, World Meteorological Organization, *Scientific Assessment of Ozone Depletion: 1994*, WMO Global Ozone Research and Monitoring Project—Report No. 37, Geneva, 1995; the executive summary of the WMO report is available at www.al.noaa.gov/WWWHD/pubdocs/Assessment94/executive-summary.html#A.

10. U.S. Environmental Protection Agency, "Ozone Science Fact Sheet," 1997, available at http://www.epa.gov/ozone/science/sc_fact.html.

11. United States Environmental Protection Agency, "What You Should Know about Refrigerants When Purchasing or Repairing a Residential A/C System or Heat Pump," April 26; 2000 available at www.epa.gov/ozone/title6/phaseout/22phaseout.html.

12. U.S. Environmental Protection Agency, "Environmental Effects of Acid Rain," April 1999; available at www.epa.gov/acidrain/effects/envben.html. For a readable and informal overview of the acid rain problem (and other environmental issues), see Bernadette West, Peter M. Sandman, and Michael R. Greenberg, *The Reporter's Environmental Handbook* (New Jersey: Rutgers Unviersity Press, 1995), pp. 33–38.

13. See B. J. Mason, *Acid Rain: Its Causes and Effects on Inland Waters* (Oxford, Clarendon Press, 1992).

14. Environmental Protection Agency, *National Air Quality and Emissions Trends Report, 1998* (EPA 454/R-00–003), March 2000, p. 81.

15. Quoted in Huey D. Johnson, ed., *No Deposit-No Return* (Reading, MA: Addison-Wesley Publishing Co., Inc., 1970), pp. 166 67.

16 Bad Air's Damage to Lungs Is Long-lasting, Study Says," *San Jose Mercury News* (29 March 1991): 1f.

17. See Philip E. Graves, Ronald J. Krumm, and Daniel M. Violette, "Issues in Health Benefit Measurement," in George S. Tolley, Philip E. Graves, and Alan S. Cohen, ed., *Environment Policy*, Volume II (Cambridge, MA: Harper & Row, Publishers, Inc., 1982).

18. Lester Lave and Eugene Seskind, *Air Pollution and Human Health* (Baltimore: Johns Hopkins University Press, 1977).

19. *Ibid.*, pp. 723–33.

20. *Ibid.*

21. Freeman, *Air and Water Pollution Control*, p. 69.

22. United States Environmental Protection Agency, "Water Quality Conditions in the United States: A Profile from the 1998 National Water Quality Inventory Report to Congress;" July 2000, summary of the *National Water Quality Inventory: 1998 Report to Congress*, available at www.epa.gov/305b/98report/98summary.html.

23. See U.S. Environmental Protection Agency, *National Air Pollutant Emission Trends, 1900– 1998*, EPA-454/R-00-002.

24. Council on Environmental Quality, *Environmental Trends*, p. 31.

25. X. M. Mackenthun, *The Practice of Water Pollution* (Washington, DC: U.S. Government Printing Office, 1969), ch. 8.

26. Wagner, *Environment*, pp. 102–7.

27. J. H. Ryther, "Nitrogen, Phosphorus, and Eutrophication in the Coastal Marine Environment," *Science*, vol. 171, no. 3975 (1971): 1008–13.

28. L. J. Carter, "Chemical Plants Leave Unexpected Legacy for Two Virginia Rivers," *Science,* vol. 198 (1977): 1015–20; J. Holmes, "Mercury Is Heavier Than You Think," *Esquire*, May 1971; T. Aaronson, "Mercury in the Environment," *Environment*, May 1971.

29. F. S. Sterrett and C. A. Boss, "Careless Kepone," *Environment*, vol. 19 (1977): 30–37.

30. L. Friberg, *Cadmium in the Environment* (Cleveland, OH: C.R.C. Press, 1971).

31. See Presson S. Shane, "Case Study-Silver Bay: Reserve Mining Company," in Thomas Donaldson and Patricia H. Werhane, eds., *Ethical Issues in Business* (Englewood Cliffs, NJ: Prentice-Hall, 1979), p. 358–61.

32. Sharon Begley, "Smothering the Waters," *Newsweek*, 10 April 1989.

33. Council on Environmental Quality, *Environmental Quality*, 1987–1988 (Washington, DC: U.S. Government Printing Office, 1989).

34. D. Burnham, "Radioactive Material Found in Oceans," *New York Times*, 31 May 1976, p. 13.

35. Council on Environmental Quality, *Environmental Trends*, p. 47.

36. *Ibid.*

37. World Bank, *World Development Indicators, 1999*, p. 119.

38. Freeman, *Air and Water Pollution Control*, p. 159.

39. For these and other similar examples, see Lewis Regenstein, *America the Poisoned* (Washington, DC: Acropolis Books, Ltd., 1982); "The Poisoning of America Continues," *Time*, 14 October, 1985, pp. 76–90.

40. Council on Environmental Quality, *Environmental Trends*, p. 139.

41. *Ibid.*, p. 140.

42. *Ibid.*

43. *Council on Environmental Quality,* Environmental Quality Report, 1987–1988 (Washington, DC: U.S. Government Printing Office, 1989), p. 3.

44. *Ibid.*

45. *Ibid.* p. 5.

46. Council on Environmental Quality, *Environmental Trends*, p. 139.

47. Council on Environmental Quality, *Environmental Trends,* p. 139.

48. *Ibid.*

49. Council on Environmental Quality, *Environmental Quality* 1983 (Washington, DC: U.S. Government Printing Office, 1984), p. 62.

50. See U.S. Nuclear Regulatory Commission, "NRC Statement on Risk Assessment and the Reactor Safety Study Report in Light of the Risk Assessment Review Group Report," 18 January 1979.

51. U.S. Nuclear Regulatory Commission, "Final Generic Environmental Statement on the Use of Plutonium Recycle in Mixed Oxide Fuel in Light Water Cooled Reactors," NUREG-0002, vol. 1, August 1976.

52. See Theodore B. Taylor and Mason Willrich, *Nuclear Theft: Risks and Safeguards* (Cambridge, MA: Ballinger Publishing Co., 1974).

53. Thomas O'Toole, "Glass, Salt Challenged as Radioactive Waste Disposal Methods," *The Washington Post*, 24 December 1978.

54. U.S. General Accounting Office, GAO Report to Congress B-164052, "Cleaning Up the Remains of Nuclear Facilities-A Multibillion Dollar Problem," EMD-77–46 (Washington, DC: U.S. Government Printing Office, 1977).

55. Sam H. Schurr, et al., *Energy in America's Future* (Baltimore: The Johns Hopkins University Press, 1979), p. 35.

56. Ellen Winchester, "Nuclear Wastes," *Sierra*, July/August 1979.

57. Charles Officer & Jake Page, *Earth and You: Tales of the Environment* (Portsmouth, NH: Peter E. Randall Publisher, 2000).

58. C. S. Wong, "Atmospheric Input of Carbon Dioxide from Burning Wood," *Science*, 200 (1978): 197–200

59. G. M. Woodwell, "The Carbon Dioxide Question," *Scientific American*, vol. 238 (1978): 34–43.

60. Mara D. Bellaby, "11,046 Plants and Animals At Risk, Report Says," *San Jose Mercury News*, September 29, 2000, p. 10A.

61. Council on Environmental Quality, *The Global 2000 Report to the President*, p. 23.

62. An exponential rate of depletion is assumed in the Club of Rome report; Donella H. Meadows, Dennis L. Meadows, Jergen Randers, and William W. Behrens III, *The Limits to Growth* (New York: Universe Books, 1972).

63. U.S. Congress Office of Technology Assessment, *World Petroleum Availability: 1980–2000* (Washington, DC: U.S. Government Printing Office, 1980).

64. M. K. Hubbert, "U.S. Energy Resources: A Review as of 1972," Document No. 93–40 (92–72) (Washington, DC: U.S. Government Printing Office, 1974).

65. *Time*, "Cheap Oil," 14 April 1986, pp. 62–78.

66. See the overview of this issue in Barry B. Hughes, *World Futures* (Baltimore: The Johns Hopkins University Press, 1985), pp. 113–23.

67. Davis, *The Seventh Year*, pp. 44–46.

68. *Ibid.*, p. 128.

69. *Ibid.*, pp. 131–132.

70. Paul R. Portney, ed., *Current Issues in Natural Resource Policy* (Washington, DC: Resources for the Future, 1982), pp. 80–81.

71. Robert B. Gordon, Tjalling C. Koopmans, William D. Nordhaus, and Brian J. Skinner, *Toward a New Iron Age?* (Cambridge, MA: Harvard University Press, 1987).

72. *Ibid.*, p. 153.

73. U.S. Geological Survey, *Minteral Commodity Summaries*, February 2000, p. 23.

74. *Ibid.*, p.107.

75. *Ibid.*, p. 109.

76. *Ibid.*, p. 57.

77. *Ibid.*, p. 87.

78. *Ibid.*, p. 97.

79. The term is Garrit Hardin's; see his "The Tragedy of the Commons," *Science*, vol.162, no. 3859 (13 December 1968): 1243–48.

80. Richard M. Stephenson, *Living with Tomorrow* (New York: John Wiley & Sons, Inc., 1981), pp. 205–8.

81. *Ibid.*, p. 204.

82. Otto Johnson, ed., *1996 Information Please Almanac* (Boston: Houghton Mifflin, 1996), p. 133.

83. Carl J. George and Daniel McKinely, *Urban Ecology: In Search of an Asphalt Rose* (New York: McGraw-Hill Book Company, 1974).

84. Barry Commoner, *The Closing Circle* (New York: Alfred A. Knopf, Inc., 1971), ch. 2.

85. See Kenneth E. F. Watt, *Understanding the Environment* (Boston: Allyn & Bacon, Inc., 1982).

86. Matthew Edel, *Economics and the Environment* (Englewood Cliffs, NJ: Prentice-Hall, 1973); for the term *spaceship earth*, see Kenneth Boulding, "The Economics of the Coming Spaceship Earth," in Henry Jarret, ed., *Environmental Quality in a Growing Economy* (Baltimore: Johns Hopkins Press for Resources for the Future, 1966).

87. George Perkins *Man and Nature*, [1864] (Cambridge: Harvard University Press, 1965), p. 76.

88. For discussions favoring this view as well as criticisms, see the essays collected in Donald Scherer and Thomas Attig, eds., *Ethics and the Environment* (Englewood Cliffs, NJ: Prentice-Hall, 1983); see also W. K. Frankena, "Ethics and the Environment," K. E. Goodpaster and K. M. Sayre, eds., *Ethics and Problems of the 21st Century* (Notre Dame, IN: University of Notre Dame Press, 1979), pp. 3–20; William T. Blackstone, "The Search for an Environmental Ethic," in Tom Regan, ed., *Matters of Life and Death* (New York: Random House, Inc., 1980), pp. 299–335; an excellent and extensive annotated bibliography is provided by Mary Anglemyer, et al., *A Search for Environmental Ethics, An Initial Bibliography* (Washington, DC: Smithsonian Institution Press, 1980).

89. Quoted in Bill Devall, *Simple in Means, Rich in Ends, Practicing Deep Ecology* (Salt Lake City, UT: Peregrine Smith Books, 1988), pp. 14–15.

90. Ted Gup, "Owl vs. Man," *Time,* 25 June 1990, pp. 56–62; Catherine Caufield, "A Reporter at Large: The Ancient Forest," *New Yorker*, 14 May 1990, pp. 46–84.

91. Devall, *Simple in Means, Rich in Ends*, p. 138.

92. Peter Singer, *Animal Liberation* (New York: Random House, Inc., 1975).

93. Tom Regan, *The Case for Animal Rights* (Berkeley, CA: University of California Press, 1983); in a similar vein, Joel Feinberg argues that animals have interests and consequently have rights in "The Rights of Animals and Unborn Generations," in William T. Blackstone, ed., *Philosophy and Environmental Crisis* (Athens, GA: University of Georgia Press, 1974).

94. See William Aiken, "Ethical Issues in Agriculture," in Tom Regan, ed., *Earthbound: New Introductory Essays in Environmental Ethics* (New York: Random House, Inc., 1984), pp. 247–88.

95. Kenneth Goodpaster, "On Being Morally Considerable," *Journal of Philosophy*, vol. 75 (1978): 308–25; see also Paul Taylor, "The Ethics of Respect for Nature," *Environmental Ethics*, vol. 3 (1981): 197–218; Robin Attfield, "The Good of Trees," *The Journal of Value Inquiry*, vol. 15 (1981): 35–54; and Christopher D. Stone, *Should Trees Have Standing? Toward Legal Rights for Natural Objects* (Boston: Houghton Mifflin, 1978).

96. Aldo Leopold, "The Land Ethic," in *A Sand County Almanac* (New York: Oxford University Press, 1949), pp. 201–26; see also J. Baird Callicott, "Animal

Liberation: A Triangular Affair," *Environmental Ethics*, vol. 2, no. 4 (Winter 1980): 311–38; John Rodman, "The Liberation of Nature?" *Inquiry*, vol. 20 (1977): 83–131; K. Goodpaster argues that the "biosphere" as a whole has moral value in "On Being Morally Considerable"; Holmes Rolston III holds a similar position in "Is There an Ecological Ethic," *Ethics*, vol. 85 (1975): 93–109; for a variety of views on this issue see Bryan G. Norton, ed., *The Preservation of Species* (Princeton, NJ: Princeton University Press, 1986).

97. Albert Schweitzer, *Out Of My Life and Thought*, trans. A. B. Lemke (New York: Holt, 1990), p. 130.

98. *Ibid.*, p. 131.

99. Paul Taylor, *Respect for Nature* (Princeton, NJ: Princeton University Press, 1986), p. 80.

100. *Ibid.*, pp. 121–2.

101. W. K. Frankena, "Ethics and the Environment," in K. E. Goodpaster and K. M. Sayre, eds., *Ethics and Problems of the 21st Century* (Notre Dame, IN: University of Notre Dame Press, 1979), pp. 3–20.

102. For other criticisms of these arguments, see Edward Johnson, "Treating the Dirt: Environmental Ethics and Moral Theory," in Tom Regan, ed., *Earthbound: New Introductory Essays in Environmental Ethics* (New York: Random House, 1984), pp. 336–65; see also the discussion between Goodpaster and Hunt in W. Murray Hunt, "Are Mere Things Morally Considerable?" *Environmental Ethics*, vol. 2 (1980): 59–65; and Kenneth Goodpaster, "On Stopping at Everything: A Reply to W. M. Hunt," *Environmental Ethics*, vol. 2 (1980): 281–84.

103. See, for example, R. G. Frey, *Interests and Rights: The Case Against Animals* (Oxford: Clarendon Press, 1980), and Martin Benjamin, "Ethics and Animal Consciousness," in Manuel Velasquez and Cynthia Rostankowski, eds., *Ethics: Theory and Practice* (Englewood Cliffs, NJ: Prentice-Hall, 1985).

104. For useful treatments of the ethics of environmental issues, see Dale Jamison, ed., *A Companion to Environmental Ethics* (New York: Blackwell Publishers, 2000); and Robin Attfield, *The Ethics of Environmental Concern* (New York: Columbia University Press, 1983).

105. William T Blackstone, "Ethics and Ecology," in William T. Blackstone, ed., *Philosophy and Environmental Crisis* (Athens, GA: University of Georgia Press, 1974); see also his later article, "On Rights and Responsibilities Pertaining to Toxic Substances and Trade Secrecy," *The Southern Journal of Philosophy*, vol. 16 (1978): 589–603.

106. *Ibid.*, p. 31; see also William T. Blackstone, "Equality and Human Rights," *Monist*, vol. 52, no. 4 (1968); and William T. Blackstone, "Human Rights and Human Dignity," in Laszlo and Grotesky, ed., *Human Dignity*.

107. Quoted in Keith Davis and William C. Frederick, *Business and Society* (New York: McGraw-Hill Book Company, 1984), pp. 403–4.

108. Robert H. Haveman and Greg Christiansen, *Jobs and the Environment* (Scarsdale, NY: Work in America Institute, Inc., 1979), p. 4.

109. Richard Kazis and Richard L. Grossman, "Job Blackmail: It's Not Jobs or Environment," p. 260, in Mark Green, ed., *The Big Business Reader* (New York: The Pilgrim Press, 1983), pp. 259–69.

110. See U.S. Department of Labor, *Mass Layoffs in 1987–1990*, Bureau of Labor Statistics Bulletins 2395, 2375, 2310; see also Goodstein, E.B. "Jobs or the Environment? No Trade-off," *Challenge* (January-February 1995): 41–45.

111. The Environmental Protection Agency's so-called "bubble policy," see *Time*, 17 December 1979, p. 71; and *Business Week*, 9 July 1984, p. 34.

112. For an analysis of the impact of this executive order, see the essays collected in V. Kerry Smith, ed., *Environmental Policy Under Reagan's Executive Order* (Chapel Hill, NC: The University of North Carolina Press, 1984).

113. There are a number of texts describing this approach. An elementary text is Tom Tietenberg, *Environmental and Natural Resource Economics* (Glenview, IL: Scott, Foresman & Company, 1984); a more compact treatment is Edwin S. Mills, *The Economics of Environmental Quality* (New York: W. W. Norton & Co., Inc., 1978), ch. 3; for several viewpoints consult Robert Dorfman and Nancy Dorman, eds., *Economics of the Environment* (New York: W. W. Norton & Co., Inc., 1977).

114. For a still useful review of the literature on external costs, see E. J. Mishan, "The Postwar Literature on Externalities: An Interpretative Essay," *Journal of Economic Literature*, vol. 9, no. 1 (March 1971): 1–28.

115. Not only is much of the electrical power industry still monopolized, but in the short run, at least, demand is relatively inelastic. Over the long run, demand may have the more elastic characteristics we assume in the example.

116. See E. J. Mishan, *Economics for Social Decisions* (New York: Praeger Publishers, Inc., 1973), pp. 85 ff.; also E. J. Mishan, *Cost Benefit Analysis*, 3rd ed. (London: Allen & Unwin, 1982).

117. S. Prakesh Sethi, *Up Against the Corporate Wall* (Englewood Cliffs, NJ: Prentice-Hall, 1977), p. 21.

118. See Mishan, "The Postwar Literature on Externalities," p. 24.

119. William J. Baumal and Wallace E. Oates, Economics, *Environmental Policy, and the Quality of Life* (Englewood Cliffs, NJ: Prentice-Hall, 1979), p. 177.

120. *Ibid.*, pp. 180–82.

121. *Ibid.*, pp. 182–84.

122. Mishan, "The Postwar Literature on Externalities," p. 24.

123. Mills, *Economics of Environmental Quality*, pp. 111–12.

124. *Ibid.*, pp. 83–91.

125. For a number of cases that apply these techniques, see Yusuf J. Ahmad, Partha Dasgupta, and Karl-Goran Maler, eds., *Environmental Decision-Making* (London: Hodder and Stoughton, 1984).

126. Thomas A. Klein, *Social Costs and Benefits of Business* (Englewood Cliffs, NJ: Prentice-Hall, 1977), p. 118.

127. Ibid., p. 119; the literature on social accounting for business firms was once vast; see U.S. Department of Commerce, *Corporate Social Reporting in the United States and Western Europe* (Washington, DC: U.S. Government Printing Office, 1979); Committee on Social Measurement, *The Measurement of Corporate Social Performance* (New York: American Institute of Certified Public Accountants, Inc., 1977).

128. See Boyd Collier, *Measurement of Environmental Deterioration* (Austin, TX: Bureau of Business Research, The University of Texas at Austin, 1971).

129. See Michael D. Boyles, "The Price of Life," *Ethics*, vol. 89, no. 1 (October 1978): 20–34; for other problems with using cost-benefit analysis in environmental areas, see Mark Sagoff, "Ethics and Economics in Environmental Law," in Regan, ed.,

Earthbound, pp. 147–78, and Rosemarie Tong, *Ethics in Policy Analysis* (Englewood Cliffs, NJ: Prentice-Hall, 1986), pp. 14–29.

130. Much of the material in this and the following paragraphs is based on the superb analysis in Robert E. Goodwin, "No Moral Nukes," *Ethics*, vol. 90, no. 3 (April 1980): 417–49.

131. Committee on Social Measurement, *The Measurement of Corporate Social Performance* (New York: American Institute of Certified Public Accountants, Inc., 1977).

132. U.S. General Accounting Office, *The Nation's Nuclear Waste* (Washington, DC: U.S. Government Printing Office, 1979), p. 12. For a criticism of this kind of policy analysis, see Tong, *Ethics in Policy Analysis*, pp. 39–54.

133. Murray Bookchin, *Defending the Earth: A Dialogue Between Murray Bookchin and Dave Foreman*, ed. Steve Chase (Boston: South End Press, 1991), p. 58.

134. Karen J. Warren, "The Power and Promise of Ecological Feminism," *Environmental Ethics*, vol. 12 (Summer 1990): 126.

135. Val Plumwood, "Current Trends in Ecofeminism," *The Ecologist*, vol. 22, no. 1 (January/February 1992): 10.

136. Nell Noddings, *Caring, A Feminine Approach to Ethics and Moral Education* (Berkeley: University of California Press, 1984), p. 14.

137. Karen J. Warren, "The Power and the Promise of Ecological Feminism," in Christine Pierce and Donald VanDeVeer, *People, Penguins, and Plastic Trees, Basic Issues in Environmental Ethics*, 2nd ed. (Belmont, CA: Wadsworth, 1995), pp. 218 and 223.

138. Martin Golding, "Obligations to Future Generations," *Monist*, vol. 56, no. 1 (1972): 85–99; Richard T. DeGeorge, "The Environment, Rights, and Future Generations," in K. E. Goodpaster and K. M. Sayre, eds., *Ethics and Problems of the 21st Century*, pp. 93–105.

139. DeGeorge, "The Environment, Rights, and Future Generations," pp. 97–98.

140. *Ibid.*

141. Martin Golding, "Obligations to Future Generations," *Monist*, vol. 56, no. 1 (1972); Gregory Kavka argues, however, that full knowledge of the needs of future people is not required to accord them moral standing in "The Futurity Problem," in Ernest Partridge, *Responsibilities to Future Generations* (New York: Prometheus Books, 1981), pp. 109–22; see also Annette Baier, "For the Sake of Future Generations," in Regan, ed., *Earthbound*, pp. 214–46.

142. John Rawls, *A Theory of Justice* (Cambridge: Harvard University Press, 1971), p. 289.

143. *Ibid.*, pp. 285 and 288.

144. Among authors who favor Rawls in their treatment of our obligations to future generations are R. and V. Routley, "Nuclear Energy and Obligations to the Future," *Inquiry*, vol. 21 (1978): 133–79; K. S. Shrader-Frechette, *Nuclear Power and Public Policy* (Dordecht, Boston and London: Reidel, 1980); F. Patrick Hubbard, "Justice, Limits to Growth, and an Equilibrium State," *Philosophy and Public Affairs*, vol. 7 (1978): 326–45; Victor D. Lippit and Koichi Hamada, "Efficiency and Equity in Intergenerational Distribution," in Dennis Clark Pirages ed., *The Sustainable Society* (New York and London: Praeger Publishers, Inc., 1977), pp. 285–99. Each of these authors, however, introduces modifications to Rawls' position.

145. Attfield adopts this "Lockean principle" from G. Kavka, *ibid.*

146. Attfield, *The Ethics of Environmental Concern*, pp. 107–10.

147. J. Brenton Stearns, "Ecology and the Indefinite Unborn," *Monist*, vol. 56, no. 4 (October 1972): 612–25; Jan Narveson, "Utilitarianism and New Generations," *Mind*, vol. 76 (1967): 62–67.

148. Robert Scott, Jr., "Environmental Ethics and Obligations to Future Generations," in R. I. Sikora and Brian Barry, eds., *Obligations to Future Generations* (Philadelphia: Temple University Press, 1978), pp. 74–90; but see Kavka, *ibid.*, who argues against discounting.

149. Joan Robinson, *Economic Philosophy* (London: Penguin Books, 1966), p. 115.

150. William G. Shepherd and Clair Wilcox, *Public Policies Toward Business*, 6th ed. (Homewood, IL: Richard D. Irwin, Inc., 1979), pp. 524–25.

151. E. F. Schumacher, *Small Is Beautiful* (London: Blond and Briggs, Ltd., 1973).

152. Herman E. Daly, ed., *Toward A Steady-State Economy* (San Francisco: W. H. Freeman & Company, Publishers, 1974), p. 152; see also Herman E. Daly, *Steady-State Economics* (San Francisco; W. H. Freeman & Company, Publishers, 1977); Herman E. Daly, ed., *Economics, Ecology, and Ethics* (San Francisco: W. H. Freeman & Company, Publishers, 1980); Robert L. Stirers, *The Sustainable Society: Ethics and Economic Growth* (Philadelphia: Westminster Press, 1976); and Lester R. Brown, *Building a Sustainable Society* (New York: ;. W. Norton & Co., Inc., 1981).

153. See, for example, Wilfred Beckerman, *In Defense of Economic Growth* (London: Jonathan Cape, 1974); Rudolph Klein, "The Trouble with Zero Economic Growth," *New York Review of Books* (April 1974); Julian L. Simon, *The Ultimate Resource* (Princeton, NJ: Princeton University Press, 1981).

154. E. J. Mishan, *The Economic Growth Debate: An Assessment* (London: George Allen & Unwin Ltd., 1977).

155. See Heilbroner, *An Inquiry into the Human Prospect, Updated for the 1980s.*

156. Several of these scenarios are reviewed in James Just and Lester Lave, "Review of Scenarios of Future U.S. Energy Use," *Annual Review of Energy*, vol. 4 (1979): 501–36; and in Hughes, *World Futures.*

157. Meadows, Meadows, Randers, and Behrens, *The Limits to Growth* (New York: Universe Books, 1974).

158. See, for example, Council on Environmental Quality, *The Global 2000 Report.*

159. *Ibid.*, p. 132.

160. H. S. D. Cole, Christopher Freeman, Marie Jahoda, and K. L. R. Pavitt, eds., *Models of Doom: A Critique of the Limits to Growth* (New York: Universe Books, 1973); William Nordhaus, "World Dynamics: Measurement Without Data," *Economic Journal*, vol. 83 (December 1973): 1156–83; Herman Kahn, William Brown, and Leon Martel, *The Next 200 Years* (New York: William Morrow & Company, Inc., 1976); Charles Maurice and Charles W. Smithson, *The Doomsday Myth* (Stanford: Hoover Institution Press, 1984); and Piers Blaikie, "The Use of Natural Resources in Developing and Developed Countries," in R. J. Johnston and P. J. Taylor, *A World in Crisis* (Cambridge, MA: Basil Blackwell, 1989), pp. 125–50.

161. In a later study, the Club of Rome has moderated its predictions; see Donella H. Meadows et al., *The Limits to Growth*, 2nd ed. (New York: Universe Books, 1974).

162. Heilbroner, *The Human Prospect.*

163. On the link between environmental resource use and the uneven distribution of world wealth, see Willy Brandt, *North-South: A Program for Survival* (Cambridge: MIT Press, 1980).

Cases for Discussion

Genetic Engineering at Monsanto/Pharmacia[1]

In March 2000, two companies—Monsanto and Pharmacia & Upjohn—merged to form a new entity named Pharmacia, the world's largest producer of genetically engineered (GE) plants and organisms, with combined sales of $16.4 billion. Scarcely 3 months later, on June 23, 2000, several stockholders of the new company asked the other shareholders of Pharmacia to vote in favor of a shareholder resolution that stated:

> Whereas:
>
> –Several of Europe's largest food retailers, including Tesco, Sainsbury Group, Carrefour, and Rewe, have committed to removing genetically engineered ingredients from their store-brand products. In the UK, three fast-food giants—McDonald's Burger King, and Kentucky Fried Chicken—are eliminating GE soya and corn ingredients from their menus;
>
> –Gerber Products Co. announced in July 1999 that it would not allow GE corn or soybeans in any of its baby foods;
>
> –Archer Daniels Midland asked its grain suppliers in August 1999 to segregate its genetically engineered crops from conventional crops;
>
> –There is increasing scientific concern that genetically engineered agricultural products may be harmful to humans, animals, or the environment;
>
> –The U.S. Department of Agriculture has acknowledged (July 13, 1999) the need to develop a comprehensive approach to evaluating long-term and secondary effects of GE products;
>
> –As early as 1989, scientist reported that GE foods may pose risks to human health;
>
> –Some GE crops have been engineered to have higher levels of toxins, such as Bacillus thuringiensis (Bt), to make them insect resistant;
>
> –In 1999, the European Union suspended approval of new genetically engineered organisms until a new safety law for genetically engineered organisms is implemented in 2002. This followed a new study that showed Bt corn pollen may harm monarch butterflies.
>
> RESOLVED: Shareholders request the Board of Directors to adopt a policy of not marketing or distributing genetically engineered agricultural products until long-term safety testing has shown that they are not harmful to humans, animals, and the environment.

Genetic engineering consists of techniques for changing the genes in the cells of plants and animals. Genes contain the blueprints that determine what characteristics an organism will have. Genetic engineering takes the genes from one species and inserts them into the genes of another species to create a new organism that shares the characteristics of both species. Genetic engineering has been used to develop soybeans that are resistant to insects, cows that produce more milk, bacteria that can consume oil accidently spilled on water, and tomatoes that do not rot for several days after being picked.

Monsanto has been at the forefront of this new biotechnology. Two of the first genetically engineered foods produced were Roundup Ready soybean and cotton plants, which were engineered in 1994 by Monsanto to be immune to the weed killer "Roundup" (so that weeds around soybean or cotton plants could be sprayed with the weed killer without harming the plants). Monsanto also used genetic engineering to develop Bt corn and Bt cotton in 1995. These plants produce a bacterium (Bt) that kills insect predators. These and other genetically engineered organisms Monsanto developed were approved by the Animal and Plant Health Inspection Service (APHIS) of the U.S. Department of Agriculture. The Federal Drug Administration (FDA) determined that it has no jurisdiction to regulate genetically modified foods.

Perhaps because it pioneered this new technology, Monsanto has been involved in a number of controversies. One controversy relates to the fact that Monsanto requires farmers who bought its Roundup Read seeds to agree not to plant any of the seeds produced by these plants, but to go back to the company to buy new seeds each year. The company explained that it had to do this or farmers would stop buying its seeds and its market would disappear. In March 1998, another company, Delta and Pine Land Company, announced it had discovered a way to make "Terminator" seeds, which are genetically engineered to be incapable of reproducing. When Monsanto announced that it was buying Delta and Pine Land Company, observers immediately concluded that Monsanto would use the new technology to ensure that farmers would have to buy new seeds from it each year.

But the worse controversies in which Monsanto became involved related to the environmental dangers of its genetically engineered crops. Critics charged that it was possible that Monsanto's "Roundup Ready" plants might cross-pollinate with weeds and spread to them their immunity to Roundup herbicide. The result could be a superweed that would be immune to weed killer and might spread rapidly.

Organic farmers feared the growing use of Monsanto's Bt soybean and Bt cotton. Bt is a bacterium that organic farmers use to protect their crops from insects. It is virtually the only natural insect killer they can use against predators. The farmers feared that as more insects are exposed to Monsanto's Bt plants—which produce Bt on their leaves so that insect predators avoid them—insects will eventually develop an immunity to Bt, much like the overuse of antibiotics by humans has created infections that are immune to these antibiotics. Monsanto scientists were quoted as saying that it was inevitable that eventually insects would become immune to Bt. Organic farmers feared that outcome because it would mark the end of their ability to defend themselves against insect predators.

In May 2000, Cornell University researchers released a study indicating that the pollen from genetically engineered Bt corn was deadly to monarch butterflies. The study, which was published in the journal *Nature*, consisted of feeding monarch butterfly caterpillars milkweed leaves dusted with pollen from Bt corn. Forty-four percent of the caterpillars died after 4 days. Bt corn is now one of the major varieties of corn being planted on farms around the United States. The EPA announced that it would study the environmental effects of Bt corn and require farmers to plant non-Bt corn together with their Bt corn to serve as a refuge for beneficial insects that may be harmed by it.

Europeans, who were staunchly opposed to moving genetically altered organisms from the laboratory into the open environment, passed a resolution through the European Union requiring that all foods containing genetically engineered organisms of any kind should be labeled as such. In February 1999, the British parliament discussed a proposal for a moratorium on planting and growing genetically modified crops in the open environment, fearing that this might accidently create a potentially dangerous new organism. Several American food companies, including Gerber Products, Heinz, and Frito-Lay, announced that they would not use genetically modified food ingredients. Whole Foods Market, a 103-store chain of natural foods supermarkets, announced in 1999 that it would lobby for required labeling of foods containing genetically modified organisms. Environmental activists argued that there was no real evidence proving indisputably that genetically engineered organisms posed no risk to the environment. The Worldwatch Institute, an environmental organization, suggested that, "Instead of requiring critics to prove that the technology poses potential dangers, the producers of a technology shoulder the burden of presenting evidence that the technology is safe."

In its defense, Monsanto insisted that its plants were perfectly safe and provided significant benefits both to the environment and people. In a statement urging stockholders to vote against the shareholder resolution quoted earlier, the company said:

> Biotechnology is facilitating fundamental changes in agricultural production methods resulting in increased yield and reduced use of traditional pesticides. Indeed, the products produced from this technology have already brought important benefits to growers and the environment after just a few years of commercial application.

> Examples include Bollgard cotton, which in 1998 in the United States allowed growers to eliminate the use of more than 1.1 million liters of chemical insecticides. Also in 1998, field tests showed YieldGard corn provided an overall yield advantage of three to seven bushels per acre over non-insect-protected corn-hybrid varieties, some of which were treated with chemical insecticides. Roudup-Ready crops help facilitate implementation of soil-saving conservation tillage farming techniques and reduce the use of other herbicides. Genetically engineered agricultural products marketed by Monsanto have undergone rigorous testing to ensure that the foods produced from such products are as save and nutritious to eat as products from other new plant varieties and that these crops are appropriate for environmental release.

The company posted an article entitled "Genetically Modified Nonsense" on its website, in which it claimed that its critics did not have an adequate understanding of the virtually nonexistent risks its plants posed to the environment. There was, it argued, no undisputed scientific evidence that genetically modified organisms are harmful to the environment or people. Moreover, Monsanto suggested, the new plant varieties it had engineered would help feed a hungry world.

QUESTIONS

1. In your judgment, what, if any, obligations does Monsanto/Pharmacia have to delay marketing genetically engineered organisms "until long-term safety testing has shown that they are not harmful to humans, animals, and the environment"? To whom does it have these obligations?
2. Analyze the actions of Monsanto/Pharmacia in terms of utilitarianism, rights, justice, and caring. In your judgment, is the company morally justified in continuing to market genetically engineered organisms?
3. How should companies deal with products like genetically engineered organisms when information about the potential risks to the environment is limited or nonexistent, but the product promises significant benefits to humans? Explain your answer.

NOTES

1. This case is based entirely on Jan Degges, "Genetically Modified Organisms," 2000 Background Report–H1 (New York: Investor Responsibility Research Center, 2000), and Jan Degges, "Pharmacia: Genetically Modified Organisms," 2000 Company Report–H1 (New York: Investor Responsibility Research Center, 2000).

The New Market Opportunity

In 1994, anxious to show off the benefits of a communist regime, the government of China invited leading auto manufacturers from around the world to submit plans for a car designed to meet the needs of its massive population.[1] A wave of rising affluence had suddenly created a large middle class of Chinese families with enough money to buy and maintain a private automobile. China was now eager to enter joint ventures with foreign companies to construct and operate automobile manufacturing plants inside China. The plants would not only manufacture cars to supply China's new internal market, but could also make cars that could be exported for sale abroad and would be sure to generate thousands of new jobs. The Chinese government specified that the new car had to be priced at less than $5000, be small enough to suit families with a single child (couples in China are prohibited from having more than one child), rugged enough to endure the poorly maintained roads that criss-crossed the nation, generate a minimum of pollution, be composed of parts that were predominantly made within China, and be manufactured through joint-venture agreements between Chinese and foreign companies. Experts anticipated that the plants manufacturing the new cars would use a minimum of automation and would instead rely on labor-intensive technologies that could capitalize on China's cheap labor. China saw the development of a new auto industry as a key step in its drive to industrialize its economy.

The Chinese market was an irresistible opportunity for General Motors, Ford, and Chrysler, as well as for the leading Japanese, European, and Korean automobile companies. With a population of 1.2 billion people and almost double-digit annual economic growth rates, China estimated that in the next 40 years between 200 and 300 million of the new vehicles would be purchased by Chinese citizens. Already cars had become a symbol of affluence for China's new rising middle class, and a craze for cars had led more than 30 million Chinese to take driving lessons despite that the nation had only 10 million vehicles, most of them government-owned trucks.

Environmentalists, however, were opposed to the auto manufacturers' eager rush to respond to the call of the Chinese government. The world market for energy, particularly oil, they pointed out, was based in part on the fact that China, with its large population, was using relatively low levels of energy. In 1994, the per-person consumption of oil in China was only one sixth of Japan's and only a quarter of Taiwan's. If China were to reach even the modest per person consumption level of South Korea, China would be consuming twice the amount of oil the United States currently uses. At the present time, the United States consumes one fourth of the world's total annual oil supplies, about half of which it must import from foreign countries.

Critics pointed out that if China were to eventually have as many cars on the road per person as Germany does, the world would contain twice as many cars as it currently does. No matter how "pollution-free" the new car design was, the cumulative environmental effects of that many more automobiles in the world would be formidable. Even clean cars would have to generate large amounts of carbon dioxide as they burned fuel, thus significantly worsening the greenhouse effect. Engineers pointed out that it would be difficult, if not impossible, to build a clean car for under $5000. Catalytic converters, which diminished pollution, alone cost over $200 per car to manufacture. In addition, China's oil refineries were designed to produce only gasoline with high levels of lead. Upgrading all its refineries so they could make low-lead gasoline would require an investment China seemed unwilling to make.

Some of the car companies were considering submitting plans for an electric car because China had immense coal reserves which it could burn to produce electricity. This would diminish the need for China to rely on oil, which it would have to import. However, China did not have sufficient coal burning electric plants nor an electrical power distribution system that could provide adequate electrical power to a large number of vehicles. Building such an electrical power system also would require a huge investment that the Chinese government did not seem particularly interested in making. Moreover, because coal is a fossil fuel, switching from an oil-based auto to a coal-based electric auto would still result in adding substantial quantities of carbon dioxide to the atmosphere.

Many government officials were also worried by the political implications of having China become a major consumer of oil. If China were to increase its oil consumption, it would have to import all its oil from the same countries that other nations relied on, which would create large political, economic, and military risks. Although the United States imported some of its oil from Venezuela and Mexico, most of its imports came from the Middle East—an oil source that China would have to turn to also. Rising demand for Middle East oil would push oil prices sharply upward, which would send major shocks reverberating through the economies of the United States and those of other nations that relied heavily on oil. State Department officials worried that China would begin to trade weapons for oil with Iran or Iraq, heightening the risks of major military confrontations in the region. If China were to become a major trading partner with Iran or Iraq, this would also create closer ties between these two major power centers of the non-Western world—a possibility that was also laden with risk. Of course, China might also turn to tapping the large reserves of oil that were thought to be lying under Taiwan and other areas neighboring its coast. However, this would bring it into competition with Japan, South Korea, Thailand, Singapore, Taiwan, the Philippines, and other nations that were already drawing on these sources to supply their own booming economies. Many of these nations, anticipating heightened tensions, were already pouring money into their military forces, particularly their navies. In short, because world supplies of oil were limited, increasing demand seemed likely to increase the potential for conflict.

QUESTIONS

1. In your judgment, is it wrong, from an ethical point of view, for the auto companies to submit plans for an automobile to China? Explain your answer.
2. Of the various approaches to environmental ethics outlined in this chapter, which approach sheds most light on the ethical issues raised by this case? Explain your answer.
3. Should the U.S. government intervene in any way in the negotiations between U.S. auto companies and the Chinese government? Explain.

NOTE

1. All information for this case is drawn from the following sources: "Is China's 'People's Car' Good or Bad?" *San Jose Mercury News*, 1 December 1996, pp. 1E, 5E; John W. Wright, ed., *The Universal Almanac* (Kansas City: Andrews and McMeel, 1996).

6

The Ethics of Consumer Production and Marketing

INTRODUCTION

Consider the nature of the consumer products discussed below:

In 1996, the Food and Drug Administration (FDA) reported that tobacco products were killing 400,000 Americans each year, more than acquired immune deficiency syndrome (AIDS), alcohol, car accidents, murders, suicides, illegal drugs, and fires combined. As their traditional markets have stopped growing, American cigarette companies—Phillip Morris, R. J. Reynolds, and American Brands—have focused on new populations. In December 1991, the *Journal of the American Medical Association* published studies showing that R. J. Reynold's Joe Camel cartoon cigarette campaign was strongly attracting children and adolescents to smoking.[1] Two other groups have been targeted by tobacco marketing campaigns: minorities and women. Minority groups in inner-city neighborhoods have lower access to health education, are less aware of the risks of smoking, are a rapidly growing population, and are particularly vulnerable and responsive to targeted advertising. Women, with greater independence and purchasing power than ever before, are the fastest growing group of smokers, and among them lung cancer has now overtaken breast cancer as the leading cause of death from cancer.

In October 1996, the EPA conducted tests of several common lawn herbicides containing toxic chemicals and found that, after outdoor spraying on house lawns, the contamination levels inside homes were between 10 and 100 times the levels on the lawn.[2] Brought into the home by foot traffic and pets, the chemicals were quickly and invisibly smeared over floors and carpets. Babies and children playing or crawling on contaminated carpets and floors picked up the chemicals on their hands, clothes, and toys and transferred them to their mouths.

After reviewing several cases in which BIC Corporation lighters were alleged to have injured children and others, the U.S. Court of Appeals, Third Circuit, ruled in 1992 that, "on balance, the high social value placed on the safety of people and property threatened by childplay fires, the high gravity of risk, the considerable probability of risk, and the likelihood of a reasonably available alternative, may outweigh BIC's interest in producing its lighters without childproofing features." In a related case, a woman, Ethel Smith, flicked on a Bic Corporation lighter to light her cigarette. It exploded in her hands, killing her and severely burning her husband. Earlier, Cynthia Littlejohn suffered severe burns about her torso that required seven painful skin grafts when a Bic lighter in her pocket spontaneously ignited and enveloped her in flames.[3] The company later confessed that its own tests showed that 1.2 percent of its lighters were faulty. Experts claimed that the defects could have been corrected for "a couple of pennies a lighter." Some 200 people a year, half of them children, are killed in lighter-related injuries.[4]

Americans are exposed daily to astonishingly high levels of risk from the use of consumer products. Each year some 20 million people suffer serious accidental injuries and about 100,000 are killed, more than half of them in accidents involving consumer products. After declining by more than 20 percent between 1979 and 1992 (when deaths reached a 68-year low of 86,777), accidental deaths began rising again in the early 1990s. The National Safety Council estimated that the total cost of these injuries in 1995 alone was $435 billion.

However, product injuries make up only one category of costs imposed on unwary consumers. Consumers must also bear the costs of deceptive selling practices, shoddy product construction, products that immediately break down, and warranties that are not honored. For example, several years ago, the engine of Martha and George Rose's Chevrolet station wagon began hissing and white smoke poured out of the tailpipe as she drove it 6 miles to work.[5] Two non-Chevrolet mechanics who then checked the car later testified that the radiator and cooling system were "in satisfactory condition," that the radiator "was not boiling over," and that the temperature light on the dashboard "was not burning." Upon taking the engine apart, a mechanic found that a hairline crack in the engine block had allowed water to enter the cylinder head, meaning that the car would need an expensive new engine. The engine was still under a "5-year or 50,000-mile" warranty, so the Roses thought the Chevrolet division of General Motors would bear the large costs of repairing what they concluded was an inherently defective engine block. However, when a Chevrolet service manager examined the dismantled car, he insisted that the problem was that the radiator thermostat had stuck shut so no coolant had reached the engine. Because the thermostat was only under a "12-month or 12,000-miles" warranty that had by then expired, and because, the Chevrolet manager claimed, the faulty thermostat had caused the engine to overheat and the engine block to crack, Chevrolet had no responsibility under the warranty. Moreover, the car had been torn down and worked on by unauthorized mechanics. Although the Roses pointed out that the other mechanics had found no evidence of overheating and that no Chevrolet mechanic had suggested replacing the thermostat at any of their regular maintenance servicings, the General Motors field manager and his superiors, both in New Orleans and Detroit, refused to honor the warranty. Without the engine, the car that General Motors had sold them was now worth only 10 percent of what they had originally paid for it. Because they could not afford an attorney for a trial they might lose, the Roses could not file suit against General Motors.

The sales practices of Pacific Bell Telephone Company, which serves California telephone customers, provide another illustration of the difficulties that face consumers. On April 23, 1986, the Pacific Utilities Commission of California released a report stating that Pacific Bell service representatives were duping new telephone customers into buying expensive optional features by quoting a fee for new telephone service that included the expensive features, but without telling the new customer that the features were optional, that the consumer was being charged extra for them, and that basic service was available at a much cheaper monthly fee. A sales representative of the telephone company described the way that she approached a new customer calling to get a new telephone hook-up:

> I'm going to tell you that "You will get unlimited local calling, Touchtone service, our four, custom-calling services and a 20 percent discount in the Pacific Bell service area; the central office fee to turn the services on is $37.50 and I have all of these things available and it's only $22.20 a month." Most customers will say, "That's fine." It really isn't a bad deal, but how many people know they don't have to buy all those things, that they can get basic service for $9.95? The company says, "People should be intelligent enough to ask; why should it be PacBell's job to tell them?" People who don't speak English, well, they end up with those services. Sometimes they call back and say, "What is this? I didn't want this." [Pacific Telephone sales representative][6]

According to the Utilities Commission report, 65 percent of Pacific Bell's phone order centers did not quote the basic $9.95 monthly rate that allowed unlimited local calls, but instead quoted only a standard price, which included extra features (such as a device that tells a customer another call is waiting, automatic forwarding of a call to another phone, equipment for three-way or conference calls, codes that automatically dial a preset number, and extra charges for call discounts at certain times or certain areas) that cost as much as $27.20 a month. The sales representatives pleaded that the company's marketing managers imposed stiff sales quotas on them and would put them on probation if they failed to meet the quotas. In one city, for example, they were expected to sell

$197 to $238 worth of services each hour they spent on the telephone with customers. A Utilities Commission staff member remarked that, "Marketing management appears to be more concerned about generating revenues than they are about ethical and fair treatment of customers."[7]

Consumers are also bombarded daily by an endless series of advertisements urging them to buy certain products. Although sometimes defended as sources of information, advertisements are also criticized on the grounds that they rarely do more than give the barest indications of the basic function a product is meant to serve and sometimes misrepresent and exaggerate its virtues. Economists argue that advertising expenditures are a waste of resources while sociologists bemoan the cultural effects of advertising.[8]

This chapter examines the many ethical issues raised by product quality and advertising. The first few sections discuss various approaches to consumer issues, and the last sections deal with consumer advertising. We begin with a focus on what is perhaps the most urgent issue: consumer product injuries and the responsibilities of manufacturers.

6.1 Markets and Consumer Protection

Consumer advocates point out that, in 1992 alone, there were more than 585,000 injuries requiring hospital treatment inflicted on youngsters and adults using toys, nursery equipment, and playground equipment; more than 322,000 people were mangled using home workshop equipment; 2,055,000 people needed emergency treatment for injuries involving home furnishings; and 3,467,000 people required treatment for injuries involving home construction materials.[9] Injuries from auto-related accidents in 1995 averaged 44,200 each week while deaths averaged 120 per day; financial losses were estimated at $479 million per day.[10]

Many people believe that consumers automatically will be protected from injury by the operations of free and competitive markets and that neither governments nor businesspeople have to take special steps to deal with these issues. As we have seen in earlier chapters (particularly in Chapter 4), free markets promote an allocation, use, and distribution of goods that are, in a certain sense, just, respectful of rights, and efficiently productive of maximum utility for those who participate in the market. Moreover, in such markets, the consumer is said to be "sovereign." When consumers want and will willingly pay for something, sellers have an incentive to cater to their wishes. If sellers do not provide what consumers want, then sellers will suffer losses. However, when sellers provide what consumers want, they will profit. As the author of a leading textbook on economics wrote, "Consumers direct by their innate or learned tastes, as expressed in their dollar votes, the ultimate uses to which society's resources are channeled."[11]

In the "market" approach to consumer protection, consumer safety is seen as a good that is most efficiently provided through the mechanism of the free market whereby sellers must respond to consumer demands. If consumers want products to be safer, they will indicate this preference in markets by willingly paying more for safer products and showing a preference for manufacturers of safe products while turning down the goods of manufacturers of unsafe products. Producers will have to respond to this demand by building more safety into their products or they risk losing customers to competitors who cater to the preferences of consumers. Thus, the market ensures that producers respond adequately to consumers' desires for safety. However, if consumers do not place a high value on safety and demonstrate neither a willingness to pay more for safety nor a preference for safer products, then it is wrong to push increased levels of safety down their throats through government regulations that force producers to build more safety into their products than consumers demand. Such government interference, as we saw earlier, distorts markets, making them unjust, disrespectful of rights, and inefficient. It is just as wrong for businesspeople to decide on their own that consumers should have more protection than they are demanding, as to force on them costly safety devices that they would not buy on their own. Only consumers can say what value they place on safety, and they should be allowed to register their preferences through their free choices in markets and not be coerced by businesses or governments into paying for safety levels they may not want.

For example, an appliance selling for $100 may indicate that it will overheat if it is used for more than an hour and a half, whereas one selling for $400 may indicate that it can be run safely all day and night continuously. Some buyers will prefer the cheaper model, willingly trading the somewhat higher risk for the $300 cut in price, whereas others will prefer the more expensive one. If government regulations forced all appliance makers to make only the safer model or if manufacturers voluntarily decided to make only the safer model, then consumers who do not feel that the increase in safety is worth $300 extra to them will be out of luck. If they cannot do without the appliance, they will be forced to pay the extra $300 even if they would have preferred spending it on something else that is more valuable to them. Thus, they are unjustly forced to pay money for something they do not want, and their resources are inefficiently wasted on something that produces little utility for them.

Critics to this market approach respond, however, that the benefits of free markets obtain with certainty only when markets have the seven characteristics that define them: (a) there are numerous buyers and sellers, (b) everyone can freely enter and exit the market, (c) everyone has full and perfect information, (d) all goods in the market are exactly similar, (e) there are no external costs, (f) all buyers and sellers are rational utility maximizers, and (g) the market is unregulated. Critics of the market approach to consumer issues argue that these characteristics are absent in consumer markets, focusing especially on characteristics (c) and (f).

Markets are efficient, critics point out, only if condition (c) obtains—that is, only if participants have full and perfect information about the goods they are buying. Obviously consumers are frequently not well informed about the products they buy simply because the sophisticated consumer products on contemporary market shelves are too complex for anyone but an expert to be knowledgeable about them. Not surprisingly, manufacturers, who are knowledgeable about their products, might not voluntarily provide information about the safety levels or defective characteristics of their products to consumers. Because gathering information is expensive, a consumer may not have the resources to acquire the information on his or her own by, for example, testing several competing brands to determine which provides the most safety for the cost.

In theory, it would be possible for consumers who want information to turn to organizations such as the Consumers Union, which make a business of acquiring and selling product information. That is, market mechanisms should create a market in consumer information if that is what consumers want. However, for two reasons related to the nature of information, it is difficult for such organizations to cover their costs by selling information to consumers. First, as several economists have pointed out, once information is provided to one person who pays for it, it is easily leaked to many others who do not pay, especially in this age of photocopiers.[12] Because people know they can become *free riders* and acquire the information compiled by others without paying for it themselves, the number of people who willingly pay for the information is too small to allow the organization to cover its costs. Second, consumers are often unwilling to pay for information because they do not know what its value to them will be until after they get it and then they no longer need to pay for it because it is already in their possession. For example, a consumer may pay for the information contained in a research report and then find that he or she already knew what was in the report, that it is about products other than those he or she wants to buy, or that it is irrelevant information about those products. Consumers cannot know in advance precisely what they are buying when they buy information, thus they are unwilling to pay the costs organizations must charge to gather the information.[13] Markets alone, then, are not able to support organizations that can provide consumers with the information they need. Instead, such organizations must rely on charitable contributions or government grants.

A second criticism of the argument that free markets can deal with all consumer issues takes aim at characteristic (f) of free markets: the assumption that the consumer is a "rational utility maximizer." As one author put it, the consumer assumed by such arguments is "a budget-minded, rational individual, relentlessly pushing toward maximizing his satisfaction . . . [who is able] to think well ahead, to 'wait,' to consider. The consumer defined by the theory watches every penny."[14] More precisely, the *rational utility maximizer* that the consumer is assumed to be is a person who has a well-defined and consistent set of preferences, and who is certain how his or her choices will affect those preferences.

Unfortunately, virtually all consumer choices are based on probability estimates we make concerning the chances that the products we buy will function as we think they will. All the research available shows that we become highly inept, irrational, and inconsistent when we make choices based on probability estimates.[15]

First, as is obvious to any observer, few of us are good at estimating probabilities. We typically underestimate the risks of personal life-threatening activities, such as driving, smoking, or eating fried foods, and of being injured by the products we use, and we overestimate the probabilities of unlikely but memorable events such as tornadoes or attacks by grizzly bears in national parks.[16] Studies have shown that our probability judgments go astray for a number of reasons, including the following:

1. Prior probabilities are ignored when new information becomes available, even if the new information is irrelevant.
2. Emphasis on "causation" results in the underweighing of evidence that is relevant to probability but is not perceived as "causal."
3. Generalizations are made on the basis of small sample findings.
4. Belief is placed in a self-correcting but nonexistent "law of averages."
5. People believe that they exert control over purely chance events.[17]

Second, as a number of researchers have shown, people are irrational and inconsistent when weighing choices based on probability estimates of future costs or payoffs. For example, one set of researchers found that when people are asked to rank probable payoffs, they inconsistently will rank one payoff as being both better and worse than another. Another investigator found that when people were asked which of two probable payoffs they preferred, they would often say that they would pay more for the payoff that, they least preferred. Another set of studies found that, in many cases, a majority of persons would prefer one probable payoff to another in one context, but reversed their preferences in a different context although the probable payoffs were identical in both contexts.[18]

Finally, as several critics have pointed out and as we saw in Chapter 4, markets often fail to incorporate the most fundamental characteristic of competitive markets: the presence of numerous buyers and sellers. Although buyers or consumers in most markets are numerous, still many, perhaps most, consumer markets are monopolies or oligopolies; that is, they are dominated by one or a few large sellers. Sellers in monopoly and oligopoly markets are able to extract abnormally high profits from consumers by ensuring that supply is insufficient to meet demand, thereby creating shortages that put upward pressures on prices.

On balance, then, it does not appear that market forces by themselves can deal with all consumer concerns for safety, freedom from risk, and value. Market failures, characterized by inadequate consumer information, irrationality in the choices of consumers, and concentrated markets, undercut arguments that try to show that markets alone can provide adequate consumer protection. Instead, consumers must be protected through the legal structures of government and through the voluntary initiatives of responsible businesspeople. We turn then to examining several views about the responsibilities of businesses toward consumers—views that have formed the basis of many of our consumer laws and of increased calls for greater acceptance of responsibility for consumer protection on the part of business.

It is clear, of course, that part of the responsibility for consumer injuries must rest on consumers. Individuals are often careless in their use of products. "Do-it-yourselfers" use power saws without guards attached or inflammable liquids near open flames. People often use tools and instruments that they do not have the skill, knowledge, or experience to handle.

Injuries also arise from flaws in product design, in the materials out of which products are made, or in the processes used to construct products. Insofar as manufacturing defects are the source of product-related injuries, consumer advocates claim, the duty of minimizing injuries should lie with the manufacturer. The producer is in the best position to know the hazards raised by a certain product and to eliminate the hazards at the point of manufacture. In addition, the producer's expertise makes the producer knowledgeable about the safest materials and manufacturing methods and enables him to build adequate safeguards into the design of the product. Finally, because the producer is intimately acquainted with the workings of the product, he or she can best inform the consumer on the safest way to use the product and on the precautions to be taken.

Where then does the consumer's duty to protect his or her own interests end, and where does the manufacturer's duty to protect consumers' interests begin? Three different theories on the ethical duties of manufacturers have been developed, each one of which strikes a different balance between the consumer's duty to him or herself and the manufacturer's duty to the consumer: the contract view, the "due care" view, and the social costs view. The contract view would place the greater responsibility on the consumer, whereas the due care and social costs views place the larger measure of responsibility on the manufacturer. We examine each of these in turn.

6.2 The Contract View of Business' Duties to Consumers

According to the contract view of the business firm's duties to its customers, the relationship between a business firm and its customers is essentially a contractual relationship, and the firm's moral duties to the customer are those created by this contractual relationship.[19] When a consumer buys a product, this view holds, the consumer voluntarily enters into a "sales contract" with the business firm. The firm freely and knowingly agrees to give the consumer a product with certain characteristics, and the consumer in turn freely and knowingly agrees to pay a certain sum of money to the firm for the product. In virtue of having voluntarily entered this agreement, the firm then has a duty to provide a product with those characteristics, and the consumer has a correlative right to get a product with those characteristics.

The contract theory of the business firm's duties to its customers rests on the view that a contract is a free agreement that imposes on the parties the basic duty of complying with the terms of the agreement. We examined this view earlier (Chapter 2) and noted the two justifications Kant provided for the view: A person has a duty to do what he or she contracts to do because failure to adhere to the terms of a contract is a practice that (a) cannot be universalized, and (b) treats the other person as a means and not as an end.[20] Rawls' theory also provides a justification for the view, but one that is based on the idea that our freedom is expanded by the recognition of contractual rights and duties: An enforced system of social rules that requires people to do what they contract to do will provide them with the assurance that contracts will be kept. Only if they have such assurance will people feel able to trust each other's word and, on that basis, to secure the benefits of the institution of contracts.[21]

We also noted in Chapter 2 that traditional moralists have argued that the act of entering into a contract is subject to several secondary moral constraints:

1. Both of the parties to the contract must have full knowledge of the nature of the agreement they are entering.
2. Neither party to a contract must intentionally misrepresent the facts of the contractual situation to the other party.
3. Neither party to a contract must be forced to enter the contract under duress or undue influence.

These secondary constraints can be justified by the same sorts of arguments that Kant and Rawls use to justify the basic duty to perform one's contracts. Kant, for example, easily shows that misrepresentation in the making of a contract cannot be universalized, and Rawls argues that if misrepresentation were not prohibited, fear of deception would make members of a society feel less free to enter contracts. However, these secondary constraints can also be justified on the grounds that a contract cannot exist unless these constraints are fulfilled. A contract is essentially a free agreement struck between two parties. Because an agreement cannot exist unless both parties know what they are agreeing to, contracts require full knowledge and the absence of misrepresentation. Because freedom implies the absence of coercion, contracts must be made without duress or undue influence.

Hence, the contractual theory of business' duties to consumers claims that a business has four main moral duties: the basic duty of (a) complying with the terms of the sales contract, and the secondary duties of (b) disclosing the nature of the product, (c) avoiding misrepresentation, and (d) avoiding the use of duress and undue influence. By acting in accordance with these duties, a business respects the right of consumers to be treated as free and equal persons—that is, in accordance with their right to be treated only as they have freely consented to be treated.

The Duty to Comply

The most basic moral duty that a business firm owes its customers, according to the contract view, is the duty to provide consumers with a product that lives up to those claims that the firm expressly made about the product, which led the customer to enter the contract freely and which formed the customer's understanding concerning what he or she was agreeing to buy. In the early 1970s, for example, Winthrop Laboratories marketed a painkiller that the firm advertised as *nonaddictive*. Subsequently, a patient using the painkiller became addicted to it and shortly died from an overdose. A court found Winthrop Laboratories liable for the patient's death because, although it had expressly stated that the drug was nonaddictive, Winthrop Laboratories had failed to live up to its duty to comply with this express contractual claim.[22]

As this example suggests, our legal system has incorporated the moral view that firms have a duty to live up to the express claims they make about their products. The Uniform Commercial Code, for example, states in Section 2-314:

> Any affirmation of fact or promise made by the seller to the buyer that related to the goods and becomes part of the basis of the bargain creates an express warranty that the goods shall conform to the affirmation or promise.

In addition to the duties that result from the express claim a seller makes about the product, the contract view also holds that the seller has a duty to carry through on any implied claims he or she knowingly makes about the product. For example, the seller has the moral duty to provide a product that can be used safely for the ordinary and special purposes for which the customer, relying on the seller's judgment, has been led to believe it can be used. The seller is morally bound to do whatever he or she knows the buyer understood the seller was promising because at the point of sale sellers should have corrected any misunderstandings of which they were aware.[23]

This idea of an implied agreement has also been incorporated into the law. Section 2-315 of the Uniform Commercial Code, for example, reads:

> Where the seller at the time of contracting has reason to know any particular purpose for which the goods are required and that the buyer is relying on the seller's skill or judgment to select or furnish suitable goods, there is . . . an implied warranty that the goods shall be fit for such purpose.

The express or implied claims that a seller might make about the qualities possessed by the product range over a variety of areas and are affected by a number of factors. Frederick Sturdivant classified these areas in terms of four variables: "The definition of product quality used here is: the degree to which product performance meets predetermined expectation with respect to (1) reliability, (2) service life, (3) maintainability, and (4) safety."[24]

Reliability Claims of reliability refer to the probability that a product will function as the consumer is led to expect that it will function. If a product incorporates a number of interdependent components, then the probability that it will function properly is equal to the result of multiplying together each component's probability of proper functioning.[25] As the number of components in a product multiplies, therefore, the manufacturer has a corresponding duty to ensure that each component functions in such a manner that the total product is as reliable as he or she implicitly or expressly claims it will be. This is especially the case when malfunction poses health or safety hazards. The U.S. Consumer Product Safety Commission lists hundreds of examples of hazards from product malfunctions in its periodic announcements.[26]

Service Life Claims concerning the life of a product refer to the period of time during which the product will function as effectively as the consumer is led to expect it to function. Generally, the consumer implicitly understands that service life will depend on the amount of wear and tear to which one subjects the product. In addition, consumers also base some of their expectations of service life on the explicit guarantees the manufacturer attaches to the product.

A more subtle factor that influences service life is the factor of obsolescence.[27] Technological advances may render some products obsolete when a new product appears that carries out the same functions more efficiently. Purely stylistic changes may make last year's product appear dated and less desirable. The contract view implies that a seller who knows that a certain product will become obsolete has a duty to correct any mistaken beliefs he or she knows buyers will form concerning the service life they may expect from the product.

Maintainability Claims of maintainability are claims concerning the ease with which the product can be repaired and kept in operating condition. Claims of maintainability are often made in the form of an express warranty. Whirlpool Corporation, for example, appended this express warranty on one of its products:

> During your first year of ownership, all parts of the appliance (except the light bulbs) that we find are defective in materials or workmanship will be repaired or replaced by Whirlpool free of charge, and we will pay all labor charges. During the second year, we will continue to assume the same responsibility as stated above except you pay any labor charges.[28]

But sellers often also imply that a product may be easily repaired even after the expiration date of an express warranty. In fact, however, product repairs may be costly, or even impossible, because of the unavailability of parts.

Product Safety Implied and express claims of product safety refer to the degree of risk associated with using a product. Because the use of virtually any product involves some degree of risk, questions of safety are essentially questions of acceptable and known evels of risk. That is, a product is safe if its attendant risks are known and judged to be "acceptable" or "reasonable" by the buyer in view of the benefits the buyer expects to derive from using the product. This implies that the seller complies with his or her part of a free agreement if the seller provides a product that involves only those risks he or she says it involves, and the buyer purchases it with that understanding. The National Commission on Product Safety, for example, characterized *reasonable risk* in these terms:

> Risk of bodily harm to users are not unreasonable when consumers understand that risks exist, can appraise their probability and severity, know how to cope with them, and voluntarily accept them to get benefits they could not obtain in less risky ways. When there is a risk of this character, consumers have reasonable opportunity to protect themselves; and public authorities should hesitate to substitute their value judgments about the desirability of the risk for those of the consumers who choose to incur it. But preventable risk is not reasonable (a) when consumers do not know that it exists; or (b) when, though aware of it, consumers are unable to estimate its frequency and severity; or (c) when consumers do not know how to cope with it, and hence are likely to incur harm unnecessarily; or (d) when risk is unnecessary in that it could be reduced or eliminated at a cost in money or in the performance of the product that consumers would willingly incur if they knew the facts and were given the choice.[29]

Thus, the seller of a product (according to the contractual theory) has a moral duty to provide a product whose use involves no greater risks than those the seller expressly communicates to the buyer or those the seller implicitly communicates by the implicit claims made when marketing the product for a use whose normal risk level is well known. If the label on a bottle, for example, indicates only that the contents are highly toxic ("Danger: Poison"), the product should not include additional risks from flammability. If a firm makes and sells skis, use of the skis should not embody any unexpected additional risks other than the well-known risks that attend skiing (e.g., it should not involve the added possibility of being pierced by splinters should the skis fracture). In short, the seller has a duty to provide a product with a level of risk that is no higher than he or she expressly or implicitly claims it to be and that the consumer freely and knowingly contracts to assume.

The Duty of Disclosure

An agreement cannot bind unless both parties to the agreement know what they are doing and freely choose to do it. This implies that the seller who intends to enter a contract with a customer has a duty to disclose exactly what the customer is buying and what the terms of the sale are. At a minimum, this means the seller has a duty to inform the buyer of any facts about the product that would affect the customer's decision to purchase the product. For example, if the product the consumer is buying possesses a defect that poses a risk to the user's health or safety, the consumer should be so informed. Some have argued that sellers should also disclose a product's components or ingredients, its performance characteristics, costs of operation, product ratings, and any other applicable standards.[30]

Behind the claim that entry into a sales contract requires full disclosure is the idea that an agreement is free only to the extent that one knows what alternatives are available: Freedom depends on knowledge. The more the buyer knows about the various products available on the market and the more comparisons the buyer is able to make among them, the more one can say that the buyer's agreement is voluntary.[31]

The view that sellers should provide a great deal of information for buyers, however, has been criticized on the grounds that information is costly and, therefore, should be treated as a product for which the consumer should either pay or do without. In short, consumers should freely contract to purchase information as they freely contract to purchase goods, and producers should not have to provide it for them.[32] The problem with the criticism is that the information on which a person bases his or her decision to enter a contract is a rather different kind of entity from the product exchanged through the contract. Because a contract must be entered into freely and free choice depends on knowledge, contractual transactions must be based on an open exchange of information. If consumers had to bargain for such information, the resulting contract would hardly be free.

The Duty Not to Misrepresent

Misrepresentation, even more than the failure to disclose information, renders freedom of choice impossible. That is, misrepresentation is coercive: The person who is intentionally misled acts as the deceiver wants the person to act and not as the person would freely have chosen to act if he or she had known the truth. Because free choice is an essential ingredient of a binding contract, intentionally misrepresenting the nature of a commodity is wrong.

A seller misrepresents a commodity when he or she represents it in a way deliberately intended to deceive the buyer into thinking something about the product that the seller knows is false. The deception may be created by a verbal lie, as when a used model is described as *new*, or it may be created by a gesture, as when an unmarked used model is displayed together with several new models. That is, the deliberate intent to misrepresent by false implication is as wrong as the explicit lie.

The varieties of misrepresentation seem to be limited only by the ingenuity of the greed that creates them.[33] A computer software or hardware manufacturer may market a product it knows contains "bugs" without informing buyers of that fact; a manufacturer may give a product a name that the manufacturer knows consumers will confuse with the brand name of a higher quality competing product; the manufacturer may write *wool* or *silk* on material made wholly or partly of cotton; the manufacturer may mark a fictitious "regular price" on an article that is always sold at a much lower "sale" price; a business may advertise an unusually low price for an object that the business actually intends to sell at a much higher price once the consumer is lured into the store; a store may advertise an object at an unusually low price, intending to "bait and switch" the unwary buyer over to a more expensive product; and a producer may solicit paid "testimonials" from professionals who have never really used the product. We return to some of these issues when we discuss advertising.

The Duty Not to Coerce

People often act irrationally when under the influence of fear or emotional stress. When a seller takes advantage of a buyer's fear or emotional stress to extract consent to an agreement that the buyer would not make if the buyer were thinking rationally, the seller is using duress or undue influence to coerce. An unscrupulous funeral director, for example, may skillfully induce guilt-ridden and grief-stricken survivors to invest in funeral services they cannot afford. Because entry into a contract requires freely given consent, the seller has a duty to refrain from exploiting emotional states that may induce the buyer to act irrationally against his or her own best interests. For similar reasons, the seller also has the duty not to take advantage of gullibility, immaturity, ignorance, or any other factors that reduce or eliminate the buyer's ability to make free rational choices.

Problems with the Contractual Theory

The main objections to the contract theory focus on the unreality of the assumptions on which the theory is based. First, critics argue, the theory unrealistically assumes that manufacturers make direct agreements with consumers. Nothing could be farther from the truth. Normally, a series of wholesalers and retailers stand between the manufacturer and the ultimate consumer. The manufacturer sells the product to the wholesaler, who sells it to the retailer, who finally sells it to the consumer. The manufacturer never enters into any direct contract with the consumer. How then can one say that manufacturers have contractual duties to the consumer?

Advocates of the contract view of manufacturers' duties have tried to respond to this criticism by arguing that manufacturers enter into *indirect* agreements with consumers. Manufacturers promote their products through their own advertising campaigns. These advertisements supply the promises that lead people to purchase products from retailers who merely function as "conduits" for the manufacturer's product. Consequently, through these advertisements, the manufacturer forges an indirect contractual relationship not only with the immediate retailers who purchase the manufacturer's product but also with the ultimate consumers of the product. The most famous application of this doctrine of broadened indirect contractual relationships is to be found in a 1960 court opinion, *Henningsen v. Bloomfield Motors*.[34] Mrs. Henningsen was driving a new Plymouth when it suddenly gave off a loud cracking noise. The steering wheel spun out of her hands and the car lurched to the right and crashed into a brick wall. Mrs. Henningsen sued the manufacturer, Chrysler Corporation. The court opinion read:

> Under modern conditions the ordinary layman, on responding to the importuning of colorful advertising, has neither the opportunity nor the capacity to inspect or to determine the fitness of an automobile for use; he must rely on the manufacturer who has control of its construction, and to some degree on the dealer who, to the limited extent called for by the manufacturer's instructions, inspects and services it before delivery. In such a marketing milieu his remedies and those of persons who properly claim through him should not depend "upon the intricacies of the law of sales. The obligation of the manufacturer should not be based alone on privity of contract [that is, on a direct contractual relationship]. It should rest, as was once said, upon 'the demands of social justice' " *Mazetti v. Armous & Co.* (1913). "If privity of contract is required," then, under the circumstances of modern merchandising, "privity of contract exists in the consciousness and understanding of all right-thinking persons. . . ." Accordingly, we hold that under modern marketing conditions, when a manufacturer puts a new automobile in the stream of trade and promotes its purchase by the public, an implied warranty that it is reasonably suitable for use as such accompanies it into the hands of the ultimate purchaser. Absence of agency between the manufacturer and the dealer who makes the ultimate sale is immaterial.

Thus, Chrysler Corporation was found liable for Mrs. Henningsen's injuries on the grounds that its advertising had created a contractual relationship with Mrs. Henningsen and this contract created an "implied warranty" about the car, which Chrysler had a duty to fulfill.

A second objection to the contract theory focuses on the fact that a contract is a two-edged sword. If a consumer can freely agree to buy a product with certain qualities, the consumer can also freely agree to buy a product without those qualities. That is, freedom of contract allows a manufacturer to be released from his or her contractual obligations by explicitly disclaiming that the product is reliable, serviceable, safe, and so on. Many manufacturers fix such disclaimers on their products. The Uniform Commercial Code, in fact, stipulates in Section 2-316:

> a. Unless the circumstances indicate otherwise, all implied warranties are excluded by expressions like "as is," "with all faults," or other language that in common understanding calls the buyer's attention to the exclusion of warranties and makes plain that there is no warranty, and
>
> b. When the buyer before entering into the contract has examined the goods or the sample or model as fully as he desired, or has refused to examine the goods, there is no implied warranty with regard to defects that on examination ought in the circumstances to have been revealed to him.

The contract view, then, implies that if the consumer has ample opportunity to examine the product and its disclaimers and voluntarily consents to buy it anyway, he or she assumes the responsibility for the defects disclaimed by the manufacturer, as well as for any defects the customer may carelessly have overlooked. Disclaimers can effectively nullify all contractual duties of the manufacturer.

A third objection to the contract theory criticizes the assumption that buyer and seller meet each other as equals in the sales agreement. The contractual theory assumes that buyers and sellers are equally skilled at evaluating the quality of a product and that buyers are able to adequately protect their interests against the seller. This is the assumption built into the requirement that contracts must be freely and knowingly entered into: Both parties must know what they are doing and neither must be coerced into doing it. This equality between buyer and seller that the contractual theory assumes derives from the laissez-faire ideology that accompanied the historical development of contract theory.[35] Classical laissez-faire ideology held that the economy's markets are competitive and that in competitive markets the consumer's bargaining power is equal to that of the seller. Competition forces the seller to offer the consumer as good or better terms than the consumer could get from other competing sellers, so the consumer has the power to threaten to take his or her business to other sellers. Because of this equality between buyer and seller, it was fair that each be allowed to try to outbargain the other and unfair to place restrictions on either. In practice, this laissez-faire ideology gave birth to the doctrine of *caveat emptor:* let the buyer take care of himself.

In fact, sellers and buyers do not exhibit the equality that these doctrines assume. A consumer who must purchase hundreds of different kinds of commodities cannot hope to be as knowledgeable as a manufacturer who specializes in producing a single product. Consumers have neither the expertise nor the time to acquire and process the information on which they must base their purchase decisions. Consequently, consumers must usually rely on the judgment of the seller in making their purchase decisions and are particularly vulnerable to being harmed by the seller. Equality, far from being the rule, as the contract theory assumes, is usually the exception.

6.3 The Due Care Theory

The "due care" theory of the manufacturer's duties to consumers is based on the idea that consumers and sellers do not meet as equals and that the consumer's interests are particularly vulnerable to being harmed by the manufacturer who has a knowledge and an expertise that the consumer lacks. Because manufacturers are in a more advantaged position, they have a duty to take special care to ensure that consumers' interests are not harmed by the products that they offer them. The doctrine of *caveat emptor* is here replaced with a weak version of the doctrine of *caveat vendor:* let the seller take care. A New York court decision neatly described the advantaged position of the manufacturer and the consequent vulnerability of the consumer:

> Today as never before the product in the hands of the consumer is often a most sophisticated and even mysterious article. Not only does it usually emerge as a sealed unit with an alluring exterior rather than as a visible assembly of component parts, but its functional validity and usefulness often depend on the application of electronic, chemical, or hydraulic principles far beyond the ken of the average consumer. Advances in the technologies of materials, of processes, of operational means have put it almost entirely out of the reach of the consumer to comprehend why or how the article operates, and thus even farther out of his reach to detect when there may be a defect or a danger present in its design or manufacture. In today's world it is often only the manufacturer who can fairly be said to know and to understand when an article is suitably designed and safely made for its intended purpose. Once floated on the market, many articles in a very real practical sense defy detection of defect, except possibly in the hands of an expert after laborious, and perhaps even destructive, disassembly. By way of direct illustration, how many automobile purchasers or users have any idea how a power steering mechanism operates or is intended to operate, with its "circulating work and piston assembly and its cross shaft splined to the Pitman arm"? We are accordingly persuaded that from the standpoint of justice as regards the operating aspect of today's products, responsibility should be laid on the manufacturer, subject to the limitations we set forth.[36]

The "due care" view holds then that, because consumers must depend on the greater expertise of the manufacturer, the manufacturer not only has a duty to deliver a product that lives up to the express and implied claims about it, but also has a duty to exercise due care to prevent others from being injured by the product even if the manufacturer explicitly disclaims such responsibility and the buyer agrees to the disclaimer. The manufacturer violates this duty and is negligent when there is a failure to exercise the care that a reasonable person could have foreseen would be necessary to prevent others from being harmed by use of the product. Due care must enter into the design of the product, the choice of reliable materials for constructing the product, the manufacturing processes involved in putting the product together, the quality control used to test and monitor production, and the warnings, labels, and instructions attached to the product. In each of these areas, according to the due care view, the manufacturer, in virtue of a greater expertise and knowledge, has a positive duty to take whatever steps are necessary to ensure that when the product leaves the plant it is as safe as possible, and the customer has a right to such assurance. Failure to take such steps is a breach of the moral duty to exercise due care and a violation of the injured person's right to expect such care—a right that rests on the consumer's need to rely on the manufacturer's expertise. Edgar Schein sketched out the basic elements of the "due care" theory several years ago when he wrote:

> [A] professional is someone who knows better what is good for his client than the client himself does . . . . If we accept this definition of professionalism . . . we may speculate that it is the *vulnerability of the client* that has necessitated the development of moral and ethical codes surrounding the relationship. The client must be protected from exploitation in a situation in which he is unable to protect himself because he lacks the relevant knowledge to do so. . . . If [a manufacturer] is . . . a professional, who is his client? With respect to whom is he exercising his expert knowledge and skills? Who needs protection against the possible misuse of these skills? . . . Many economists argue persuasively . . . that the consumer has not been in a position to know what he was buying and hence was, in fact, in a relatively vulnerable position. . . . Clearly, then, one whole area of values deals with the relationship between the [manufacturer] and consumers.[37]

The due care view, of course, rests on the principle that agents have a moral duty not to harm or injure other parties by their acts, and that this duty is particularly stringent when those other parties are vulnerable and dependent on the judgment of the agent. This principle can be supported from a variety of different moral perspectives, but it is most clearly implied by the requirements of an ethic of care. The principle follows almost immediately, in fact, from the requirement that one should care for the well-being of those with whom one has a special relationship, particularly a relationship of dependence, such as a child has on its mother. Moreover, an ethic of care imposes the requirement that one should carefully examine the particular needs and characteristics of the person with whom one has a special relationship to ensure that one's care for that person is tailored to that person's particular needs and qualities. As we see, this emphasis on carefully examining the specific needs and characteristics of a vulnerable party is also an explicit and critically important part of the due care view.

Although the demands of an ethic of care are aligned with the due care principle that manufacturers have a duty to protect vulnerable consumers, the principle has also been defended from other moral perspectives. Rule utilitarians have defended the principle on the grounds that if the rule is accepted, everyone's welfare will be advanced.[38] The principle has been argued for on the basis of Kant's theory because it seems to follow from the categorical imperative that people should be treated as ends and not merely as means—that is, that they have a positive right to be helped when they cannot help themselves.[39] Rawls has argued that individuals in the "original position" would agree to the principle because it would provide the basis for a secure social environment.[40] The judgment that individual producers have a duty not to harm or injure vulnerable parties, therefore, is solidly based on several ethical perspectives.

The Duty to Exercise Due Care

According to the due care theory, manufacturers exercise sufficient care only when they take adequate steps to prevent whatever injurious effects they can foresee that the use of their product may have on consumers after having conducted inquiries into the way the product will be used and after having attempted to anticipate any possible misuses of the product. A manufacturer then is not morally negligent when others are harmed by a product and the harm was not one that the manufacturer could have possible foreseen or prevented. Nor is a manufacturer morally negligent after having taken all reasonable steps to protect the consumer and ensure that the consumer is informed of any irremovable risks that might still attend the use of the product. For example, a car manufacturer, cannot be said to be negligent from a moral point of view when people carelessly misuse the cars the manufacturer produces. A car manufacturer would be morally negligent only if it had allowed unreasonable dangers to remain in the design of the car that consumers cannot be expected to know about or cannot guard against by taking their own precautionary measures.

What specific responsibilities does the duty to exercise due care impose on the producer? In general, the producer's responsibilities would extend the to following three areas:[41]

Design The manufacturer should ascertain whether the design of an article conceals any dangers, whether it incorporates all feasible safety devices, and whether it uses materials that are adequate for the purposes the product is intended to serve. The manufacturer is responsible for being thoroughly acquainted with the design of the item, and to conduct research and tests extensive enough to uncover any risks that may be involved in employing the article under various conditions of use. This requires researching consumers and analyzing their behavior, testing the product under different conditions of consumer use, and selecting materials strong enough to stand up to all probable usages. The effects of aging and wear should also be analyzed and taken into account in designing an article. Engineering staff should acquaint themselves with hazards that might result from prolonged use and wear, and it should warn the consumer of any potential dangers. There is a duty to take the latest technological advances into account in design a product, especially where advances can provide ways to design a product that is less liable to harm or injure its users.

Production The production manager should control the manufacturing processes so as to eliminate any defective items, identify any weaknesses that become apparent during production, and ensure that short-cuts, substitution of weaker materials, or other economizing measures are not taken during manufacture that would compromise the safety of the final product. To ensure this, there should be adequate quality controls over materials that are to be used in the manufacture of the product and over the various stages of manufacture.

Information The manufacturer should fix labels, notices, or instructions on the product that will warn the user of all dangers involved in using or misusing the item and that will enable the user to adequately guard him or herself against harm or injury. These instructions should be clear and simple, and warnings of any hazards involved in using or misusing the product should also be clear, simple, and prominent. In the case of drugs, manufacturers have a duty to warn physicians of any risks or dangerous side effects that research or prolonged use have revealed. It is a breach of the duty not to harm or injure if the manufacturer attempts to conceal or down play the dangers related to drug usage.

In determining the safeguards that should be built into a product, the manufacturer must also take into consideration the capacities of the persons who will use the product. If a manufacturer anticipates that a product will be used by persons who are immature, mentally deficient, or too inexperienced to be aware of the dangers attendant on the use of the product, the manufacturer owes them a greater degree of care than if the anticipated users were of ordinary intelligence and prudence. For example, children cannot be expected to realize the dangers involved in using electrical equipment. Consequently, if a manufacturer anticipates that an electrical item will probably be used by children, steps must be taken to ensure that a person with a child's understanding will not be injured by the product.

If the possible harmful effects of using a product are serious or if they cannot be adequately understood without expert opinion, then sale of the product should be carefully controlled. A firm should not oppose regulation of the sale of a product when regulation is the only effective means of ensuring that the users of the product are fully aware of the risks its use involves.

Problems with "Due Care"

The basic difficulty raised by the "due care" theory is that there is no clear method for determining when one has exercised enough "due care." That is, there is no hard and fast rule for determining how far a firm must go to ensure the safety of its product. Some authors have proposed this general utilitarian rule: The greater the probability of harm and the larger the population that might be harmed, the more the firm is obligated to do. However, this fails to resolve some important issues. Every product involves at least some small risk of injury. If the manufacturer should try to eliminate even low-level risks, this would require that the manufacturer invest so much in each product that the product would be priced out of the reach of most consumers. Moreover, even attempting to balance higher risks against added costs involves measurement problems: For example, how does one quantify risks to health and life?

A second difficulty raised by the "due care" theory is that it assumes that the manufacturer can discover the risks that attend the use of a product before the consumer buys and uses it. In fact, in a technologically innovative society, new products whose defects cannot emerge until years or decades have passed will continually be introduced into the market. Only years after thousands of people were using and being exposed to asbestos, for example, did a correlation emerge between the incidence of cancer and exposure to asbestos. Although manufacturers may have greater expertise than consumers, their expertise does not make them omniscient. Who, then, is to bear the costs of injuries sustained from products whose defects neither the manufacturer nor the consumer could have uncovered beforehand?

Third, the due care view appears to some to be paternalistic: It assumes that the manufacturer should be the one who makes the important decisions for the consumer, at least with respect to the levels of risks that are proper for consumers to bear. One may wonder whether such decisions should not be left up to the free choice of consumers who can decide for themselves whether they want to pay for additional risk reduction.

6.4 The Social Costs View of the Manufacturer's Duties

A third theory on the duties of the manufacturer would extend the manufacturer's duties beyond those imposed by contractual relationships and beyond those imposed by the duty to exercise due care in preventing injury or harm. This third theory holds that a manufacturer should pay the costs of any injuries sustained through any defects in the product, even when the manufacturer exercised all due care in the design and manufacture of the product and has taken all reasonable precautions to warn users of every foreseen danger. According to this third theory, a manufacturer has a duty to assume the risks of even those injuries that arise out of defects in the product that no one could reasonably have foreseen or eliminated. The theory is a strong version of the doctrine of *caveat vendor:* let the seller take care.

This third theory, which has formed the basis of the legal doctrine of *strict liability*, is founded on utilitarian arguments.[42] The utilitarian arguments for this third theory hold that the "external" costs of injuries resulting from unavoidable defects in the design of an artifact constitute part of the costs society must pay for producing and using an artifact. By having the manufacturer bear the external costs that result from these injuries as well as the ordinary internal costs of design and manufacture, all costs are internalized and added on as part of the price of the product. Internalizing all costs in this way, according to proponents of this theory, will lead to a more efficient use of society's resources. First, because the price will reflect all the costs of producing and using the artifact, market forces will ensure that the product is not overproduced and resources are not wasted on it. (Whereas if some costs were not included in the price, then manufacturers would tend to produce more than is needed.) Second, because manufacturers have to pay the costs of injuries, they will be motivated to exercise greater care and thereby reduce the number of accidents. Therefore, manufacturers will strive to cut down the social costs of injuries, and this means a more efficient care for our human resources. To produce the maximum benefits possible from our limited resources, therefore, the social costs of injuries from defective products should be internalized by passing them on to the manufacturer even when the manufacturer has done all that could be done to eliminate such defects. Third, internalizing the costs of injury in this way enables the manufacturer to distribute losses among all the users of a product instead of allowing losses to fall on individuals who may not be able to sustain the loss by themselves.

Underlying this third theory on the duties of the manufacturer are the standard utilitarian assumptions about the values of efficiency. The theory assumes that an efficient use of resources is so important for society that social costs should be allocated in whatever way will lead to a more efficient use and care of our resources. On this basis, the theory argues that a manufacturer should bear the social costs for injuries caused by defects in a product even when no negligence was involved and no contractual relationship existed between the manufacturer and user.

Problems with the Social Costs View

The major criticism of the social costs view of the manufacturer's duties is that it is unfair.[43] It is unfair, the critics charge, because it violates the basic canons of compensatory justice. Compensatory justice implies that a person should be forced to compensate an injured party only if the person could have foreseen and prevented the injury. By forcing manufacturers to pay for injuries they could neither foresee nor prevent, the social costs theory (and the legal theory of "strict liability" that flows from it) treats manufacturers unfairly. Moreover, insofar as the social costs theory encourages passing the costs of injuries on to all consumers (in the form of higher prices), consumers are also being treated unfairly.

A second criticism of the social costs theory attacks the assumption that passing the costs of all injuries on to manufacturers will reduce the number of accidents.[44] On the contrary, critics claim, by relieving consumers of the responsibility of paying for their own injuries, the social costs theory will encourage carelessness in consumers. An increase in consumer carelessness will lead to an increase in consumer injuries.

A third argument against the social costs theory focuses on the financial burdens the theory imposes on manufacturers and insurance carriers. Critics claim that a growing number of consumers successfully sue manufacturers for compensation for any injuries sustained while using a product even when the manufacturer took all due care to ensure that the product was safe.[45] Not only have the number of "strict liability" suits increased, critics claim, but the amounts awarded to injured consumers have also escalated. Moreover, they continue, the rising costs of the many liability suits that the theory of "strict liability" has created have precipitated a crisis in the insurance industry because insurance companies end up paying the liability suits brought against manufacturers. These high costs have imposed heavy losses on insurance companies and have forced many insurance companies to raise their rates to levels that are so high that many manufacturers can no longer afford insurance. Thus, critics claim, the social costs or "strict liability" theory wreaks havoc with the insurance industry, forces the costs of insurance to climb to unreasonable heights, and forces many valuable firms out of business because they can no longer afford liability insurance nor can they afford to pay for the many and expensive liability suits they must now face.

Defenders of the social costs view, however, have replied that in reality the costs of consumer liability suits are not large. Studies have shown that the number of liability suits filed in state courts has increased at a fairly low rate.[46] Less than 1 percent of product-related injuries results in suits, and successful suits average payments of only a few thousand dollars.[47] Defenders of the social costs theory also point out that insurance companies and the insurance industry as a whole have remained quite profitable; they also claim that higher insurance costs are due to factors other than an increase in the amount of liability claims.[48]

The arguments for and against the social costs theory deserve much more discussion than we can give them here. The theory is essentially an attempt to come to grips with the problem of allocating the costs of injuries between two morally innocent parties: The manufacturer who could not foresee or prevent a product-related injury and the consumer who could not guard him or herself against the injury because the hazard was unknown. This allocation problem will arise in any society that, like ours, has come to rely on technology whose effects do not become evident until years after the technology is introduced. Unfortunately, it is also a problem that may have no "fair" solution.

6.5 Advertising Ethics

The advertising industry is a massive business. Over $150 billion was spent in 1994 on advertising.[49] More than $30 billion was spent on television advertising alone; another $32 billion was spent on newspaper advertisements.[50] There are over 6000 advertising agencies doing business in the United States, many of which employ several thousand people.

Who pays for these advertising expenditures? In the end, advertising costs must be covered by the prices consumers pay for the goods they buy: The consumer pays. What does the consumer get for his or her advertising dollar? According to most consumers, they get very little. Surveys have shown that 66 percent of consumers feel that advertising does not reduce prices, 65 percent believe it makes people buy things they should not buy, 54 percent feel advertisements insult the intelligence, and 63 percent feel advertisements do not present the truth.[51] However, defenders of the advertising industry see things differently. Advertising, they claim, "is, before all else, communication."[52] Its basic function is to provide consumers with information about the products available to them—a beneficial service.[53]

Is advertising then a waste or a benefit? Does it harm consumers or help them?

A Definition

Commercial advertising is sometimes defined as a form of "information" and an advertiser as "one who gives information." The implication is that the defining function of advertising is to provide information to consumers. This definition of advertising, however, fails to distinguish advertisements from, say, articles in publications like *Consumer Reports*, which compare, test, and objectively evaluate the durability, safety, defects, and usefulness of various products. One study found that more than half of all television ads contained no consumer information whatsoever about the advertised product, and that only half of all magazine ads contained more than one informational cue.[54] Consider how much information is conveyed by the following advertisements:

"Got Milk?" (America's Dairy Farmers and Milk Processors")
"Be late" (Neiman Marcus watches)
"Embrace your demons" (Cinnamon flavored Altoids)
"For the way it's made" (KitchenAid home applicances)
"Connect with style" (Nokia cell phones)
"Inside every woman is a glow just waiting to come out" (Dove soap)
"It is, in the end, the simple idea that one plus one can, and must, equal more than two" (Chrysler cars)
"Marlboro Country" (Marlboro cigarettes)
"Before there was a Land Rover there was a dream" (Land Rover S.U.V.)

Advertisements often do not include much objective information for the simple reason that their primary function is not that of providing unbiased information. The primary function of commercial advertisements, rather, is to sell a product to prospective buyers, and whatever information they happen to carry is subsidiary to this basic function and usually determined by it.

A more helpful way of characterizing commercial advertising is in terms of the buyer–seller relationship: Commercial advertising can be defined as a certain kind of communication between a seller and potential buyers. It is distinguished from other forms of communication by two features. First, it is publicly addressed to a mass audience as distinct from a private message to a specific individual. Because of this public feature, advertising necessarily has widespread social effects.

Second, advertising is intended to induce several members of its audience to buy the seller's products. An advertisement can succeed in this intent in two main ways: (a) by creating a desire for the seller's product in consumers, and (b) by creating a belief in consumers that the product is a means of satisfying some desire the buyer already has.

Discussion of the ethical aspects of advertising can be organized around the various features identified in the prior definition: its social effects, its creation of consumer desires, and its effects on consumer beliefs. We begin by discussing the social effects of advertising.

Social Effects of Advertising

Critics of advertising claim that it has several adverse effects on society: It degrades people's tastes, it wastes valuable resources, and it creates monopoly power. We examine these criticisms one by one.

Psychological Effects of Advertising A familiar criticism of advertising is that it debases the tastes of the public by presenting irritating and aesthetically unpleasant displays.[55] To be effective, advertisements must often be intrusive, strident, and repetitive. Therefore, so that they are understood by the most simple-minded person, advertisements are often boring, insipid, and insult the intelligence of viewers. In illustrating the use of toothpaste, mouthwashes, deodorants, and undergarments, for example, advertisements sometimes employ images that many people find vulgar, offensive, disgusting, and tasteless. However, although these sorts of criticisms may be quite accurate, they do not seem to raise important ethical issues. It is certainly unfortunate that advertisements do not measure up to our aesthetic norms, but this does not imply that they also violate our ethical norms.

More to the point is the criticism that advertising debases the tastes of consumers by gradually and subtly inculcating materialistic values and ideas about how happiness is achieved.[56] Because advertising necessarily emphasizes the consumption of material goods, people are led to forget the importance of their other, more basic, needs and of other more realistic ways of achieving self-fulfillment. As a result, personal efforts are diverted from "nonmaterialistic" aims and objectives, which are more likely to increase the happiness of people, and are instead channeled into expanded material consumption. Consumer advocate Mary Gardiner Jones wrote:

> The conscious appeal in the television commercial is essentially materialistic. Central to the message of the TV commercial is the premise that it is the acquisition of things that will gratify our basic and inner needs and aspirations. It is the message of the commercial that all of the major problems confronting an individual can be instantly eliminated by . . . the use of a product. . . . A second inescapable premise of these ads is that we are all externally motivated, concerned to do and be like our neighbors or to emulate popular successful individuals. . . . Personal success in the TV ad is externally contrived, not the product of years of study and training. . . . In addition, . . . the TV commercial presents a very special and limited view of American society. Here, according to the TV commercial . . . is what the young and successful are wearing and how they furnish their homes. . . . [But] the TV world [is] typically that of the white suburban middle-income, middle-class family.[57]

The difficulty with this criticism, however, is that it is uncertain whether advertising actually has the large psychological effects the criticism attributes to it.[58] A person's beliefs and attitudes are notoriously difficult to change without there being a willingness to accept the message being offered. Thus, the success of advertising may depend more on its appeal to the values consumers already possess than on its ability to instill new values. If this is so, then advertising does not so much create society's values as reflect them.

Advertising and Waste A second major criticism brought against advertising is that it is wasteful.[59] Economists sometimes distinguish between *production costs* and *selling costs*. Production costs are the costs of the resources consumed in producing or improving a product. Selling costs are the additional costs of resources that do not go into changing the product, but are invested instead in persuading people to buy the product. The costs of resources consumed by advertising, critics claim, are essentially "selling costs": They are not used to improve the product, but to merely persuade people to buy it. The resources consumed by advertisements do not add anything to the utility of the product. Such resources, critics conclude, are "wasted" because they are expended without adding to consumer utility in any way.

One reply made to this argument is that advertising does in fact produce something: It produces and transmits information on the availability and the nature of products.[60] Yet as many have pointed out, even in these respects, the information content of advertisements is minimal and could be transmitted by substantially less expensive means.[61]

Another more persuasive reply to the argument is that advertising serves to produce a beneficial rise in demand for all products. This rising general demand in turn makes mass production possible. The end result is a gradually expanding economy in which products are manufactured with ever greater efficiency and ever more cheaply. Advertising adds to consumer utility by serving as an incentive to greater consumption and thereby indirectly motivating a greater productivity and efficiency and a lower price structure.[62]

However, there is substantial uncertainty surrounding the question of whether advertising is responsible for a rise in the total consumption of goods.[63] Studies have shown that advertising frequently fails to stimulate consumption of a product, and consumption in many industries has increased despite minimal advertising expenditures. Thus, advertising appears to be effective for individual companies not because it expands consumption, but only because it shifts consumption away from one product to another. If this is true, then economists are correct when they claim that, beyond the level needed to impart information, advertising becomes a waste of resources because it does nothing more than shift demand from one firm to another.[64]

Moreover, even if advertising were an effective spur to consumption, many authors have argued, this is not necessarily a blessing. E. F. Schumacher, Herman E. Daly, and other economists have claimed that the most pressing social need at present is finding ways of decreasing consumption.[65] Increasing consumption has led to a rapid industrial expansion that has polluted much of the natural environment and has rapidly depleted our nonrenewable resources. Unless we limit consumption, we will soon outrun the finite natural resources our planet possesses with disastrous consequences for us all. If this is so, then the claim that advertising induces ever higher levels of consumption is not in its favor.

Advertising and Market Power For many decades, Nicholas Kaldor and others have claimed that the massive advertising campaigns of modern manufacturers enable them to achieve and maintain a monopoly (or oligopoly) power over their markets.[66] Monopolies, as we have seen, lead to higher consumer prices. Kaldor's argument was simple. Large manufacturers have the financial resources to mount massive and expensive advertising campaigns to introduce their products. These campaigns create in consumers a "loyalty" to the brand name of the manufacturer, giving the manufacturer control of a major portion of the market. Small firms are then unable to break into the market because they cannot finance the expensive advertising campaigns that would be required to get consumers to switch their brand loyalties. As a result, a few large oligopoly firms emerge in control of consumer markets from which small firms are effectively barred. Advertising then is supposed to reduce competition and raise barriers to entry into markets.

However, is there a connection between advertising and market power? If advertising does raise costs for consumers by encouraging monopoly markets, there should be a statistical connection between the amount of advertising revenues spent by an industry and the degree of market concentration in that industry. The more concentrated and less competitive industries should exhibit high levels of advertising, whereas less concentrated and more competitive industries should exhibit correspondingly lower levels. Unfortunately, the statistical studies aimed at uncovering a connection between advertising intensity and market concentration have been inconclusive.[67] Some concentrated industries (soaps, cigarettes, breakfast cereals) expend large amounts on advertising, but others (drugs, cosmetics) do not. Moreover, in at least some oligopoly industries (e.g., the auto industry), smaller firms spend more per unit on advertising than the large major firms. Whether advertising harms consumers by diminishing competition is an interesting but unsettled question.

The criticisms of advertising based on its social effects are inconclusive. They are inconclusive for the simple reason that it is unknown whether advertising has the capacity to produce the effects that the criticisms assume it has. To establish the case for or against advertising on the basis of its effects on society will require a great deal more research on the exact nature of the psychological and economic effects advertising has.

Advertising and the Creation of Consumer Desires

John K. Galbraith and others have long argued that advertising is manipulative: It is the creation of desires in consumers for the sole purpose of absorbing industrial output.[68] Galbraith distinguished two kinds of desires: those that have a "physical" basis, such as desires for food and shelter; and those that are "psychological in origin," such as the individual's desires for goods that "give him a sense of personal achievement, accord him a feeling of equality with his neighbors, direct his mind from thought, serve sexual aspiration, promise social acceptability, enhance his subjective feeling of health, contribute by conventional canons to personal beauty, or are otherwise psychologically rewarding."[69]

The physically based desires originate in the buyer and are relatively immune to being changed by persuasion. The psychic desires, however, are capable of being managed, controlled, and expanded by advertising. Because the demand created by physical needs is finite, producers soon produce enough to meet these needs. If production is to expand, therefore, producers must create new demand by manipulating the pliable psychic desires through advertising. Advertising is therefore used to create psychic desires for the sole purpose of "ensuring that people buy what is produced"—that is, to absorb the output of an expanding industrial system.

The effect of this management of demand through advertising is to shift the focus of decision in the purchase of goods from the consumer where it is beyond control to the firm where it is subject to control.[70] Production is not molded to serve human desires; rather, human desires are molded to serve the needs of production.

If this view of Galbraith's is correct, then advertising violates the individual's right to choose for him or herself: Advertising manipulates the consumer. The consumer is used merely as a means for advancing the ends and purposes of producers, and this diminishes the consumer's capacity to freely choose for him or herself.[71]

It is not clear that Galbraith's argument is correct. As we have already seen, the psychological effects of advertising are still unclear. Consequently, it is unclear whether psychic desires can be manipulated by advertising in the wholesale way that Galbraith's argument assumes.[72]

Moreover, as F. A. von Hayek and others have pointed out, the "creation" of psychic wants did not originate with modern advertising.[73] New wants have always been "created" by the invention of novel and attractive products (such as the first bow and arrow, the first painting, the first perfume), and such a creation of wants seems harmless enough.

However, although it is unclear whether advertising as a whole has the massive manipulative effects that Galbraith attributes to it, it is clear that some particular advertisements are at least intended to manipulate. They are intended, to arouse in the consumer a psychological desire for the product without the consumer's knowledge and without the consumer being able to rationally weigh whether the product is in his or her own best interests. Advertisements that intentionally rely on "subliminal suggestion," or that attempt to make consumers associate unreal sexual or social fulfillment with a product, fall into this class, as do advertisements that are aimed at children.

Suppa Corporation in Fallbrook, California, for example, briefly tested candy advertisements printed on paper on which the word *buy* was written so it would register subconsciously but could not be consciously perceived unless one specifically sought it out. Subsequent tests showed that the ads created more of a desire to buy candy than those printed on paper on which the word *no* appeared in a similar subliminal manner.[74] Manipulative ads aimed at children are exemplified by a criticism The National Advertising Division of the Council of Better Business Bureaus recently leveled at a Mattel, Inc., television commercial aimed at children, which mixed animation sequences with group shots of dolls. Children who are still learning to distinguish between fantasy and reality, the Council felt, would not be given "an accurate depiction of the products" pictured in the advertisements.[75] The Council also criticized a Walt Disney Music Co. advertisement of a limited-time offer that conveyed a "sense of urgency" that children might find "overwhelming." Critics have also claimed that television shows of animated characters who resemble toy dolls and figures that are advertised on the same show are in effect prolonged advertisements for these toys. The effect of such "half-hour advertisements," they allege, is to manipulate the vulnerable child by feeding him commercials under the guise of entertainment.[76] Moreover, such *advertisement programs* often contain high levels of violence because their cartoon superhero characters, such as "He-Man," "Rambo," "She-Ra," "GI Joe," and "Transformers," are violent. Advertising which promotes toys modeled on violent characters or promotes military toys indirectly promotes aggression and violent behavior in children who are highly suggestible and easily manipulated, critics claim, and it is therefore unethical.[77] Advertisements of this sort are manipulative insofar as they circumvent conscious reasoning and seek to influence the consumer to do what the advertiser wants and not what is in the consumer's interests.[78] They violate, that is, the consumer's right to be treated as a free and equal rational being.

Advertising and Its Effects on Consumer Beliefs

The most common criticism of advertising concerns its effect on the consumer's beliefs. Because advertising is a form of communication, it can be as truthful or deceptive as any other form of communication. Most criticisms of advertising focus on the deceptive aspects of modern advertising.

Deceptive advertising can take several forms. An advertisement can misrepresent the nature of the product by using deceptive mock-ups, using untrue paid testimonials, inserting the word *guarantee* where nothing is guaranteed, quoting misleading prices, failing to disclose defects in a product, misleadingly disparaging a competitor's goods, or simulating well-known brand names. Some fraudulent forms of advertising involve more complex schemes. For example, bait advertisements announce the sale of goods that later prove not to be available or to be defective. Once the consumer is lured into the store, he or she is pressured to purchase another more expensive item.

A long ethical tradition has consistently condemned deception in advertising on the grounds that it violates consumers' rights to choose for themselves (a

Kantian argument) and on the grounds that it generates a public distrust of advertising that diminishes the utility of this form and even of other forms of communication (the utilitarian argument).[79] The central problem then is not understanding why deceptive advertising is wrong, but understanding how it becomes deceptive and, therefore, unethical.

All communication involves three terms: (a) the author(s) who originates the communication, (b) the medium that carries the communication, and (c) the audience who receives the communication. Because advertising is a form of communication, it involves these three terms, and the various ethical problems raised by the fact that it is a form of communication can be organized around the following three elements.

The Authors Deception involves three necessary conditions in the author of a communication: (a) The author must intend to have the audience believe something false, (b) the author must know it is false, and (c) the author must knowingly do something that will lead the audience to believe the falsehood. This means that the deliberate intent to have an audience believe something false by merely implying it is as wrong is an express lie. It also means, however, that the advertiser cannot be held morally responsible for misinterpretations of an advertisement when these are the unintended and unforeseen results of unreasonable carelessness on the part of the audience. The "author" of an advertisement includes, of course, not only the heads of an advertising agency, but also the persons who create advertising copy and those who "endorse" a product. By offering their positive cooperation in the making of an advertisement, they become morally responsible for its effects.

The Medium Part of the responsibility for truth in advertising rests on the media that carry advertisements. As active participants in the transmission of a message, they also lend their positive cooperation to the success of the advertisement and so they, too, become morally responsible for its effects. Therefore, they should take steps to ensure that the contents of their advertisements are true and not misleading. In the drug industry, retail agents who serve as company sales agents to doctors and hospitals are in effect advertising "media" and are morally responsible for not misleading doctors with respect to the safety and possible hazards of the drugs they promote.

The Audience The meaning attributed to a message depends in part on the capacities of the person who receives the message. A clever and knowledgeable audience, for example, may be capable of correctly interpreting an advertisement that may be misleading to a less knowledgeable or less educated group. Consequently, the advertiser should take into account the interpretive capacities of the audience when he or she determines the content of an advertisement. Most buyers can be expected to be reasonably intelligent and possess a healthy skepticism concerning the exaggerated claims advertisers make for their products. Advertisements that will reach the ignorant, credulous, immature, and unthinking, however, should be designed to avoid misleading even those potential buyers whose judgment is limited. When matters of health or safety, or the possibility of significant injury to buyers is involved, special care should be exercised to ensure that advertisements do not mislead users into ignoring possible dangers.

The third category of issues ("The Audience") raises what is perhaps the most troubling problem in advertising ethics: To what extent do consumers possess the capacity to filter out the *puffery* and bias most advertising messages carry? When an advertisement for a Norelco electric shaver proclaims "You can't get any closer," do consumers automatically discount the vague, nonspecific, and false implication that Norelco was tested against every possible method of shaving and was found to leave facial hair shorter than any other method? Unfortunately, we have little knowledge of the extent to which consumers are able to filter out the exaggerations advertisements contain.

The moral issues raised by advertising are complex and involve several still unsolved problems. However, the following summarizes the main factors that should be taken into consideration when determining the ethical nature of a given advertisement:

Social Effects

1. What does the advertiser intend the effect of the advertisement to be?
2. What are the actual effects of the advertisement on individuals and on society as a whole?

Effects on Desire

1. Does the advertisement inform or does it also seek to persuade?
2. If it is persuasive, does it attempt to create an irrational and possibly injurious desire?

Effects on Belief

1. Is the content of the advertisement truthful?
2. Does the advertisement have a tendency to mislead those to whom it is directed?

6.6 Consumer Privacy

Advances in computer processing power, database software, and communication technologies have given us the power to collect, manipulate, and disseminate personal information about consumers on a scale unprecedented in the history of the human race. This new power over the collection, manipulation, and dissemination of personal information has enabled mass invasions of the privacy of consumers and has created the potential for significant harms arising from mistaken or false information. For example, a pair of British investigators reported that in England, where companies register with the government the kind of information they will collect, businesses were collecting highly detailed and very personal information about their customers:

> The Midland Bank has approval to hold details about the sex lives of potential customers seeking insurance; BNLF is registered to store sexual and political information for "business and technical intelligence"; W. H. Smith, the high street retailer, has official sanction to hold sexual data for "personnel and employee administration" as well as for marketing purposes; Grand Metropolitan, the leisure company, is entitled to hold similar information for use by corporate lawyers; BT is licensed to hold information about political party membership "as a reference tool."[80]

In the United States, fairly complete files on the medical history of consumers is maintained by the Medical Information Bureau (MIB), a company founded in 1902 to provide insurance companies with information about the health of individuals applying for life insurance to detect fraudulent applications. The MIB currently has medical histories on about 15 million people. Information is collected from the forms consumers fill out when applying for life insurance, the applicant's physician, hospitals, employment records, the Department of Motor Vehicles, and even interviews with employers or friends. The information kept by the MIB is translated into certain codes (e.g., the code "45GTY" might refer to lung cancer) to lessen the chance that unauthorized persons who see the records will be able to interpret them. Information in these files is sometimes inaccurate. One individual was erroneously reported to have AIDS and to be gay, whereas another was wrongly reported to be an alcoholic.[81]

The most complete files on consumers are those maintained by credit bureaus. Credit bureaus provide credit reports about specific individuals to banks, retailers, employers, and other businesses who ask for information about specific customers. These credit reports include information about a person's credit card accounts, mortgages, bank loans, student loans, history of payments on these with special notes on late payments, foreclosures, bankruptcies, details about loan amounts, nonpayment of property taxes, personal or property liens, divorce proceedings, marriage licenses, driver licenses, civil lawsuits, present and past employers, present and previous addresses, and other personal information compiled from various sources. There are currently three main bureaus—TRW Credit Data, Equifax, and Trans Union Corp.—that together compile information on about 150 million consumers. Every day fresh credit data come into each bureau that must be entered into the appropriate files. Equifax has estimated that its staff must input some 65 million updates each day. Not surprisingly, a 1991 study by Consumer Reports found errors in 43 percent of the reports they analyzed.[82] These errors can result in being refused a loan, credit card, or job. Beyond the problems created by errors in the data files maintained on them, consumers worry that the detailed information that credit bureaus compile on them will be given to inappropriate parties. For example, until a few years ago, credit bureaus would sell names from their files to junk mailers. The potential for invading consumers' privacy is clearly quite high. To discuss this issue, however, it is important to have a clearer idea about what privacy is and why consumers and others have a right to privacy.

Speaking broadly, the right to privacy is the right to be left alone. We do not discuss this broad characterization of the right to privacy, however, but concentrate on privacy as the right of a person not to have others spy on his or her private life. In this more narrow sense, the right to privacy can be defined as the right of persons to determine what, to whom, and how much information about themselves will be disclosed to other parties.[83]

There are two basic types of privacy: *psychological* and *physical*.[84] Psychological privacy is privacy with respect to a person's inner life. This includes the person's thoughts and plans, personal beliefs and values, feelings, and wants. These inner aspects of a person are so intimately connected with the person that to invade them is almost an invasion of the very person. Physical privacy is privacy with respect to a person's physical activities. Because people's inner lives are revealed by their physical activities and expressions, physical privacy is important in part because it is a means for protecting psychological privacy. However, many of our physical activities are considered "private" apart from their connection to our inner life. What kinds of activities are considered private depends to some extent on the conventions of one's culture. For example, a person in our culture normally feels degraded if forced to disrobe publicly or perform biological or sexual functions in public. Physical privacy, therefore, is also valued for its own sake.

The purpose of rights, as analyzed in Chapter 2, is to enable the individual to pursue his or her significant interests and to protect these interests from the intrusions of other individuals. To say that persons have a moral right to something is to say at least that they have a vital interest in that "something." Why is privacy considered important enough to surround it with the protection of a right?[85] To begin with, privacy has several protective functions. First, privacy ensures that others do not acquire information about us that, if revealed, would expose us to shame, ridicule, embarrassment, blackmail, or other harm. Second, privacy also prevents others from interfering in our plans simply because they do not hold the same values we hold. Our private plans may involve activities that, although harming no one, might be viewed with distaste by other people. Privacy protects us against their intrusions and thereby allows us the freedom to behave in unconventional ways. Third, privacy protects those whom we love from being injured by having their beliefs about us shaken. There may be things about ourselves that, if revealed, might hurt those whom we love. Privacy ensures that such matters are not made public. Fourth, privacy also protects individuals from being led to incriminate themselves. By protecting their privacy, people are protected against involuntarily harming their own reputations.

Privacy is also important because it has several enabling functions. First, privacy enables a person to develop ties of friendship, love, and trust. Without intimacy, these relationships could not flourish. Intimacy, however, requires both sharing information about oneself that is not shared with everyone and engaging in special activities with others that are not publicly performed. Therefore, without privacy, intimacy would be impossible and relationships of friendship, love, and trust could not exist. Second, privacy enables certain professional relationships to exist. Insofar as the relationships between doctor and patient, lawyer and client, and psychiatrist and patient all require trust and confidentiality, they could not exist without privacy. Third, privacy also enables a person to sustain distinct social roles. The executive of a corporation, for example, may want, as a private citizen, to support a cause that is unpopular with his or her firm. Privacy enables the executive to do so without fear of reprisal. Fourth, privacy enables people to determine who they are by giving them control of the way they present themselves to society in general and of the way that society in general looks on them. At the same time, privacy enables people to present themselves in a special way to those whom they select. In both cases, this self-determination is secured by the right of the individual to determine the nature and extent of disclosure of information about oneself.

It is clear then that our interest in privacy is important enough to recognize it as a right that all people have, including consumers. However, this right must be balanced against the rights and legitimate needs of others. If banks are to provide loans to consumers, for example, they need to know something about the credit history of the individuals to whom they are providing loans and how diligent they have been in repaying previous loans. Consumers ultimately benefit from such a banking system. Insurance companies that want to provide life insurance to individuals need to know whether such individuals have any life-threatening illnesses, and so they must have access to their medical information. Consumers benefit from having life insurance available to them. Thus there are significant consumer benefits that businesses can provide, but that they can provide only if there exist agencies that can collect information about individuals and make that information available to those businesses. Thus, consumers' rights to privacy have to be balanced with these legitimate needs of businesses. Several considerations have been suggested as key to balancing legitimate business needs with the right to privacy including: (a) relevance, (b) informing, (c) consent, (d) accuracy, (e) purpose, and (f) recipients and security.

Relevance Databases containing information on consumers should include only information that is directly relevant to the purpose for which the database is being compiled. Thus, credit information provided to banks or credit card issuing agencies should not include information about sexual orientation, political affiliations, medical history, or other information not directly relevant to determining an individual's credit worthiness.

Informing Entities collecting information on consumers should inform consumers that the information is being collected and inform them about the purpose for which the information is being collected. This enables consumers to voluntarily choose not to engage in those transactions that will result in revealing information about themselves that they do not want to reveal.

Consent A business should collect information about an individual person only if that person has explicitly or implicitly consented to provide that information to that business and only if the information is to be used for the purpose for which the person consented to have it used. Consent may be explicit, such as when a person provides information on a credit card application. But consent may be implicit, such as when a person makes a purchase with a credit card knowing that a record of that purchase will be kept by the company issuing the credit card and the record will be collected by a credit bureau. In the latter case, the very act of using the credit card constitutes acceptance of the conditions the credit card company imposes on use of the card, particularly if the credit card company has explicitly advised the consumer that such information will be collected and reported to a credit bureau.

Accuracy Agencies collecting information on a person must take reasonable steps to ensure that the information they store is accurate and that any inaccuracies called to their attention are corrected. Toward this end, agencies should allow individuals to see what information they have collected on them and allow them to bring inaccuracies to their attention.

Purpose The purpose for which information about specific consumers is collected must be legitimate. In this context, a purpose is legitimate if it results in benefits that are generally enjoyed by the people about whom the information is being collected. Consumers benefit, for example, if banks are generally willing to extend loans, insurers are generally willing to insure them, and credit card companies are generally willing to provide credit. This does not mean that a specific individual will benefit from having information about him or herself available to, say, a bank because the bank may refuse to give that specific person a loan on the basis of his or her credit record. It merely means that consumers benefit generally from having available a banking system (or credit card or insurance companies) that is willing to provide loans, and such a system requires a mechanism for collecting information on its potential customers.

Recipients and Security Agencies that collect information on specific individuals must ensure that information is secure and not available to parties that the individual has not explicitly or implicitly consented to be a recipient of that information. If an individual provides information about herself to one business so that the business can better serve her, it is wrong for the business to sell that information to another business without the individual's consent.

Questions for Review and Discussion

1. Define the following concepts: contractual theory (of a seller's duties), duty to comply, implied claim, reliability, service life, maintainability, product safety, reasonable risk, duty of disclosure, duty not to misrepresent, duty not to coerce, manufacturer's implied warranty, disclaimer, caveat emptor, due care theory (of a seller's duties), caveat vendor, professional, manufacturer's duty to exercise due care, social costs theory (of a seller's duties), advertisement, production costs, selling costs, to expand consumption, to shift consumption, Kaldor's theory of advertising and market power, brand loyalty, Galbraith's theory of the creation of consumer desires, bait advertisements, deception.
2. Discuss the arguments for and against the three main theories of a producer's duties to the consumer. In your judgment, which theory is most adequate? Are there any marketing areas where one theory is more appropriate than the others?
3. Who should decide (a) how much information should be provided by manufacturers, (b) how good products should be, and (c) how truthful advertisements should be? The government? Manufacturers? Consumer groups? The free market? Explain your views.
4. "Advertising should be banned because it diminishes a consumer's freedom of choice." Discuss this claim. Review the materials available in your library and decide whether you agree that "criticisms of advertising based on its social effects are inconclusive."
5. Carefully examine two or more advertisements taken from current newspapers or magazines and assess the extent to which they meet what you would consider adequate ethical standards for advertising. Be prepared to defend your standards.
6. A manufacturer of electric coffee pots recalled the pots (through newspaper announcements) when he found that the handles would sometimes fall off without warning and the boiling contents would spill. Only 10 percent of the pots were returned. Does the manufacturer have any additional duties to those who did not return the pots? Explain your answer.

Web Resources

Readers wishing to conduct research on consumer issues through the Internet might begin by turning to the websites of the following organizations: The National Safety Council (http://www.nsc.org), the Consumer Product Safety Commission (gopher://cpsc.gov), The Consumer Law Page (http://www.alexanderlaw.com), the Federal Trade Commission (http://www.ftc.gov). Articles on consumer law can be found at the Alexander law firm (http://tsw.ingress.com/tsw/talf/talf.html) and The

Nolo Press (http://gnn.com/gnn/bus/nolo). The Consumer Law Page provides links and articles for consumers (http://starbase.ingress.com/tsw/talf/txt/intro.html).

Notes

1. Indiana Prevention Resource Center, "Alcohol, Tobacco Campaigns Frequently Aim at Women, Children, Minorities," *Prevention Newsline*, Spring 1992; see also "Poll Shows Camel Ads Are Effective with Kids," *Advertising Age*, April 27, 1992, p. 12.
2. CNN news report, October 1996.
3. Frederick D. Sturdivant and Heidi Vernon-Wortzel, *Business and Society: A Managerial Approach*, 4th ed. (Homewood, IL: Irwin, 1990), pp. 310–11.
4. *Ibid.*
5. The facts summarized in this paragraph are drawn from Penny Addis, "The Life History Complaint Case of Martha and George Rose: 'Honoring the Warranty,'" in Laura Nader, ed., *No Access to Law* (New York: Academic Press, Inc., 1980), pp. 171–89.
6. Quoted in Ed Pope, "PacBell's Sales Quotas," *San Jose Mercury News*, 24 April 1986, p. 1C; see also "PacBell Accused of Sales Abuse," *San Jose Mercury News*, 24 April 1986, p. 1A; "PacBell Offers Refund for Unwanted Services," *San Jose Mercury News*, 17 May 1986, p. 1A.
7. *Ibid.*, p. 134.
8. Several of these criticisms are surveyed in Stephen A. Greyser, "Advertising: Attacks and Counters," *Harvard Business Review*, vol. 50 (10 March 1972): 22–28.
9. U.S. Bureau of the Census, *Statistical Abstract of the United States, 1995*, Table 206.
10. National Safety Council, *Accident Facts*, 1996.
11. Paul A. Samuelson and William D. Nordhaus, *Macroeconomics*, 13th ed. (New York: McGraw-Hill Book Company, 1989), p. 41.
12. See Robert N. Mayer, *The Consumer Movement: Guardians of the Marketplace* (Boston Twayne Publishers, 1989), p. 67; and Peter Asch, *Consumer Safety Regulation* (New York: Oxford University Press, 1988), p. 50.
13. Peter Asch, *Consumer Safety Regulation*, p. 51.
14. Lucy Black Creighton, *Pretenders to the Throne: The Consumer Movement in the United States* (Lexington, MA: Lexington Books, 1976), p. 85.
15. For an overview of the research on irrationality in decision making, see Max Bazerman, *Judgment in Managerial Decision Making*, 3rd ed. (New York: John Wiley & Sons, Inc., 1994), pp. 12–76.
16. Peter Asch, *Consumer Safety Regulation*, pp. 74, 76.
17. *Ibid.*
18. For references to these studies see *ibid*, pp. 70–73.
19. See Thomas Garrett and Richard J. Klonoski, *Business Ethics*, 2nd ed. (Englewood Cliffs, NJ: Prentice-Hall, 1986), p. 88.
20. Immanual Kant, *Groundwork of the Metaphysic of Morals*, H. J. Paton, ed. (New York: Harper & Row, Publishers, Inc., 1964), pp. 90, 97; see also, Alan Donagan, *The Theory of Morality* (Chicago: The University of Chicago Press, 1977), p. 92.

21. John Rawls, *A Theory of Justice* (Cambridge: Harvard University Press, Belknap Press, 1971), pp. 344–50.

22. Crocker v. Winthrop Laboratories, Division of Sterling Drug, Inc., 514 Southwestern 2d 429 (1974).

23. See Donagan, *Theory of Morality*, p. 91.

24. Frederick D. Sturdivant, *Business and Society*, 3rd ed. (Homewood, IL: Richard D. Irwin, Inc., 1985), p. 392.

25. *Ibid*., p. 393.

26. The U.S. Consumer Products Safety Commission's notices of dangerous consumer products are accessible on the Commission's Web page at gopher://cpsc.gov.

27. A somewhat dated but still incisive discussion of this issue is found in Vance Packard, *The Wastemakers* (New York: David McKay Co., Inc., 1960).

28. Quoted in address by S. E. Upton (vice-president of Whirlpool Corporation) to the American Marketing Association in Cleveland, OH: 11 December 1969.

29. National Commission on Product Safety, Final Report, quoted in William W. Lowrance, *Of Acceptable Risk* (Los Altos, CA: William Kaufmann, Inc., 1976), p. 80.

30. See Louis Stern, "Consumer Protection via Increased Information," *Journal of Marketing*, vol. 31, no. 2 (April 1967).

31. Lawrence E. Hicks, *Coping with Packaging Laws* (New York: AMACOM, 1972), p. 17.

32. See the discussions in Richard Posner, *Economic Analysis of Law*, 2nd ed. (Boston: Little, Brown and Company, 1977), p. 83; and R. Posner, "Strict Liability: A Comment," *Journal of Legal Studies*, vol. 2, no. 1 (January 1973): 21.

33. See, for example, the many cases cited in George J. Alexander, *Honesty and Competition* (Syracuse, NY: Syracuse University Press, 1967).

34. *Henningsen v. Bloomfield Motors, Inc*., 32 New Jersey 358, 161 Atlantic 2d 69 (1960).

35. See Friedrich Kessler and Malcolm Pitman Sharp, *Contract*s (Boston: Little, Brown and Company, 1953), pp. 1–9.

36. *Codling v. Paglia*, 32 New York 2d 330, 298 Northeastern 2d 622, 345 New York Supplement 2d 461 (1973).

37. Edgar H. Schein, "The Problem of Moral Education for the Business Manager," *Industrial Management Review*, vol. 8 (1966): 3–11.

38. See W. D. Ross, *The Right and the Good* (Oxford: The Clarendon Press, 1930), ch. 2.

39. Donagan, *Theory of Morality*, p. 83.

40. Rawls, *Theory of Justice*, pp. 114–17, 333–42.

41. Discussions of the requirements of due care may be found in a variety of texts, all of which, however, approach the issues from the point of view of legal liability: Irwin Gray, Product *Liability: A Management Response* (New York: AMACOM, 1975), ch. 6; Eugene R. Carrubba, *Assuring Product Integrity* (Lexington, MA: Lexington Books, 1975); Frank Nixon, *Managing to Achieve Quality and Reliability* (New York: McGraw-Hill Book Co., 1971).

42. See, for example, Michael D. Smith, "The Morality of Strict Liability In Tort," *Business and Professional Ethics*, vol. 3, no. 1 (December 1979): 3–5; for a review of the rich legal literature on this topic, see Richard A. Posner, "Strict Liability: A Comment," *The Journal of Legal Studies*, vol. 2, no. 1 (January 1973): 205–21.

43. George P. Fletcher, "Fairness and Utility in Tort Theory," *Harvard Law Review*, vol. 85, no. 3 (January 1972): 537–73.

44. Posner, *Economic Analysis of Law*, pp. 139–42.

45. See "Unsafe Products: The Great Debate Over Blame and Punishment," *Business Week*, 30 April 1984; Stuart Taylor, "Product Liability: the New Morass," *New York Times*, 10 March 1985; "The Product Liability Debate," *Newsweek*, 10 September 1984.

46. "Sorting Out the Liability Debate," *Newsweek*, 12 May 1986.

47. Ernest F. Hollings, "No Need for Federal Product-Liability Law," *Christian Science Monitor*, 20 September 1984; see also Harvey Rosenfield, "The Plan to Wrong Consumer Rights," *San Jose Mercury News*, 3 October 1984.

48. Irvin Molotsky, "Drive to Limit Product Liability Awards Grows as Consumer Groups Object," *New York Times*, 6 March 1986.

49. John W. Wright, General Editory, *The Universal Almanac, 1996* (Kansas City: Andrews and McMeel, 1996) p. 270.

50. *Ibid.*

51. Raymond A. Bauer and Stephen A. Greyser, *Advertising in America: The Consumer View* (Cambridge: Harvard University Press, 1968), p. 394

52. Walter Weir, *Truth in Advertising and Other Heresies* (New York: McGraw-Hill Book Company, 1963), p. 154.

53. See also, J. Robert Moskin, ed., *The Case for Advertising* (New York: American Association of Advertising Agencies, 1973), passim.

54. See "Ads Infinitum," *Dollars & Sense*, May/June 1984. For an ethical analysis of the information content of advertising, see Alan Goldman, "Ethical Issues in Advertising," pp. 242–49 in Tom Regan, ed., *New Introductory Essays in Business Ethics* (New York: Random House, Inc., 1984), pp. 235–70; The view that advertising is justified by the "indirect" information it provides is advanced in Phillip Nelson, "Advertising and Ethics," in Richard T. DeGeorge and Joseph A. Pichler, eds., *Ethics, Free Enterprise, and Public Policy* (New York: Oxford University Press, 1978), pp. 187–98.

55. See Stephen A. Greyser, "Irritation in Advertising," *Journal of Advertising Research*, vol. 13, no. 3 (February 1973): 7–20.

56. See Michael Schudson, *Advertising, the Uneasy Persuasion* (New York: Basic Books, Inc., Publishers, 1984), p. 210; David M. Potter, *People of Plenty* (Chicago: The University of Chicago Press, 1954), p. 188; International Commission for the Study of Communication Problems, *Many Voices, One World* (London: Kogan Page, 1980), p. 110.

57. Mary Gardiner Jones, "The Cultural and Social Impact of Advertising on American Society," in David Aaker and George S. Day, eds., *Consumerism*, 2nd ed. (New York: The Free Press, 1974), p. 431.

58. Stephen A. Greyser, "Advertising: Attacks and Counters," *Harvard Business Review*, vol. 50 (10 March 1972): 22–28.

59. For an overview of the economic literature on this issue, see Mark S. Albion and Paul W. Farris, *The Advertising Controversy, Evidence on the Economic Effects of Advertising* (Boston, MA: Auburn House Publishing Company, 1981), pp. 69–86,

153–70; for an informal discussion of the issue, see Jules Backman, "Is Advertising Wasteful?" *Journal of Marketing* (January 1968): 2–8.

60. Phillip Nelson, "The Economic Value of Advertising," in Yale Brozen, *Advertising and Society* (New York: New York University Press, 1974), pp. 43–66.

61. Richard Caves, *American Industry: Structure, Conduct, Performance* (Englewood Cliffs, NJ: Prentice-Hall, Inc., 1972), p. 101.

62. David M. Blank, "Some Comments on the Role of Advertising in the American Economy-A Plea for Reevaluation," in L. George Smith, ed., *Reflections on Progress in Marketing* (Chicago: American Marketing Association, 1964), p. 151.

63. See the discussion in Thomas M. Garrett, *An Introduction to Some Ethical Problems of Modern American Advertising* (Rome: The Gregorian University Press, 1961), pp. 125–30.

64. *Ibid.*, p. 177.

65. See E. F. Schumacher, *Small Is Beautiful* (London: Blond and Briggs, Ltd., 1973); and Herman E. Daly, ed., *Toward a Steady-State Economy* (San Francisco: W. H. Freeman, 1979), "Introduction."

66. Nicholas H. Kaldor, "The Economic Aspects of Advertising," *The Review of Economic Studies*, vol. 18 (1950–51): 1–27; see also William S. Comanor and Thomas Wilson, *Advertising and Market Power* (Cambridge: Harvard University Press, 1975). A readable review of the economic literature on this issue can be found in Albion and Farris, *The Advertising Controversy*, pp. 45– 68.

67. See L.G. Telser, "Some Aspects of the Economics of Advertising," *Journal of Business* (April 1968), pp. 166–73; for a survey of studies on this issue, see James M. Ferguson, *Advertising and Competition: Theory Measurement and Fact* (Cambridge, MA: Ballinger Publishing Company, 1974), ch. 5.

68. See John Kenneth Galbraith, *The Affluent Society* (Boston: Houghton Mifflin Company, 1958).

69. John Kenneth Galbraith, *The New Industrial State* (New York: New American Library, 1967), p. 211.

70. *Ibid.*, p. 215.

71. See the discussion of manipulation in advertising in Tom L. Beauchamp, "Manipulative Advertising," *Business & Professional Ethics Journal*, vol. 3, nos. 3 & 4 (Spring/Summer 1984): 1–22; see also in the same volume the critical response of R. M. Hare, "Commentary," pp. 23–28.

72. See George Katova, *The Mass Consumption Society* (New York: McGraw-Hill Book Company, 1964), pp. 54–61.

73. F. A. von Hayek, "The Non Sequitur of the 'Dependence Effect,'" *Southern Economic Journal* (April 1961).

74. Vance Packard, "Subliminal Messages: They Work; Are They Ethical?" *San Francisco Examiner*, 11 August, 1985; see also W. B. Key, *Media Sexploitation* (Englewood Cliffs, NJ, Prentice-Hall, 1976).

75. "Ads Aimed at Kids Get Tough NAD Review," *Advertising Age,* 17 June 1985.

76. Cynthia Kooi, "War Toy Invasion Grows Despite Boycott," *Advertising Age*, vol. 3 (March 1986).

77. Howard LaFranchi, "Boom in War Toys Linked to TV," *Christian Science Monitor*, vol. 7 (January 1986). LaFranchi notes that the average child watches 800 ads for war toys and 250 war-toy television segments in a year, or the equivalent of 22 days in the classroom. See also Glenn Collins, "Debate on Toys and TV Violence," *New York Times*, 12 December 1985.

78. See the discussion of manipulation in advertising in Tom L. Beauchamp, "Manipulative Advertising," *Business & Professional Ethics Journal*, vol. 3, nos. 3 & 4 (Spring/Summer 1984): 1–22; and in the same volume the critical response of R. M. Hare, "Commentary," pp. 23–28; see also Alan Goldman, "Ethical Issues in Advertising," pp. 253–60; and Robert L. Arrington, "Advertising and Behavior Control," pp. 3–12, in *Journal of Business Ethics* vol. 1, no. 1 (February 1982).

79. A critical discussion of several definitions of deception in advertising is found in Thomas L. Carson, Richard E. Wokutch, and James E. Cox, "An Ethical Analysis of Deception in Advertising." *Journal of Business Ethics*, vol. 4 (1985): 93–104.

80. Greg Hadfield and Mark Skipworth, "Firms Keep 'Dirty Data' on Sex Lives of Staff," *Sunday Times* (London), July 25, 1993; quoted in John Weckert and Douglas Adeney, *Computer and Information Ethics* (Westport, CT: Greenwood Press, 1997), p. 75.

81. Jeffrey Rothfeder, *Privacy for Sale* (New York: Simon & Schuster, 1992).

82. Richard A. Spinello, *Case Studies in Information and Computer Ethics* (Upper Saddle River, NJ: Prentice-Hall, 1997), pp. 108–9.

83. See Charles Fried, *An Anatomy of Values: Problems of Personal and Social Choice* (Cambridge: Harvard University Press, 1970), p. 141.

84. See Garrett, *Business Ethics*, pp. 47–49, who distinguishes these two types of privacy (as well as a third kind, "social" privacy).

85. The analyses in this paragraph and the following are drawn from Fried, *Anatomy of Values*, pp. 137–52; Richard A. Wasserstrom, "Privacy" in Richard A. Wasserstrom, ed., *Today's Moral Problems*, 2nd ed. (New York: Macmillan, Inc., 1979); Jeffrey H. Reiman, "Privacy, Intimacy and Personhood," *Philosophy and Public Affairs*, vol. 6, no. 1 (1976): 26–44; and James Rachels, "Why Privacy Is Important," *Philosophy and Public Affairs*, vol. 4, no. 4 (1975): 295–333.

Cases for Discussion

*AIDS and Needles**

Becton Dickinson, one of the largest manufacturers of medical supplies, dominates the market in disposable syringes and needles. In 1992, a nurse, Maryann Rockwood (a fictional name), used a Becton Dickinson 5 cc syringe and needle to draw blood from a patient known to be infected with AIDS. Ms. Rockwood worked in a clinic that served AIDS patients, and she drew blood from these patients several times a day. After drawing the blood on this particular day, she transferred the AIDS-contaminated blood to a sterile test tube called a *Vacutainer tube* by sticking the needle through the rubber stopper of the test tube, which she was holding with her other hand. She accidently pricked her finger with the contaminated needle. She is now HIV positive.

A few years earlier, in 1986, Becton Dickinson had acquired exclusive rights to a patent for a new syringe invented by Charles B. Mitchell that had a moveable protective sleeve around it. The plastic tube around the syringe could slide down to safely cover the needle. The Becton Dickinson 5 cc syringe used by Maryann Rockwood in 1992, however, did not yet have such a protective guard built into it.

The AIDS epidemic has posed peculiarly acute dilemmas for health workers, including doctors and nurses. Doctors performing surgery on AIDS patients can easily prick their fingers with a scalpel, needle, sharp instrument, or even bone fragment and can become infected with the virus. The greatest risk is to nurses, who, after routinely removing an intravenous system, drawing blood, or delivering an injection to an AIDS patient, can easily stick themselves with the needle they were using. "Rarely a day goes by in any large hospital where a needlestick incident is not reported."[1] In fact, needlestick injuries account for about 80 percent of reported occupational exposures to the AIDS virus among health care workers. [2] It was conservatively estimated in 1991 that about 64 health care workers were then being infected with the AIDS virus each year as a result of needlestick injuries. [3]

Although the fear of AIDS had heightened concerns over needlestick injuries, AIDS was not the only risk posed by needlestick injuries. Hepatitis B can also be contracted through an accidental needlestick. In 1990, the Centers for Disease Control (CDC) estimated, on the basis of hospital reports, that each year at least 12,000 health care workers are exposed to blood contaminated with the Hepatitis B virus, and of these 250 die as a consequence.[4] Due to underreporting, however, the actual numbers may be higher. In addition to Hepatitis B, needlestick injuries can also transmit numerous other viral, bacterial, fungal, and parasitic infections, as well as toxic drugs or other agents that are delivered through a syringe and needle.

The total statistics on needlestick injuries in 1992 are disturbing, although the exact incidence of contamination is unclear. It was estimated that each year, in the United States alone, between 800,000 and 1 million needlestick injuries occurred in hospitals Of these, between 60,000 and 300,000 resulted in Hepatitis B. By one estimate, the risk of contracting HIV (the virus that causes AIDS) from a known contaminated needle could be as high as 1 in 1000, and the risk of contracting Hepatitis B, a serious and often life-threatening condition, could be as high as 1 in 6. These estimates would imply that as many as 600 to 1000 health care workers were at risk of contracting HIV and as many as 100,000 were at risk of contracting Hepatitis B. Another estimate suggested that as many as 6000 needle sticks had resulted in HIV infection by 1992. The cost of all such injuries is estimated at $400 million to $1 billion a year.[5]

Several agencies stepped in to set guidelines for nurses, including the American Nursing Association, the CDC, the Environmental Protection Agency (EPA), and the Food and Drug Administration (FAD),who all developed such guidelines. The most comprehensive guidelines were issued by the Occupational Safety and Health Administration (OSHA), who on December 6, 1991, required hospitals and other employers of health workers to (a) make sharps containers (safe needle containers) accessible to workers, (b) prohibit the practice of recapping needles by holding the cap in one hand and inserting the needle with the other, and (c) provide information and training on needlestick prevention to employees.[6]

The usefulness of these guidelines was controversial.[7] Nurses work in high-stress emergency situations requiring quick action, and they are often pressed for time both because of the large number of patients they must care for and the highly variable needs and demands of these patients. In such workplace environments, it is difficult to adhere to the guidelines recommended by the agencies. For example, a high risk source of needle sticks is the technique of replacing the cap on a needle (after it has been used) by holding the cap in one hand and inserting the needle into the cap with the other hand. OSHA guidelines warned against this two-handed technique of recapping and recommended instead that the cap be placed on a surface and the nurse use a one-handed spearing technique to replace the cap. However, nurses were often pressed for time and, believing (correctly) that carrying an exposed contaminated needle is extremely dangerous, yet seeing no ready surface on which to place the needle cap, they will recap the needle using the two-handed technique.

Several analysts suggested that the peculiar features of the nurse's work environment made it unlikely that needlesticks would be prevented through mere guidelines: The problem was not the worker, but the design of the needle and syringe. Dr. Janine Jaegger, an expert on needlestick injuries, argued that, "Trying to teach health care workers to use a hazardous device safely is the equivalent of trying to teach someone how to drive a defective automobile safely. . . . Until now the focus has been on the health care worker, with finger wagging at mistakes, rather than focusing on the hazardous product design. . . . We need a whole new array of devices in which safety is an integral part of the design."[8] In 1987, the Department of Labor and Department of Health and Human Services in a joint advisory issued that, "Whenever possible, engineering controls should be used as the primary method to reduce worker exposure to harmful substances. The preferred approach . . . is to use, to the fullest extent feasible, intrinsically safe substances, procedures, or devices."[9] The manufacturer of needles and syringes, it was urged, must provide the health care worker with devices "in which safety is an integral part of the design."

The risks of contracting life-threatening diseases by the use of needles and syringes in health care settings have been well documented since the early 1980s.

Articles in medical journals in 1980 and 1981, for example, reported on the "problem" of "needlestick and puncture wounds" among health care workers.[10] Several articles in 1983 reported on the growing risk of injuries hospital workers were sustaining from needles and sharp objects.[11] Articles in 1984 and 1985 were sounding alarms on exposure to Hepatitis B and AIDS resulting from needlesticks.[12]

Well over half of all the needles and syringes used by U.S. health care workers since 1980 were being manufactured by Becton Dickinson. Despite the emerging crisis, however, Becton Dickinson decided not to modify its syringes, although it did include in each box of needled syringes an insert warning of the danger of needlesticks and of the dangers of two-handed recapping.

ICU Medical Inc., also a major supplier of medical devices, however, responded to the growing needlestick crisis by marketing a needle in the early 1980s that sat on a long strawlike sheath that could be raised to cover the needle after use. However, ICU's device was extremely awkward to use because the long sheath effectively doubled the length of the needle, making the needle somewhat wobbly and difficult to control during insertion.

On December 23, 1986, the U.S. Patent office issued patent number 4,631,057 to Charles B. Mitchell for a syringe with a tube surrounding the body of the syringe that could be pulled down to cover and protect the needle on the syringe. At the time, at least four other patents for needle-shielding devices existed. As Mitchell noted in his patent application, those devices all suffered from serious drawbacks. One of them would not lock the protective cover over the exposed needle, one was extremely complex, another was much longer than a standard syringe and difficult to use, and a fourth was designed primarily for use on animals.[13] It was Mitchell's assessment that his invention was the only effective, easily usable, and easily manufactured device capable of protecting users from needlesticks, particularly in "emergency periods or other times of high stress." Unlike other syringe designs, Mitchell's was shaped and sized like a standard syringe so nurses already familiar with standard syringe design would have no difficulty adapting to it.

Shortly after Mitchell patented his syringe, Becton Dickinson purchased from him an exclusive license to manufacture it. A few months later, Becton Dickinson began field tests of early models of the syringe using a 3 cc model. Nurses and hospital personnel were enthusiastic when shown the product. However, they warned that if the company priced the product too high, hospitals, with pressures on their budgets rising, could not buy the safety syringes. With concerns about AIDS rising fast, the company decided to market the product.

In 1988, with the field tests completed, Becton Dickinson had to decide which syringes would be marketed with the protective sleeves. Sleeves could be put on all of the major syringe sizes, including 1 cc, 3 cc, 5 cc, and 10 cc syringes. However, the company decided to market only a 3 cc version of the protective sleeve. The 3 cc syringes account for about half of all syringes used, although the larger sizes—5 cc and 10 cc syringes—are preferred by nurses when drawing blood.

This 3 cc syringe was marketed in 1988 under the trademarked name *Safety-Lok Syringe*. It was promoted as a device that "virtually eliminates needlesticks." The 3 cc safety syringe with the protective sleeve was sold in 1988 to hospitals and doctors' offices for between 50 and 75 cents. By 1991, the company had dropped the price to 26 cents a unit. At the time, a regular syringe without any protective device was priced at 8 cents a unit and cost 4 cents to make. Information about the cost of manufacturing the new safety syringe is proprietary, but an educated guess would put the costs of manufacturing each "Safety-Lok" syringe in 1991 at perhaps 13 to 20 cents.[14]

The difference between the price of a standard syringe and the price of the safety syringe was an obstacle for customers. To switch to the new safety syringe would increase the hospital's costs for 3 cc syringes by a factor of three to seven. An equally important impediment to adoption was the fact that the syringe was available in only one 3 cc size, and so, as one study suggested, it had "limited applications."[15] Hospitals are reluctant to adopt and adapt to a product that is not available for the whole range of applications the hospital must confront. In particular, hospitals often needed the larger 5 cc and 10 cc sizes to draw blood, and Becton Dickinson had not made these available with a sleeve.

For 5 years, Becton Dickinson manufactured only 3 cc safety syringes. During that period, Becton Dickinson did not license its new safety syringe technology to another manufacturer that might have produced a full range of syringe sizes. Most hospitals and clinics, including the medical facility where Maryann Rockwood worked at drawing blood from many patients with Hepatitis B or AIDS, did not stock the Becton Dickinson safety syringe. Most nurses in the United States continued to use unprotected syringes.

Maryann Rockwood sued Becton Dickinson, alleging that, because it alone had an exclusive right to Mitchell's patented design, the company had a duty to provide the safety syringe in all its sizes, and that by withholding other sizes from the market it had contributed to her injury. The case was settled out of court.

In 1993, a major competitor of Becton Dickinson announced that it was planning to market a safety syringe based on a new patent that was remarkably like Becton Dickinson's. Unlike Becton Dickinson, however, the competitor indicated that it would market its safety device in all sizes and that it would be priced well below what Becton Dickinson had been charging. Shortly after the announcement, Becton Dickinson declared that it, too, had decided to provide its Safety-Lok syringe in the full range of common syringe sizes. Becton Dickinson also announced that it was lowering its prices. The new prices made the devices more affordable to hospitals.

QUESTIONS

1. In your judgment, did Becton Dickinson have an obligation to provide the safety syringe in all its sizes? Explain your position using the materials from this chapter and the principles of utilitarianism, rights, justice, and caring.
2. Assume that when Maryann Rockwood sued Becton Dickinson, the case had gone to trial and that Maryann Rockwood had won. What would this imply for the duties that other manufacturers would then have? Do you think that such an outcome would be desirable? Explain.
3. Should manufacturers be held liable for failing to market all the products for which they hold exclusive patents when someone's injury would have been avoided if they had marketed those products? Explain your answer.
4. In your judgment, who was morally responsible for Maryann Rockwood's accidental needlestick: Maryann Rockwood? The clinic that employed her? The government agencies that merely issued guidelines? Becton Dickinson?

NOTES

1. J. R. Roberts, "Accidental Needle Stick," *EM & ACM*, May 1987, pp. 6–7.
2. R. Marcus, "Surveillance of Health Care Workers Exposed to Blood from Patients Infected with the Human Immunodeficiency Virus," *N. Eng. J. Med.,* vol. 319, no. 17 (October 1988): 1118–23
3. "Special Report and Product Review; Needlestick-Prevention Devices," *Health Devices*, vol. 20, no. 5 (May 1991): 155
4. "Special Report," *Health Devices*, 1991: p. 155.
5. Kathy Sullivan and Diana Schnell, "Needleless Systems," *Infusion*, October 1994, pp. 17–19.
6. "Rules and Regulations," *Federal Register*, vol. 58, no. 235 (December 6, 1991): 64175–64182.
7. "Needlestick Injuries Tied to Poor Design," *Internal Medicine*, December 1, 1987.
8. *Ibid.*
9. Quoted in *Health Devices*, p. 154.
10. J.S. Reed et al., "Needlestick and Puncture Wounds: Definition of the Problem," *Am. J. Infect. Control*, 1980, 8:101–6; RD McCormick et al., "Epidemiology of Needlestick Injuries in hospital personnel," *Am J. Med.*, 1981, 70:928–32.
11. J.T. Jacobson et al., "Injuries of Hospital Employees from Needles and Sharp Objects," *Infectious Control*, 1983, 4:100–2; F. L. Reuben et al., Epidemiology of Accidental Needle Puncture Wounds in Hospital Workers," *American J. Med. Sci.*, 1983; 286(1): 26–30.
12. B. Kirkman-Liff et al., "Hepatitis B—What Price Exposure?" *Am J. Nurs*, August 1984, pp. 988–990; S.H. Weiss et al., "HTLV-III Infection Among Health Care Workers: Association with Needle-Stick Injuries," *JAMA*, 1985; 254(15): 2089–93.
13. U.S. Patent 4,631,057, Mitchell.

14. In 1991, the device carried a published list price of 26 cents; see *Health Devices*, p. 170; assuming an extremely conservative 20 percent margin, this would imply a manufacturing cost of about 20 cents; assuming a margin similar to its regular syringes of 50 percent would imply a manufacturing cost of about 12 cents.

15. *Health Devices*, p. 170.

Toy Wars[1]

Early in 1986, Tom Daner, president of the advertising company Daner Associates, was contacted by Mike Teal, the sales manager of Crako Industries. Crako Industries is a family-owned company that manufactures children's toys and had long been a favorite and important client of Daner Associates. The sales manager of Crako Industries explained that the company had just developed a new toy helicopter. The toy was modeled on the military helicopters that had been used in Vietnam and that had appeared in the "Rambo" movies. Mike Teal explained that the toy was developed in response to the craze for military toys that had been sweeping the nation in the wake of the Rambo movies. The family-owned toy company had initially resisted moving into military toys because members of the family objected to the violence associated with such toys. However, as segments of the toy market were increasingly taken over by military toys, the family came to feel that entry into the military toy market was crucial for their business. Consequently, they approved development of a line of military toys, hoping that they were not entering the market too late. Mike Teal now wanted Daner Associates to develop a television advertising campaign for the toy.

The toy helicopter Crako designers had developed was about one and one-half feet long, battery operated, and made of plastic and steel. Mounted to the sides were detachable replicas of machine guns and a detachable stretcher modeled on the stretchers used to lift wounded soldiers from a battlefield. Mike Teal of Crako explained that they were trying to develop a toy that had to be perceived as "more macho" than the top-selling "G.I. Joe" line of toys. If the company were to compete successfully in today's toy market, according to the sales manager, it would have to adopt an advertising approach that was even "meaner and tougher" than what other companies were doing. Consequently, he continued, the advertising clips developed by Daner Associates would have to be "mean and macho." Television advertisements for the toy, he suggested, might show the helicopter swooping over buildings and blowing them up. The more violence and mayhem the ads suggested, the better. Crako Industries was relying heavily on sales from the new toy, and some Crako managers felt that the company's future might depend on the success of this toy.

Tom Daner was unwilling to have his company develop television advertisements that would increase what he already felt was too much violence in television aimed at children. In particular, he recalled a television ad for a tricycle with a replica machine gun mounted on the handle bars. The commercial showed the tricycle being pedaled through the woods by a small boy as he chased several other boys fleeing before him over a dirt path. At one point, the camera closed in over the shoulder of the boy, focused through the gunsight, and showed the gunsight apparently trying to aim at the backs of the boys as they fled before the tricycle's machine gun. Ads of that sort had disturbed Tom Daner and had led him to think that advertisers should find other ways of promoting these toys. Therefore, he suggested that instead of promoting the Crako helicopter through violence it should be presented in some other manner. When Teal asked what he had in mind, Tom was forced to reply that he didn't know. At any rate, Tom pointed out, the three television networks would not accept a violent commercial aimed at children. All three networks adhered to an advertising code that prohibited violent, intense, or unrealistic advertisements aimed at children.

This seemed no real obstacle to Teal, however. Although the networks might turn down children's ads when they were too violent, local television stations were not as squeamish. Local television stations around the country regularly accepted ads aimed at children that the networks had rejected as too violent. The local stations inserted the ads as spots on their non-network programming, thereby circumventing the advertising codes of the three national networks. Daner Associates would simply have to place the ads they developed for the Crako helicopter through local television stations around the country. Mike Teal was firm: If Daner Associates would not develop a mean and tough ad campaign, the toy company would move their account to an advertiser that would. Reluctantly, Tom Daner agreed to develop the advertising campaign. Crako Industries accounted for $1 million of Daner's total revenues.

Like Crako Industries, Daner Associates was also a family-owned business. Started by his father almost 50 years ago, the advertising firm that Tom Daner now ran had grown dramatically under his leadership. In 1975, the business had grossed $3 million; 10 years later, it had revenues of $25 million and provided a full line of advertising services. The company was divided into three departments (creative, media, and account executive), each of which had about 12 employees. Tom Daner credited much of the company's success to the many new people he had hired, especially a group with MBAs who had developed new marketing strategies based on more thorough market and consumer analyses. Most decisions, however, were made by a five-person executive committee consisting of Tom Daner, the senior accountant, and the three department heads. As owner-president, Tom's views tended to color most decisions, producing what one member of the committee called a "benevolent dictatorship." Tom was an enthusiastic, congenial, intelligent, and well-read person. During college he had considered becoming a missionary priest, but had changed his mind and was now married and the father of three daughters. His personal heroes included Thomas Merton, Albert Schweitzer, and Tom Doley.

When Tom Daner presented the Crako deal to his executive committee, he found that they did not share his misgivings. The other committee members felt that Daner Associates should give Crako exactly the kind of ad Crako wanted: one with a heavy content of violence. Moreover, the writers and artists in the creative department were enthused with the prospect of letting their imaginations loose on the project, several feeling that they could easily produce an attention-grabbing ad by "out-violencing" current television programming. The creative department, in fact, quickly produced a copy script that called for videos showing the helicopter "flying out of the sky with machine-guns blazing" at a jungle village below. This kind of ad, they felt, was exactly what they were being asked to produce by their client.

After viewing the copy, Tom Daner refused to use it. They should produce an ad, he insisted, that would meet their client's needs but that would also meet the guidelines of the national networks. The ad should not glorify violence and war, but should somehow support cooperation and family values. Disappointed and somewhat frustrated, the creative department went back to work. A few days later, they presented a second proposal: an ad that would show the toy helicopter flying through the family room of a home as a little boy plays with it; then the scene shifts to show the boy on a rock rising from the floor of the family room; the helicopter swoops down and picks up the boy as if rescuing him from the rock where he had been stranded. Although the creative department was mildly pleased with their attempt, they felt it was too "tame." Tom liked it, however, and a version of the ad was filmed.

A few weeks later, Tom Daner met with Mike Teal and his team and showed them the film. The viewing was not a success. Teal turned down the ad. Referring to the network regulations that other toy advertisements were breaking as frequently as motorists broke the 55-mile-per-hour speed law, he said, "That commercial is going only 55 miles an hour when I want one that goes 75." If the next version was not "tougher and meaner," Crako Industries would be forced to look elsewhere.

Disappointed, Tom Daner returned to the people in his creative department and told them to go ahead with designing the kind of ad they had originally wanted: "I don't have any idea what else to do." In a short time, the creative department had an ad proposal on his desk that called for scenes showing the helicopter blowing up villages. Shortly afterwards, a small set was constructed depicting a jungle village sitting next to a bridge stretching over a river. The ad was filmed using the jungle set as a background.

When Tom saw the result, he was not happy. He decided to meet with his creative department and air his feelings. "The issue here," he said, "is basically the issue of violence. Do we really want to present toys as instruments for beating up people? This ad is going to promote aggression and violence. It will glorify dominance and do it with kids who are terrifically impressionable. Do we really want to do this?" The members of the creative department, however, responded that they were merely giving their client what the client wanted. That client, moreover, was an important account. The client wanted an aggressive "macho" ad, and that was what they were providing. The ad might violate the regulations of the television networks, but there were ways to get around the networks. Moreover, they said, every other advertising firm in the business was breaking the limits against violence set by the networks. Tom made one last try: Why not market the toy as an adventure and fantasy toy? Film the ad again, he suggested, using the same jungle backdrop. But instead of showing the helicopter shooting at a burning village, show it flying in to rescue people from the burning village. Create an ad that shows excitement, adventure, and fantasy, but no aggression. "I was trying," he said later, "to figure out a new way of approaching this kind of advertising. We have to follow the market or we can go out of business trying to moralize to the market. But why not try a new approach? Why not promote toys as instruments that expand the child's imagination in a way that is positive and that promotes cooperative values instead of violence and aggression?"

A new film version of the ad was made, now showing the helicopter flying over the jungle set. Quick shots and heightened background music give the impression of excitement and danger. The helicopter flies dramatically through the jungle and over a river and bridge to rescue a boy from a flaming village. As lights flash and shoot haphazardly through the scene, the helicopter rises and escapes into the sky. The final ad was clearly exciting and intense. It promoted the saving of a life instead of violence against life.

It was clear when the final version was shot, however, that it would not clear the network censors. Network guidelines require that sets in children's ads must depict things that are within the reach of most children so that they do not create unrealistic expectations. Clearly the elaborate jungle set (which cost $25,000 to construct) was not within the reach of most children, and consequently most children would not be able to re-create the scene of the ad by buying the toy. Moreover, network regulations stipulate that in children's ads scenes must be filmed with normal lighting that does not create undue intensity. Again clearly the helicopter ad, which created excitement by using quick changes of light and fast cuts, did not fall within these guidelines.

After reviewing the film, Tom Daner reflected on some last-minute instructions Crako's sales manager had given him when he had been shown the first version of the ad: The television ad should show things being blown up by the guns of the little helicopter and perhaps even some blood on the fuselage of the toy; the ad had to be violent. Now Tom had to make a decision. Should he risk the account by submitting only the rescue mission ad? Or should he let Teal also see the ad that showed the helicopter shooting up the village, knowing that he would probably prefer that version if he saw it? Was the rescue mission ad really that much different from the ad that showed the shooting of the village? Did it matter that the rescue mission ad still violated some of the network regulations? What if he offered Teal only the rescue mission ad and Teal accepted the rescue approach, but demanded he make it more violent. Should he give in? Should Tom risk launching an ad campaign that was based on this new untested approach? What if the ad failed to sell the Crako toy? Was it right to experiment with a client's product, especially a product that was so important to the future of the client's business? Tom was unsure what he should do. He wanted to show Teal only the rescue mission commercial, but he felt he first had to resolve these questions in his own mind.

Questions

1. From a moral point of view, what, in your judgment, should Tom Daner's final decision be? Justify your answer. What should Tom do if he is asked to make the final ad more violent than the rescue ad he had filmed?
2. Answer the questions Tom Daner asked himself: Was the rescue mission ad really that much different from the ad that showed the shooting of the village? Did it matter that the rescue mission ad still violated some of the network regulations? Was it right to experiment with a client's product, especially a product that was so important to the future of the client's business?

Notes

1. Copyright, 1986, by Manuel Velasquez. Although the events described in this case are real, all names of the individuals and the companies involved are fictitious; in addition, several details have been altered to disguise the identity of participants.

PART FOUR

Business and Its Internal Constituencies

Employee Issues

The process of producing goods forces businesses not only to engage in external exchanges, but also to coordinate the activities of the various internal constituencies that must be brought together and organized into the processes of production. Employees must be hired and organized, stockholders and creditors must be solicited, and managerial talent must be tapped. Inevitably conflicts arise within and between these internal constituencies as they interact with each other and as they seek to distribute benefits among themselves. The next two chapters explore some of the ethical issues raised by these internal conflicts. Chapter 7 discusses the issue of job discrimination. Chapter 8 discusses the issue of conflicts between the individual and the organization.

7

The Ethics of Job Discrimination

Introduction

In a major speech entitled "Mend It, Don't End It," former President Bill Clinton said:

> Beyond all else, our country is a set of convictions: "We hold these truths to be self-evident, that all men are created equal; that they are endowed by their Creator with certain unalienable rights; that among these are life, liberty, and the pursuit of happiness." Our whole history can be seen first as an effort to preserve these rights and then as an effort to make them real in the lives of all our citizens. . . .
>
> The purpose of affirmative action is to give our nation a way to finally address the systematic exclusion of individuals of talent on the basis of their gender or race from opportunities to develop, perform, achieve, and contribute. Affirmative action is an effort to develop a systematic approach to open the doors of educational, employment, and business development opportunities to qualified individuals who happen to be members of groups that have experienced long-standing and persistent discrimination.
>
> Now there are those who say that even good affirmative action programs are no longer needed . . . because there is no longer any systematic discrimination in our society. Let us consider the facts.
>
> According to the recently completed report of the Glass Ceiling Commission, sponsored by Republican members of Congress, in the nation's largest companies only 0.6 percent of senior management positions are held by African-Americans, 0.4 percent by Hispanic-Americans, and 0.3 percent by Asian-Americans; women hold between 3 and 5 percent of these positions. White men make up 43 percent of our workforce, but they hold 95 percent of these jobs. . . .

Just last week, the Chicago Federal Reserve Bank reported that black home loan applicants are more than twice as likely to be denied credit as whites with the same qualifications, and that Hispanic applicants are more than one and a half times as likely to be denied loans as whites with the same qualifications. Evidence abounds in other ways of the persistence of the kind of bigotry that can affect the way we think even if we're not conscious of it, in hiring and promotion and business. . . .

There are people who honestly believe that affirmative action always amounts to group preferences over individual merit; that affirmative action always leads to reverse discrimination; and that ultimately, therefore, it demeans those who benefit from it and discriminates against those who are not helped by it. . . . But I believe that if there are no quotas-if we give no opportunities to unqualified people-if we have no reverse discrimination-and if, when the problem ends, the program ends-then the criticism is wrong.

Today I am directing all federal agencies to . . . apply the four standards of fairness that I have already articulated to all our affirmative action programs: no quotas, in theory or in practice; no illegal discrimination of any kind, including reverse discrimination; no preference for people who are not qualified for jobs or other opportunities; and as soon as a program has succeeded, it must be retired. Any program that doesn't meet these four principles must be eliminated or reformed to meet them. . . .[1]

A few days later, Pete Wilson, then governor of California, responded to the president in a speech that highlighted his support of legislation designed to end affirmative action programs, which he referred to as *preferential treatment*:

Thomas Jefferson first described the American ideal more than two hundred years ago when he declared "equal rights for all, special privileges for none." The pursuit of that ideal has been the key to American success since 1776. . . .

But today that fundamental American principle of equality is being eroded, eroded by a system of preferential treatment that awards public jobs, public contracts, and seats in our public universities, not based on merit and achievement but on membership in a group defined by race, ethnicity, or gender. That's not right. It's not fair. It is, by definition, discrimination. . . .

What we owe the people is not to ignore the unfairness and pretend it doesn't exist. We owe them the leadership and courage to change what's wrong and set it right. The question shouldn't be, How can we justify the current quagmire of race and gender based preferences? The question should be, How can we reset our moral compass and get back on the road to equality and fairness under the law?

If President Clinton believes in Thomas Jefferson's maxim of "equal rights for all, special privileges for none," did he have the courage to change the programs that don't meet that test? Or did he instead try to placate and buy off the vocal apologists for unfair racial and gender preferences who are determined to keep the status quo in place? . . .

My friends, we are again a house divided against itself. We are divided by a system that offers preferences and privileges to some at the expense of others. We are divided by a system that flies in the face of the American notion of fairness and justice. . . .

> We can't endure divided. We can't endure by canceling the contest and awarding the prize based on race or gender. That's not the American way.[2]

The debates over what equality is and how it should be secured have been prolonged and acrimonious. Controversy has swirled around the nature of the plight of racial minorities, the inequality of women, and the *harm* that White males have suffered as a result of the preference shown to women and minorities. These continuing debates over racial and sexual equality have been focused largely on business. This is inevitable: Racial and sexual discrimination have had a long history in business, and it is in this area that discriminatory practices have the most substantial and long-lasting consequences.

Perhaps more than any other contemporary social issue, public discussions of discrimination have clearly approached the subject in ethical terms: The words *justice*, *equality*, *racism*, *rights*, and *discrimination* inevitably find their way into the debate. This chapter analyzes the various sides of this ethical issue. The chapter begins by examining the nature and extent of discrimination. It then turns to discussing the ethical aspects of discriminatory behavior in employment and ends with a discussion of affirmative action programs.

7.1 Job Discrimination: Its Nature

Although many more women and minorities are entering formerly male-dominated jobs, they still face problems that they would characterize as forms of discrimination. A few years ago, for example, the American Broadcasting Company (ABC) sent a male and female, Chris and Julie, on an "experiment" to apply in person for jobs several companies were advertising. Chris and Julie were both blonde, trim, neatly dressed college graduates in their 20s, with identical resumes indicating management experience. Unknown to the companies, however, both were secretly wired for sound and had hidden cameras. One company indicated in its help-wanted ad that it had several open positions. However, when the company recruiter spoke with Julie, the only job he brought up was a job answering phones. A few minutes later, the same recruiter spoke with Chris. He was offered a management job. When interviewed afterward by ABC, the company recruiter indicated that he would never want a man answering his phone. Another company had advertised positions as territory managers for lawn-care services. The owner of the company gave Julie a typing test, discussed her fiance's business with her, and then offered her a job as a receptionist at $6 an hour. When the owner interviewed Chris, however, he gave him an aptitude test, chatted with him about how he kept fit, and offered him a job as territory manager paying $300 to $500 a week. When the owner was later interviewed by ABC, he commented that women "do not do well as territory managers, which involves some physical labor." According to the owner, he had also hired one other woman as a receptionist and had hired several other males as territory managers.[3]

The experience of young Chris and Julie suggest that sexual discrimination is alive and well. Similar experiments suggest that racial discrimination also continues to thrive. During the early 1990s, researchers at the Urban Institute published a study in which they paired several young Black men with similar young White men, matching them in openness, energy level, articulateness, physical characteristics, clothing, and job experience. In the same way, young Hispanic males fluent in English were matched with young White males. Each member of each pair was trained and coached in mock interviews to act exactly like the other. Each member of each pair then applied in person for the same jobs, ranging from general laborer to management trainee in manufacturing, hotels, restaurants, retail sales, and office work. Despite that all were equally qualified for the same jobs, Blacks and Hispanics were offered jobs 50 percent fewer times than the young White males.[4]

The root meaning of the term *discriminate* is "to distinguish one object from another," a morally neutral and not necessarily wrongful activity. However, in modern usage, the term is not morally neutral: It is usually intended to refer to the wrongful act of distinguishing illicitly among people not on the basis of individual merit but on the basis of prejudice or some other invidious or morally reprehensible attitude.[5] This morally charged notion of *invidious* discrimination, as it applies to employment, is what is at issue in this chapter.[6] In this sense, to discriminate in employment is to make an adverse decision (or set of decisions) against employees (or prospective employees) who belong to a certain class because of morally unjustified prejudice toward members of that class. Thus, discrimination in employment must involve three basic elements. First, it is a decision against one or more employees (or prospective employees) that is not based on individual merit, such as the ability to perform a given job, seniority, or other morally legitimate qualifications. Second, the decision derives solely or in part from racial or sexual prejudice, false stereotypes, or some other kind of morally unjustified attitude against members of the class to which the employee belongs. Third, the decision (or set of decisions) has a harmful or negative impact on the interests of the employees, perhaps costing them jobs, promotions, or better pay.

Employment discrimination in the United States historically has been directed at a surprisingly large number of groups. These have included religious groups (such as Jews and Catholics), ethnic groups (such as Italians, Poles, and Irish), racial groups (such as Blacks, Asians, and Hispanics), and sexual groups (such as women and homosexuals). We have an embarrassingly rich history of discrimination.

Forms of Discrimination: Intentional and Institutional Aspects

A helpful framework for analyzing different forms of discrimination can be constructed by distinguishing the extent to which a discriminatory act is intentional and isolated (or noninstitutionalized) and the extent to which it is unintentional and institutionalized.[7] First, a discriminatory act may be part of the isolated (noninstitutionalized) behavior of a single individual who intentionally and knowingly discriminates out of personal prejudice. In the ABC experiment described, for example, the attitudes that the male interviewer is described as having may not be characteristic of other company interviewers: His behavior toward female job seekers may be an intentional but isolated instance of sexism in hiring. Second, a discriminatory act may be part of the routine behavior of an institutionalized group, which intentionally and knowingly discriminates out of the personal prejudices of its members. The Ku Klux Klan, for example, is an organization that historically has intentionally institutionalized discriminatory behavior. Third, an act of discrimination may be part of the isolated (noninstitutionalized) behavior of a single individual who unintentionally and unknowingly discriminates against someone because he or she unthinkingly adopts the traditional practices and stereotypes of his or her society. If the interviewer quoted in the ABC experiment described, for example, acted unintentionally, then he would fall into this third category. Fourth, a discriminatory act may be part of the systematic routine of a corporate organization or group that unintentionally incorporates into its formal institutionalized procedures practices that discriminate against women or minorities. The two companies examined in the ABC experiment, for example, described organizations in which the best-paying jobs are routinely assigned to men and the worst-paying jobs are routinely assigned to women—on the stereotypical assumption that women are fit for some jobs and not for others. There may be no deliberate intent to discriminate, but the effect is the same: a racially or sexually based pattern of preference toward White males.

During the last century, an important shift in emphasis occurred—from seeing discrimination primarily as an intentional and individual matter to seeing it as a systematic and not necessarily intentional feature of institutionalized corporate behavior. Later, in some quarters, the emphasis shifted back again to seeing it as an intentional and individual matter. During the early 1960s, employment discrimination was seen primarily as an intentional, calculated act performed by one individual on another. Title VII of the Civil Rights Act of 1964, for example, seems to have had this notion of discrimination in mind when it stated:

> It shall be an unlawful employment practice for an employer (1) to fail or refuse to hire or to discharge any individual, or otherwise discriminate against any individual

> with respect to his compensation, terms, conditions, or privileges of employment because of such individual's race, color, religion, sex, or national origin; or (2) to limit, segregate, or classify his employees or applicants for employment in any way that would deprive or tend to deprive any individual of employment opportunities or otherwise adversely affect his status as an employee because of such individual's race, color, sex, or national origin.[8]

However, in the late 1960s, the concept of discrimination was enlarged to include more than the traditionally recognized intentional forms of individual discrimination. By the early 1970s, the term *discrimination* was being used regularly to include disparities of minority representation within the ranks of a firm regardless of whether the disparity had been intentionally created. An organization was engaged in discrimination if minority group representation within its ranks was not proportionate to the group's local availability. The discrimination would be remedied when the proportions of minorities within the organization were made to match their proportions in the available workforce by the use of "affirmative action" programs. For example, a Department of Labor guidebook for employers issued in February 1970 stated:

> An acceptable affirmative action program must include an analysis of areas within which the contractor is deficient in the utilization of minority groups and women, and further, goals and timetables to which the contractor's good faith efforts must be directed to correct the deficiencies and thus to increase materially the utilization of minorities and women at all levels and in all segments of his work force where deficiencies exist. . . . "Underutilization" is defined as having fewer minorities or women in a particular job classification than would reasonably be expected by their availability.[9]

Many people subsequently came to criticize the view that an institution is "discriminatory" if a minority group is underrepresented within its ranks. Discrimination is the act of individuals, these critics argued, and it is individual women and minorities whom it mistreats. Consequently, we should not say discrimination exists until we know that a specific individual was discriminated against in a specific instance. The problem with this criticism is that it is generally impossible to know whether a specific individual was discriminated against. People compete with each other for jobs and promotions; whether a person wins a specific job or promotion depends to a large extent on chance factors, such as who his or her competitors happened to be, what abilities his or her competitors happened to have, how interviewers happened to see him or her, and how he or she happened to perform at the crucial moments. Consequently, when a minority individual loses in this competitive process, there is generally no way of knowing whether that individual's loss was the result of chance factors or systematic discrimination. The only way of knowing whether the process is systematically discriminating is by looking at what happens to minorities as a group: If minorities as a group regularly lose out in a competitive process in which their abilities as a group match those of nonminorities, then we may conclude that the process is discriminatory.[10]

Nevertheless, during the 1980s, government policy under the Reagan administration shifted toward the view that the focus of society should not be on discrimination in its institutionalized forms. Starting in about 1981, the federal government began to actively oppose affirmative action programs based on statistical analyses of systematic discrimination. The administration held that only individuals who could prove that they had been the victims of discrimination aimed specifically and intentionally at them should be eligible for special treatment in hiring or promotions. Although the Reagan administration was largely unsuccessful in its efforts to dismantle affirmative action programs altogether, it did succeed in naming a majority of Supreme Court justices who rendered decisions that tended to undermine some legal supports of affirmative action programs. These trends were reversed once again in the 1990s, when Bush became president and pledged to "knock down the barriers left by past discrimination." Moreover, Congress stepped in to propose legislation that would support affirmative action programs and that would reverse the Supreme Court rulings that had undermined them. However, when a Republican majority was elected to the House of Representatives in 1992, Congress began to discuss legislation that would prohibit affirmative action programs. In California, legislation was passed in 1996 prohibiting all state government agencies from using "preferential treatment" programs. As their speeches (quoted earlier) indicate, former President Clinton opposed such legislation, whereas former California Governor Pete Wilson supported it. No legislation similar to California's has been enacted at the federal level of government. Thus, our society has wavered and continues to waver on the question of whether discrimination should be seen only as an intentional and isolated act or also as an unintentional and institutionalized pattern revealed by statistics, and whether we should bend our efforts to combating only the former or also the latter.

For purposes of analysis, it is important to keep separate the ethical issues raised by policies that aim at preventing individuals from discriminating intentionally against other individuals, from those raised by affirmative action policies that aim at achieving a proportional representation of minorities within our business institutions. We discuss each of these issues separately. First, however, we must examine the extent to which our business institutions today are discriminatory. It is a commonly held belief that, although business used to be discriminatory, this is no longer the case because of the great strides minorities and women have made during the last few years. If this belief is correct—and it is at least challenged by the experiments described, in which matched pairs of male and female or White and minority people applied for the same job—then there is not much point in discussing the issue of discrimination. But is it correct?

7.2 Discrimination: Its Extent

How do we estimate whether an institution or a set of institutions is practicing discrimination against a certain group? We do so by looking at statistical indicators of how the members of that group are distributed within the institution. A prima facie indication of discrimination exists when a disproportionate number of the members of a certain group hold the less desirable positions within the institutions despite their preferences and abilities.[11] Three kinds of comparisons can provide evidence for such a distribution: (a) comparisons of the average benefits the institutions bestow on the discriminated group with the average benefits the institutions bestow on other groups; (b) comparisons of the proportion of the discriminated group found in the lowest levels of the institutions with the proportions of other groups found at those levels; and (c) comparisons of the proportions of that group that hold the more advantageous positions with the proportions of other groups that hold those same positions. If we look at American society in terms of these three kinds of comparisons, it becomes clear that some form of racial and sexual discrimination is present in American society as a whole. It is also clear that for some segments of the minority population (such as young college-educated Black males) discrimination is not as intense as it once was.

Average Income Comparisons

Income comparisons provide the most suggestive indicators of discrimination. If we compare the average incomes of non-White American families, for example, with the average incomes of White American families, we see that White family incomes are substantially above those of non-Whites, as Table 7.1 indicates.

Contrary to a commonly held belief, the income gap between Whites and minorities has not decreased. Since 1970, in fact, even during periods when the real incomes of Whites have gone up, real minority incomes have not kept up. In 1970, the average income for a Black family was 65 percent of a White family's average income; in 1998, the average Black family's income was 63 percent of the average White family's income.[12]

Income comparisons also reveal large inequalities based on sex. A comparison of average incomes for men and women shows that women receive only a portion of what men receive. A recent study found, in fact, that firms employing mostly men paid their workers on average 40 percent more than those employing mostly women.[13] As Table 7.2 shows, the earnings gap between men and women has narrowed. But in 1998 women earned only about 68 cents for every dollar that men earned (albeit an improvement over the 59 cents of the

TABLE 7.1 AVERAGE FAMILY INCOMES BY RACE AND AS PERCENT OF WHITE (IN 1998 DOLLARS)

Year	Non-Hispanic White ($)	Black ($)	Black as Percent of White (%)	Hispanic ($)	Hispanic as Percent of White (%)
1998	65,338	38,563	59	39,727	61
1997	63,281	37,069	59	38,368	60
1996	60,899	36,293	60	36,976	61
1995	59,864	36,377	61	34,925	58
1994	59,011	36,104	61	35,580	60
1993	58,056	33,881	58	35,092	60
1992	55,881	32,507	58	34,826	62
1991	55,907	32,996	59	35,901	64
1990	57,278	34,363	60	36,555	64
1989	58,722	34,723	59	38,380	65
1988	57,144	34,882	61	37,651	66
1987	56,818	34,109	60	37,091	65
1986	55,630	33,876	61	36,346	65
1985	53,437	32,356	61	35,072	66
1984	52,031	31,028	60	35,405	68
1983	50,350	30,108	60	33,422	66
1982	49,753	29,427	59	33,652	68
1981	49,604	30,205	61	35,042	71
1980	50,304	31,305	62	34,888	69
1979	52,001	31,957	61	36,946	71
1978	51,194	32,380	63	35,394	69
1977	49,826	30,851	62	34,284	69
1976	48,878	30,943	63	33,094	68
1975	47,470	30,167	64	32,182	68

Source: U.S. Census Bureau, *Current Population Reports*, Series P60-206, Table B-4.

male's dollar that they earned in 1980) and had total annual incomes equal to only 56 percent of men's incomes. However, much of the improvement in the ratio of female and male earnings has come about not as a result of declining discrimination, but as a result of declines in the average earnings of men because of downsizing in manufacturing occupations traditionally occupied by men.[14] Between 1979 and 1992, for example, women's median hourly wage rose only 31 cents while men's median hourly wage fell by $1.84. Thus, the decline in male earnings is responsible for 86 percent of the improvement in the ratio of female-to-male earnings between 1979 and 1992.

The disparities in earnings between men and women begin as soon as men and women graduate from school, contrary to the optimistic belief held by each

TABLE 7.2 AVERAGE ANNUAL EARNINGS OF FULL-TIME MALE AND FEMALE WORKERS (IN 1998 DOLLARS) AND AVERAGE ANNUAL INCOMES OF MEN AND WOMEN (NOT ALL WORKING FULL TIME, IN 1994 DOLLARS)

Year	Men's Annual Earnings ($)	Women's Annual Earnings ($)	Women's Earnings as Percent of Men's (%)	Men's Annual Income ($)	Women's Annual Income ($)	Women's Income as Percent of Men's (%)
1998	44,866	30,660	68	36,315	20,462	56
1997	44,358	29,700	67	35,336	19,815	56
1996	43,684	29,457	67	34,075	19,083	56
1995	43,166	28,376	66	33,642	18,466	55
1994	43,185	28,896	67	33,400	18,124	54
1993	42,896	28,542	67	32,644	17,779	54
1992	41,214	27,802	67	31,148	17,336	56
1991	41,114	27,465	67	31,558	17,292	55
1990	41,572	27,408	66	32,477	17,351	53
1989	43,392	27,656	64	33,844	17,386	51
1988	42,842	27,356	64	33,143	16,963	51
1987	42,928	27,056	63	32,712	16,555	51
1986	42,798	26,621	62	32,454	15,974	49
1985	41,529	25,795	62	31,285	15,411	49
1984	40,571	25,148	62	30,495	15,036	49
1983	40,249	24,805	62	29,636	14,369	48
1982	40,302	24,428	61	29,635	13,973	47
1981	40,155	23,721	59	29,877	13,460	45
1980	40,643	23,842	59	30,382	13,412	44

Sources: U.S. Census Bureau (www.census.gov), Historical Income Tables—People, Table P-3; "Race and Hispanic Origin of People by Mean Income and Sex: 1947 to 1998," <http://www.census.gov/hhes/income/histinc/p03.html>, and Table P-39; "Full-Time, Year-Round Workers (All Races) by Mean Earnings and Sex: 1967 to 1998,"<http://www.census.gov/hhes/income/histinc/p39.html>.

generation of graduating women that "my generation will be different." An early study in 1976—ten years after "affirmative action" was instituted—found that the average starting salary offered to female college graduates majoring in marketing was $9768, whereas male marketing graduates were offered average starting salaries of $10,236.[15] A 1980 census bureau study of men and women ages 21 to 22 found that White women's starting salaries were 83 percent of White men's—an actual decline from 1970, when White women of that age earned 86 percent of what White men earned.[16] The same study found that, between 1970 and 1980, White women had substantially increased their job qualifications relative to men. In 1998, as Table 7.3 indicates, a young woman ages 18 to 24 who had just finished college with a bachelor's degree will have been given a job with a salary of $17,558, whereas her male counterpart will have been given a job

TABLE 7.3 AVERAGE EARNINGS OF WORKING MEN AND WOMEN RECENTLY OUT OF SCHOOL, 1998

	Average Earnings of 18- to 24-Year-Olds		Average Earnings of 25 to 34-Year-Olds	
Education	Men ($)	Women ($)	Men ($)	Women ($)
Elementary	22,210	7516	15,269	10,878
High school				
some, no diploma	8983	5776	20,062	10,844
diploma	16,507	10,873	27,333	16,538
College				
some, no degree	11,321	9216	32,399	19,396
associate degree	23,609	13,453	35,504	22,448
bachelor's degree	21,677	17,558	43,477	30,036
master's degree	NA	NA	45,118	37,969
professional degree	NA	NA	69,275	40,320

Source: U.S. Census Bureau (www.census.gov), Historical Income Tables—People; Table P-28, "Educational Attainment—Workers 18 Years Old and Over by Mean Earnings, Age, and Sex: 1991 to 1998," <http://www.census.gov/hhes/income/histinc/p28.html>.

with a salary of $21,677; a young woman with a new master's degree, ages 25 to 34, could expect to earn only $37,969, whereas her male classmate would be given a job earning $45,118. If she had a professional degree (as a lawyer or an MBA), she would be earning $40,320, whereas her male counterpart would be getting $69,275. As Table 7.4 shows, female college graduates on average still have lower earnings than male graduates; in fact, on average a woman would have to graduate from college before she could hope to have the average income of a male high school graduate. A male with an undergraduate college degree earns substantially more ($55,832) than an average female with a graduate master's degree ($46,072). Not surprisingly, as Table 7.5 shows, women's incomes fall predominantly into the lower income brackets, whereas men tend to occupy the higher income brackets. Although almost twice as many women as men have incomes under $5000, about five times as many men as women have incomes over $100,000. Moreover, the earning disparities between men and women cut across all occupations, as Table 7.6 indicates. In every single occupational group, women's weekly earnings are only a portion of men's, ranging from sales occupations, where women earn only 60 percent of what men earn, to farming, forestry, and fishing, where the few women employed in those occupations earn only 85 percent of what men earn.

TABLE 7.4 AVERAGE ANNUAL EARNINGS OF YEAR-ROUND FULL-TIME WORKERS, 18 YEARS OLD AND OVER, BY EDUCATION, 1998

			Both Sexes		
Education	Men's Average Earnings ($)	Women's Average Earnings ($)	Whites' Average Earnings ($)	Blacks' Average Earnings ($)	Hispanics' Average Earnings ($)
5th to 8th grade	23,435	15,140	21,245	18,231	18,902
High school					
some, no diploma	27,638	18,594	25,809	18,921	21,440
diploma	32,611	22,656	29,306	24,055	24,209
College					
some, no degree	39,367	26,562	35,093	28,151	27,608
associate degree	40,465	29,776	36,091	30,915	30,154
bachelor's degree	55,832	37,319	49,566	36,190	38,622
master's degree	71,225	46,072	62,130	44,408	53,101
professional degree	120,052	74,077	109,705	60,438	80,969
doctorate degree	93,106	60,468	87,470	(NA)	(NA)

Source: U.S. Census Bureau, (www.census.gov), Current Population Reports, Population Characterisitcs, Series P20-513, Table 9; "Earnings by Educational Attainment for Persons 18 Years Old and Over, by Age, Sex, Race, and Hispanic Origin: March 1998," <http://www.census.gov/prod/3/98pubs/p20-513u.pdf>.

TABLE 7.5 DISTRIBUTION OF INCOME AMONG WORKING MEN AND WOMEN, 1998

Income ($)	Percent of Men with That Income (%)	Percent of Women with That Income (%)
1 to 4999	10	17
5000 to 9999	7	13
10,000 to 14,999	8	13
15,000 to 24,999	17	22
25,000 to 49,999	35	27
50,000 to 74,999	14	6
75,000 to 99,999	4	1
100,000 and over	5	1

Source: U.S. Census Bureau, *Current Population Reports*, Series P60-206, Table 10.

TABLE 7.6 MEDIAN WEEKLY EARNINGS OF MEN AND WOMEN BY OCCUPATIONAL GROUP, 2000 (FIRST QUARTER)

Occupational Group	Median Weekly Earnings: Men ($)	Median Weekly Earnings: Women ($)	Women's as Percent of Men's (%)
Executive, administrative, managerial	981	674	69
Professional specialty	972	725	75
Technicians and related support	747	524	70
Sales occupations	679	410	60
Administrative support, including clerical	588	443	75
Service occupations	418	317	76
Precision production, craft, repair	623	421	68
Machine operators, assemblers, inspectors	495	349	71
Transportation and material moving	548	399	73
Handlers, equipment cleaners, laborers	395	320	81
Farming, forestry, fishing	329	279	85

Source: U.S. Bureau of Labor Statistics, *Employment and Earnings*, April 2000, Table D-22.

Blacks do not fare much better than females. Although young Black college male graduates (between the ages of 22 and 27) now earn close to what young White male graduates of the same age earn, there is little improvement in the relative earnings of older Blacks.[17] Overall, Black unemployment in 1998 was running at twice the White unemployment rate. In 1998, unemployment among Whites ages 16 to 24 was 8.8 percent, whereas unemployment among Blacks the same age was 20.7 percent. Thus, the disadvantaged situation of the vast majority of Blacks more than overshadows the advances made by the small percentage (11 percent) of young Blacks who graduate from college.[18]

Lowest Income Group Comparisons

The lowest income group in the United States consists of those people whose annual income falls below the poverty level. In 1999, the poverty level was set at $16,895 for a family of four with two children (by comparison, the average tuition, room, and board fees for one person to attend college during the 1998 to 1999 school year were about $20,000 at private colleges and about $8,000 at public colleges).[19] As Table 7.7 shows, poverty began to increase in America during the 1970s, particularly among Black, Hispanic, and Asian minorities, and continued to rise until 1994. As the table indicates, the poverty rate among minorities

TABLE 7.7 PERCENT OF WHITES, BLACKS, HISPANICS, AND ASIANS BELOW POVERTY LEVEL

Year	Non-Hispanic Whites Below Poverty Level (%)	Blacks Below Poverty Level (%)	Hispanics Below Poverty Level (%)	Asians Below Poverty Level (%)
1998	8	26	26	13
1997	9	27	27	14
1996	9	28	29	15
1995	9	29	30	15
1994	9	31	31	15
1993	10	33	31	15
1992	10	33	30	13
1991	9	33	29	14
1990	9	32	28	12
1985	10	31	29	NA
1980	9	33	26	NA
1975	9	31	27	NA

Source: U.S. Census Bureau, (www.census.gov), Historical Poverty Tables—People, "Table 2. Poverty Status of People, by Family Relationships, Race, and Hispanic Origin: 1959–1998," <http://www.census.gov/hhes/poverty/histpov/hstpov2.html>.

has consistently been two to three times higher than among Whites. This is not surprising because minorities have lower average incomes.

In view of the lower average incomes of women, it also comes as no surprise that families headed by single women fall below the poverty level much more often than families headed by single men. As Table 7.8 indicates, families headed by women are almost three times more likely to be poor than families headed by men. Table 7.8 also shows that this pattern has endured for several decades.

The bottom income groups in the United States are statistically correlated with race and sex. In comparison with Whites and male-headed families, larger proportions of minorities and female-headed families are poor.

Desirable Occupation Comparisons

The evidence of racial and sexual discrimination provided by the quantitative measures we have so far cited can be filled out qualitatively by examining the occupational distribution of racial and sexual minorities. As the figures in Table 7.9 suggest, in every major occupational group, larger percentages of White males move into the higher paying occupations, while minorities and women end up in those that pay less and so are less desirable.

TABLE 7.8 POVERTY IN FAMILIES HEADED BY MALES AND FEMALES

Year	Percent of Families Headed by Females Below Poverty Level (%)	Percent of Families Headed by Males Below Poverty Level (%)
1998	30	12
1997	32	13
1996	33	14
1995	32	14
1994	35	17
1993	36	17
1992	35	16
1991	36	13
1990	33	12
1989	32	12
1988	33	12
1987	34	12
1986	35	11
1985	34	13

Source: U.S. Bureau of the Census (www.census.gov), Historical Poverty Tables—Families, "Table 4. Poverty Status of Families by type of Family, Presence of Related Children, Race, and Hispanic Origin: 1959 to 1998," <http://www.census.gov/hhes/poverty/histpov/histpov4.html>.

Just as the most desirable occupations are held by Whites while the less desirable are held by Blacks, so also the most well-paying occupations tend to be reserved for men and the remainder for women. As the occupations selected as illustrations in Table 7.10 indicate, the more women working in an occupation, the lower the pay for that occupation. Although there are a large number of exceptions, there is still a very close direct correlation between the proportion of men in an occupation and the salary level of that occupation. Moreover, studies indicate that, despite two decades of women entering the workforce in record numbers, women managers still are not being promoted from middle-management positions into senior or top-management posts because they encounter an impenetrable *glass ceiling* through which they may look but not enter.[20] Consequently, although many women have moved into middle-management positions in recent years, they have not yet been allowed into the top-paying executive positions.

The fact that women and minorities earn less than White males is not wholly explainable in terms of the lower educational levels of minorities and women.[21] In 1998, the average full-time year-round working male who had some college but never graduated earned $39,367—more than the $37,319 earned by a similar female who graduated from college (Table 7.4). The same year, a White

TABLE 7.9 MEDIAN WEEKLY EARNINGS OF SELECTED OCCUPATIONS AND PERCENTOF MEN AND WOMEN IN EACH OCCUPATION, 1998

Occupations	Weekly Earnings ($)	Percent Men (%)	Percent Women (%)
Executive, administrative, managerial			
Managers, marketing	960	62	38
Managers, medicine	716	21	79
Professional speciality			
Lawyers and judges	1218	66	34
Teachers, kindergarten	397	2	98
Technical sales, administrative support			
Airplane pilots and navigators	1383	99	1
Licensed practical nurses	473	5	95
Service occupations			
Police and detectives	646	84	16
Cleaners and servants	235	5	95
Precision production, craft, repair			
Electrical power installers	789	99	1
Electrical equipment assemblers	381	32	68
Operators, laborers			
Welders and cutters	518	95	5
Sewing machine operators	280	17	83
Transportation			
Rail occupations	849	92	8
Bus drivers	428	59	41
Farming, forestry, and fishing			
Supervisors, agricultural	469	94	6
Graders and sorters	259	25	75

Source: U.S. Bureau of Labor Statistics, *Employment and Earnings*, January 1999, Table 39.

full-time year-round worker who attended high school but never graduated made $25,809, whereas a Black full-time year-round worker who likewise attended high school but never graduated made $18,921; and whereas a White worker with a college degree made $49,566, a Black worker with a college degree made only $36,190 (Table 7.4).

Nor can the large disparities between White males and women or minorities be wholly accounted for by the preferences of the latter.[22] It is sometimes suggested that women *voluntarily choose* to work in those jobs that have relatively low pay and low prestige. It is suggested sometimes, for example, that women believe only certain jobs (such as secretary or kindergarten teacher) are

TABLE 7.10 MEDIAN WEEKLY EARNINGS OF SELECTED OCCUPATIONS AND PERCENT OF MEN AND WOMEN IN THOSE OCCUPATIONS, 1999

		Percent of Total in Occupation Who Are	
Occupation	Weekly Earnings ($)	Men (%)	Women (%)
Child-care workers	211	1	99
Receptionists	374	4	96
Typists	454	4	96
Licensed practical nurses	498	6	94
Bank tellers	346	7	93
Legal assistants	589	14	86
Dietitians	577	15	85
Financial processing supervisors	678	19	81
Clinical lab technicians	623	26	74
Social workers	601	31	69
Accountants	723	40	60
Physicians' assistants	908	50	50
Management analysts	908	52	48
Operations analysts	864	53	47
Marketing managers	1036	63	37
Lawyers	1168	67	33
Computer systems analysts	1008	71	29
Aerospace engineers	1201	88	12
Electrical engineers	1073	91	9
Airplane pilots	1048	97	3

Source: U.S. Bureau of Labor Statistics, Employment and Earnings, January 2000, Table 39.

appropriate for women; many women choose courses of study that suit them only for such jobs; many women choose those jobs because they plan to raise children and these jobs are relatively easy to leave and reenter; many women choose these jobs because they have limited demands and allow them time to raise children; and many women defer to the demands of their husbands' careers and choose to forgo developing their own careers. Although choice plays some role in pay differentials, however, researchers who have studied the differences in earnings between men and women have all concluded that wage differentials cannot be accounted for simply on the basis of such factors. One study found that only half of the earnings gap might be accounted for by women's choices, whereas other studies have found it could account for a bit more or a bit less.[23] All studies, however, have demonstrated that only a portion of the gap can be accounted for on the basis of male and female differences in education, work experience, work continuity, self-imposed work restrictions, and absenteeism.[24] These studies show that, even after taking such differences into account, a gap between the earnings of men and women remains that can only be accounted for by discrimination in the labor market. A report of the National Academy of Sciences concluded that, "about 35 to 40 percent of the disparity in average earnings is due to sex segregation because women are essentially steered into lower-paying 'women's jobs.' "[25] Some studies have shown that perhaps only one tenth of the wage differences between men and women can be accounted for by differences in their personalities and tastes.[26] Similar studies have shown that half of the earning differences between White and minority workers cannot be accounted for by differences of work history, on-the-job training, absenteeism, or self-imposed restrictions on work hours and location.[27]

Several trends that emerged in the early 1990s have increased the difficulties facing women and minorities in job markets. To begin with, most new workers now entering the labor force are not White males, but women and minorities. Although two decades ago White males held the largest share of the job market, between 1985 and 2000, White males comprised only 15 percent of all new workers entering the labor force. Their place has been taken by women and minorities. Three fifths of all new entrants coming into business between 1985 and 2000 were women—a trend created by sheer economic necessity as well as cultural redefinitions of the role of women. Native minorities and immigrants now make up some 40 percent of all new workers.[28]

This large influx of women and minorities has encountered major difficulties in the job market. First, as we saw, a sizable proportion of women are still steered into traditionally female jobs that pay less than traditionally male jobs. Second, as women advance in their careers, they encounter barriers (the so-called *glass ceiling*) when attempting to advance into top-paying top-management positions. Surveys have found that over 90 percent of newly promoted corporation chairmen, presidents, and vice presidents are men. In fact, some studies have suggested that the percentage of women being promoted to the vice presidential level was declining. Less than 2 percent of all officers of Fortune 500 companies today are women. Third, married women who want children, unlike married men who want children, currently encounter major difficulties in their career advancement. One survey found that 52 percent of the few married women who were promoted to vice president remained childless, whereas only 7 percent of the married men had no children. Another survey found that, during the 10 years following their graduation, 54 percent of those women who had made significant advances up the corporate ladder had done so by remaining childless. Several studies have found that women with professional careers are six times more likely than their husbands to have to be the one who stays home with a sick child; even women at the level of corporate vice president report that they must carry a greater share of such burdens than their husbands.[29]

The large numbers of minorities entering the workforce also encounter significant disadvantages. As these large waves of minorities hit the labor market, they find that most of the good jobs awaiting them require levels of skill and education far higher than they have. Of all the new jobs that have been created during the past decade, more than half require some education beyond high school and almost a third require a college degree. Among the fastest-growing fields are professions with extremely high education requirements, such as technicians, engineers, social scientists, lawyers, mathematicians, scientists, and health professionals. In contrast, jobs that require relatively low levels of education and skills, such as machine tenders and operators, blue collar supervisors, assemblers, hand workers, miners, and farmers, have actually been declining in number. Even jobs that require relatively low levels of skill now have tough requirements: Secretaries, clerks, and cashiers need the ability to read and write clearly, understand directions, and use computers; assembly-line workers are being required to learn statistical process control methods employing basic algebra and statistics. Thus, most good new jobs demand more education and higher levels of language, math, and reasoning skills.

Unfortunately, minorities are currently the least advantaged in terms of skill levels and education. Studies have shown that only about three fifths of Whites, two fifths of Hispanics, and one fourth of Blacks could find information in a news article or almanac; only 25 percent of Whites, 7 percent of Hispanics, and 3 percent of Blacks could interpret a bus schedule; and only 44 percent of Whites, 20 percent of Hispanics, and 8 percent of Blacks could figure out the change they were owed from buying two items.[30] Minorities are also much more disadvantaged in terms of education. In 1998, when 94 percent of White students graduated from high school, only 88 percent of Blacks, and 63 percent of Hispanics did.[31] That same year 28 percent of Whites ages 25 to 29 had graduated from college, but only 16 percent of Blacks that age and 10 percent of Hispanics had.[32] Thus, although future new jobs will require steeply increasing levels of skills and education, minorities are falling behind in their educational attainment.

Moreover, recent years have brought to light an especially troublesome obstacle that working women face in the workplace. Forty-two percent of all women working for the federal government reported that they had experienced some form of uninvited and unwanted sexual attention, ranging from sexual remarks to attempted rape or assault. Women working as executives, prison guards, and even rabbis have reported being sexually harassed.[33] Victims of verbal or physical forms of sexual harassment were most likely to be single or divorced, between the ages of 20 and 44, have some college education, and work in a predominantly male environment or for a male supervisor.[34] An early study of sexual harassment in business found that 10 percent of 7000 people surveyed reported that they had heard of or observed a situation in their organizations as extreme as: "Mr. X has asked me to have sex with him. I refused, but now I learn that he's given me a poor evaluation. . . ."[35] A federal court vividly described the injuries that sexual harassment can inflict on a person:

> Cheryl Mathis's relationship with Mr. Sanders began on terms she described as good, but it later became clear that Sanders sought some kind of personal relationship with her. Whenever Mathis was in his office he wanted the door to outside offices closed, and he began discussing very personal matters with her, such as the lack of a sexual relationship with his wife. He then began bombarding her with unwelcome invitations for drinks, lunch, dinner, breakfast, and asking himself to her house. Mathis made it clear that she was not interested in a personal relationship with her married boss. . . . Sanders also commented on Mathis's appearance, making lewd references to parts of her body. As Mathis rejected Sanders's advances, he would become belligerent. By the spring of 1983 Mathis began to suffer from severe bouts of trembling and crying which became progressively worse and eventually caused her to be hospitalized on two separate occasions, once for a week in June, 1983, and again in July for a few days. During this entire summer Mathis remained out on sick leave, not returning to work until September, 1983. . . . As soon as she returned to work, Sanders's harassment resumed . . . and once again she was forced to seek medical help and did not work. . . . The harassment not only tormented . . . Mathis, it created hostility between her and other members of the department who apparently resented the plaintiff's familiarity with Sanders.[36]

Every year thousands of complaints of sexual harassment are filed with the federal government's Equal Employment Opportunity Commission, and thousands of other complaints are lodged with state civil rights commissions.

It is clear then that women and minorities, who now comprise the bulk of new workers entering the workforce, find themselves in highly disadvantaged positions as they enter the workforce. What are these disadvantages if not an additional form of systematic institutionalized discrimination?

The various statistical comparisons that we have examined, together with the extensive research showing that these differences are not due in any simple way to differences in the preferences or abilities of women and minorities, indicate that American business institutions incorporate some degree of systematic discrimination, much of it, perhaps, an unconscious relic of the past. Whether we compare average incomes, proportional representation in the highest economic positions, or proportional representation in the lowest economic positions, it turns out that women and minorities are not equal to White males, and the last 20 years have seen only relatively small narrowings of the racial and sexual gaps. Moreover, a number of ominous trends indicate that, unless we embark on some major changes, the situation for minorities and women will not improve.

Of course, finding that our economic institutions as a whole still embody a great deal of discrimination does not show that any particular business is discriminatory. To find out whether a particular firm is discriminatory, we would have to make the same sorts of comparisons among the various employment levels of the firm that we made earlier among the various economic and occupational levels of American society as a whole. To facilitate such comparisons within firms, employers today are required to report to the government the numbers of minorities and women their firm employs in each of nine categories: officials and managers, professionals, technicians, sales workers, office and clerical workers, skilled craftworkers, semiskilled operatives, unskilled laborers, and service workers.

7.3 Discrimination: Utility, Rights, and Justice

Given the statistics on the comparative incomes and low-status positions of minorities and women in the United States, the question we must ask ourselves is this: Are these inequalities wrong, and if so, how should they be changed? To be sure, these inequalities directly contradict the fundamental principles on which the United States was founded: "We hold these truths to be self-evident: that all men are created equal and endowed by their creator with certain inalienable rights."[37] However, historically we have often tolerated large discrepancies between these ideals and reality. The ancestors of most Black Americans living today, for example, were brought to this country as slaves, treated like cattle, and lived out their lives in bondage, Despite our ideals of equality. As the personal property of a White owner, Blacks prior to the Civil War were not recognized as people and consequently had no legal powers, no claims on their bodies or their labors, and were regarded by the Supreme Court in one of its opinions as "beings of an inferior order . . . and so far inferior that they had no rights that the White man was bound to respect."[38] Women were treated comparably. Through much of the 19th century, women could not hold office, could not vote, could not serve on juries, nor bring suit in their own names; a married woman lost control over her property (which was acquired by her husband), she was considered incapable of making binding contracts, and, in a major opinion, she was declared by the Supreme Court to have "no legal existence, separate from her husband, who was regarded as her head and representative in the social state."[39] Why are these forms of inequality wrong? Why is it wrong to discriminate?

The arguments mustered against discrimination generally fall into three groups: (a) utilitarian arguments, which claim that discrimination leads to an inefficient use of human resources; (b) rights arguments, which claim that discrimination violates basic human rights; and (c) justice arguments, which claim that discrimination results in an unjust distribution of society's benefits and burdens.

Utility

The standard utilitarian argument against racial and sexual discrimination is based on the idea that a society's productivity will be optimized to the extent that jobs are awarded on the basis of competency (or "merit").[40] Different jobs, the argument goes, require different skills and personality traits if they are to be carried out in as productive a manner as possible. Furthermore, different people have different skills and personality traits. Consequently, to ensure that jobs are maximally productive, they must be assigned to those individuals whose skills and personality traits qualify them as the most competent for the job. Insofar as jobs are assigned to individuals on the basis of other criteria unrelated to competency, productivity must necessarily decline. Discriminating among job applicants on the basis of race, sex, religion, or other characteristics unrelated to job performance is necessarily inefficient and, therefore, contrary to utilitarian principles.[41]

Utilitarian arguments of this sort, however, have encountered two kinds of objections. First, if the argument is correct, then jobs should be assigned on the basis of job related qualifications only so long as such assignments will advance the public welfare. If, in a certain situation, the public welfare would be advanced to a greater degree by assigning jobs on the basis of some factor not related to job performance, then the utilitarian would have to hold that in those situations jobs should not be assigned on the basis of job-related qualifications, but on the basis of that other factor. For example, if society's welfare would be promoted more by assigning certain jobs on the basis of need (or sex or race) instead of on the basis of job qualifications, then the utilitarian would have to concede that need (or sex or race), and not job qualifications, is the proper basis for assigning those jobs.[42]

Second, the utilitarian argument must also answer the charge of opponents who hold that society as a whole may benefit from some forms of sexual discrimination. Opponents might claim, for example, that society will function most efficiently if one sex is socialized into acquiring the personality traits required for raising a family (nonaggressive, cooperative, caring, submissive, etc.) and the other sex is socialized into acquiring the personality traits required for earning a living (aggressive, competitive, assertive, independent).[43] One might hold that one sex ends up with the traits suited for raising a family as a result of its inborn biological nature, whereas the other sex ends up with the traits suited for earning a living as a result of its own biology. In either case, whether sexual differences are acquired or natural, one might argue that jobs that call for one set of sexually based traits rather than another should be assigned on the basis of sex because placing people in jobs that suit their personality traits promotes society's welfare.[44]

The utilitarian argument against discrimination has been attacked on several fronts. None of these attacks, however, seems to have defeated its proponents.

Utilitarians have countered that using factors other than job-related qualifications never provides greater benefits than the use of job-related qualifications.[45] Moreover, they claim, studies have demonstrated that there are few, or no, morally significant differences between the sexes.[46]

Rights

Nonutilitarian arguments against racial and sexual discrimination may take the approach that discrimination is wrong because it violates a person's basic moral rights.[47] Kantian theory, for example, holds that human beings should be treated as *ends* and never used merely as *means*. At a minimum, this principle means that each individual has a moral right to be treated as a free person equal to any other person, and that all individuals have a correlative moral duty to treat each individual as a free and equal person. Discriminatory practices violate the principle in two ways. First, discrimination is based on the belief that one group is inferior to other groups: that Blacks, for example, are less competent or less worthy of respect than Whites or perhaps that women are less competent or worthy of respect than men.[48] Racial and sexual discrimination, for instance, may be based on stereotypes that see minorities as "lazy" or "shiftless" and see women as "emotional" and "weak." Such degrading stereotypes undermine the self-esteem of those groups against whom the stereotypes are directed and thereby violate their right to be treated as equals. Second, discrimination places the members of groups that are discriminated against in lower social and economic positions: Women and minorities have fewer job opportunities and are given lower salaries. Again, the right to be treated as a free and equal person is violated.[49]

A group of Kantian arguments, related to those mentioned, holds that discrimination is wrong because the person who discriminates would not want to see his or her behavior universalized.[50] In particular, the person would not want to be discriminated against on the basis of characteristics that have nothing whatever to do with the person's own ability to perform a given job. Because the person who discriminates would not want to see his or her own behavior universalized, according to Kant's first categorical imperative, it is morally wrong for that person to discriminate against others.

Justice

A second group of nonutilitarian arguments against discrimination views it as a violation of the principles of justice. For example, John Rawls argued that among the principles of justice that the enlightened parties to the "original position" would choose for themselves is the principle of equal opportunity: "Social and economic inequalities are to be arranged so that they are attached to offices and positions open to all under conditions of fair equality of opportunity."[51] Discrimination violates this principle by arbitrarily closing off to minorities the more desirable offices and positions in an institution, thereby not giving them an opportunity equal to that of others. Arbitrarily giving some individuals less of an opportunity to compete for jobs than others is unjust, according to Rawls.

Another approach to the morality of discrimination that also views it as a form of injustice is based on the formal "principle of equality": Individuals who are equal in all respects relevant to the kind of treatment in question should be treated equally even if they are dissimilar in other nonrelevant respects. To many people, as indicated in Chapter 2, this principle is the defining feature of justice.[52] Discrimination in employment is wrong because it violates the basic principle of justice by differentiating between people on the basis of characteristics (race or sex) that are not relevant to the tasks they must perform. A major problem faced by this kind of argument against discrimination, however, is that of defining precisely what counts as a *relevant respect* for treating people differently and explaining why race and sex are not relevant, whereas something like intelligence or war service may be counted as relevant.

Discriminatory Practices

Regardless of the problems inherent in some of the arguments against discrimination, it is clear that there are strong reasons for holding that discrimination is wrong. It is consequently understandable that the law has gradually been changed to conform to these moral requirements, and that there has been a growing recognition of the various ways in which discrimination in employment occurs. Among the practices now widely recognized as discriminatory are the following:[53]

Recruitment Practices Firms that rely solely on the word-of-mouth referrals of present employees to recruit new workers tend to recruit only from those racial and sexual groups that are already represented in their labor force. When a firm's labor force is composed of only White males, this recruitment policy will tend to discriminate against minorities and women. Also, when desirable job positions are only advertised in media (or by job referral agencies) that are not used by minorities or women (such as in English newspapers not read by Spanish-speaking minorities) or are classified as *for men only*, recruitment will also tend to be discriminatory.

Screening Practices Job qualifications are discriminatory when they are not relevant to the job to be performed (e.g., requiring a high school diploma or a credential for an essentially manual task in places where minorities statistically have had high secondary school drop-out rates). Aptitude or intelligence tests used to screen applicants become discriminatory when they serve to disqualify members from minority cultures who are unfamiliar with the language, concepts, and social situations used in the tests but who are in fact fully qualified for the job. Job interviews are discriminatory if the interviewer routinely disqualifies women and minorities by relying on sexual or racial stereotypes. These stereotypes may include assumptions about the sort of occupations "proper" for women, the sort of work and time burdens that may fittingly be "imposed" on women, the ability of a woman or minority person to maintain "commitment" to a job, the propriety of putting women in "male" environments, the assumed effects women or minorities would have on employee morale or on customers, and the extent to which women or minorities are assumed to have personality and aptitude traits that make them unsuitable for a job. Such generalizations about women or minorities are not only discriminatory, they are also false.

Promotion Practices Promotion, job progression, and transfer practices are discriminatory when employers place White males on job tracks separate from those open to women and minorities. Seniority systems will be discriminatory if past discrimination has eliminated minorities and women from the higher, more senior positions on the advancement ladder. To rectify the situation, individuals who have specifically suffered from discrimination in seniority systems should be given their rightful place in the seniority system and provided with whatever training is necessary for them. When promotions rely on the subjective recommendations of immediate supervisors, promotion policy will be discriminatory to the extent that supervisors rely on racial or sexual stereotypes.

Conditions of Employment Wages and salaries are discriminatory to the extent that equal wages and salaries are not given to people who are doing essentially the same work. If past discrimination or present cultural traditions result in some job classifications being disproportionately filled with women or minorities (such as secretarial, clerical, or part-time positions), steps should be taken to make their compensation and benefits comparable to those of other classifications.

Discharge Firing an employee on the basis of his or her race or sex is a clear form of discrimination. Less blatant but still discriminatory are layoff policies that rely on a seniority system, in which women and minorities have the lowest seniority because of past discrimination.

Sexual Harassment

Women, as noted earlier, are victims of a particularly troublesome kind of discrimination that is both overt and coercive: They are subjected to sexual harassment. Although males are also subjected to some instances of sexual harassment, it is women who are by far the most frequent victims. For all its acknowledged frequency, sexual harassment still remains difficult to define and to police and prevent. In 1978, the Equal Employment Opportunity Commission published a set of "guidelines" defining sexual harassment and setting out what, in its view, was prohibited by the law. In their current form, the guidelines state:

> Unwelcome sexual advances, requests for sexual favors and other verbal or physical contact of a sexual nature constitute sexual harassment when (1) submission to such conduct is made either explicitly or implicitly a term or condition of an individual's employment, (2) submission to or rejection of such conduct by an individual is used as the basis for employment decisions affecting such individual, or (3) such conduct has the purpose or effect of unreasonably interfering with an individual's work performance or creating an intimidating, hostile or offensive working environment.[54]

The guidelines state, further, that sexual harassment is prohibited, and that an employer is responsible for all sexual harassment engaged in by employees, "regardless of whether the employer knew or should have known" the harassment was occurring and regardless of whether it was "forbidden by the employer."

In several major respects, the guidelines are clearly morally justified. They are intended to outlaw those situations in which an employee is coerced into giving in to another employee's sexual demands by the threat of losing some significant job benefit, such as a promotion, raise, or even the job. This kind of degrading coercion exerted on employees who are vulnerable and defenseless inflicts great psychological harms on the employee, violates the employees' most basic rights to freedom and dignity, and is an outrageously unjust misuse of the unequal power that an employer can exercise over the employee. It is thus a crude violation of the moral standards of utilitarianism, rights, justice, and care.

However, several aspects of these guidelines merit further discussion. First, the guidelines prohibit more than particular acts of harassment. In addition to prohibiting harassing acts, they also prohibit conduct that "creates" an "intimidating, hostile or offensive working environment." That means that an employer is guilty of sexual harassment when the employer allows an environment that is hostile or offensive to women even in the absence of any particular incidents of sexual harassment. This raises some difficult questions. If the mechanics in a garage are accustomed to placing pin-ups in their place of work and are accustomed to recounting off-color jokes and using off-color language, are they guilty of creating an environment that is "hostile and offensive" to a female coworker? In a well-known case, for example, a federal court described the following real situation:

> For seven years the [female] plaintiff worked at Osceola as the sole woman in a salaried management position. In common work areas [she] and other female employees were exposed daily to displays of nude or partially clad women belonging

> to a number of male employees at Osceola. One poster, which remained on the wall for eight years, showed a prone woman who had a gold ball on her breasts with a man standing over her, golf club in hand, yelling "Fore!" And one desk plaque declared "Even male chauvinist pigs need love. . . . " In addition, Computer Division Supervisor Dough Henry regularly spewed anti-female obscenity. Henry routinely referred to women as "whores," "cunt," "pussy," and "tits. . . . " Of plaintiff, Henry specifically remarked, "All that bitch needs is a good lay" and called her "fat ass."[55]

Should this kind of situation count as the kind of "intimidating, hostile or offensive working environment" that the guidelines prohibit as sexual harassment? The answer to this legal question is unclear, and different courts have taken different positions on the question. But a different question and one that is more relevant to our inquiry is this: Is it morally wrong to create or allow this kind of environment? The answer to this question seems in general to be "yes" because such an environment is degrading, it is usually imposed by more powerful male parties upon more vulnerable female employees, and it imposes heavy costs on women because such environments tend to belittle them and make it more difficult for them to compete with males as equals.

Nevertheless, some critics object that these kinds of environments were not created to intentionally degrade women, that they are part of the "social mores of [male] American workers," that it is hopeless to try to change them, and that they do not unjustly harm women because women have the power to take care of themselves.[56] A *Forbes* magazine article, for example, asked rhetorically, "Can women really think they have the right to a pristine work environment free of rude behavior?"[57] Such sentiments are indicative of the uncertainties surrounding this issue.

A second important point to note is that the guidelines indicate that, "verbal or physical contact of a sexual nature" constitutes sexual harassment when it has the "effect of unreasonably interfering with an individual's work performance." Many critics have argued that this means that what counts as sexual harassment depends on the purely subjective judgments of the victim. According to the guidelines, verbal contacts—presumably conversations—of a sexual nature count as prohibited sexual harassment when they "unreasonably" interfere with work performance. But sexual conversations that are "unreasonable" interferences to one person, critics claim, may be well within reasonable limits to another person because people's tolerance, even enjoyment, of sexual conversations differs. What one person believes is innocent innuendo, flirting, or an enjoyable sexual joke may be taken by another as an offensive and debilitating "come-on." The critics claim that a person who in all innocence makes a comment that is taken wrongly by another person may find himself the target of a sexual harassment complaint. However, supporters of the guidelines reply that our law courts are well experienced with defining what is *reasonable* in the more or less objective terms of what an average competent adult would feel to be reasonable, so this concept should present no major difficulties. Critics, however, have countered that this still leaves open the question of whether the guidelines should prohibit sexual conversations that the average woman would find unreasonable or that the average man would find unreasonable—two standards, they claim, that would have drastically different implications.

A more fundamental objection to the prohibition of "verbal conduct" that creates an "intimidating, hostile, or offensive working environment" is that these kinds of prohibitions in effect violate people's right to free speech. This objection is frequently made on university campuses, where prohibitions of speech that creates a hostile or offensive environment for women or minorities are not unusual, and where such prohibitions are generally characterized as requiring "politically correct speech." Students and faculty alike have objected that free speech must be preserved on university campuses because truth is found only through the free discussion and examination of all opinions, no matter how offensive, and truth is the objective of the university. Similar claims cannot usually be made about a business corporation, of course, because its objective is not the attainment of truth through the free discussion and examination of all opinions. Nevertheless, it can be argued that employees and employers have a right to free speech, and that prohibitions of speech that create an environment that some feel to be offensive are wrong even in corporate contexts because such prohibitions violate this basic right. The reader will have to decide whether such arguments have much merit.

A third important feature of the guidelines to note is that an employer is guilty of sexual harassment even if the employer did not know and could not have been expected to know that it was going on, and even if the employer had explicitly forbidden it. This violates the common moral norm that a person cannot be held morally responsible for something of which they had no knowledge and which they had tried to prevent. Many people have suggested that the guidelines are deficient on this point. However, supporters reply that the guidelines are morally justified from a utilitarian point of view for two reasons. First, over the long run, they provide a strong incentive for employers to take steps that will guarantee that the harm of sexual harassment is eradicated from their companies, even in those areas of the company of which they usually have little knowledge. Moreover, the harms inflicted by sexual harassment are so devastating that any costs imposed by such steps will be balanced by the benefits. Second, the guidelines in effect ensure that the harms inflicted by sexual harassment are always transferred to the shoulders of the employer, thereby making such harms part of the costs of doing business that the employer will want to minimize to remain competitive with other businesses. Thus, the guidelines in effect internalize the costs of sexual harassment so that competitive market mechanisms can deal with them efficiently. The guidelines are also just, supporters claim, because the employer is usually better able to absorb the costs of sexual harassment than the innocent injured employee who would otherwise have to suffer the losses of harassment alone.

Beyond Race and Sex: Other Groups

Are there other groups that deserve protection from discrimination? The Age Discrimination in Employment Act of 1967 prohibited discriminating against older workers merely because of their age, until they reached age 65. This act was modified in 1978 to prohibit age discrimination until workers reach age 70.[58] On October 17, 1986, new legislation was enacted prohibiting forced retirement at any specific age. Thus, in theory, older workers are protected against discrimination by federal laws. The disabled are also now protected by the Americans with Disabilities Act of 1990, which bars discrimination on the basis of disability and which requires that employers make reasonable accommodation for their disabled employees and customers. Nevertheless, because of widespread stereotypes about the abilities and capacities of older workers and the disabled, subtle and overt discrimination against these groups continues to pervade America.[59]

Although older and disabled workers at least have some legal protections against discrimination, such protections are rare for workers with unusual sexual preferences. There are no federal laws that prohibit discrimination on the basis of sexual orientation, and only a few states and cities have laws prohibiting discrimination against gays or transexuals. A court held, for example, that Liberty Mutual Insurance Company was not acting illegally when it refused to hire a male merely on the grounds that he was "effeminate," and a court also cleared Budget Marketing, Inc., of acting illegally when that company fired a male who began to dress as a female prior to a sex-change operation.[60]

Although it is illegal to do so, many companies have found reasons to fire or cancel the health benefits of workers found to have the virus for acquired immune deficiency syndrome (AIDS).[61] Between 1981 and 1998, over 688,200 individuals were diagnosed with AIDS in the United States, although only a portion of them had yet suffered symptoms or debilitation that affected their ability to perform well on the job.[62] Several court decisions have held that AIDS qualifies as a "handicap" (under the federal Vocational Rehabilitation Act of 1973 and, more recently, under the Americans with Disabilities Act), and federal law prohibits federal contractors, subcontractors, or employers who participate in federally funded programs from firing such handicapped persons, so long as they can perform their jobs if some "reasonable" accommodation is made. Some states and cities have enacted local laws to prevent discrimination against AIDS victims, but many employers are not monitored, and some continue to discriminate against the victims of this terrible disease.

Many companies also have policies against hiring overweight persons—a class of people that most state laws do not protect. For example, Philadelphia Electric Company refused to hire Joyce English solely on the grounds that she weighed 300 pounds and not because she was unable to perform the duties of the position for which she applied.[63] Should any of these groups—gays, transsexuals, obese persons—be protected against job discrimination? Some have argued that they should be protected on the same grounds that women and ethnic minorities are currently protected.[64] At the present time, these groups remain as vulnerable as women, minorities, and older workers once were.

7.4 Affirmative Action

All of the equal opportunity policies discussed are ways of making employment decisions blind with respect to sex and race. These policies are all negative: They aim to prevent any further discrimination. Therefore, they ignore the fact that, as a result of past discrimination, women and minorities do not now have the same skills as their White male counterparts; because of past discrimination, women and minorities are now underrepresented in the more prestigious and desirable job positions. The policies discussed so far do not call for any positive steps to eliminate these effects of past discrimination.

To rectify the effects of past discrimination, many employers have instituted affirmative action programs designed to achieve a more representative distribution of minorities and women within the firm by giving preference to women and minorities. Affirmative action programs, in fact, are now legally required of all firms that hold a government contract. What does an affirmative action program involve? The heart of an affirmative action program is a detailed study (a "utilization analysis") of all the major job classifications in the firm.[65] The purpose of the study is to determine whether there are fewer minorities or women in a particular job classification than could be reasonably expected by their availability in the area from which the firm recruits. The utilization analysis will compare the percentage of women and minorities in each job classification with the percentage of those minority and female workers available in the area from which the firm recruits who have the requisite skills or who are capable of acquiring the requisite skills with training the firm could reasonably supply. If the utilization analysis shows that women or minorities are underutilized in certain job classifications, the firm must then establish recruiting goals and timetables for correcting these deficiencies. Although the goals and timetables must not be rigid and inflexible quotas, they must nonetheless be specific, measurable, and designed in good faith to correct the deficiencies uncovered by the utilization analysis within a reasonable length of time. The firm appoints an officer to coordinate and administer the affirmative action program, and it undertakes special efforts and programs to increase the recruitment of women and minorities so as to meet the goals and timetables it has established for itself.

Supreme Court decisions have not been clear about the legality of affirmative action programs. A large number of federal court decisions have agreed that the use of affirmative action programs to redress imbalances that are the result of previous discriminatory hiring practices is legitimate. Moreover, in 1979, the U.S. Supreme Court ruled that companies legally can use affirmative action programs to remedy a "manifest racial imbalance" regardless of whether the imbalance resulted from past discriminatory job practices.[66] In June 1984, however, the Court ruled that companies may not set aside the seniority of White workers during layoffs in favor of women and minority workers hired under affirmative action plans so long as the seniority system was adopted without a discriminatory motive. Thus, although affirmative action programs that give preferences to women or minorities as a group were not declared illegal, their effects could disappear during hard times because *the last hired, first fired* rule of seniority would hit strongest at women and minorities recently hired through the programs.[67] The 1984 Supreme Court decision also included a nonbinding advisory statement that,

> If individual members of a . . . class demonstrate that they have been actual victims of the discriminatory practice, they may be awarded competitive seniority and given their rightful place on the seniority roster. However, . . . mere membership in the disadvantaged class is insufficient to warrant a seniority award; each individual must prove that the discriminatory practice had an impact on him.[68]

To many this seemed to imply that affirmative action programs that awarded jobs on the basis of membership in a disadvantaged class were not completely legal. However, others interpreted the "advisory" more narrowly to mean merely that awarding seniority could not be based on mere membership in a disadvantaged class.[69] This latter interpretation seemed to be supported by another Supreme Court ruling on May 19, 1986, which held that, although layoffs based on race were unconstitutional, racial hiring goals were a legally allowable means to remedy past discrimination. The 1986 Supreme Court majority opinion stated that layoffs based on race "impose the entire burden of achieving racial equality on particular (White) individuals, often resulting in serious disruption of their lives. . . . On the other hand, racial preferences in hiring merely deny a future employment opportunity, not the loss of an existing job, and may be used to cure the effects of past discrimination."[70]

In 1989, the Supreme Court issued several decisions that interpreted previous civil rights laws in a manner that substantially weakened the ability of minorities and women to seek redress against discrimination, particularly through affirmative action programs. In 1991, however, Congress passed the

Civil Rights Act of 1991, which stated explicitly how those laws should be interpreted and in effect overruled the Supreme Court decisions of 1989. One important decision was left standing, however. In January 1989, in *City of Richmond v. J. A. Croson Co.*, the Court ruled that the affirmative action plan of a state or local government that operates by setting aside a certain percentage of its public monies for minority contractors is unconstitutional. Such set-aside programs, the Court ruled, could be used by public bodies only as "a last resort" in an "extreme case" and only if there was hard and specific proof of previous racial bias by that governmental body. *Adarand Construction, Inc. v. Pena*, a case the Supreme Court heard in 1995, reinforced this decision when it ruled that the federal government is also bound by its ruling in *City of Richmond v. J. A. Croson Co.*

Thus, the Supreme Court has vacillated on the constitutionality of affirmative action programs. Depending on the period in question, the issue at stake, and the current makeup of the Court, it has tended to support and then undermine affirmative action programs. Like the public, which remains deeply divided on the issue, the Supreme Court has had trouble making up its mind whether to support or attack these programs.[71]

Affirmative action programs have been attacked mainly on the grounds that, in attempting to correct the effects of past discrimination, these programs have become racially or sexually discriminatory.[72] By showing preference to minorities or women, the programs institute a form of reverse discrimination against White males.[73] A 45-year-old electrical worker at a Westinghouse plant, for example, is quoted as saying:

> What does bother me is the colored getting the preference because they're black. This I am against. I say, I don't care what his color is. If he has the ability to do the job, he should get the job—not because of his color. They shouldn't hire 20 percent just because they're black. This is discrimination in reverse as far as I'm concerned. . . . If they want it, they can earn it like I did. I am not saying deprive them of something—not at all.[74]

Affirmative action programs are said to discriminate against White males by using a nonrelevant characteristic—race or sex—to make employment decisions, and this violates justice by violating the principles of equality and equal opportunity.

The arguments used to justify affirmative action programs in the face of these objections tend to fall into two main groups.[75] One group of arguments interprets the preferential treatment accorded to women and minorities as a form of compensation for past injuries they have suffered. A second set of arguments interprets preferential treatment as an instrument for achieving certain social goals. Whereas compensation arguments for affirmative action are backward looking insofar as they focus on the wrongness of past acts, the instrumentalist arguments are forward looking insofar as they focus on the goodness of a future state (and the wrongness of what happened in the past is irrelevant).[76] We begin by examining the compensation arguments and then turn to the instrumentalist arguments.

Affirmative Action as Compensation

Arguments that defend affirmative action as a form of compensation are based on the concept of compensatory justice.[77] Compensatory justice, as noted in Chapter 2, implies that people have an obligation to compensate those whom they have intentionally and unjustly wronged. Affirmative action programs are then interpreted as a form of reparation by which White male majorities now compensate women and minorities for unjustly injuring them by discriminating against them in the past. One version of this argument holds, for example, that Blacks were wronged in the past by American Whites and that consequently the former should now receive compensation from Whites.[78] Programs of preferential treatment provide that compensation.

The difficulty with arguments that defend affirmative action on the basis of the principle of compensation is that the principle requires that compensation should come only from those specific individuals who intentionally inflicted a wrong, and it requires them to compensate only those specific individuals whom they wronged. For example, if five red-haired persons wrongfully injure five Black-haired persons, then compensatory justice obligates only the five red-haired persons to give to only the five Black-haired persons whatever the Black-haired persons would have had if the five red-heads had not injured them. Compensatory justice, however, does not require that compensation should come from all the members of a group that contains some wrongdoers, nor does it require that compensation should go to all the members of a group that contains some injured parties. In this example, although justice requires that the five red-haired persons must compensate the five Black-haired persons, it does not require that all red-haired persons should compensate all Black-haired persons. By analogy, only the specific individuals who discriminated against minorities or women in the past should now be forced to make reparation of some sort, and they should make reparation only to those specific individuals against whom they discriminated.[79] Although affirmative action programs usually benefit all the members of a racial or sexual group, regardless of whether they specifically were discriminated against in the past, and because these programs hinder every White male regardless of whether he specifically discriminated against someone in the past, it follows that such preferential programs cannot be justified on the basis of compensatory justice.[80] In short, affirmative action programs are unfair because the beneficiaries of affirmative action are not the same individuals who were injured by past discrimination, and the people who must pay for their injuries are usually not the ones who inflicted those injuries.[81]

Various authors have tried to counter this objection to the "affirmative action as compensation" argument by claiming that actually *every* Black person (or every woman) living today has been injured by discrimination and that *every* White person (or every male) has benefited from those injuries. For example, Judith Jarvis Thomson wrote:

> But it is absurd to suppose that the young blacks and women now of an age to apply for jobs have not been wronged. . . . Even young blacks and women have lived through downgrading for being black or female. . . . And even those who were not themselves downgraded for being black or female have suffered the consequences of the downgrading of other blacks and women: lack of self-confidence and lack of self-respect.[82]

Martin Redish wrote:

> It might also be argued that, whether or not the [White males] of this country have themselves participated in acts of discrimination, they have been the beneficiaries—conscious or unconscious—of a fundamentally racist society. They thus may be held independently "liable" to suppressed minorities for a form of unjust enrichment.[83]

It is unclear whether these arguments succeed in justifying affirmative action programs that benefit groups (all Blacks and all women) instead of specific injured individuals and that penalize groups (White males) instead of specific wrongdoers.[84] Has every minority and woman really been injured, as Thomson claims, and are all White males really beneficiaries of discrimination as Redish implies? Even if a White male happens (through no fault of his own) to benefit from someone else's injury, does this make him "liable" for that injury?

Affirmative Action as an Instrument for Achieving Social Goals

A second set of justifications advanced in support of affirmative action programs is based on the idea that these programs are morally legitimate instruments for achieving morally legitimate ends. For example, utilitarians have claimed that affirmative action programs are justified because they promote the public welfare.[85] They have argued that past discrimination has produced a high degree of correlation between race and poverty.[86] As racial minorities were systematically excluded from better paying and more prestigious jobs, their members have become impoverished. The kinds of statistics cited earlier in this chapter provide evidence of this inequality. Impoverishment in turn has led to unmet needs, lack of self-respect, resentment, social discontent, and crime. Therefore, the public welfare is promoted if the position of these impoverished persons is improved by giving them special educational and employment opportunities. If opponents object that such affirmative action programs are unjust because they distribute benefits on the basis of an irrelevant criterion such as race, the utilitarian can answer that *need*, not race, is the criterion by which affirmative action programs distribute benefits. Race provides an inexpensive *indicator* of need because past discrimination has created a high correlation between race and need. Need, of course, is a just criterion of distribution.[87] Appealing to the reduction of need is consistent with utilitarian principles because reducing need will increase total utility.

The major difficulties encountered by these utilitarian justifications of affirmative action have concerned, first, the question of whether the social costs of affirmative action programs (such as the frustrations felt by White males) outweigh their obvious benefits.[88] The utilitarian defender of affirmative action, of course, will reply that the benefits far outweigh the costs. Second, and more important, opponents of these utilitarian justifications of affirmative action have questioned the assumption that race is an appropriate indicator of need. It may be inconvenient and expensive to identify the needy directly, critics argue, but the costs might be small compared to the gains that would result from having a more accurate way to identify the needy.[89] Utilitarians answer this criticism by arguing that all minorities (and women) have been impoverished and psychologically harmed by past discrimination. Consequently, race (and sex) provide accurate indicators of need.

Although utilitarian arguments in favor of affirmative action programs are quite convincing, the most elaborate and persuasive array of arguments advanced in support of affirmative action have proceeded in two steps. First, they argue that the end envisioned by affirmative action programs is equal justice. Second, they argue that affirmative action programs are morally legitimate means for achieving this end.

The end that affirmative action programs are supposed to achieve is phrased in various ways. In our present society, it is argued, jobs are not distributed justly because they are not distributed according to the relevant criteria of ability, effort, contribution, or need.[90] Statistics show that jobs are in fact still distributed according to race and sex. One end of affirmative action is to bring about a distribution of society's benefits and burdens that is consistent with the principles of distributive justice, and that eliminates the important position race and sex currently have in the assignment of jobs.[91]In our present society, women and minorities do not have the equal opportunities that White males have and that justice demands. Statistics prove this. This lack of equal opportunity is because of subtle racist and sexist attitudes that bias the judgments of those (usually White males) who evaluate job applicants and that are so deeply entrenched that they are virtually ineradicable by good faith measures in any reasonable period of time.[92] A second end of affirmative action programs is to neutralize such conscious and unconscious bias to ensure equal opportunity to women and minorities. The lack of equal opportunity under which women and minorities currently labor has also been attributed to the privations they suffered as children. Economic privation hindered minorities from acquiring the skills, experience, training, and education they needed to compete equally with White males.[93] Furthermore, because women and minorities have not been represented in society's prestigious positions, young men and women have had no role models to motivate them to compete for such positions as young White males have. Few Black youths, for example, are motivated to enter the legal profession:

> Negro youth in the north, as well as the south, have been denied an inspiring image of the Negro lawyer, at least until recent years. On the contrary, they have been made sharply aware of the lack of respect and dignity accorded the Negro lawyer . . . Negro youth also know in what lack of regard the Negro, if employed in law enforcement at all, is held. . . . Such knowledge does little to inspire Negroes to do anything but avoid involvement with the law whatever its form.[94]

A third end of affirmative action programs is to neutralize these competitive disadvantages with which women and minorities are currently burdened when they compete with White males, and thereby bring women and minorities to the same starting point in their competitive race with others. The aim is to ensure an equal ability to compete with White males.[95]

The basic end that affirmative action programs seek is a more just society—a society in which an individual's opportunities are not limited by his or her race or sex. This goal is morally legitimate insofar as it is morally legitimate to strive for a society with greater equality of opportunity. The means by which affirmative action programs attempt to achieve a just society is giving qualified minorities and females preference over qualified White males in hiring and promotion and instituting special training programs for minorities and females that will qualify them for better jobs. By these means, it is hoped, the more just society outlined will eventually be born. Without some form of affirmative action, it is argued, this end could not be achieved.[96] But is preferential treatment a morally legitimate means for attaining this end? Three reasons have been advanced to show that it is not.

First, it is often claimed that affirmative action programs "discriminate" against White males.[97] Supporters of affirmative action programs, however, have pointed out that there are crucial differences between the treatment accorded to Whites by preferential treatment programs and immoral discriminatory behavior.[98] To discriminate, as we indicated earlier, is to make an adverse decision against the member of a group because members of that group are considered inferior or less worthy of respect. Preferential treatment programs, however, are not based on invidious contempt for White males. On the contrary, they are based on the judgment that White males are currently in an advantaged position and that others should have an equal opportunity to achieve the same advantages. Moreover, racist or sexist discrimination is aimed at destroying equal opportunity. Preferential treatment programs are aimed at restoring equal opportunity where it is absent. Thus, preferential treatment programs cannot accurately be described as "discriminatory" in the same immoral sense that racist or sexist behavior is discriminatory.

Second, it is sometimes claimed that preferential treatment violates the principle of equality ("Individuals who are equal in all respects relevant to the kind of treatment in question should be treated equally") by allowing a nonrelevant characteristic (race and sex) to determine employment decisions.[99] Defenders of affirmative action programs have replied that sexual and racial differences are now relevant to making employment decisions. These differences are relevant because when society distributes a scarce resource (such as jobs), it may legitimately choose to allocate it to those groups that will best advance its legitimate ends. In our present society, allocating scarce jobs to women and minorities will best achieve equality of opportunity, thus race and sex are now relevant characteristics to use for this purpose. Moreover, as we have seen, the reason that we hold that jobs should be allocated on the basis of job-related qualifications is that such an allocation will achieve a socially desirable (utilitarian) end: maximum productivity. When this end (productivity) conflicts with another socially desirable end (a just society), it is legitimate to pursue the second end even if doing so means that the first end will not be as fully achieved.

Third, some critics have objected that affirmative action programs actually harm women and minorities because such programs imply that women and minorities are so inferior to White males that they need special help to compete.[100] This attribution of inferiority, critics claim, is debilitating to minorities and women and ultimately inflicts harms that are so great that they far outweigh the benefits provided by such programs. In a widely read and much-acclaimed book, for example, the Black author Shelby Steele criticized affirmative action programs in business and education:

> [I]n theory, affirmative action certainly has all the moral symmetry that fairness requires—the injustice of historical and even contemporary White advantage is offset with black advantage; preference replaces prejudice, inclusion answers exclusion. It is reformist and corrective, even repentant and redemptive. . . . But after twenty years of implementation, I think affirmative action has shown itself to be

> more bad than good and that blacks . . . now stand to lose more from it than they gain. . . . I think that one of the most troubling effects of racial preferences for blacks is a kind of demoralization, or put another way, an enlargement of self-doubt. Under affirmative action the quality that earns us preferential treatment is an implied inferiority. However, this inferiority is explained—and it is easily enough explained by the myriad deprivations that grew out of our oppression—it is still inferiority. . . . Even when the black sees no implication of inferiority in racial preferences, he knows that Whites do, so that—consciously or unconsciously—the result is virtually the same. The effect of preferential treatment—the lowering of normal standards to increase black representation—puts blacks at war with an expanded realm of debilitating doubt, so that the doubt itself becomes an unrecognized preoccupation that undermines their ability to perform, especially in integrated situations.[101]

Steele's eloquently expressed view is one that many other minorities have come to hold.[102]

This third objection to affirmative action programs has been met in several ways. First, although many minorities concede that affirmative action carries some costs for minorities, they also hold that the benefits of such programs still outweigh the costs. For example, a Black worker who won several jobs through affirmative action is reported as saying, "I had to deal with the grief it brought, but it was well worth it."[103]

Second, proponents of affirmative action programs also argue that these programs are based not on an assumption of minority or female inferiority, but on a recognition of the fact that White males, consciously or unconsciously, will bias their decisions in favor of other White males. The only remedy for this, they argue, is some kind of affirmative action program that will force White males to counter this bias by requiring them to accept that proportion of minority applicants that research shows are qualified and willing to work. As studies repeatedly show, even when women and minorities are more qualified, White males are still granted higher salaries and positions by their White male counterparts. Moreover, they claim, the unjustified attributions of inferiority that many minorities experience are the result of lingering racism on the part of coworkers and employees, and such racism is precisely what affirmative action programs are meant to eradicate.

A third response that supporters of affirmative action make is that, although a portion of minorities may be made to feel inferior by current affirmative action programs, nevertheless many more minorities were made to feel much more devastatingly inferior by the overt and covert racism that affirmative action is gradually eroding. The overt and covert racism that pervaded the workplace prior to the implementation of affirmative action programs systematically disadvantaged, shamed, and undermined the self-esteem of all minorities to a much higher degree than is currently the case.

Finally, proponents argue that it is simply false that showing preference toward a group makes members of that group feel inferior: For centuries, White males have been the beneficiaries of racial and sexual discrimination without apparent loss of their self-esteem. If minority beneficiaries of affirmative action programs are made to feel inferior, it is because of lingering racism, not because of the preference extended to them and their fellows.

Strong arguments can be made in support of affirmative action programs, and strong objections can be lodged against them. Because there are such powerful arguments on both sides of the issue, the debate over the legitimacy of affirmative action programs continues to rage without resolution. However, the review of the arguments seems to suggest that affirmative action programs are at least a morally permissible means for achieving just ends, even if they may not show that they are a morally required means for achieving those ends.

Implementing Affirmative Action and Managing Diversity

Opponents of affirmative action programs have argued that other criteria besides race and sex have to be weighed when making job decisions in an affirmative action program. First, if sex and race are the only criteria used, this will result in the hiring of unqualified personnel and a consequent decline in productivity.[104] Second, many jobs have significant impacts on the lives of others. Consequently, if a job has significant impact on, say, the safety of others (such as the job of flight controller or surgeon), then criteria other than race or sex should have a prominent place and should override affirmative action.[105] Third, opponents have argued that affirmative action programs, if continued, will turn us into a more racially and sexually conscious nation.[106] Consequently, the programs should cease as soon as the defects they are meant to remedy are corrected.

The following guidelines have been suggested as a way to fold these sorts of considerations into an affirmative action program when minorities are underrepresented in a firm:[107]

1. Both minorities and nonminorities should be hired or promoted only if they reach certain minimum levels of competency or are capable of reaching such levels in a reasonable time.
2. If the qualifications of the minority candidate are only slightly less (or equal to or higher) than those of the nonminority, then the minority should be given preference.
3. If both the minority and nonminority candidates are adequately qualified for a position but the nonminority candidate is much more qualified, then:
    - **a.** if performance in the job directly affects the lives and safety of people (such as a surgeon or an airline pilot) or if performance on the job has a substantial and critical effect on the entire firm's efficiency (such as head comptroller), then the more qualified nonminority should be given preference; but
    - **b.** if the position (like most positions in a firm) does not directly involve safety factors and does not have a substantial and highly critical effect on a firm's efficiency, then the minority person should be given preference.

4. Preference should be extended to minority candidates only so long as their representation throughout the various levels of the firm is not proportional to their availability.

The success or failure of an affirmative action program also depends in part on the accommodations a company makes to the special needs of a racially and sexually diverse workforce. Both women and minorities encounter special workplace problems, and companies need to devise innovative means for addressing these needs. The major problems faced by women relate to the fact that a large number of married couples have children, and it is women who physically bear children and who in our culture carry most of the burden of raising and caring for them. Some people have suggested that companies respond by creating two career tracks for women: one track for women who indicate that they plan to have and actively participate in raising their own children while pursuing their careers, and the other track for women who either plan not to have children or plan to have others (husbands or child-care providers) raise their children while they devote themselves to pursuing their careers by putting in extra hours, making sacrifices in their personal lives, traveling, transferring, and relocating to advance their careers, and taking every opportunity for professional development.[108]

This approach, however, has been criticized as unjust because it may force women, unlike men, to choose between their careers and their families, and it may result in a lower status cohort of *mommies* who are discriminated against in favor of a high-status cohort of *career females*. Others have suggested that so long as our culture continues to put child-care tasks primarily on women, companies should help women by providing more generous family leave policies (IBM provides up to 8 weeks of paid maternity leave, up to an additional year of unpaid leave for a new parent with the option of part-time work during that year and a guarantee of their jobs when they return, and pays up to $1750 of adoption expenses); more flexible work schedules (allowing parents to schedule their arrival and departure times to fit the needs of their children's schedules or work four 10-hour days in a week instead of five 8 hour days, allowing mothers of school-age children to work full time during the school year and either rely on temporary replacements during vacations or allow mothers to only work part time); sick leave for parents whose children are sick (or for nonparents who have special needs); special job arrangements for parents (letting new parents spend several years working part time while their children are growing up and guaranteeing their jobs when they return, or letting two parents share the same job); and child care support (setting up a child-care facility at or near the workplace, reimbursing employees for child-care expenses, setting up a child-care referral service, providing special day-care personnel who can care for employees' sick children, or providing an onsite clinic that can care for sick children while parents work).[109]

The special needs of minorities differ from those of women. Minorities are much more economically and educationally disadvantaged than nonminorities, with fewer work skills, fewer years of formal education, poor quality educations, and poor or nonexistent English language skills. To meet their needs, companies have to begin providing on-the-job education in work skills, basic reading, writing, and computational skills, and English language skills. Newark, New Jersey's Prudential Insurance, for example, provides computer-assisted training in reading and math for entry-level applicants. Northeast Utilities in Hartford, Connecticut, provides 5 weeks of training in vocational skills and English language skills for its Hispanic recruits. Amtek Systems in Arlington, Virginia, provides similar programs for Asians. Minorities often have cultural values and beliefs that can give rise to misunderstandings, conflicts, and poor work performance. To deal with this issue, companies have to train their managers to manage a culturally diverse workforce by educating them on those minority cultures represented in their workforce and helping managers learn to become more aware of, to listen to, communicate with, and understand people from diverse backgrounds.[110]

The controversy over the moral propriety of affirmative action programs has not yet died. The Supreme Court has ruled that such programs do not violate the Civil Rights Act of 1964. It does not follow that these programs do not violate any moral principles. If the arguments examined are correct, however, then affirmative action programs are at least consistent with moral principles. However, the arguments continue to be the subject of intense debate.

Comparable Pay for Jobs of Comparable Worth

During the past decade, some groups have advanced a proposal to deal with sexual discrimination that is much more radical and far reaching than affirmative action programs. Affirmative action programs attempt to increase the proportions of women in positions where they are underrepresented, but they leave untouched the wages and salaries that attach to the positions women already tend to hold. That is, affirmative action programs do not address the problem posed by the fact that jobs women historically have filled tend to pay low wages and salaries, and merely ensure that more women are hired into those jobs with higher wages and salaries. In contrast to this, the new so-called *comparable worth* programs that many groups have advocated to deal with sexually biased earnings attempt to alter the low wages and salaries that market mechanisms tend to assign to jobs held by women. Unlike affirmative action programs, a comparable worth program does not attempt to place more women into those positions that have higher salaries. Instead, it attempts to place higher salaries on those positions that most women already hold.

Comparable worth programs proceed by measuring the value of each job to an organization (in terms of skill requirements, educational requirements, tasks involved, level of responsibility, and any other features of the job that the employer thinks deserve compensation) and ensuring that jobs of equal value are paid the same salary regardless of whether external labor markets pay the same rates for those jobs.[111] For example, studies have shown that legal secretaries and instrument repair technicians hold jobs that have the same relative value for a firm in terms of problem solving, know how, and accountability.[112] Nevertheless, legal secretaries, who are virtually all female, command $9432 less on the job market than instrument repair technicians, who are predominantly male. A comparable worth program in a firm would adjust the salaries of these two occupations so that they are paid approximately the same.

Thus, in a comparable worth program, each job is assigned a certain number of points for difficulty, skill requirements, experience, accountability, work hazards, knowledge requirements, responsibility, working conditions, and any other factors that are deemed worthy of compensation. Jobs are then assumed to deserve equal pay if they score equal points and higher (or lower) pay if they have higher (or lower) scores. Job market considerations are used to determine the actual salary to be paid for jobs with a given number of points. However, when jobs have the same scores, they are paid the same salaries. For example, because the job market pays instrument repair technicians $9432 more than legal secretaries (although these jobs have approximately equal values), a comparable pay program might raise the salaries of the secretaries by $9432 or perhaps lower the salaries of technicians by the same amount, or it might raise the salaries of secretaries by half that amount and lower that of technicians by the same amount. Thus, job market considerations play a small role in setting comparable worth salaries, but they do not determine the salary of one job relative to another.

The fundamental argument in favor of comparable worth programs is one based on justice: Justice requires that equals should be treated as equals.[113] Proponents of comparable worth programs argue that, at present, jobs filled by women are paid less by job markets than jobs filled by men even when the jobs involve equal responsibilities and require equal abilities. Once jobs are objectively evaluated, they claim, it is clear that many women's jobs are equivalent to men's jobs and, in justice, should be paid the same even if discriminatory job markets place them on different wage scales. That certain jobs involve equal responsibilities and abilities is evident, proponents claim, from an examination of the jobs.

The main arguments against comparable worth programs focus on the appropriateness of markets as determinants of salaries.[114] Opponents of comparable worth argue that there is no "objective" way to evaluate whether one job is "equivalent" to another than by appealing to labor markets that register the combined evaluations of hundreds of buyers and sellers.[115] Only the market forces of supply and demand can determine the "true" worth of a job, and only market forces can achieve an approximate capitalist justice by ensuring that each laborer receives a price for her labor that exactly equals the value both she and the buyer places on it. Assigning salaries by assigning "points" to a job is much more arbitrary and less objective than doing so by relying on market forces. Moreover, opponents argue, if the job market pays those who enter a certain occupation a low salary, this is because there is a large supply of workers who want that occupation relative to the demand for that occupation. So-called *women's jobs* have low salaries because there are too many women bidding for those jobs and they thereby drive those salaries down. The solution is not to distort markets by assigning higher "comparable worth" salaries for jobs that are already overcrowded. It is much better to allow the low salaries to stand so they can channel women into other areas of the economy where demand is lower as indicated by the existence of higher salaries. Finally, opponents say, the higher paying "male jobs" are as open to women as to men. If women choose to enter the lower paying jobs instead of the higher paying ones, this is because they derive some utility from (i.e., get some benefits from) the lower paying jobs that they do not get from the higher paying ones: Perhaps the lower paying jobs are "cleaner," more personally rewarding, or less arduous. Thus, women do receive some compensation from the jobs they continue to select even though this might not be in the form of a salary.

Defenders of comparable worth programs answer these criticisms by replying that job markets are not "objective." Women's jobs are paid less, proponents claim, because current job markets are discriminatory: They arbitrarily assign lower salaries to "women's" jobs precisely because they are filled by women. As proof that job markets assign lower salaries to some jobs precisely because they are filled with women, proponents of comparable worth programs point to figures such as those in Table 7.10, which show that there is a consistent relationship between the percentage of women in an occupation and that occupation's salary: The more an occupation is dominated by women, the less it pays. A pattern this consistent indicates that the low wages of women's jobs are not a matter of chance overcrowding of women into this or that occupation. Instead, it is an indication that women are consistently perceived by those in the labor markets as being less capable, skilled, or committed than men. Because of these subjective and discriminatory biases, buyers in job markets systematically underprice the talents of women. As a result, job markets undervalue the jobs women take. Consequently, job markets are not adequate indicators of appropriate wage scales for women's jobs.

Like affirmative action, comparable worth continues to be a highly controversial issue.

Conclusions

Earlier sections examined several future trends that will affect the future status of women and minorities in the workforce. Of particular significance is the fact that only a small proportion of new workers will be White males. Most new workers will be women and minorities. Unless major changes are made to accommodate their needs and special characteristics, they will not be incorporated smoothly into the workplace.

We have reviewed a number of programs that provide special assistance to women and minorities on moral grounds. However, it should be clear, in view of the future demographic trends, that enlightened self-interest should also prompt business to give women and minorities a special hand. The costs of not assisting the coming influx of women and minorities with their special needs will not be borne entirely by women and minorities. Unfortunately, if businesses do not accommodate themselves to these new workers, American businesses will not be able to find the workers they need and they will suffer recurrent and crippling shortages over the next decade. The pool of traditional White male workers simply will be so small that businesses will not be able to rely on them to fill all their requirements for skilled and managerial positions.

Many businesses, aware of these trends, have undertaken programs to prepare themselves now to respond to the special needs of women and minorities. To respond to women's needs, for example, many companies have instituted day-care services and flexible working hours that allow women with children to care for their children's needs. Other companies have instituted aggressive affirmative action programs aimed at integrating large groups of minorities into their firms where they are provided with education, job training, skills, counseling, and other assistance designed to enable them to assimilate into the workforce. The belief of such companies is that if they act now to recruit women and minorities, they will be familiar with their special needs and will have a large cadre of women and minorities capable of bringing other women and minorities along. James R. Houghton, chairman of Corning Glass Works, is quoted as saying:

> Valuing and managing a diverse work force is more than ethically and morally correct. It's also a business necessity. Work force demographics for the next decade make it absolutely clear that companies which fail to do an excellent job of recruiting, retaining, developing and promoting women and minorities simply will be unable to meet their staffing needs.[116]

QUESTIONS FOR REVIEW AND DISCUSSION

1. Define the following concepts: job discrimination, institutionalized/isolated discrimination, intentional/nonintentional discrimination, statistical indicators of discrimination, utilitarian argument against discrimination, Kantian arguments against discrimination, formal principle of "equality," discriminatory practices, affirmative action program, utilization analysis, "reverse discrimination," compensation argument for preferential treatment, instrumental argument for preferential treatment, utilitarian argument for preferential treatment, the end goals of affirmative action programs, invidious contempt, comparable pay.

2. In your judgment, was the historical shift in emphasis from intentional/isolated discrimination to nonintentional/institutionalized discrimination good or bad? Justify your judgment.
3. Research your library or the Internet (e.g., the Census Bureau puts its statistics on the World Wide Web at http://www.census.gov) for statistics published during the last year that tend to support or refute the statistical picture of racism and sexism developed in Section 7.2 of the text. In view of your research and the materials in the text, do you agree or disagree with the statement, "There is no longer evidence that discrimination is widely practiced in the United States"? Explain your position fully.
4. Compare and contrast the three main kinds of arguments against racial and sexual job discrimination. Which of these seem to you to be the strongest? The weakest? Can you think of different kinds of arguments not discussed in the text? Are there important differences between racial discrimination and sexual discrimination?
5. Compare and contrast the main arguments used to support affirmative action programs. Do you agree or disagree with these arguments? If you disagree with an argument, state clearly which part of the argument you think is wrong and explain why it is wrong. (It is not enough to say, "I just don't think it is right.")
6. "If employers only want to hire [the best qualified young White males, then they have a right to do so without interference, because these are their businesses." Comment on this statement.

Web Resources

Readers interested in researching the topic of discrimination might want to begin by accessing the web page of the U.S. Census Bureau for current detailed statistics on income, earnings, poverty, and other topics (http://www.census.gov). The legal aspects of discrimination can be researched by searching the resources provided by Hieros Gamos (http://www.hg.org) and the American Bar Association (http://www.abanet.org). Information on sexual harassment is provided by VIX (http://www.vix.com/pub/men/harass/harass.html). Information on minority business is provided by the Minority Information Service (http://web.fed.com/web/fed/aid).

Notes

1. From Bill Clinton, "Mend It, Don't End It," in George Curry, *The Affirmative Action Debate* (Reading, MA: Addison-Wesley Publishing Company, Inc., 1996).
2. Pete Wilson, "The Minority-Majority Society," in George Curry, *The Affirmative Action Debate* (Reading, MA: Addison-Wesley Publishing Company, Inc., 1996).
3. 4. ABC, *Prime-Time Live*, October 7, 1993.
4. Michael Fix and Raymond J. Strucyk, eds., *Clear and Convincing Evidence: Measurement in America* (Washington, DC: Urban Institute Press, 1993).

5. This morally charged meaning is now perhaps the dominant meaning given to the term *discrimination* and is found in any relatively recent dictionary; see, for example, *Webster's New Collegiate Dictionary* (Springfield, MA: G. & C. Merriam Company, 1974), p. 326, where a main meaning attributed to the term *discriminate* is "to make a difference in treatment or favor on a basis other than individual merit," and where a meaning attributed to *discrimination* is "prejudiced or prejudicial outlook, action, or treatment."

6. For a somewhat lengthy discussion of the meaning of discrimination, see Barry R. Gross, *Discrimination in Reverse* (New York: New York University Press, 1978), pp. 6–28. Although modern dictionaries all attest to the morally charged meaning of *discrimination*, Gross tries to provide an argument to the effect that the term should retain its morally neutral meaning so that it can be used to apply to "discrimination against White males" that is not based on racial prejudice. In the text, however, I rely more on the morally laden notion of *invidious discrimination* that has been used by the Supreme Court and is developed, for example, in Ronald Dworkin, "Why Bakke Has No Case," *New York Review of Books*, 10 November 1977, p. 15.

7. Joe R. Feagin and Clairece Booker Feagin, *Discrimination American Style*, 2nd ed. (Malabar, FL: Robert E. Krieger Publishing Company, 1986), pp. 23–33.

8. U.S. Congress, Senate, Subcommittee on Labor of the Committee on Labor and Public Welfare, *Compilation of Selected Labor Laws Pertaining to Labor Relations*, Part II, 93rd Congress, 2nd Session, 6 September 1974, p. 610.

9. U.S. Equal Employment Opportunity Commission, *Affirmative Action and Equal Employment: A Guidebook for Employers*, II (Washington, DC: Government Printing Office, 1974), p. D-28.

10. The necessity of basing analyses of discrimination on statistical grounds and the uselessness of attempting an individual case-by-case procedure are discussed by Lester Thurow in "A Theory of Groups and Economic Redistribution," *Philosophy and Public Affairs*, vol. 9, no. 1 (Fall 1979): 25–41.

11. Walter B. Connolly, Jr., *A Practical Guide to Equal Employment Opportunity*, 2 vols. (New York: Law Journal Press, 1975), 1:231–42; for a discussion of the relevance of statistics, see Tom Beauchamp, "The Justification of Reverse Discrimination," in W. T. Blackstone and R. Heslep, *Social Justice and Preferential Treatment* (Athens, GA: The University of Georgia Press, 1977), pp. 84–110.

12. U.S. Census Bureau, Current Population Reports, P60–206, *Money Income in the United States, 1998* (Washington, DC: U.S. Government Printing Office, 1999), Table 2, p. 5.

13. William J. Carrington and Kenneth R. Troske, *Gender Segregation in Small Firms*, (Washington, DC: Center for Economic Studies of the U.S. Census Bureau, October 1992), [CES Report No. 92–13]; a short version of this report is available from the Bureau of the Census as a Statistical Brief entitled "Two Different Worlds: Men and Women From 9 to 5" (SB/94–24), issued February 1995.

14. Barbara Reskin and Irene Padavic, *Women and Men at Work* (Thousand Oaks, CA: Pine Forge Press, 1994), p. 106.

15. U.S. Dept. of Labor, *The Earnings Gap Between Women and Men* (Washington, DC: U.S. Government Printing Office, 1979), p. 6.

16. Robert Pear, "Women's Pay Lags Further Behind Men's," *New York Times*, 16 January 1984, p. 1; see also, "Gender Gap/Dollar Gap," *Los Angeles Times*, 25 January 1984.
17. Daniel S. Hamermesh and Albert Rees, *The Economics of Work and Pay*, 3rd ed. (New York: Harper & Row Publishers, Inc., 1984), p. 319.
18. Of 3572 Blacks ages 18 to 24 sampled in March 1998, 107 reported having graduated from college. See U.S. Department of Education (http://nces.ed.gov), National Center for Education Statistics, *Digest of Education Statistics, 1999*, NCES 2000–031, by Thomas D. Snyder. Production Manager, Charlene M. Hoffman. Washington, DC: 2000, table 9, p. 18.
19. Poverty level figures are from U.S. Census Bureau (www.census.gov), *Current Population Survey, Poverty 1999*, <http://www.census.gov/hhes/poverty/threshld/thresh99.html>; college costs are from U.S. Department of Education, National Center for Education Statistics, *Digest of Education Statistics, 1999*, NCES 2000–031, by Thomas D. Snyder, production manager, Charlene M. Hoffman, Washington, DC: 2000.
20. Barbara Reskin and Irene Padavic, *Women and Men At Work* (Thousand Oaks, CA: Pine Forge Press, 1994), pp. 82–84 and U.S. Department of Labor, Office of Federal Contract Compliance Programs, Glass Ceiling Commission, *Good for Business: Making Full Use of the Nation's Human Capital* (Washington, DC: Government Printing Office, 1995), pp. 11–12.
21. Bradley R. Schiller, *The Economics of Poverty & Discrimination*, 6th ed. (Englewood Cliffs, NJ: Prentice-Hall, 1995), pp. 193–94.
22. Reskin and Padavic, *Women and Men at Work*, pp. 39–43.
23. Jacob Mincer and Solomon W. Polachek, "Family Investments in Human Capital: Earnings of Women," *Journal of Political Economy*, vol. 82 (March/April, 1982, Part II): s76–s108; see also Reskin and Padavic, *Women and Men at Work*, pp. 39–43.
24. See Mary Corcoran, Greg J. Duncan, and Martha S. Hill, "The Economic Fortunes of Women and Children," in Micheline R. Malson, Elisabeth Mudimbe-Boyi, Jean F. O'Barr, and Mary Wyer, eds., *Black Women in America* (Chicago: The University of Chicago Press, 1988), pp. 97–113; Mary Corcoran, "A Longitudinal Approach to White Women's Wages," *Journal of Human Resources*, vol. 18, no. 4 (Fall 1983): 497–520; and Paula England, "The Failure of Human Capital Theory to Explain Occupational Sex Segregation," *Journal of Human Resources*, vol. 17, no. 3 (Summer 1982): 358–70.
25. "Study Blames Barriers, Not Choices, For Sex Segregation," *San Jose Mercury News*, 20 December 1985, p. 21E.
26. Randall K. Filer, "Sexual Differences in Earnings: The Role of Individual Personalities and Tastes," *The Journal of Human Resources*, vol. 18, no. 1 (Winter 1983).
27. Mary Corcoran and Greg J. Duncan, "Work History, Labor Force Attachment, and Earnings Differences Between the Races and Sexes," *The Journal of Human Resources*, vol. 19, no. 1 (Winter 1979): 3–20; see also Gerald Jaynes and Robin Williams, eds., *A Common Destiny: Blacks and American Society* (Washington, DC: National Academy Press, 1989), pp. 319–23.
28. The data in this paragraph are drawn from William B. Johnston and Arnold E. Packer, *Workforce 2000: Work and Workers for the Twenty-first Century* (Indianapolis, IN: Hudson Institute, 1987).

29. All of the studies in this paragraph are cited in Clint Bolick and Susan Nestleroth, *Opportunity 2000* (Indianapolis, IN: Hudson Institute, 1988), pp. 21–22.

30. *Ibid.*, p. 67.

31. U.S. Department of Education, National Center for Education Statistics, *The Condition of Education, 1999*, NCES 1999–022 (Washington, DC: U.S. Government Printing Office, 1999), p. 152.

32. U.S. Census Bureau (www.census.gov), *Current Population Reports, Population Characteristics, Series P20–513*, "Educational Attainment in the United States, March 1998," Table 1, <http://www.census.gov/prod/3/98pubs/p20–513u.pdf>.

33. Dick Lilly, "City Staff Survey Finds Harassment," *Seattle Times*, 8 October 1991, p. B3; "Female Execs See Marketing as Fastest Track," Sales & Marketing Management, August 1993, p. 10; "Survey Finds Most Women Rabbis Have Been Sexually Harassed on Job," *United Press International*, August 28, 1993; "Female Jail Guards Fight Against Harassment by Male Colleagues," *Houston Chronicle*, 17 October 1993, p. A5.

34. Reported in Terry Halbert and Elaine Inguilli, eds., *Law and Ethics in the Business Environment* (St. Paul, MN: West Publishing Co., 1990), p. 298.

35. Eliza G. C. Collins and Timothy B. Blodgett, "Sexual Harassment . . . Some See It . . . Some Won't," *Harvard Business Review*, vol. 59, no. 2, March/April 1981.

36. Charlotte Lynn Rawlins Yates and Cheryl Jenkins Mathis v. Avco Corporation, 814 F. 2d 630 (1987), U.S. Court of Appeals, Sixth Circuit.

37. Thomas Jefferson, *Declaration of Independence*.

38. *Dred Scott v. Sanford*, 60 U.S (19 How) (1857) at 407 and 421. See Don E. Fehrenbacher, *The Dred Scott Case* (New York: Oxford University Press, 1978).

39. *Bradwell v. Illinois*, 83 U.S. (16 Wall) (1873). See Leo Kanowitz, *Women and the Law* (Albuquerque, NM: University of New Mexico Press, 1969), p. 36.

40. Norman Daniels, "Merit and Meritocracy," *Philosophy and Public Affairs*, vol. 7, no. 3 (Spring 1978): 208–9.

41. For economic analyses of the costs and benefits associated with discrimination, see Gary S. Becker, *The Economics of Discrimination*, 2nd ed. (Chicago: The University of Chicago Press, 1971); Janice Fanning Madden, *The Economics of Sex Discrimination* (Lexington, MA: D.C. Heath and Company, 1973). For a critical review of this literature, see Annette M. LaMond, "Economic Theories of Employment Discrimination," in Phyllis A. Wallace and Annette M. LaMond, eds., *Women, Minorities, and Employment Discrimination* (Lexington, MA: D.C. Heath and Company, 1977), pp. 1–11.

42. *Ibid.*, p. 214.

43. See the discussion of this view in Sharon Bishop Hill, "Self-Determination and Autonomy," in Richard Waserstrom, eds., *Today's Moral Problems*, 2nd ed. (New York: Macmillan, Inc., 1979), pp. 118–33.

44. On this issue, see Janet S. Chafetz, *Masculine, Feminine, or Human?: An Overview of the Sociology of Sex Roles* (Itasca, IL: Peacock, 1974); and Joyce Trebilcot, "Sex Roles: The Argument from Nature," *Ethics*, vol. 85, no. 3 (April 1975): 249–55.

45. See, for example, Thomas Nagel, "Equal Treatment and Compensatory Discrimination," *Philosophy and Public Affairs*, vol. 2 (1973): 360; and Ronald Dworkin, *Taking Rights Seriously* (Cambridge: Harvard University Press, 1977), pp. 232–37.

46. Susan Haack, "On the Moral Relevance of Sex," *Philosophy*, vol. 49: 90–95; Jon J. Durkin, "The Potential of Women," in Bette Ann Stead, ed., *Women in Management* (Englewood Cliffs, NJ: Prentice-Hall, 1978), pp. 42–46.

47. Richard Wasserstrom, "Rights, Human Rights, and Racial Discrimination," *The Journal of Philosophy*, vol. 61 (29 October 1964): 628–41.

48. Richard Wasserstrom, "Racism, Sexism, and Preferential Treatment: An Approach to the Topics," *UCLA Law Review*, vol. 24 (1977): 581–622.

49. This is, for example, the underlying view in John C. Livingston, *Fair Game?* (San Francisco: W. H. Freeman and Company, 1979), pp. 74–76.

50. Richard M. Hare, *Freedom and Reason* (New York: Oxford University Press, 1963), pp. 217–19.

51. John Rawls, *A Theory of Justice* (Cambridge: Harvard University Press, Belknap Press, 1971), pp. 83–90.

52. Feagin and Feagin, *Discrimination American Style*, pp. 43–77.

53. Charles Perelman, *The Idea of Justice and the Problem of Argument* (London: Routledge and Kegan Paul, 1963).

54. Equal Employment Opportunity Commission, Title 29 Code of Federal Regulations, Section 1604.11, Sexual Harassment.

55. *Rabidue v. Osceola Refining Company*, 805 F. 2d 611 (1986), U.S. Court of Appeals, Sixth Circuit, Circuit Judge Keith, Dissenting in Part, quoted in Terry Halbert and Elaine Inguilli, eds., *Law and Ethics in the Business Environment* (St. Paul, MN: West Publishing Co., 1990), p. 301.

56. This was, for example, the position of the majority opinion in *Rabidue vs. Osceola Refining Company.*

57. Gretchen Morgenson, "Watch That Leer, Stifle That Joke," *Forbes*, 15 May 1989, p. 72.

58. Barbara Lindemann Schlei and Paul Grossman, *Employment Discrimination Law*, 1979 Supplement (Washington, DC: The Bureau of National Affairs, Inc., 1979), pp. 109–20.

59. John Lawrie, "Subtle Discrimination Pervades Corporate America," *Personnel Journal*, January 1990, pp. 53–55.

60. See *Smith v. Liberty Mutual Insurance Company*, 395 F. Supp., 1098 (1975), and *Sommers v. Budget Marketing Inc.*, 667 F. 2d 748 (1982).

61. Terence Roth, "Many Firms Fire AIDS Victims, Citing Health Risk to Co-Workers," *Wall Street Journal*, 12 August 1985; Dorothy Townsend, "AIDS Patient Sues Kodak Over Firing, Claims Bias," *Los Angeles Times*, 2 April 1986; Jim Dickey, "Firing Over AIDS Test Claimed," *San Jose Mercury News*, 11 October 1985, p. 1B.

62. U.S. Census Bureau, *Statistical Abstract of the United States, 1999*, Table 228, p. 148.

63. Robert N. Webner, "Budding Movement Is Seeking to Stop Fat Discrimination," *Wall Street Journal*, 8 October 1979, p. 33.

64. See Richard D. Mohr, "Gay Rights," in Patricia H. Werhane, A. R. Gini, and David Ozar, eds., *Philosophical Issues in Human Rights* (New York: Random House, Inc., 1986), pp. 337–41; David Margolick, "Court Blocks Job Denials for Obesity," *New York Times*, 8 May 1985, p. 18; Cris Oppenheimer, "A Hostile Marketplace Shuts Out Older Workers," *San Jose Mercury News*, 9 December 1985.

65. On the requirements of affirmative action programs, see Connolly, Jr., *A Practical Guide to Equal Employment Opportunity*, 1:359–73.

66. United Steelworkers of America v. Weber, 99 S. Ct. 2721 (1979).

67. Rogene A. Buchholz, *Business Environment and Public Policy* (Englewood Cliffs, NJ: Prentice-Hall, 1982), pp. 287–88.

68. Quoted in "High Court Dumps Quotas in Labor Case," *Washington Times*, 13 June 1984, p. 1.

69. "A Right Turn on Race?" *Newsweek*, 25 June 1984, pp. 29–31; Stuart Taylor, "Reagan Attack on Quotas in Jobs Goes to High Court," *New York Times*, 6 August 1985, p. 17.

70. Aaron Epstein, "Layoffs Can't Favor Minority Workers," *San Jose Mercury News*, 20 May 1986, p. 1a.

71. See, for example, "The New Politics of Race" and "A Crisis of Shattered Dreams," in *Newsweek*, 6 May 1991, pp. 22–26, 28–31.

72. See, for example, Barry R. Gross, *Discrimination in Reverse: Is Turnabout Fair Play*?; for a contrasting view, see also Alan H. Goldman, *Justice and Reverse Discrimination* (Princeton: Princeton University Press, 1979).

73. See, for example, the articles collected in Barry R. Gross, ed., *Reverse Discrimination* (Buffalo: Prometheus Books, 1977).

74. Theodore V. Purcell and Gerald F. Cavanagh, *Blacks in the Industrial World* (New York: The Free Press, 1972), p. 164.

75. See Bernard Boxill, *Blacks and Social Justice* (Totowa, NJ: Rowman & Allanheld, 1984), pp. 147–72; see also the essays collected in Marshall Cohen, Thomas Nagel, and Thomas Scanlon, eds., *Equality and Preferential Treatment* (Princeton: Princeton University Press, 1977); and William T. Blackstone and Robert D. Heslep, eds., *Social Justice & Preferential Treatment* (Athens, GA: The University of Georgia Press, 1977).

76. George Sher, "Reverse Discrimination, the Future, and the Past," in *Ethics,* vol. 90 (October 1979): 81–87; and George Sher, "Preferential Hiring," in *Just Business*, Tom Regan, ed. (New York: Random House, Inc., 1984), pp. 32–59. An excellent discussion of affirmative action programs is Robert K. Fullinwider, *The Reverse Discrimination Controversy* (Totowa, NJ: Rowman and Littlefield, 1980).

77. Paul W. Taylor, "Reverse Discrimination and Compensatory Justice," *Analysis*, vol. 33 (1973): 177–82; see also Anne C. Minas, "How Reverse Discrimination Compensates Women," *Ethics,* vol. 88, no. 1 (October 1977): 74–79.

78. Bernard Boxhill, "The Morality of Reparations," *Social Theory and Practice*, vol. 2, no. 1 (1972): 113–22.

79. Alan H. Goldman, "Limits to the Justification of Reverse Discrimination," *Social Theory and Practice*, vol. 3, no. 3.

80. See Karst and Horowitz, "Affirmative Action and Equal Protection," *Virginia Law Review*, vol. 60 (1974).

81. There are innumerable discussions of this objection to the compensation justification; see, for example, the series: Michael Bayles, "Reparations to Wronged Groups," *Analysis,* 33, no. 6 (1973); L. J. Cowan, "Inverse Discrimination," *Analysis*, 33, no. 10 (1972); Roger Shiner, "Individuals, Groups, and Inverse Discrimination," *Analysis*, 33 (June 1973); Paul Taylor, "Reverse Discrimination and Compensatory Justice," *Analysis*, 33 (June 1973); James

Nickel, "Should Reparations Be to Individuals or Groups?" *Analysis*, 34, no. 9: 154–160; Alan H. Goldman, "Reparations to Individuals or Groups?" *Analysis*, 35, no. 5: 168–70.

82. Judith Jarvis Thomson, "Preferential Hiring," *Philosophy and Public Affairs*, vol. 2, no. 4 (Summer 1973): 381; for a similar claim with respect to Blacks, see Graham Hughes, "Reparation for Blacks?" *New York University Law Review*, vol. 43 (1968): 1072–73.

83. Martin H. Redish, "Preferential Law School Admissions and the Equal Protection Clause: An Analysis of the Competing Arguments," *University of California at Los Angeles Review* (1974), p. 389; see also Bernard R. Boxill, "The Morality of Preferential Hiring," *Philosophy and Public Affairs*, vol. 7, no. 3 (Spring 1978): 246–68.

84. Robert Simon, "Preferential Hiring: A Reply to Judith Jarvis Thomson," *Philosophy and Public Affairs*, vol. 3, no. 3 (Spring 1974): 312–20; Gertrude Ezorsky, "It's Mine," *Philosophy and Public Affairs*, vol. 3, no. 3 (Spring 1974): 321–30; Robert K. Fullinwider, "Preferential Hiring and Compensation," *Social Theory and Practice*, vol. 3, no. 3 (Spring 1975): 307–20.

85. For examples of utilitarian arguments, see Thomas Nagel, "Equal Treatment and Compensatory Discrimination," *Philosophy and Public Affairs*, vol. 2, no. 4 (Summer 1973): 348–63; James W. Nickel, "Preferential Policies in Hiring and Admissions, A Jurisprudential Approach," *Columbia Law Review*, vol. 75: 534–58; Ronald Dworkin, "The De Funis Case: The Right to Go to Law School," *New York Review of Books*, vol. 23, no. 1 (5 February 1976): 29–33.

86. Owen M. Fiss, "Groups and the Equal Protection Clause," *Philosophy and Public Affairs*, vol. 5, no. 2 (Winter 1976): 150–51.

87. James W. Nickel, "Classification of Race in Compensatory Programs," *Ethics,* vol. 84, no. 2 (1974): 146–50.

88. Virginia Black, "The Erosion of Legal Principles in the Creation of Legal Policies," *Ethics,* vol. 84, no. 3 (1974); William T. Blackstone, "Reverse Discrimination and Compensatory Justice," in Blackstone and Heslep, eds., *Social Justice and Preferential Treatment* (Athens, GA: University of Georgia Press, 1977).

89. Robert K. Fullinwider, "On Preferential Hiring," in Mary Vetterling-Braggin, Frederick A. Elliston, and Jane English, eds., *Feminism and Philosophy* (Totowa, NJ: Littlefield, Adams and Company, 1978), pp. 210–24.

90. See Nickel, "Preferential Policies."

91. Nagel, "Equal Treatment and Compensatory Discrimination."

92. Lawrence Crocker, "Preferential Treatment," in *Feminism and Philosophy*, Vetterling-Braggin et al., eds., pp. 190–204.

93. George Sher, "Justifying Reverse Discrimination in Employment," *Philosophy and Public Affairs*, vol. 4, no. 2 (Winter 1975): 159–70.

94. Carl and Callahan, "Negroes and the Law," *Journal of Legal Education*, vol. 17 (1965): 254.

95. Kaplan, "Equal Justice in an Unequal World," *N.W.U. Law Review*, vol. 61 (1966): 365.

96. Theodore V. Purcell and Gerald F. Cavanagh, *Blacks in the Industrial World* (New York: The Free Press, 1972), pp. 30–44. See also the articles on alternative feminist futures collected in Carol Gould, ed., *Beyond Domination* (Totowa, NJ: Rowman and Allenheld, 1983).

97. Carl Cohen, "Race and the Constitution," *The Nation*, 8 February 1975; Lisa H. Newton, "Reverse Discrimination as Unjustified," *Ethics*, vol. 83 (1973): 308–12.

98. Ronald Dworkin, "Why Bakke Has No Case."

99. *Ibid.*

100. For example, Glenn C. Loury, "Performing Without a Net," in Curry, ed., *Affirmative Action Debate.*

101. Shelby Steele, *The Content of Our Character: A New Vision of Race in America* (New York: St. Martin's Press, 1990), pp. 112, 113, 117–118.

102. Sonia L. Nazario, "Many Minorities Feel Torn by Experience of Affirmative Action," *Wall Street Journal*, 27 June 1989, pp. A1, A7.

103. *Ibid.*

104. Sidney Hook, "Discrimination Against the Qualified?" *New York Times*, 1971.

105. See Nickel, "Preferential Policics," p. 546.

106. For example, Gross, *Discrimination in Reverse*, p. 108; for a reply to Gross, see Boxill, "The Morality of Preferential Hiring."

107. Theodore V. Purcell, "A Practical Way to Use Ethics in Management Decisions," Paper for the Drew-Allied Chemical Workshop, June 26–27, 1980; and Nickel, "Preferential Policics."

108. Felice N. Schwartz, "Management Women and the New Facts of Life," *Harvard Business Review* (January-February, 1989), pp. 65–76.

109. Bolick and Nestleroth, *Opportunity 2000*, pp. 28–50.

110. Ibid., pp. 65–94; see also, Beverly Geber, "Managing Diversity," *Training*, pp. 23–30.

111. See Donald J. Trieman and Heidi I. Harmann, eds., *Women, Work, and Wages: Equal Pay for Jobs of Equal Value* (Washington, DC: National Academy Press, 1981); and *Comparable Worth: A Symposium on the Issues and Alternatives* (Washington, DC: Equal Employment Advisory Council, 1981).

112. Darla Miller, "On the Way to Equitable Pay," *San Jose Mercury News*, 15 July 1981, pp. 1C, 3C.

113. For these and other arguments, see "Paying Women What They're Worth," *Report from the Center for Philosophy & Public Policy*, University of Maryland, vol. 3, no. 2 (Spring 1983): 1–5.

114. See *Pay Equity: Equal Pay for Work of Comparable Value*, Joint Hearings before the Subcommittees on Human Resources, Civil Service, and Compensation and Employee Benefits of the Committee on Post Office and Civil Service, House of Representatives, September 16, 21, 30, and December 2, 1982 (Washington, DC: U.S. Government Printing Office, 1983); Caroline E. Mayer, "The Comparable Pay Debate," *The Washington Post National Weekly Edition*, 6 August 1984; Nina Totenberg, "Why Women Earn Less," *Parade Magazine*, 10 June 1984.

115. Joanne Jacobs, "Only the Market Can Establish Comparable Worth," *San Jose Mercury News*, 12 October 1984, p. 7B.

116. Quoted in Investor Responsibility Research Center, "Equal Employment Opportunity, 1990 Analysis E" (Washington, DC: Investor Responsibility Research Center, Inc., 1990.), pp. 3–4.

CASES FOR DISCUSSION

Wage Differences at Robert Hall

Robert Hall Clothes, Inc., owned a chain of retail stores that specialized in clothing for the family.[1] One of the chain's stores was located in Wilmington, Delaware. The Robert Hall store in Wilmington had a department for men's and boys' clothing and another department for women's and girl's clothing. The departments were physically separated and were staffed by different personnel: Only men were allowed to work in the men's department and only women in the women's department. The personnel of the store were sexually segregated because years of experience had taught the store's managers that, unless clerks and customers were of the same sex, the frequent physical contact between clerks and customers would embarrass both and would inhibit sales.

The clothing in the men's department was generally of a higher and more expensive quality than the clothing in the women's department. Competitive factors accounted for this: There were few other men's stores in Wilmington so the store could stock expensive men's clothes and still do a thriving business, whereas women's clothing had to be lower priced to compete with the many other women's stores in Wilmington. Because of these differences in merchandise, the store's profit margins on the men's clothing was higher than its margins on the women's clothing. As a result, the men's department consistently showed a larger dollar volume in gross sales and a greater gross profit, as is indicated in Table 7.11.

Because of the differences shown in Table 7.11, women personnel brought in lower sales and profits per hour. In fact, male salespersons brought in substantially more than the females did (see Tables 7.12 and 7.13).

TABLE 7.11

	Men's Department			Women's Department		
Year	Sales ($)	Gross Profit ($)	Percent Profit (%)	Sales ($)	Gross Profit ($)	Percent Profit (%)
1963	210,639	85,328	40.5	177,742	58,547	32.9
1964	178,867	73,608	41.2	142,788	44,612	31.2
1965	206,472	89,930	43.6	148,252	49,608	33.5
1966	217,765	97,447	44.7	166,479	55,463	33.3
1967	244,922	111,498	45.5	206,680	69,190	33.5
1968	263,663	123,681	46.9	230,156	79,846	34.7
1969	316,242	248,001	46.8	254,379	91,687	36.4

TABLE 7.12

Year	Male Sales Per Hour ($)	Female Sales Per Hour ($)	Excess M Over F (%)
1963	38.31	27.31	40
1964	40.22	30.36	32
1965	54.77	33.30	64
1966	59.58	34.31	73
1967	63.14	36.92	71
1968	62.27	37.20	70
1969	73.00	41.26	77

As a result of these differences in the income produced by the two departments, the management of Robert Hall paid their male salespersons more than their female personnel. Management learned after a Supreme Court ruling in their favor in 1973 that it was entirely legal for them to do this if they wanted. Wages in the store were set on the basis of profits per hour per department, with some slight adjustments upward to ensure wages were comparable and competitive to what other stores in the area were paying. Over the years, Robert Hall set the wages given in Table 7.14. Although the wage differences between males and females were substantial, they were not as large as the percentage differences between male and female sales and profits. The management of Robert Hall argued that their female clerks were paid less because the commodities they sold could not bear the same selling costs that the commodities sold in the men's department could bear. However, the female clerks argued, the skills, sales efforts, and responsibilities required of male and female clerks were "substantially" the same.

TABLE 7.13

Year	Male Gross Profits Per Hour ($)	Female Gross Profits Per Hour ($)	Excess M Over F (%)
1963	15.52	9.00	72
1964	16.55	9.49	74
1965	23.85	11.14	114
1966	26.66	11.43	134
1967	28.74	12.36	133
1968	29.21	12.91	127
1969	34.16	15.03	127

TABLE 7.14

Year	Male Earnings Per Hour ($)	Female Earnings Per Hour ($)	Excess M Over F (%)
1963	2.18	1.75	25
1964	2.46	1.86	32
1965	2.67	1.80	48
1966	2.92	1.95	50
1967	2.88	1.98	45
1968	2.97	2.02	47
1969	3.13	2.16	45

QUESTIONS

1. In your judgment, do the managers of the Robert Hall store have any ethical obligations to change their salary policies? If you do not think they should change, then explain why their salary policy is ethically justified; if you think they should change, then explain why they have an obligation to change and describe the kinds of changes they should make. Would it make any difference to your analysis if, instead of two departments in the same store, it involved two different Robert Hall stores, one for men and one for women? Would it make a difference if two stores (one for men and one for women) owned by different companies were involved? Explain each of your answers in terms of the relevant ethical principles upon which you are relying.
2. Suppose that there were very few males applying for clerks' jobs in Wilmington while females were flooding the clerking job market. Would this competitive factor justify paying males more than females? Why? Suppose that 95 percent of the women in Wilmington who were applying for clerks' jobs were single women with children who were on welfare while 95 percent of the men were single with no families to support. Would this *need* factor justify paying females more than males? Why? Suppose for the sake of argument that men were better at selling than women; would this justify different salaries?
3. If you think the managers of the Robert Hall store should pay their male and female clerks equal wages because they do "substantially the same work," then do you also think that ideally each worker's salary should be pegged to the work he or she individually performs (such as by having each worker sell on commission)? Why? Would a commission system be preferable from a utilitarian point of view considering the substantial bookkeeping expenses it would involve? From the point of view of justice? What does the phrase *substantially the same* mean to you?

NOTE

1. Information for this case is drawn entirely from *Hodgson v. Robert Hall Clothes, Inc.*, 473 F. 2nd 589, cert. denied, 42 U.S.L.W. 3198 (9 October 1973) and 326 F. Supp. 1264 (D. Del. 1971).

Brian Weber[1]

The Kaiser Aluminum plant in Gramercy, Louisiana, opened in 1958. From the beginning, the Kaiser Gramercy plant had relatively few Black workers. By 1965, although 39 percent of the local work force was Black, Kaiser had hired only 4.7 percent Blacks. In 1970, a federal review of Kaiser employment practices at the Gramercy plant found that of 50 professional employees, none were Black; of 132 supervisors, only 1 was Black; and of 246 skilled craftworkers, none were Black. A 1973 federal review found that, although Kaiser had allowed several Whites with no prior craft experience to transfer into the skilled craft positions, Blacks were not transferred unless they possessed at least 5 years of prior craft experience. Since Blacks were largely excluded from the crafts unions, they were rarely able to acquire such experience. As a result, only 2 percent of the skilled craftworkers at Gramercy were Black. A third federal review in 1975 found that 2.2 percent of Kaiser Gramercy's 290 craftworkers were Black; that of 72 professional employees, only 7 percent were Black; and that of 11 draftsmen, none were Black. Moreover, although the local labor market in 1975 was still 39 percent Black, the Kaiser Gramercy plant's overall work force was only 13.3 percent Black. Only the lowest-paying category of jobs—unskilled laborers—included a large proportion (35.5 percent) of Blacks, a proportion that was brought about by implementing a 1968 policy of hiring one Black unskilled worker for every White unskilled worker.

By 1974, Kaiser was being pressured by federal agencies to increase the number of Blacks in its better paying skilled crafts positions. Moreover, the U.S. Steelworkers Union was simultaneously pressing Kaiser to institute a program for training its own workers in the crafts, instead of hiring all its crafts workers from outside the company. As a response to both of these pressures, Kaiser agreed in 1974 to set up a training program that was intended to qualify its own workers (both White and Black) for crafts positions, and that was also intended to eliminate the manifest racial imbalance in its crafts positions. According to the agreement with the union, Kaiser workers would be trained for crafts positions, in order of seniority, at Kaiser's own expense ($15,000–20,000 per year per trainee). One half of the slots in the crafts training program would be reserved for Blacks until the percentage of Black skilled craftworkers in the Gramercy plant approximated the percentage of Blacks in the local labor force. Openings in the program would be filled by alternating between the most senior qualified White employee and the most senior qualified Black employee.

During the first year of the program, 13 workers were selected for the training program: seven Blacks and six Whites. Brian Weber, a young White worker who had applied to the program, was not among those selected. Brian, a talkative, likeble southerner and father of three, had been working as a blue-collar lab analyst in the Gramercy plant. His position was rated as *semiskilled*. He wanted very much to enter one of the skilled jobs. On investigation, Weber found that he had several months more seniority than two of the Black workers who had been admitted into the training program. Forty-three other White workers who were also rejected had even more seniority than he did. Junior Black employees were thus receiving training in preference to more senior White employees. Weber later found that none of the Black workers who had been admitted to the program had been the subject of any prior employment discrimination by Kaiser.[2]

Questions

1. In your judgment, was the Kaiser plant practicing discrimination? If you believe it was discriminating, explain what kind of discrimination was involved and identify the evidence for your judgment. If you believe it was not discriminatory, prepare responses to the strongest objections to your own view. Was Kaiser management morally responsible for the situation in its plant? Why?
2. In your judgment, did the management of Kaiser act rightly when it implemented its preferential treatment program? Explain your judgment in terms of the ethical principles that you think are involved. Does the fact that none of the Black workers had been subject to any prior employment discrimination by Kaiser absolve Kaiser from any ethical duty to rectify the racial imbalance in its workforce? What policies would you have recommended for Kaiser?
3. Was Brian Weber treated fairly or unfairly? Explain your judgment on the basis of the moral principles that you think are involved. What is the value of seniority relative to equality of opportunity? As a manager, how would you have dealt with Brian and others who felt as he did? Should seniority serve as a basis for deciding who gets trained for a job? What kinds of qualifications do you believe should be taken into account?

Notes

1. See Rick Harris and Jack Hartog, "The Catch-22 Case," Civil Rights Digest, vol. 11, no. 2 (Winter 1979): 2–11.
2. Weber subsequently sued Kaiser and the case was eventually heard by the U.S. Supreme Court. The Court ruled that Kaiser's affirmative action program was not in violation of the Civil Rights Act of 1964.

8

The Individual in the Organization

Introduction

What are organizations like? Here are some descriptions of life inside organizations by three people positioned at different organizational levels.

Spot-Welder at a Ford Assembly Plant:

> I start the automobile, the first welds. . . . The welding gun's got a square handle, with a button on the top for high voltage and a button on the bottom for low. . . . We do about thirty-two jobs per car, per unit. Forty-eight units an hour, eight hours a day. Thirty-two times forty-eight times eight. Figure it out. That's how many times I push that button. . . . It don't stop. It just goes and goes and goes. . . . I don't like the pressure, the intimidation. How would you like to go up to someone and say, "I would like to go to the bathroom?" If the foreman doesn't like you, he'll make you hold it, just ignore you. . . . Oh, yeah, the foreman's got somebody knuckling down on him, putting the screws to him. But a foreman is still free to go the bathroom, go get a cup of coffee. He doesn't face the penalties. . . . When a man becomes a foreman, he has to forget about even being human, as far as feelings are concerned. You see a guy there bleeding to death. So what, buddy? That line's gotta keep goin'.[1]

PLANT MANAGER AT FORD ASSEMBLY PLANT:

I'm usually here at seven o'clock. . . . Then I go out on the floor, tour the plant. . . . I'll change my tour so they can't tell every day I'm going to be in the same place at the same time. The worst thing I could do is set a pattern where they'll always know where I'll be. I'm always stopping to talk to foremen or hourly fellas. . . . I may see a water leak, I say to the foreman, "Did you call maintenance?" Not do it myself, let him go do it. By the time I get back in the office, I have three or four calls, "Can you help me on this?" This is how you keep in contact. . . . The operating committee meets usually every other day: my assistant plant managers; an operations manager, he has two production managers; a controller; an engineering manager; a quality control manager; and a materials manager. That's the eight key figures in the plant. . . . You can't run a business sitting in the office 'cause you get divorced too much from the people. The people are the key to the whole thing. If you aren't in touch with the people they think he's too far aloof, he's distant. It doesn't work.[2]

EX-PRESIDENT OF CONGLOMERATE:

I don't know of any situation in the corporate world where an executive is completely free and sure of his job from moment to moment. . . . The danger starts as soon as you become a district manager. You have men working for you and you have a boss above. You're caught in a squeeze. The squeeze progresses from station to station. I'll tell you what a squeeze is. You have the guys working for you that are shooting for your job. The guy you're working for is scared stiff you're gonna shove him out of his job. . . . There's always the insecurity. You bungle a job. You're fearful of losing a big customer. You're fearful so many things will appear on your record, stand against you. You're always fearful of the big mistake. You've got to be careful when you go to corporation parties. Your wife, your children have to behave properly. You've got to fit in the mold. You've got to be on guard. When I was president of this big corporation . . . [the] corporation specified who you could socialize with, and on what level. . . . The executive is a lonely animal in the jungle who doesn't have a friend.[3]

Not everyone experiences organizations as these three people have. Nonetheless, these three descriptions of organizational life touch on many of the most problematic characteristics of business organizations: the alienation experienced by workers doing repetitive work, the feelings of oppression created by the exercise of authority, the responsibilities heaped on the shoulders of managers, the power tactics employed by managers anxious to advance their career ambitions, and the pressures felt by subordinates and superiors as they both try to get their jobs done. Other problems could be added to the list: health problems created by unsafe working conditions, conflicts of interest created by an employee's allegiance to other causes, absence of due process for nonunionized employees, and invasion of privacy by management's legitimate concern to know its own workers. The list could go on.

This chapter explores these and other problems raised by life within business organizations. The chapter is divided into three main parts. The first part begins by describing the traditional model of the organization: the organization as a "rational" structure. The following sections then discuss the employee's duties to the firm as defined by this traditional model, and the employer's duties to the employee, again as defined by this model. The second main part of the chapter turns to describing a more recent view of the organization: the organization as a "political" structure. The sections in this part of the chapter discuss the two main ethical issues raised by this more recent "political" analysis of the firm: employee rights and organizational politics. The third main part of the chapter discusses a new view of the organization: the organization as a network of personal relations focused on caring. The discussion of this third, most recent, and still emerging view is, of necessity, much briefer than the earlier discussions, which have a much longer history of development.

8.1 The Rational Organization

The more traditional, "rational" model of a business organization defines the organization as a structure of formal (explicitly defined and openly employed) relationships designed to achieve some technical or economic goal with maximum efficiency.[4] E. H. Schein provides a compact definition of an organization from this perspective:

> An organization is the rational coordination of the activities of a number of people for the achievement of some common explicit purpose or goal, through division of labor and function and through a hierarchy of authority and responsibility.[5]

If the organization is looked at in this way, then the most fundamental realities of the organization are the formal hierarchies of authority identified in the organizational chart that represents the various official positions and lines of authority in the organization. Figure 8.1 provides a simplified example.

At the bottom of the organization is the "operating layer": those employees and their immediate supervisors who directly produce the goods and services that constitute the essential outputs of the organization. The work of the Ford spot-welder quoted at the beginning of this chapter was located at this level. Above the operating layer of laborers are ascending levels of "middle managers" who direct the units below them and who are in turn directed by those above them in ascending formal lines of authority. The plant manager quoted earlier worked within these middle levels of the organization. At the apex of the pyramid

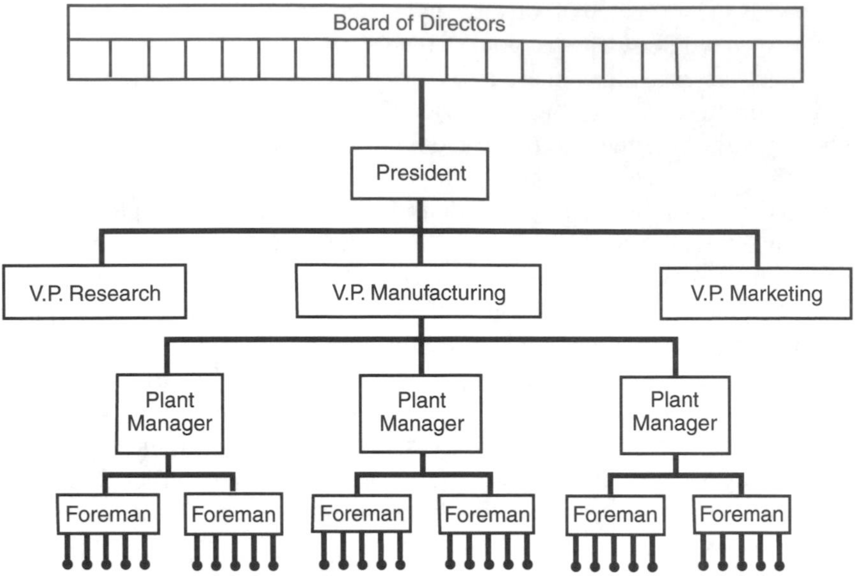

Figure 8.1

is top management: the board of directors, the chief executive officer, and his or her staff. The ex-president quoted earlier inhabited these upper levels of the organization.

The rational model of an organization supposes that most information is collected from the operating layers of the organization, rises through the various formal management levels, each of which aggregates the information, until it reaches top-management levels. On the basis of this information, the top managers make general policy decisions and issue general commands, which are then passed downward through the formal hierarchy, where they are amplified at each managerial level until they reach the operating layer as detailed work instructions. These decisions of the top managers are assumed to be designed to achieve some known and common economic goal such as efficiency, productivity, profits, maximum return on investment, and so on. The goal is defined by those at the top of the hierarchy of authority, who are assumed to have a legitimate right to make this decision.

What is the glue that holds together the organization's many layers of employees and managers and that fixes these people onto the organization's goals and formal hierarchy? Contracts. The model conceives of the employee as an agent who freely and knowingly agreed to accept the organization's formal authority and to pursue its goals in exchange for support in the form of a wage and fair working conditions. These contractual agreements cement each employee into the organization by formally defining each employee's duties and scope of authority. By virtue of this contractual agreement, the employee has a moral responsibility to obey the employer in the course of pursuing the organization's goals, and the organization in turn has a moral responsibility to provide the employee with the economic supports it has promised. As we have already discussed at some length, when two persons knowingly and freely agree to exchange goods or services with each other, each party to the agreement acquires a moral obligation to fulfill the terms of the contract. Utilitarian theory provides additional support for the view that the employee has an obligation to loyally pursue the goals of the firm: Businesses could not function efficiently and productively if their employees were not single-mindedly devoted to pursuing their firm's goals. If each employee were free to use the resources of the firm to pursue his or her own ends, chaos would ensue and everyone's utility would decline.

The basic ethical responsibilities that emerge from these "rational" aspects of the organization focus on two reciprocal moral obligations: (a) the obligation of the employee to obey organizational superiors, pursue the organization's goals, and avoid any activities that might threaten that goal; and (b) the obligation of the employer to provide the employee with a fair wage and fair working conditions. These duties in turn are presumed to be defined through the organization's formal lines of authority and through the contracts that specify the employee's duties and working conditions. We examine these two reciprocal duties in turn.

8.2 The Employee's Obligations to the Firm

In the rational view of the firm, the employee's main moral duty is to work toward the goals of the firm and avoid any activities that might harm those goals. To be unethical, basically, is to deviate from these goals to serve one's own interests in ways that, if illegal, are counted as a form of "white collar crime."[6]

As administrator of the company's finances, for example, the financial manager is entrusted with its funds and has the responsibility of managing those funds in a way that will minimize risk while ensuring a suitable rate of return for the company's shareholders. Financial managers have this contractual duty to the firm and its investors because they have contracted to provide the firm with their best judgment and to exercise their authority only in the pursuit of the goals of the firm and not for their own personal benefit. Financial managers fail in their contractual duty to the firm when they misappropriate funds, when they waste or squander funds, when they are negligent or fraudulent in the preparation of financial statements, when they issue false or misleading reports, and so on.

These traditional views of the employee's duties to the firm have, of course, made their way into the "law of agency"—that is, the law that specifies the legal duties of "agents" (employees) toward their "principals."[7] The "restatement" of the law of agency, for example, states in Section 385 that, "an agent is subject to a duty to his principal to act solely for the benefit of the principal in all matters connected with his agency"; and Section 394 prohibits the agent from acting "for persons whose interests conflict with those of the principal in matters in which the agent is employed."[8] In short, the employee must pursue the goals of the firm and must do nothing that conflicts with those goals while he or she is working for the firm.

There are several ways in which the employee might fail to live up to the duty to pursue the goals of the firm: The employee might act on a "conflict of interest," the employee might steal from the firm, or the employee might use his or her position as leverage to force illicit benefits out of others through extortion or commercial bribery. We turn now to examine the ethical issues raised by these tactics.

Conflicts of Interest

Conflicts of interest in business arise when an employee or officer of a company is engaged in carrying out a task on behalf of the company and the employee has a private interest in the outcome of the task that is (a) possibly antagonistic to the best interests of the company, and (b) substantial enough that it does or reasonably might affect the independent judgment the company expects the employee to exercise on its behalf.[9] More simply, conflicts of interest arise when the self-interest of employees in positions of trust leads them to discharge their offices in ways that may not be in the best interests of the firm. An official of a corporation, for example, is involved in a conflict of interest if he holds stock in one of the companies submitting bids for a construction contract. His interest in seeing the value of the stock improve may tempt him to give the contract to the building company in which he holds stock, although it did not offer the best terms to the corporation for which he works.

Conflicts of interest need not be financial. For example, if my daughter-in-law is a saleswoman for a firm that manufactures the type of tools that my company purchases, I have an interest in seeing her succeed and may be motivated to give her my company's business even although other firms may offer better terms.

Conflicts of interest can also arise when officers or employees of one company hold another job or consulting position in an outside firm with which their own company deals or competes. An employee of one bank, for example, could be involved in a conflict of interest if he or she took a job serving a competing bank or took a job serving an insurance company that leased the employee's own bank's equipment or facilities. At the very least, the employee's loyalties would be divided between serving the interests of each competing firm.

Similarly, a conflict of interest would be created if an accountant working for an insurance company also provides "independent" auditing services for some of the firms the insurance company insures: The accountant might be tempted to pass on to the insurance company some of the private information gathered when auditing the books of those other firms.

Conflicts of interest may be actual or potential.[10] An actual conflict of interest occurs when a person actually discharges his or her duties in a way that is prejudicial to the firm and does it out of self-interest. A potential conflict of interest occurs when a person is merely motivated or tempted by self-interest to act in a way that is prejudicial to the firm. In the first case cited, for example, the official of the corporation is involved in a merely potential conflict of interest, so long as his judgment is not biased by his stockholdings and he gives the contract to the construction company that offers his employer the best terms. The conflict of interest becomes actual if his judgment is biased toward the construction company in which he holds stock, and he acts on this bias.

If we accept the view (outlined in Chapter 2) that agreements impose moral duties, then actual conflicts of interest are unethical because they are contrary to the implied contract that a worker freely accepts when taking a job with a firm. The administrative personnel of a firm are hired to use their unbiased judgment to advance the goals of the firm. By accepting the position within the firm, the employee contracts to administer the assets of the firm in accordance with these goals and in return takes the salary connected with fulfilling this administrative task. To break this contractual relation violates the rights and duties created by the contract.

Potential conflicts of interest may or may not be ethical depending on the probability that the employee's judgment will be affected by the conflicting interest or will appear to be affected. Obviously, there are no general rules for determining whether an employee's private and conflicting interests are significant enough to affect his or her judgment: Much depends on the employee's personal psychology and intentions, the employee's position in the firm and the nature of his or her job, how much he or she stands to gain from the transactions involved, and the impact the employee's actions will have on others inside and outside the firm. To avoid problems, many companies (a) specify the amount of stock that the company will allow employees to hold in supplier firms; (b) specify the relationships with competitors, buyers, or suppliers that the company prohibits employees from having; and (c) require key officers to disclose all their outside financial investments.

Conflicts of interest can be created by a variety of different kinds of situations and activities. Two kinds of situations and activities demand further attention: bribes and gifts.

Commercial Bribes and Extortion A commercial bribe is a consideration given or offered to an employee by a person outside the firm with the understanding that, when the employee transacts business for his or her own firm, the employee will deal favorably with that person or that person's firm. The consideration may consist of money, tangible goods, the "kickback" of part of an official payment, preferential treatment, or any other kind of benefit. A purchasing agent, for example, is accepting a bribe when he or she accepts money from a supplier who gives it to the agent to receive favored treatment in the agent's purchasing decisions. In contrast, an employee is engaged in commercial extortion if the employee demands a consideration from persons outside the firm as a condition for dealing favorably with those persons when the employee transacts business for his or her firm. For example, purchasing agents who will buy only from those salespeople who give them certain goods or services are involved in extortion. Extortion and the acceptance of bribes obviously create a conflict of interest that violates the moral duty that the employee's work contract establishes—that is, the duty to use one's unbiased judgment in the pursuit of the employer's legitimately established goals.

Gifts Accepting gifts may or may not be ethical. The purchasing agent, for example, who accepts gifts from the salesperson with whom he or she deals without asking for the gifts and without making such gifts a condition of doing business with them may be doing nothing unethical. If the agent does not give favored treatment to those from whom he or she accepts gifts and is not prejudiced against those who fail to give a "gift," no actual conflict of interest is created. A potential conflict of interest, however, may exist and the act may encourage a practice that in some instances becomes an actual conflict of interest or that may be subtly affecting the independence of a person's judgment. Vincent Barry suggests that the following factors should be considered when evaluating the morality of accepting a gift:[11]

1. What is the value of the gift? That is, is it substantial enough to influence one's decisions?
2. What is the purpose of the gift? That is, is the gift intended or accepted as a bribe?
3. What are the circumstances under which the gift was given? That is, was the gift given openly? Was it given to celebrate a special event (Christmas, a birthday, a store opening)?
4. What is the position of the recipient of the gift? That is, is the recipient in a position to influence his own firm's dealings with the giver of the gift?
5. What is the accepted business practice in the area? That is, is the gift part of an open and well-known industry practice?
6. What is the company's policy? That is, does the company forbid acceptance of such gifts?
7. What is the law? That is, is the gift forbidden by a law, such as a law prohibiting gifts in sports recruiting?

Employee Theft and Computers

The employee of a firm has a contractual agreement to accept only certain specified benefits in exchange for his labor and to use the resources and goods of the firm in pursuit only of the legitimate aims of the firm. For the employee to appropriate additional benefits for him or herself or to convert company resources to the employee's own use are forms of theft because to do either is to take or use property that belongs to another (the employer) without the consent of its rightful owner.

Employee theft is often petty, involving the theft of small tools, office supplies, or clothing. At the managerial level, petty theft sometimes occurs through the manipulation or padding of expense accounts, although the amounts involved are sometimes substantial. Other forms of managerial theft, sometimes referred to as *white collar crime*, are embezzlement, larceny, fraud in the handling of trusts or receiverships, and forgery. The ethics of these forms of theft, however, are relatively clear. Not always as clear are some particularly modern kinds of theft: thefts involving various forms of information and the use of computers.

Computer Theft What are the ethics of using a computer to gain entry into a company's data bank? Of copying a company's computer programs? Of using or copying a company's computerized data? Of using a company computer during one's own time? Unless authorized explicitly or through a company's formal or informal policies, all such activities are unethical forms of theft because they all involve taking or using property that belongs to someone else without the consent of its rightful owners. Of course, the information contained in a data bank and the programs provided by a company are not tangible property, and the employee who examines, uses, or copies such information or programs might leave the original information or programs unchanged (the company might never even realize what the employee did). Nevertheless, unauthorized examination, use, or copying of computer information or programs constitutes theft. It is theft because information gathered in a computer bank by a company and computer programs developed or purchased by a company are the property of that company.

Such theft is best understood by considering the nature of property, which we examined in Chapter 3: Property consists of a bundle of rights that attach to some identifiable asset. The most important of these rights are the right to exclusive use of the asset; the right to decide whether and how others may use the asset; the right to sell, trade, or give away the asset; the right to any income generated by the asset; and the right to modify or change the asset.[12] (These rights, of course, are limited by the rights of others, such as the right not to be harmed.) All of these rights can and do attach to those computers, computer data, and computer programs that a company used its own resources to develop or that the company purchased with its own resources. Consequently, such information or programs are the property of the company, and only the company has the right to its use or benefits. To usurp any of the rights that attach to property, including the rights pertaining to use, is a form of property theft and is, therefore, unethical.

Trade Secrets "Proprietary information" or "trade secrets" consist of nonpublic information that (a) concerns a company's own activities, technologies, future plans, policies, or records and that, if known by competitors, would materially affect the company's ability to compete commercially against those competitors; (b) is owned by the company (although it might not be patented or copyrighted) because it was developed by the company for its private use from resources it owns or was purchased for its private use from others with its own funds; and (c) the company indicates through explicit directives, security measures, or contractual agreements with employees that it does not want anyone outside the company to have that information. For example, if a company, using its own engineering and laboratory resources, develops a secret process to manufacture computer diskettes that can carry more computer data than any other company's disks, and it takes explicit measures to ensure that process is not known to anyone else, detailed information about that process is a *trade secret.* Similarly, lists of suppliers or customers, research results, formulas, computer programs, computer data, marketing and production plans, and any other information developed by a company for its own private use from its own resources can all constitute trade secrets. Because employees, especially those involved in company research and development, often have access to trade secrets that the company must entrust to them if it is to carry on its business, they often have the opportunity to use such secrets for their own advantage by dealing with competitors. Such use of trade secrets by employees is unethical because it is using the property of another agent for a purpose not sanctioned by that other agent, and because the employee has an implied (or even, in some cases, an explicit) contract not to use company resources for purposes not sanctioned by the company.[13] For example, a female engineering employee who is hired to oversee the development of a secret manufacturing process that gives her company a competitive edge over others acts wrongly if she decides to leave that company to work for a competitor that promises her a higher salary in exchange for setting up the same process she developed while being paid to do so by her former employer.

However, skills that an employee acquires by working for a company do not count as trade secrets because trade secrets consist of information and not skills. The skills that an employee develops are considered part of his or her own person and are not the property of an employer, as is proprietary information. Unfortunately, it is not always easy to distinguish skills from trade secrets. The situation, for example, might resemble that of Donald Wohlgemuth, a general manager dissatisfied with his salary and his working conditions, who oversaw a B. F. Goodrich secret technology for making spacesuits for the government.[14]

Wohlgemuth subsequently negotiated a job with International Latex, a Goodrich competitor, at a much higher salary. At Latex, however, he was to manage a division that involved, among other things, the manufacture of spacesuits for the government. Goodrich managers objected to his working for a competitor where he might use the information and skills Goodrich had paid to develop. When they questioned the ethics of his decision, Wohlgemuth heatedly replied that, "loyalty and ethics have their price and International Latex has paid the price." The Ohio Court of Appeals ruled that Goodrich could not keep Wohlgemuth from selling his skills to another competitor, but it imposed on Wohlgemuth an injunction restraining him from disclosing to Latex any of the trade secrets of B. F. Goodrich. However, the court did not explain how Wohlgemuth, Goodrich, or Latex were to distinguish between the information and the skills Wohlgemuth had acquired while working for Goodrich.

Some companies have tried to avoid the problem of trade secrets by having employees sign contracts agreeing not to work for competitors for 1 or 2 years after leaving the company, but courts have generally rejected the validity of such contracts. Other companies have dealt with these problems by agreeing to provide departing employees with continuing remuneration or future retirement benefits in exchange for their not revealing proprietary information.

The ethical issue of misusing proprietary information has become much more prominent in the last decade as new "information technologies" (such as the computer) have increasingly turned information into a valuable asset to which employees have regular access. As information technologies continue to develop, this issue will continue to grow in importance.

Before leaving the subject of proprietary information, it is worth recalling that a company's property rights over proprietary information are not unlimited. In particular, they are limited by the rights of other agents, such as the rights of employees to know the health risks associated with their jobs. A company's right to keep information secret is not absolute, but must be balanced against the legitimate rights of others.

Insider Trading

As a start, we can define *insider trading* as the act of buying and selling a company's stock on the basis of "inside" information about the company. "Inside" or "insider" information about a company is confidential or proprietary information about a company that is not available to the general public outside the company, but that would have a material or significant impact on the price of the company's stock. For example, the president of a defense company may learn that the company is about to receive a multibillion-dollar contract from the government before any member of the outside public is aware of this. This president may then purchase a large block of the stock of her company, knowing that its value will rise when the news of the contract becomes public and other buyers and sellers of stock bid up its price. The purchase of stock is insider trading. The president may also tip off one's father, who also hurries out to buy some stock before the general public learns about the contract. His purchase is also insider trading.

Insider trading is illegal. During the past decade, a large number of stockbrokers, bankers, and managers were prosecuted for insider trading. Insider trading is also unethical—not merely because it is illegal, but because, it is claimed, the person who trades on insider information in effect "steals" this information and thereby gains an unjust or unfair advantage over the member of the general public.[15] However, several people have argued that insider trading is actually socially beneficial and, on utilitarian grounds, should not be prohibited but encouraged.[16]

First, it is sometimes argued, the insider and his friends bring their inside information to the stock market and, by trading on it, bid up the price of the stock (or bid it down) so that its stock market price rises (or falls) to reflect the true underlying value of the stock. Experts on the stock market tell us that the stock market functions most efficiently when the market price of each company's stock equals the true underlying value of the stock as determined by the information available. When insiders trade stocks on their inside information and bid up (or down) the value of stocks, they in effect bring their information to the market and, by their purchases, "signal" to others the information they have about what those stocks are really worth. So insider traders perform the valuable service of making their inside information available to the stock market, thereby ensuring that the market value of stocks more accurately reflects their true underlying value and securing a more efficient market.

Second, it is argued, insider trading does not harm anyone. Critics of insider trading sometimes claim that the insider who has special "inside" information somehow harms those people who unwittingly sell their stocks to him or her, not realizing that he or she knows their stocks are worth more than he or she is paying them for the stock. But those who defend the ethics of insider trading point out that when people sell their stocks it is because they need or want the money at that moment. Regardless of whether they sell to the insider or some other party, they will get whatever the current market price of their stock is. Later, of course, when the insider's information becomes available to everyone, they will regret selling because the value of the stock they sold will rise. Yet at the moment they wanted to sell their stock, they would not have gotten more for their stock from others than what the insider gave them. Moreover, the defenders of insider trading argue, when insiders begin buying up stock on the basis of their inside information, the price of the stock gradually begins to rise. This means that people who need to sell their stocks during that period of rising prices will get more for their stock than they would have received if the insider had not stepped in to raise the price. Therefore, not only does the insider not harm those who sell stocks to him right from the beginning, he also benefits those who sell stocks to him or others later.

Third, the defenders of insider trading argue, it is untrue that the insider trader has an unfair advantage over others who do not have access to his inside information. The fact is that many of the people who buy and sell stocks on the stock market have more or better information than others. For example, experts tell us that they can analyze and research coming economic trends, future industry events, probable new discoveries, and other occurrences, and that they can use their analyses to generate information about the value of certain stocks not generally available to the public. There is clearly nothing wrong or unfair about this. More generally, there is nothing basically unethical or unfair about having an information advantage over others in the stock market.

Those who claim that insider trading is unethical, however, point out that the defenders of insider trading conveniently ignore several important facts about insider trading. First, the information that the insider trader uses does not belong to him. The executives, managers, employees, and others who work inside a company and who are aware of inside events that will affect the price of the company's stock do not own the company. The resources they work with, including the information that the company makes available to them, are resources that belong collectively to the shareholders. Employees have an ethical (or "fiduciary") duty to refrain from using company information to benefit themselves or their friends. Just as all employees have an ethical duty to use company resources only for the benefit of the shareholder-owners, so also do they have an ethical duty to use company information only for the benefit of shareholder-owners. Therefore, an insider who takes confidential inside company information and uses it to enrich himself is in effect a thief stealing what is not his. Like any common thief who violates the moral rights of those from whom he steals, the insider trader is violating the moral rights of all shareholders, especially those who unwittingly sell him their stock.

Second, argue those who hold that insider trading is unethical, the information advantage of the insider really is unfair or unjust. Because the information of the insider is information that he stole, it is quite unlike the information advantage of stock experts or analysts. The information advantage of the insider is unfair because it is unjustly stolen from others—the company's owners—who made the investments that ultimately produced the information he stole. The insider's advantage ultimately comes from stealing the fruits of someone else's labor or resources. This is quite unlike the information advantage of the analyst who owns the information he uses because it was produced through his own labors or purchases.

Third, argue those who claim that insider trading is unethical, it is untrue that no one is harmed by insider trading. Both empirical and theoretical studies have shown that insider trading has two effects on the stock market that are harmful to everyone in the market and to society in general. First, insider trading tends to reduce the size of the market, and this harms everyone. Everyone knows that the insider has an advantage over others, so the more inside trading that people suspect is going on in the market, the more they will tend to leave the market and the smaller it will get. The reduced size of the market will have a number of harmful effects, including (a) a decline in the liquidity of stocks because it is harder to find buyers and sellers for stock; (b) an increase in the variability of stock prices because small variations will make relatively larger differences in the smaller market; (c) a decline in the market's ability to spread risk because there are fewer parties among whom to spread risks; (d) a decline in market efficiency due to the reduced number of buyers and sellers; and (e) a decline in the utility gains available to traders because of the decline in available trades.[17]

The second effect of insider trading is that it increases the costs of buying and selling stocks in the market (i.e., the transaction costs), and this is also harmful. Stocks in the New York stock market are always bought and sold through an intermediary called a *specialist*, who charges a small fee for purchasing the stocks of those who want to sell and for holding the stocks for those who want to buy them later. When a specialist senses that insiders are coming to him, he will realize that the stocks insiders are selling to him and, which he will have to hold for others, might later turn out to be worth far less (otherwise why would the insiders with their inside information have gotten rid of them?). Therefore, to cover himself from potential future losses, he will start to raise the fee he charges for his services as an intermediary (by increasing the bid-ask spread). The more insiders there are, the more the specialist must raise his fees, and the more costly it becomes to make stock exchanges. Although in the extreme case the costs may rise so high that the market in a stock breaks down completely, in the less extreme case the rising costs will merely make the stock market just that much more inefficient. In either case, insider trading has a harmful effect on the market.[18]

There are then good reasons supporting the view that insider trading is unethical on the grounds that it violates people's rights, that it is based on an unjust informational advantage, and that it harms society's overall utility. In short, insider trading violates our standards of rights, justice, and utility. But the issue continues to be greatly debated and is still not completely settled.

The law on insider trading, however, is fairly settled, although its exact scope is unclear. The Securities and Exchange Commission (SEC) has prosecuted a large number of insider trading cases, and court decisions in these cases have tended to establish that insider trading is illegal. It has been determined that it consists of trading in a security while in possession of nonpublic information that can have a material effect on the price of the security, and that was acquired, or was known to have been acquired, in violation of a person's duty to keep the information confidential.[19] As this definition indicates, it is not just company employees who can be guilty of insider trading, but anyone who knowingly buys or sells stock using information that they know was acquired by a person who had a duty to keep that information confidential. That is, anyone is guilty who trades on stock knowingly using stolen private information that can affect the stock's price.

8.3 The Firm's Duties to the Employee

The basic moral obligation that the employer has toward employees, according to the rational view of the firm, is to provide them with the compensation they have freely and knowingly agreed to receive in exchange for their services. There are two main issues related to this obligation: the fairness of wages and the fairness of employee working conditions.[20] Both wages and working conditions are aspects of the compensation employees receive from their services, and both are related to the question of whether the employee contracted to take a job freely and knowingly. If an employee was "forced" to accept a job with inadequate wages or inadequate working conditions, then the work contract would be unfair.

Wages

From the employee's point of view, wages are the principal (perhaps the only) means for satisfying the basic economic needs of the worker and the worker's family. From the employer's point of view, wages are a cost of production that must be kept down lest the product be priced out of the market. Therefore, every employer faces the dilemma of setting fair wages: How can a fair balance be struck between the employer's interests in minimizing costs and the workers' interest in providing a decent living for themselves and their families?

Unfortunately, there is no simple formula for determining a "fair wage." The fairness of wages depends in part on the public supports that society provides the worker (social security, Medicare, unemployment compensation, public education, welfare, etc.), the freedom of labor markets, the contribution of the worker, the needs of the worker, and the competitive position of the firm.

Although there is no way to determine fair salaries with mathematical exactitude, we can at least identify a number of factors that should be taken into account in determining wages and salaries.[21]

1. *The going wage in the industry and the area* Although labor markets in an industry or an area may be manipulated or distorted (e.g., by job shortages), they generally provide at least rough indicators of fair wages if they are competitive and if we

assume competitive markets are just. In addition, the cost of living in the area must be taken into account if employees are to be provided with an income adequate to their families' needs.

2. *The firm's capabilities* In general, the higher the firm's profits, the more it can and should pay its workers; the smaller its profits, the less it can afford. Taking advantage of cheap labor in captive markets when a company is perfectly capable of paying higher wages is exploitation.
3. *The nature of the job* Jobs that involve greater health risks, offer less security, require more training or experience, impose heavier physical or emotional burdens, or take greater effort should carry higher levels of compensation.
4. *Minimum wage laws* The minimum wages required by law set a floor for wages. In most circumstances, wages that fall beneath this floor are unfair.
5. *Relation to other salaries* If the salary structure within an organization is to be fair, workers who do roughly similar work should receive roughly similar salaries.
6. *The fairness of wage negotiations* Salaries and wages that result from "unfree" negotiations in which one side uses fraud, power, ignorance, deceit, or passion to get its way will rarely be fair. For example, when the management of a company uses the threat of relocation to force wage concessions out of a wholly dependent community, or when a union "blackmails" a failing company with a strike that is certain to send the firm into bankruptcy, the resulting wages have little likelihood of being fair.
7. *Local costs of living* The goods and services that a family needs to meet their basic needs (food, housing, clothing, transportation, child care, and education) differ from one geographical region to another. Wages should be sufficient to enable a family of four to meet their basic needs (taking into account whether families in the region are traditionally one- or two-wage families), even if such wages would be above the minimum wage.

Working Conditions: Health and Safety

Each year more than 5000 workers are killed and over 3,000,000 are seriously injured as a result of job accidents.[22] Ten percent of the job force suffers a job-related injury or illness each year, for a loss of over 31 million work days annually. Delayed occupational diseases resulting from exposure to chemical and physical hazards kill off additional numbers. Annual costs of work-related deaths and injuries were estimated to be $119 billion in 1995.[23]

Workplace hazards include not only the more obvious categories of mechanical injury, electrocution, and burns, but also extreme heat and cold, noisy machinery, rock dust, textile fiber dust, chemical fumes, mercury, lead, beryllium, arsenic, corrosives, poisons, skin irritants, and radiation.[24] A government description of occupational injuries is dismaying:

> Three and a half million American workers exposed to asbestos face a dual threat: Not only do they risk falling victim to the lung-scarring pneumoconiosis of their trade, asbestosis, but they are endangered by lung cancer associated with inhalation

> of asbestos fibers. Recent studies of insulation workers in two states showed 1 in 5 deaths were from lung cancer, seven times the expected rate; half of those with twenty years or more in the trade had x-ray evidence of asbestosis; 1 in 10 deaths were caused by mesothelioma, a rare malignancy of the lung or pleura which strikes only 1 in 10,000 in the general working population. Of 6000 men who have been uranium miners, an estimated 600 to 1100 will die during the next twenty years as a result of radiation exposure, principally from lung cancer. Fifty percent of the machines in industry generate noise levels potentially harmful to hearing. Hundreds of thousands of workers each year suffer skin diseases from contact with materials used in their work. The dermatoses are the most common of all occupational illnesses. Even the old, well-known industrial poisons, such as mercury, arsenic, and lead, still cause trouble.[25]

In 1970, Congress passed the Occupational Safety and Health Act and created the Occupational Safety and Health Administration (OSHA) "to assure as far as possible every working man and woman in the nation safe and healthful working conditions."[26] Unfortunately, from the beginning, OSHA found itself embroiled in controversy. Despite the severe criticism it has received,[27] an inadequate number of field inspectors (800), and often inefficient forms of regulation, the existence of OSHA has led many firms to institute their own safety programs. One poll revealed that 36 percent of the firms surveyed had implemented safety programs as a result of OSHA, and 72 percent said that the existence of OSHA had influenced them in their safety efforts.[28]

Although more attention is now being paid to worker safety, occupational accident rates have not all been declining. Between 1960 and 1993, the number of workers killed on the job declined dramatically from 21 deaths per 100,000 workers to 8 deaths per 100,000. However, the number of disabling injuries rose from 2.0 million in 1960 to 3.2 million in 1993.[29]

Risk is, of course, an unavoidable part of many occupations. A race-car driver, a circus performer, and a rodeo cowboy all accept certain hazards as part of their jobs. So long as they (a) are fully compensated for assuming these risks, and (b) freely and knowingly choose to accept the risk in exchange for the added compensation, then we may assume that their employer has acted ethically.[30]

The basic problem, however, is that in many hazardous occupations, these conditions do not obtain.

1. Wages will fail to provide a level of compensation proportional to the risks of a job when labor markets in an industry are not competitive or when markets do not register risks because the risks are not yet known. In some rural mining areas, for example, a single mining company may have a monopoly on jobs. The health risks involved in mining a certain mineral (such as uranium) may not be known until many years afterward. In such cases, wages will not fully compensate for risks.
2. Workers might accept risks unknowingly because they do not have adequate access to information concerning those risks. Collecting information on the risks of handling

certain chemicals, for example, takes a great deal of time, effort, and money. Therefore, workers acting individually may find it too costly to collect the information needed to assess the risks of the jobs they accept.

3. Workers might accept known risks out of desperation because they lack the mobility to enter other less risky industries or because they lack information on the alternatives available to them. Low-income coal miners, for example, may know the hazards inherent in coal mining. However, because they lack the resources needed to travel elsewhere, they may be forced to either take a job in a coal mine or starve.

When any of the three conditions obtain, the contract between employer and employee is no longer fair. The employer has a duty, in such cases, to take steps to ensure that the worker is not being unfairly manipulated into accepting a risk unknowingly, unwillingly, or without due compensation. In particular:

1. Employers should offer wages that reflect the risk–premium prevalent in other similar but competitive labor markets.
2. To insure their workers against unknown hazards, the employer should provide them with suitable health insurance programs.
3. Employers should (singly or together with other firms) collect information on the health hazards that accompany a given job and make all such information available to workers.

Working Conditions: Job Satisfaction

The rational parts of the organization put a high value on efficiency: All jobs and tasks are to be designed so as to achieve the organization's goals as efficiently as possible. When efficiency is achieved through specialization, the rational aspects of organizations tend to incorporate highly specialized jobs.[31]

Jobs can be specialized along two dimensions.[32] Jobs can be specialized horizontally by restricting the range of different tasks contained in the job and increasing the repetition of this narrow range of tasks. The spot-welder quoted in the introduction to this chapter, for example, does nothing but apply welds to car bodies, "thirty-two jobs per car, forty-eight (cars) an hour, eight hours a day." Jobs can also be specialized vertically by restricting the range of control and decision making over the activity that the job involves. Whereas the job of the spot-welder is highly specialized vertically, the job of the plant manager is much less vertically specialized.

Job specialization is most obvious at the operating levels of organizations. Assembly-line work usually consists of closely supervised, repetitive, and simple tasks. Low-level clerical jobs also tend to be fragmented, repetitive, dull, and closely monitored, as this example shows:

> I worked for a while at the Fair Plan Insurance Company, where hundreds of women sat typing up and breaking down sextuplicate insurance forms. My job was in endorsements: *First, third, and fourth copies staple together/place the pink sheet in back of the yellow/If the endorsement shows a new mortgagee/stamp the fifth copy "certificate needed. . . ."* Other sections, like coding, checks, filing, and endorsement typing, did similar subdivided parts of the paperwork. The women in the other sections sat at steel desks like mine, each working separately on a stack of forms or cards. Every section had a supervisor who counted and checked the work. She recorded the number of pieces we completed, and the number of errors we made, on our individual production sheets. These production sheets were the basis for our periodic merit raises. Aside from counting and checking, the supervisor also tried to curtail talking and eating at desks.[33]

The debilitating effects that job specialization can have on workers were first noted over 200 years ago by Adam Smith:

> In the progress of the division of labor, the employment of the far greater part of those who live by labor, that is, of the great body of the people, comes to be confined to a few very simple operations, frequently to one or two. But the understandings of the greater part of men are necessarily formed by their ordinary employments. The man whose whole life is spent in performing a few simple operations has no occasion to exert his understanding. . . . He naturally loses, therefore, the habit of such exertion and generally becomes as stupid and ignorant as it is possible for a human creature to become. . . . It corrupts even the activity of his body, and renders him incapable of exerting his strength with vigor and perseverance, in any other employment than that to which he has been bred.[34]

More recent research on the mental health of assembly-line workers has tended to corroborate Smith's early suspicions. In a study of auto workers, for example, A. W. Kornhauser found that about 40 percent suffered some sort of mental health problem and only 18 percent could be considered to have "good mental health."[35] A later study found that many American workers suffered from ulcers, lack of self-esteem, anxiety, and other psychological and psychosomatic diseases.[36] In a survey of 15 years of research on job satisfaction, Stanislav Kasl found that, among other factors, low job satisfaction was related to "lack of control over work; inability to use skills and abilities; highly fractionated, repetitive tasks involving few diverse operations; no participation in decision-making," and that poor mental health was related to similar factors.[37]

Not all workers are equally affected by job specialization. Older workers and workers in large urban areas seem to show more tolerance for routine monotonous jobs apparently because older workers scale down their expectations over the years, wheras urban workers reject the Puritan work ethic and prefer not to become involved in their work.[38] Nonetheless, only 24 percent of all blue collar workers would choose the same type of work if they could start all over again—an indication that a substantial portion of workers do not find their jobs intrinsically satisfying.[39]

The injuries that highly specialized work has on the well-being of workers poses an important problem of justice for employees. The most narrowly specialized forms of work are those that require the least skills (because one of the functions of specialization is to dispense of the need for training). Unskilled labor, of course, commands the lowest levels of compensation. As a consequence, the psychological costs of dull, meaningless, and repetitive work tend to be borne by the group of workers that is paid least: unskilled laborers.

Not only may the injuries of specialization be inequitable, they are also often related to a lack of freedom. Unskilled workers often have no real freedom of choice: They must either accept work that is meaningless and debilitating or else not work at all. Therefore, the freedom that is essential to a fair work contract is often absent.

Excessive job specialization is undesirable for other reasons than that it places unjust burdens on workers. There is also considerable evidence that it does not contribute to efficiency. Research findings have demonstrated that there is a linkage between worker productivity and programs that improve the quality of work life for workers by giving workers greater involvement in and control over a variety of work tasks.[40]

How should these problems of job dissatisfaction and mental injury be dealt with? Hackman, Oldham, Jansen, and Purdy have argued that there are three determinants of job satisfaction:

> *Experienced Meaningfulness.* The individual must perceive his work as worthwhile or important by some system of values he accepts.
>
> *Experienced Responsibility.* He must believe that he is personally accountable for the outcome of his efforts.
>
> *Knowledge of Results.* He must be able to determine, on some regular basis, whether the outcomes of his work are satisfactory.[41]

To influence these three determinants, the authors claim, jobs must be expanded along five dimensions:

1. *Skill Variety* The degree to which a job requires the worker to perform activities that challenge his skills and abilities.
2. *Task Identity* The degree to which the job requires a completion of a whole and identifiable piece of work—doing a job from beginning to end with a visible outcome.
3. *Task Significance* The degree to which the job has a substantial and perceivable impact on lives of other people, whether in the immediate organization or the world at large.

4. *Autonomy* The degree to which the job gives the worker freedom, independence, and discretion in scheduling work and determining how he will carry it out.
5. *Feedback* The degree to which a worker, in carrying out the work activities required by the job, gets information about the effectiveness of his efforts.[42]

In short, the solution to job dissatisfaction is perceivable enlargement of the narrowly specialized jobs that give rise to dissatisfaction: broadening the job "horizontally" by giving the employee a wider variety of tasks and deepening the job "vertically" by allowing the employee more perceivable control over these tasks. For example, jobs can be horizontally enlarged by replacing single workers performing single repetitive tasks with teams of three or four who are jointly responsible for the complete assembly of a certain number of machines.[43] Such team jobs can be vertically enlarged by delegating to the team the responsibility of determining their own work assignments, work breaks, and inspection procedures.[44]

8.4 The Political Organization

To anyone who has ever worked within a large organization, the goal-directed and efficient structure that the rational model of the organization attributes to business firms will seem a bit incomplete if not altogether unreal. Although much of the behavior within organizations accords with the orderly picture drawn by the rational model, a great deal of organizational behavior is neither goal directed nor efficient nor even rational. Employees within organizations often find themselves embroiled in intrigues, ongoing battles for organization resources, feuding between cliques, arbitrary treatment by superiors, scrambles for career advancement, controversies over what the organization's "real" goals are or should be, and disagreements over strategies for pursuing goals. Such behaviors do not seem to fit within the orderly pattern of the rational pursuit of organizational goals.[45] To understand these behaviors and the ethical issues they raise, we must turn to a second model of the firm—one that focuses less on its rational aspects and more on its political features: the political model of the organization.[46]

The political analysis of the organization that we now sketch is a more recently developed view of organizations than the rational analysis. Unlike the rational model, the political model of the organization does not look merely at the formal lines of authority and communication within an organization nor does it presume that all organizational behavior is rationally designed to achieve an objective and a given economic goal such as profitability or productivity. Instead the political model of the organization sees the organization as a system of competing power coalitions and formal and informal lines of influence and communication that radiate from these coalitions.[47] In place of the neat hierarchy of the rational model, the political model postulates a messier and more complex network of clustered power relationships and criss-crossing communication channels (see Fig. 8.2).

In the political model of the organization, individuals are seen as grouping together to form coalitions that then compete with each other for resources, benefits, and influence. Consequently, the "goals" of the organization are those established by the historically most powerful or dominant coalition.[48] Goals are not given by "rightful" authority, but are bargained for among more or less powerful coalitions. The fundamental organizational reality, according to this model, is not formal authority or contractual relationships, but power: the ability of the individual (or group of individuals) to modify the conduct of others in a desired way without having one's own conduct modified in undesired ways.[49] An example of an organizational coalition and the nonformal power it can exert even over formal authorities is provided by this account of life in a government agency:

> We had this boss come in from Internal Revenue [to run this OEO department]. He wanted to be very, very strict. He used to have meetings every Friday—about people comin' in late, people leavin' early, people abusin' lunch time. . . . Every Friday,

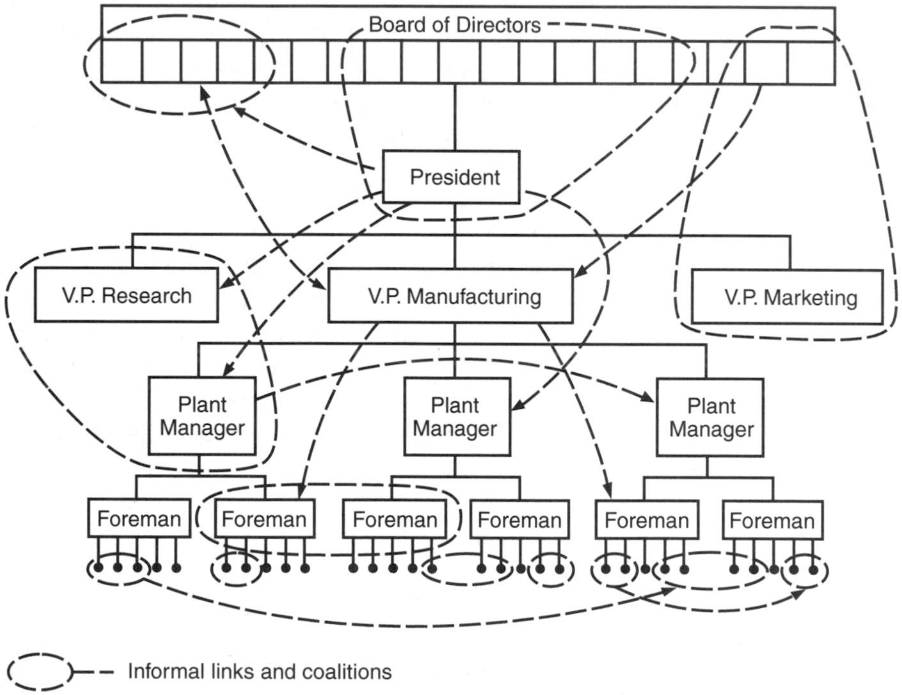

Figure 8.2

> everyone would sit there and listen to this man. And we'd all go out and do the same thing again. Next Friday he'd have another meeting and he would tell us the same thing. (Laughs.) We'd all go out and do the same thing again. (Laughs.) He would try to talk to one and see what they'd say about the other. But we'd been working all together for quite awhile. You know how the game is played. Tomorrow you might need a favor. So nobody would say anything. If he'd want to find out what time someone came in, who's gonna tell 'em? He'd want to find out where someone was, we'd always say, "They're at the Xerox." Just anywhere. He couldn't get through.[50]

As this example shows, behavior within an organization may not be aimed at rational organizational goals such as efficiency or productivity, and both power and information may travel completely outside (even contrary to) formal lines of authority and communication. Nonetheless, formal managerial authority and formal communication networks provide rich sources of power. The spot-welder quoted earlier was referring to the power of formal authority when he said, "I don't like the pressure. . . . If the foreman doesn't like you, he'll make you hold it. . . . Oh, yeah, the foreman's got somebody knuckling down on him, putting the screws to him." The ex-president of the conglomerate whom we also quoted earlier was in part referring to the power of formal authority when he said, "You have men working for you and you have a boss above. You're caught in a squeeze. The squeeze progresses from station to station." The formal authority and sanctions put in the hands of superiors are a basic source of the power they wield over subordinates.

If we focus on power as the basic organizational reality, then the main ethical problems we will see when we look at an organization are problems connected with the acquisition and exercise of power. The central ethical issues will focus not on the contractual obligations of employers and employees (as the rational model would focus them), but on the moral constraints to which the use of power within organizations must be subjected. The ethics of organizational behavior as seen from the perspective of the political model focus on this question: What are the moral limits, if any, to the exercise of power within organizations? In the sections that follow, we discuss two aspects of this question: (a) What, if any, are the moral limits to the power managers acquire and exercise over their subordinates? (b) What, if any, are the moral limits to the power employees acquire and exercise on each other?

8.5 Employee Rights

Observers of corporations have repeatedly pointed out that the power of modern corporate management is much like that of a government.[51] Governments are defined in terms of four features: (a) a centralized decision-making body of officials who (b) have the power and recognized authority to enforce their decisions on subordinates (citizens); these officials (c) make decisions that determine the public distribution of social resources, benefits, and burdens among their subordinates, and (d) they have a monopoly on the power to which their subordinates are subject. These same four features, observers have argued, also characterize the managerial hierarchies that run large corporations: (a) Like a city, state, or federal government, the top managers of a corporation constitute a centralized decision-making body; (b) these managers wield power and legally recognized authority over their employees—a power that is based on their ability to fire, demote, or promote employees and an authority that is based on the law of agency that stands ready to recognize and enforce managerial decisions; (c) the decisions of managers determine the distribution of income, status, and freedom among the corporation's constituencies; and (d) through the law of agency and contract, through their access to government agencies, and through the economic leverage they possess, managers of large corporations effectively share in the monopoly on power that political governments possess.[52]

These analogies between governments and managements, several observers have held, show that the power managers have over their employees is fully comparable to the power government officials have over their citizens. Consequently, if there are moral limits to the power government officials may legitimately exercise over citizens, then there are similar moral limits that should constrain the power of managers.[53] In particular, these authors argue, just as the power of government should respect the civil rights of citizens, so the power of managers must respect the moral rights of employees. What are these employee rights? The moral rights of employees would be similar to the civil rights of citizens: the right to privacy, the right to consent, the right to freedom of speech, and so on.[54]

The major objection to this view of employee rights is that there are a number of important differences between the power of corporate managers and the power of government officials, and these differences undercut the argument that the power of managers should be limited by employee rights comparable to the civil rights that limit the power of government. First, the power of government officials (in theory at least) is based on consent, whereas the power of corporate managers is (in theory again) based on ownership. Government officials rule because they have been elected or because they have been appointed by someone who has been elected; corporate managers *rule* (if that is the right word) because they own the firm for which workers freely choose to work or because they have been appointed by the owners of the firm. Consequently, because the power of government rests on the consent of the governed, that power can legitimately be limited when the governed choose to limit it. However, because the power of managers rests on ownership of the firm, they have the right to impose whatever conditions they choose to impose on employees, who freely and knowingly contracted to work on their firm's premises.[55] Second, the power of corporate managers, unlike that of most government officials, is effectively limited by unions: Most blue collar and some white collar workers belong to a union that provides them with a degree of countervailing power that limits the power of management. Accordingly, moral rights need not be invoked to protect the interests of employees.[56] Third, whereas a citizen can escape the power of a particular government only at great cost (by changing citizenship), an employee can escape the owner of a particular management with considerable ease (by changing jobs). Because of the relatively high costs of changing citizenship, citizens need civil rights that can insulate them from the inescapable power of government. They do not need similar employee rights to protec them from the power of a corporation whose influence is easily escaped.[57]

Advocates of employee rights have responded to these three objections in a number of ways: First, they claim, corporate assets are no longer controlled by private owners; they are now held by a dispersed and almost powerless group of stockholders. This kind of dispersed ownership implies that managers no longer function as agents of the firm's owners, and, consequently, that their power no longer rests on property rights.[58] Second, although some workers are unionized, many are not, and these nonunionized workers have moral rights that managers do not always respect.[59] Third, changing jobs is sometimes as difficult and traumatic as changing citizenship, especially for the employee who has acquired specialized skills that can be used only within a specific organization.[60]

There is then a continuing controversy over the adequacy of the general argument that, because managements are like governments, the same civil rights that protect citizens must also protect employees. Regardless of whether this general argument is accepted, a number of independent arguments have been advanced to show that employees have certain particular rights that managers should respect. We look at these arguments next.[61]

The Right to Privacy

As indicated in Chapter 6, the *right to privacy* can be defined as the right people have to determine what, to whom, and how much information about themselves shall be disclosed to others. The employee's right to privacy has become particularly vulnerable with the development of recent technologies, particularly computer technologies.[62] Employees who use phones and computers can be legally monitored by their employer, who may wish to check how fast they are working, whether they are engaged in personal or business-related activities, or simply what they are doing. Polygraph or "lie detector" machines, although generally prohibited by federal law in most industries, are still allowed during internal investigations of suspected employee theft or economic loss and in a number of "exempt" industries. Computerized methods of obtaining, storing, retrieving, collating, and communicating information have made it possible for employers to collect and keep personal information about their employees, such as company medical records, credit histories, criminal and arrest histories, FBI information, and employment histories. Genetic testing, although not yet widely used by many companies, already allows employers to test an employee for about 50 genetic traits that indicate that the employee will be more likely than others to develop certain diseases (such as cystic fibrosis or sickle-cell anemia) or be affected by certain workplace toxins or occupational hazards. It is expected that, in the future, genetic tests of workers and job candidates will enable employers to screen out a wide range of workers whose genes indicate that they are likely to add to the company's medical insurance costs or add to the costs of installing workplace protections. Urine tests allow companies to screen out employees who take drugs, drink alcohol, or smoke tobacco at home. Written psychological tests, personality inventory tests, and *honesty* tests make it possible for an employer to uncover a wide range of personal characteristics and tendencies that most persons would rather keep private, such as their level of honesty or their sexual orientation.

Not only have these innovations made a person's privacy more vulnerable, but they have come at a time when managers are particularly anxious to learn more about their employees. Advances in industrial psychology have demonstrated relationships between an employee's private home life or personality traits and on-the-job performance and productivity.

As discussed in Chapter 6, there two types of privacy: psychological privacy, which is privacy regarding one's inner thoughts, plans, beliefs, values, feelings, and wants; and physical privacy, which is privacy with respect to one's physical activities, particularly those that reveal one's inner life and those that involve physical or personal functions that are culturally recognized as private.[63] Each of us has a significant interest in privacy, which justifies protecting privacy by surrounding it with the protection of a right. Privacy protects us: It lets us protect information about ourselves that could embarrass or shame us, it protects us from having others interfere in our lives merely because they disagree with our values, it lets us protect those we love from knowledge about ourselves that might hurt them, and, more generally, it protects our reputation. Privacy also empowers or enables us: It enables us to have intimacy, which lets us develop personal relationships of love, friendship, and trust; it enables us to maintain confidential relationships with professionals such as doctors, lawyers, and psychiatrists; it enables us to maintain private social roles that are distinct from our public roles; and it enables us to determine our self-identity by letting us control the way that society in general and selected individuals will look on us.

Hence, it is clear that employees, like others, have a significant interest in maintaining privacy over information about themselves, and so employees must be recognized as having a right to privacy. However, this right must be balanced against the rights and needs of others. In particular, employers sometimes have a legitimate right to inquire into the activities of employees or prospective employees. The employer is justified in wanting to know, for example, what a job candidate's past work experience has been and whether the candidate has performed satisfactorily on previous jobs. An employer may also be justified in wanting to identify the culprits when the firm finds itself the subject of pilferage or employee theft, and of subjecting employees to on-the-job surveillance to discover the source of thefts. How are these rights to be balanced against the right to privacy? Three elements must be considered when collecting information that may threaten the employee's right to privacy: relevance, consent, and method.[64]

Relevance The employer must limit inquiry into the employee's affairs to those areas that are directly relevant to the issue at hand. Although employers have a right to know the person whom they are employing and to know how the employee is performing, employers are not justified in inquiring into any areas of the employee's life that do not affect the employee's work performance in a direct and serious manner. To investigate an employee's political beliefs or social life, for example, is an invasion of privacy. Moreover, if a firm acquires information about an employee's personal life in the course of a legitimate investigation, it has an obligation to destroy the information, especially when such data would embarrass or otherwise injure the employee if it were leaked. The dividing lines between justified and unjustified investigation are fairly clear with respect to lower level employees: There is clearly little justification for investigating the marital problems, political activities, or emotional characteristics of clerical workers, sales workers, or factory laborers. The dividing line between what is and is not relevant, however, becomes less clear as one moves higher in the firm's management hierarchy. Managers are called on to represent their company before others, and the company's reputation can be significantly damaged by a manager's private activities or emotional instability. A vice president's drinking problem or membership in a disreputable association, for example, will affect the vice president's ability to adequately represent the firm. In such cases, the firm may be justified in inquiring into an officer's personal life or psychological characteristics.

Consent Employees must be given the opportunity to give or withhold their consent before the private aspects of their lives are investigated. The firm is justified in inquiring into the employee's life only if the employee has a clear understanding that the inquiry is being made and clearly consents to this as part of the job or can freely choose to refuse the job. The same principle holds when an employer undertakes some type of surveillance of employees for the purpose of, say, uncovering or preventing pilferage. Employees should be informed of such surveillance so they can ensure they will not inadvertently reveal their personal lives while under surveillance.

Methods The employer must distinguish between methods of investigation that are both ordinary and reasonable, as well as methods that are neither. Ordinary methods include the supervisory activities that are normally used to oversee employees' work. Extraordinary methods include devices like hidden microphones, secret cameras, wiretaps, lie detector tests, personality inventory tests, and spies. Extraordinary methods are unreasonable and unjustified unless the circumstances are extraordinary. Extraordinary methods of investigation might be justified if a firm is suffering heavy losses from employee theft that ordinary supervision has failed to stop. Extraordinary devices, however, are not justified merely because the employer hopes to be able to pick up some interesting tidbits about employee loyalties. In general, the use of extraordinary devices is justified only when the following conditions have been met: (a) The firm has a problem that can be solved in no other manner than by employing such extraordinary means; (b) the problem is serious and the firm has well-founded grounds for thinking that the use of extraordinary means will identify the culprits or put an end to the problem; (c) the use of the extraordinary devices is not prolonged beyond the time needed to identify the wrongdoers or after it becomes clear that the devices will not work; (d) all information that is uncovered but not directly relevant to the purposes for which the investigation was conducted is disregarded and destroyed; and (e) the failure rate of any extraordinary devices employed (such as lie detectors, drug tests, or psychological tests) is taken into account, and all information derived from devices with a known failure rate is verified through independent methods that are not subject to the same failure rates.

Freedom of Conscience

In the course of performing a job, an employee may discover that a corporation is doing something that he or she believes is injurious to society. Indeed, individuals inside a corporation are usually the first to learn that the corporation is marketing unsafe products, polluting the environment, suppressing health information, or violating the law.

Employees with a sense of moral responsibility who find that their company is injuring society in some way will normally feel an obligation to get the company to stop its harmful activities and consequently will often bring the matter to the attention of their superiors. Unfortunately, if the internal management of the company refuses to do anything about the matter, the employee today has few other legal options available. If, after being rebuffed by the company, the employee has the temerity to take the matter to a government agency outside the firm or, worse, to disclose the company's activities to a public medium, the company has the legal right to punish the employee by firing him or her. Furthermore, if the matter is serious enough, the company can reinforce this punishment by putting the matter on the employee's record and, in extreme cases, seeing to it that the employee is black-balled by other companies in the industry.[65]

Several authors have argued that this is in effect a violation of an individual's right to freedom of conscience.[66] It is a violation of the right to freedom of conscience because the individual is forced to cooperate with an activity that violates the individual's personal moral beliefs. What is the basis of this right? The right to freedom of conscience derives from the interest that individuals have in being able to adhere to their religious or moral convictions.[67] Individuals who have religious or moral convictions commonly see them as absolutely binding and can transgress them only at great psychological cost. The right to freedom of conscience protects this interest by requiring that individuals may not be forced to cooperate in activities that they conscientiously believe are wrong.

These arguments, however, have not yet had a substantial effect on the law, which still by and large reinforces the employee's duty of maintaining loyalty and confidentiality toward the employer's business.[68] In the absence of legal protections of the employee's right to freedom of conscience, some authors have supported the practice of *whistleblowing*.[69]

Whistleblowing

Whistleblowing is an attempt by a member or former member of an organization to disclose wrongdoing in or by the organization. Mr. Mackowiak, for example, was hired as a welding inspector by University Nuclear Systems, Inc. (UNSI), a firm responsible for installing the heating, ventilating, and air conditioning system at a nuclear power plant owned by the Washington Public Power Supply system. Mackowiak was supposed to inspect the work of UNSI employees and make sure it conformed to federal quality and safety standards—a task that was mandated by federal regulations requiring builders of nuclear power plants to give their inspectors the authority and organizational freedom they needed to fulfill their role as independent observers of the construction process. However, Mackowiak claimed, some UNSI employees would not give him access to areas in which work was not up to federal specifications. Mackowiak brought the problem to his superiors. When he was unable to get them to respond to his concerns, Mackowiak *blew the whistle* on the company. He met with officials of the Nuclear Regulatory Commission (NRC) at his home and disclosed to them his concerns about the safety and quality control of the work of UNSI. The NRC took his allegations seriously, acted on them, and conducted a full investigation of UNSI that rectified the problems. However, the company, found out that Mackowiak had talked to federal agents and early the following year he was fired because, the company said, he had a "mistrustful attitude toward management," although his "inspection qualifications/expertise is excellent and he is a good inspector."[70]

Whistleblowing can be internal or external. If the wrongdoing is reported only to those higher in the organization, as Mackowiak initially did, it is internal whistleblowing. When the wrongdoing is reported to external individuals or bodies such as government agencies, newspapers, or public interest groups, the whistleblowing is said to be external.

As Mackowiak's experience shows, blowing the whistle is often a brave act of conscience that can carry heavy personal costs. A study of whistleblowers found that the average whistleblower is a 47-year-old family man who has been a conscientious employee for 7 years and who has strong belief in universal moral principles.[71] The same study reported that 100 percent of the whistleblowers surveyed who worked for private businesses were fired by their employers, 20 percent could still not find work at the time of the survey, 25 percent had suffered increased financial burdens on their family, 17 percent lost their homes, 54 percent had been harassed by their peers at work, 15 percent viewed their subsequent divorce as a result of their whistleblowing, 80 percent suffered physical deterioration, 86 percent reported emotional stress including feelings of depression, powerlessness, isolation, and anxiety, and 10 percent reported having attempted suicide. Nevertheless, most of the whistleblowers surveyed had few regrets and would do it again. Typical of the comments they made to the survey team were the following: "This has turned out to be the most frightening thing I have ever done. But it has also been the most satisfying. I think I did the right thing, and I have caused some changes to be made in the plant," "Do what is right. Lost income can be replaced. Lost self-esteem is more difficult to retrieve," and "Finding honesty within myself was more powerful than I expected."

It is sometimes argued that external whistleblowing is always wrong because employees have a contractual duty to be loyal to their employer and to keep all aspects of the business confidential. When an employee accepts a job, the argument goes, the employee implicitly agrees to keep all aspects of the business confidential and to singlemindedly pursue the best interests of the employer. The whistleblower violates this agreement and thereby violates the rights of his or her employer.

Although part of what this argument asserts is true, the conclusion is false. It is true that an employee enters an agreement to act on behalf of his or her employer in all matters pertaining to the business and that the employee also implicitly agrees to keep trade secrets and other proprietary information secret. However, this agreement is not unqualified, and it does not impose on the employee unlimited obligations toward his or her employer. As we saw in an earlier discussion, agreements and contracts are void if they require a person to do something immoral. Consequently, if an employee has a moral obligation to prevent other people from being harmed and the only way to prevent the harm is by blowing the whistle on one's employer, an employment agreement cannot require the employee to remain silent. In such a situation, the employment agreement would be void because it would require the employee to immorally fail to do what he is morally obligated to do. Thus, external whistleblowing is justified if it is necessary to prevent a wrong that one has a moral right or duty to prevent, or if it will yield a benefit that one has a moral right or duty to provide.

It is also false, as it is sometimes argued, that external whistleblowing is always morally justified on the grounds that all persons, including employees, have a right to freedom of speech. When employees disclose what is going on in a firm to external parties, the argument holds, they are merely exercising their right to freedom of speech, and their act is, therefore, morally justified. However, this argument ignores the fact that the right to freedom of speech, like all other rights, is limited by the rights of other persons. In particular, an employee's right to freedom of speech is limited by the rights of the employer and other parties. Because of the employment contract, the employer has a right to have employees keep proprietary matters secret and to have the employee pursue the employer's best interests, provided the employee is not thereby forced to do anything immoral. Moreover, other parties—such as stockholders or fellow employees—who can be injured by external whistleblowing also have a right to not be subjected to such injuries needlessly or without a proportionately serious reason. Thus, external whistleblowing can be justified only if other means—such as internal whistleblowing—of preventing a wrong have been tried but have failed, and only if the harm that is to be prevented is much more serious than the harm that will result to other parties.

External whistleblowing is morally justified if:

1. there is clear, substantiated, and reasonably comprehensive evidence that the organization is engaged in some activity that is seriously wronging or will seriously wrong other parties;
2. reasonably serious attempts to prevent the wrong through internal whistleblowing have been tried and have failed;
3. it is reasonably certain that external whistleblowing will prevent the wrong; and
4. the wrong is serious enough to justify the injuries that external whistleblowing will probably inflict on oneself, one's family, and other parties.

To say that external whistleblowing is justified is not the same as saying that it is obligatory. Although it may be morally permissible for a person to blow the whistle on a company, this does not mean that the person also has a moral duty or moral obligation to do so.[72] Under what conditions is it not only permissible but obligatory for a person to engage in external whistleblowing? Whistleblowing is merely a means to an end—the end of correcting or preventing a wrong—therefore, a person has an obligation to take this means only to the extent that he or she has an obligation to achieve the end. Clearly, a person has a moral obligation to engage in whistleblowing only when he or she has a moral obligation to prevent the wrong that whistleblowing will prevent. When does a person have an obligation to prevent a wrong? Assuming that Conditions 1 to 4 are met, so that whistleblowing is at least permissible, a person also has an obligation to blow the whistle when (a) that specific person has a moral duty to prevent the wrong, either because it is part of the person's specific professional responsibilities (e.g., as an accountant, environmental officer, professional engineer, lawyer, etc.) or because no one else can or will prevent the wrong in which the company is involved; and (b) the wrong involves serious harm to society's overall welfare, serious injustice against a person or group, or serious violation of the basic moral rights of one or more people. For example, when a company is involved in activities that can result in substantial health injuries to many people who have a right to be protected from such injuries, and no one else in the company is willing to bring these activities to a halt, then I have an obligation to prevent the wrong even if this means resorting to whistleblowing.

It must be recognized, however, that the occurrence of justified external whistleblowing generally indicates a failure in an organization's internal communication system. External whistleblowing is a symptom of a structural problem: the absence of company mechanisms that enable concerned employees to effectively voice their concerns through internal whistleblowing. Most companies have no clear policies or procedures that allow employees to voice their moral concerns outside the standard chain of command. When employees encounter waste, fraud, abuse, or managerial ineptitude, they have no way of taking their concerns to those within the organization who can do something about the issue. Moreover, even when companies have open door policies that say that employees can take concerns to those higher in the organization, fear of reprisal will often prevent them from going over the head of their immediate supervisor. As a result, frustrated and morally conscientious employees either leave the organization or take to external whistleblowing.[73]

To overcome these problems, many companies have implemented programs that provide channels and procedures that facilitate internal whistleblowing. For example, FMC corporation has an "ethics hotline"—a toll-free telephone number—that any employee can call to report suspected legal or ethical violations to an "ethics officer" whose full-time responsibility is responding to any calls that come in.[74] If the employee wishes to remain anonymous, he or she is assigned a number that can be used for identification in any future communications. The ethics officer is empowered to conduct a full investigation of the allegations and to take the results of the investigation to higher management, including, if necessary, the audit committee of the board of directors. To ensure that employees are not penalized for using the hotline, it is a company policy that any supervisor who retaliates against an employee who reports a violation is subject to punishment. To ensure that employees are aware of the hotline and encouraged to use it, FMC regularly reminds employees of the hotline in the company paper and in other company documents, and calls it to the attention of new employees in their initial orientation training sessions.

The Right to Participate and Participatory Management

A democratic political tradition has long held that government should be subject to the consent of the governed because individuals have a right to liberty, and this right implies that they have a right to participate in the political decisions that affect them. Within a democracy, therefore, decision making usually has two characteristics: (a) Decisions that affect the group are made by a majority of its members, and (b) decisions are made after full, free, and open discussion.[75] Either all the members of the group participate in these decision-making processes or they do so through elected representatives.

A number of authors have proposed that these ideals of democracy should be embodied in business organizations.[76] Some have argued that enabling the individual employee within the organization to participate in the decision-making processes of the organization is an "ethical imperative."[77] As a first step toward such democracy, some have suggested that, although decisions affecting workers should not be made by workers, they should, nonetheless, be made only after full, free, and open discussion with workers. This would mean open communication between workers and their supervisors and the establishment of an environment that encourages consultation with workers. Employees would be allowed to freely express criticism, receive accurate information about decisions that will affect them, make suggestions, and protest decisions.

A second step toward "organizational democracy" would give individual employees not only the right to consultation, but also the right to make decisions about their own immediate work activities. These decisions might include matters such as working hours, rest periods, organization of work tasks, and scope of responsibility of workers and supervisors.

A third step toward extending the ideals of democracy into the workplace would allow workers to participate in the major policy decisions that affect the general operations of the firm. European firms, for example, particularly in West Germany, have adopted the concept of *codetermination*.[78] Since 1951, German law has required that each firm in the basic industries (coal, iron, and steel) should be administered by an 11-member board of directors composed of 5 directors elected by stockholders, 5 directors elected by employees, and 1 director elected by the other 10. Further extension of the law to firms with more than 20 workers required such firms to have 12-member boards composed of 8 directors elected by stockholders and 4 directors elected by employees. These "work councils" decide issues such as plant shut-down or relocation, mergers with other firms, substantial product diversification, or introduction of fundamentally new labor methods.

Full organizational democracy has not been particularly popular in the United States. Part of the reason, perhaps, is that employees have not shown a great deal of interest in participating in the firm's broader policy decisions. A more important reason, however, is that American ideology distinguishes sharply between the power exercised in political organizations and the power exercised within economic organizations: Power in political organizations should be democratic, whereas power in economic organizations should be left in the private hands of managers and owners.[79] Whether this ideological distinction is valid is something the reader must decide. Many authors continue to argue that, given the large and dominant role that business organizations are now playing in our daily lives, democracy will soon touch only the peripheral areas of our lives if it continues to be restricted to political organizations.[80]

Moreover, some management theories have urged managers to adopt a leadership style characterized as *participative leadership*, on the utilitarian grounds that such a leadership style will increase worker satisfaction and favorably affect the organization's performance and productivity. Such theories are heavily dependent on assumptions about human nature and human motivation. One of the earliest such theories, for example, that of Douglas McGregor, described two theories or sets of assumptions managers can make about employees.[81] In one theory, Theory X, managers assume that employees are naturally indolent and self-centered, prefer to be led, are resistant to change, and need to be rewarded, punished, and controlled to get them to achieve organizational objectives. Managers who subscribe to Theory X tend to be more authoritarian, directive, controlling, and less consultative. In the other theory, Theory Y, managers assume that employees want and can develop the capacity to accept responsibility, have an inherent readiness to support organizational goals, and can determine for themselves the best means for achieving these goals and willingly direct their efforts toward those means. Theory Y, McGregor held, is a more accurate description of the modern workforce, and managing according to Theory Y means that the manager would delegate decisions, enlarge job responsibilities, use a participative and consultative style of management, and allow employees to evaluate themselves on the basis of their achievement of objectives they had set for themselves as means toward broader company objectives. Theory Y leadership, McGregor held, will create a more effective and ultimately more productive organization.

A later theory, that of Raymond Miles, largely agreed with McGregor's, but went a step beyond his by distinguishing not two but three "models" or sets of assumptions managers can make about employees.[82] The "traditional" model assumes that most employees dislike work, most neither want nor are capable of being creative or self-directed, and most care more about how much they earn than what they do. Under these assumptions, the manager must provide all direction, closely supervise and control employees, and establish all work routines and procedures. The second and more enlightened "human relations" model assumes that most employees want to belong and be recognized, feel useful and important, and that meeting these needs is more important to them than what they earn. The human relations manager tries to keep employees informed, listens to them, allows them some self-direction and self-control, and tries to make each feel useful and important. The third and most enlightened model is the "human resources" model, which assumes that most employees do not find work inherently distasteful, people want to contribute to meaningful goals that they helped establish, and most employees can be creative and responsible and can exercise more self-direction and self-control than they presently have. The human resources manager tries to create an environment in which everyone can contribute to the limits of their ability, encourages full employee participation on important matters, continually expands employee self-direction and self-control, and tries to make use of "untapped" human resources. Miles held that worker satisfaction and organizational effectiveness and productivity would all be increased by the use of human resources management.

Yet another theory, developed by Rensis Likert, went one more step beyond Miles' theory to posit not three but four "systems of organization": System 1, the "exploitive authoritative"; System 2, the "benevolent authoritative"; System 3, the "consultative"; and System 4, the "participative."[83] As their titles suggest, these systems of leadership range from the absence of trust in System 1 to complete mutual trust between manager and employee in System 4; from lack of employee freedom to discuss problems to complete freedom; from no use of employee ideas to constant use; from no employee involvement in decisions to full involvement; from absolute management control of work to employee self-control; from no teamwork to a substantial amount of cooperative teamwork; from all influence and decisions coming from the top to influence and decisions flowing upward, downward, and laterally. Likert argues that System 4, which incorporates the highest levels of employee participation and self-direction, is likely to yield the highest levels of organizational effectiveness and productivity.

If participative management styles like those advocated in different ways by McGregor, Miles, and Likert do make organizations more effective and productive, then on utilitarian grounds, managers would have a moral obligation to seek to implement these styles. However, the research that has been conducted on whether participative management is more effective and productive has not come to firm conclusions. In some cases, participative management has been spectacularly successful, enabling entire plants to be turned from unproductive "disasters" into highly efficient dynamos.[84] In other cases, participative management has not had substantial positive effects on performance or productivity.[85] Moreover, critics of the participative approach to management have argued both that people are different and do not all want or can participate in management decision making, and that organizations and organizational tasks are different and not all suited to participatory management. If this is correct, then the utilitarian argument in favor of participative management can at most show that managers have an obligation to use participative management with the right people and in the right organizational contexts.

The Right to Due Process versus Employment at Will

When a General Motors internal investigation uncovered what it considered sufficient evidence of a secret employee scheme to defraud the company, without consulting the employees the team felt were involved, GM quickly doled out what one journalist called "an almost ruthless brand of corporate justice" in his description of the subsequent firings at GM's Tarrytown, New York, offices:

> Only a few days remained until Christmas, and the General Motors employees working in the modern Chevrolet Division office here were looking forward to the long paid holiday—totally unprepared for the ordeal most of them were about to face. Suddenly, without warning, about 25 salaried employees were summoned, one-by-one. They each were funneled through a three-room "assembly line" where solemn-faced GM officials from Detroit fired them, stripped them of their company cars and other benefits, and gave them cab fare home. One worker, with more than 20 years of service, recalls watching in disbelief as a GM functionary with a map and a ruler measured off the distance to his home and handed him $15. Within a few hours it was over. GM had all but wiped out the staff of the zone sales and service office that supervises the Chevrolet dealers in the New York City area.[86]

Until recently, American labor law has given a prominent position to the principle of *employment at will*, the doctrine that, unless employees are protected by an explicit contract (such as union employees), employers "may dismiss their employees at will . . . for good cause, for no cause, or even for causes morally wrong, without being thereby guilty of legal wrong."[87] The doctrine of employment at will is based on the assumption that, as owner of a business, the employer has a right to decide freely who will work for the business so long as the employee freely accepts and freely can reject that work. As owner of the property constituting the business, therefore, the employer has the right to hire, fire, and promote employees of the business on whatever grounds the employer chooses. In this view, the employee has no right to object to or contest the employer's decisions: As a nonowner, the employee has no right to determine how the business will be run and because, as a free agent, the employee freely agreed to accept the authority of the employer and always remains free to work elsewhere.

The doctrine of employment at will has come under considerable attack.[88] First, employees often are not free to accept or reject employment without suffering considerable harm because often they have no other job available. Moreover, even when they are able to find alternative employment, workers pay the heavy costs involved in engaging in a job search and of going unpaid while they are doing so. Consequently, one of the fundamental assumptions on which employment at will is based—that employees "freely" accept employment and are "free" to find employment elsewhere—is erroneous. Second, employees generally make a conscientious effort to contribute to the firm, but do so with the understanding that the firm will treat them fairly and conscientiously in return. Workers surely would not freely choose to work for a firm if they believed the firm would treat them unfairly. Therefore, there is a tacit agreement that the firm makes to treat workers fairly, and workers, therefore, have a quasicontractual right to such treatment. Third, workers have a right to be treated with respect as free and equal persons. Part of this right is the right to nonarbitrary treatment and the right not to be forced to suffer harm unfairly or on the basis of false accusations. Because firings and reductions in pay or status obviously harm employees—particularly when they have no other job alternatives—these violate the employee's right when they are arbitrary or based on false or exaggerated accusations. For these reasons, a recent trend away from the doctrine of employment at will has developed and been replaced gradually by the view that employees have a right to "due process."[89]

For many people, the most critical right of employees is the right to due process. For our purposes, *due process* refers to the fairness of the process by which decision makers impose sanctions on their subordinates. An ideal system of due process would be one in which individuals were given clear antecedent notice of the rules they were to follow, which gave a fair and impartial hearing to those who are believed to have violated the rules, which administered all rules consistently and without favoritism or discrimination, which was designed to ascertain the truth as objectively as possible, and which did not hold people responsible for matters over which they had no control.

It is obvious why the right to due process is seen by many people as the most critical right of employees: If this right is not respected, employees stand little chance of seeing their other rights respected. Due process ensures that individuals are not treated arbitrarily, capriciously, or maliciously by their superiors in the administration of the firm's rules, and it sets a moral limit on the exercise of the superior's power.[90] If the right to due process were not operative in the firm, then even if the rules of the firm protect the employee's other rights, these protections might be enforced sporadically and arbitrarily.

The most important area in which due process must play a role is in the hearing of grievances. By carefully spelling out a fair procedure for hearing and processing employee grievances, a firm can ensure that due process becomes an institutionalized reality. Here is an example of one company's fairly simple set of procedures for ensuring due process in grievances:

> All problems should be taken up initially with the employee's immediate supervisor. Most of the problems will be settled at this point to the satisfaction of the employee. There may be times, however, when the nature of the problem is such that the supervisor may not be able to give an immediate answer. In those instances where the immediate supervisor is unable to solve the problem within two working days following the date of presentation by the employee, the employee may review the problem with his departmental manager or superintendent. In situations where, after having discussed his problem with his immediate supervisor and departmental manager or superintendent, an employee still has questions, he may take the problem to the personnel manager for disposition.[91]

Trotta and Gudenberg identify the following features as the essential components of an effective grievance procedure:

1. Three to five steps of appeal depending on the size of the organization. Three steps usually suffice.
2. A written account of the grievance when it goes past the first level. This facilitates communication and defines the issues.
3. Alternate routes of appeal so that the employee can bypass his supervisor if he desires. The personnel department may be the most logical alternate route.
4. A time limit for each step of the appeal so that the employee has some idea of when to expect an answer.
5. Permission for the employee to have one or two co-workers accompany him at each interview or hearing. This helps overcome fear of reprisal.[92]

Employee Rights and Plant Closings

During the last two or three decades, American manufacturing plants have been closing while the manufacturing capacity of foreign nations has been increasing.[93] In 1960, for example, American car companies had 95 percent of the domestic automobile market; by 1994, their share had shrunk to 72 percent, foreign competitors having taken the rest. Although 24.8 percent of all vehicles sold all over the world were made in the United States in 1986, by 1992, the U.S. share had declined to 20.7 percent—a decline of almost 17 percent. Similarly, whereas 95 percent of our domesticly consumed steel came from American plants in 1960, by 1994, U.S. companies provided only 82 percent of the steel we use domestically.

A number of factors have contributed to the transfer of the United States' manufacturing capacity to foreign countries. First, blue collar wages tend to be much lower in other countries: American steelworkers earn $23 an hour including benefits, whereas Latin-American workers earn $2 an hour. Second, some foreign competitors (e.g., Japanese steelmakers) have invested in more efficient equipment, cultivated more productive employer–employee relations, applied more cooperative employee work rules, and instituted other programs that have raised worker productivity relative to the United States. Third, governments of some foreign manufacturing industries (e.g., the government of the French steel industry) have provided planning, financial subsidies, protective tariffs, favorable tax rates, and other "industrial policies" designed to nurture and support their industrial base, whereas the U.S. government has done little in this direction. Overall, these three factors have shifted the United States from a "manufacturing" to a "service economy." In a service economy, most employees are engaged in so-called *service industries* where work consists largely of providing services to others, such as the banking, restaurant, legal, educational, software design, fashion design, and medical industries. This contrasts with a manufacturing economy, in which most employees are engaged in work that is aimed at producing manufactured products, such as the auto or steel industries.

As American manufacturing plants have become less viable, many have been shut down, throwing their employees out of work. Between 1987 and 1994, the U.S. shoe manufacturing industry, for example, closed nearly 100 plants and lost nearly one third of its jobs. In total, between 1980 and 1993, the Fortune 500 industrial companies shed almost 4.4 million jobs, more than one fourth of the 1980 total (incidently, the compensation of the average CEO during this same period increased by a factor of 6).[94] Between 1993 and 1995, 12 percent of college-educated male workers lost their jobs. Although the national average unemployment rate in 1995 hovered around 6 percent (about 8 million people), cities and towns formerly dependent on manufacturing facilities that had shut down continued to face double-digit unemployment.

The loss of competitiveness is not the only reason plants shut down, of course. Plants also close because their products become obsolete (e.g., facilities manufacturing kerosene lamps); their manufacturing technology becomes obsolete (e.g., a mill using water power); demand shifts away from a certain product design before the plant has time to retool (e.g., in 1973, a gas shortage within months shifted demand away from large American cars to the smaller cars being manufactured abroad); the plant is taken over in a merger and the new managers decide to consolidate operations in a few large facilities (e.g., a small profitable steel operation may be closed down after a merger and its operations shifted to another plant that is more efficient and has higher profit margins); or managers make the wrong decisions or put short-term profits ahead of long-term investment (e.g., a team of managers might put off buying new equipment to show higher earnings on their quarterly report).

Whatever the cause—foreign competition, changes in domestic demand, or mismanagement—plant closings impose high costs on workers and their communities. Workers' life savings are exhausted. Many lose their homes to foreclosure, are forced to accept menial jobs with drastically lower salaries and status, lose their pension rights, and suffer acute mental distress resulting in feelings of worthlessness and self-doubt, psychosomatic illnesses, alcoholism, family quarrels, child and spouse abuse, divorce, and suicide.[95] Communities are harmed because closed plants mean declining tax revenues, loss of business from unemployed workers, and increased revenues that must be spent to provide social services for the unemployed.[96] In some cases, entire towns have been reduced to ghost towns when the plant on which most of the local labor force depended left.

Plant closings are not always avoidable in a market economy such as ours. However, although shutdowns are sometimes necessary, the moral rights of workers involved should continue to be respected, even when a business is forced to close.[97] Among the rights that must be respected are the workers' right to be treated only as they freely and knowingly consent to be treated—a right that requires they be informed about impending shutdowns that will affect them.

Other countries, such as Sweden, Germany, and Great Britain, all require extended advance notice of impending plant closures. As the laws of these same countries also recognize, workers have a right, too, to participate (e.g., through their unions) in closure decisions perhaps even by being given the opportunity to purchase the plant and operate it themselves. Moreover, utilitarian principles imply that the harm caused by layoffs should be minimized, and this in turn means that the costs of plant closings should be absorbed by those parties who have the greater resources and who would therefore be harmed the least by having to pay the costs. Consequently, because the corporate owner of a plant scheduled for shutdown often has greater resources than the workers, it should bear much of the costs of retraining, transfer, relocation, and so forth by developing and paying for programs to deal with these. Many companies have successfully implemented such programs. Finally, considerations of justice imply that workers and communities that have made substantial contributions to a plant during its operating life should be repaid by company assurances that it will not unjustly abandon worker pension plans, worker health plans, worker retirement plans, and community reliance on tax revenues.

These ethical considerations are nicely embodied in the suggestions that William Diehl, a former senior vice president in the steel industry, makes concerning eight steps that companies can take to minimize the harmful effects of plant closings:[98]

1. *Advance Notice* If the company can notify workers of a closing date 12 to 18 months in advance, they would have time to prepare for it. . . . One day's notice of closing is totally unjust and unacceptable.
2. *Severance Pay* A commonly suggested formula is for each worker to receive severance pay equal to 1 week's earnings for every year of service. . . .
3. *Health Benefits* Worker's health benefits should be covered by the company for at least 1 additional year after the employee is dismissed.
4. *Early Retirement* Workers who are within 3 years of normal retirement should be retired on full pension, with years of service computed as if they had worked until age 65.
5. *Transfer* In the case of a multiplant corporation, all workers at the facility should have the opportunity to transfer to an equally paying job at another plant, with full moving expenses covered by the employer.
6. *Job Retraining* Company-sponsored training programs should be established to train and place workers in other jobs in the local community. These programs should also include family counseling for all employees.
7. *Employee Purchase* Workers and the local community should be given the opportunity to purchase the plant and operate it under an employee Stock Ownership Plan (ESOP) . . . [if] viable. . . .
8. *Phasing Out of Local Taxes* Companies should phase out their local taxes over a 5-year period. This may involve a voluntary contribution to the local taxing authority if the plant and equipment are disposed of in a way that will severely reduce property taxes.

Unions and the Right to Organize

Just as owners have the right to freely associate with each other to establish and run a business for the achievement of their morally legitimate ends, so also workers have the right to freely associate with each other to establish and run unions for the achievement of their morally legitimate common ends. The same rights of free association that justify the formation and existence of corporations also underlie the worker organizations we call *unions*.[99]

The worker's right to organize into a union also derives from the right of the worker to be treated as a free and equal person. Corporate employers, especially during periods of high unemployment or in regions where only one or a few firms are located, can exert an unequal pressure on an employee by forcing the employee to accept their conditions or go without an adequate job. Unions have traditionally been justified as a legitimate countervailing means for balancing the power of the large corporation so that the worker in solidarity with other workers can achieve an equal negotiating power against the corporation.[100] Thus, unions achieve an equality between worker and employer that the isolated worker could not secure, and they thereby secure the worker's right to be treated as a free and equal person in job negotiations with powerful employers.

Not only do workers have a right to form unions, but their unions also have a right to strike.[101] The right of unions to call a strike derives from the right of each worker to quit his or her job at will so long as doing so violates no prior agreements or the rights of others. Union strikes are therefore morally justified so long as the strike does not violate a prior legitimately negotiated agreement not to strike (which the company might have negotiated with the union) and so long as the strike does not violate the legitimate moral rights of others (such as citizens whose right to protection and security might be violated by strikes of public workers such as firefighters or police).

Despite the well-accepted view that unions and union strikes are legitimate, there has been a good deal of dissatisfaction toward them. Although unions represented 35 percent of the workforce in 1947, by the early 1990s, they represented only 16 percent.[102] From an earlier record of winning 75 percent of all union elections, unions must now be satisfied with winning only about 45 percent of worker votes.[103] By 2000, unions represented only about 15 percent of the labor force.

There are a variety of factors responsible for this decline in union membership, including an increase in white collar and female workers, a shift from manufacturing to service industries, and a decline in public confidence in unions. One of the major causes is rising opposition to unions on the part of managers and a disturbing increase in the use of illegal tactics to defeat union organizing campaigns.[104] This is unfortunate and shortsighted because the decline in the effectiveness of unions has been accompanied by a consequent increase in the appeal to legislatures and the courts to establish rigid legal protections against the abuses that unions were originally established to secure. As the effectiveness of workers' rights to unionize and strike continues to shrink, we can count on a proliferation of laws to secure the rights that worker organizations can no longer accomplish.

8.6 Organizational Politics

The discussion so far has focused primarily on formal power relationships within organizations—that is, the ethical issues raised by the power that the formal structure of the organization allows managers to exercise over their subordinates. These power relations are sanctioned and overt: They are spelled out in the firm's "organizational chart," inscribed in the contracts and job descriptions that define the employee's duties to the firm, recognized by the law (of agency), openly employed by superiors, and largely accepted as legitimate by subordinates.

The ethical constraints on the use of this formal power that we reviewed have also been approached from a largely formal perspective. The rights to privacy, due process, freedom of conscience, and consent can all be formalized within the organization (by formulating and enforcing rules, codes, and procedures) just as the power relationships they constrain are formalized.

However, as we have already seen, organizations also contain informal pockets and channels of power: sources of power that do not appear on organizational charts and uses of power that are covert and perhaps not recognized as legitimate. We turn now to look at this underbelly of the organization: organizational politics.

Political Tactics in Organizations

There is no settled definition of *organizational politics*. For our purposes, however, we can adopt the following definition: the processes in which individuals or groups within an organization use nonformally sanctioned power tactics to advance their own aims; we call such tactics *political tactics*.[105]

A word of caution is necessary, lest the reader interpret *their own aims* to mean "aims in conflict with the best interests of the organization." Although the aims of a coalition in a firm may conflict with the best interests of the firm (a problem we examine later), such conflict is neither inevitable nor even, perhaps, frequent. Two factors tend to suppress such conflicts: (a) The careers of individuals often depend on the health of their organizations, and (b) long-time association with an organization tends to generate bonds of loyalty to the organization. Often, therefore, what one person perceives as a conflict between a certain group's aims and the best interests of the organization is in fact a conflict between the beliefs of that person and the beliefs of the group concerning what the "best interests" of the organization are. The group may genuinely believe that X is in the best interests of both the organization and itself, whereas the person may genuinely believe instead that Y, which conflicts with X, is what is in the best interests of the organization.

Because organizational politics aim at advancing the interests of one individual or group (such as acquiring promotions, salary or budget increases, status, or even more power) by exerting nonformally sanctioned power over other individuals or groups, political individuals tend to be covert about their underlying intents or methods.[106] Virginia E. Schein, for example, gave this illustration of a department head intent on strengthening her position in an organization:

> The head of a research unit requests permission to review another research group's proposal in case she can add information to improve the project. Her covert intent is to maintain her current power, which will be endangered if the other research group carries out the project. Using her informational power base, her covert means are to introduce irrelevant information and pose further questions. If she sufficiently confuses the issues, she can discredit the research group and prevent the project from being carried out. She covers these covert intents and means with the overt ones of improving the project and reviewing its content.[107]

The fact that political tactics are usually covert means that they can easily become deceptive or manipulative. This is evident if we examine more examples of organizational political tactics. In a recent study of managerial personnel, respondents were asked to describe the political tactics they had experienced most frequently in the organizations in which they had worked.[108] The following kinds of tactics were reported:

Blaming or attacking others Minimizing one's association with plans or results that are failing or have failed and blaming one's rivals for the failure or "denigrating their accomplishments as unimportant, poorly timed, self-serving, or lucky."

Controlling information Withholding information detrimental to one's aims or distorting information "to create an impression by selective disclosure, innuendo," or overwhelming the subject with "objective" data (graphs, formulas, tables, summations) designed to create an impression of rationality or logic and to obscure important details harmful to one's interests.

Developing a base of support for one's ideas Getting others to understand and support one's ideas before a meeting is called.

Image building Creating the appearance of being thoughtful, honest, sensitive, on the inside of important activities, well liked, and confident.

Ingratiation Praising superiors or those with power and making them feel that one admires them or developing good rapport with them.

Associating with the influential Trying to get one's superiors or those with power to feel that one is a friend.

Forming power coalitions and developing strong allies Forming or joining groups that are already formed and that can help one in pursuing one's interests.

Creating obligations Making others feel obligated to oneself by performing services or favors for them.

Some researchers have argued that the basic source of power is the creation of dependency: A acquires power over B by making B dependent on A for something. Some authors identify the following two categories of political tactics as encompassing the main kinds of tactics by which such dependencies can be created:[109]

Getting control over scarce resources desired by others Controlling employees, buildings, access to influential persons, equipment, and useful information.

Establishing favorable relationships Getting others to feel obligated to oneself, making others think one is a friend, building a reputation as an expert, and encouraging others to believe that one has power and that they are dependent on that power.

Anyone who has ever worked within organizations can undoubtedly think of many examples of the use of political tactics in organizational life. Here is a former executive's description of the use of some "ploys" he encountered during his corporate career:

> [This is] a ploy for many minor executives to gain some information: I heard that the district manager of California is being transferred to Seattle. He knows there's been talk going on about changing district managers. By using this ploy—"I know something"—he's making it clear to the person he's talking to that he's been in on it all along. Therefore, it's all right to tell him. Gossip is another way of building up importance within a person who starts the rumor. He's in, he's part of the inner circle. . . . When a top executive is let go. . . . suddenly everybody in the organization walks away and shuns him because they don't want to be associated with him. In corporations, if you back the wrong guy, you're in his corner and he's fired, you're guilty by association. . . . A guy in a key position, everybody wants to talk to him. All his subordinates are trying to get an audience with him to build up their own positions.[110]

The Ethics of Political Tactics

Obviously, political behavior in an organization can easily become abusive: Political tactics can be used to advance private interests at the expense of organizational and group interests, they can be manipulative and deceptive, and they can seriously injure those who have little or no political power or expertise. However, political tactics can also be put at the service of organizational and social goals, they may sometimes be necessary to protect the powerless, and they are sometimes the only defense a person has against the manipulative and deceptive tactics of others. The dilemma for the individual in an organization is knowing where the line lies that separates morally legitimate and necessary political tactics from those that are unethical.

Very few authors have examined this dilemma.[111] This is unfortunate because, although few organizations are totally pervaded by political behavior, it is also the case that no organization is free of it. We are all political animals even if our political campaigns are largely confined to the office. Here we only start to analyze the many complex ethical issues raised by the political maneuvering that inevitably goes on within organizations. The issues can best be approached by addressing four questions that can focus our attention on the morally relevant features of using political tactics: (a) The utilitarian question: Are the goals one intends to achieve by the use of the tactics socially beneficial or socially harmful? (b) The rights question: Do the political tactics used as means to these goals treat others in a manner consistent with their moral rights? (c) The justice question: Will the political tactics lead to an equitable distribution of benefits and burdens?[112] (d) The caring question: What impact will the political tactics have on the web of relationships within the organization?

The Utility of Goals Utilitarian principles require that managers pursue those goals that will produce the greatest social benefits and the least social harm. If we assume that business organizations generally perform a socially beneficial function and that activities that harm the organization will probably diminish these social benefits, then utilitarianism implies that the individual manager should avoid harming the organization and the manager should work to ensure that the organization carries out its beneficial social functions as efficiently as possible. For example, the basic function of most businesses is to produce goods and services for consumers. Insofar as a business organization is serving this function in a socially beneficial and nonharmful way, the employee should avoid harming the business and should strive to ensure that the business carries on its productive function with a minimum of waste.

Two kinds of political tactics directly contradict this norm and are, therefore, typically judged unethical: political tactics that involve the pursuit of personal goals at the expense of the organization's productive goals, and political tactics that knowingly involve inefficiency and waste. Suppose, for example, that the head of a research unit secretly withholds critical information from other research units in the same company so that his own unit will look better than the others. As a result, his career ambitions are advanced and his unit gets a larger budget allocation the following year. Was his tactic of withholding information to gain an edge on others morally legitimate? No. The tactic was clearly inconsistent with the efficient pursuit of the company's productive functions.

Of course, businesses do not always have socially beneficial and nonharmful goals. Pollution, planned obsolescence, price fixing, and the manufacture of hazardous products are some obvious organizational goals that utilitarianism would condemn. To the extent that a business pursues such goals, the employee has a duty not to cooperate (unless, perhaps, the employee is threatened with personal losses of such magnitude that he or she is in effect coerced to comply). Utilitarian principles imply that to voluntarily pursue goals that are socially harmful or to voluntarily cooperate in such a pursuit is immoral, regardless of what kinds of political tactics one uses.

Unfortunately, organizational goals are not always clear because there may be no consensus over what the organization's goals actually are. This is especially the case, for example, when a company is in the process of undergoing a change in management or a change in organization and more or less widespread bargaining erupts over what the new goals should be. When organizational goals are in the process of being redefined in this way, the various coalitions and individuals within the organization will usually attempt to use political tactics to install the goals that each wants, either through a unilateral exercise of power (e.g., a new management may try to get rid of all the old staff and hire its own team) or through political compromise (e.g., the new management may try to persuade the old staff to accept new goals). In such fluid situations, the individual has no choice but to examine the goals being proposed by the various coalitions and make a conscientious attempt to determine which goals are in the long run the most socially beneficial. Whereas the use of political tactics to install illegitimate organizational goals would be unethical, political tactics may be used to ensure the installation of morally legitimate goals provided that the tactics meet the following two criteria.

The Consistency of Political Means with Moral Rights Some political tactics are obviously deceptive, as when a person creates the impression that he or she has an expertise that the person does not in fact have. Other tactics are manipulative. For example it is manipulative, to feign love to extract favors from a person. Deception and manipulation are both attempts to get a person to do (or believe) something that that person would not do (or believe) if he or she knew what was going on. These sorts of political tactics are unethical to the extent that they fail to respect a person's right to be treated not merely as a means, but also as an end; that is, they fail to respect a person's right to be treated only as he or she has freely and knowingly consented to be treated. Such moral disrespect is exhibited in many of those political tactics that take advantage of our emotional dependencies and vulnerabilities, both of which provide others with the cheapest and most reliable levers for acquiring power over us. For example, a skilled administrator can become adept at pretending friendship and concern, and adept at getting others to look on him or her with affection, respect, loyalty, indebtedness, trust, gratitude, and so on. The administrator can then exploit these feelings to get subordinates to do things for him or her that they ordinarily would not do, especially if they knew the deception involved and knew the covert motives on which the administrator acted. A skillful administrator might also learn to take advantage of particular individuals' personal vulnerabilities such as vanity, generosity, sense of responsibility, susceptibility to flattery, gullibility, naivete, or any of the other traits that can lead a person to unwittingly put him or herself at the mercy of others. By covertly taking advantage of these vulnerabilities, the manager can get employees to serve the manager's aims, although they would not do so if they knew the covert motives on which the manager acted.

However, are deceptive and manipulative political tactics always wrong? What if I am forced to work in an organization in which others insist on using deceptive and manipulative tactics against me? Must I remain defenseless? Not necessarily. If the members of an organization know that certain kinds of covert political tactics are in common use within an organization, and if they nonetheless freely choose to remain within the organization and become skillful in using and defending themselves against these tactics, then one can presume that these organizational members have tacitly consented to having those kinds of covert political tactics used against themselves. They have freely agreed to play an organizational game, as it were, in which everyone knows that fooling the other players and maneuvering them out of winning positions is all part of the game. Dealing with them on the basis of this tacit consent would not violate their right to be treated as they have freely and knowingly chosen to be treated.

However, the use of deceptive or manipulative political tactics is clearly unethical when: they are used against persons who (a) do not know or do not expect that these kinds of tactics will be used against themselves, (b) are not free to leave the organization in which these tactics are being used, or (c) are not skilled at defending themselves against these tactics. Using a deceptive or manipulative tactic in any of these instances violates the moral respect due to persons, especially if the tactic injures a person by maneuvering the person into unknowingly acting against his or her own best interests.

The Equity of the Consequences Political tactics can create injustices by distorting the equality of treatment that justice demands. An individual who controls an organization's budget or information system, for example, may covertly administer that system unjustly by showing favoritism to those persons or groups who can advance the individual's career. Such political tactics blatantly violate the basic principle of distributive justice discussed earlier: Individuals who are similar in all relevant respects should be treated similarly, and individuals who are dissimilar in relevant respects should be treated dissimilarly in proportion to their dissimilarity.

Political tactics can also create injustices among those employees who have few or no political skills. Those without political skills are easily maneuvered into accepting a smaller share of the organization's benefits than their abilities or needs may merit in comparison to others. Benefits are then no longer distributed to these people on the basis of their relevant characteristics: An injustice is committed against them.

Not only can political tactics leave others better or worse off than they deserve, but politics can also be used to gain unjust advantages for oneself. An engineer who is competing with another engineer for promotion to department head, for example, may cultivate and flatter her superiors while using innuendo to discredit her rival. As a result, she may get the promotion, although the other engineer was more qualified. Using political tactics in this way to acquire advantages on the basis of nonrelevant characteristics is also unjust.

The Impact on Caring In addition to these inequities, the prolonged prevalence of political tactics within an organization can have long-term and debilitating effects on the quality of the personal relationships that pervade the organization. Several researchers have found that the use of power in organizations tends to routinize the dehumanized treatment of less powerful individuals. David Kipnis, for example, found that individuals who exercise power find themselves increasingly tempted to (a) increase their attempts to influence the behavior of the less powerful, (b) devalue the worth of the performance of the less powerful, (c) attribute the cause of the less powerful's efforts to power controlled by themselves rather than to the less powerful's motivations to do well, (d) view the less powerful as objects of manipulation, and (e) express a preference for the maintenance of psychological distance from the less powerful.[113] Power, in short, corrupts.

Chris Argyris and others have maintained that those who are controlled by the powerful "tend to feel frustration, conflict, and feelings of failure"; that they "adapt" by leaving the organization, trying to climb the organization's ladder, retreating to aggression, daydreaming, regression, or simple apathy; and that the organization becomes characterized by competition, rivalry, and hostility.[114] Therefore, in deciding whether to use political tactics, one should seriously consider the long-range consequences that the exercise of power implied by these tactics can have on oneself and one's relationships with those in the organization.

8.7 The Caring Organization

So far we have looked at organizations as having two aspects. First, we have considered organizations as hierarchical collections of autonomous individuals who are connected to each other and to the organization by contractual agreements. The employee signs a contract agreeing to carry out the tasks spelled out in the "job description" in return for a wage that the employer agrees to pay him or her. Employees take their orders from ranked tiers of managers arranged in a hierarchy of authority, at the top of which sit the CEO and his or her top-management staff and at the bottom of which stand the workers who perform the actual labor of the organization. The whole organization pursues the goal of profit. We have called this aspect of the organization the *rational* organization. Criss-crossing the rational organization's formal lines of authority is a second system of power, which we have called the *political* organization. The political elements of the organization consist of the network of power relationships, coalitions, and informal lines of communication through which individuals seek to achieve their personal goals and seek to get others to help them achieve their personal goals through the exercise of power.

It is possible to conceive of organizations as consisting of yet another quite different set of relationships. Recent thinkers have suggested that organizations can and should be thought of as networks of relationships in which "connected selves" form webs of ongoing personal relationships with other "connected selves." In this aspect of the organization, the focus of employees is not on the pursuit of profit personal goals, but on caring for those particular individuals who make up the organization and those with whom the organization interacts. We encounter this aspect of the organization when we make friends with the people with whom we work, come to care for them, look out for their well-being, and seek to deepen and preserve these caring relationships. Employers, too, may grow close to their employees, deepening their relationships with employees and coming to seek ways of caring for the particular needs of these particular individuals and of developing their full potential. When a fire destroyed the main plant of Malden Mills, for example, the CEO, Aaron Feuerstein, refused to lay off the idled workers, but continued to pay them from his own pocket although they were not working, saying that they were "part of the enterprise, not a cost center to be cut. They've been with me for a long time. We've been good to each other, and there's a deep realization of that." The members of an organization may befriend even their clients and customers, truly caring for them and genuinely seeking to develop and improve the well-being of those particular customers whom they encounter. Such caring for the well-being of customers is most evident perhaps in organizations of professionals that provide services for their clients, such as hospitals, law firms, and consulting firms that have ongoing relationships with their clients, as well as pharmaceutical companies that provide life-saving medicines for people. Merck, Inc., a very successful pharmaceutical company, for example, developed ad gave away at no charge a cure for river blindness that it saw one group of customers desperately needed but could not afford.

This aspect of organizational life is not adequately described by the contractual model that underlies the "rational" organization, nor by the power notions that underlie the "political" organization. Perhaps, it is best described as *the caring organization*, in which the dominant moral concepts are those that arise from an ethic of care. Jeanne M. Liedtka described the caring organization as that organization, or part of the organization, in which caring is:

> (a) focused entirely on persons, not "quality," "profits," or any of the other kinds of ideas that much of today's "care-talk" seems to revolve around;
> (b) undertaken as an end in and of itself, and not merely a means toward achieving quality, profits, etc.;
> (c) essentially personal, in that it ultimately involves particular individuals engrossed, at a subjective level, in caring for other particular individuals;
> (d) growth-enhancing for the cared-for, in that it moves them towards the use and development of their full capacities, within the context of their self-defined needs and aspirations.[115]

It has been argued that business organizations in which such caring relationships flourish will exhibit better economic performance than the organization that restricts itself to the contractual and power relationships of the rational and political organization.[116] In the caring organization, trust flourishes because "one needs to be trusting if one sees oneself as interdependent and connected."[117] Because trust flourishes in the caring organization, the organization does not have to invest resources in monitoring its employees and trying to make sure that they do not violate their contractual agreements. Thus, caring lowers the costs of running an organization and reduces the "costs of disciplinary actions, theft, absenteeism, poor morale and motivation."[118] (In the genuinely caring organization, of course, caring is not motivated by the desire to reduce such costs, but is pursued for its own sake.) It has also been argued that business organizations in which caring flourishes develop a concern for serving the customer and creating customer value that in turn enables such organizations to achieve a competitive advantage over other organizations. In such a business organization, the focus is not on producing differentiated or low cost products for growing markets, but on creating value for particular customers and remaining tuned to their evolving needs. Such a focus on knowing and serving the customer, it is argued, enables the company to continually adapt to the rapid changes that characterize most markets today. Moreover, the caring that gives rise to a focus on the customer can also inspire and motivate employees to excel in a way that contractual and power relations do not. Bartlett and Ghoshal, for example, argued:

> But . . . contractually based relationships do not inspire the extraordinary effort and sustained commitment required to deliver consistently superior performance. For that, companies need employees who care, who have a strong emotional link with the organization.[119]

There may be few, perhaps even no, organizations that perfectly embody the caring organization, but some well-known firms come close. W. L. Gore & Associates, Inc., for example, the extremely successful company that invented and now manufactures the well-known "GORE-TEX" line of fabrics, is an organization that has no managers, no titles, no hierarchy.[120] Instead, every employee is trusted to such an extent that he or she is left free to decide for him or herself what job each will voluntarily commit to do according to where each feels he or she can make the best contribution. Leaders emerge when employees are willing to follow them because they are convinced the leader has a worthwhile idea or project. Every employee has one or more "sponsors" who work closely as coaches to help the employee develop to his or her full potential, and who serve as the employee's "advocates" when a "compensation team" (consisting of fellow employees) reviews the contribution the employee has made to decide what compensation the employee should receive the following year. Company units are kept small (under 200 people) so that everyone can get to know everyone else and so that all communications are open, direct, and person to person. In such an unstructured and unmanaged organization, all work done within the organization must ultimately rely on the relationships that employees form with each other. Over time, employees come to care for each other and for the customers for whom they are trying to create value.

Although organizations like W. L. Gore are rare, still most organizations, to a greater or lesser extent, have aspects of the caring organization. In some organizations, such as W. L. Gore, the caring organization dominates the rational and political aspects of the organization. In most others, however, the contractual and political aspects are more prominent. Yet in many, there are at least some employees and managers who respond to the demands of caring by nurturing the relationships they have with each other and by attending to the concrete and particular needs of each other and of their customers.

In the contractual model, the key ethical issues arise from the potential for violations of the contractual relation. In the political model, the key ethical issues arise from the potential for the misuse of power. What are the key ethical issues from the perspective of the caring organization? the potential for caring too much and the potential for not caring enough.

The moral problems of caring too much The needs of those for whom we care can demand a response from us that can overwhelm us, leading, eventually to "burnout."[121] Here the conflict is between the needs of others and the needs of the self. Several writers have argued that the ethic of care requires achievement of a mature balance between caring for the needs of others and caring for one's own needs.[122] Others have argued that "burnout" occurs not because people are overwhelmed by the needs of others, but because organizations place bureaucratic burdens on caregivers and limit their autonomy and influence in decision making.[123] In addition to conflicts between the needs of the self and the needs of others, the demands of caring can lead to a different kind of conflict: The needs of those for whom we care can demand a response that conflicts with what we may feel we owe others. This is the problem of balancing partiality toward those for whom we care, with the impartial demands of other moral considerations, such as the impartial demands of fairness or of moral rights.[124] For example, a person may be torn between caring for a friend who is violating company policy and fairness toward the company that requires that such violations be reported. Which demand should be satisfied: the demands of caring partiality or the demands of impartial morality?

The moral problems of not caring enough More pressing, however, are failures to live up to the demands of caring. This may happen on a personal basis or an organizational level. We may personally see a fellow employee or customer in need, but fatigue, self-interest, or simply disinterest may lead us to ignore that need. On a broader organizational level, the entire organization may systematically drive out caring through indiscriminate layoffs, the creation of large impersonalized bureaucracies, the use of managerial styles that see employees as disposable costs, or the use of reward systems that discourage caring and reward competitiveness.

How should these kinds of moral issues be resolved? Unfortunately, at this time the answers are not clear. Research and thinking on the caring organization and caring in organizations is so recent that no clear consensus has emerged on how issues such as these should be resolved. We have come here to the very edges of current thinking in ethics.

Questions for Review and Discussion

1. Define the following concepts: the rational model of the organization, employee's obligations to the firm, law of agency, conflict of interest, actual/potential conflicts of

interest, commercial bribe, commercial extortion, morality of accepting gifts, insider information, theft, fair wage, OSHA, unfairly imposed employee risk, horizontal/vertical job specialization, job satisfaction, the political model of the organization, power, government–management analogy, right to privacy, physical/psychological privacy, relevance, consent, extraordinary methods, right to freedom of conscience, whistleblowing, right to participate, right to due process, organizational politics, political tactics.

2. Relate the theory of the employee's obligations to the firm in this chapter to the discussion on contractual rights and duties in Chapter 2. Relate the six criteria for just wages in this chapter to the various standards of justice developed in Chapter 2. Relate the problems of job satisfaction described in this chapter to the discussion of alienation in Chapter 3. Relate the discussions of employee rights in this chapter to the theory of moral rights developed in Chapter 2.
3. Compare and contrast the rational model of the organization with the political model of the organization and the caring model of the organization. Would you agree with the following statement: "The rational model of the organization implies that the corporation is based on consent, while the political model implies that the corporation is based on force, and the caring model implies that the corporation is based on interpersonal relationships"? Which of the two models do you think provides the more adequate view of organizations you are familiar with, such as the university or companies you have worked for? Explain your answers.
4. In view of the contractual agreement that every employee makes to be loyal to the employer, do you think whistleblowing is ever morally justified? Explain your answer.
5. Do you agree or disagree with the claim that corporate managements are so similar to governments that employees should be recognized as having the same "civil rights" as citizens have?
6. Evaluate the desirability of the "caring organization."

Web Resources

Readers interested in researching the topic of organizational life including worker safety might want to start with the Occupational Safety and Health Association Web Page (http://www.osha.gov); the National Institute for Occupational Safety and Health (http://www.cdc.gov/niosh/homepage.html); the labor organizations listed by the Essential Organization (http://essential.org); the topics of labor and employment law at Hieros Gamos (http://www.hg.org); the American Bar Association (http://www.abanet.org); the Legal Information Institute at Cornell Law School (http://fatty.law.cornell.edu/topics/topics2.html#employment_law); and the 'Lectric Law Library (http://www.inter=law.com/temp.html). The Employee Ownership Page provides cases and information on employee empowerment (http://www.fed.org/fed). Information on firings is available at When You Have to Let Someone Go (http://nearnet.gnn.com/gnn/bus/nolo/letgo.html). Resources on labor law can be found at the Institute of Labor Relations at Cornell University (http://www.ilr.cornell.edu/othersites). Information on Unions is provided by the American Federation of Labor-Congress of Industrial Organizations (http://www.aflcio.org) and Labornet (http://www.igc.apc.org/labornet). The Campaign for Labor Rights provides information on labor issues (http://www.compugraph.com/clr).

NOTES

1. Studs Terkel, *Working: People Talk About What They Do All Day and How They Feel About What They Do* (New York: Pantheon Books, Inc., 1979), pp. 159, 160, 161.
2. *Ibid.*, pp. 178, 179.
3. *Ibid.*, pp. 405, 406.
4. See James D. Thompson, *Organizations in Action* (New York: McGraw-Hill Book Company, 1967), pp. 4–6; see also, John Ladd, "Morality and the Ideal of Rationality in Formal Organizations," *Monist*, vol. 54 (1970).
5. E. H. Schein, *Organizational Psychology* (Englewood Cliffs, NJ: Prentice-Hall, 1965), p. 8.
6. The classic analysis of white collar crime is Edwin H. Sutherland, *White Collar Crime* (New York: Holt, Rinehart and Winston, Inc., 1949); see also U.S. Chamber of Commerce, "White Collar Crime: The Problem and Its Import," in Sir Leon Radzinowicz and Marvin E. Wolfgang, *Crime and Justice, vol. I, The Criminal in Society*, 2nd ed. (New York: Basic Books, Inc., 1977), pp. 314–55; and Donald R. Cressey, *Other People's Money* (Glencoe, IL: The Free Press, 1953). The most extensive analysis of white collar crime is Marshall B. Clinard, Peter C. Veager, Jeanne Brissette, David Petrashek, and Elizabeth Harries, *Illegal Corporate Behavior* (Washington, DC: U.S. Government Printing Office, 1979).
7. See Philip I. Blumberg, "Corporate Responsibility and the Employee's Duty of Loyalty and Obedience: A Preliminary Inquiry," in Dow Votaw and S. Prakash Sethi, eds., *The Corporate Dilemma* (Englewood Cliffs, NJ: Prentice-Hall, 1973), pp. 82–113.
8. Quoted in *ibid.*, pp. 87 and 88.
9. Conflicts of interest are discussed in M. Davis, "Conflict of Interest," *Business and Professional Ethics Journal*, vol. 1, no. 4 (Summer 1982): 17–29; see also Twentieth Century Fund, ed., *Abuse on Wall Street: Conflicts of Interest in the Securities Markets* (Westport, CT: Quorum Books, 1980).
10. Thomas M. Garrett and Richard J. Klonoski, *Business Ethics*, 2nd ed. (Englewood Cliffs, NJ: Prentice-Hall, 1986), p. 55.
11. Vincent Barry, *Moral Issues in Business* (Belmont, CA: Wadsworth Publishing Company, Inc., 1986), pp. 237–38.
12. See Lawrence C. Becker, *Property Rights* (London: Routledge & Kegan Paul, 1977), p. 19.
13. For more extended discussion of the ethics of trade secrets, see DeGeorge, *Business Ethics*, pp. 292–98.
14. This case is recounted in Michael S. Baram, "Trade Secrets: What Price Loyalty?" *Harvard Business Review* (November/December 1968).

15. See, for example, Patricia H. Werhane, "The Ethics of Insider Trading," *Journal of Business Ethics*, vol. 8, no. 11 (November 1989): 841–45.

16. See Bill Shaw, "Should Insider Trading Be Outside the Law?" *Business and Society Review*, Summer 1988, pp. 34–37; the main defender of insider trading along the lines sketched later is Henry G. Manne, *Insider Trading and the Stock Market* (New York: The Free Press, 1966) and "In Defense of Insider Trading," *Harvard Business Review*, vol. 113 (November/December 1966): 113–22. A defense of insider trading who also provides a useful bibliography of Manne's work is Robert W. McGee, "Insider Trading: An Economic and Philosophical Analysis," *The Mid-Atlantic Journal of Business*, vol. 25, no. 1 (November 1988): 35–48.

17. See H. Mendelson, "Random Competitive Exchange: Price Distributions and Gains from Trade," *Journal of Economic Theory* (December 1985): 254–80.

18. See L. R. Glosten and P. R. Milgrom, "Bid, Ask, and Transaction Prices in a Specialist Market with Heterogeneously Informed Traders," *Journal of Financial Economics* (March 1985): 71–100; T. Copeland and D. Galai, "Information Effects on the Bid-Ask Spread," *Journal of Finance* (December 1983): 1457–69; G. J. Bentson and R. Hagerman, "Determinants of Bid-Ask Spreads in the Over-the-Counter Market," *Journal of Financial Economics* (January–February 1974): 353–64; P. Venkatesh and R. Chiang, "Information Asymmetry and the Dealer's Bid-Ask Spread: A Case Study of Earnings and Dividend Announcements," *Journal of Finance* (December 1986): 1089–1102.

19. Gary L. Tidwell and Abdul Aziz, "Insider Trading: How Well Do You Understand the Current Status of the Law?" *California Management Review*, vol. 30, no. 4 (Summer 1988): 115–23.

20. The following analysis of wages and working conditions draws from Garrett, *Business Ethics*, pp. 53–62.

21. See Garrett, *Business Ethics*, pp. 38–40; and Barry, *Moral Issues in Business*, pp. 174–75.

22. National Safety Council, *Accident Facts*, 1996.

23. *Ibid.*

24. William W. Lowrance, *Of Acceptable Risk* (Los Altos, CA: William Kaufmann, Inc., 1976), p. 147.

25. U.S. Department of Health, Education and Welfare, "Occupational Disease . . . The Silent Enemy," quoted in *ibid.*, p. 147.

26. Occupational Safety and Health Act of 1970, Public Law, 91-596.

27. See, for example, Robert D. Moran, "Our Job Safety Law Should Say What It Means," *Nation's Business*, April 1974, p. 23.

28. Peter J. Sheridan, "1970–1976: America in Transition-Which Way Will the Pendulum Swing?" *Occupational Hazards* (September 1975): 97.

29. National Safety Council, *Accident Facts*, 1994.

30. See Russell F. Settle and Burton A. Weisbrod, "Occupational Safety and Health and the Public Interest," in Burton Weisbrod, Joel F. Handler, and Neil K. Komesar, eds., *Public Interest Law* (Berkeley: University of California Press, 1978), pp. 285–312.

31. Thompson, *Organizations in Action*, pp. 51–82.

32. Henry Mintzberg, *The Structuring of Organizations* (Englewood Cliffs, NJ: Prentice-Hall, 1979), pp. 69–72.

33. Barbara Garson, *All the Livelong Day: The Meaning and Demeaning of Routine Work* (Garden City, NY: Doubleday & Co., Inc., 1975) p. 157. Reprinted by permission of Doubleday & Co.

34. Adam Smith, *The Wealth of Nations* (New York: Modern Library, 1937), p. 734.

35. A. W. Kornhauser, *Mental Health of the Industrial Worker: A Detroit Study* (Huntington, NY: R. E. Krieger, 1965).

36. H. Sheppard and N. Herrick, *Where Have All the Robots Gone?* (New York: The Free Press, 1972).

37. Stanislav Kasl, "Work and Mental Health," in W. J. Heisler and John W. Houck, eds., *A Matter of Dignity* (Notre Dame, IN: University of Notre Dame Press, 1977).

38. See J. L. Pierce and R. B. Dunham, "Task Design: A Literature Review," *Academy of Management Review* (October 1976): 83–97.

39. *Work in America: Report of a Special Task Force to the Secretary of Health, Education, and Welfare* (Washington, DC: Congressional Quarterly, Inc., 1973), p. 15.

40. See the review of the research on this issue in John Simmons and William Mares, *Working Together* (New York: Alfred A. Knopf, Inc., 1983).

41. Richard Hackman, Grey Oldham, Robert Jansen, and Kenneth Purdy, "A New Strategy for Job Enrichment," *California Management Review*, vol. 17, no. 4 (Summer 1975): 58.

42. *Ibid.*, p. 59.

43. Lars E. Bjork, "An Experiment in Work Satisfaction," *Scientific American* (March 1975): 17–23.

44. For a study of how one company set up such programs, see Michael Maccoby, "Helping Labor and Management Set Up a Quality-Of-Worklife Program," *Monthly Labor Review* (March 1984).

45. For a compact contrast of rational and political behaviors, see Robert Miles, *Macro Organizational Behavior* (Santa Monica, CA: Good Year Publishing, 1980), pp. 156–61. A fuller and more historical discussion of the "rational" and "political" approaches to organization is Henry Mintzberg, *Power In and Around Organizations* (Englewood Cliffs, NJ: Prentice-Hall, 1983), pp. 8–21.

46. For more recent analyses of the firm based on the "political" model, see Mintzberg, *Power In and Around Organizations*; Samuel B. Bacharach and Edward J. Lawler, *Power and Politics in Organizations* (San Francisco: Jossey-Bass, Inc., Publishers, 1980); James G. March, "The Business Firm as a Political Coalition," *Journal of Politics*, vol. 24 (1962): 662–68; Tom Burns, "Micropolitics: Mechanisms of Institutional Change," *Administrative Science Quarterly*, VI (1962–62): 255–81; Michael L. Tushman "A Political Approach to Organizations: A Review and Rationale," *Academy of Management Review* (April 1977): 206–16; Jeffrey Pfeffer, "The Micropolitics of Organizations," in Marshall W. Meyer et al., eds., *Environments and Organizations* (San Francisco: Jossey-Bass, Inc., Publishers, 1978), pp. 29–50.

47. See R. M. Cyert and J. G. March, *A Behavioral Theory of the Firm* (Englewood Cliffs, NJ: Prentice-Hall, 1963); H. Kaufman, "Organization Theory and Political Theory," *The American Political Science Review*, vol. 58, no. 1 (1964): 5–14.

48. Walter R. Nord, "Dreams of Humanization and the Realities of Power," *Academy of Management Review* (July 1978): 674–79.

49. On the primacy of power in organizations, see Abraham Zaleznik, "Power and Politics in Organizational Life," *Harvard Business Review* (May–June 1970): 47–60. The definition of *power* in the text is derived from Virginia E. Schein, "Individual Power and Political Behaviors in Organizations: An Inadequately Explored Reality," *Academy of Management Review* (January 1977): 64–72. Definitions of power are, of course, controversial.

50. Terkel, *Working*, p. 349. Many more examples of political behaviors can be found in Samuel A. Culbert and John J. McDonough, *The Invisible War* (New York: John Wiley & Sons, Inc., 1980).

51. For example, Richard Eells, *The Government of Corporations* (New York: The Free Press of Glencoe, 1962); and Arthur Selwyn Miller, *The Modern Corporate State* (Westport, CT: Greenwood Press, 1976).

52. See Earl Latham, "The Body Politic of the Corporation," in Edward S. Mason, ed., *The Corporation in Modern Society* (Cambridge: Harvard University Press, 1960).

53. See, for example, David W. Ewing, *Freedom Inside the Organization* (New York: McGraw-Hill Book Company, 1977), pp. 3–24; Garrett, *Business Ethics*, pp. 27–30.

54. David W. Ewing, "Civil Liberties in the Corporation," *New York State Bar Journal* (April 1978): 188–229.

55. This ownership and contract argument is the basis of traditional legal views on the employee's duty to obey and be loyal to his employer. See Blumberg, "Corporate Responsibility," pp. 82–113.

56. Donald L. Martin, "Is an Employee Bill of Rights Needed?" in M. Bruce Johnson, ed., *The Attack on Corporate America* (New York: McGraw-Hill Book Company, 1978).

57. *Ibid.*

58. The classic exposition of this view is Adolf Berle and Gardner Means, *The Modern Corporation and Private Property*, 1932; a more recent exposition of similar themes is Adolf Berle, *Power without Property* (New York: Harcourt Brace Jovanovich, Inc., 1959); see also John Kenneth Galbraith, "On the Economic Image of Corporate Enterprise," in Ralph Nader and Mark J. Green, eds., *Corporate Power in America* (Middlesex, England: Penguin Books, 1977); and John J. Flynn, "Corporate Democracy: Nice Work if You Can Get It," in *ibid.*

59. Jack Stierber, "Protection Against Unfair Dismissal," in Alan F. Westin and Stephen Salisbury, eds., *Individual Rights in the Corporation* (New York: Pantheon Books, Inc., 1980).

60. David W. Ewing, *Freedom Inside the Organization* (New York: McGraw-Hill Book Company, 1977), pp. 36–41.

61. Several of these arguments are summarized in Patricia H. Werhane, *Persons, Rights, and Corporations* (Englewood Cliffs, NJ: Prentice-Hall, 1985), pp. 108–22.

62. See John Hoerr, "Privacy in the Workplace," *Business Week*, 28 March 1988, pp. 61–65, 68; Susan Dentzer, "Can You Pass the Job Test?" *Newsweek*, 5 May 1986; Sandra N. Hurd, "Genetic Testing: Your Genes and Your Job," Employee

Responsibilities and Rights Journal, vol. 3, no. 4 (1990): 239–52; U.S. Congress, Office of Technology Assessment, *Genetic Monitoring and Screening in the Workplace*, OTA-BA-455 (Washington, DC: U.S. Government Printing Office, October 1990); Arthur R. Miller, *The Assault on Privacy: Computers, Data Banks and Dossiers* (Ann Arbor: University of Michigan Press, 1971).

63. See Garrett, *Business Ethics*, pp. 47–49, who distinguishes these two types of privacy (as well as a third kind, "social" privacy).

64. The remarks that follow are based in part on Garrett, *Business Ethics*, pp. 49–53; for a more stringent view, which concludes that polygraphs, for example, should not be used at all by employers, see George G. Brenkert, "Privacy, Polygraphs, and Work," *Business and Professional Ethics Journal*, vol. 1, no. 1 (Fall 1981): 19–35.

65. For examples, see Alan F. Westin, *Whistle Blowing, Loyalty and Dissent in the Corporation* (New York: McGraw-Hill Book Company, 1981); and Frederick Elliston, John Keenan, Paula Lockhart, and Jane van Schaick, *Whistleblowing, Managing Dissent in the Workplace* (New York: Praeger Publishers, Inc., 1985).

66. For example, Ewing, *Freedom Inside the Organization*, pp. 115–27.

67. See John Rawls, *A Theory of Justice* (Cambridge: Harvard University Press, 1971), pp. 205–11.

68. See Blumberg, "Corporate Responsibility."

69. For example, Ralph Nader, Peter J. Petkas, and Kate Blackwell, *Whistle Blowing* (New York: Grossman Publishers, 1972); and Charles Peters and Taylor Branch, *Blowing the Whistle: Dissent in the Public Interest* (New York: Praeger Publishers, Inc., 1972); for a recent comprehensive study of whistleblowing, see Frederick Elliston, John Keenan, Paula Lockhart, and Jane van Schaick, *Whistleblowing Research, Methodological and Moral Issues* (New York: Praeger Publishers, Inc., 1985).

70. *Mackowiak v. University Nuclear Systems, Inc.*, 753 F. 2d 1159 (9th Cir. 1984).

71. C. H. Farnsworth, "Survey of Whistleblowers Finds Retaliation but Few Regrets," *New York Times*, 21 February 1988.

72. Richard T. DeGeorge, *Business Ethics*, 3rd ed. (New York: Macmillan Publishing Company, 1990) p. 211; see also Richard DeGeorge, "Whistleblowing: Permitted, Prohibited, Required," in F. A. Elliston, ed., *Conflicting Loyalties in the Workplace* (Notre Dame, IN: University of Notre Dame Press, 1985). My discussion draws heavily on DeGeorge.

73. See Rowe and Baker, "Are You Hearing Enough Employee Concerns?" *Harvard Business Review*, May–June 1984.

74. For a description of these and other effective corporate ethics programs, see Manuel G. Velasquez, "Corporate Ethics: Losing It, Having It, Getting It," pp. 228–44; Peter Madsen and Jay M. Shafritz, eds., *Essentials of Business Ethics* (New York: Meridian Books, 1990).

75. Robert G. Olson, *Ethics* (New York: Random House, Inc., 1978), pp. 83–84.

76. Martin Carnoy and Derek Shearer, *Economic Democracy, the Challenge of the 1980s* (White Plains, NY: M. E. Sharpe, Inc., 1980); Warren G. Bennis and Philip E. Slater, *The Temporary Society* (New York: Harper & Row, Publishers, Inc., 1968); Vincent P. Mainelli, "Democracy in the Workplace," *America* (15 January 1977): 28–30; see also the essays in Ichak Adizes and Elizabeth Mann Borgese, eds., *Self-Management: New Dimensions to Democracy* (Santa Barbara, CA: Clio Books, 1975).

77. Marshall Sashkin, "Participative Management Is an Ethical Imperative," *Organizational Dynamics*, vol. 12, no. 4 (1984): 4–22.

78. David P. Baron, *Business and Its Environment*, 3rd ed. (Upper Saddle River, NJ: Prentice-Hall, Inc., 2000) p. 472.

79. See Robert A. Dahl, *After the Revolution? Authority in a Good Society* (New Haven: Yale University Press, 1970), pp. 117–18.

80. C. Pateman, "A Contribution to the Political Theory of Organizational Democracy," *Administration and Society*, vol. 7 (1975): 5–26.

81. Douglas McGregor, *The Human Side of Enterprise* (New York: McGraw-Hill, 1960).

82. Raymond E. Miles, *Theories of Management: Implications for Organizational Behavior and Development* (New York: McGraw-Hill, 1975), p. 35.

83. Rensis Likert, "From Production- and Employee-Centeredness to Systems 1–4," *Journal of Management*, vol. 5 (1979): 147–56.

84. See, for example, William F. Dowling, "At General Motors: System 4 Builds Performance and Profits," *Organizational Dynamics*, vol. 3, no. 3 (1975): 26–30.

85. For a review of the literature, see Edwin A. Locke, David M. Schweiger, and Gary P. Latham, "Participation in Decision Making: When Should It Be Used?" *Organizational Dynamics*, vol. 14, no. 3 (1986): 58–72.

86. Greg Conderacci, "Motorgate: How a Floating Corpse Led to a Fraud Inquiry and Ousters by GM," *Wall Street Journal*, 24 April 1982, pp. 1, 16.

87. Quoted in Lawrence E. Blades, "Employment at Will versus Individual Freedom," *Columbia Law Review*, vol. 67 (1967): 1405.

88. See, for example, Patricia H. Werhane, *Persons, Rights, and Corporations*, pp. 81–93; Richard DeGeorge, *Business Ethics*, pp. 204–7.

89. Robert Ellis Smith, *Workrights* (New York: E. P. Dutton, 1983), pp. 209–15.

90. See T. M. Scanlon, "Due Process," in J. Roland Pennock and John W. Chapman, eds., *Due Process* (New York: New York University Press, 1977), pp. 93–125.

91. Quoted in Maurice S. Trotta and Harry R. Gudenberg, "Resolving Personnel Problems in Nonunion Plants," in Westin and Salisbury, *Individual Rights*, p. 306.

92. *Ibid.*, pp. 307–8.

93. All data in this paragraph are drawn from International Trade Administration, U.S. Department of Commerce, *U.S. Industrial Outlook, 1994* (Washington, DC: Government Printing Office, 1994).

94. David C. Korten, *When Corporations Rule the World* (West Hartford, CT: Kumarian Press, 1995), p. 218.

95. Barry Bluestone and Bennett Harrison, *The Deindustrialization of America* (New York: Basic Books, Inc., Publishers, 1982), pp. 140–90.

96. Don Stillman, "The Devastating Impact of Plant Relocations," in *The Big Business Reader*, Mark Green, ed. (New York: The Pilgrim Press, 1983), pp. 137–48.

97. For a discussion of the ethical issues involved in plant closings, see Judith Lichtenberg, "Workers, Owners, and Factory Closings," *Philosophy and Public Policy* (January 1985).

98. William E. Diehl, *Plant Closings* (New York: Division for Mission in North America, Lutheran Church in America, 1985), pp. 14–16.

99. Richard DeGeorge, *Business Ethics*, p. 192.

100. J. K. Galbraith, *American Capitalism: The Concept of Countervailing Power* (Boston: Houghton Mifflin, 1952).

101. Douglas Fraser, "Strikes: Friend or Foe of American Business and the Economy?" *Los Angeles Times*, 3 November 1985.

102. John Wright, ed., *The Universal Almanac*, 1996, p. 260.

103. "Beyond Unions," *Business Week*, 8 July 1985.

104. *Ibid.*

105. This definition is from Bronston T. Mayes and Robert W. Allen, "Toward A Definition of Organizational Politics," *Academy of Management Review* (October 1977): 672–78; for a popular overview of the issues raised by organizational politics, see "Playing Office Politics," *Newsweek*, 16 September 1985, pp. 54–59.

106. Miles, *Macro Organizational Behavior*, pp. 161–64.

107. Schein, "Individual Power and Political Behaviors," p. 67.

108. Robert W. Allen, Dan L. Madison, Lyman W. Porter, Patricia A. Renwick, and Bronston T. Mayes, "Organizational Politics," *California Management Review*, vol. 22, no. 1 (Fall 1979): 77–83.

109. These are culled from the pages of John P. Kotter, *Power in Management* (New York: American Management Association, 1979), a book that argues that "skillfully executed power-oriented behavior" is the mark of the "successful manager."

110. Terkel, *Working*, pp. 407, 409, 410.

111. See John R. S. Wilson, "In One Another's Power," *Ethics*, vol. 88, no. 4 (July 1978): 299–315; L. Blum, "Deceiving, Hurting, and Using," in A. Montefiore, ed., *Philosophy and Personal Relations* (London: Routledge and Kegan Paul, 1973).

112. Gerald F. Cavanagh, Dennis J. Moberg, and Manuel Velasquez, "The Ethics of Organizational Politics," *Academy of Management Review* (July 1980); Manuel Velasquez, Dennis J. Moberg, and Gerald F. Cavanagh, "Organizational Statesmanship and Dirty Politics: Ethical Guidelines for the Organizational Politician," *Organizational Dynamics* (Autumn 1983): 65–80.

113. David Kipnis, "Does Power Corrupt?" *Journal of Personality and Social Psychology*, vol. 24, no. 1 (1972): 33.

114. Chris Argyris, *Personality and Organization* (New York: Harper & Brothers, 1957), pp. 232–37.

115. Jeanne M. Liedtka, "Feminist Morality and Competitive Reality: A Role for an Ethic of Care?" *Business Ethics Quarterly*, vol. 6, no. 2 (April 1996): 185.

116. Thomas I. White, "Business Ethics" and Carol Gilligan's "Two Voices," *Business Ethics Quarterly*, vol. 2, no. 1 (January 1992).

117. John Dobson and Judith White, "Toward the Feminine Firm: An Extension to Thomas White," *Business Ethics Quarterly*, vol. 5, no. 3 (July 1995): 466.

118. *Ibid.*

119. C. Bartlett and S. Ghoshal, "Changing the Role of Top Management: Beyond Strategy to Purpose," *Harvard Business Review* (November/December 1994): 81.

120. There are several case studies of W. L. Gore & Associates. See, for example, Frank Shipper and Charles C. Manz, "W. L. Gore & Associates, Inc.—1993," in

Alex Miller and Gregory G. Dess, *Strategic Management*, 2nd ed. (New York: McGraw-Hill, 1996).

121. See Nell Noddings, *Caring*, pp. 73 ff.

122. For example, Carol Gilligan, *In a Different Voice: Psychological Theory and Women's Development* (Cambridge, MA: Harvard University Press, 1982), chaps. 3 and 4.

123. R. Scott, A. Aiken, D. Mechanic, and S. Moravcsik, "Organizational Aspects of Caring," *Milbank Quarterly*, vol. 73, no. 1 (1995): 77–95.

124. An overview of the literature on this topic can be found in Marilyn Friedman, *What Are Friends For?* (Ithaca, NY: Cornell University Press, 1993), chap. 3, entitled "The Social Self and the Partiality Debates."

CASES FOR DISCUSSION

The Gap

On Monday, July 24, 1995, Stanley Raggio, senior vice president for international sourcing and logistics for The Gap, Inc., opened a copy of *The New York Times* and found the article on the Gap. There, in a story by Bob Herbert, he saw his boss, Donald G. Fisher, being castigated for sourcing practices that he, Stan Raggio, was charged with managing.

The hundreds of thousands of young (and mostly female) factory workers in Central America who earn next to nothing and often live in squalor have been an absolute boon to American clothing company executives like Donald G. Fisher, the chief executive of the Gap and Banana Republic empire, who lives in splendor and paid himself more than $2 million last year.

Judith Viera is an 18-year-old who worked at a maquiladora plant in El Salvador that made clothing for the Gap and other companies. She was paid a pathetic 56 cents an hour.

Donald Fisher should meet Judith Viera, spend some time with her, and listen to her as she describes in a still-childish voice her most innocent of dreams. She would like to earn enough money to buy a little more food for her mother and two sisters. She would like to go to high school. But Donald Fisher is a busy man. It takes a great deal of time to oversee an empire balanced on the backs of youngsters like Ms. Viera (and her counterparts in Asia).[1]

The article in the *New York Times* was one of hundreds that were to appear in newspapers across the United States during the next few months describing human rights violations and subsistence-level wages at suppliers in Central America from which the Gap and other clothing retailers sourced their apparel.

The Gap, Inc. is a chain of retail stores that sell casual apparel, shoes, and accessories for men, women, and children. Headquartered in San Francisco, the stores operate under a variety of names including: Gap, Banana Republic, Old Navy Clothing Company, GapKids, and babyGap. All merchandise sold by the chain is private label.[2]

The Gap was founded in 1969 when Donald Fisher and his wife, Doris, opened a small clothing store near San Francisco State University. By 1971 they were operating six Gap stores. In 1983, Fisher enticed Millard Drexler, former president of Ann Taylor, into taking over as the new president of the Gap while Fisher became chief executive officer and chairman of the company. Drexler transformed the company by replacing the drab lines of clothing the store had been stocking with new brightly colored lines of rugged, high-quality cotton clothes.

In 1995, Fisher retired as CEO and Drexler, now age 50, took over the title. By now the Gap had 1348 well-located stores in the United States and Puerto Rico, 72 in Canada, 49 in the United Kingdom, and 3 in France. Competition was intense, and earlier R. H. Macy and Federated stores had been forced to file chapter 11 bankruptcy. The Gap, however, had been doing very well, with 1994 profits of $258 million on sales of $3.723 billion.[3]

Apparel stores like the Gap purchased their clothes from manufacturers in the United States and around the world. Some 20,000 contractors in the United States, most employing 5 to 50 workers, sewed clothes for companies like the Gap. The apparel manufacturing industry in the United States was under intense pressure from imports because the work was so labor-intensive, and labor was less regulated and much cheaper in many developing countries, depressing both wages and working conditions in the United States. For example, it is estimated that in China, wage rates in the apparel industry are approximately one twentieth of U.S. rates. Since 1990, the United States had lost more than a half a million textile and apparel jobs, and companies struggling to survive in the United States often had working conditions as bad as anything to be found in developing countries. A 1989 study by the General Accounting Office discovered that two thirds of the 7000 garment shops in New York City were sweatshops.[4] A spot check by the Labor Department in Southern California had found that 93 percent of the shops checked had health and safety violations.

The Gap contracted with over 500 manufacturers around the world that made the company's private-label apparel according to Gap's specifications. Gap, Inc. purchased about 30 percent of its clothes from manufacturers located in the United States and 70 percent from vendors located in 46 foreign countries. No single supplier provided more than 5 percent of its merchandise.

On May 10, 1993, a toy-factory fire in Thailand killed over 200 workers and injured 500. The toy factory was owned by Kader Industries, which made toys at the plant for some of the largest toy companies in the United States, including Toys R Us, Fisher-Price, and Tyco. U.S. Customs Service documents revealed that during the first 3 months of 1993, U.S. companies had imported more than 270 tons of toys from the Thai factory. The accident drew attention not only to the responsibilities of the toy industry, but to the responsibilities of all U.S. industries and consumers in ensuring that products are made under safe and humane working conditions regardless of where they are produced.

In the wake of concern over Third World working conditions, the Gap also adopted a set of Sourcing Principles and Guidelines. These provided standards that vendors had to meet including: engage in no form of discrimination, use no forced or prison labor, employ no children under 14 years of age, provide a safe working environment for employees, pay the legal minimum wage or the local industry standard—whichever is greater, meet all applicable local environmental regulations and comply with the Gap's own more stringent environmental standards, neither threaten nor penalize employees for their efforts to organize or bargain collectively, and uphold all local customs laws. To ensure compliance with its standards, the Gap sent a Gap Field Representative to conduct an in-depth interview with a prospective supplier prior to the initiation of a business relationship.

Among the suppliers from whom the Gap sourced its clothes was one in El Salvador run by Mandarin International, a Taiwanese-owned company that operated apparel assembly plants around the world. The Gap had begun contracting with the Mandarin plant in El Salvador in 1992. A worker there was paid approximately 12 cents for assembling a Gap three-quarter sleeve T-shirt or turtleneck, which retailed at about $20 in the United States. Wages at the Mandarin plant averaged 56 cents an hour—a level that was claimed to provide only 18 percent of the amount needed to support a family of four but that was consistent with the industry standard for the region.[5]

El Salvador is now a constitutional democracy.[6] In 1992, the country finally ended a 12-year civil war that tore the country apart with massacres and death squad killings and that left 70,000 people dead. Despite dramatic declines, the level of violence in El Salvador remained high, particularly murder, assaults, and robberies, including crimes against women and children. About 40 percent of the population was living below the poverty level. Despite increases in the average monthly wage, inflation had brought about a decline in real wages. This in turn had encouraged foreign apparel makers to set up apparel factories there.

The government maintained six *free trade zones*, where foreign countries are allowed to import and export goods for assembly within the country without paying tariffs. Foreign companies operating within the free trade zones are called *maquiladoras*, and they often paid better than companies outside the zones. Although the law prohibits employers from firing or harrassing employees who are trying to start a union, government authorities sometimes do not enforce this requirement. The Labor Code also prohibits minors between 14 and 18 years of age from being worked more than 6 hours a day, and the maximum normal workweek for adults is set at 44 hours unless overtime rates are paid. However, these rules are also not always enforced.

Troubles erupted at the Mandarin plant, which was located in one of the free trade zones, in early February 1995 when workers notified the company of their intent to form a union, a right authorized by the Salvadoran labor code.[7] The Ministry of Labor granted the union legal status, the first union to be recognized in a free trade zone in El Salvador.

The Mandarin company was notified of the legal status of the union on February 7. It responded by closing down the plant on February 8. Workers spent that day and night camped out in front of the factory. The next morning company security guards attacked and beat some of the female workers.[8] An emergency commission met, and the evening of February 9, the company agreed to end the lock-out, recognize the union, and comply with the Salvadoran Labor Code. A few days later, however, Mandarin fired over 150 union members and supporters.[9]

In late March 1995, managers at the Gap became aware of claims that the management of the Mandarin factory was resisting union efforts to organize, in violation of Gap guidelines. Events at the plant were starting to receive publicity in the media, particularly with legislation now pending in Congress that would affect imports from the area. A Gap executive, Stan Raggio, went to El Salvador to investigate the situation.[10] While there, he interviewed a number of workers regarding conditions at the factory. At the conclusion of his visit, he reported that he had found no human rights abuses or other violations of the company's corporate sourcing policies. The company would, however, continue to monitor the situation at Mandarin. In April, the Gap suspended placement of new orders at the Mandarin plant and announced it would not place more orders until it had determined whether the allegations were well founded.[11]

On Monday, May 15, the workers' union called a work stoppage to protest the continued firings of union people. Company guards are said to have physically attacked and beat union leaders when they stood up to announce the work stoppage.[12] Mandarin again closed the plant and fired all of the union leadership. An emergency commission was again convened and it again reached an agreement with the company; the next morning the company reopened its doors. The company, however, refused to hire back the union leaders the next day. In May, the Gap's Stanley P. Raggio again went to El Salvador to investigate the situation and was again unable to get clear testimony from workers interviewed at the plant that their union rights were being violated.

American unions, such as the International Ladies' Garment Workers Union, had long been concerned with conditions in offshore apparel sweatshops like the Mandarin plant, with which American apparel manufacturers had to compete. Until the conditions of apparel workers in those countries improved, the plight of apparel workers in the United States would probably also remain unchanged because American companies could not afford worker amenities when they were competing against foreign companies that provided their workers with the barest minimum. Union leadership, therefore, had turned increasing attention to improving the conditions of labor in countries outside the United States with whom U.S. workers were now competing.

The National Labor Relations Committee, a coalition of 25 labor unions, now made plans to launch a national campaign early in the summer of 1995 protesting harsh conditions faced by workers in Caribbean and Central American apparel contracting plants. The union decided to focus attention on workers' attempts to unionize the Mandarin plant, the subsistence wages prevalent in the area, and the sweatshop conditions at the plant.

During the summer of 1995, the National Labor Committee arranged to have two young maquiladora workers—Judith Viera, an 18-year-old former employee at Mandarin, and Claudia Molina, a 17-year-old former employee at Orion Apparel, a Korean-owned maquiladora in Choloma, Honduras—spend 59 days criss-crossing the United States and Canada, visiting over 20 cities to criticize the Gap and other companies at press conferences and public meetings arranged by the National Labor Committee. At press conferences, the two women and representatives of the National Labor Committee accused the Gap of a "cover-up" of the situation at Mandarin; they described in detail long hours of work for 56 cents an hour, violence against union supporters, sexual harassment from supervisors, lack of clean drinking water, not being allowed to use rest rooms, and being forced to sweep the factory grounds under a torrid sun as a punishment. The publicity focused enormous attention on the Gap and its vendor in El Salvador. Major articles based on interviews with the two employees appeared in all major newspapers in the country.[13] The National Labor Relations Committee urged consumers to boycott the Gap and to telephone or write to Gap executives voicing their displeasure about conditions at their vendor's factory. Union officials demanded that the Gap undertake a joint investigation, with the National Labor Relations Committee, of the situation at Mandarin, should pressure Mandarin to reinstate the fired union workers, and should commit itself to third party, independent monitoring of contractors' compliance with the Gap code of conduct. The union noted plans to begin a "broader range of coordinated actions at Gap stores across the United States and Canada–leafleting consumers, etc.," starting the day after Thanksgiving, when the critical Christmas buying season began.[14]

The week of August 27, Stanley Raggio once again visited El Salvador and met with U.S. and El Salvadoran government officials as well as several current and former factory workers in an attempt to objectively assess conditions at the factory. In a public statement issued after the visitation, the company stated that, "Despite this intensive effort our investigation has not uncovered any significant evidence supporting the allegations or indicating that there has been any serious violations of our sourcing guidelines. Based on our investigation, we have determined with confidence that the Mandarin factory treats its workers well and meets our standards of fairness and decency."[15] The National Labor Relations Committee responded with news releases stating that several human rights organizations had verified its accusations and that workers had not spoken with the Gap out of fear.

On the evening of Wednesday, August 2, Stanley Raggio met with Charles Kernaghan, executive director of the National Labor Committee, to discuss the charges against the plant that the National Labor Committee was making in its summer campaign. Earlier that same day, the National Labor Committee had held a demonstration at the Gap's distribution center in San Francisco. Both sides felt the discussions were productive, but there were no immediate changes.[16]

Two months later, Bob Herbert, writer for the *New York Times*, visited El Salvador to investigate the situation for himself. On October 9 and October 13, the *New York Times* published articles by him that were harshly critical of the Gap for continuing to claim that there was no evidence to corroborate the charges of the National Labor Committee.[17] Herbert claimed to have interviewed over 30 women in El Salvador who had been fired for being union members. He had interviewed the president of the Mandarin plant who had confirmed that the women had worked at the plant but had "left" in late June. Interviews with local church groups and with the Government's Office for the Defense of Human Rights, he said, had also confirmed the mass firing of union workers.

The question that now faced Stan Raggio and his fellow managers was: what to do?

Questions

1. What course of action would you recommend to Stanley Raggio? Should the Gap give in to the Union's demand that the Gap "undertake a joint investigation, with the National Labor Relations Committee, of the situation at Mandarin, should pressure Mandarin to reinstate the fired union workers, and should commit itself to third party, independent monitoring of contractors' compliance with the Gap code of conduct?"
2. Should companies like the Gap attempt to get their suppliers to pay more than the local industry standard when it is insufficient to live on? Should they pay wages in the Third World that are equivalent to U.S. wages? Should they provide the same levels of medical benefits that are provided in the United States? The same levels of workplace safety?
3. Is a company like the Gap morally responsible for the way its suppliers treat their workers? Explain your answer.

Notes

1. Bob Herbert, "Sweatshop Beneficiaries," *New York Times*, July 24, 1995.
2. Patrick J. Spain and James R. Talbot, eds., *Hoover's Handbook of American Companies, 1996* (Austin, TX: The Reference Press, 1996), p. 394.

3. The Gap, *Annual Report*, 1995.

4 "Look Who's Sweating Now: How Robbert Reich is Turning Up the Heat on Retailers," *Business Week*, 16 October 1995.

5. Letter of Charles Kernaghan, Executive Director, National Labor Committee Education Fund In Support of Worker and Human Rights in Central America, 15 Union Square, New York, NY 10003; dated May 18, 1995.

6. Information in this and the following paragraphs is drawn from: U.S. Department of State, *Country Reports on Human Rights Practices for 1994* (Washington: U.S. Government Printing Office, 1995.

7. Richard Rothstein, "USAID Teaching El Salvador How to Suppress Labor," The Sacramento Bee (Final Edition), 8 June 1995.

8. National Labor Committee, News Release, 28 June 1995.

9. "Free Trade Zone Organizers Told 'Blood Will Flow,' " LaborLink, June–August, 1995, no. 4.

10. The Gap, Press Release, reported in *Business Wire Information Services*, 28 July 1995.

11. Joyce Barrett, "Caribbean Rights Group Heading for Gap Offices," *Women's Wear Daily*, 2 August, 1995.

12. *Ibid.*

13. Articles appeared in: the *New York Times* (July 21, 24), the *Washington Post* (July 24), the *Los Angeles Times* (July, date unknown), The *Miami Herald* (July 1), The *Toronto Star* (August 16), The *Toronto Globe and Mail* (August 16), the *Twin Cities' Star Tribune* (July 7), the *Hartford Journal* (July 12), the *Toledo Blade* (July 31), the *San Francisco Examiner* (August 2), the *San Francisco Chronicle* (August 1), the *Sacramento Bee* (June 8, August 1), the *New York Newsday* (June 27), the *New York Daily News*, the *Women's Wear Daily* (August 2, 4, 9, 11), and dozens of other major metropolitan newspapers around the United States.

14. Letter entitled "Outline/Proposal, The GAP Campaign, A Strategy to Win" from National Labor Committee Education Fund in Support of Worker and Human Rights in Central America, 15 Union Square, New York, NY 10003, dated October 18, 1995.

15. Letter of Dotti Hatcher, Director, Sourcing & Trade Compliance, The Gap, dated September 11, 1995.

16. "Gap Meets Rights Group on Salvador," *Women's Wear Daily*, 4 August 1995.

17. Bob Herbert, "Not a Living Wage," (Op-Ed), *New York Times*, 9 October 1995, and "In Deep Denial," (Op-Ed), *New York Times*, 13 October 1995.

Working for Eli Lilly & Company[1]

Eli Lilly, the discoverer of Erythromycin, Darvon, Ceclor, and Prozac, is a major pharmaceutical company that sold $6.8 billion of drugs all over the world in 1995, giving it profits of $2.3 billion. Headquartered in Indianapolis, Minnesota, the company also provides food, housing, and compensation to numerous homeless alcoholics who perform short-term work for the company. The work these street people perform, however, is a bit unusual.

Before approving the sale of a newly discovered drug, the U.S. Food and Drug Administration requires that the drug be put through three phases of tests after being tested on animals. In Phase I, the drug is taken by healthy human individuals to determine whether it has any dangerous side effects. In Phase II, the drug is given to a small number of sick patients to determine dosage levels. In Phase III, the drug is given to large numbers of sick patients by doctors and hospitals to determine its efficacy.

Phase I testing is often the most difficult to carry out because most healthy individuals are reluctant to take a new and untested medication that is not intended to cure them of anything and that may have potentially crippling or deadly side effects. To secure test subjects, companies must advertise widely and offer to pay them as much as $250 a day. Eli Lilly, however, does not advertise as widely and pays its volunteers only $85 a day plus free room and board, the lowest in the industry. One of the reasons that Lilly's rates are so low is because, as a long-time nurse at the Lily Clinic is reported to have indicated, "the majority of its subjects are homeless alcoholics" recruited through word of mouth that is spread in soup kitchens, shelters, and prisons all over the United States. Because they are alcoholics, they are fairly desperate for money. Because Phase I tests can run several months, test subjects can make as much as $4500—an enormous sum to people who are otherwise unemployable and surviving on handouts. Interviews with several homeless men who have participated in Lilly's drug tests and who describe themselves as alcoholics who drink daily suggest that they are, by and large, quite happy to participate in an arrangement that provides them with "easy money." When asked, one homeless drinker hired to participate in a Phase I trail said he had no idea what kind of drug was being tested on him even though he had signed an informed-consent form. An advantage for Lilly is that this kind of test subject is less likely to sue if severely injured by the drug. The tests run on the homeless men, moreover, provide enormous benefits for society. It has been suggested, in fact, that in light of the difficulty of securing test subjects, some tests might be delayed or not performed at all if it were not for the large pool of homeless men willing and eager to participate in the tests.

The Federal Drug Administration requires that people who agree to participate in Phase I tests must give their "informed consent" and must make a "truly voluntary and uncoerced decision." Some have questioned whether the desperate circumstances of alcoholic and homeless men allow them to make a truly voluntary and uncoerced decision when they agree to take an untested potentially dangerous drug for $85 a day. Some doctors claim that alcoholics run a higher risk because they may carry diseases that are undetectable by standard blood screening and that make them vulnerable to being severely harmed by certain drugs. One former test subject indicated in an interview that the drug he had been given in a test several years before had arrested his heart and "they had to put things on my chest to start my heart up again." The same thing happened to another subject in the same test. Another man indicated that the drug he was given had made him unconscious for 2 days while others told of excruciating headaches.

In earlier years, drug companies used prisoners to test drugs in Phase I tests. During the 1970s, drug companies stopped using prisoners when critics complained that their poverty and the promise of early parole in effect were coercing the prisoners into "volunteering." When Lilly first turned to using homeless people during the 1980s, a doctor at the company is quoted as saying, "We were constantly talking about whether we were exploiting the homeless. But there were a lot of them who were willing to stay in the hospital for four weeks." Moreover, he adds, "Providing them with a nice warm bed and good medical care and sending them out drug- and alcohol-free was a positive thing to do."

A homeless alcoholic indicated in an interview that when the test he was participating in was completed, he would rent a cheap motel room where "I'll get a case of Miller and an escort girl and have sex. The girl will cost me $200 an hour." He estimated that it would take him about two weeks to spend the $4650 Lilly would pay him for his services. The manager at another cheap motel said that when test subjects completed their stints at Lilly, they generally arrived at his motel with about $2500 in cash: "The guinea pigs go to the lounge next door, get drunk and buy the house a round. The idea is, they can party for a couple of weeks and go back to Lilly and do the next one."

QUESTIONS

1. Discuss this case from the perspectives of utilitarianism, rights, justice, and caring. What insight does virtue theory shed on the ethics of the events described in this case?
2. "In a free enterprise society all adults should be allowed to make their own decisions about how they choose to earn their living." Discuss this statement in light of the Lilly case.
3. In your judgment, is the policy of using homeless alcoholics for test subjects morally appropriate? Explain the reasons for your judgment. What does your judgment imply about the moral legitimacy of a free market in labor?
4. How should the managers of Lilly handle this issue?

NOTE

1. The information for this case is drawn entirely from Laurie P. Cohen, "Stuck for Money," *Wall Street Journal*, 14 November 1996, pp. 1, 10. All quotations are drawn from this article.

Index

A

D

F

G

N

O

P

T

U

V